BIOLOGICAL PSYCHOLOGY

BIOLOGICAL PSYCHOLOGY

SUZANNE HIGGS, ALISON COOPER,
JONATHAN LEE AND MIKE HARRIS

Los Angeles | London | New Delhi
Singapore | Washington DC

Los Angeles | London | New Delhi
Singapore | Washington DC

SAGE Publications Ltd
1 Oliver's Yard
55 City Road
London EC1Y 1SP

SAGE Publications Inc.
2455 Teller Road
Thousand Oaks, California 91320

SAGE Publications India Pvt Ltd
B 1/I 1 Mohan Cooperative Industrial Area
Mathura Road
New Delhi 110 044

SAGE Publications Asia-Pacific Pte Ltd
3 Church Street
#10-04 Samsung Hub
Singapore 049483

Editor: Michael Carmichael
Development editor: Christopher Kingston
Assistant Editor: Keri Dickens
Production editor: Imogen Roome
Copyeditor: Kate Harrison; Bryan Campbell
Indexer: Martin Hargreaves
Marketing manager: Alison Borg
Cover design: Wendy Scott
Typeset by: C&M Digitals (P) Ltd, Chennai, India
Printed in India at Replika Press Pvt Ltd

Library of Congress Control Number: 2014933962

British Library Cataloguing in Publication data

A catalogue record for this book is available from the British Library

ISBN 978-0-85702-261-5
ISBN 978-0-85702-262-2 (pbk)

At SAGE we take sustainability seriously. Most of our products are printed in the UK using FSC papers and boards. When we print overseas we ensure sustainable papers are used as measured by the Egmont grading system. We undertake an annual audit to monitor our sustainability.

CONTENTS

'FOCUS ON METHODS' BOXES

GUIDED TOUR

CHAPTER BREAKDOWN

Each chapter sets out clearly at its beginning what key information you should soon understand, so you can easily track your progress.

ROADMAP

These introductions start each chapter off by describing the key issues that will be thoroughly covered during the chapter.

FOCUS ON METHODS: BOXES

The key research methods used by biological psychologists are described in these boxes, explaining how psychologists have uncovered the workings of the brain.

INSIGHT BOXES

Particularly interesting issues are highlighted in Insight boxes that give you a deeper picture of some of the most important issues in biological psychology.

KEY POINTS

Throughout the chapters, Key Points offer markers of which points you need to understand from the previous section and help you navigate quickly to the most important information.

CHAPTER SUMMARY

Review the contents of each chapter in the Summary, an easy-to-read reminder of the most important information you've read.

FURTHER READING

If a chapter has inspired you to read more widely on that topic, look at the Further Reading section for suggestions of relevant and interesting books or articles.

 # SPOTLIGHT

Each chapter is accompanied by one or two spotlights – extensive sections focusing on particular areas of research that are designed to stretch your understanding of the major issues in biological psychology.

KEY STUDY

Seminal or particularly interesting pieces of research are described and evaluated in Key Study boxes, along with full citation information so you know where to find the original article.

GLOSSARY

Definitions of key terms are collected at the back of the book, so if you're drowning in jargon or not sure of the meaning of a particular phrase, you can easily find an explanation here. Terms that appear in the glossary are highlighted throughout the book.

REFERENCES

Extensive references offer you a library of further reading sources to deepen your understanding of seminal literature or find sources for your own research project.

Be sure to visit the ⑤SAGE edge™ website at **edge.sagepub.com/higgs** to find a range of free tools and resources that will enhance the learning experience.

⑤SAGE edge™ **for Students** provides a personalised approach to help you accomplish your coursework goals in an easy-to-use learning environment and features elements such as:

- Mobile-friendly **eFlashcards** which strengthen understanding of key terms and concepts
- Mobile-friendly practice **quizzes** that allow you to assess your understanding of course material
- Links to online **videos, animations** and **podcasts** that offer a new perspective and an alternative learning style
- An online **action plan** including tips and feedback on progress through the course and materials which allows you to individualise your learning experience
- **Summaries** and **learning objectives** for each chapter that reinforce the most important material

$SAGE edge **for Instructors** supports teaching by making it easy to integrate quality content and create a rich learning environment for students. **$SAGE edge** instructor sites include tools and elements such as:

- **Test banks** that provide a diverse range of pre-written options as well as the opportunity to edit any question and/or insert personalised questions to effectively assess students' progress and understanding

- Editable, chapter-specific **PowerPoint® slides** that offer complete flexibility for creating a multimedia presentation

FOREWORD

This new textbook on biological psychology from the University of Birmingham provides an informative guide for psychology students on the study of brain and behaviour. The University of Birmingham is highly rated for both teaching and research and this is evident in the reassuringly authoritative tone of the book. The writing is informative, fast-moving, and succinct. At a time when neuroscience is emerging as one of the most exciting and influential sciences, there has never been more need for a text that excites students about biological foundations of behaviour.

This book marks itself out from other books on biological psychology because it is a text in which behaviour is at the fore and the relevance of biology to psychology and neuroscience is clear. It also takes a progressive approach to learning and takes students on a journey in biopsychology from basic principles to 'hot' research topics. It is scholarly and challenging but has an accessible narrative style that will help students see links between topics.

The book is organised around broad sections that cover the major themes in biological psychology but each theme is covered at both introductory and more advanced level. Introductory sections provide breadth via an accessible overview of each theme and emphasise guiding principles rather than technical details. Depth is provided by the spotlight chapters that provide detailed coverage at a more advanced level. The 'spotlight' topics also discuss contemporary issues in biological psychology and neuroscience and provide guided reading and critical analysis of key papers.

For students, the spotlights provide a stepping stone from secondary sources to independent reading. The book will be attractive to students because it will be a book that will be useful to them throughout their undergraduate careers. The transition from textbook based courses to courses that rely on reading of primary sources can be difficult for students and this book will help bridge this gap. The critical approach taken in advanced chapters will equip students with the confidence to move from working with textbook material to engagement with original material. For lecturers, the spotlights provide a secure basis for teaching at advanced undergraduate level. Biological psychology is a core subject on all undergraduate psychology courses. Many departments teach biological psychology at introductory level and at honours level but there is no one text currently that can support courses at these different levels. This text is different because it can support teaching at introductory level and will be an excellent reference for higher level courses too. I hope you enjoy reading it and do indeed find it to be of use in this way.

Kimron Shapiro

ACKNOWLEDGEMENTS

The authors and publishers would like to thank the following reviewers, and others who chose to remain anonymous, for their comments and suggestions that have helped to shape the writing of this book:

Dr Laura Brown, University of Manchester

Dr Hans Crombag, University of Sussex

Professor Håkan Fischer, Stockholm University

Professor Paul Gilbert, San Diego State University

Professor Eef Hogervorst, Loughborough University

Dr Sue McHale, Sheffield Hallam University

Dr Maarten Milders, Heriot Watt University

Professor Suvobrata Mitra, University of Warwick

Drew Munn, University of Northampton

Dr Sonia Tucci, University of Liverpool

Dr Heather Woods, University of Glasgow

Dr Andrew Young, University of Leicester

The authors and publishers would like to thank Professor Phil Terry, Kingston University, for his contribution to the companion website materials.

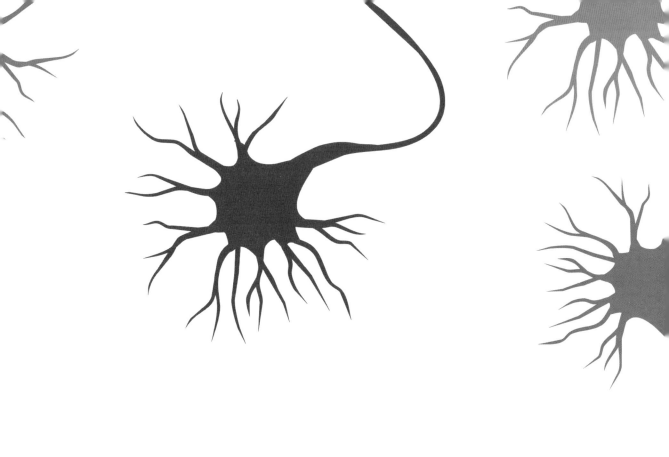

INTRODUCTION

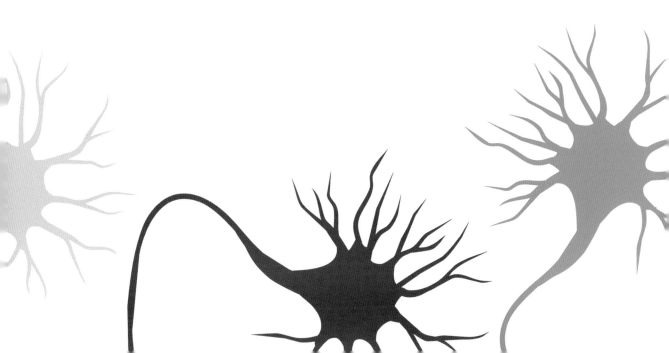

Biological psychology is the study of the brain and human behaviour – primarily of how the brain brings about behaviour but also of how behaviour can alter the brain as we learn from experience. This ambitious undertaking requires an unusually broad approach, ranging from the 'hard' science typical of biology to the 'softer' techniques favoured by psychologists. In practice, many psychologists are content to confine themselves to trying to understand behaviour without worrying about the additional complexities involved in trying to understand the brain. They might, in their more gloomy moments, even argue that trying to understand behaviour by studying the brain is about as likely to succeed as trying to understand a computer program by poking about inside a computer with a screwdriver. But biological psychologists are made of sterner stuff. They believe that brain activity and behaviour are no more than different levels of the same multi-layered phenomenon, so that every observable action has an observable underlying neural cause. And they hope that, even though the two levels require different styles of thinking, understanding one will help us to understand the other. This book is a progress report on the extent to which this hope has so far been fulfilled. It reviews recent theories and evidence in a wide variety of topics, from how nerves work to the likely causes of depression.

Wide though this range may be, it has some obvious omissions. In particular, there is little mention of the more sophisticated behaviours, such as language, that characterise human beings. Why is this? Nowadays we can use relatively non-invasive human imaging techniques to 'see' which brain areas are active during a task, and we can also examine the behavioural consequences of temporarily 'lesioning' particular areas using rTMS. But before these methods were developed, there were few ways to study the working human brain. We could place electrodes on the scalp and use EEG to record overall patterns of neural activity, but the results were often complex and it was very difficult to figure out where in the brain the activity was located. And we could study the behavioural deficits of patients with localised brain damage, but the damage often involved more than one functional area so that the deficits were sometimes confusing and, because the brain may reconfigure itself over time to minimise problems, potentially misleading. Nonetheless, both techniques have had their successes – for example, the different brain rhythms picked up by EEG led to the identification of the different stages of sleep, and we have learned a good deal about memory from brain-damaged patients like HM (see Chapter 4).

Despite these successes from the direct study of people, biological psychologists have traditionally relied upon animal studies, which allow them to use a much wider range of techniques. Of course, this approach also has important limitations. For example, animals don't show the full range of human behaviour – we can't hope to learn very much from them about language, for example. Consequently, biological psychology has traditionally focused upon the more basic aspects of behaviour, such as motivation or emotion, which animals do display. Even with the modern techniques mentioned above, which allow us directly to study the human brain, animal studies still play an important role. TMS and some imaging techniques currently work best near the surface of the brain and are less effective in deeper areas. Happily, the areas that control higher human functions like language are conveniently located in the cerebral cortex, close to the brain's surface. But the areas controlling the more basic functions studied by biological psychologists lie much deeper in the brain and are more easily studied in animals.

A second, perhaps more important, concern is that understanding the neural mechanisms that underpin animal behaviour might not provide much insight into how our own behaviour is controlled. We might, after all, have evolved completely different ways of doing things. At least at the most basic level, this does not seem to be the case. For example, our understanding of how nerves work is based almost entirely upon the squid, an invertebrate that happens to have very large diameter nerves which are easy to record from. Nevertheless, all vertebrates, including people, seem to work essentially the same way. The many examples of animal studies described throughout this book will allow you to judge for yourself how useful and how valid animal work has been in helping us to understand more sophisticated systems and, ultimately, human behaviour.

We are all to some extent already familiar with human behaviour, but it is probably worthwhile giving a brief overview of the brain and of neural function before launching into the more specialist chapters. The brain receives input from sensory receptors that respond to some feature of the internal or external environment, and generates the output signals that control muscles and glands. Between these two stages lies a complex network of neurons. Neurons are electrically active – in common with almost all types of cell, there is a tiny electrical potential, or voltage, between the inside and outside of the cell – and they work simply by rapidly varying this voltage.

Though there are many variations in form, a 'typical' neuron has many dendrites (branch-like fibres that spread out from the cell body), and a single axon (a longer fibre that can rapidly conduct tiny spikes of electricity, called action potentials, away from the cell body). Each neuron receives inputs from the axons of many other neurons, which form connections called synapses on the neuron's dendrites. Synapses are either inhibitory or excitatory, tending slightly to increase or decrease the neuron's electrical potential. All the tiny signals from active synapses are added together across the cell body and the resulting overall potential determines the neuron's response – the rate at which it generates action potentials, which are transmitted to the neurons making up the next stage of the network. Synapses provide an important key to understanding how the brain works. They communicate using chemicals called neurotransmitters, and specific neurotransmitters are often associated with particular aspects of behaviour. Moreover, the strengthening and weakening of synaptic connections provides the basis of learning and memory.

But how can such an essentially simple system control behaviour? Imagine a very simple animal that swims around in ponds using two, paddle-like cilia, one on each side of its body. Each paddle is controlled by a single neuron; the faster its firing rate, the faster the paddle rows. Suppose our animal needs light to survive and is also equipped with two light-sensitive receptors, again one on each side of the body. To make the animal turn towards the light, we could connect each light receptor to the neuron on the opposite side of the body using an excitatory connection. Faster paddling on that side would then turn the animal towards the light. Alternatively, we could connect each light receptor to the neuron on the same side of the body using an inhibitory connection. This would slow the paddle down and again produce the required turn.

In fact, making both these excitatory and inhibitory connections would be even better. Each neuron would then receive excitation from one sensor and inhibition from the other. Summing these two inputs would be like subtracting one from the other and, in effect, the neuron's output would depend on the difference in lighting on the two sides of the body; the bigger the difference, the faster the animal would turn in the required direction.

This system is by no means perfect – it would send a moth spiralling in towards a bright light, for example – but it does illustrate three essential principles that are thought to apply to the brain. First, the response of any given neuron seems always to have the same meaning; firing of the neurons connecting the receptors to the motor neuron in the above model means 'the amount of light from this side', for example. This is why, when you very gently press your eyeball, you see a flash of light; the pressure stimulates retinal cells, and retinal response always means 'light' even though, in this case, it was provoked by touch.

Second, neurons process information simply by combining the meaningful signals brought to them by excitatory and inhibitory synapses. For example, the combination of excitatory and inhibitory synapses in the above model does some simple arithmetic. In fact, simply by subtracting signals from two spatially offset receptors, the model computes the gradient of the lightness change across the animal's body – it is actually doing something very like differential calculus.

Third, while the cell body and synapses are the main information processors, the axon transmits the results of that processing rapidly to where it's needed. For example, axons can transmit information about a rapid rise in temperature at the big toe all the way to the brain, and transmit the command to move all the way back to the leg muscles, quickly enough to avoid seriously burning the skin.

You might like to explore these principles a little further by constructing a simple model, like the one above, which would allow the animal to turn towards a nutritious chemical source. And then you might try to build in a way to choose between light coming from one direction and the promise of food in the other. The point of these exercises is to illustrate how a few connections among even fewer neurons can, at least in principle, achieve rather complicated behaviour. Try to imagine what might be achieved by the estimated 100 billion (10^{11}, or 100 000 000 000) neurons present in the brain – each of which, on average, makes an estimated 1,000 connections, giving a total of 100 trillion (10^{14}, or 100 000 000 000 000) synapses.

This unimaginable complexity has the great advantage of making our own, very sophisticated behaviour possible. But it also has the considerable disadvantage, for the biological psychologist, of making the task of unravelling all the connections particularly formidable. In some cases, most often in the extreme periphery of the nervous system, we can trace and figure out the function of simple circuits that are remarkably like the theoretical ones described for our simple pond-dweller. Examples include the spinal reflex described in Chapter 6 and the retinal circuitry described in Chapter 5. But this type of circuit is a far cry from the complex neural mechanisms that must underpin much of our everyday experience and behaviour. Unlike our pond-dweller, drawn automatically towards the light or a promising food source, we seem to exercise free choice over a very wide range of sophisticated behaviours. We might decide upon a snack, pause the TV, negotiate the complicated and potentially dangerous sequence of actions involved in tea-making while day-dreaming about what to wear the next day, remind ourselves to buy more tea, and then return to the sofa to pick up the programme we were watching seamlessly from where we left it. Or we might thrill to the sight of beautiful countryside or to the sound of a symphony. Or 'simply' read a book.

Biological psychologists believe that, just as these sophisticated abilities gradually evolved from simpler behaviours in our evolutionary past, so the neural systems that support them gradually evolved from simpler circuits like the ones in our theoretical pond-dweller. Over hundreds of thousands of years, the brain seems gradually to have built upon and combined existing circuits into a complex hierarchy, consisting of layer upon layer of wiring, and making new behaviours and abilities possible.

In the human brain, the cerebral cortex – the convoluted outer layer of the forebrain that is the brain's most obvious visual feature – forms the topmost layer of this hierarchy. It can be divided anatomically into discrete areas, many of which seem to form distinct functional 'modules', concerned with a particular aspect of behaviour, such as the ability to plan and perform actions, or to formulate a grammatical sentence. Consequently, rather than worrying about basic, low-level circuits, current biological psychologists tend to focus on how these high-level modules work and how they are connected together. This is by no means a simple task, as illustrated by Figure I.1, which shows a schematic representation of the pathways between the cortical modules thought to contribute to visual processing.

Of course, this teasing apart of the brain's wiring needs to be carried out in parallel with questions about the various problems that the brain has evolved to solve. How do sensory receptors work and what information about the environment do they provide (Chapter 5)? How do muscles work and how do nerves control them (Chapter 6)? How are neurons originally wired up to form functioning circuits (Chapter 1) and how are the circuits modified by experience (Chapter 4)? As the nervous system becomes more complicated so that it has to prioritise conflicting demands, how are the conflicts resolved (Chapter 8), and how can the overall system be

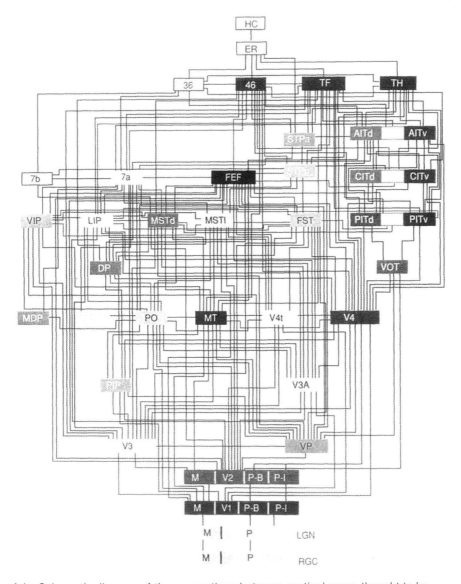

Figure I.1 Schematic diagram of the connections between cortical areas thought to be concerned with vision, illustrating both the number of relevant areas and the complexity of the neural wiring between them. There is no need to remember either the names of the areas or their interconnections

Source: Felleman and Van Essen (1991)

flexibly controlled so that it can be adapted to a particular context (Chapter 8)? And what happens when the system goes wrong and what can we do to repair it (Chapter 9)?

Each of the following chapters provides a general review of a particular topic, addressing fundamental questions like those listed above, highlighting important controversies, and outlining up-to-date theories and relevant evidence. Taken together, the chapters will provide you with a solid knowledge and understanding of contemporary biological psychology. In addition, the coverage of each topic includes an associated 'spotlight', which tackles a specific issue in more depth and aims to give you some insight into the type of work that biological psychologists actually do in developing, testing, and choosing amongst ideas about how the brain underpins behaviour. We begin by considering the structure of the nervous system and how nerves and synapses function in a little more detail.

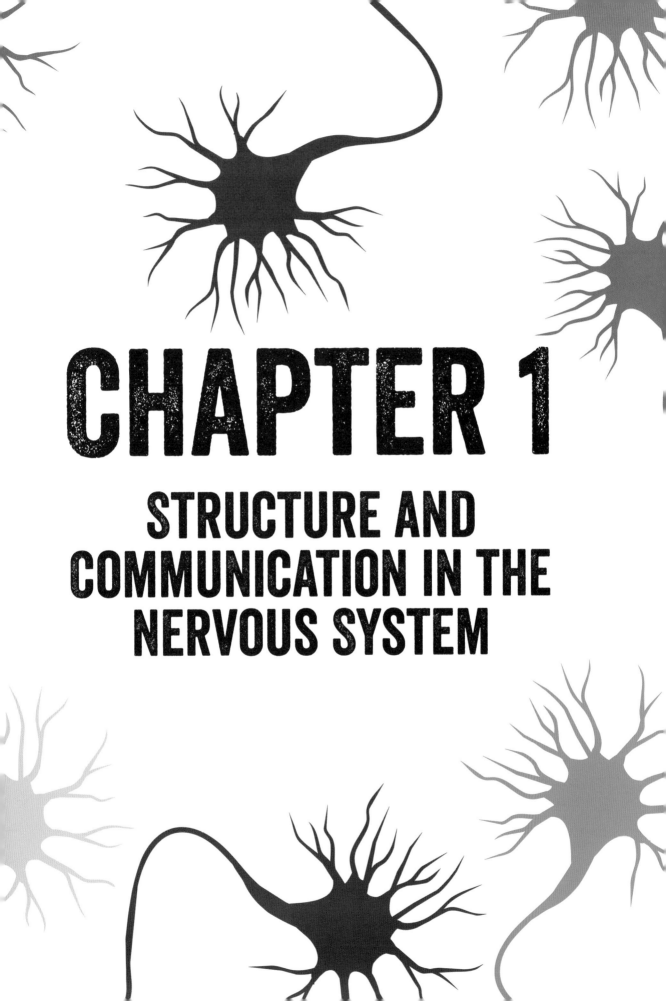

CHAPTER 1

STRUCTURE AND COMMUNICATION IN THE NERVOUS SYSTEM

CHAPTER BREAKDOWN

- An introduction to some key terminology in the field.
- A basic introduction to the components of the human nervous system.
- Overview of the organisation of the human nervous system.
- Overview of the key processes that underlie neuronal function.

ROADMAP

As with all areas of science, the field of neuroscience is full of terminology and it will be important to be familiar with some key terminology in order to get the most out of subsequent chapters, where this knowledge will be assumed. Throughout the chapter, the relationship between the structure and function of the nervous system, from cellular level right up to the whole system, will be emphasised. This is important as it will enable us to understand how the ability of the nervous system to change and adapt enables it to perform the functions that will be described in subsequent chapters and how these processes may be interrupted, resulting in dysfunction of the nervous system.

From the early part of the section it will be clear that the brain and its individual cellular components are highly organised. What is also evident is that, because of their unique structural features, the neuronal cells need a form of *intra*cellular communication that allows for the faithful transfer of information over relatively long distances from one end of the cell to another. This intracellular communication is achieved using electrical signals, and the production and transmission of these will be addressed in this chapter. Another key issue that emerges from studying the structure of the human brain is that there needs to be extensive *inter*cellular communication to allow the networks of neurons that need to cooperatively act to underpin brain function to form; this takes the form of chemical signalling processes, and the many ways that these processes can occur will be discussed. An understanding of these processes is necessary as the importance of them in determining normal neuronal function and as targets for modification both by physiological processes and exogenous substances such as drugs will be discussed in subsequent chapters. Clearly, these processes and their modification are critical for determining behaviour.

ORGANISATION OF THE NERVOUS SYSTEM

Although the brain is the key part of the nervous system for determining human behaviour, before we can consider the function/dysfunction of the brain we need to have some understanding of how the whole human nervous system is organised and the role that the rest of the

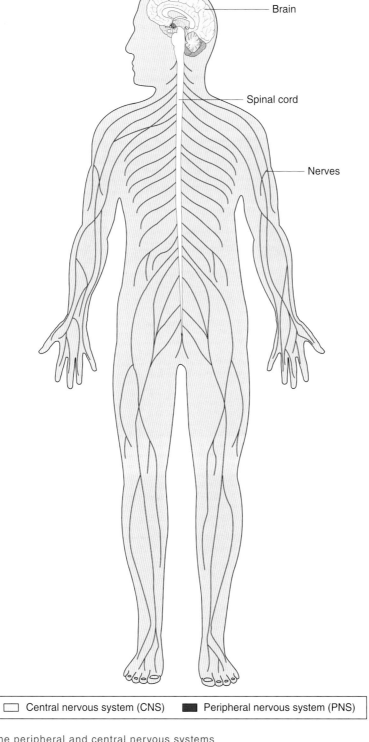

Central nervous system (CNS)   Peripheral nervous system (PNS)

Figure 1.1 The peripheral and central nervous systems

nervous system plays in both providing the brain with information and also carrying out actions determined by it.

So, we'll start with some very basic neuroanatomy for orientation. Traditionally, the nervous system is divided into two major parts: the central nervous system (CNS) and the peripheral nervous system (PNS) (Figure 1.1). The **central nervous system** comprises the brain and spinal cord, and everything else is considered the **peripheral nervous system**. This terminology arose from centuries of anatomical studies where observation suggested that the brain and spinal cord gave rise to thin string-like projections which went all over the body. However, this division into central and peripheral is rather artificial and is, in fact, unhelpful if we are trying to consider the nervous system as a single, functionally integrated system.

Central nervous system (CNS)

The brain

Humans have been fascinated by the brain and what it does for centuries – a question for which we still do not have a complete answer. The brain inherently attracts interest because of its somewhat bizarre appearance. It is the largest structure in the human body to be almost entirely encased in a hard bony structure, the skull, which indicates a critical need to protect it from damage. In life the human brain is rather variable from individual to individual but consists of approximately 1.5kg of a pink-beige substance with a jelly-like consistency and with a folded appearance.

Visual inspection of the intact human brain shows that it consists of three distinct parts, illustrated in Figure 1.2:

1. A stalk which joins the brain to the spinal cord, known as the **brainstem**.

2. A large domed structure of uniform appearance (if folded) known as the **cerebrum**. When viewed from above we can see that the cerebrum consists of two mirror-image halves known as hemispheres. If a cut is made along the midline of the hemispheres and the cut surface viewed, it is clear that each hemisphere consists of the folded outer surface, known as the cortex, but also a collection of structures beneath the cortex which are not visible in the intact brain; these structures are collectively known as subcortical regions.

3. A smaller version of the cerebrum, found at the back and tucked in underneath the cerebrum, known as the **cerebellum**.

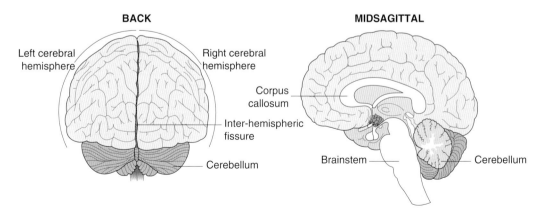

Figure 1.2   Key features of the human brain. Left: view from the rear, showing the two hemispheres. Right: internal features visible when the brain is cut along the middle

Over the centuries of studying the brain in a variety of species, it became apparent that brains of mammals, at least, had the same basic structure. Detailed descriptions and drawings of the appearance of the human brain appeared during the 17th century and what was clear was that the unique structural feature of the human brain was the relatively large size and highly folded appearance of the cortex when compared to, for example, the small, smooth brain of a rodent. When comparing across species it became clear that the reason that the cortex became progressively more folded as the brain became bigger was that this allowed for a more efficient packing of the steadily increasing number of neurons into the confined space of the skull. You can observe the effect for yourself by simply taking a sheet of paper and introducing folds into it (see Figure 1.3).

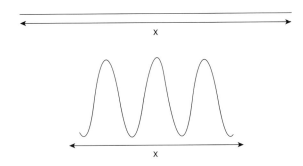

Figure 1.3 The folding of the cortex as it expanded allowed for more efficient packing of neurons

Observation of a large number of human brains resulted in the finding that some of the fissures, known as sulci (singular: **sulcus**), that result from the folding can be identified readily in the brains from many individuals. It followed that the cerebral cortex could be subdivided into regions based on their location relative to these sulci. These regions are known as **lobes** and this terminology is often used in relation to particular functions, described later in this book. Figure 1.4 illustrates the lobes that can be seen on the external surface of the brain.

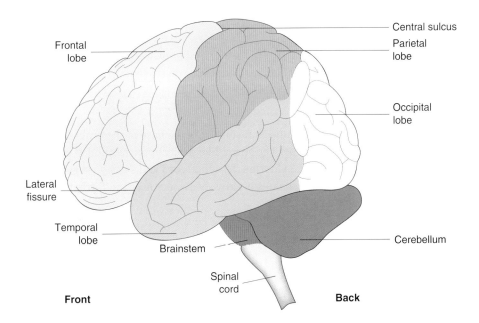

Figure 1.4 The lobes of the brain with key landmark structures that are common in all humans

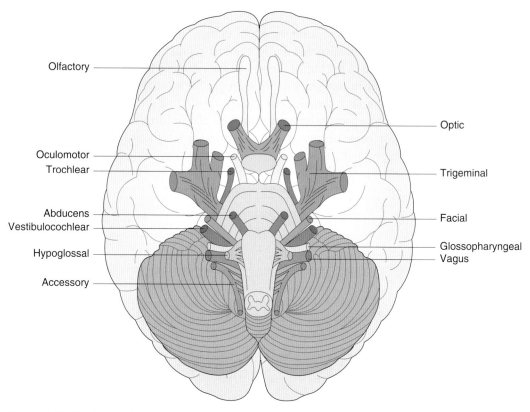

Figure 1.5   The base of the brain showing the cranial nerves

Source: Barnes (2013)

Interestingly, although the major sulci are generally readily identifiable in nearly all normal human brains, the minor ones, and the folds between them, known as gyri (singular: **gyrus**), are quite variable between individuals, which may well reflect functional differences. The positions of the gyri and sulci are determined during brain development, which is considered in Chapter 3.

When viewed from below (Figure 1.5) we can see a number of fine projections leaving the base of the brain; these are known as cranial nerves and will be discussed further below.

The spinal cord

The spinal cord is a tube-shaped structure that runs from the base of the brain down through a series of bony rings known as vertebrae. The string-like projections mentioned earlier, technically known as spinal nerves, can be seen leaving the spinal cord and exiting via gaps between the vertebrae. For this reason the tube becomes progressively narrower the further away from the brain we look at it.

Peripheral nervous system (PNS)

It has been recognised for many years that there are long, fine structures emanating from the brain and spinal cord. The cranial/spinal nerves are collections of individual neuronal cells bundled together and as they travel away from the CNS they give rise to the extensive network of neural cells that travel to the extremities, allowing the CNS to communicate with the various

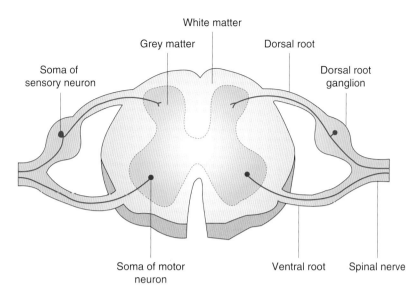

Figure 1.6   Spinal cord with spinal nerves carrying neurons entering or leaving the spinal cord

Based on Dr Jennifer Tobin's illustration for the Accelerated Cure Project at www.acceleratedcure.org/msresources/neuroanatomy

organs and tissues all over the body. It is important to recognise that this information flows in both directions, that is, both towards and away from the CNS. As a general rule, where information is flowing towards the CNS we term this **afferent** or sensory activity. Sensory information can be in many forms: some we are consciously aware of such as vision, smell or hearing; others, which are perhaps less familiar such as pH (level of acidity) or degree of skeletal muscle tension, we are not generally conscious of. Where information is flowing away from the CNS we term this **efferent** or secretomotor activity. The efferent nerves of the PNS are generally further categorised as belonging to the somatic nervous system or the autonomic nervous system.

Somatic nervous system

The somatic nervous system controls the skeletal muscles of the body, that is, those muscles which are attached to the skeleton and allow us to move our bodies in space. This includes both large-scale movements, for example when we walk across a room, to fine, delicate movements such as texting on a mobile phone. In Chapter 6 we will see how different parts of the brain control movements. The somatic nervous system is sometimes called the voluntary nervous system because we associate it with making choice, such as deciding to pick up a pen. However, this is a misnomer because it gives the impression that we *always* control its activity consciously; when you do walk across a room you do not have to think about which of your muscles needs to work or the sequence that they work in; this can all occur subconsciously.

Autonomic nervous system

The autonomic nervous system (ANS) is so-named because it was originally believed that it was entirely independent from the brain. We now know that this is not the case and that, like the rest of the peripheral nervous system, the activity of the ANS is ultimately controlled by the brain. In contrast to the somatic nervous system, the ANS innervates the cardiac muscle of the heart, smooth muscle and glandular tissue. Smooth muscle is found, for example, in the walls of the digestive tract and blood vessels. The ANS is sometimes termed the involuntary system, implying that its actions all occur subconsciously, but this is a misnomer too because there is mounting evidence to suggest that we can have a small degree of conscious influence over autonomic activity. The ANS is further divided into three divisions: sympathetic, parasympathetic and enteric nervous systems.

The sympathetic (SNS) and parasympathetic nervous systems act in conjunction; in general terms we can consider that they have opposing actions on the smooth/cardiac muscle and glands that they innervate. So, for example, whilst the sympathetic increases heart rate, the parasympathetic decreases it. This is, however, a gross over-simplification and there are examples where tissues are only affected by one or the other, e.g. the sweat glands are only innervated by the SNS.

The enteric nervous system (ENS), as the name suggests, is involved in the control of the digestive tract and associated structures. Although this seems far removed from the goal of understanding the role of the brain in human behaviour, the ENS is, in fact, a useful research tool. The complexity of the functioning and interactions of the cells that we find in the ENS has resulted in it being termed the 'little brain' and it has acted as a useful model for studying brain function at the cellular and network level.

These three interacting autonomic systems allow the state of physiological homeostasis – where the internal environment is stable and appropriate for the conditions that the body finds itself in. Clearly, if there is any dysfunction in the parts of the brain that control ANS activity, this may cause symptoms in the periphery that a patient is aware of. Although this may seem like a long way from the focus of this book, many psychological disorders include changes to ANS function. So, for example, a patient who has an anxiety disorder (see Chapter 9) may report a variety of diverse symptoms but these might include evidence of an increase in sympathetic activity such as an increase in heart rate (often described as palpitations) and changes in gut function.

KEY POINTS

- The brain is part of the central nervous system and coordinates body-wide activity via the peripheral nervous system.
- The brain isn't homogeneous structurally but has distinct parts, of which one, the cerebrum, can be divided up into regions known as lobes.

CELLS OF THE NERVOUS SYSTEM

Before going on to consider how the nervous system actually works we need to consider what it is made of. Only relatively recently in the mid-19th century was it recognised and accepted that the brain was a conglomerate of individual cellular elements. The pivotal work was conducted by the histologist Ramon y Cajal, whose original drawings are readily recognisable as neurons, and the importance of his work was recognised by the award of a Nobel prize (see Figure 1.7b for an example of his work).

Our current understanding is that, like any other structure in the human body, the entire nervous system is made up of cells, that is, self-contained units of biological activity. Clearly, cells which belong in different organs and tissues perform different functions and therefore have to be specialised to have different properties; we wouldn't expect a cell in the brain to behave in the same way as a cell in the liver. Within the mammalian nervous system we can find two basic types of cells known as neurons and glia. Both of these cell types are microscopic, being only perhaps 10–20 micrometres in diameter. Immediately this tells us that the human brain must be made up of billions of these cells. Estimating the number of neurons contained within the normal brain of the modern human is technically very difficult and attempts over the years have produced widely different values. However, a relatively recent attempt suggests that there is something in the order of 10^{11}. Estimates for the total number of glia and the glia to neuron ratio have been even more controversial, with values for the latter ranging from 1:1 to 10:1 (Azevedo et al., 2009). Furthermore, we need to take into account at what stage in the brain's life we are making these estimates. For many years the dogma was that the number of neurons an individual had at birth was the maximum number they could ever have. However, as we shall see in Chapter 3, current evidence suggests the adult brain retains some capacity for producing new neurons.

Neurons

These are generally considered to be the critical cell type as they are the computational units that process information and initiate a response. When looked at individually, the striking feature is their intricate cellular structure. If we look in different parts of the human nervous system, or even different regions of the brain, we can see that, although there are subtle variations in this cellular structure, all neurons appear to have the same structural elements. Furthermore, if we look at the nervous systems of other organisms, neurons are clearly identifiable. Evolutionary principles tell us that the persistence of this basic structure must be important for function. Figure 1.7a below shows a cartoon representation of the common structural features of the typical neuron.

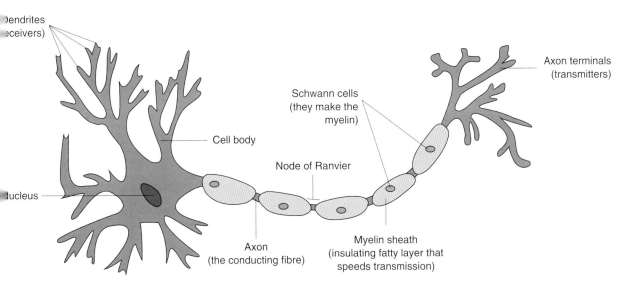

Figure 1.7a   The traditional representation of a neuron

Source: Quasar Jarosz/Wikimedia Commons

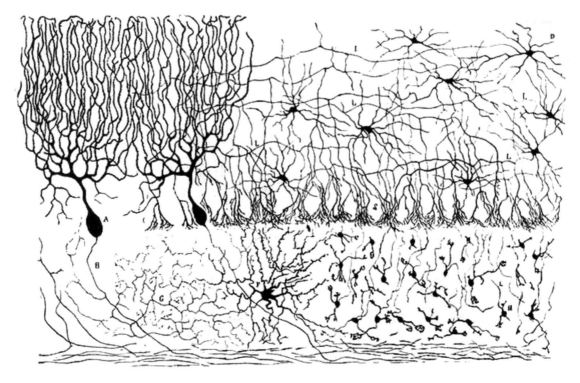

b. Drawing of brain neurons by Cajal

Figure 1.7   The structure of the neuron

In common with most cell types, neurons contain the DNA of the individual, enveloped in a nucleus. The region of neurons where the nucleus is found is known as the cell body or **soma** (plural: somata) and it also contains various components required for basic cell maintenance such as protein production. Projecting from the soma are a variable number of thin processes known as **dendrites** and **axons**.

The dendrites get their name from their tree-like appearance. Close inspection of dendrites shows that they are covered in minute projections that are known as dendritic spines. This means that the membrane area of the dendritic tree for any one neuron is very large and must have functional significance. We now know that the dendrites and their spines act like aerials receiving incoming information. The extent of the dendritic tree can vary enormously between neurons in different parts of the human nervous system and this reflects the volume of information that those neurons receive and process. The Purkinje cells of the cerebellum (Figure 1.8). The information flows along the dendrites in the form of small electrical signals to the soma where all the incoming signals are integrated.

The term 'dendritic tree', coupled with the static drawings of textbooks, gives the impression that dendrites and their spines are permanent structures with fixed morphology. In fact, a large body of evidence suggests that dendritic trees, and in particular the dendritic spines, are dynamic and undergoing remodelling throughout the lifespan of the organism; a feature that enables them to contribute to the functional adaptability of individual neurons that ultimately underlies behavioural adaptation of the whole individual (Trachtenberg et al., 2002).

The result of the computational activity in the soma in response to the incoming information from the dendrites leaves the soma via the axon. Mammalian neurons possess a single axon although this may branch to communicate with multiple regions of the nervous system. Axons, although extremely small in cross-sectional area, can be very long. In the human peripheral nervous system the longest axons belong to neurons that run in the sciatic nerves. These neurons have somata which lie at the base of the spinal cord and axons that project all the way to the ends of the toes. Clearly, this is not the limit of axonal length since in larger mammals such as giraffes and whales there are axons that are even longer. The information that travels along axons is in the form of electrical signals which are self-regenerating, thus allowing faithful communication over long distances. At the ends of the axons are the appropriately named synaptic terminals – once the electrical signals reach here, they can trigger the release of chemical substances known as **neurotransmitters**. These allow one neuron to communicate with other neurons to form a network.

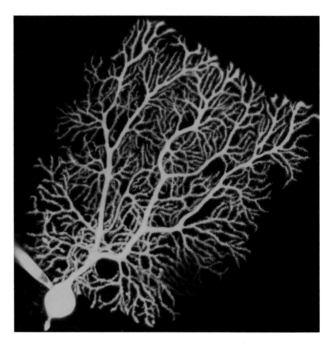

Figure 1.8 Purkinje neuron of the cerebellum with a massive dendritic tree

Source: Testuya Tatsukawa, RIKEN, Unearthing the pathways of plasticity, *RIKEN Research*

| Day 1 | Day 2 | Day 3 | Day 4 | Day 5 | Day 6 | Day 7 | Day 8 |

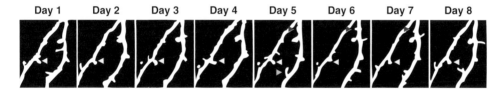

Figure 1.9 Experimental work monitoring dendritic form has demonstrated that dendritic morphology can change over time

Source: Trachtenberg et al. (2002)

In both the peripheral and central nervous systems, axons often travel bundled together. In the periphery these are the spinal and cranial nerves mentioned previously. In the CNS these bundles are named **tracts** and are visible within the substance of the brain and spinal cord. If, for example, the brain is cut coronally, that is, perpendicularly to the midline that runs from front to back, then we can discern internal structure, as shown in Figure 1.10. This internal structure appears as lighter and darker regions which were termed white and grey matter by the anatomists centuries ago.

Closer microscopic inspection reveals that grey matter is made up mostly of somata, dendrites and terminals, whereas white matter is made up of axons. The lighter colour of white matter occurs because many of the axons of the CNS are wrapped in a pale-coloured lipid substance called **myelin** which is produced by a type of glial cell.

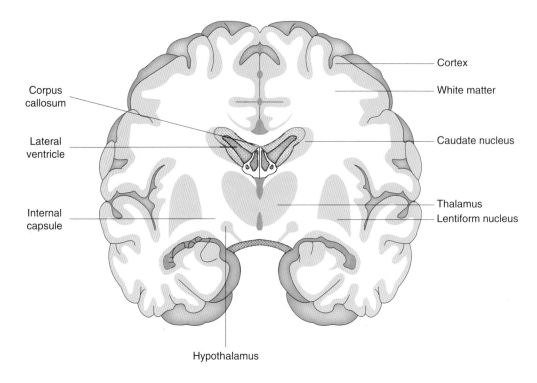

Cortex

White matter

Corpus callosum

Lateral ventricle

Caudate nucleus

Internal capsule

Thalamus
Lentiform nucleus

Hypothalamus

Figure 1.10   Coronal section through the brain showing white and grey matter

Glia

The brief introduction to neurons given might suggest that all that was needed for a functioning nervous system was an interconnected set of neurons. However, histological study of both CNS and PNS suggests that there are other cells present which collectively are known as glia or neuroglia (from the Greek for 'glue'). This collective term is convenient but does not convey the diversity of functions that have been attributed to these cells. The major types of glia found in the human brain are oligodendrocytes, astrocytes and microglia.

FOCUS ON METHODS: HISTOLOGY

Histology is the study of body tissues at the microscopic level. Neural tissue, such as that of the brain, is sliced extremely thinly to allow visible light or a beam of electrons to pass through it. Usually it is also necessary to treat the tissues with chemicals so that particular cell types or features of the cells are visible. This technique allows us to observe the unique structural features of individual neurons. We can also examine the relationships between neurons, which can help us to work out how regions of the brain are connected together to form circuits. To do this we may have to use a tract-tracing technique where we inject a dye-like substance into one region of the brain that can be transported via the axons to other regions. When we use histological techniques, we can work out how one region is connected to another.

Originally it was considered that glia had a rather passive role, providing physical and metabolic support to the neurons. However, in recent years it has been recognised that the glia play a more important role than had previously been realised in enabling normal neuronal activity. Consequently, they are sometimes now implicated in disease and disorder of the nervous system, as both a cause of neuronal dysfunction and also a target for therapeutic intervention.

Oligodendrocytes have a critical role in enabling axons to faithfully and rapidly transmit electrical signals. It is these cells that produce the myelin that gives the white matter its colour. In the peripheral nervous system a similar job is performed by the Schwann cells. The oligodendrocytes and Schwann cells wrap themselves around the axon resulting in a sheath which is formed of multiple layers of cell membrane.

Cell membrane is made of a kind of lipid and as such is electrically insulating. As a consequence the electrical signals that travel down the axons are forced to jump between regions of axons which are not ensheathed by myelin, known as nodes of Ranvier, as illustrated in Figure 1.7a.

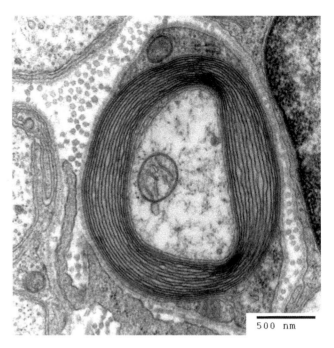

500 nm

Figure 1.11 Electronmicrograph of transverse section through a myelinated axon showing the multiple layers of the glial cell membrane wrapped around the central axon

Source: Roadnottaken, Wikimedia Commons

Astrocytes are large cells and, as the name suggests, are star-shaped. They perform a number of functions depending upon where they are located. Some are found closely associated with blood capillaries forming the blood–brain barrier. As the name suggests, these astrocytes serve to limit the exchange of substances between the blood and the brain. This is beneficial in relation to, for example, excluding toxic substances from the brain but is actually a hindrance in relation to access of therapeutic drugs into the brain. Other astrocytes are found in amongst the somata of neurons and it is these that probably perform the newly recognised functions mentioned above. For example, it is believed that these cells can help to regulate the concentrations of ions, known to be important for electrical signalling and even to regulate the extracellular concentration of chemical substances used to signal between neurons – an idea we shall come back to later in this chapter.

Microglia are very small cells found throughout the brain and are mostly inactive. However, they can become activated if the brain is damaged or infectious organisms are present, when they release substances that may help with repair processes and act as scavengers phagocytosing cell debris.

KEY POINTS

- The brain contains two types of cell, with differing functions: neurons and glia.
- The cellular structure of neurons has evolved to optimise integration of information and communication with other cells.

BUILDING A BRAIN

Communication and neuronal networks

Our current understanding allows us to conclude that the neurons of the human brain are highly specialised, having the structural features that enable them to perform a computational function, ably supported by the glia. However, what is clear from the estimates of the numbers of cells present in the human brain is that for these cells to function effectively they must be organised in a highly coordinated way as networks of neurons which contribute to controlling the same function. This simple statement may lead us to believe that the more neurons that we have the smarter we would be. However, there are organisms with larger (by volume) brains than humans. The sperm whale, for example, has a brain that weighs 8kg; does this mean that it is more than four times smarter than us? As there is no evidence to support this we must find an alternative index for what determines 'smartness'. If we remember back to the diagram of the coronal section through the brain (Figure 1.10), we noted the white matter tracts that contained the axons and therefore represented the paths of communication between neurons. Measurement of the ratio of grey to white matter in the brains of a range of species suggests that humans have a much higher proportion of white matter than other species. Thus, the ability of our neurons to communicate extensively with each other, coupled with the ability at a cellular level for the intimate connections between neurons to subtly change, allows the human brain to be constantly adapting to our environment, for example learning a new skill. However, sometimes this ability to adapt leads to dysfunction and it does leave open the possibility of exogenous substances, i.e. drugs, being able to alter brain function, although, of course, this includes therapeutic as well as illegal drugs.

Structure: Function relationship

It has long been recognised that damage to the human brain results in a change to the way the individual functions. Even early studies of the human brain, where only correlation between the region damaged and the effect on the individual could be observed, suggested that there was consistency of location of function between different individuals' brains. We now have far more sophisticated and expensive imaging equipment that allows us to observe the living brain in action, but in general, the conclusion is the same: some functions appear to be localised to particular parts of the brain in all humans. The combined efforts of thousands of studies has allowed us to produce functional maps of the human brain, such as that illustrated in Figure 1.12. In subsequent chapters you will meet some of these regions in detail and the functions that they appear to perform, for example Chapter 6 which looks at motor control and the role that various brain regions have in controlling it.

The production of functional maps leads us to be able to make a number of predictions which, in some cases, can be useful both medically and scientifically. So, for example, if we see someone with a functional change we might be able to predict where we may see pathological change in their brain. Conversely, if someone is subject to, for example, traumatic brain injury, we may be able to predict what changes in function they might experience thereafter.

However, whilst it would be tempting to think that we have the entire brain 'mapped out' functionally, this is far from the truth. The reality is that this map primarily holds true for overtly observable or describable functions such as an ability to move a leg or hear basic sounds. However,

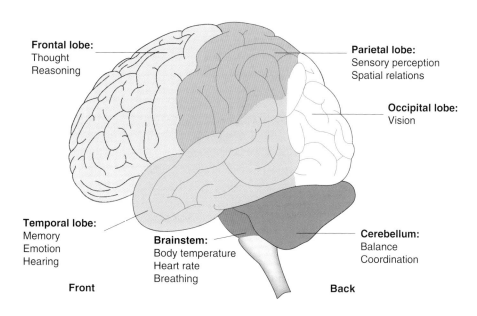

Frontal lobe:
Thought
Reasoning

Parietal lobe:
Sensory perception
Spatial relations

Occipital lobe:
Vision

Temporal lobe:
Memory
Emotion
Hearing

Brainstem:
Body temperature
Heart rate
Breathing

Cerebellum:
Balance
Coordination

Front

Back

Figure 1.12 Lateral view of the brain showing areas that have been associated with particular functions

it is not the case that in all situations where we see functional change do we see gross structural change that is reproducible in all patients; for example, in clinical depression (Chapter 9) we cannot observe gross pathology in the same brain region in all individuals. Furthermore, and rather intriguingly, there are individuals who can have structural abnormalities identifiable through imaging studies of their brains but yet do not appear to have obvious functional changes. This latter observation has lead to such scientific myths as 'Humans only need a minority percentage of their brain to function'. Clearly, evolutionary principles tell us that this can't be the case; we simply would not be able to justify the resources to produce masses of brain tissue that had no use. In fact, as we study human behaviour in ever-more detail it is becoming clear that some regions are responsible for rather more subtle functions such as an ability to take a two-dimensional image and 'see' it as three dimensional, which, of course, would be less obvious to a casual observer than, say, the ability to see at all. What is also becoming clear is that for some functions, including learning and memory (Chapter 4), a large number of brain regions are involved such that the function could be said to be distributed across the brain, rather than localised within it.

Electrical conduction

All cells in the human body use a variety of intracellular chemical molecules as signalling systems to ensure that the cells' activities are coordinated. Neurons are no different, but they face an additional problem in that they may extend over relatively large distances. The observation that thin wire-like structures ran all over the body, coupled to the observation that electricity appeared to be able to influence muscle activity, was recognised some time ago at the end of the 18th century by Galvani who coined the term 'animal electricity'. This led to the suggestion that these wire-like structures might act like cables to convey electrical signals around the body.

INSIGHT: HISTORICAL PERSPECTIVE ON RESEARCH IN NEUROSCIENCE

Luigi Galvani is generally credited as the first person to recognise that electricity could influence biology. Working in Italy at the end of the 18th century, he observed that the muscles of a dead frog could be made to twitch if electrical current was made to flow through them. Although his initial assumptions about how this 'animal electricity' was being generated were incorrect, this eventually led to the concept of electrophysiology, the study of which is still prevalent today in helping us understand the activity of the brain. Furthermore, Galvani's observations are also important in the underpinnings of the physics of electricity; he is revered by the physics and electrical engineering community as the work on frogs led ultimately to the production of batteries.

As the nervous system evolved to enable communication between cells and thus support the increase in size of multicellular organisms, a means of enabling signals to pass throughout a single neuron relatively rapidly was required. Thus the property of electrical excitability evolved, peculiar to neurons and muscle cells.

FOCUS ON METHODS: ELECTROPHYSIOLOGY

Electrophysiology involves the electrical recording of neurons. Electrophysiology can be carried out in the intact brain (*in vivo*) or in slices of an extracted brain (*in vitro*). One or more electrodes are inserted into the brain tissue to record the electrical activity generated by action potentials. Using a single recording electrode, a field potential can be recorded that reflects the overall activity generated by the neurons in the area. Alternatively, a tetrode can be used that consists of four intertwined electrodes of very slightly different lengths. By comparing the response recorded in each electrode, the activity of single neurons can be deduced. While electrophysiology is most commonly used in experimental animals, it is also employed in some clinical populations (e.g. epileptic patients).

Resting membrane potential

All cells in the human body exhibit basic electrical properties. Our understanding of the bio-physical properties of cells that bring these about and their functional significance is now very advanced. A detailed description is beyond the scope of this text but a simplified explanation will enable the key features relevant to neuronal function to be understood. This is useful because it will allow us to make predictions about how pathological processes or exogenous drugs may affect brain function and thus behaviour.

We shall start by considering how these basic electrical properties come about in *all* human cells before discussion of the special case of excitable cells. Cells are bounded by a structure known as a cell membrane formed of various lipid-like substances and, for this reason, often described as the phospholipid bilayer. The phospholipid bilayer can be considered as a sack which contains liquid known as cytosol or cytoplasm which contains a wide range of signalling molecules. In addition, the sack contains some larger structures such as the nucleus and other specialised structures known as organelles whose functions are vital for cells to be considered alive, for example the nucleus, which contains DNA and the mitochondria which produce the energy to drive cell processes. Clearly there is an advantage in packaging these cell contents up as it means that molecules and structures can interact more easily. However a major disadvantage of this arrangement is that the phospholipid bilayer forms a physical barrier to the essential movement of substances in and out of the cell; for example oxygen and glucose need to move in and waste products need to move out. The passage of these substances requires the presence of specific proteins which span the bilayer. One type of these proteins, called transporters, bind to substances and physically translocate them across the membrane. The other type is known as channels, which form pores allowing continuous contact between the extra- and intracellular environments.

One consequence of this arrangement is that large proteins, which act as anions as they carry a negative electrical charge, are 'trapped' within the cytosol. This has physiological consequences because both the extracellular environment and the cytosol contain other charged entities, namely ions such as Na^+, K^+ and Cl^-. However, the concentrations of these ions differ between the extra- and intracellular environments because of the continuous activity of the transporters. The most important transporter in this case is the Na^+K^+-ATPase, the activity of which produces a higher concentration of Na^+ outside cells than in and the opposite situation for K^+. This concentration difference means that these ions will continuously tend to move down their concentration gradients through ion channels, known as leak channels, which are highly permeable to K^+. This set-up is illustrated in Figure 1.13. We might expect that, eventually, a point would be reached whereby the movement of the ions due to the activity of the Na^+K^+-ATPase pumping ions in one direction

Outside neuron

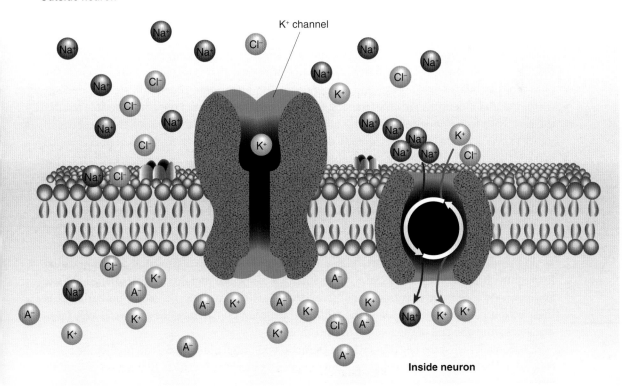

Inside neuron

Figure 1.13   A representation of the neuronal cell membrane with a K^+ channel and the Na^+K^+-ATPase

Adapted from Garrett (2011)

would be matched by their movement through the channels in the other. However, what also has to be taken into account is that these ions are charged and so there will be an interaction with the negatively charged proteins inside the cells mentioned above. The effect of this interaction with K^+ ions is of particular note since it forms the basis of the resting membrane potential measurable in all cells of the body. The forces acting on K^+ are acting in opposite directions; whilst the higher concentration of K^+ intracellularly compared to extracellularly tends to favour movement of K^+ out of the cell (known as efflux), the electrical attraction between the K^+ and the negatively charged proteins inside the cell opposes the K^+ efflux. At some point these forces balance each other out such that there is no net movement of K^+ ions across the bilayer. At this point the distribution of the charged entities means that there is an electrical potential difference across the bilayer such that the inside is negative relative to the outside. We can measure this potential difference which has a value of about −80mV. For many cells in the human body this is exactly the situation that we see. However, for excitable cells the situation is a little more complicated.

Action potential

A key difference between cells which are electrically active like neurons and those that are not is that the former are able to alter their membrane potential. To understand what it means for neurons to be electrically active, we have to consider what these cells contain that electrically *in*active cells do not.

The first difference is that, for neurons, the resting membrane potential is determined by the movement of Na^+ as well as K^+. At rest, leak channels have some permeability to Na^+ (though not as great as for K^+). Remember that the concentration of Na^+ is higher outside than inside cells, so Na^+ will tend to enter down its concentration gradient and will also be electrically attracted to the inside of the cell by the negatively charged proteins. The overall effect is that the point at which the movement of Na^+ and K^+ are balanced results in a less negative resting membrane potential compared to non-excitable cells of about −65mV.

A key feature of excitable cells like neurons is their ability to change their membrane potential. Clearly, even from the brief description above, it is clear that the ability of ions to cross the phospholipid bilayer has a profound influence on the membrane potential. We can deduce, therefore, that if neurons are able to change their membrane potential they must be able to alter the ease with which ions can cross the bilayer and, as we know, this requires the presence of ion channels. The leak channels already discussed were portrayed as fixed, open pores, which is inconsistent with the idea that the neuronal membrane potential can change. Thus, the special ion channels that neurons possess must have the key property that they can be opened and closed in a highly controlled way.

We now know that there are a large number of ion channels which can be opened in response to particular conditions, such as the value of the membrane potential or the binding of another signalling molecule to the protein complex that forms the ion channel. Those that are sensitive to membrane potential, in particular a voltage-gated sodium channel and a voltage-gated potassium channel, are the critical components that allow the membrane potential to change and generate a self-perpetuating signal in excitable cells known as the action potential. It is these action potentials which allow the faithful transmission of a message over relatively large distances from one end of the neuron to the other.

If we consider what the key properties of the action potential must be, we can predict the properties that the neurons and its channels must possess. Clearly, it is critical that action potentials are generally only produced when the neurons have been excited. Thus, a mechanism needs to be in place to minimise the occurrence of random action potentials. The voltage-dependency of the chances of the Na$^+$ and K$^+$ channels opening is key here since it means that the channels will only rarely open randomly. The membrane potential at which the channels open is more positive than that of the resting membrane potential (remember: about −65mV) and movement in this less negative direction is known as depolarisation. Once this potential is reached and the channels start to open, the ion flux through them will contribute to changes in membrane potential which promote further channel opening. Clearly a point will be reached when the number of ion channels open and the consequent ion flux is such that the system becomes self-sustaining; this point is termed the threshold potential and once it is reached an action potential will occur. Hence, action potentials are often described as being all-or-none since if the threshold is not reached then this self-sustaining point is not reached and no action potentials will occur, whereas if it *is* reached then action potentials *will* occur. Our current knowledge of the precise role that individual types of voltage-gated channels play in underpinning the action potential is now very detailed. For the purposes of this text, it will suffice to know that the depolarising phase in neurons can be attributed to the opening of voltage-gated Na$^+$ channels. If we record membrane potential during an action potential, we can see that the depolarising phase is immediately followed by a repolarising phase when the membrane potential returns to a more negative state, ultimately attaining the resting membrane potential. Detailed analysis has shown that this repolarising phase occurs as a result of the closing of the voltage-gated Na$^+$ channels coupled to the opening of voltage-gated K$^+$ channels. This process is shown diagrammatically in Figure 1.14.

The diagram shows how the membrane potential (Vm) changes with time. From the initial resting potential, the membrane depolarises before repolarising and eventually returning to the resting value.

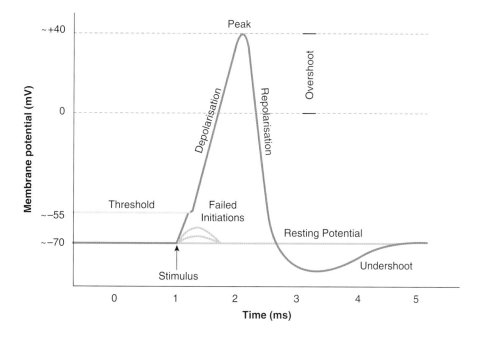

Figure 1.14   The action potential

Source: Chris 73 and Diberri, Wikimedia Commons

The self-sustaining nature of action potentials means that, once one has been triggered and starts to travel along the axon, it will depolarise the region of axon in front of it, initiating the same regenerative process as before. In this way, action potentials can travel along the whole length of axons without any need for any kind of 'boosting' or amplification process.

Histological examination of nervous tissue in which axons can clearly be seen, for example in the white matter tracts of the brain, also frequently shows that axons are enveloped by the processes of other cells. These cells are the glial subtype known as oligodendrocytes that were covered earlier in this chapter. The function of these glia is to increase the speed at which action potentials can travel along axons – clearly an important property for allowing the very rapid transmission of electrical signals.

At this point it may be reasonable to ask the question: 'What causes the initial depolarisation that allows the membrane to come to threshold in the first place?' The easiest example for this is to consider the role that sensory receptors play. We have already considered that information needs to get into the brain from the environment and that sensory afferent neurons are the conduit for this information. Environmental stimuli are very diverse in nature and might be, for example, touch on the skin or the pattern of light falling on the retina. Clearly a means of encoding this diverse information into a language that the nervous system can process is needed. A whole variety of processes have evolved which enable the conversion of the stimuli into electrical signals, a process known as signal transduction, and more details on this will be found in the later chapters that consider the specifics of these sensory processes. However, for now it is sufficient to recognise that signal transduction processes all share the property that the stimuli can produce graded changes in the membrane potentials of specialised sensory cells. The strength of the stimulus, i.e. whether a touch is gentle or hard, is encoded by the size of the graded potential; clearly if this graded potential is sufficiently large that the membrane potential of the neuron reaches threshold then action potentials can be produced and the regenerative process described above can carry this information from the periphery to the central nervous system. Furthermore, if the stimulus is very large, then the membrane of the sensory receptor will depolarise well beyond the threshold potential. A common misconception is that this would somehow lead to larger action potentials but in fact this is not biologically possible because action potentials are all-or-none. Instead, it is the *number* of action potentials that changes with stimulus intensity such that a larger number of action potentials would be produced. This is the concept of frequency coding whereby the number of action potentials produced is directly related to the strength of the stimulus: the stronger the stimulus the higher the frequency of action potentials.

Whilst this example provides a neat explanation of how action potentials can be generated by stimuli originating outside of the body, there must be an alternative explanation that explains how, for example, neurons deep within the brain which are not directly connected to sensory cells can be depolarised. To understand this process we need to consider the process by which one neuron can communicate with another.

Chemical conduction at the synapse

At the start of this chapter, when the basic cellular structure of neurons was discussed, we saw that axons end in structures named synaptic terminals. Hence, if we can understand what happens once action potentials arrive at these terminals we will have an understanding of how one neuron can talk to another.

Structure of the synapse

If we look at brain tissue with an electron microscope that can visualise subcellular structures, we can observe that axon terminals exist in very close proximity to dendrites (described earlier in the chapter). The term **synapse** is used to describe the whole of this structural arrangement, comprising the cell providing the information and the cell receiving it (see Figure 1.15). In fact, the 'input' and 'output' cells are named according to their position relative to the synapse. Hence, the cell bringing the information to the synapse, and which the terminals are part of, is termed the *presynaptic* cell; the one that receives the information and acts as the output from the synapse is known as the *postsynaptic* cell. It is important to remind ourselves that postsynaptic cells may be neurons, the arrangement found in the brain, but may be other cell types such as skeletal or smooth muscle as we find in the rest of the body.

The description above may give us the impression that the number of synapses between neurons in the brain is limited and even just a one-to-one arrangement. In fact, any single neuron will make hundreds if not thousands of connections with other neurons which means that a postsynaptic neuron is 'computing' all of its inputs to determine its own activity; it is this property that gives the human brain its incredible computational power.

If we study the structure of synapses we see that they have some reproducible features. Within each of the terminals a large number of membrane-bound vesicles can be seen and, under certain circumstances, these vesicles appear to fuse with the main plasma membrane. We now know that

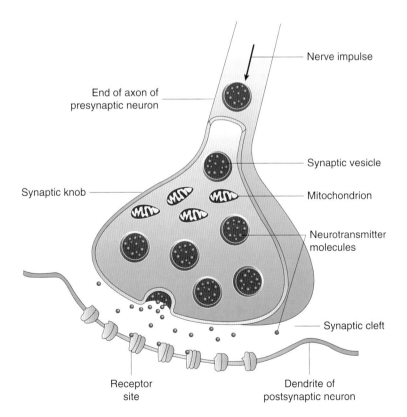

Figure 1.15   The key structures of the synapse

Source: Barnes (2013)

these vesicles contain chemical substances which can be released into the extracellular environ-ment when vesicle fusion with the cell membrane occurs. The chemical substances that can be released in this way are chemically rather diverse and so are collectively known as neurotransmit-ters to reflect their function. Historically, there were two types of chemical substances defined, neurotransmitters and neuromodulators, which had subtle differences in the effects they had on the postsynaptic cells. Increasingly the complexity of this chemical signalling process means that this distinction in definition is becoming less useful. Later in this chapter, where specific examples of neurotransmitters are discussed, this subtle distinction between neuromodulators and neurotransmitters will be highlighted. However, for the purposes of the following section, the term neurotransmitter will be used to keep it simple. Intuitively we might expect that the released neurotransmitters will be able to act as message carriers from one neuron to the next (neuron or other cell). It also follows, therefore, that the distance between cells across which these neurotransmitters need to travel should be very small to optimise the efficiency of this process. Indeed, using the electron microscope it has been estimated that the gap, known as the synaptic cleft, is in the order of 20nm, which, to put it in context, is smaller than the estimated diameter of the virus responsible for the common cold.

Postsynaptic events

Release of the neurotransmitter into the narrow synaptic cleft is of little consequence unless the postsynaptic cell can detect the presence of the neurotransmitter and initiate appropriate responses within the cell. Furthermore, the existence of multiple neurotransmitters suggests a degree of specificity; that is, that the postsynaptic cell should only respond to particular mes-sages and not *all* neurotransmitters released by any presynaptic cell in the vicinity. This spe-cificity is brought about by the existence of receptors on the postsynaptic cell which are highly specific to a particular neurotransmitter. Receptors are large protein molecules which are usu-ally embedded within the phospholipid bilayer. These proteins have a highly developed struc-ture to mean that they can only interact with molecules (neurotransmitters in this case) of a particular shape. This is somewhat analogous to the concept of locks and keys: whilst keys look essentially the same, their unique structure means that they only fit one particular lock. As a consequence postsynaptic cells are only affected by the neurotransmitters for which they have the relevant receptors.

So, assuming we have a synapse at which the presynaptic cell releases a particular neuro-transmitter and the postsynaptic cell has the relevant receptors, what happens next? In fact there isn't one answer to this and we are still discovering new ways in which neurotransmitters can affect postsynaptic cells. However, for the purposes of this textbook there are two key post-synaptic effects that it will be useful for you to understand. We will consider these in general before moving on to some actual examples of neurotransmitters, their receptors and the post-synaptic consequences of the two coming together.

First, binding of the neurotransmitter to its receptors may result in a change in the protein structure of the receptor which allows the temporary opening of an ion channel. This type of receptor is classified as ionotropic or a ligand-gated ion channel. As we saw earlier, allowing ions to move in and/or out of neurons has a profound effect on the membrane potential, and this may be sufficient to bring the membrane potential of the postsynaptic cell to threshold and hence the cell may fire action potentials. Neurotransmitters that have this effect on postsyn-aptic cells are termed *excitatory*. However, it is important to recognise at this point that the membrane potential need not become *less* negative and therefore closer to threshold but may become *more* negative and further from threshold. This has the rather counter-intuitive effect of making the postsynaptic neuron less likely to fire; these neurotransmitters are thus termed *inhibitory*.

Alternatively, binding of the neurotransmitter to its receptor may again produce a change in the protein structure of the receptor but this time this affects an interaction between the receptor and an intracellular molecule known as a G protein. Consequently, this type of receptor is classified as a G-protein-coupled receptor, which is a type of metabotropic receptor. There are many types of G protein but the common feature of receptor-G protein interaction is initiation of an intracellular signalling cascade that can result in changes in a diverse range of processes. For example, this may ultimately result in short-term effects on ion channels which can affect the membrane potential of the postsynaptic cell, affecting its excitability. Alternatively, G protein activation may result in longer-term cellular changes including protein synthesis in the postsynaptic cell.

In practice it is common for any one neurotransmitter to have more than one receptor type that it can bind to. The importance of this is that the individual receptor types can have different functions. Thus a single neurotransmitter may bring about quite different effects on target neurons depending upon which subtypes of receptor those target cells possess. To distinguish these receptor types, they are usually named according to substances other than the main neurotransmitter, which each bind exclusively to a subset of a neurotransmitter's receptors. Examples of this are given below when individual neurotransmitters are considered.

Synaptic transmission: The reality

Although the account given above covers the basic process of neurotransmission at the synapse, it is far from complete. We are now aware of a number of instances, particularly in the brain, where these basic processes are not sufficient to explain what we can observe about brain activity in health and/or disease. Some key examples of this additional complexity will be covered next, though this is by no means the full story.

Molecular diversity of neurotransmitter receptors

We have already seen that a single neurotransmitter may interact with more than one type of receptor. However, with the advent of advanced molecular biology techniques it has become clear that a receptor may actually be formed of individual subunits and that the subunit composition of receptor complexes can vary. Thus the potential molecular diversity of receptors that a single type of neurotransmitter can bind to is large. Whilst this may explain subtle differences in function of neurotransmitters in different brain regions in the normal state, it is of particular interest in relation to the development of therapeutic drugs since this opens the possibility of producing drugs that are highly selective for receptors of particular subunit composition. Clearly, targeting drugs so specifically should help to minimise unwanted effects at non-targeted sites throughout the brain, or even the periphery. A good example of this is seen for the benzodiazepine class of drugs that have some therapeutic use for anxiety disorders, as will be discussed in the chapter on psychological disorders (Chapter 9).

Retrograde signalling

In the simple description of synaptic transmission given above, there was a unidirectional flow of information from the pre- to the postsynaptic cell. It is now clear that this is not necessarily the case and that the presynaptic terminals are not just releasers of neurotransmitters but have a more integrated role in synaptic function. Two examples of the additional role that the presynaptic terminals play will be considered.

We now know that there are neurotransmitter receptors present presynaptically as well as postsynaptically. Functionally, this means that a neurotransmitter can influence the level of its own release through a negative feedback process. A particularly good example of this is the neurotransmitter serotonin and the arrangement of its receptors, which we will meet below.

A more radical process involves the release of a substance from the postsynaptic cell which can act on the presynaptic cell and consequently change the activity of it. One of the first to be discovered was nitric oxide (NO). Production of NO by the postsynaptic cell can be induced following activation of a subtype of glutamate receptor, known as an NMDA receptor (discussed in more detail below), due to the resultant elevation in intracellular calcium levels. This process has been linked to long-term potentiation (LTP), a process which has been linked to learning (see Chapter 4) whereby patterns of activity at synapses result in changes in so-called synaptic strength through changes to both pre- and postsynaptic neurons. Whilst the molecular details are complex and not yet fully understood, part of the process of synaptic change involves NO diffusing from the postsynaptic neuron and acting on the presynaptic cell to ultimately result in changes in neurotransmitter release which, of course, then affects the level of activity in the postsynaptic neuron (Garthwaite, 2008).

The tripartite synapse

Earlier in this chapter, we saw that recent studies have indicated a more critical role for glia than the traditional view that they provide rather passive support. One of the lines of research

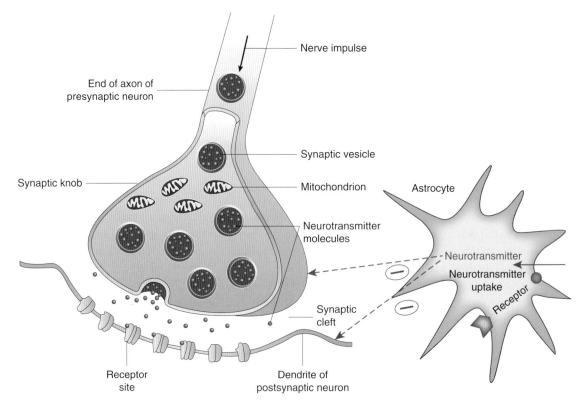

Figure 1.16   The tripartite synapse, showing the involvement of a glial cell with the pre- and postsynaptic cells

Adapted from Barnes (2013)

into neuronal–glial interaction has resulted in the proposal of the concept of the tripartite synapse, composed of the presynaptic terminal, the postsynaptic dendrite and glial cells, specifically astrocytes. One of the emerging findings from these studies is that the glia play a role in determining synaptic levels of neurotransmitter, since there is evidence that they can both take up and release transmitter substances, thus modulating the degree of synaptic transmission between the pre- and postsynaptic neurons. Clearly, therefore, glial dysfunction may result in inappropriate neurotransmission which may lead to functional and hence behavioural changes. Furthermore, the activity of glia may be a future therapeutic drug target.

Neurotransmitters and their receptors

In this section we are going to look at some specific examples of neurotransmitters and their receptors. This is by no means an exhaustive list, but it will act as a primer for later chapters where we will investigate the pathways that utilise specific neurotransmitters and the actions of these neurotransmitters and any drug which can interfere with their production, transmission or reception in more detail.

Traditionally neurotransmitters have been classified according to their chemical nature, e.g. if they are derivatives of amino acids. Whilst this tells us little about their function it does give us a way of grouping them systematically. In recent years a large number of substances have been proposed as neurotransmitters and this can sometimes raise controversy because it can be hard to prove that a substance found in many cell types has such a specific function in neurons. Indeed in many instances some aspect of the production, storage or control of the substance does not fit with our general and rather simplistic understanding of the process of neurotransmission. Furthermore, experimental studies began to show that whilst some substances clearly had a profound impact on driving neuronal activity, others only seemed to adjust it. To address this issue, the term neuromodulator was proposed. However, it is now clear that a definitive distinction between a neurotransmitter and a neuromodulator can't be made and so for this reason it is no longer possible to give a strict definition of what parameters are necessary for a substance to be classifiable as a neurotransmitter.

Amino acid derivatives

Glutamate and GABA are often described as the classical neurotransmitters because they are the best understood and their actions can be described as the prototype for our understanding of synaptic transmission in the brain.

Glutamate   Glutamate is the most abundant excitatory neurotransmitter in the human brain. Glutamate is actually a fairly abundant substance in all cell types, being derived from the amino acid glutamic acid and therefore a common cellular metabolic substance. However, in the brain it is packaged into presynaptic vesicles and released as a neurotransmitter into the synaptic cleft. As described above, it is able to interact with receptors, and these are found both post- and presynaptically. In fact, glutamate does not bind to a single type of receptor but to a family of receptors of both ionotropic and metabotropic types, and the evidence suggests that there are at least eight different receptors for glutamate.

Clearly a highly abundant neurotransmitter is going to have widespread effects on brain function and therefore influence behaviour. It is unsurprising, therefore, that disruptions in glutamate-based neurotransmission have been implicated in a variety of disorders of behaviour, some of which are covered in this text.

One of the most well known effects of glutamate is on the processes of learning and memory. Here, two types of ionotropic glutamate receptors are significantly involved: AMPA (α-amino-3-hydroxy-5-methyl-4-isoxazolepropionic acid) receptors which bind glutamate and AMPA, and NMDA (N-methyl-D-aspartate) receptors which bind glutamate and NMDA. The role that glutamate and its receptors play in learning and memory is considered in more detail in Chapter 4.

Glutamate dysfunction is also proposed to play a role in psychotic disorders such as schizophrenia. This is discussed in greater detail in Chapter 9 but of note is that the widespread nature of glutamate in the human brain means that it will be a challenge to produce drugs that alter glutamate transmission only within selective brain areas to, for example, improve psychotic symptoms but without affecting learning/memory.

Finally, in relation to human behaviour, it appears that glutamatergic transmission in particular has the potential to be influenced by glial activity, and a number of studies have suggested that glia may play a prominent role both in pathophysiology and as a therapeutic target for, for example, mood disorders; these are considered in Chapter 9 (Machado-Vieira et al., 2009)

GABA   GABA (gamma-aminobutyric acid) is the most abundant inhibitory neurotransmitter found in the human brain. As we saw above, the term inhibitory means that when it binds to its receptors it reduces the chances of the neuron firing. GABA is produced from glutamate by a specific enzyme family which is not universally expressed in all neurons. Like glutamate, GABA binds to multiple receptors of both the ionotropic (GABAA) and metabotropic (GABAB) types.

From a functional perspective it may at first seem counterintuitive that the human brain should have evolved to produce a substance that reduces the chances of neurons firing action potentials. However, as our understanding of how neurons link up to form circuits in the brain has developed, it has become clear that this is in fact a very useful function. This is because it enables activity within circuits to be self-limiting and also reduces the chance that 'random' firing of action potentials can set off a train of events in the brain which is, in fact, not required.

Functionally, like glutamate, the widespread nature of GABA within the brain means that the functions that it has been linked to are rather diverse. For example, in Chapter 9 the therapeutic use of drugs which target GABAergic neurotransmission for anxiety disorders implies that increasing the level of inhibition in the brain may be beneficial in these disorders.

Glycine   Glycine is an unusual substance in that it appears to have two quite distinct roles in the central nervous system. First, it can act as a neurotransmitter in its own right, its actions mirroring in the spinal cord that of GABA in the brain. Indeed its receptors are ionotropic and are functional equivalents of GABAA receptors. However, it also has a critical role to play as part of glutamatergic neurotransmission. In particular, it can be considered as a co-agonist for NMDA receptors which means that both glycine and glutamate are required to bind in order to activate the NMDA receptors. Thus it could be said that glycine can be seen as either an excitatory or inhibitory neurotransmitter depending upon the exact receptors that we are considering.

Monoamines

This group of neurotransmitters are grouped together because of a shared chemical composition. This group contains a number of substances of which serotonin and dopamine are examples to be met later in this book. The actions and functions of this group mark them out as distinctly different from the widespread glutamate and GABA. For example, they cannot easily be described as excitatory or inhibitory because they can have either action dependent upon the precise subtype of receptor they act upon or even whether the receptor is located pre- or postsynaptically. Most of the receptors for the monoamines are G-protein coupled, although there are a small number of exceptions to this. Furthermore, although the receptors for these neurotransmitters are widespread in the brain, if we look at the distribution of the neurons that produce these substances we see that it is usually a relatively small number of neurons, often grouped into distinct collections of similar cells and often located in the evolutionarily older parts of the brain. Functionally, the monoamines have particular interest in the context of behaviour in what we might consider as both normal and abnormal states. However, if we consider the postsynaptic neurons that contain monoaminergic receptors, we can see that, generally, these neurons also contain receptors for the more classical glutamate or GABA. This suggests that the main driver for determining the activity of these neurons is a classical neurotransmitter but that the monoamine can somehow either enhance or suppress this drive. It is for this reason that the term neuromodulator arose and was originally applied to neurotransmitters of this kind, although, as noted above, it is now recognised that this is too simplistic a view.

Dopamine   Dopamine has been implicated in a diverse range of actions. It was first associated with control of motor activity, and its role in determining the activity of the basal ganglia is considered in Chapter 6. However, a seemingly different function has been associated with it more recently, namely the processes associated with reward, and its relationship to addiction which will be addressed in more detail in Chapter 8. In parallel with motor control, the basal ganglia, albeit different subregions, are also implicated here and it would appear that the two different functions are mediated by dopamine-producing cells originating in different, though adjacent, parts of the brain.

Serotonin   Serotonin (alternatively termed 5-hydroxytryptamine or 5-HT) is found in neuronal terminals throughout the central nervous system even though the number of neurons that synthesise it is probably only in the order of a few hundred thousand in the adult human; functionally, this means that a relatively small number of neurons can have widespread influence on brain regions and, therefore, on a diverse range of functions. The number of serotonergic receptors and subtypes is also notably large with at least 13 being recognised. The location of these receptors appears to be inconsistent in the brain with some types being widespread but others only being found in a small number of locations. Furthermore, others have particular pre- or postsynaptic locations or occasionally both. Functionally, it is considered that serotonin has fundamental actions since it is found in the protobrains of rather primitive organisms and in anatomically equivalent places to humans. From a behavioural perspective it is interesting because of the long association it has had with psychological disorders such as depression and its treatment, and this is considered in more detail in Chapter 9.

Neuropeptides   There is an ever-growing list of neuropeptides considered to have a neurotransmitter function. As with previous examples, they appear to have specific receptors, sometimes multiple receptors, which mediate their actions; and some of them are found in very highly restricted regions of the brain where communication via them is conducted between maybe as little as a few thousand neurons. A particularly high density of a number of neuropeptides is found in the hypothalamus, which is one of the regions that has been implicated in feeding and its regulation (see Spotlight 8b). An important family of neuropeptides is the opioids; these consist of a number of endogenous substances which can bind to one of a number of receptor subtypes. Physiologically, they are believed to have diverse roles and therapeutically are key targets for pain management. Of particular relevance to this text, opioids also have psychotropic effects, including profound abuse potential. Similarly to the monoamines, it is often the case that their receptors are found on neurons that also contain receptors for the classical transmitters. In addition, most terminals that release neuropeptides also release one of the classical transmitters so that a terminal may contain, for example, the neuropeptide enkephalin and GABA.

Substances with unusual properties

In recent years, a number of highly unusual substances have been proposed as neurotransmitters. They can be unusual for a variety of reasons but most often it is their chemical nature. For example the gas nitric oxide, which we have already met as a retrograde signalling molecule, and certain derivatives from the phospholipid bilayer, such as the endocannabinoids, all demonstrate some properties which enable us to classify them as neurotransmitters.

Lipids   In the light of the descriptions of the general properties of neurotransmitters and their receptors it may seem a surprise that substances which are chemically lipid in nature should qualify and act as neurotransmitters. Of historical interest is that cannabinoid receptors were found before any endogenous ligand was found, when it was recognised that the cannabis plant must contain substances that acted on the brain to bring about its psychotropic effects. Later, anandamide was identified as an endogenous ligand and subsequently several others have also been proposed. The lipophilic nature of the endocannabinoids challenges our concept of a neurotransmitter for several reasons. First, the lipophilic nature of the molecules means it cannot be readily contained or stored within membrane-bound vesicles. Instead it is produced 'to order' and can then simply diffuse out of the terminal. This might suggest that the endocannabinoid could have very widespread effects on a large number of cells. However, we must remember that the extracellular environment is aqueous and so the lipophilicity of the endocannabinoid will inhibit its ability to travel any great distance.

It is now established that there are at least two receptors for endocannabinoids, CB1 and CB2. CB1 seems to be primarily located in the central nervous system whilst CB2 is primarily found peripherally, associated with cells of the immune system. However, there is some evidence to suggest that this dichotomy is not absolute. Of note, the CB1 receptors in the brain are primarily located presynaptically, and the endocannabinoid is produced by the postsynaptic cell and diffuses retrogradely to activate these presynaptic receptors

Synaptic plasticity

The account of the structure and events that occur at synapses given above may give the impression that these are fixed processes and that once a synapse forms, it continues to operate in an unchanging way. It is worth remembering when earlier we saw that the dendritic trees of neurons are not static but undergo continual remodelling. As the dendrites are the postsynaptic portions of synapses, this implies that synapses are also not fixed. In fact there is considerable evidence to suggest that synapses are dynamic and adaptable throughout the life of the human, from the formation of the first circuits in the foetus until death. This dynamic process is termed **synaptic plasticity**. Functionally this is important because it allows the individual to change and acquire new functionality, particularly in relation to their behaviour. The most intuitive example of this process occurring is seen with learning and memory; we have all consciously experienced the process whereby we can acquire and later retrieve knowledge; the precise details of these processes are discussed later in Chapter 4. However, synaptic plasticity has been implicated in a whole variety of behavioural responses which might occur rather more subconsciously and may well account, for example, for the ability of the mood state of a human to change, resulting in clinical depression.

Clearly, the ability of the fetal brain to form such highly specialised neurons with precise connectivity involves a great deal of synaptic plasticity; almost certainly at least as many synapses form and then degrade as form and survive. We shall in Chapter 3 investigate how these processes occur and what their importance is in producing an adult brain. There is also considerable evidence to suggest that the impact of early-life experience has a considerable effect on synaptic production, the effects of which on behaviour may not be entirely clear until later in life; a good example is schizophrenia where, as we shall see later in the book, there is evidence to suggest that early-life events may predispose an individual to become schizophrenic many years later.

KEY POINTS

- Neurons use electrical forms of signalling to convey messages within the cell.
- Neurons in the brain use neurotransmitter chemicals to convey messages from one neuron to the next at synapses.
- Each neuron makes a large number of synapses which underpins the potential computing power of the brain.
- There are a large number of neurotransmitters, each of which can act at multiple receptors, which means that drugs can have a specific site of action in the brain.
- Synaptic plasticity is an important process occurring in the brain throughout life and is critical in allowing the brain to continually adapt functionally.

CHAPTER SUMMARY

The brain is the key component of the human nervous system for determining behaviour. Our understanding of the anatomical arrangement of neurons in the brain and the electrical and chemical signalling processes used by individual neurons is now extensive. Clearly these simple processes underlie the complex behaviours, both normal and abnormal, that have been described in humans. However, the extraordinarily large numbers and vast connectivity of neurons means that we are only just beginning to understand the biological bases of human behaviour.

FURTHER READING

Crossman, A. R. and Neary, D. (2010). *Neuroanatomy: An illustrated colour text*. Edinburgh: **Churchill Livingstone.**

This is an exhaustive text which provides much greater detail on the basic neuroanatomy that is covered in this chapter.

Bear, M. F., Connors, B. W. and Paradiso, M. A. (2007). *Neuroscience: Exploring the brain*. **Baltimore: Lippincott Williams and Wilkins.**

This text focuses on the physiology of the nervous system and includes clear descriptions and explanations of the basic principles of neuronal cell biology.

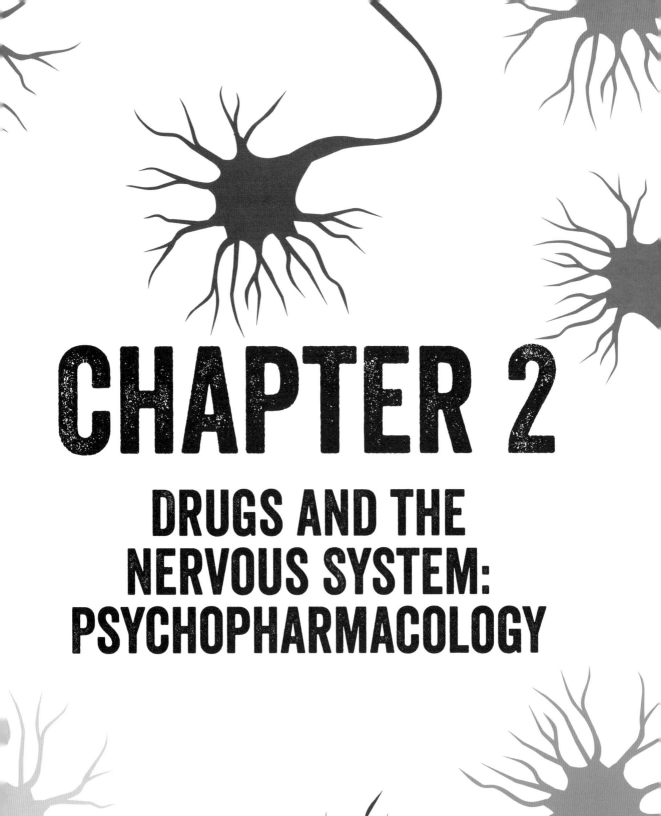

CHAPTER 2

DRUGS AND THE NERVOUS SYSTEM: PSYCHOPHARMACOLOGY

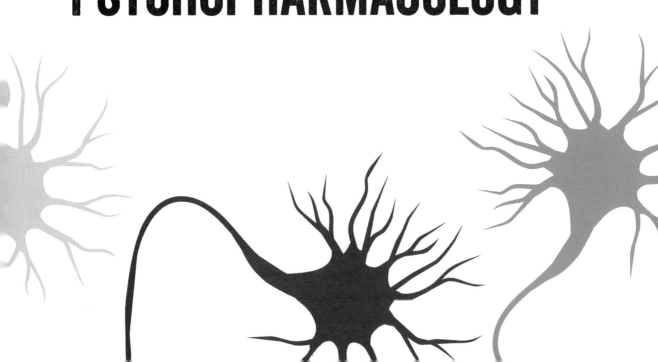

CHAPTER BREAKDOWN

- Introduction to psychopharmacology and the study of psychoactive drugs.
- How psychoactive drugs are handled by the body.
- The effect of psychoactive drugs on neurotransmission.
- Neuroplastic responses to repeated administration of drugs.
- The effects of commonly used psychoactive drugs on behaviour and their pharmacological mechanisms of action.

ROADMAP

The topic of this chapter is **psychopharmacology**, which is the study of **psychoactive drugs** and how they affect brain and behaviour. Psychoactive drugs are compounds that are not naturally present in the body but which can nevertheless act on the body to produce changes in mood and/or behaviour. Psychoactive drugs may be found in plants or they may be compounds that have been synthesised in a chemical laboratory. In this chapter we will be exploring the effects of drugs that alter neurotransmission. We will be finding out about the many ways that drugs get from outside to inside the body to affect brain function. We will examine how drugs are eventually removed from the body and how we respond to the effects of repeated drug administration. The specific ways in which drugs alter neurotransmission will be explored and we will look in detail at the effects of commonly used recreational drugs.

Why might we be interested in studying the effects of drugs on the brain? One reason is that studying how drugs affect the brain tells us something about how the brain works. We can use drugs as tools to find out about the role of specific transmitters and receptors in psychological processes. For example, if we have a drug that we know alters serotonin neurotransmission then we can examine the effects of this drug on behaviour and infer something about the role of serotonin in the behaviours observed. In this way, we might also learn something about the changes in brain function that underlie psychiatric disorders and this knowledge can help in developing better treatments. If a drug mimics the symptoms of the disorder then this give clues as to changes in neurotransmission that might be giving rise to psychological problems. Recreational drug use is also widespread in many societies and is associated with personal and societal problems. Studying how drugs affect the brain helps us understand and deal with problematic drug use.

We will draw on knowledge gained from reading other chapters to help our understanding. We will use our understanding of neurotransmission to think about how drugs alter synaptic communication (Chapter 1). Knowledge of perceptual processes will also be important for understanding some of the effects of drugs (Chapter 5). In addition, there are links to learning and memory processes and their role in the propensity of some psychoactive drugs to engender dependence (Chapter 4).

The first step in understanding the effects of psychoactive drugs is to consider how the body handles them. How do drugs get to their sites of action and why don't they just build up in the body if we keep taking them? Pharmacokinetics is the term given to studying how drugs are handled by the body and how they are eliminated.

HOW DRUGS ARE HANDLED BY THE BODY: PHARMACOKINETICS

When we take a drug it is only able to have its effects if it is absorbed into the bloodstream and distributed throughout the body to reach its site of action. After a while, the effects of the drug disappear because it is transformed (metabolised) into a compound that can be eliminated from the body. Pharmacokinetics is the study of these processes of absorption, distribution, metabolism and elimination. We will look at each process in turn and what is involved at each step, considering the implications for understanding the effects of drugs and the design of effective treatments.

Absorption

Drugs can enter the bloodstream in many different ways, referred to as routes of administration. Routes of administration are important to consider because some drugs can only be taken via a particular route and this may affect compliance with the taking of therapeutic drugs. People would generally rather swallow a tablet than have to inject a drug.

Some routes of administration such as smoking can also be harmful. The amount of drug that gets delivered to the site of action also varies on the route of administration. For some routes of administration the drug has to cross biological membranes such as the lining of the intestine or mucous membranes in the mouth. Biological membranes are primarily made of fat (lipids) and so drugs need to be lipid soluble to cross them. The extent to which a drug is able to reach its sites of action is referred to as **bioavailability**.

Routes of administration

The most common form of drug administration is to swallow a tablet or a capsule containing a liquid form of the drug (Figure 2.1). This is known as oral administration. Once swallowed, the tablet or capsule dissolves in the stomach and passes from the stomach to the intestines where it can travel across the intestinal membranes and enter the bloodstream. Not all drugs can be administered this way though because some are destroyed by acids in the stomach and others induce vomiting, meaning the drug is unable to reach the small intestines for absorption. If a drug does not

Figure 2.1 Oral administration of drugs is often preferred to other routes of administration because it is most convenient and usually the safest and least expensive

© Djomas/Shutterstock.com

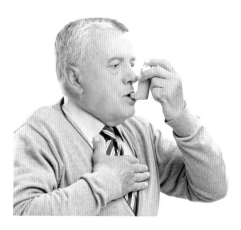

Figure 2.2   Some drugs can be inhaled but specialised equipment may be needed and inhalation should be monitored to ensure the right amount of drug is delivered

© Ljupco Smokovski/Shutterstock.com

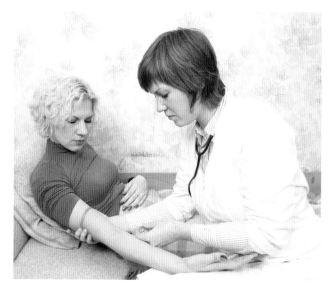

Figure 2.3   When a drug is administered intravenously, is goes directly into the bloodstream and tends to take effect more quickly than when given by any other route of administration

© Iakov Filimonov/Shutterstock.com

get into the bloodstream it is said to have low bioavailability.

Another issue is that once the drug enters the bloodstream from the intestines it is carried directly to the liver via the hepatic portal vein. In the liver, the drug may undergo substantial metabolism, which is a process known as the **first pass effect**. Some drugs may be almost completely inactivated in this way and so may never reach their sites of action. However, an advantage of oral administration is that it is relatively safe and an overdose can be dealt with by pumping the stomach to remove the drug before too much of it enters the system. However, absorption after oral administration can be unpredictable because it is affected by factors such as how much food is in the stomach. This is why some drugs are directed to be taken on an empty stomach.

An alternative to oral administration for drugs that cause stomach upset is to use a suppository that is inserted in the rectum. The rectal route may be used if a person is unable to take a drug orally, for example if they are unconscious; but absorption from rectal membranes can be incomplete and unpredictable and the suppository may cause irritation.

Drugs can also be absorbed via other membranes in the body including mucous membranes in the mouth and nose. Drug tabs can be placed under the tongue to dissolve, which is known as sublingual administration, or they may be absorbed via the cheek membrane, which is known as buccal administration. An example would be nicotine replacement therapies formulated as sublingual tabs or chewing gums. Some drugs can be administered topically via patches on the skin (transdermal route). These patches contain reservoirs that allow the drug to be released slowly over a long period. The drug diffuses through the skin into blood circulation. Some opioid agonists used for pain relief can be administered this way.

Inhaling drugs (inhalation route) is a fast route of administration because once a drug is inhaled it is carried quickly to the lungs, which are richly supplied with blood capillaries (Figure 2.2). From the lungs, the blood travels in arterial blood directly to the left side of the heart to be pumped to the brain. Inhaled drugs are suspended as small droplets or particles in a gas or aerosol. Cigarette smoke is an example of an aerosol but some medical drugs are taken using inhalers or nebulisers that create a fine mist containing the drug. A problem is that lung damage can be caused by drug inhalation.

Drugs can also be injected directly into a vein (intravenous route) (Figure 2.3). Intravenous injection is a fast route of administration that allows for precise control over the amount of drug that enters circulation. However, it can be dangerous because of the risk of infection from dirty needles and the fact that there is little time to respond to overdose or allergic reactions. There may also be issues with collapsed veins with repeated injections. Drugs can also be injected directly into muscles (intramuscular injection) or under the skin (subcutaneous injection). Subcutaneous injections are limited by the fact that only small volumes of drug can be administered into the space under the skin without causing pain but they are useful for drugs that require slow release.

Distribution

Once in the bloodstream, drugs circulate around the body and enter tissue sites where they bind to receptors to exert their effects. One thing to bear in mind is that although psychoactive drugs bind to receptors in the brain, they may also have effects at receptors at sites outside of the brain because the blood plasma that carries the drugs reaches all parts of the body. This explains some of the side effects of psychoactive drugs, for example their effects on the heart.

To get to brain receptor sites, drugs have to cross the **blood brain barrier**. Large or non-lipid soluble drug molecules cannot cross the blood brain barrier. Unlike other capillaries in the body, the blood capillaries that supply the brain are not very porous and are separated from the brain by tightly packed glia cells that act to keep out potentially toxic substances. This is an issue for the design of new therapeutic drugs targeting the brain because creating effective drugs that can cross the blood brain barrier is not easy.

Another factor that affects distribution of drugs around the body is that some drugs bind to proteins that are present in the blood plasma. When a drug molecule is bound to a plasma protein it is effectively stuck in the blood circulation because the drug-protein complex is too large to move through capillary pores into tissue. This limits the amount of drug that can reach receptor sites and is known as depot binding. The action of very fat soluble drugs can also be limited by depot binding in fat tissue. Fat soluble drugs reach the brain very quickly but then they are rapidly taken out of circulation into body fat, where they are effectively inactivated for a time. Eventually, the drug is released slowly from the fat back into circulation to be metabolised. This slow release of low levels of a drug can cause a hangover effect. An example of a very fat soluble drug is tetrahydrocannabinol (THC), the active constituent in cannabis.

Metabolism and elimination

The process of drug metabolism allows us to eliminate drugs from the body. In this way, drugs do not stay in the body forever. The main way the body gets rid of drugs is in urine, but only water soluble compounds can be eliminated in this manner. This is why most drugs have to be metabolised before they can eliminated. The main site of action for drug metabolism is the liver. The liver contains many different metabolic enzymes that allow fat soluble molecules to be changed into water soluble molecules that can be excreted in urine produced by the kidneys.

Metabolism of drugs can result in the production of a new compound that is inactive. However, metabolism can also result in production of a compound that is just as active or even more active than the parent compound. The activity of some drugs is mainly due to the effects

Figure 2.4   After drinking alcohol, there is alcohol in the blood stream, and when the blood passes through the lungs some of the alcohol moves across the membranes of the lung's air sacs (alveoli) into the air. As the alcohol in the air in the lungs is exhaled, it can be detected by a breath alcohol testing device. Because the alcohol concentration in the breath is related to that in the blood, measuring alcohol on the breath provides a measure of the amount of alcohol in the blood. This can be used by police officers to detect whether someone is drunk driving, instead of using a blood test

© papa1266/Shutterstock.com

of a metabolite. For example, the opioid agonist codeine is metabolised to morphine. A drug may have to undergo several transformations before it can be eliminated.

Drugs may also be excreted via the lungs untransformed, as is the case with alcohol. The excretion of alcohol in the breath forms the basis of the alcohol breathalyser test (Figure 2.4). Alcohol and other drugs such as cocaine can also be excreted in sweat via the skin. Some of the drug in the sweat is incorporated into hair, which is why hair analysis is also used as a basis for drug testing. Drugs can also be transferred to the breast milk of nursing mothers.

The time course of drug effects

Knowledge about drug pharmacokinetics tells us about the likely time course of a drug effect. This is important because the onset and offset of the action of a drug affects its therapeutic use. For some drugs it might be critical to have a quick and short-lived effect, say for an anaesthetic. For other drugs, it may be important that the effects last for a long time. This is true for psychiatric drugs that people may have to take chronically. Responses to recreational drugs are also affected by the time course of their effects as we will discover later.

It is important to remember that the effect of a drug depends upon the amount that is available at receptor sites. This is an important principle of drug action: drug effects are related to the dose of the drug. For most psychoactive drugs the amount of drug at the receptor sites equates to the amount that is present in the blood plasma. When drugs are administered intravenously, peak plasma levels will be achieved immediately and so the onset of the drug effect is very quick (Figure 2.5). For drugs that have to cross biological membranes to get into the bloodstream, the onset of the drug effect will depend on factors relating to absorption. The time taken to reach peak plasma levels can affect the response to drugs. For the same dose of drug, a faster onset of effect is associated with greater behavioural and subjective effects (de Wit et al., 1993). After peak plasma levels are reached, the amount of drug reaching receptors is affected by the distribution of drug around the body and the rate of metabolism and elimination. For most drugs, distribution is quite rapid and so the main factor is how long it takes to detoxify the drug for elimination. Metabolism to an active compound before elimination will prolong the drug action. The **half-life** of a drug is a measure of the duration of action of the drug, and is defined as the time taken for the levels in the plasma to fall by a half. Some drugs have, a half-life of hours whereas others have a half-life of days. Drugs with short half-lives have to be administered more frequently to maintain their effects. If a therapeutic drug, has a very short half-life then this may affect compliance with taking the drug because of the burden associated with frequent dosing.

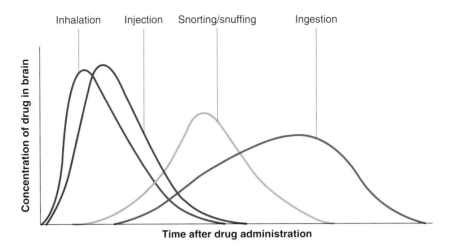

Figure 2.5 The route of administration affects the onset, intensity, and duration of a drug's effect. Methamphetamine, for example, can be smoked, snorted, taken orally, or injected. If the drug is smoked or injected, the user almost immediately experiences an intense rush that lasts a few minutes. Snorting methamphetamine produces feelings of euphoria within three to five minutes, while oral ingestion produces effects within 15 to 20 minutes

KEY POINTS

- Psychoactive drugs achieve their effects by interacting with receptor sites in the brain.
- To reach these receptor sites drugs must enter the bloodstream to be distributed around the body.
- The route of administration of a drug affects how much of the drug is absorbed and the onset of its effects.
- The duration of action of a drug is affected by the rate at which it is metabolised and eliminated from the body.

EFFECTS OF DRUGS ON NEUROTRANSMISSION: PHARMACODYNAMICS

Pharmacokinetics is the effect that the body has on drugs (how drugs are handled by the body) whereas pharmacodynamics is the effect that drugs have on the body. Psychoactive drugs bring about their effects by altering neurotransmission. Generally speaking, drugs either act to enhance or dampen the effects of neurotransmitters by increasing or decreasing the number of receptors that are activated. Drugs that enhance neurotransmission are called **agonists** and those that dampen are called **antagonists**. We can think of agonists and antagonists as turning up or toning down on-going neural transmission.

One thing to bear in mind is that drug agonism is not the same as neuronal excitation. Remember that some neurotransmitters have inhibitory effects on neurotransmission and so agonists of these neurotransmitters enhance inhibitory neurotransmission. Similarly, an antagonist could be acting to reduce inhibitory neurotransmission. The outcome would be an increase in neuronal activity and so antagonism is not the same as neuronal inhibition. In addition, the effects of drugs on behaviour will depend upon the distribution of receptors in different areas of the brain and the specificity and affinity of the drug for particular types of receptor. Drugs act to modulate activity in the brain circuits that underlie behaviour and so, depending upon the dose administered, it is possible for a drug to have effects that both stimulate some behaviours and depress other behaviours.

Agonists either mimic the effects of a particular neurotransmitter by binding to postsynaptic receptors in a similar way and producing a similar response in the postsynaptic neuron (direct agonist) or they enhance the action of a natural neurotransmitter via other actions that do not involve direct interaction with postsynaptic receptors (indirect agonists). For example, heroin is a direct agonist in that it resembles the brain's natural opioids sufficiently to activate opioid receptors. Similarly, nicotine attaches to receptors for acetylcholine, the neurotransmitter for the cholinergic system. Indirect agonist actions include: blocking the transporter proteins that remove neurotransmitters from the synapse; causing release of neurotransmitters from the presynaptic neuron; or inactivating the enzymes that normally break down the neurotransmitter. All of these actions increase the amount of neurotransmitters available in the synapse thus enhancing the action of the neurotransmitter. Cocaine is an example of a re-uptake inhibitor. It attaches to the dopamine transporter and as long as cocaine occupies the transporter, dopamine cannot re-enter the cell by this route and it builds up in the synapse.

Direct antagonists compete with the neurotransmitter for binding at the same receptor site. They reduce the action of the neurotransmitter because they bind to the receptor but they do not induce any response. In other words, by sitting on the receptor and having no effect (blocking the receptor), the antagonist reduces the number of receptors available for the neurotransmitter to activate. Antagonists also block the effect of agonist drugs, which is why antagonists can be administered as antidotes to the effects of agonists. For example, an opioid antagonist can be used to reverse the effect of overdose on an opioid agonist like morphine. Indirect antagonist actions involve inactivation of the enzymes that synthesise neurotransmitters or inhibition release of a neurotransmitter.

Some drugs alter neurotransmission by modulating the activity of the neurotransmitter when it is bound to the receptor. Benzodiazepines, such as diazepam, enhance the responses that occur when the neurotransmitter GABA binds to receptors. Benzodiazepines bind to a different receptor site than GABA but they change the shape of the receptor so that when GABA binds to its receptor site a greater than usual response is elicited. This is known as **allosteric modulation**.

A rarer type of drug action is inverse agonism. As its name suggests, these compounds actually have the opposite effect of the natural neurotransmitter. So, rather than mimicking the effects of the neurotransmitter, they bind to the same receptors but bring about an opposite cellular response. One way of thinking about the effects of agonists, antagonists and **inverse agonists** is to picture their effects along a continuum: agonists are at one end, inducing the same response as the neurotransmitter when they bind to receptors; antagonists are in the middle, having no effects when they bind; and inverse agonists are at the other end, inducing an opposite effect to the neurotransmitter.

The extent to which a drug activates a receptor is known as its efficacy. Antagonists have no efficacy because they do not induce a response in the receptor, whereas full agonists induce a response that is maximal relative to the effects of the neurotransmitter, and full inverse agonists induce a maximal response in the opposite direction. In between there are partial agonists and inverse agonists. These compounds activate receptors but even at very high doses the maximal response is not achieved.

Partial agonists are interesting because their effects depend upon the background level of neurotransmitter activity and for this reason they may be useful for treatment in disorders where stabilisation of neurotransmission is required. For example, in the case of low levels of the neurotransmitter, partial agonists raise activity back up to more normal levels. In a situation where there may be excess levels of neurotransmission then a partial agonist would actually have antagonist properties and might be useful in toning down activity. This is because the partial agonist would be competing with the neurotransmitter for the same receptors but would be eliciting a submaximal response on binding relative to the neurotransmitter. This would effectively reduce over-stimulation by the high levels of neurotransmitter.

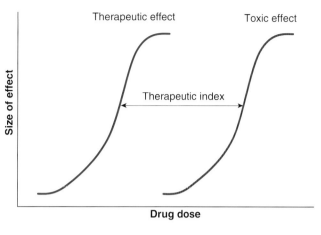

Figure 2.6 The concept of therapeutic index refers to the relationship between toxic and therapeutic dose. The therapeutic index determines the safety of a drug. Drugs with a large therapeutic index are preferred (a large difference between the toxic and clinical dose) because there is less likelihood of a person being able to overdose or experience toxic effects if they accidentally take too much of the drug

We have been talking so far as if all drugs are very specific in their actions and have one type of action to alter neurotransmission. Some drugs do primarily disrupt one neurotransmitter or class of neurotransmitters but others interact with many neurotransmitters. For example, morphine primarily acts as an agonist at a particular type of opioid receptor in the brain and so is quite selective, whereas cocaine acts as an indirect agonist for monoamine neurotransmitters; it inhibits re-uptake of dopamine, serotonin and noradrenaline. Alcohol is even less specific and has effect to alter GABA, glutamate, dopamine, serotonin, cannabinoid and opioid neurotransmission. Even if a drug is selective for a particular receptor then it is likely to have more than one effect on behaviour because of the fact that receptors in different areas of the brain control different functions. Opioid receptors in some brain areas are important in pain responses but in other areas are involved in control of basic physiological functions such as breathing.

The relationship between the dose of a drug and its effects on behaviour usually vary according to the affected behaviour. The pain relieving effects of opioids occur at lower doses than the effects to depress breathing. The gap between desired and undesired or even fatal effects of drugs is obviously critical for therapeutic drugs because of the possibility of overdose. Ideally there should be a very large difference in the therapeutic versus lethal doses. This margin is known as the **therapeutic index** and is calculated as the dose of drug that elicits a lethal response in 50% of a sample (known as the lethal dose or LD50) divided by the dose that elicits a desired response in 50% of a sample (known as the effective dose or ED50) (Figure 2.6).

EFFECTS OF REPEATED CONSUMPTION OF DRUGS

The acute effects of taking a psychoactive drug are often different to the effects that are experienced after a drug has been taken repeatedly. Neuronal systems adapt to drug-induced changes in neurotransmission. An adaptive response might be that numbers of receptors are

down-regulated in response to increases in activation by drugs. This can lead to tolerance, whereby with repeated administration of drugs a higher dose is required to achieve the same effects. **Tolerance** can also be due to drug-induced changes in the synthesis and release of neurotransmitters. As a result of these neuroplastic changes, if a person stops taking a drug they may experience **withdrawal** symptoms because once the drug is taken away the effects of down regulation become apparent.

In other cases, the adaptive response to repeated drug administration is an increase in receptor numbers or sensitivity to a drug. This is known as **sensitisation**, meaning that the same dose of a drug elicits a greater response over time. A drug can invoke tolerance in some systems but not others. Also, one behaviour might show tolerance while another shows sensitisation. This can lead to problems because if there is tolerance to some of the effects of a recreational drug and a person increases their dose to overcome the tolerance, they might be more likely to overdose if there is no tolerance to the lethal effects.

FOCUS ON METHODS: PSYCHOPHARMACOLOGY

Psychopharmacology is the study of the effects of drugs on the brain and behaviour. In some psychopharmacology studies, drugs are administered that either enhance (agonists) or dampen down (antagonists) the effects of neurotransmitters, and the effect on physiological and behavioural responses is examined. If we know about the specific action of the drug then we make inferences about the biological basis of the affected behaviour. For example, if a serotonin agonist improves mood then we might infer that serotonin neurotransmission is important for positive mood states. Another approach is to examine brain chemistry in behaving animals to find out about the neurochemical basis of psychological experiences. This can be done via in vivo dialysis which involves implanting a tube into the brain of a rat so that neurotransmitters that are released in a specific area can be collected and stored for later analysis.

KEY POINTS

- Drugs affect behaviour by altering synaptic transmission in various ways.
- Agonist drugs enhance the effects of neurotransmitters whereas antagonist drugs dampen their effects.
- Drugs vary in their selectivity: some alter the activity of specific neurotransmitters whereas others affect multiple neurotransmitters.
- Repeated administration of a drug can alter the drug response via adaptive neuroplastic processes known as tolerance and sensitisation.

USE OF PSYCHOACTIVE DRUGS

Humans have used psychoactive drugs throughout history. As hunter gatherers, early humans would have been exposed to psychoactive substances contained in plants (Johns, 1990). Drugs like caffeine, nicotine and cocaine are plant neurotoxins that likely evolved because they defend the plant from consumption by plant-eating animals (Karban and Baldwin, 1997). As part of the co-evolution of plants and animals, humans found ways of dealing with plant chemical defences including the ability to metabolise them (Karban and Agrawal, 2002). While the consumption of these plants may have some beneficial effccts that promoted their consumption, the pure forms of the drug extracted from plants have powerfully reinforcing effects on behaviour and induce long-term adaptations in brain reward systems that can create serious problems for individuals and society (Nesse and Berridge, 1997).

We will examine the effects on the brain and behaviour of commonly used psychoactive drugs. The focus is on drugs that are used recreationally for their mind-altering effects. Some of these drugs also have medicinal uses that will be discussed but drugs that are primarily used in treatment of psychological disorders will be discussed in Chapter 9.

ALCOHOL

When we speak of alcohol, we are referring to a particular type of alcohol, ethanol, which is present in alcoholic beverages and foodstuffs. Alcohol consumption is part of many cultures today and historical records suggest that dilute alcoholic beverages were probably the most common daily drink among people in Western civilisation for thousands of years. Drinking alcohol, which is an antiseptic, would have been much safer than risking consuming contaminated water from unsafe supplies. In the East, the problem of safe drinking water was solved in a different way by boiling water for tea (Vallee, 1998).

Initial human encounters with alcohol were probably accidental via the consumption of fermented fruits. As fruits ripen, the sugar they contain is eventually converted to alcohol by yeast on the skin. Humans foraging for fruit would have been exposed to alcohol in this way but probably only in small amounts (Dudley, 2004). With the development of agriculture came the introduction to the human diet of beer and wine, made from cultivated wheat and grapes. But it was not until the invention of distillation processes, to create high-alcohol-content spirits, that alcoholic beverages resembled the strong drinks on offer today (Vallee, 1998). While many societies approve of moderate alcohol use, excessive drinking is considered detrimental to health and public safety.

Alcohol is usually classed as a depressant drug because its overall effect on brain function is inhibitory. But anyone who has observed the behaviour of someone consuming alcohol might note that, at low doses, alcohol stimulates behaviour (Babor et al., 1983). People become more talkative and less anxious in social situations when they drink alcohol (Pohorecky, 1981). This is because alcohol dampens the processes that normally restrain our behaviour in social contexts. In other words, alcohol reduces inhibitory control or produces what is known as disinhibition. Imagine a neural circuit that normally keeps emotional responses in check. If activity in this circuit is depressed then an increase in emotional responses would be observed via disinhibition, as is the case with alcohol. In this way alcohol can also produce an increase in risky behaviours that a person would not normally engage in when sober. These activities include risky sexual practices and aggressive behaviours.

There are strong links between alcohol use and violence reported in many countries (Graham and West, 2001), although the extent of the problem varies according to cultural factors such as expectations about how people should behave when intoxicated (Jones et al., 2001). Alcohol-related aggression might also be due to other effects of alcohol on cognitive processing such as a reduced ability to process information and problem solve in social situations or a narrowing of attention focus on certain aspects of a situation (Steele and Josephs, 1990). An effect of alcohol to limit a person's ability to attend to and make use of all the available cues of information in a social situation might also explain why alcohol induces such a wide range of effects across individuals but also within the same person. For example, a person might be aggressive after alcohol at certain times but other times feel depressed.

At higher doses of alcohol there are widespread effects on the brain, and general inhibition of activity overwhelms any initial disinhibitory effects in specific circuits. Drinkers become sedated and their ability to react to things is impaired, as is their balance and coordination, which is why drunk driving is so dangerous. As the dose of alcohol increases still further then a person might lose consciousness and eventually their breathing may stop (Figure 2.7). Death from too much alcohol can also occur if a comatose person vomits and then breathes in the vomit and chokes. A person may vomit because toxic levels of alcohol in the body are detected by the brain. The vomit reflex is an attempt to remove any unabsorbed alcohol from the system.

The effects of alcohol on the brain are due to its modulation of various neurotransmitters, including the main inhibitory and excitatory neurotransmitters GABA and glutamate (Nestoros, 1980). Alcohol enhances GABA transmission by binding to the GABAA receptor and increasing the flow of Cl$^-$ ions through the ion channel in response to GABA binding to the receptor (Ticku et al., 1986). Conversely, alcohol inhibits ion flow through the NMDA glutamate receptors (Lovinger et al., 1989). Both these actions have the effect of inhibiting neurotransmission. The ability of alcohol to affect GABA and glutamate receptors depends upon the composition of

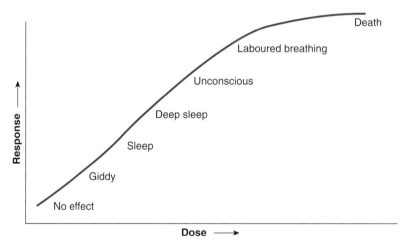

Figure 2.7 Different effects of alcohol are experienced according to the dose administered. At low doses, there is behavioural disinhibition but at higher doses there is sedation. At very high doses breathing will be depressed and the person may die

Source: Marczewski and Kamrin (1991)

the receptors, and some receptor subtypes are sensitive to the effects of alcohol whereas others are not (Crews et al., 1996).

Alcohol also affects neurotransmission in serotonin, opioid and dopamine systems in the brain (Gessa et al., 1985; Froehlich and Li, 1994; Le Marquand et al., 1994). These effects likely relate to the rewarding effects of alcohol and its potential for abuse. Alcohol can increase neurotransmission in the mesolimbic dopamine system and these effects may be in part due to an effect of alcohol on cannabinoid receptors (Hungund et al., 2003).

The long-term effects of consuming alcohol depend on the amounts consumed. There is some suggestion that moderate consumption of alcohol does not induce harmful changes to the body and may even have some beneficial effects (Grønbæk et al., 1998). Moderate drinkers tend to suffer less from heart disease than those who drink heavily or abstain (Rimm et al., 1996). But a problem with studying the relationship between drinking and health is factoring out the influence of other lifestyle factors (Naimi et al., 2005). In addition, some people who abstain from drinking may do so because they had problems with alcohol, and their poorer health makes the moderate drinkers look good by comparison (Fillmore et al., 2007). So experts disagree about whether it is possible to say that moderate drinking has health benefits.

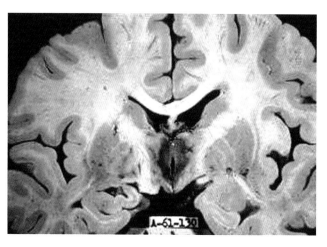

Figure 2.8 Korsakoff's syndrome is caused by lack of thiamine (vitamin B1) and this causes damage to the thalamus and hypothalamus, which leads to memory problems and a dementia-like syndrome. Note the pigmentation of the grey matter around the third ventricle

Heavy consumption of alcohol (usually defined as more than 2–3 drinks per day) is associated with health problems such as cirrhosis of the liver and brain damage. Liver cirrhosis is a condition in which scar tissue replaces healthy liver tissue, preventing the liver from working properly. This happens because alcohol is metabolised by the liver and some of the products of alcohol metabolism are harmful to the liver. **Korsakoff's syndrome** is a type of dementia caused by a lack of vitamin B1. Heavy drinkers who are dependent on alcohol usually have a poor diet that lacks essential vitamins, which can cause problems like Korsakoff's (Figure 2.8).

Heavy drinking is also a risk factor for cancer (Schütze et al., 2011). The brain adapts to chronic heavy consumption of alcohol which means that when someone stops drinking they experience serious withdrawal effects when alcohol is no longer having a depressing effect on the brain. In withdrawal, the brain is in a state of rebound hyperexcitability which can manifest as anxiety, tremor, disorientation, and seizures. Severe withdrawal is marked by a syndrome called **delirium tremens**, which involves hallucinations and irrational behaviour.

Heavy alcohol consumption is harmful to unborn babies. Alcohol consumed by a mother during pregnancy goes across the placenta to the foetus via the bloodstream. Because the foetus's liver is not fully formed, it cannot metabolise the alcohol quickly enough. The high blood alcohol concentration in the foetus affects development and is known as **fetal alcohol syndrome**. Babies born with this syndrome have distinctive features including a small head and a smooth area between the nose and the lips as well as a thin upper lip. They are smaller than other babies and have learning difficulties (Clarren and Smith, 1978).

STIMULANTS

The term stimulant is used to describe various drugs that increase activity, alertness and mood. Drugs such as cocaine, nicotine and caffeine have different primary mechanisms of action but they share a common effect to increase dopamine neurotransmission in the brain and this likely underlies their energising effects.

Cocaine

The leaves of the plant *Erythroxylum coca* contain cocaine, which is released when the leaves are chewed (Figure 2.9). Coca leaves have been used in religious ceremonies and medicine in South America, where the bushes grow abundantly, for thousands of years. Cocaine in purified form was extracted from coca leaves in the mid-1800s and used as a local anaesthetic. It was present in many tonics around that time (including Coca-Cola) and was advocated as a treatment for depression by, among others, Sigmund Freud. Freud later changed his mind about the benefits of cocaine once he became aware of its dependence-inducing effects.

Powdered cocaine is in the form of a hydrochloride salt that can be snorted because it is water soluble. It cannot be smoked because the salt is destroyed by heat. The pure non-salt form of cocaine is known as free-base and is the smokable form of the drug. Crack is a form of free-base cocaine that is made by combining cocaine hydrochloride with baking powder (sodium bicarbonate) and water then heating the paste to remove the hydrochloride. When smoked, the rocks that are cut from the cocaine precipitate make a popping sound, from which crack gets its name.

The short-term effects of cocaine include increased alertness, heightened sensations and a desire for further drug taking. The need for sleep is reduced and appetite is suppressed. These effects come on very quickly if the drug is smoked and last for about 10 minutes. If the drug is snorted there is a slower onset of action but the effects are also prolonged owing to the slower absorption of the drug, and they may last for 30 minutes. Large doses may cause symptoms similar to schizophrenia such as paranoia, and hallucinations. One type of hallucination experienced is the feeling of bugs crawling under the skin, known as formication. Knowledge about the effects of cocaine on brain and behaviour has informed theories of schizophrenia (see Chapter 9).

At high doses, the cardiovascular effects of cocaine can result in sudden death from heart attack. Taking alcohol with cocaine increases the stimulant effects experienced (Andrews, 1997) but also increases the risk of immediate death (Harris et al., 2003). This is because the combination of cocaine and alcohol produces a new compound called cocaethylene, which has similar effects to cocaine but is more toxic. The long-term consequences of taking cocaine include dependence and malnourishment due to the appetite-suppressant effects of the drug. Snorting cocaine can lead to loss of sense of smell, nosebleeds and damage of the nasal septum.

Figure 2.9 *Erythroxylum coca* is a densely leafed plant native to the eastern slopes of the Andes. The leaves contain cocaine

© iStock.com/rchphoto

Cocaine inhibits re-uptake of dopamine, serotonin and noradrenaline by binding to presynaptic transporter proteins thus enhancing monoamine neurotransmission. The reinforcing effects of cocaine are likely mediated by its action to increase serotonin and dopamine transmission in reward pathways in the brain (Rocha et al., 1998; Volkow et al., 1997). Longer-term changes in these systems are implicated in cocaine dependence (Pelloux et al., 2012; Robinson and Berridge, 1993).

Amphetamines

Amphetamines are synthetic drugs that were originally developed in the 1920s to treat asthma and narcolepsy (Piness et al., 1930). They were used as antidepressants and diet pills in the 1940s and given to soldiers during World War II to prevent fatigue (Rasmussen, 2008). The effects of amphetamines are similar to those of cocaine. Amphetamines increase dopamine and noradrenaline neurotransmission by acting primarily to release these neurotransmitters from nerve terminals but also inhibiting re-uptake (Fleckenstein et al., 2007).

Methamphetamine is very similar to amphetamine but its effects are longer lasting and come on more quickly because it is more lipid soluble than amphetamine and so is partitioned into the brain more quickly. This might explain why methamphetamine has been noted to have a high potential for abuse since rapid delivery of a drug to the brain is thought to facilitate adaptive changes in neuronal circuits that underlie addiction (Samaha and Robinson, 2005). Long-term use of methamphetamine causes structural changes to the brain, only some of which are reversed upon cessation of drug taking (Thompson et al., 2004).

Nicotine

Nicotine is the drug found in cigarettes and other tobacco products such as chewing tobacco and snuff. The plant *Nicotiana tabacum*, which is native to the Americas, is the source of nicotine for tobacco products. Tobacco has been used throughout human history. The first archaeological evidence for tobacco use dates back to 1400 BC in New Mexico (Gilman and Xun, 2004). In indigenous American culture, tobacco smoking was important in medicine and ceremonies and features in creation stories (Robicsek, 2004). Sir Walter Raleigh introduced tobacco to England in the late 1500s. As there were no other smokers at the time, a servant seeing Raleigh smoking is reputed to have thrown water on him, thinking he was on fire!

The way in which tobacco is used is subject to cultural influences: pipe smoking has been popular at certain times and snuff taking at others. However, the mass manufacture of cigarettes in the 1800s led to cigarettes becoming the predominant mode of consumption and widespread use of nicotine throughout the world. Smoking in some parts of the world is still very high but is declining in many developed countries owing to awareness about the health problems associated with tobacco use (Shafey et al., 2003).

Smoking causes many illnesses that shorten life, such as cancer and cardiovascular disease (Doll et al., 1994).This is due to the inhalation of smoke and carcinogens that are formed in the burning of tobacco. Nicotine itself is very toxic at high doses but can be safely used in products that replace the use of tobacco.

Although nicotine is probably responsible for most of the effects of tobacco use it is possible that other compounds play a role. Tobacco smoke contains many other compounds that could either have a direct effect themselves on behaviour or potentiate the effects of nicotine. There is not much known about other active constituents of tobacco smoke but one compound – the enzyme monoamine oxidase (MAO) – could potentiate the effects of nicotine on the brain because it is responsible for breaking down the neurotransmitters dopamine, noradrenaline and serotonin (Lewis et al., 2007).

The rate of absorption of nicotine varies depending on the route of administration. Nicotine reaches the brain quickly after cigarette smoke inhalation but is much slower if nicotine is delivered by patch, gum, nasal spray, or inhaler, as used in nicotine replacement therapies for smoking cessation.

Nicotine is an acetylcholine agonist and it binds to specific receptors called nicotinic acetylcholine receptors or nAChRs. Activation of presynaptic nAChRs causes release of various neurotransmitters including acetylcholine, dopamine noradrenaline, serotonin GABA, glutamate, and endogenous opioids (Wonnacott, 1997). Like other stimulants, nicotine causes release of dopamine in the nucleus accumbens by acting at nAChRs located on dopamine neurons that project from the VTA to the nucleus accumbens (Nestler, 2005). However, nicotine can desensitise rather than activate neurons. This means the receptors adopt a conformation that means they are unable to be activated by nicotine. Desensitisation can occur minutes after drug binding but some subtypes of nAChR are more prone to desensitisation than others (Martin-Ruiz et al., 2000). A consequence is that neurotransmitter release by nicotine is more likely to occur after periods of abstinence, such as during overnight sleeping, because after the first cigarette, the receptors will be desensitised (Brody et al., 2006). Desensitisation of receptors may underlie the short-term tolerance that occurs to the effects of nicotine and may play a role in withdrawal and craving (Benowitz, 1996). A longer-term adaptive response to repeated desensitisation of nAChR is an increase in their receptor number as observed in regular smokers that could underlie chronic tolerance (Wang and Sun, 2005).

As with other stimulants, nicotine increases heart rate and blood pressure owing to increases in dopamine and noradrenaline in the periphery. It increases reaction times and other cognitive functions although some of the effects observed in smokers are likely related to the reversal of withdrawal symptoms (Heishman et al., 1994). Some smokers may use nicotine to improve their concentration and mood (Pomerleau and Pomerleau, 1985). People with depression and schizophrenia are more likely to take up smoking than people without depression (Lasser et al., 2000) and this may be because of antidepressant and cognitive enhancing effects of nicotine (Malpass and Higgs, 2007; Warburton, 1994).

Regular smokers also show changes in cognitive processing characterised by biases towards smoking related cues (Mogg et al., 2003). This is also true for other drugs of abuse (Field and Cox, 2008) but seems especially strong for nicotine associated stimuli (Caggiula et al., 2001). It has been suggested that an important factor maintaining smoking behaviour is that cues such as the sight and smell of smoking, and objects and places associated with smoking, trigger smoking behaviour and satisfy cravings (O'Brien et al., 1998). So smoking a cigarette that does not actually contain nicotine can be almost as satisfying as smoking a real cigarette, whereas infusion of nicotine directly into the bloodstream is not effective at all in reducing cravings (Rose et al., 2000). This might explain why smokers continue to smoke even when nicotine receptors are desensitised.

Caffeine

Caffeine is present in a wide variety of food and drinks from coffee to energy drinks and chocolate. Many people say they can't get by first thing in the morning without a shot of caffeine in their favourite beverage, and around 80% of the world's population consume the drug (James, 1997). Caffeine has mild stimulant effects to increase mood and alertness (Lieberman et al., 1987) which probably explains its popularity.

Some people are very sensitive to the effects of caffeine and experience negative effects. In particular, patients with panic disorders experience increases in anxiety after caffeine and so they tend to avoid it (Charney et al., 1985; Lee et al., 1988). This may be due to variation in genes coding for the receptors where caffeine acts in the brain (Alsene et al., 2003).

Studying the effects of caffeine in the laboratory is quite difficult for two reasons. First, people often come to the studies with clear expectations about how they will feel after consuming caffeine. Second, even short-term abstinence from caffeine results in a feeling of fatigue and lack of concentration (Juliano and Griffiths, 2004) and so it is difficult to separate direct effects of caffeine to improve mood and cognition from an effect of a caffeine shot to reverse the negative effects of withdrawal from the drug (James and Rogers, 2005).

It is possible to design studies to overcome these problems but such studies are not easy to carry out. Participants must not be aware that they have been given caffeine, and the influence of expecting to feel better after caffeine should be controlled for. Ideally one would want to test the effects of caffeine in people who have never had caffeine but this poses ethical issues because non-consumers or low consumers are unlikely to wish to consume caffeine

Another approach is to test people who consume very little coffee but this can be problematic because such individuals are hard to recruit. In addition, they may be avoiding caffeine consumption because they have had an atypical reaction in the past and so are not representative of how most other people would respond to the drug. Overall, research on the effects of caffeine on cognition and mood suggests that most of the effects of caffeine observed in the laboratory are likely explained by withdrawal reversal but some studies do report some direct effects of caffeine in low consumers (Childs and de Wit, 2006). It may be that the stimulant effects of caffeine motivate its initial use but thereafter everyday use is maintained to avoid the unpleasant effects of not having consumed caffeine for a while.

Caffeine binds to adenosine receptors that are distributed throughout the body, including the brain. It is an adenosine antagonist. Generally speaking, the physiological effects of caffeine are the opposite to those of adenosine. For example, adenosine is a vasodilator whereas caffeine constricts blood vessels. This is why it is often used in conjunction with other drugs for treatment for headaches. Caffeine is a diuretic, meaning it increases urination, whereas adenosine decreases urine output. In the brain, adenosine is an inhibitory neuromodulator that influences the release of several neurotransmitters and is involved in the regulation of sleep (see Chapter 8).

Direct binding of caffeine to adenosine receptors in the brain underlies its behavioural effects but it is likely that indirect effects on dopamine neurotransmission also play a role. Adenosine receptors are located near to dopamine D2 receptors in reward areas of the brain and probably interact with them (Ferré et al., 1992). Caffeine may remove the inhibitory effect of adenosine from dopamine receptors via its antagonist action thereby increasing dopamine activity. In support of this idea, people find the effects of low doses of amphetamine to be somewhat similar to the effects of caffeine (Chait and Johanson, 1988).

Interestingly, there is also some suggestion that regular coffee drinking is associated with reduced incidence of Parkinson's disease, perhaps because of the effect of caffeine on dopamine transmission (Chen et al., 2001). A relationship has also been noted between coffee consumption and Alzheimer's disease although the underlying mechanism is unclear (Eskelinen and Kivipelto, 2010).

OPIATES

Opiates come from the poppy flower *Papaver somniferum*. Two opiates contained in poppy sap are morphine and codeine. Dried poppy sap is referred to as opium and has been used for centuries for pain relief and for its mood altering properties. A combination of opium and alcohol, known as laudanum, was widely available in the 1800s. It was used by many writers and artists including the poet Samuel Taylor Coleridge, who became dependent on it, but its use was not confined to a particular social class (Berridge, 1977). Around the same time, morphine was extracted from opium and sold commercially.

The use of morphine was dramatically affected by the invention of the hypodermic syringe which allowed for a more rapid effect of the drug. This method of drug delivery was used by medics for pain relief in minor surgical procedures and the management of post-operative and chronic pain, but it was also used by people for self-medication.

In trying to create a less addictive analgesic, chemists modified the structure of morphine to create heroin. Heroin crosses the blood brain barrier more easily than morphine because it is more lipid soluble. It is then converted to morphine and another potent active compound and so it is actually no less addictive than morphine. Many other **opioid** drugs that mimic the effects of morphine have been synthesised since but they all have abuse potential. Drugs such as fentanyl and oxycodone are used in pain management today but they too are addictive. Methadone is another synthetic opioid that is similar to morphine but its effects last for much longer and it can be taken orally. For these reasons methadone is given to people dependent upon opiates as a safer substitute for heroin or morphine. When taking methadone, withdrawal symptoms are experienced less frequently because the drug levels are more stable and there are fewer drug cravings (Ward et al., 1999).

The brain contains opioid receptors that bind opiate drugs and naturally occurring brain chemicals known as endogenous opioids (Pert and Snyder, 1973). Opioid agonists like morphine have similar effects to the endogenous opioids, and opioid antagonists like naltrexone bind to the receptor but do not elicit any changes to cellular function. The major effects of opioid agonists on the brain is to inhibit neurotransmitter release.

Morphine binds specifically to the mu type of opioid receptor. An effect of morphine binding to the mu receptor is to increase dopamine release in the nucleus accumbens, which is an area of the brain important for motor function and reward. This happens indirectly via an effect on GABA interneurons in the ventral tegmental area. GABA interneurons exert an inhibitory influence on dopamine neurons that project to the nucleus accumbens. There are opioid receptors located on the GABA interneurons and when they bind morphine this reduces the amount of GABA that is released, which tones down the inhibitory influence on the dopamine neurons. As a result, more dopamine is released in the nucleus accumbens (Di Chiara and North, 1992).

Morphine and other opioid agonists supress the cough reflex, which explains why they were used historically in cough syrups. They are also sedating and have a constipating effect. On first use of the drug many people experience nausea and vomiting. Tolerance occurs to many of the effects of opioid agonists, and overdose can result in a person stopping breathing because the brain becomes less sensitive to the signals that maintain respiration (Bailey et al., 2000). The treatment for opioid overdose is to administer an opioid antagonist. Administration of opioid agonists causes long-term changes in receptor signalling mechanisms in the locus coeruleus which is thought to underlie tolerance (Carlezon et al., 2005).

CANNABIS

Cannabis is the most widely used illicit drug in the world (UNODC, 2012). About 147 million people, or 2.5% of the world population, consume cannabis. Various parts of cannabis plants are used recreationally for their mood and perception altering effects. The dried crushed plant is known as marijuana whereas the crushed tops of the female plants are known as ganja. Hashish is a dried resin from the female plants. The effects of cannabis on the brain are due primarily to a chemical component called delta-9-tetrahydrocannabinol, which we refer to as THC (Mechoulam and Gaoni, 1967).

The amount of THC varies according to the type of drug preparation and plant type. Hashish has more THC than marijuana. Some plant strains have a high THC content and are known as skunk. Cannabis is usually smoked as a joint or using a water pipe (sometimes with tobacco added), which delivers THC rapidly to the brain. It may also be consumed orally in fat containing foods or drunk as a tea, in which case the peak plasma concentration is reached after about an hour (Agurell et al., 1986). THC is taken up into fat and slowly released to maintain low levels in blood. Levels of THC can be detected in plasma for up to six days after smoking, in frequent users.

THC is an agonist at cannabinoid receptors in the brain. There are two types of cannabinoid receptors: CB1 and CB2 (Devane et al., 1988; Munro et al., 1993). The psychological effects of cannabis are due to the actions of THC at CB1 receptors (Heishman et al., 1989). Drugs that block the effects of THC also block the effects of cannabis. THC mimics the effects of endogenous cannabinoids like anandamide (Devane et al., 1992). The most commonly reported effects of cannabis in users are relaxation, happiness, increased sensory perception and laughter (Green et al., 2003). Some users report negative responses such as feelings of paranoia and anxiety (Atha and Blanchard., 1997). Cannabis users also experience time as passing quickly (Hicks et al., 1984). The effects experienced depend on whether a person is experienced with cannabis and on the set and setting in which the drug is taken.

Cannabinoid receptors are distributed all over the brain but are present in high numbers in the **hippocampus**, the cerebellum, the basal ganglia and the neocortex (Herkenham et al., 1990). Effects of THC binding in these areas include memory impairment and disruption of motor function (Chevaleyre and Castillo, 2004; Glass et al., 1997). Many studies have shown significant effects on short-term memory (Abel, 1971). Cannabis, like alcohol, impairs balance (Greenberg et al., 1994) and performance on tasks that require fine coordination (Manno et al., 1970). Effects on perceptual–motor coordination can increase the risk of accidents if users drive while intoxicated, although the effects of cannabis may be less harmful than alcohol because people drive more slowly and take fewer risks under the influence of cannabis (Terry and Wright, 2005).

Cannabinoid receptors are also abundant in the mesolimbic dopamine system and actions at these receptors underlies the rewarding effects of THC (Maldonado et al., 2006). THC is effective in animal models of addiction such as self-administration and conditioned place preference. Experimental studies in people show that they are able to discriminate between cigarettes containing different levels of THC and readily choose higher concentration of THC over lower concentrations or placebo (Haney et al., 1997). THC selectively activates dopaminergic neurons in the ventral tegmental area, which causes release of dopamine in the nucleus accumbens (Tanda et al., 1997).

There are also interactions between cannabinoid and opioid systems in the brain. Administration of a mu opioid antagonist blocks the ability of THC to induce accumbens dopamine release (Tanda et al., 1997).

Tolerance develops to the mood, memory, motor, and performance effects of the THC with repeated administration at high doses (Abood and Martin, 1992). The mechanism of this tolerance is likely to be a desensitisation of the CB1 receptor and/or a decrease in receptor numbers

(Pertwee, 2006). Repeated administration of cannabis can also give rise to some subtle withdrawal symptoms when use is ceased abruptly. The withdrawal syndrome is not particularly pronounced, probably because THC is very lipid soluble and so disappears only very slowly from its sites of action.

Various claims have been made for using cannabis and cannabinoid drugs as treatments for medical conditions such as glaucoma, multiple sclerosis and chronic pain. Of course cannabis itself has been used for medical reasons for centuries (Mechoulam, 1986) but it is only more recently that specific synthetic forms of cannabinoid agonists and antagonists have been developed for therapeutic use. An issue is that some people who say they benefit from cannabis medically argue to be allowed to smoke the drug rather than take synthetic formulations either orally or as a mouth spray. Doctors are reluctant to endorse smoking cannabis because of the adverse effects of smoking on health. Cannabis smoke contains the same carcinogens as does tobacco smoke (Moir et al., 2007).

There is interest in whether the other constituents of cannabis may be important for medical use of cannabis. For example, the cannabis based medicine Sativex contains THC and another cannabis constituent cannabidiol. Cannabis also contains many other compounds known as phytocannabinoids and these compounds are only just being fully characterised. They could prove to be useful therapeutics in the future (Russo, 2011). Dronabinol is a synthetic THC given to patients with AIDS because it increases appetite and counteracts the weight loss associated with AIDS (Beal et al., 1997). Nabilone, a synthetic drug similar to THC has been used to treat nausea and vomiting associated with cancer chemotherapy (Vincent et al., 1983). There is not much evidence that cannabis can alleviate acute pain, but it can help with some forms of chronic pain such as experienced with multiple sclerosis (Zajicek et al., 2003). Sativex has been reported to help with the spasticity (muscle stiffness) associated with multiple sclerosis (Wade et al., 2004).

Synthetic forms of THC have also recently become common on the street in the form of 'spice' drugs that are sold as legal alternatives to marijuana. There are more than 140 different spice products that can be bought on the internet or in 'head shops' and they are often marketed as herbal or natural products. There is limited knowledge of the exact chemical composition of spice ingredients but tests have shown that they contain variable amounts of synthetic cannabinoid agonists, alongside other additive and plant materials of unknown pharmacology and toxicology. The formulation of the drugs also changes regularly to avoid regulation and detection (Seely et al., 2012). Some spice blends contain non-cannabinoid ingredients as in the herbal blend krypton that contains a mu opioid agonist and has been associated with unintentional overdose (Kronstrand et al., 2011).

PSYCHEDELIC DRUGS

Some drugs alter consciousness by distorting perception, cognition and mood in a manner described as 'mind expanding'. Thoughts appear less constrained than normal and the world seems stranger under the influence of these drugs. For this reason they are known as 'psychedelic' which means 'mind-manifesting'. **Psychedelic drugs** are also known as hallucinogens but this term is somewhat misleading because at the doses that most users experience, psychedelics rarely produce visual hallucinations. The actual effects experienced also depend upon the mind-set of the person taking the drug (expectations) and the setting in which the drug is taken, for example whether the context is familiar or unfamiliar. A person may experience pleasant mystical-like experiences or feelings of anxiety because of a sense of disconnection from external reality.

Psychedelic drugs derived from plants have been used throughout human history in healing ceremonies and religious rituals because of their consciousness altering effects (Schultes and Hofmann, 1979). As we will discover it is perhaps not surprising that psychedelic drugs were regarded as sacred by many civilizations since the experiences they engender are so other-worldly. Imagine how early humans would have felt after ingesting hallucinogenic plants and then sought to explain their experiences.

Research into psychedelics began in the 1950s with clinical trials reporting promising effects of psychedelics for the treatment of anxiety and depression. However, in the 1970s, use of the drugs became more widespread and associated with counterculture. Psychedelic drug use then became illegal and research was almost impossible. But recently interest in how psychedelic drugs act to alter consciousness has grown, sparking new debate about their potential use as therapeutics. In addition, studying the effects of psychedelics is providing new insights into the neurobiological understanding of consciousness. Psychedelic drugs are varied in the primary way in which they alter neurotransmission but recent research suggests that they may have similar effects on patterns of brain connectivity, which could explain their common behavioural effects (Isbell, 1959).

Lysergic acid diethylamide

Lysergic acid diethylamide (LSD) is a compound that was first synthesised by the scientist Albert Hofmann. He was actually investigating the potential therapeutic effects of compounds derived from a fungus called ergot that grows on cereals like rye grass (Figure 2.10) and was not interested in psychedelic drugs at all. Initially, LSD seemed of little interest until one afternoon Hofmann accidentally experienced its effects after some of the very potent compound got on his skin (Hofmann, 1994). What he experienced was an LSD trip characterised by perceptual distortions and out-of-body experiences. LSD also has physiological effects to dilate the pupils, increase heart rate and blood pressure and induce dizziness and drowsiness.

The effects of LSD on perception are thought to be mediated by action at the 5-HT2A receptor (Sadzot et al., 1989). It was noted that some of the effects of LSD resemble perceptual distortion seen in schizophrenia and this led to the idea that serotonin dysfunction may play a role in psychotic states (Geyer and Vollenweider, 2008). Some of the effects of LSD may also be mediated by an action of the drug at dopamine receptors (Marona-Lewicka et al., 2005).

LSD is taken orally and its effects typically begin within 30 to 90 minutes of ingestion and may last as long as 6–8 hours. Tolerance develops rapidly to the effects of LSD and is likely due to a reduction in 5-HT2A receptors (Smith et al., 1999). The drug itself is not very toxic and one would have to consume massive amounts to overdose and die. LSD and other similar drugs are not considered addictive because they do not have effects in animal models of drug abuse (Griffiths et al., 1980; Fantegrossi et al., 2004). But that is not to say that there are no dangers associated with taking LSD and other psychedelic

Figure 2.10 Ergot of rye is a plant disease that is caused by the fungus *Claviceps purpurea*. Poisoning attributed to ergot of rye is referred to as ergotism and the symptoms can include convulsions and mania. It has been suggested that some victims of ergotism in the dark ages were thought to be bewitched and that this spurred witch trials

© Carmen Rieb/Shutterstock.com

drugs. Fatal accidents have occurred after recreational, unsupervised use of LSD (Jaffe, 1990), and use of hallucinogens can contribute to the onset of psychosis in a small number of users (McGlothlin and Arnold, 1971).

An adverse effect of LSD use is what is known as a flash back, which involves re-experiencing the effects of drug when no longer under the influence (also known as hallucinogen persisting perception disorder). However, cases are rare and the underlying mechanism unclear, but may relate to some people having especially vivid memories of the drug taking experience (Halpern and Pope, 2003).

Figure 2.11 Peyote is a small cactus that contains mescaline as its primary active chemical. It has a long history of use among the indigenous people of northern Mexico and south-west United States

© iStock.com/Oakwoodimages

Mescaline

Mescaline is one of the oldest known psychedelic drugs and it is found in the Peyote cactus that grows commonly in Mexico and the south-western United States (Figure 2.11). Mescaline has been used in religious ceremonies for centuries for the mystical experiences it invokes (Steelman et al., 2006), as described by Aldous Huxley in his book *The Doors of Perception*. Like LSD, mescaline also acts at the 5-HT2A receptor and repeated taking of mescaline will result in tolerance to LSD, which is consistent with a common pharmacological mechanism (Winter, 1971).

Psilocybin

Most recent research on psychedelics has been conducted on the effects of psilocybin, which is found in magic mushrooms. When the mushrooms are eaten, psilocybin is transformed into psilocin which is a potent psychedelic. In a well-controlled study in which psilocybin was administered in a supportive environment, participants reported mystical like experiences that had a profound spiritual significance to them. The participants had not taken psilocybin before and were unaware that they had taken the drug due to the double blind placebo design helping to rule out any effects of drug expectancies on the results (Griffiths et al., 2006). In another study, high doses of psilocybin increased scores on the personality trait of 'openness' and these scores remained high even a year later for participants who had a mystical experience under the drug (MacLean et al., 2011). The effects of psilocybin to alter perception are reversed by giving participants a drug that blocks 5-HT2A receptors (an antagonist). This tells us that the psychedelic effects of psilocybin are due to activity at the 5-HT2A receptors (Vollenweider, Vollenweider-Scherpenhuyzen et al., 1998).

Insight into how psilocybin might alter perception has been gained from studying the effect of the drug on neural activity at rest (Carhart-Harris et al., 2012). Areas of the brain that are normally quite active when we are just lying resting and not thinking about anything in particular are depressed after psilocybin. These areas are part of what is called the 'default mode network' that has been suggested to underlie the sense of self (Raichle and Snyder, 2007).

One possibility is that psilocybin and other psychedelic agents induce mystical experience because of its effects to reduce activity in this key brain network. These findings have sparked interest in the use of psilocybin to treat psychological disorders such as depression that are associated with hyperactivity in the default mode network (Sheline et al., 2010). In support of the idea that positive effects may be gained by patients even months after drug exposure, psilocybin was reported to reduce the distress associated with advanced stage cancer (Grob et al., 2011).

Phencyclidine and ketamine

Phencyclidine (PCP) was originally developed as an anaesthetic in the 1950s but patients coming round from the anaesthesia experienced negative psychological effects such as agitation and delirium and so it was never approved for use. Ketamine was developed to replace PCP. It has a similar chemical structure to PCP, but it is much less potent. Both drugs are known as dissociative anaesthetics because they have analgesic effects but they do not produce the sleep-like state seen with other anaesthetics (Corssen and Domino, 1966). Under ketamine, patients do not move or feel pain but they may still have their eyes open and appear to be awake. In other words the patient appears to be dissociated from their immediate environment. Indeed, out-of-body experiences and near-death experiences are reported when under the influence of dissociative drugs (Curran and Morgan, 2000; Jansen, 1997). Ketamine is still used today as an anaesthetic for humans and in veterinary practice. The acute effects of PCP and ketamine have been suggested to resemble schizophrenic psychosis (Krystal et al., 1994).

PCP and ketamine are used recreationally and can be ingested by snorting a powdered form of the drug or compressing the powder into pills. PCP is commonly smoked. Tablets containing ketamine are often sold as 'ecstasy'. When used therapeutically, ketamine is usually administered intravenously or intramuscularly.

PCP and ketamine are both non-competitive NMDA receptor antagonists. They attach to a binding site within the NMDA receptor ion channel and inhibit the flow of calcium ions through the channel which is thought to underlie their dissociative effects. They also have effects on opioid neurotransmission which likely contribute to their analgesic effects (Freo and Ori, 2002), and effects to enhance dopamine neurotransmission which may contribute to their ability to induce a psychosis-like state (Hancock and Stamford, 1999).

Acute dosing with ketamine causes impairment in various cognitive functions (Malhotra et al., 1996). Long-term use can induce memory problems even when not on the drug and some of these impairments are still present when drug use has ceased (Morgan et al., 2004). Tolerance develops to the effects of ketamine and PCP. The tolerance is lost when the drug use stops but returns if use is restarted (Kamaya and Krishna, 1987). Both drugs have effects in animal models of drug addiction (Carroll and Stotz, 1983; Carroll et al., 2000) consistent with reports of compulsive use from some users (Jansen, 2000).

Salvinorin A

A type of mint plant, *Salvia divinorum*, contains the active ingredient salvinorin A, which is a potent psychedelic (Siebert, 1994). Salvinorin A binds to a type of opioid receptor known as the Kappa opioid receptor (Roth et al., 2002). The leaves of the plant were traditionally chewed by the Mazatec people of Oaxaca, Mexico and used in healing ceremonies (Valdés, 1994). In recreational usage dried leaves are usually smoked (Giroud et al., 2000). The effects experienced are similar to other psychedelics but are shorter lived and there are no effects on heart rate or blood pressure (Addy, 2012; Johnson et al., 2011).

MDMA

MDMA (ecstasy) is sometimes classed as a psychedelic drug although we can perhaps best view it as a drug that has both stimulant and psychedelic properties. In fact it is similar in structure to that of both amphetamine and mescaline. Ecstasy is taken recreationally for its ability to induce feelings of euphoria and self-confidence and heighten sensory awareness (Figure 2.12). Ecstasy users often report that they feel more open and closer to other people after the drug, although this response is not universal and some users report feelings of anxiety or aggression and paranoia (Baylen and Rosenberg, 2006). There are also strong changes in physiological function including increased body temperature, sweating, faster heart rate, dry mouth, teeth grinding and jaw-clenching (Vollenweider, Gamma et al., 1998).

MDMA is an indirect serotonin agonist, inducing serotonin release from neurons and inhibiting re-uptake of serotonin at a serotonin transporter (SERT). In addition, MDMA causes release of dopamine and noradrenaline (Green et al., 2003). If we compare ecstasy to methamphetamine then we see that causes greater serotonin release and somewhat lesser dopamine release. Another difference between ecstasy, amphetamine and other psychedelics is that it also is an agonist at specific 5-HT and dopamine receptors (Battaglia et al., 1988). The rapid release of 5-HT after ecstasy leads to a depletion of serotonin in neurons. This may explain reports that ecstasy users experience low mood after taking the drug (Curran and Travill, 1997), although some of these effects may be explained by alterations in sleep patterns (Pirona and Morgan, 2010).

Figure 2.12   Ecstasy is the colloquial name used to describe the psychedelic drug 3,4-methylenedioxymethamphetamine (MDMA). Ecstasy increases emotional sensitivity and empathy and has been referred to as the 'love drug'. In the UK in the 1980s ecstasy was the drug of choice for people attending rave parties. However, a large percentage of the tablets that are sold as ecstasy, do not actually contain MDMA

© dwphotos/Shutterstock.com

Ecstasy use can be fatal, although compared to the total number of users the numbers of deaths are relatively small. Most deaths are due to the effects of hyperthermia, which can induce organ failure. To combat increases in temperature some users drink too much water and this can disturb the salt content of the body and lead to swelling of the brain and death (Schifano et al., 2003). These dangers are minimised when the drug is taken by study participants under controlled conditions with medical support.

The popularity of ecstasy has raised concerns over the possible long-term effects of taking the drug on the brain and there has been vigorous debate about the dangers by scientists and policy-makers. There is some evidence that learning and memory abilities may be slightly impaired in chronic users of ecstasy (Morgan, McFie et al., 2002) but there has been debate about the interpretation of studies that compare the cognitive function of groups of drug users and non-users at a single point in time (cross-sectional studies). One debatable issue is who should we compare ecstasy users with? Just comparing to non-drug users is a problem because their lifestyles might differ from drug users in all sorts of ways, not just in their use of ecstasy. Many studies address this issue by including a group of people who use drugs generally and might have similar lifestyles to ecstasy users (poly-drug users). Users of ecstasy often take other drugs, particularly cannabis, and so controlling for poly-drug use in studies is very important. When lifestyle factors and other drug use are taken into account, there seems to be little difference between ecstasy users and poly-drug users although both show subtle impairments in learning and memory compared to non-drug-using participants. This might suggest that recreational drug use in general, and not ecstasy use in particular, is associated with cognitive problems.

Of course, rather than rely on cross-sectional studies, preferably, we would want to study the cognitive function of people who have never used drugs and then go on to see if any later drug use is associated with declines in performance (longitudinal study). Some recent studies that have done just that and followed young people from not having taken ecstasy to using ecstasy at low levels for a year. Young people who went on to take ecstasy were not as good at some learning tasks as similar young people who did not go on to use ecstasy (Wagner et al., 2013). Both groups performed similarly at the study baseline. A downside of these studies is that the ecstasy users may have thought they were taking in ecstasy but in fact the pills they took were not ecstasy at all. Ecstasy is often mixed with other compounds and so users are unlikely to be taking pure MDMA. For example, one study found that many ecstasy tabs contained caffeine or amphetamine instead of or as well as MDMA (Vogels et al., 2009). Also, we don't know if the effects would reverse if the young people stopped taking the drug although there is some evidence that this might be the case. Most of the impairments also recover if people stop taking the drug (Gouzoulis-Mayfrank et al., 2005).

To investigate the long term effects of ecstasy, researchers have examined the brains of users using imaging techniques alongside assessing cognitive function. These studies suggest that there are changes in serotonin and dopamine function in the brains of people who report using ecstasy that include alterations in receptor numbers and neurotransmitter levels (Buchert et al., 2004; Tai et al., 2010). Such changes could underlie alterations in cognitive function seen in ecstasy users but caution should still be applied because the imaging studies also suffer from the same limitations as the behavioural studies.

So what can we conclude about the long-term effects of ecstasy? We might conclude that there is some evidence of long-term changes to brain and behaviour in ecstasy users but many of these effects could be due to concurrent use of other drugs. What we don't yet know is the extent to which other factors like the setting in which the drug is taken and genetic factors might affect whether or not a person suffers long lasting damage. It may be that a genetic variation in serotonin genes affects vulnerability to MDMA (Roiser et al., 2006). It is also possible that taking ecstasy with other drugs might have toxic effects on the brain. However, many scientists conclude that if low doses of MDMA are given intermittently in a controlled setting then toxic effects are unlikely (Sessa and Nutt, 2007). In fact some scientists are proposing that MDMA could be helpful in the treatment of disorders like post-traumatic stress disorder because promoting empathy with other people could help patients 'open up' and gain the most from therapy (Mithoefer et al., 2011).

KEY POINTS

- Alcohol is a depressant drug that affects many systems in the brain to inhibit neurotransmission.
- Stimulant drugs like cocaine, amphetamine, nicotine and caffeine increase energy levels and arousal and have a common effect to increase dopamine neurotransmission.
- Opiates and cannabis are drugs that have medical uses today but are also used recreationally. They mimic the effects of naturally occurring opioids and cannabinoids in the brain and have mood altering and analgesic effects.
- Psychedelic drugs like LSD, mescaline, psilocybin and MDMA induce distortions in perception, cognition and mood via alteration in serotonin neurotransmission.

CHAPTER SUMMARY

Drugs that alter psychological functioning do so by interacting with receptor sites in the brain and modulating the effects of neurotransmitters. They enhance or dampen the effects of neurotransmitters. Most drugs have effects on more than one neurotransmitter system to bring about diverse effects on behaviour, some of which may be desirable in a therapeutic context and some of which may be undesirable side effects. The effect of drugs on behaviour can vary with chronic use as adaptation occurs to the drug action. Responding can increase over time (sensitisation) or decrease such that more of a drug is required to achieve the desired effects (tolerance). Humans have taken drugs recreationally throughout history. Stimulant drugs enhance dopamine and serotonin neurotransmission and increase arousal and alertness. Depressant drugs such as alcohol enhance GABA transmission and increase glutamate transmission to inhibit neurotransmission. Other drugs such as psychedelics are taken for their ability to alter mood and perception. They act at specific serotonin receptors in the brain. There are significant risks associated with most recreational drugs and many have the potential for abuse.

FURTHER READING

Benowitz, N. L. (2010). Nicotine Addiction. *New England Journal of Medicine, 362*, 2295–303.
This reviews the brain mechanisms underlying the psychoactive effects of nicotine, and provides details on clinical aspects of nicotine addiction.

Murray, R. M., Morrison, P. D., Henquet, C. et al. (2007). Science and society – Cannabis, the mind and society: The hash realities. *Nature Reviews Neuroscience, 8*, 885–95.

This provides more detail on the effect of cannabis on the brain and on cannabis in society, and discusses the relationship between cannabis use and psychiatric illness. It also discusses the clinical uses of cannabis.

Nesse, R. M. and Berridge K. C. (1997). Psychoactive drug use in evolutionary perspective. *Science, 278,* 63.
This provides an evolutionary perspective on the universal human vulnerability to the effects of psychoactive drugs.

Schuckit, M. A. (2009). Alcohol-use disorders. *Lancet, 373,* 492–501.
This provides an overview of the epidemiology, diagnosis, pathophysiology and treatment of alcohol-use disorders.

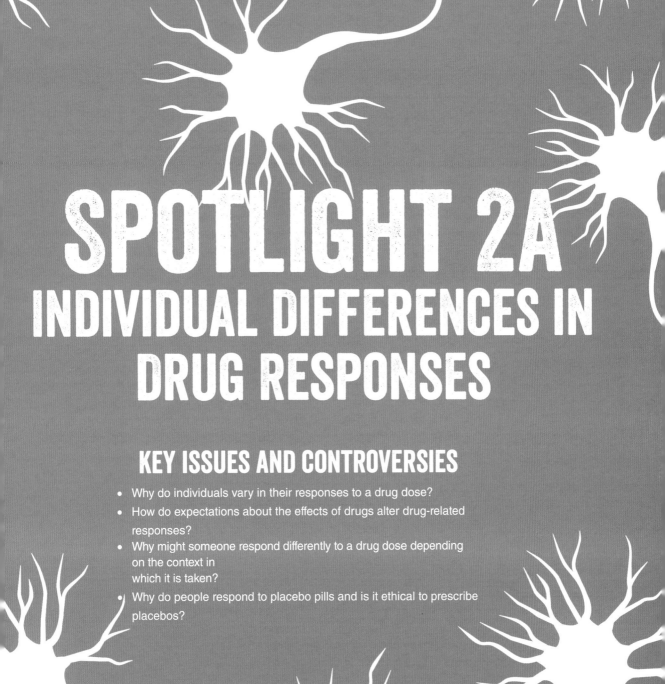

SPOTLIGHT 2A
INDIVIDUAL DIFFERENCES IN DRUG RESPONSES

KEY ISSUES AND CONTROVERSIES

- Why do individuals vary in their responses to a drug dose?
- How do expectations about the effects of drugs alter drug-related responses?
- Why might someone respond differently to a drug dose depending on the context in which it is taken?
- Why do people respond to placebo pills and is it ethical to prescribe placebos?

INTRODUCTION

In Chapter 2 we considered the effects of psychoactive drugs on behaviour, emphasising the population effects of drugs. In reality, the specific effects experienced by individuals vary quite a lot; the way in which one person responds to a drug may be very different from another person's reaction. Imagine two friends are out drinking beer. At the end of the evening one friend may be feeling much more intoxicated than the other even though they have consumed the same amount of alcohol. Let's say one of the friends goes out again but this time to another friend's house where they have never been before. They may drink an amount of alcohol that they think will not be overly intoxicating but they end up feeling a little more drunk than they had intended. In this spotlight we will find out why this might be the case. We will investigate differences between people in how they handle and respond to drugs and how environmental factors have an impact on drug responding both across and within individuals. Understanding individual differences in drug responding can help us figure out why some people do not respond well to therapeutic drugs and why some people may experience unexpected or adverse responses to drugs.

INDIVIDUAL DIFFERENCES IN DRUG RESPONDING

For the same dose of a drug, two people might experience different effects because different amounts of the drug reach the receptor sites; in other words they differ in drug pharmacokinetics. People also differ in pharmacodynamics, for example the number of drug receptors they have or their physiological response to a particular concentration of drug at the site of action. Some of these differences are inherited and relate to the genetics of drug metabolising enzymes or receptor types and some are acquired as a person ages or suffers from a disease.

A major influence on drug responding is body size. Large people have a bigger vascular system than smaller people. This means that a particular dose of drug will be distributed in a greater blood volume and will therefore be more diluted in the blood stream of a large person versus a small person. Less of the drug will be available at the target site to have its effects and so the drug effect will be smaller. This is why drug doses are usually scaled for body weight. Body composition (the amount of fat versus muscle a person has) is also a factor and this is becoming more of an issue with increasing numbers of obese people in many countries. The effect of body composition depends upon the drug. Obese people may respond more strongly to a drug than leaner people of a similar size if that drug is not very fat soluble. This is because fat is less richly supplied with blood than muscle and so a drug that is not taken up into fat will be more concentrated in the blood plasma of the obese than the muscular person. On the other hand, fat soluble drugs, including most psychoactive drugs, will be taken up into the body fat. This can extend the duration of action of a fat soluble drug in obese relative to lean people.

Age is another major factor affecting drug responding. In general, older people tend to need lower doses of drug than younger people to achieve the same effects and drug effects are prolonged in older people. One of the changes that occur with age is an increase in fat relative to lean tissue and this change in body composition may in part explain why older people respond differently to drugs than younger people. Aging is also associated with changes in drug metabolism and excretion. The size and effectiveness of the liver is reduced with age and the kidneys are less able to excrete drugs into urine. Older people may also be more sensitive to effects of drugs due to changes in receptor sensitivity. For example, much smaller doses of benzodiazepines are required in elderly than young people to achieve sedative effects (Albrecht et al., 1999). Aging is also associated with greater likelihood of chronic disease that can affect drug metabolising and excreting organs.

Men and women respond differently to drugs for various reasons. On average, men are bigger than women and they have a lower proportion of body fat than women. As we know, these factors affect the distribution of drugs in the body. Men and women also differ in the way in which they metabolise some drugs. Alcohol is a good example of sex differences in drug pharmacokinetics. Even allowing for size, women have higher blood alcohol content than men after consuming the same amount of an alcoholic beverage because women have a lower amount of an enzyme that breaks down alcohol. Alcohol is converted to acetaldehyde by the enzyme alcohol dehydrogenase. Alcohol dehydrogenase is present in the stomach and so some alcohol is metabolised in the stomach before it can enter the bloodstream. Women have less gastric alcohol dehydrogenase than men and so ingestion of the same amount of alcohol will result in greater blood levels of alcohol in women than men (Frezza et al., 1990).

Changes in female sex hormones across the menstrual cycle can also affect response to drugs via interactions between hormones and neurotransmitter systems like dopamine. For example, responses to stimulant drugs like amphetamine and cocaine are similar in men and in women who are in the follicular phase of the menstrual cycle, but men report stronger drug effects than women who are in the luteal phase of the menstrual cycle (Justice and de Wit, 1999).

Genetic differences between people can affect drug metabolism. The genes coding for the enzymes that metabolise drugs can exist in slightly different forms known as polymorphisms and these polymorphisms can affect the activity of the enzyme. In most cases, the polymorphisms result in slight changes to the activity of the enzyme

Figure 2a.1 Older people are more likely to experience drug-related side effects. Older people have a smaller amount of water in the body and a higher percentage of fat than younger people. This means that in older people, drugs that dissolve in water reach higher concentrations, because there is less water to dilute them, and drugs that dissolve in fat accumulate more because there is more storage in fat. With age, the kidneys are less able to excrete drugs into urine, and the liver is less able to break down many drugs, and so drugs are not eliminated from the body in the same way as for younger people

© berna namoglu/Shutterstock.com

but in some cases the enzyme may be inactivated (Evans and Johnson, 2001). Drug enzyme polymorphisms often differ in frequency among ethnic and racial groups. One example is polymorphisms in the alcohol metabolising enzyme aldehyde dehydrogenase, which converts the first product of alcohol metabolism, acetaldehyde, into acetic acid. Some Asian groups of people have a polymorphism that results in the production of aldehyde dehydrogenase with reduced activity (Cook et al., 2005). This means that when alcohol is consumed, acetaldehyde builds up because it is not metabolised properly. Acetaldehyde is a pretty nasty compound and an unpleasant reaction is associated with a build-up of acetaldehyde that includes nausea and flushing of the skin (Wall et al., 1992). If you have not experienced this effect then to give you an idea, acetaldehyde build up is thought to be partly to blame for the unpleasant effects of an alcohol

Figure 2a.2 For the same dose of alcohol, women will usually experience greater levels of intoxication than men because they are on average smaller, have a larger percentage of body fat, and lower levels of an alcohol metabolising enzyme in their stomach. These factors affect how alcohol is handled by the body

© Deborah Kolb/Shutterstock.com

hangover. A treatment for alcoholism, called antabuse, also has a similar effect because it blocks the actions aldehyde dehydrogenase.

There are also ethnic differences in other enzymes that metabolise drugs (Bertilsson et al., 2002). A small proportion of Caucasians have a polymorphism of a liver enzyme that means they metabolise some drugs very quickly and so therefore have a poor clinical response (Johansson et al., 1993). On the other hand there are genetic variants that result in poor metabolism of some drugs and a higher likelihood of an adverse drug reaction (Bertilsson et al., 2002).

There is similar genetic variation in the genes that encode drug receptor targets. Polymorphisms in the dopamine transporter are associated with differences in response to amphetamine (Hamidovic et al., 2010) and polymorphisms of the adenosine receptor affect responses to caffeine (Yang et al., 2010). Treatment response to antidepressant drugs is also affected by genotype (Serretti et al., 2006). Patients with a particular variant of the serotonin transporter respond better to treatment with serotonin re-uptake inhibitors like Prozac.

Whether or not a patient experiences side effect of drugs is also influenced by genotype. Antipsychotic medication is more likely to induce the side effect of weight gain in individuals who have a particular variant of a gene that is associated with the control of food intake (Malhotra et al., 2012). Variations in dopamine genes may be associated with a motor side effect of antipsychotics, tardive dyskinesia (Bakker et al., 2006).

Implications

Research into genetic differences in drug responding is leading to a new approach to prescribing psychiatric drugs. The idea is that with genetic testing, health professionals can avoid prescribing drugs that patients are unlikely to respond to or may be likely to induce an adverse reaction. This approach to treatment is known as pharmacogenomics and is part of a wider move towards personalised medicine. At the moment many people are prescribed drugs like antidepressants that are not effective for them and it is only after several medications have been tried out that the right drug is found. With pharmacogenomics, this process will be speed up greatly. Patients will not even have to take the drug to see if it works because doctors will be able to perform a simple and quick DNA test that will let them know how they are likely to respond.

PERSONALITY AND DRUG RESPONSES

Personality can influence placebo responding as it has been reported that people with a more optimistic disposition show a greater pain relieving response to a placebo than people with a more pessimistic outlook on life (Geers et al., 2010).

Acute responses to stimulant drugs vary according to personality traits. People differ in their reports of arousal and euphoria after taking amphetamines, with some people expecting stronger effects than others (White et al., 2005). One reason for this has been suggested to relate to similarities in neurochemical mechanisms that underlie drug effects and personality traits. (Depue and Collins, 1999; Drevets et al., 2001). For example, individuals who score high on a personality measure of reward sensitivity experience much greater effects of amphetamine on ratings of euphoria, vigour, arousal, elation and friendliness (White et al., 2005). One reason why this might be is that dopamine neurotransmission underlies both the subjective responses to amphetamine and trait reward sensitivity (Depue and Collins, 1999; Drevets et al., 2001). This may be significant because it is possible that individuals who respond more strongly to the acute effects of drugs like amphetamine are more likely to end up abusing them (Gabbay, 2003).

Variations in the response to alcohol have been linked to high rates of alcohol use disorders. In one study, young men with bipolar disorder reported less intoxication after alcohol than healthy controls even though they had similar breath alcohol levels. The authors suggest that the lower response to alcohol may contribute to the increased rates of alcohol misuse in young people at-risk for bipolar disorder (Yip et al., 2012). Evidence from animal models suggests that a low response to alcohol may be related to variation in serotonin genes but may also depend on early life experiences (Barr and Goldman, 2006).

STRESS AND DRUG RESPONSES

There are links between stress and drug responses. A strong association has been noted between early life stress and later alcohol abuse (Pilowsky et al., 2009). There is supporting evidence from studies of laboratory animals in which exposure to a stressor can be carefully controlled. A stressful environment increases the reinforcing effects of drugs of abuse whereas exposure to a stimulating environment reduces the reinforcing effects of drugs like cocaine (Stairs and Bardo, 2009). The effects of harsh environments early in life can have long lasting effects on drug responses (Kosten et al., 2000). However, social status is also important and is likely to interact with stressful conditions to determine drug responses. Animals of low social status within a group hierarchy are more likely to self-administer drugs of abuse (Miczek et al., 2008). In addition, social context modifies the propensity of monkeys to self-administer cocaine and this is related to changes in dopamine D2 receptors (Morgan, Grant et al., 2002). The effects of manipulating environmental conditions on drug responses has been conducted mainly with laboratory animals but there are implications for individual differences in responses of people to drugs of abuse.

Implications

Research into the role of personality, stress and social environment suggests that these factors interact to affect drug responding. Perceptions of stress that are mediated by individual differences in personality traits affect responses to drugs, especially drugs of abuse, and this may be exacerbated by the effects of poor social environment. High levels of anxiety combined with early life stressors might affect how a person first responds to taking a drug and then whether they carry on taking that drug. Understanding how different people respond to drugs and what makes some people more sensitive to the effects of drugs of abuse is likely to be helpful in predicting if someone is at risk of substance abuse and in designing more effective treatments for drug abuse.

ENVIRONMENTAL FACTORS THAT AFFECT DRUG RESPONSES

Genes are an important factor influencing drug responding and some but not all genetic effects map onto ethic group status. However, some differences between ethnic groups in drug responding may be due to environmental factors such as diet. We will next discuss the role of these kinds of factors in drug responding. Let's take two people who are very similar in body size, age, sex and ethnicity. These two people might still respond very differently to a drug. Why is this? There are many factors such as diet, drug taking history, the setting in which the drug is taken and the expectations they have about the drug, which will affect how they react.

Drug–drug and drug–food interactions

People usually do not take just one type of drug. This is often the case for patients who are being prescribed more than one type of psychiatric medication. For example, patients with depression often suffer from anxiety too and may be taking both antidepressant and antianxiety drugs. Recreational drug users also rarely take just one substance. Indeed, poly-drug use is the norm. This means that how a person responds to a drug may be influenced by interactions between drugs. Drug interaction is defined as the modification of the effects of one drug by the prior or concomitant use of another drug. Drugs can also interact with food constituents and herbal preparations in a similar way. Such interactions may occur accidentally or due to lack of knowledge about substances being taken.

There are three types of interaction that can occur. The effects can simply add together so that the total effect is the sum of the individual effects. This kind of interaction has been noted with alcohol and some benzodiazepine drugs that are used to treat anxiety (Linnoila, 1990). Taking alcohol on top of a benzodiazepine may be dangerous for driving because both drugs impair motor coordination and the combination can result in increased likelihood of an accident (Maxwell et al., 2010). Some interactions are synergistic: the presence of a drug or food constituent actually potentiates the effect of another drug. In other words the effect of the drugs add up to more than the sum of their parts. Synergistic: drug reactions occur between antidepressant medications and an amino acid found in some foods called tyramine. Tyramine increases levels of noradrenaline in the body but these increases are normally dealt with by the enzyme monoamine oxidase that breaks down dietary tyramine in the gut. However, when someone is taking monoamine oxidase inhibitors as a treatment for depression, their ability to handle tyramine in the diet is vastly reduced and a small amount of tyramine can induce harmful increases in blood pressure (Da Prada et al., 1989). This is why people taking a monoamine oxidase inhibitor are advised to monitor their diet and avoid foods that are high in tyramine such as aged cheese and Marmite. Another type of interaction is where one drug reduces the effect of another, which is an antagonistic interaction. For example, the memory impairing effects of the main active constituent in cannabis, THC, are inhibited by another compound found in cannabis, cannabidiol (Morgan, Schafer et al., 2010)

Drug interactions can occur due to pharmacokinetic effects. For example, a drug or food constituent can alter the effectiveness of metabolic enzymes. Some fruits such as grapefruit contain compounds that inhibit enzymes that metabolise drugs like caffeine and benzodiazepines. This means that if grapefruit is consumed alongside these drugs then their effects are greater because their metabolism is reduced (Bailey et al., 1994).

There are also pharmacodynamic interactions. If two drugs interact with the same neurotransmitter system then toxicity can result because of the combined effects. An example is the serotonin syndrome that can result if antidepressant medications like serotonin re-uptake inhibitors (SSRIs) are taken with St. Johns Wort, an over-the-counter medication for depression that also increases serotonin neurotransmission (Fugh-Berman, 2000). Serotonin syndrome involves sweating, tremor, flushing, confusion and agitation and is potentially life threatening.

DRUG EXPECTATIONS AND PLACEBO EFFECTS

A person's history of drug taking can affect responses due to processes of tolerance and/or sensitisation as we discussed in Chapter 2. But a history of taking drugs can also have effects to alter expectations about the effects of a drug. So how someone thinks they will be affected by a drug is important in determining how they actually respond. In addition, these drug expectancies can become dependent on the context in which a drug is taken, meaning that the same person can experience different drug effects depending on where they take the drug.

People bring to a drug experience ideas about how they will react. This may be based on prior experience with taking the drug or on folklore and cultural beliefs. One person may have an expectation that they will be happy and sociable after alcohol whereas someone else might believe that alcohol makes them reflective and subdued. These expectations can affect how a person behaves. Similarly, someone who believes that a pill is a pain killer will experience more of an analgesic effect than someone who does not have that same expectation. This is known as the **placebo effect**. Beliefs about expected drug effects can affect responses in a positive manner whereby the drug can produce a greater response if it is believed to be effective, but they can also be negative such that people will experience less of a drug effect if they have low expectations. For example, negative expectations can increase pain sensitivity and attenuate the effects of analgesic drugs (Tracey, 2010). This is known as a nocebo effect.

KEY STUDY
Levine, J., Gordon N. and Fields, H. (1978). The mechanism of placebo analgesia. *The Lancet*, 312(8091), 654–7

Placebo effects can explain individual variation in drug responding because the expectations about the drug add to the pharmacological effects of the drug and may even involve activation of the same pharmacological systems. A classic study on this topic is the report by Levine and colleagues on the role of opioids in placebo effects. To understand this study we need to first know that opioids are involved in pain relief. Brain opioids are important in natural responses to painful stimuli, and synthetic opioids are used medicinally as analgesics. Levine and colleagues were interested in whether the expectation that a pill will provide pain relief is due to activity in the brain opioid systems that mediate actual pain relief. To do this, they decided to study the effect of placebos on real pain. The

(Continued)

(Continued)

patients in the study by Levine and colleagues certainly had a painful experience because they had a tooth removed! This was not done for the experiment of course: it needed to happen anyway. The experiment was actually about what the patients were given after the surgery. They were told that they might receive morphine, placebo, or naloxone. Two hours after the surgery, some of the patients were actually given morphine, some naloxone, and some placebo. All the doses were given double-blind so that neither the participants nor the experimenters knew who had what treatment. Then, another hour later, some of the placebo patients received naloxone and some of the naloxone patients received placebo. Most of the participants stayed the course of the study and what happened was very interesting. At first, the patients receiving the placebo reported less pain than those who received the naloxone. However, on closer inspection only some of the placebo patients experienced less pain than the naloxone group; in other words there were placebo responders and non-responders.

In the next phase of the study, when some of the participants who had received placebo in the first phase were given naloxone, those participants who were placebo responders reported an increase in pain. The placebo non-responders were not affected when they subsequently got naloxone. The critical findings from this study are: 1) that some participants report pain relief even though they have been given a placebo; and 2) that the placebo effect is blocked by an opioid antagonist. These results

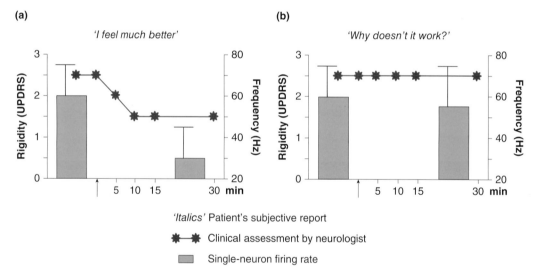

'*Italics*' Patient's subjective report

✴✴ Clinical assessment by neurologist

▢ Single-neuron firing rate

Figure 2a.3   An interesting example of a placebo effect has been observed in Parkinson's disease patients. Patients were given a placebo pill and told that it was an antiparkinsonian drug which would help with their movement control. The researchers found that when the patients took the placebo and expected their motor control to be improved, there was a release of dopamine in their striatum that was measured with PET scanning. In another study, the activity of single neurons in the subthalamic nucleus was recorded before and after a placebo was administered to patients. Patients who responded to the placebo showed a significant decrease of neuronal discharge and a reduction of bursting activity of subthalamic neurons, whereas the placebo non-responders did not. The figure shows the responses for two representative patients (a placebo responder and a non-responder). The reports of the patients correlated with both the clinical assessment of a neurologist, and the activity of single neurons. These results suggest that the expectation of a benefit affects brain reward mechanisms and this may underlie some of the effects of placebos

Source: Benedetti et al. (2005)

tell us that the expectation of pain relief is pain relieving because it involves the release of endogenous opioids. In other words, the response to the placebo was exactly the same as the effect of a real analgesic: activation of the brain's opioid system.

More recently, brain imaging studies have confirmed that expectation of pain relief has effects in systems in the brain associated with pain responding (Wager et al., 2004; Zubieta et al., 2005). In addition, the expectation of receiving a stimulant drug enhances its effects, suggesting that expectations are likely to contribute generally to the effects of a variety of drug responses (Volkow et al., 2003). Furthermore, if a person has no expectations about the effects of the drug then the response may be reduced (Benedetti et al., 2011).

CONDITIONED DRUG RESPONSES

Learning about the effects of drugs on the body is one process that underlies placebo effects. When a person takes a drug they associate cues such as the sight of a pill or other drug paraphernalia, like needles, with the drug effects. After several pairings between the cues and the drug effects, the cues themselves can elicit drug-like responses. Pavlov was the first scientist to observe that stimuli that had been paired with morphine injections could elicit learned drug responses in dogs (Pavlov, 1927). Similar effects occur in cocaine addicts who experience cocaine-like effects when they have only received a placebo injection (Muntaner et al., 1989). This kind of effect may also explain why drug addicts often report craving in the presence of drug-related cues in real-world situations (Siegel, 1999). The cues trigger a drug-like effect that is experienced as a desire to take the drug. Seeing someone else taking a drug can also be a powerful cue and this makes it hard for people to give up drug taking if they are surrounded by others who are not abstaining (Childress et al., 1993). The importance of social context is also underlined by the finding that seeing someone else benefit from a pain relieving treatment increases placebo responses (Colloca and Benedetti, 2009).

Sometimes, exposure to drug-related cues does not elicit a response that is similar to the drug effect itself but triggers physiological responses that oppose the drug effect. In this case, when the drug is administered with drug-associated cues, its effects are reduced by the compensatory responses, and tolerance is observed (Siegel, 1977). An example would be compensatory response that develops to cues associated with alcoholic drinks. Most people are used to drinking alcohol in beverages like beer and the taste of the alcoholic drink elicits compensatory reactions that reduce the effects of alcohol. This means that when alcohol is served without these cues, say in a novel soft drink, the person is more affected by the alcohol than they would have been if they drank their usual beverage (Birak et al., 2010). This kind of

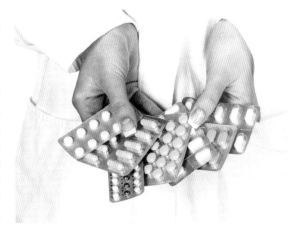

Figure 2a.4 The size, colour, shape, taste and even the name of a pill can have an effect on how a person responds to taking the tablet. How a pill is formulated is important in determining placebo effects and may affect compliance

© Lisa S./Shutterstock.com

learned tolerance can also be specific to the context in which the drug is taken. Indeed the effects of alcohol on behaviour are stronger in a familiar drinking environment than an environment in which alcohol has not previously been consumed (Birak et al., 2011; Shapiro and Nathan, 1986).

Learned tolerance may also explain some cases of overdose among drug abusers (Siegel, 2001). Taking a drug in an environment different from the one in which it is normally taken can lead to an overdose because the unfamiliar environment fails to elicit the compensatory responses that normally oppose the drug effect in the usual context.

Expectations about the effects of drugs are influenced by factors such as the colour, taste, and size of tablets. Red pills are associated with stimulant effects whereas blue pills are associated with tranquilising effects (de Craen et al., 1996). The more expensive a pill is thought to be then the more effective it is (Waber et al., 2008). This might explain why more expensive and invasive procedures are thought to be very effective placebos (Kaptchuk et al., 2006) and why people say that they get better pain relief from branded than non-branded pain killers (Branthwaite and Cooper, 1981).

Implications

Recent research on placebos suggests that expectations about a drug effect can bring about the same neurobiological responses as the drug itself. This suggests that drug-like effects can be elicited in the absence of any active pharmacological agent if the context suggests that a response will occur. This has implications for the clinical use of drugs because it suggests that the therapeutic context could enhance any patient response. So, having a positive interaction with a doctor and believing that a pill will offer symptom relief may result in changes in the brain that alter behaviour. The placebo effect also offers explanation as to why some people respond to magic charms and talismans. If someone expects to feel pain relief by following a ritual then it is likely that they will. An ethical dilemma that arises is whether doctors should be allowed to prescribe placebo pills without patients' consent. Could placebo research be used to justify the existence of healing practice based on strange rituals? Some evidence suggests that the patient–doctor relationship is a more important part of certain placebo effects than the ritual of having an injection (Kaptchuk et al., 2008). So, even social interaction can have a powerful effect on drug responses. As we discover more about the nature of placebo effects and nocebo affects, the potential for the misuse of placebos and nocebos is obvious and is an important topic for debate.

FURTHER READING

Colloca, L. and Benedetti, F. (2005). Placebos and painkillers: Is mind as real as matter? *Nature Reviews Neuroscience, 6,* 545–52.
  This reviews the mechanisms underlying the placebo effect and discusses ethical issues associated with the use of placebos.

Morgan, D., Grant, K. A., Gage, H. D. et al. (2002). Social dominance in monkeys: Dopamine D-2 receptors and cocaine self-administration. *Nature Neuroscience, 5,* 169–74.
  This provides evidence of the importance of social hierarchy in drug responding.

Siegel, S., Hinson, R. E., Krank, M. D. et al. (1982). Heroin 'overdose'death: The contribution of drug-associated environmental cues. *Science, 216*, 436–7.
This presents a model to test the role of drug-associated environmental cues in drug responses.

Yang, A., Palmer, A. A., & de Wit, H. (2010). Genetics of caffeine consumption and responses to caffeine. *Psychopharmacology, 211*, 245–57.
This provides a comprehensive review of a range of evidence on the genetics of reponses to caffeine. It also provides a useful overview of the pharmacology of caffeine.

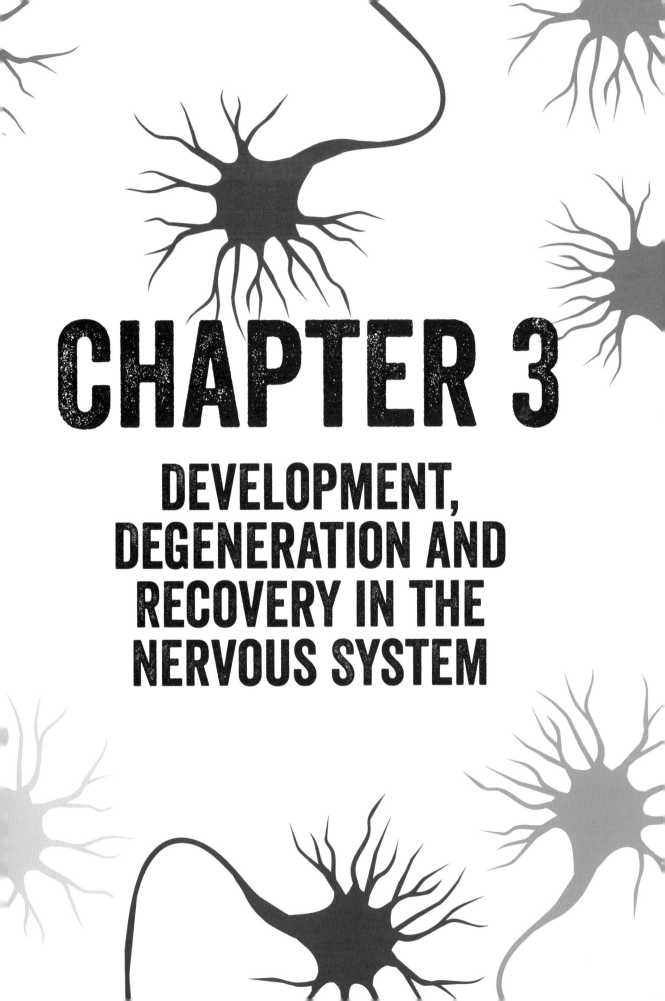

CHAPTER 3

DEVELOPMENT, DEGENERATION AND RECOVERY IN THE NERVOUS SYSTEM

CHAPTER BREAKDOWN

- An overview of the processes which convert the fertilised single cell into a multi-cellular embryo.
- Increasing cell number (proliferation), getting neurons to the correct locations (migration) and differentiation of potential neurons.
- Synaptic modelling; from initial formation of synapses, through loss of synapses (pruning) to life-long plasticity.
- Consequence of loss and potential for renewal of neurons in neurodegenerative disease.

ROADMAP

All humans start out life as a single cell yet the adult is composed of billions of cells of different types. Clearly the processes which underpin this transformation are complex and highly regulated. The building of a functioning brain requires two fundamental processes; first the cells of the brain have to be produced and organised to be in the right place within the brain structure as a whole. However, this alone is not enough to produce the brain that underpins the complex human behaviours explored in this book. We have already established that the brain is formed of millions/billions of individual cellular units and that they need to be organised very precisely. So, second, the connections between the cells have to form to allow the neurons of the brain to communicate with each other, as we have explored in Chapter 1, to form functional networks. In this chapter we will cover the developmental processes involved in these two fundamental processes that are required for building a brain.

Our understanding of the processes involved in brain development and the factors that control them may help us to explain both disorders which can have a behavioural component and become apparent during early childhood such as autism or dyslexia, and disorders that don't emerge until later in life, even in adulthood, such as schizophrenia, which is discussed in more depth in Chapter 9.

Once the brain is fully formed it would be tempting to consider it as a static structure. However, the continuous requirement for the organism to adapt its behaviour to its environment means that elements of the structure must change and the key elements here are the synapses and the neurotransmission processes that occur here. The brain also changes during the lifespan of the organism with considerable degeneration occurring over time. Yet its ability to repair and regenerate in response to the loss of neurons is very limited. Why this should be and the impact and extent of degeneration and regeneration on human behaviour will be discussed.

DEVELOPMENT

Much of our understanding of brain development has come from studying non-human organisms. Many of these studies use organisms that we would think of as considerably more simple than a human, such as fruit flies (*Drosophila melanogaster*) and microscopic nematode worms (*Caenorhabditis elegans*). However, what is now clear is that the underpinning principles of early brain development are conserved across species and are evolutionarily ancient (Arendt and Nübler-Jung, 1996). In the later stages of brain development some of the processes are almost unique to humans and, as our understanding improves, so does our ability to propose new interventions or therapies that may help not only to prevent maldevelopment of the brain but also how to encourage it to effectively rebuild itself after insult in adulthood.

Our current understanding of the development of the human brain, whilst not complete, is extensive and a detailed account of the molecules and processes involved is beyond the scope of this book. However, an appreciation of the basic principles and how they may impact on the adult brain will provide a useful underpinning to understand how behaviour may be influenced by brain structure.

Forming the embryonic nervous system

The fertilised egg undergoes a period of massive cell proliferation where repeated cell division results in a rapid increase in cell numbers within the embryo. Initially these cells appear to be virtually identical but in humans, by about week 3 after fertilisation, the uniform ball of cells has begun to take on shape and a layer of cells that are destined to produce the nervous system, called the ectoderm, can be identified; a process known as gastrulation. During the gastrulation phase the combination of differential gene expression and cell-to-cell interactions results in a process known as neural induction whereby a region of ectoderm transforms into a structure known as the neural plate; as the name suggests this is the first sign that a nervous system will ultimately be formed. The embryo then enters the **neurulation** phase, shown in Figure 3.1, which begins with the embryo elongating and the neural plate becoming a groove along the longitudinal axis of the embryo. As the cell numbers of the groove rapidly expand and the embryo elongates, the groove deepens until the top edges come together to fuse and form a hollow tube-like structure running the length of the embryo; the **neural tube**. Even at this stage it is known that cells along the longitudinal axis express particular genes which mark them as belonging to one end of the embryo or another such that the fate of cells destined to produce the brain is already determined. Genetic manipulation of primitive species suggests that the factors that determine cell fate are not just determined by the activity within the cell itself but also include environmental influences on the cell such that cell position can determine which genes are expressed. Hence, by about week 4, at the end of neurulation, the embryonic regions which will form the central nervous system have been established; the posterior part of the neural tube will form the spinal cord and the anterior region will go on to form the brain.

Clearly, the processes that have been described so far are entirely reliant on the right genes and subsequent proteins being expressed in the right place and at the right time within the rapidly developing embryo. Any error in this process is therefore likely to have profound effects on the structure and function of the embryo as a whole. Congenital defects in neural tube formation vary from those which are compatible with a good quality of life, such as mild forms of spina bifida, to anencephaly where the foetus fails to develop a substantial part, if not all, of the cerebral cortex and may be still born or die within a few days of birth (Sadler, 1998).

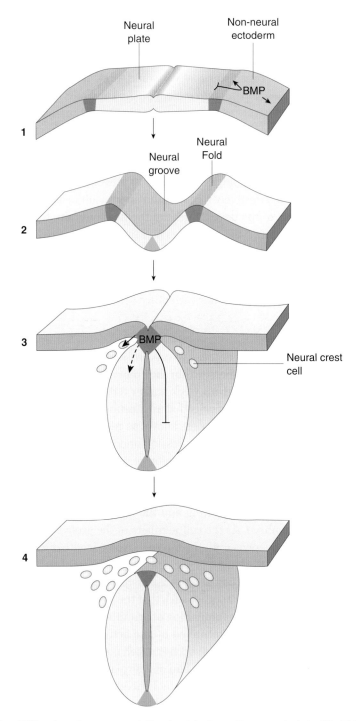

Figure 3.1   The CNS arises from a specialised epithelium, the neural plate (1). This process relies on the inhibition of bone morphogenetic protein (BMP) signalling. Folding of the neural plate to produce the neural groove is triggered by the formation of a distinct hinge point in the ventral region (the floor plate; 2). At the end of neurulation, the lateral edges of the neural plate fuse (3) and segregate from the non-neural epithelium to form a neural tube (4). The roof plate and floor plate form at the dorsal and ventral midline of the neural tube, respectively. The roof plate becomes a new organising centre that produces BMPs, which provide dorsal patterning information. Neural crest cells derive from the dorsal neural tube and migrate out to form the PNS, as well as melanocytes and cartilage in the head. Neural crest cells have been shown to form at an intermediate level of BMP signalling

Source: Liu and Niswander (2005)

Clearly the, sometimes subtle, differences we may see in adult behaviour are more likely to arise from events subsequent to neurulation whereby the highly organised structure of the brain is established.

Forming the fetal brain

At the end of neurulation, the anterior end of the embryo is not just a tube but has swellings known as vesicles. Each of these five vesicles will go on to form a predictable region of the brain. Continuing proliferation of stem cells coupled with specific protein expression and cell-to-cell interactions continues with the cells gradually differentiating to form ever-more specialised and neuron-like cells and can ultimately dictate what type of neuron is produced, including the neurotransmitters it will produce.

Migration and differentiation

Within the forming brain, progenitor neurons are produced at the same location, a region that borders the fluid-filled interior space known as the ventricular zone, but must then travel to their ultimate destination to group together with other neurons of the same type. The evidence suggests that once cells move away from the ventricular zone they lose the capability to divide, thus preventing inappropriate proliferation, and can be said to be entering a phase where they are committed to become neurons.

The processes involved in controlling this migration have been studied most in the cerebral cortex since this region contains a vast number of neurons in the adult and these can be observed histologically to show very precise organisation throughout the depth of the cortex, indicating

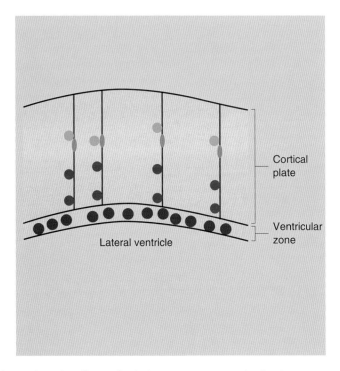

Figure 3.2 Inside-out layering. Post-mitotic immature neurons (red) migrate away from the ventricular zone along the radial glial cells (green). The earliest cells to migrate settle closest to the ventricular zone (dark red) whilst later cells migrate progressively further towards the surface of the brain (progressively lighter red)

a highly precise process has occurred during development. In brief, the newly produced neurons travel from their place of birth in the ventricular zone towards the outer surface and to their ultimate destination via a scaffolding-like network of specialised glial cells known as radial glia. The human cerebral cortex is greatly enlarged when compared to other species and is therefore considered to underpin the enhanced behavioural repertoire of humans. Hence, it should come as no surprise that any disruption to this migratory process would result in serious disruption to behaviour. Studies suggest that a whole range of factors from genetic mutations to exposure of the developing foetus to chemical substances can have profound effects on the developing brain, including through disruption of migration (Liu, 2011). An environmental substance which disrupts normal development is known as a **teratogen**. Many teratogens are found by chance when the correlation between maternal exposure and fetal developmental abnormality is observed; substances which have teratogenic effects on brain development include alcohol and even some prescription drugs; see box below. The observation that teratogens can produce brain abnormalities has been turned to scientific advantage to produce animal models of human disorders where developmental effects have been implicated. For example, if pregnant rats are exposed to methylazoxymethanol (MAM) at a particular point in their pup's gestation, then this agent interferes with the proliferation of neurons (Hradetzky et al., 2012). The pups are born appearing to be relatively normal but detailed analysis shows that they have some of the histological and behavioural characteristics which are seen in schizophrenia, making them a potential neurodevelopmental model of this condition (see Chapter 9).

INSIGHT: FETAL ALCOHOL SYNDROME

An example of a known potent teratogen is alcohol (ethanol) which, if consumed in large quantities, may result in a variety of developmental problems, including of the brain. As we have seen above, the very early stages of brain development occur in the embryo and within a matter of a few weeks post-fertilisation. At this time the mother may not even be aware that she is pregnant and alcohol consumption can result in irreparable damage being done to the developing embryo. Remarkably the embryo can survive and continue through subsequent fetal stages of development. However, if the damage was done in the early developmental stages, i.e. during neurulation, then the baby may be born with brain abnormalities such as a small forebrain. If the damage occurred later, for example, during the migration phase, then problems such as learning impairments may result due to cortical malformation.

Even if we take the situation where the potential neurons are all produced and migrate to their required final destinations, there is still some considerable activity required to produce a functioning brain. The cells can now start to differentiate and take on the physical and functional characteristics of neurons; this will require the development of processes such as dendrites and axons. These axons will need to travel through the surrounding tissue to find their intended targets and form synapses. To be functional, these synapses will need to be able to release a particular type of neurotransmitter and the postsynaptic cells will need to express the corresponding neurotransmitter receptors to ensure that communication between the pre- and postsynaptic cells can occur.

INSIGHT: GENETIC MUTATIONS IN DISC-1

The clear importance of appropriate protein expression for cell production and migration means that any error in this process will have profound effects. One of the sources of these errors is in genetic mutation. Mutations which result in a lack of protein production at this early stage in development are unlikely to be compatible with life. However, mutations where a protein is produced, but either at lower or higher levels or in a slightly different form, are more likely to be compatible with life but with some disruption of function. An example of a gene which has been implicated in underlying psychiatric disorders is DISC-1 (*Disrupted In Schizophrenia 1*). Despite its name, this gene has been implicated in a number of human psychiatric conditions within a single family including schizophrenia but also major depression, bipolar disorder and autistic spectrum disorders (Brandon et al., 2009). Experimental studies have demonstrated that the normal protein product produced by this gene is involved in supporting normal neuronal progenitor cell proliferation as well as migration of potential neurons (Mao et al., 2009). The involvement of it in different disorders implies that other factors, possibly environmental in nature, must be involved in determining exactly what the behavioural profile of the affected individual is.

Connection formation – Axon guidance

Prospective neurons being produced and making it to the appropriate location is not enough to produce a functioning brain. We have previously covered in Chapter 1 that the formation of circuits of interlinked neurons is what is required to produce a brain capable of determining behaviour. The formation of these circuits is not trivial however and requires the accurate execution of a number of processes. The first of these is that neurons that form a circuit may have their cell bodies some distance away from each other. At this point in developmental time, these prospective neurons are fairly featureless cells but, as we saw in Chapter 1, fully differentiated neurons are characterised by having long extensions from their cell bodies known as axons which can allow an individual cell to communicate with other cells some distance away via the use of regenerative action potentials. The question then arises as to how these axons are able to extend their processes in the right direction to find their intended target neurons.

   Our knowledge of this process is incomplete but appears to involve the growing tip of the axon, known as a growth cone, 'tasting' the environment through which it is travelling using receptor molecules which it expresses on its surface. The environment contains molecules which may be fixed on other cells or floating free within the intracellular environment. It should be noted that the growth cones can be repelled as well as attracted by these interactions. Thus axons are guided along a path by a combination of physical contact and concentration gradients of released molecules. This process of axon guidance appears to be highly evolutionarily preserved which is notable for two reasons. First, it suggests that solving the problem of axon targeting was key to the ability of organisms to evolve ever-more complex brains to support complex behaviour. Furthermore, it is useful for our ability to study the process since it means we can use rather more primitive organisms than humans to dissect out the details of the process.

Connection formation – Synaptogenesis

Once axons reach their intended target they will need to form synapses to allow neuron-to-neuron communication to occur. Whilst clearly this must involve the correct type of target cell, there is also a requirement for the presynaptic cell to target the right part of the post-synaptic cell. As we saw in Chapter 1, these synapses tend to form on dendrites of the postsynaptic cell. However, the precise point on the dendrites that particular synapses form, e.g. close to or away from the cell body, seems to be important. Furthermore, some synapses will need to form on the cell body of the postsynaptic cell rather than the dendrites, all of which suggest some sort of precise targeting mechanism must exist.

In Chapter 1 we saw that synapses consist of regions of the presynaptic cell that are specialised to release the neurotransmitter. The postsynaptic part of the synapse also has specialisations and the formation of these requires the exchange of reciprocal messages between the two neurons. The molecules that underpin these pre- and postsynaptic specialisations are mostly protein-based and are therefore subject to the influence of genetic mutations and other epigenetic factors that affect gene expression (discussed in more detail in Spotlight 3a). Clearly, minor changes in these proteins or their expression could still be compatible with synaptic activity but may change its character somewhat. The recognition that these changes may be important in disorders of brain function, including those where behaviour is changed, has led to the emergence of the term **synaptopathy**. Two recent candidates as synaptopathies are autism and attention deficit hyperactivity disorder (ADHD). Here individuals have a range of seemingly diverse functional impairments which emerge during the early years of life. Extensive study of the neurobiology of autism has long implicated a neurodevelopmental problem relating to basic developmental processes such as proliferation and migration. However, more recently, in-depth genetic studies have suggested that the major problem is centred around the formation and maintenance of synapses (Bourgeron, 2009). Similarly, dysfunction in synapse function has been implicated as a contributing factor in ADHD (Feng et al., 2005). Hence, the inability to associate disorders such as autism or ADHD, which appear to run in families, with any single gene may have come about because so many proteins are involved in synaptic formation. Since the synapse is the functional unit in neuronal communication then any problem with any of the contributing proteins would potentially result in the disorder.

Neurochemistry

As we saw in Chapter 1, neurons produce and release a range of neurotransmitters. Clearly, precisely which neurotransmitters a neuron releases will be determined by the suite of proteins, including enzymes necessary for synthesising the neurotransmitter which an individual neuron is producing. It seems that a multitude of factors determines the precise nature of this suite of proteins and one of the more surprising findings is that it would appear that the cells that the neuron is just beginning to make contact with can influence this process through the production of releasable substances from the postsynaptic cell which impact upon the presynaptic cell.

Optimising brain function

The processes described so far have led us to the point of having made all the necessary components of the brain and to begin to connect them together. However, this is not the end of the developmental process for there needs to be refinement to optimise the functionality of this emerging new brain.

Neuronal death and synaptic modelling

Perhaps one of the more surprising findings to have emerged from studying development of the brain is how much resource is put into processes and elements which are not ultimately found in the adult brain. For example, some estimates suggest that only approximately half of the neurons born make it into the adult brain. However, this loss appears not to be an accident or in any way random but occurs in a highly targeted and organised way via a process known as programmed cell death or **apoptosis**. This process is distinct from that which occurs as a result of direct damage to cells, e.g. trauma, which is known a **necrosis**. The mechanisms that determine whether or not a neuron will undergo apoptosis are multifactorial but include such processes as whether the neuron receives appropriate messages from the target cells it is attempting to form synapses with. Interestingly it would appear that neurons maintain their ability to undergo apoptosis and that this process can be reactivated inappropriately in later life, resulting in neurodegenerative disease as discussed below.

Synaptic formation is clearly a critical process with resource implications. So critical is it that accurate connections are formed, that many of the ones formed in the initial phases of brain development are then subsequently lost: a process known as **refinement**. In short, this process involves ensuring that connections are functional by maintaining only those that are active and therefore forming useful circuits.

Clearly, circuits are most likely to be initiating activity postnatally, once the individual is beginning to interact with its environment. It would logically follow that a human infant would produce and maintain more synapses if the input into the brain in the form of experience is higher. Evidence for this is provided by studies in experimental animals whereby those which spent their early life in simple environments had fewer connections than those that had an enriched environment which provided opportunities for, for example, exploration and play. This work, started in the 1940s by Hebb (1947), has produced a vast literature (see Van Praag et al., 2000 for a review).

One of the findings to emerge from this work is that during postnatal development there are short stretches of time during which synaptic remodelling is at its peak; these are known as **critical periods** – so named because the high level of synaptic attrition during these periods appears to be critical for subsequent functioning throughout life. It is therefore clear that if the right signals and environment are absent during a critical period, the young human will have potentially life-long impairments in function. Most of the original work on critical periods centred around sensory systems like the visual system, which is still today considered the model system for this process (Hensch, 2004). Much of this work is carried out in non-human mammals, such as the work on whisker stimulation indicating that the 'maps' of the body surface that arise in the somatosensory regions of the cerebral cortex do so according to the patterns of activity of the various inputs such that over time individual whiskers are associated with discrete regions of cortex and, concurrently, inactive synapses retract (Fox and Wong, 2005).

However, what has become clear is that critical periods exist for even complex behaviours such as emotional state and language acquisition and use. Indeed, it has been argued that the observation that disorders of adulthood, such as anxiety or schizophrenia, come about due to events and experiences (or the lack of them) that happen in the adolescent years, could therefore imply that adolescence should be seen as another critical period in brain remodelling (Blakemore, 2008).

Myelination

In Chapter 1 we saw that neurons are reliant on interactions with glial cells for optimal functioning in a number of ways. One of these ways is in the determination of the speed that axons can convey action potentials. The ensheathing of the axons by the spiral wrapping of the membranous processes of oligodendrocytes greatly enhances the speed of electrical signal conduction. This process does not occur until late on in brain development and is certainly not complete until axons have reached their targets. Indeed it has been estimated that myelination is not fully complete in the human brain until the late teenage years.

Synaptic plasticity

It would be tempting to think that once the individual has reached late adolescence that the brain could be considered to have become optimally organised with all the right synapses in the right places, analogous to the wiring diagram of a computer or a map of bus routes in a city, and with complete myelination. However, it appears that the initial connectivity plan does not persist for the lifetime of the individual. As stated above, the adolescent phase appears to have a second wave of intense synaptic remodelling seemingly critical in determining adult brain function. Some degree of on-going synaptic remodelling occurs throughout life and the importance of this fluid process cannot be underestimated. It is this process that allows us to form new memories and learn from our experience right up until old age and this is explored in more depth in Chapter 4 on learning and memory.

However, a price has to be paid for this fluidity; first it allows for inappropriate connections to be made which may result in unwanted memories or behaviours emerging at any point throughout the life of the individual. Alternatively, the coincidence of intense experience may result in a reduced ability to form memories, which may be the mechanism that explains why soldiers who are seriously injured in battle may have little recollection of the time period around the time of their injury.

INSIGHT: SYNAPTIC PLASTICITY AND THERAPY

Interestingly, whilst synaptic plasticity in the adult brain may be held responsible for a detrimental change in behaviour leading, for example, to symptoms of depression, it may also be exploited therapeutically. Many of the drug therapies used in psychological disorders, which we will meet in detail in Chapter 9, have unusual elements to the effects that they have on patients which seem to defy simple molecular biological explanations. Also, for some patients they are much more or much less effective than the so-called 'talking therapies'. Nonetheless, the evidence is gathering to suggest that for *any* therapeutic approach to be effective requires that the brain undergo plastic changes, almost certainly at the level of synaptic activity, which in effect reverses the processes that initiated the onset of the disorder in the first place (Castren, 2005).

DEGENERATION

Human brain degeneration is often thought of in the context of the mass loss of neurons following a traumatic insult such as a car accident or stroke. However, somewhat alarmingly, what is clear is that brain material is lost fairly continuously from not long after we might consider the human brain to be complete! Brain size changes during life, getting larger until about 20 years of age before steadily declining such that an 80-year-old has a brain of approximately equivalent size to a 4-year-old (Courchesne et al., 2000).

So what is lost during this natural process of degeneration? This is a difficult question to answer since it is impossible to know the precise number of neurons at any one particular time in an adult brain and to then be able to track them over subsequent time. However, what is clear from the previous section on plasticity is that natural degeneration does not necessarily have to involve loss of neurons but may involve the loss of synapses, such that considerable loss of processing power could be lost without any significant reduction in the number of neuronal cells themselves. Accumulating evidence suggests, for example, that synaptic loss can account for the reduction in cognitive power seen in normal aging. An attractive proposition therefore, is to understand the processes by which synapses are lost in order to develop means to slow or prevent this and thus maintain cognitive power with advancing years (Morrison and Baxter, 2012).

Pathological loss

The mass loss of neuronal populations through injury or pathological processes will clearly result in significant loss of function whereby the precise functions that are lost will depend on which neurons are lost. In Chapter 1 we met the concept that some functions appear to be localised within predictable regions of the brain, so to some extent we should be able to predict the functional consequences of damage to particular areas and, in reverse, predict the area of damage according to the observed functional disorder following, for example, trauma.

The mechanisms that result in neuronal death are very variable. At one extreme, neuronal death may occur in otherwise healthy neurons if, for example, the basic requirements of the cells are no longer met. This is the situation seen in stroke patients whereby disruption of the blood supply to neurons and the resultant reduction in oxygen and glucose supply and waste removal result in cell death. Neurons contain very little by way of reserves and so even temporary disruption for a few minutes can lead to cell death. If we look at the brain tissue of someone who has had a stroke at the cellular level, we see that there has been a mass breakdown of the cells in the affected area. It is difficult to discern individual neurons and there is a massive increase in glial numbers. In particular large numbers of microglia will be seen and these will have a different appearance to the ones that can be found in the normal brain. Their job is to clean up the debris of the disintegrated neurons, presumably to stop the spilled intracellular contents affecting neighbouring neurons.

Whilst the disruption to the blood supply of significant areas of the brain can lead to the extensive and diverse symptomatology of stroke, it is possible for smaller scale neuronal death to cause problems. For example, it is now recognised that transient ischaemic attacks (TIAs), whereby a relatively small region may have diminished blood supply and for a very short period of time, can, with repeated episodes over time, result in a gradual decline in function related to the region of brain affected. The most obvious situation is where an individual gradually loses cognitive power, such that tasks that they may have previously done easily become more challenging or even impossible. However, sometimes more subtle changes in behaviour may occur whereby relatives of those in this situation may notice that the individual appears to be, for example, becoming more irritable or aggressive or even takes on a more negative view of the world where previously they had been generally optimistic.

Alternatively, neurons might die due to intracellular pathological processes, where normal cellular biochemistry is disrupted. This is clearly a different situation to that described above where mass necrosis is responsible for neuronal loss. Accumulating evidence suggests that in this situation the neuronal death that we can observe is very like the apoptosis that occurs as part of normal brain development as described above. For some reason, which might be in response to a genetic mutation or an environmental insult or some combination of the two, the machinery of the cell switches into a degenerative mode that results in the death of the neurons. A striking feature of these neurodegenerative diseases is that it is often specific populations that are affected rather than some random, diffuse process throughout the brain. This suggests that for some reason the affected cells are more vulnerable to the environmental agent or are more reliant on the normal function of whichever gene(s) are dysfunctional. As we shall see in Spotlight 3a, most behavioural characteristics and disorders are complex and almost certainly involve both environmental as well as genetic influences. Furthermore, the evidence is accumulating that the number of genes involved is often extensive such that we are not, for example, going to identify a single 'Parkinson's' gene which is mutated in all patients. However, an exception to this is Huntington's disease which is monogenetic and appears to be influenced very little by environmental factors.

INSIGHT: HUNTINGTON'S DISEASE

Huntington's disease (HD) occurs approximately equally in males and females and usually only becomes apparent in adulthood. When the disorder was first being investigated it was notable that, whilst rare in any location worldwide, it was seen at highest levels in the UK and regions settled during the exploration phases of the 17th and 18th centuries. This implied that the cause of HD may be some form of genetic mutation which had originated in the UK and had 'travelled' to each of the new settlements in an individual who then gave rise to a pedigree of affected individuals. Experimental work has now shown that HD is indeed monogenetic and the protein produced by the mutated gene, called huntingtin, appears to be critical for all normal cells, including brain neuronal activity, although its precise normal function is still debated. The nature of the mutation is that a region of the genetic sequence is repeated more frequently than is found in the normal version of the gene. This so-called trinucleotide repeat is translated into the mutant protein and as a consequence the protein is processed differently, in some cells at least, forming aggregates which interfere with normal neuronal activity. For some reason, the mutated huntingtin has devastating effects on a subset of neurons found in the caudate-putamen of the basal ganglia, although as the disease progresses it affects other neuronal populations too. The earliest signs and symptoms are consistent with basal ganglia dysfunction (see Chapter 6) affecting motor activity, cognitive ability and also behaviour.

In many cases, our understanding of the cause of neurodegenerative disease remains rather poor, even though we may be able to characterise the signs and symptoms and the cellular changes that occur in the brains of individuals affected. For example, the prion diseases such as the human Creutzfeldt–Jacob disease and the form of dementia known as Alzheimer's disease result from the gradual accumulation of protein aggregates inside cells which eventually results in their death. However, we are still not certain, in either case, what starts this accumulation process or why the neurons finally die. It is likely that there won't be a single mechanism for all situations, but we will investigate in more detail the proposed causes of selective cell death seen in neurodegenerative disorders like Alzheimer's and Parkinson's disease in Spotlight 3b.

KEY POINTS

- Neurons can die by two processes: necrosis and apoptosis.
- Cause of neuronal death may be genetic, environmental or a combination of the two.
- Functional effects of neuronal loss are related to the anatomical site of the loss.

REPAIR AND RECOVERY

From time to time we may all injure ourselves in some way but then, dependent upon the nature and severity of the injury we would generally expect to recover often leaving no trace of injury. For example, a skin wound or muscle tear will heal in a matter of weeks and even a broken bone can repair itself to give normal functionality within months. The human nervous system, however, appears to behave differently whereby some parts of the nervous system can show considerable recovery but other regions show almost none. Thus if a peripheral nerve in the finger is severed it may not necessarily result in the permanent loss of sensation but, as long as the cell bodies remain alive, sensation may gradually return as the cut end of the axons regrow to innervate the area. In contrast, the extent of capacity for recovery of the adult human brain appears to be limited, since otherwise we may expect to see at least some degree of recovery in degenerative disorders such as Parkinson's disease or following acute traumatic injury. Nonetheless, increasing our understanding of what potential the adult brain has for recovery and repair is attractive in the context of reversing human conditions with a behavioural component in which neuronal loss is a key feature such as the personality changes observed alongside the decline seen in cognitive function in dementias (Emsley et al., 2005)

The rather limited capacity of the adult brain to regenerate seems rather at odds with its critical role in the survival of the individual. However, if we consider what would be required to regenerate damaged regions of the brain, it may be less surprising. In a case akin to the severed finger nerve described above, we would still need to be able to recreate the environment that was present in the developing fetal brain to enable appropriate axon extension, target finding and **synaptogenesis**. Clearly this is unlikely to be the case in the complex structure of the brain, and perhaps the prospect of regeneration resulting in inappropriate connections is a greater problem than the prospect of repairing damaged circuits. Study of the damaged adult brain indeed suggests that the lack of axonal regeneration when the cell bodies survive is not due to lack of capability of the neurons but rather that there are mechanisms in place to actively inhibit the attempts of axonal regrowth within the CNS (reviewed in Yiu and He, 2006). These mechanisms include released factors and molecules expressed by glia which often form a scar-like structure surrounding the injury site. Experimental studies, in which damaged neurons from the brain are exposed to a peripheral nervous system-like environment, have shown considerable axonal regrowth underlying the assertion that it is the nature of the environment and not some intrinsic capacity of the cells which determines the extent of regeneration.

Neurogenesis

The requirements for full regeneration to replace dead neurons would require two main features. First, there would be a need to have a pool of undifferentiated stem cells that could undergo proliferation, and second, these newly formed cells would need to undertake migration before beginning the process of differentiating into neuronal cells and therefore would need to be able to overcome the inhibitory nature of the environment described above. Up until fairly recently, the dogma was that new neurons could not be produced in the adult mammalian brain under any circumstances. However, experimental work, begun in the 1960s, has now shown this not to be true in a variety of species, including humans, and there appears to be on-going neurogenesis in the normal brain, although it would appear that the capacity for neurogenesis is generally limited to a small number of regions and that this capacity declines with age (reviewed in Ming and Song, 2005). Although the extent of intrinsic neurogenesis appears to be limited, this does bring an unexpected benefit.

FOCUS ON METHODS: EXPERIMENTAL EVIDENCE FOR NEUROGENESIS IN ADULTS

Identifying newly produced neurons in adult brain tissue is not easy because, to some degree, they will look identical to the old neurons. The fact that adult neurons have lost the capacity to divide is, however, very useful. Any newly produced neuron will contain newly-formed DNA and so it follows that if we could find a way of labelling newly-formed DNA we could identify newly-born neurons from older ones. This is possible using bromodeoxyuridine (BrdU) which can be incorporated into DNA but which is not naturally found in the DNA. Hence, if we inject adult animals with BrdU and some short while later we examine their brains for the presence of the BrdU, we can conclude that any neurons containing BrdU must have been produced after the animal was given the BrdU injection.

Elsewhere in the body, the capacity of cells to reproduce themselves or for pools of stem cells to act as almost limitless sources of new cells is subject to dysregulation which may result in the inappropriate production of high numbers of cells. This is the situation we find in cancers. Thus tumours found within the adult brain are not produced from fully developed neurons but may be glial in origin or, more likely, they have spread from other parts of the body.

Although there is now strong evidence to suggest that neurogenesis occurs throughout life in the mammalian adult brain, there is considerable debate over the extent to which this occurs and whether it is important functionally in humans (Lazarini and Lledo, 2011). The neurogenic capacity appears to be largely restricted to certain populations of neurons – the best evidence existing for neurons of the olfactory (smell) system and a subset of neurons in a structure found in the temporal lobe called the hippocampus. Considerable research effort is going into understanding why this is limited to just a small number of locations and how these regions are able to continue undertaking neurogenesis throughout life. A detailed analysis of the many factors involved in this process is beyond the scope of this chapter, but a clear picture is emerging that glial cells – which, as described in Chapter 1 have long been considered as only having a simple role in physical support – are key as they produce factors, for example, which induce progenitor cells to differentiate into neurons.

Olfactory neurons are born continuously throughout life within a vestige of the developmentally important proliferative zone which is found in the lining of the lateral ventricle, known as the subventricular zone as described above. The neurons born here follow a defined path forwards to the olfactory bulb where they integrate into the existing circuitry. Studies of the molecular basis of the migratory process have indicated that many of these mimic the processes observed during early development. In contrast, parts of the process of differentiation of the new neurons in the adult are different to that occurring in development and whilst the functional consequence of this is unknown, it is possible that this reflects the fact that in the adult these new cells are integrating into already functioning circuitry as opposed to producing circuitry *de novo*. However, this is an interesting observation for any future attempt to use stem cells therapeutically for neurodegenerative disorders. In rodents, the loss of olfaction is linked with behavioural despair and, indeed, one of the early models for clinical depression involved removing the olfactory bulbs of rodents. Furthermore, there is evidence to suggest that olfactory processes are impaired in human psychological disorders, for example during episodes of clinical depression, and that this can be reversed by the use of antidepressant drugs. It is tempting therefore to conclude that antidepressants are somehow coupled to the restarting of the neurogenesis process and that interventions that maintain or enhance olfactory neurogenesis may be novel therapeutic targets (Perera et al., 2008).

The studies concerning neurogenesis in the dentate gyrus of the hippocampus indicate that a group of stem cells give rise to immature neurons which can migrate a short distance before extending dendrites and axons, the latter travelling some distance before forming functional synapses. The key role that the hippocampus has in mediating learning and memory (see Chapter 4) makes it tempting to speculate that neurogenesis is a key contributor to these functions. The evidence to support this is accumulating with manipulations that increase neurogenesis in the dentate gyrus being linked to increases in specific aspects of learning, whilst those that decrease neurogenesis are linked to decreases in learning (reviewed in Ming and Song, 2005).

Despite our current acknowledgement that neurogenesis in the adult brain is possible, the role that neurogenesis might play in recovery from insult is still unknown. Two key questions are:

- whether the two stem cell populations described above can be induced to supply new progenitor neurons to the damaged areas even if they are distant to the sources of the new neurons; and

- whether other regions of the brain can be induced to begin neurogenesis in response to insult.

Either way, clearly an ability to manipulate the rate and extent of neurogenesis would potentially allow intervention to halt or even reverse neuronal loss following traumatic injury or as seen in neurodegenerative conditions where substantial numbers of neurons are lost (see Spotlight 3b).

KEY POINTS

- The brain retains some limited capacity to produce new neurons throughout life.
- Experimental studies in animals suggest that effectiveness of pharmacological and non-pharmacological antidepressant therapies may require neurogenesis.

CHAPTER SUMMARY

The production of a fully and normally functioning brain requires intricate and precisely timed processes which are determined by the genetic make-up of the individual and which are influenced by environmental factors. The production of the basic structure of the brain is then further altered to allow early life experiences to impact upon its structure and function. These may have immediate effects on the functioning of the individual or may, to some degree, lie dormant until later in life when they subsequently go on to have profound effects on the adult individual. The neurons of the brain remain relatively vulnerable to a variety of insults which may result in their death, although the likelihood of this increases with age. The brain appears to retain some capacity for production of new neurons throughout life, although the frequency with which neurodegenerative disorders occur suggests that this is limited. Any approach to artificially increase the regenerative capacity of the brain will need to be able to do more than just increase cell numbers; enabling the correct environmental conditions for appropriate connections to form and restore circuit functions will be critical for success.

FURTHER READING

Blakemore, S. J. (2008). The social brain in adolescence. *Nature Reviews Neuroscience, 9, 267–77.*

A review of the importance of understanding the plastic changes occurring in the brain during adolescence for determining both immediate and adult behaviour.

Castrén, E. (2005). Is mood chemistry? *Nature Reviews Neuroscience, 6,* 241–6.

A discussion, using depression as the example, of how the property of life-long synaptic plasticity might explain how behaviour can change over an individual's lifetime and whether interventions such as pharmacological agents and cognitive behavioural therapies might both rely on this property for effectiveness.

Stiles, J., & Jernigan, T. L. (2010). The Basics of Brain Development. *Neuropsychology Review,* 20, 327–48.

A comprehensive survey of all of the major processes that occur during development including a more detailed account of the role of specific genes in the processes.

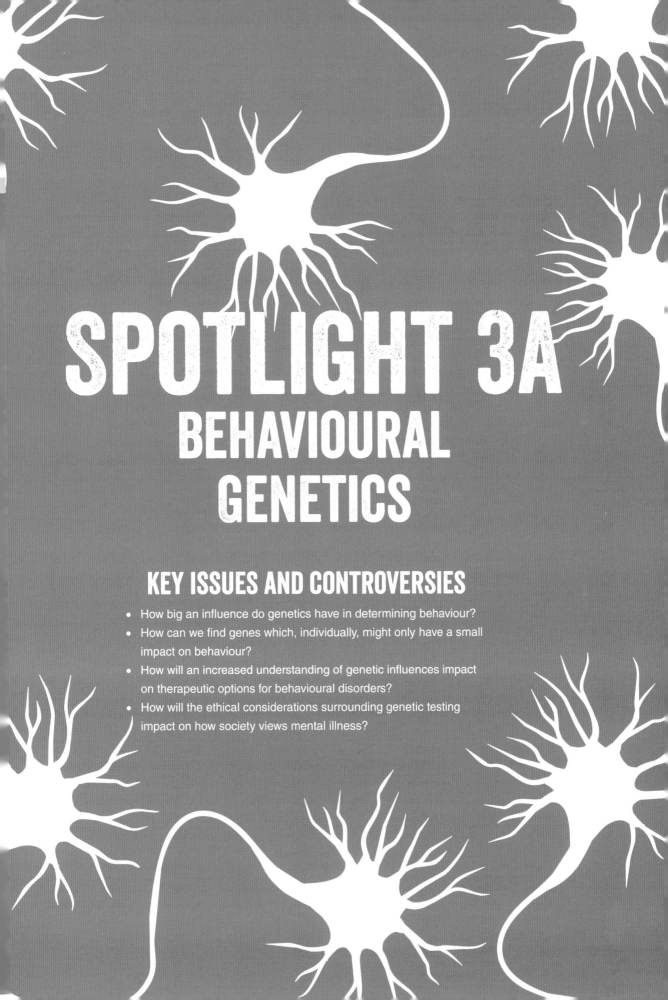

SPOTLIGHT 3A
BEHAVIOURAL GENETICS

KEY ISSUES AND CONTROVERSIES

- How big an influence do genetics have in determining behaviour?
- How can we find genes which, individually, might only have a small impact on behaviour?
- How will an increased understanding of genetic influences impact on therapeutic options for behavioural disorders?
- How will the ethical considerations surrounding genetic testing impact on how society views mental illness?

INTRODUCTION

Like any individuals in a species, humans share a considerable number of anatomical, biochemical and behavioural features. Yet we can recognise individuals because of subtle differences in, for example, their appearance and behaviour. The reasons for these differences have been a matter of debate for millennia and form the basis of the 'nature versus nurture' question. The answer to this question is still far from being explained although the consensus opinion is that, in broad terms, the differences can be attributed to differences in individuals' genetic make-up, differences in the environment and experiences that those individuals have been exposed to, and probably most commonly, a combination of the two. Hence, the response an individual makes to their experiences and environment may depend upon their genetic make-up implying that it is not 'nature versus nurture' but nature *AND* nurture that forms us as individuals, determining everything from our basic cell biology to our behavioural profile. One added complication is that differences in behavioural profiles can occur within a range; for example mood is not in one state or another but occurs across a range. This means that we have to define what is the 'normal' range with the implication that if an individual falls outside of the normal range then we might then classify them as having a disorder.

The purpose of this spotlight is to examine the evidence for a role for genetic differences in determining behavioural profiles using a few examples to illustrate the concept. We will also consider how scientific investigations have progressed to determine the extent to which genetics may be influencing behaviours and to then go on to find the genes and associated genetic control sequences within the individual's DNA.

THE GENETIC SEQUENCE

The genetic material, or **genome**, of all organisms is highly organised and our understanding of the biology and chemistry of genetic material is now highly detailed but beyond the scope of this text. However, suffice to say that in humans the genome has two major layers of organisation. First, the whole genome is divided up into chromosomes – in most cells in the human body there are 23 individual chromosomes and we have two versions of each one; one inherited from our mother and the other from our father. Second, within each of these chromosomes are the functional units which appear to be of two types: **gene**s, each of which can be considered to act as the blueprint for the production of a particular protein; and the rest of the DNA, which was once considered 'junk' but now is acknowledged as containing units which regulate the expression of the genes. Consequently, we could describe the difference between species as reflecting the fact that any one species contains a unique set of genes and control regions which is different from the set of genes and control regions found in any other species. However, what this does not explain is how differences between individual members of a species arise. To explain this we need to look at the detailed make-up of the individual genes and control regions. What becomes apparent is that each of these can exist in slightly different forms. For genes, these forms are known as **alleles**, whereby the same protein is produced in all individuals but the detailed nature of that protein can be subtly different between individuals. For example, if the protein were a receptor for a neurotransmitter, then two different alleles may produce receptors which bind the same neurotransmitter as an agonist but perhaps for different amounts of time, thereby resulting in subtle differences in the effect that the neurotransmitter has on the neurons possessing the receptor; this in turn may affect the properties of the neural network that these neurons belong to and, ultimately, the behaviour of the organism. Darwinian principles imply that only the versions of genes which make the organism the most successful amongst its peers should dominate. So the observation of difference between individuals of a species suggests that it is possible for different alleles to confer no particular extreme advantage. A well understood example in human biology is the different blood types seen in humans which are conferred by possession of different alleles, yet there is no evidence to suggest that, across the global population, possession of any one blood type is greatly advantageous over possession of the others. The coexistence of multiple types of allele or control region is known as **polymorphism** and the complete set of alleles an individual possesses is termed its **genotype**. In the context of behaviour, we can see that polymorphisms which influence neuronal function right from the development of the human brain to on-going responses and activity in adulthood are likely to produce differences in behavioural expression, known as the **phenotype** of the individual. If these differences reach such a level that they fall outside of the normal range seen in the human population, then we might expect to see a functional behavioural disorder of the type described in Chapter 9.

Genes and human behaviour

Even a basic understanding of genetics is sufficient to understand the potential implications of alterations in the genetic code, known as mutations. These mutations can range from a change in a single nucleotide (one of the four that make up the letter code of DNA) which produces a new allele, through to whole gene deletions or replications or even errors in chromosome number such as the trisomy seen in Down's syndrome. Here, the individual has three copies of one of the chromosomes (21), rather than the usual two, in each of its cells. Clearly the larger the scale of the mutation the larger the impact is likely to be and it may even be sufficient, for example, to result in spontaneous abortion during development since, as we saw in Chapter 3, proteins play a critical role in normal brain development.

So to what extent might behavioural differences either within the normal human range, or that which can be classified as disordered, be due to genetic changes/ differences? In theory, we might see situations whereby mutation in a single gene can dramatically alter behaviour or perhaps only alter the degree to which an individual exhibits a particular behaviour, for example by influencing their intelligence. In contrast, it might be that multiple genes influence a particular behaviour, and changes in any one can result in the variability we see across the normal population. In this case, behavioural disorders may require the combined effects of small scale changes in multiple genes, any one of which may have low impact in isolation. In practice, accumulating evidence suggests that human behaviour is so complex that any one behaviour is influenced by multiple genes so that we generally see gradations in behaviour rather than the presence or absence of behaviour. Although, having said that, there are some examples where single gene mutation is responsible; for example in Chapter 3 we looked at Huntington's disease where mutation in the *HTT* gene that produces the huntingtin protein results in a diverse array of severe neurological and psychiatric disturbances in affected individuals.

Epigenetics

Clearly we can see that there might be a link between the genes an individual possesses (its genotype) and how these enable the individual to interact with its environment and to assimilate experiences to produce its phenotype including its behavioural profile. However, if this was all there was to it, we might expect individuals to be 'hard-wired' behaviourally with no opportunity for their behaviour to change. To extrapolate to the full, we might then predict that, in the future, we will be able to predict how a newborn human will behave as an adult according to the alleles it possesses. Yet, this is not and never will be the case, because what we have not taken into account is how the environment impacts upon the genes. What has become clear is that possession of a particular set of gene alleles is not sufficient to explain the phenotype of any one cell, let alone an individual. All cells in an individual's body contain the same genetic material but we have a whole variety of cell types, including neurons, which are different to each other because of the particular complement of proteins that each expresses. To explain how this differential protein expression occurs, we have to take into account how and when the genes are activated to produce their related protein products. We have an ever-expanding understanding of these control processes and we now know a lot of detailed information about how the protein-product of one gene may regulate the expression of the protein-product of another. However, one of the most interesting findings in recent years has been that the control of expression of a particular gene can be influenced by factors independent from the actual genetic sequence itself. These factors are collectively known as epigenetic factors (Feinberg, 2007). We now have some understanding of the nature of these epigenetic factors and it is clear that there are a number of diverse processes involved, some of which control the permanent switching off of genes in early development, whilst others have the capacity to control gene activity in response to environmental conditions encountered throughout the life of the organism. This latter property is very attractive when thinking about behaviour because we know that human behaviour can change over time and in some cases with profound deleterious effects. So, the possibility that changes in epigenetic activity may be leading to psychiatric disorders is of obvious relevance for this text (Tsankova et al., 2007). A detailed consideration of all of these processes is beyond the scope of this spotlight, but by looking at a few examples which have been linked to behavioural traits and disorders we can get a sense of the potential impact epigenetics might have.

Genomic imprinting

One of the simplest ways of illustrating the impact of epigenetic factors is by considering the fact that all cells contain two versions of each chromosome, one from each parent. With the exception of the sex chromosomes, these two versions are considered to be equivalent such that each chromosome of the pair contains different alleles of the same genes. So the first question we could ask is 'Are both alleles expressed and if not which of the two alleles is expressed and determines the protein complement of a cell?' This would immediately lead us to a second question, 'Is the parental origin of the expressed allele random?' What has become clear is that for some proteins there is a particular pattern whereby usually either the maternal or the paternal version of the allele is silenced, allowing the other to dominate. This phenomenon, known as **imprinting**, requires a long-term modification of the DNA by methylation and is illustrated by the example of Prader–Willi and Angelman syndromes (see the Insight box below).

INSIGHT: ANGELMAN AND PRADER–WILLI SYNDROMES

Individuals with Angelman and Prader–Willi syndromes exhibit rather different characteristics. Prader–Willi syndrome is characterised by, amongst other things, learning difficulties, repetitive behaviours, hypotonia and obesity. In contrast, individuals with Angelman syndrome develop late, communicate poorly and show a high propensity for epilepsy although they are generally of a happy demeanor. Intense genetic studies showed that individuals in both cases had the same part of chromosome 15 missing, meaning that protein expression could only be determined by the allele on the other chromosome without the deletion. However, what differs between the syndromes is whether the chromosome with the deletion was inherited from the mother or father; if from the mother then the child developed Angelman syndrome, if from the father then the child had Prader–Willi syndrome. The deleted region contains a number of genes and normally either the maternal or paternal allele is turned off by an epigenetic mechanism; a phenomenon known as imprinting. So, an individual develops Angelman syndrome because the paternal allele has been silenced and the maternal allele, which would normally be active, is missing due to the deletion, and the converse is the case for Prader–Willi syndrome.

The Prader–Willi/Angelman situation is a rather extreme example of imprinting and we might ask how this phenomenon might relate to complex behavioural profiles where multiple genes from a variety of locations in the genome have been implicated. In fact, where studies have been conducted, there is gathering evidence that epigenetic control of allelic expression extends beyond early development and does not even have to occur in a predictable pattern for any one gene. Hence, some recent evidence has shown that which of the maternal/paternal alleles is expressed may switch during development as cells start to differentiate, including into neurons, suggesting that less permanent epigenetic control is possible (Lin et al., 2012).

Epigenetic effects and behaviour

The relevance of epigenetic factors in allowing the precise silencing of one allele or switching on and off genes to produce the myriad of cell types during development, is undeniable. However, the potential that epigenetics might be able to explain how the experience an individual has when young can influence behavioural expression later in life is very attractive and arguably provides the link between nature and nurture. Furthermore, epigenetics may help to explain a number of observations which have been used as arguments against evidence for genetic involvement in certain traits. For example, how it is possible that **monozygotic** twins with identical genetic material may express differences in behavioural profiles? Or how may disorders not be manifest from birth but only emerge in later life, such as appears to be the case for schizophrenia? For these processes to occur, a more flexible means of turning genes on and off is needed and again we have now got some way towards explaining these processes. Most of them seem to involve modification of a set of proteins known as histones which associate with DNA to form **chromatin** and thus allow the DNA to have a highly ordered structure that allows it to pack into the relatively small volume of the cell nucleus. Modification of these histones is required in order to allow the chromatin to open up to allow **transcription** of the genes and so it can easily be imagined that, even in normally functioning neurons, the chromatin is undergoing constant change relating to which regions are transcriptionally active and therefore which proteins a cell can produce. Chromatin remodelling processes have been implicated in mediating changes of behaviour, for example those seen in response to drugs of abuse, such as cocaine (Kumar et al., 2008). Furthermore, chromatin remodelling at any point in the life of the organism seems to be possible and might well allow the experiences of the individual to influence their gene expression. This might benefit the individual if they are, for example, forming new memories and this might partly explain the findings of the impact of environmental enrichment on synapse formation that we met in Chapter 3. Conversely, epigenetic mechanisms might also explain how negative early experiences can lead to behavioural disorders such as clinical depression (as discussed in Chapter 9) in later life (Sweatt, 2009).

INSIGHT: ADVERSE EARLY-LIFE EXPERIENCES

It has long been recognised that adult individuals with behavioural disorders such as those of mood or anxiety are more likely to have suffered adverse experiences when young than those who do not. This situation can be replicated in experimental animals of a wide range of species suggesting a common cross-species mechanism. The considerable research effort, utilising a wide range of experimental approaches from molecular studies to human family pedigrees, has converged on the physiological system that controls production of the so-called stress hormone cortisol as being of critical import-ance. It would appear that these early-life experiences could somehow alter how this system worked many years hence. In 2012, Tyrka et al. published results which indicate that the epigenetic state of the control regions of a gene that encodes a receptor for cortisol in human adults is different in those that experienced childhood adversity, suggesting a possible epigenetic mechanism by which experience ('nurture') can influence genetic activity ('nature') which might then manifest behaviourally many years after the precipitating factor was encountered.

Studying the degree of genetic influence on behaviour in the general population

So how do we go about investigating whether or not particular behaviours in the human popu-lation are influenced by genetics and, conversely, if we can identify genes in the laboratory, how can we work out whether they can influence behaviour?

For centuries it has been recognised that behavioural traits and disorders can run in families or have high prevalence in isolated communities. This implies that something can be passed on from one generation to the next and, of course, what we now know is that it is genetic mater-ial which is inherited by the offspring from the parent. Investigating the role that our genetic material has in influencing any particular trait requires a number of factors. First, we need to be able to define a particular behaviour which is not trivial; for example what exactly is extrovert behaviour and how do we categorise degrees of it? Second, we need to be able to accurately and reproducibly measure the behaviour. This is not trivial either because we will be assessing the behaviour in individuals being studied under particular environmental circumstances and if we accept that nature and nurture interact, then clearly changing the environment could influ-ence their behaviour. Nonetheless, being able to derive an estimate of how much an individual's genetics influences their behaviour has been a long-standing goal.

The concept that human behaviour may be influenced by something other than the envir-onment and experiences of the individual is not new. In the middle of the 19th century the Englishman Francis Galton was studying heredity in humans, particularly in relation to what we would now call cognitive function. The fact that he shared a grandfather with Charles Darwin now, in hindsight, seems rather poignant. This extraordinary man had wide scientific interests and looking back on his work now we can see that he was the pioneer of behavioural genetics. He introduced some key statistical processes for analysing non-binary data sets where the like-lihood of a factor having influence could be assessed – something critical for our ability to now analyse the degree of influence that genetic make-up can have on an individual's characteristics.

Where there is a suspicion that a trait can be inherited, insight into this can be gained by pro-ducing a pedigree or family tree which could indicate, for example, that a trait could be seen in a number of family members over several generations; an example is shown in Figure 3a.1. An obvious criticism is that it is impossible to disentangle genetic from environmental factors as members of the family are likely to share both genetic but also environmental factors.

So, how could we design human studies to disentangle the relative contribution of genetic from the environmental factors? Again Francis Galton provided an answer; a report of his work in 1875 suggests that he thought that twins were ideal study subjects to address the nature versus nurture question. Twins that are brought up together can be useful since there are two forms: identical twins are known as monozygotic as they arise due to the cleavage of a single fertilised egg and therefore have identical genetic make-ups; whilst those that are fraternal are no different genetically to siblings born at different times and so are **dizygotic**. Hence, these studies assume equivalent environmental experience for each twin but by collating data from many sets of twins and comparing the relative incidence of a behavioural trait for identical twins versus fraternal twins we can calculate how likely a particular trait is to arise due to genetics rather than the environment. So, if we observe that the likelihood of both identical twins having a behavioural trait is higher than both fraternal twins having the trait, then we can conclude that there is very likely to be a genetic component determining that trait.

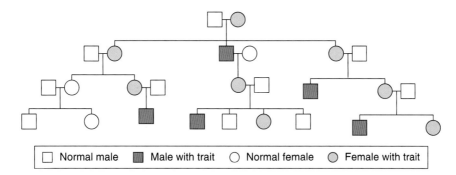

| Normal male | Male with trait | Normal female | Female with trait |

Figure 3a.1 Example of a genetic pedigree. Females are represented by circles and males by squares. Normal individuals are represented by open symbols and those with a particular trait or disease with filled-in symbols

INSIGHT: TWIN STUDIES IN AUTISM

For many years autism was considered to simply be an issue of bad parenting, but a study published in 1977 by Folstein and Rutter exploded this myth and provided the first evidence for a genetic influence in autism using a twin study. Since then, there have been a large number of studies from different parts of the world which have looked at ever-more detailed aspects of autism and related conditions as our knowledge of the disorder has increased, and most have reinforced this idea (reviewed in Ronald and Hoekstra, 2011). However, despite this weight of evidence, a relatively recent study provided evidence to suggest that the genetic component may have been over-estimated (Hallmeyer, 2011). The reason for this discrepancy in the literature is not clear. It is possible that the intricate details of study design may differ or maybe this is just a reflection of the problem highlighted earlier; the complexity of behaviour results in difficulties in providing precise definitions such that the point at which the boundary is made between the range of normal and abnormal behaviours is arbitrary, and the impact on these studies is potentially sufficient to explain these discrepancies.

Clearly we could estimate the environmental influence indirectly as everything that is not due to genetic influence, but is it possible to *directly* estimate environmental influence? Theoretically the ideal study design would be the opposite of that just described; that is, we need to have a constant genetic situation but a varying environmental one. This can be achieved where monozygotic twins are adopted into different families, but as you might imagine, this situation is relatively rare and it is difficult to get enough sets of twins for a big enough data set for meaningful analysis. A less perfect, but more achievable, study design would be to analyse differences between adopted children and their biological parents (so some shared genetics but different environment) with their adopted parents (different genetics but shared environment). However, these studies are not without difficulty either; for example, a full history of the biological parents may not be available. Also, now that we understand something about epigenetics, it is clear that the age of adoption will be important, since the later that occurs the more the chance that an environmental influence has already impacted on the behaviour, either at the time or at some point in the future, of the adopted child.

Although these types of studies can tell us the extent of influence genetics might have on a behavioural trait, they can't tell us anything about the nature of the genes involved; for this we will need to look closely at the differences in genetic material at the molecular level.

Finding genes linked to human behaviour

A good place to start to find the genes implicated by the kind of studies described above may be to ask the question as to whether we know the genetic make-up of a 'standard' human being, since this may allow comparison with someone with a different behavioural profile, even if that difference is not so great that we would consider the individual to have a disorder.

In 2003, the human genome project produced the first full sequencing of the human genome; we became aware that humans contain approximately 25–30,000 genes and it would appear that we are more than 99% identical to each other. One theoretical possibility, therefore, would be to sequence the entire genome of each of a group of individuals with a particular diagnosis and compare the sequences to look for this minuscule difference when compared to so-called normal individuals. This, however, is generally impractical as this would involve an enormous amount of work, taking a very long time; a more efficient approach is required.

INSIGHT: HUMAN GENOME PROJECT

The Human Genome Project was an initiative to determine the sequence of the nucleotide base pairs in the DNA in a number of people. This has produced a reference map of all of the genes, enabling us to localise genes to regions of particular chromosomes. It also allows us to assess the degree of variability that we may see amongst those defined as normal which means that we can compare the sequence of a gene from individuals with a trait or disorder with the reference genome to seek evidence that the gene may have a role in the trait/disorder.

A sensible approach would be to start by trying to find which of our 23 pairs of chromosomes carries the gene(s) we are looking for. For the most part our chromosomes are indistinguishable, but one pair, the so-called sex chromosomes that are either X or Y, are considerably different from the others. This means that if the gene that is associated with a trait/disorder that we are looking for resides on one of these we would expect to see a predictable pattern of inheritance in individuals of a particular gender in family pedigrees. For non-sex linked disorders though we will need to adopt a different approach.

Over the years a number of methods have been used to try and locate a gene for a disease or trait on the chromosomes. The original methods were described as **linkage analyses** as they usually relied on comparing the frequency with which an identifiable stretch of DNA (the location of which is known and is termed a marker) occurs in related affected individuals compared to non-affected individuals. These identifiable parts of DNA may be stretches of DNA which are highly variable in the general population known as **single nucleotide polymorphisms** (SNP or 'snip') or regions of tandem repeats, which are notable because they are composed of very many repeats of the same sequence. Statistically, the higher the incidence that one of these marker regions is found in affected individuals compared to unaffected individuals, the more likely it is that the gene being looked for occurs close to the location of the marker. Although this approach does not allow the precise location of the gene linked to a particular diagnosis, it does allow us to narrow down the location to a relatively restricted region of DNA.

The linkage analysis approach is very successful where a disease/trait is monogenetic, such as for Huntington's disease, which we met in Chapter 3. However, as we have already established, behaviour is most often attributed to the activity of multiple genes in different locations (loci) which might each have a minor role to play, so this approach would only be successful if we can track multiple genes and markers simultaneously. The advancement of technology has meant that we can do just that – an approach known as **quantitative trait locus analysis** (QTL; Miles and Wayne, 2008). However, these studies only tell us information about the trait loci in the pedigrees that have been studied and it may not be the case that this data can be extrapolated to the whole population of individuals with a particular trait or disorder. However, technological advances have also helped here because we now have the ability to look for subtle differences in the genomes of large numbers of non-related individuals with or without a particular trait/disorder using **genome-wide association studies** (GWAS; Stranger et al., 2011). These highly computerised studies systematically assess the variation in SNPs in affected and unaffected individuals on a chromosome by chromosome basis. The results of these studies can then highlight which locations show an association between particular SNP variants and the disease in question. Genome-wide association studies are a technological advancement of linkage analysis to enable potential genes linked to traits/disorders to be identified. The technological improvements mean that whereas linkage analyses use related individuals and focus on a limited number of markers, a genome-wide association study can compare multiple markers and in a large number of unrelated individuals. As a consequence these studies are more likely to identify genes which only have a minor contribution to a trait/disorder.

The results are usually presented as a Manhattan plot, an example of which is shown in Figure 3a.2, where the strength of the association is represented on the y axis and the location of the SNP according to chromosome is shown on the x axis. The name is derived from the similarity of the plot appearance to the Manhattan skyline. However, it is still important for us to recognise that at this stage all we have been able to do is to associate small regions of a chromosome with a trait; identifying the actual gene or control region involved still requires further investigation.

The large-scale nature of these studies, with many thousands of individuals' DNA to be tested, means that they are expensive to organise and run and so many of them can only be conducted by well-funded organisations and with very many research collaborators. Frustratingly, the relatively few large studies that have been done so far have sometimes

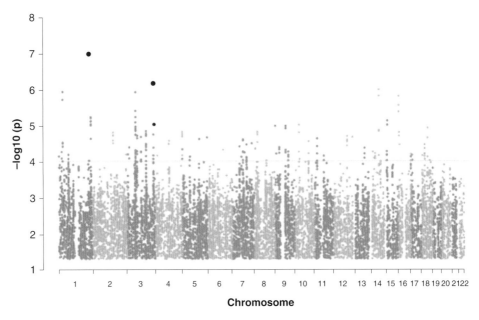

Figure 3a.2 Manhattan plot for a GWAS study examining genetic involvement in major depression (Wray et al., 2012). The data show that a large number of SNPs on many chromosomes appear to have some association with depression

produced equivocal or differing results for specific disorders. Early indications suggest that this may be due to a number of factors including the numbers of individuals which are included and also precisely how they are categorised as 'affected' or 'unaffected', further reinforcing the idea that behavioural traits may be a common endpoint for a number of unique sets of genetic variabilities. Nonetheless, an ever-advancing understanding of the key factors and statistical processing required in designing such studies will doubtless lead to more productive studies in the future.

Of course, finding genes which might have some involvement in determining behaviour is one thing, but it is the protein products of these genes which actually underpin the function. So, once candidate genes have been found we need to find out something about their activity by looking at the profile of their expression. Again new technology has massively speeded up this process, such that we can realistically assess the relative activity of all 20,000 or so human genes in individuals simultaneously using a DNA or protein microarray and comparing the patterns of activity in affected versus non-affected individuals. This will allow us to gain insights into the role these proteins play in behavioural traits and disorders.

One of the criticisms of association studies like QTL and GWAS studies has been that only a region of a chromosome linked to a trait is identified and not the actual gene itself. However, an interesting finding to emerge from QTL studies is that some regions implicated in being responsible for behavioural traits or disorders do not contain genes and so might previously have been classified as 'junk' DNA. However, an emerging picture is that these regions may encode small pieces of RNA which do not themselves encode proteins but which can interfere with protein production and thus alter the level of expression of proteins which are themselves perfectly normal. Our understanding of the role of these RNAs is still very primitive but these regions and the RNA that they produce could one day be of interest as future therapeutic targets.

Studying the role of a known gene in human behaviour

Candidate proteins and hence genes can be proposed on the basis of observation of the effect of exogenous substances on animal behaviour. For example, observing the effect that an abused drug may have or the serendipitous observation that a drug developed for one purpose may influence, perhaps entirely unexpectedly, a particular behaviour can lead us to suggest that particular forms of genes encoding proteins responsible for mediating the pharmacology of these agents may have a role in determining a particular behaviour. If we know the approximate location of such a gene then we can do an association study whereby a number of individuals, not necessarily related to each other, can be screened to see if there is a correlation between exhibition of a trait/disorder and possession of a particular gene allele which is different to that in the general population (Bird et al., 2001).

From decades of research on a variety of non-human species, we have acquired considerable knowledge of their behaviours, which appear to have some correlate with human behaviour. There are of course a large number of assumptions to be made here about how comparable animal and human behaviours are. Once we track the gene down in the animal's genome we can do two things: first, we can look to see whether humans with a behavioural disorder that seems to correlate with the change in animal behaviour possess equivalent genes. Second, we can undertake genetic manipulation studies where we alter or even delete the gene in, for example, mice, and observe the effect this has on the animals. One of the problems with this type of approach is that the mice may not be able to develop properly and so we can learn nothing about the role this gene may have after birth in the young or adult mouse when it can be subject to epigenetic influences. This problem has been solved by the creation of conditional **transgenic** animals where we have the ability to control the turning on and off of the expression of a gene at will, thus producing an animal model of the disorder.

Implications: What have behavioural genetics studies told us?

Humans have speculated that behaviours, in particular those that may be classed as disordered, have had a heritable component for decades. Over time our ability to rigorously study to what degree genes might influence our behaviour has greatly improved and we have seen that current technology allows us to study even genes which may individually have a very minor influence. So what is the current view on how much our behaviour, disordered or otherwise, is influenced by our genetics? In order to give some sense of how this huge body of work can be coherently brought together, we will take schizophrenia as our example. As covered in detail in Chapter 9, schizophrenia is an example of a human disorder with behavioural features which have been studied extensively in order to better understand the underlying biology, and in the hopes of finding therapeutic interventions to either prevent it or negate its effects should they emerge. Clearly we can see that if one goal may be to explain the cause of schizophrenia then we may have to return to the nature versus nurture debate and ask the question about what behavioural genetic studies have to tell us about the potential extent of a genetic influence. Decades of research have led to the conclusion that there is a significant genetic component to schizophrenia. So how might these various genes influence brain function to result in schizophrenic symptoms? Clearly, if genes are dysfunctional at the point of fertilisation then initial brain development in early life may be disrupted. However, the notable feature of schizophrenia is that it isn't obviously manifest in the very young but most often emerges during the early adult years. This suggests that either the dysfunctional genes are relatively unimportant during early brain development or that some other factor impacts upon the brain during adolescence which allows the dysfunction to then become apparent. Of course, as we saw earlier in this spotlight, we cannot discount the possibility that the dysfunction of genes themselves may not be the issue but rather some epigenetic factor relating to the experiences of the individual which may influence gene function. Given all of these possibilities, what have the various studies actually provided evidence for? A detailed analysis of the many thousands of studies is impractical here and reviews of this field are published frequently (for example, see Tiwari et al., 2010), but some examples to illustrate how the various approaches to studying the role of genes in schizophrenia will be covered.

The traditional types of population studies as described above have suggested that genetic factors may account for a variable likelihood that an individual would develop schizophrenia; for example, Lichtenstein et al. (2009) calculated a figure of 64%, although others have suggested as high as 81% (Sullivan et al., 2003). However, it has also become clear that this genetic influence does not follow the simple rules of genetics that were first described by Mendel following his studies of the inheritance of individual characteristics of peas. Instead exactly what trait is inherited and how it is seen in successive generations is complex and almost certainly involves multiple genes which may well not be entirely independent of each other. As described above, there are a number of methodological strategies that have been employed and improved upon over the decades to identify candidate genes. The simplest studies involve looking for relatively large scale chromosomal abnormalities and a number have been reproducibly identified. For example, a deletion from chromosome 22 containing very many genes has been linked with a syndrome which includes schizophrenia-like manifestations (Murphy, 2002). A less dramatic effect on chromosomal material involving chromosomes 1 and 11 has also been reported. Here, material is not lost but a portion of one chromosome is moved to the other, a phenomenon known as a **translocation**. The consequence of the translocation is that gene function is affected, either directly or because the gene has been separated from its control regions. Two genes, appropriately named 'disrupted in schizophrenia' 1 and 2 (DISC1 and DISC2) have thus far been identified as being affected by the translocation (Millar et al., 2004). Functional studies in animal models have linked normal DISC1 function to glutamatergic neurotransmission (Maher and LoTurco, 2012) and neuronal proliferation during development (Mao et al., 2009). As discussed in depth in Spotlight 9a, both of these processes have been implicated in the pathogenesis of schizophrenia.

A variety of linkage and, more recently, GWAS of the types described above have resulted in the proposal of a number of candidate genes implicated in schizophrenia. The proteins produced by these genes are involved in a very diverse range of processes, from brain development to neurotransmission. Some of these results for candidate genes have proven to be non-reproducible in subsequent studies or are linked to a number of psychiatric conditions suggesting common pathological mechanisms for aspects of these conditions (for example, see Fatemi et al., 2000). Candidate genes have been linked to critical processes involved in brain development (see Chapter 3), such as proliferation (Mao et al., 2009), migration (Kähler et al., 2008), and dendrite maturation reliant on the protein reelin (Förster et al., 2010) thus adding weight to the idea that schizophrenia is a multi-factorial neurodevelopmental disorder.

Multiple studies have implicated genes whose protein-products are involved in some way with neurotransmission such as those for neurotransmitter receptors, e.g. serotonergic and dopaminergic receptors or those that influence neurotransmission via poorly understood mechanisms, for example, dysbindin, which is postulated to influence glutamate release (Voisey et al., 2010) or GABAergic transmission (Bullock et al., 2008). Synaptic neurotransmitter levels are also influenced by the rate of their breakdown, and the gene encoding the enzyme COMT (catechol-O-methyltransferase), a catecholamine degradation enzyme, has been implicated in such studies (Williams et al., 2007). However, some association studies have implicated genes involved in less neurotransmitter–specific processes, for example activity of myelinating oligodendrocytes which would have the potential to have widespread effects in the brain (Tkatchev et al., 2003).

Although there is now evidence for individual genes being directly linked to schizophrenia, the differences between individuals even within families and the sometimes irreproducible results of separate studies suggest that there may be highly variable 'nurture' factors to take into account. As we saw above, epigenetic factors can have profound influences on expression of even normal genes. In the context of schizophrenia there is now evidence for epigenetic effects at various points during the life of affected individuals. For example, *in utero* viral infection may affect activity of enzymes responsible for the methylation, and consequent inactivation, of control regions for genes involved in GABAergic neurotransmission (Costa et al., 2007). There is also accumulating evidence to suggest that hypoxia occurring during birth can also

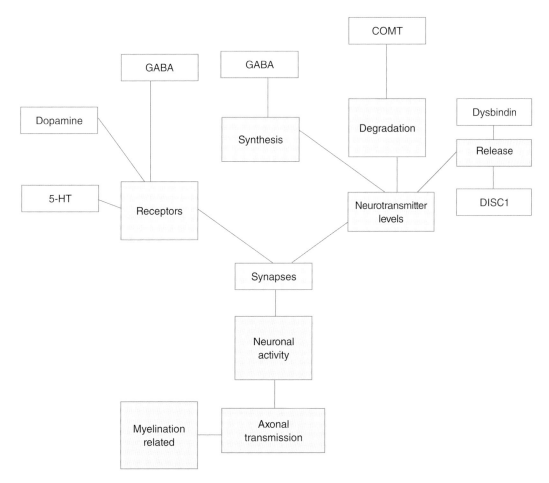

Figure 3a.3 Examples of some genes with neurotransmission-related functions implicated in schizophrenia

initiate epigenetic-mediated effects on expression of a number of genes (Schmidt-Kastner et al., 2006). Evidence of epigenetic effects but with unknown cause can also be seen in post-mortem brains of normal versus schizophrenic brains, whereby the degree of chromatin modification of some candidate genes is altered in schizophrenic brains, implying altered levels of protein expression (Tang et al., 2011). Epigenetic mechanisms of this kind may explain the results from a plethora of studies conducted on post-mortem brains where differences in the levels of mRNA or proteins for neurotransmission-related processes have been compared in normal versus schizophrenic (untreated and treated) brains; for example levels of dopamine D2 receptors.

Implications: Behavioural genetics and therapeutics

So where has all of this experimental work got us? We may not yet have the fruits of these research approaches in terms of effective therapeutic interventions but for some behavioural traits and disorders we are developing a long list of potentially implicated genes or chromosomal regions and an understanding of the factors that determine whether these bits of DNA are expressed as proteins. Clearly, this knowledge has the potential to allow us to develop a detailed understanding of the underlying biology of the disorder and therefore how to prevent manifestation of a disorder through altering protein expression.

A long-held criticism of a molecular genetic approach to research into behavioural disorders is that knowing that a single or set of genes can, if mutated, produce the disorder might be interesting but is unlikely to result in simple therapeutic strategies. For example, we might want to think about the impracticalities of gene therapy as an attempt to replace defective genes in neurons in the brain. However, with the recognition of epigenetics as a key player in the control of protein production, there is a potential new therapeutic angle. Taking as an example the case of genetic imprinting, we can see that if we could turn on a 'normal' but silenced allele in an individual carrying a mutation/deletion of the expressed allele then we should in theory be able to restore normal protein production. Early forays into this area using experimental animals have produced some exciting results where an agent was able to reactivate the silenced allele in a mouse model of Angelman syndrome (Huang et al., 2011).

Controversy surrounding behavioural genetics

Scientific research into the biological basis of behaviour can be seen as ranging from idle curiosity in attempting to explain normal variation in humans to a serious attempt to gain a better understanding of a behavioural disorder which may then form the basis for improved therapies. However, the subject is not without controversy since it raises a number of ethical issues. For example, if we can define desirable behavioural characteristics should we only allow those possessing at least a subset of those characteristics to breed? This quickly gives rise to unpalatable thoughts about Naziism and eugenics. Even at a lower level, we might ask the question as to how far genetic testing of a foetus *in utero* or in embryos used for *in vitro* fertilisation should go. Whilst it is currently acceptable to test for, for example, Down's syndrome, would it be acceptable to test for a particular set of alleles which has been shown to produce an increased likelihood of developing mental illness?

FURTHER READING

Bazzett, T. J. (2008). *An Introduction to Behavior Genetics.* **Sunderland, MA: Sinauer Associates.**
A comprehensive text discussing the issues and practicalities of behavioural genetics in much more detail.

Tsankova, N., Renthal, W., Kumar, A., & Nestler, E. J. (2007). Epigenetic regulation in psychiatric disorders. *Nature Reviews Neuroscience, 8,* **355–67.**
A review of the role that epigenetic mechanisms may play in behaviour, especially disorders such as addiction and schizophrenia.

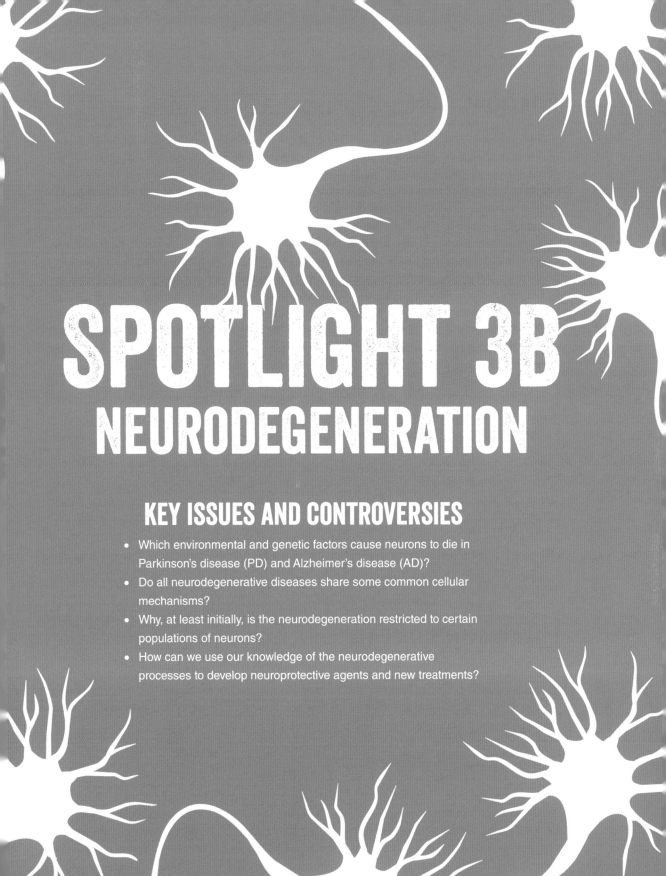

SPOTLIGHT 3B
NEURODEGENERATION

KEY ISSUES AND CONTROVERSIES

- Which environmental and genetic factors cause neurons to die in Parkinson's disease (PD) and Alzheimer's disease (AD)?
- Do all neurodegenerative diseases share some common cellular mechanisms?
- Why, at least initially, is the neurodegeneration restricted to certain populations of neurons?
- How can we use our knowledge of the neurodegenerative processes to develop neuroprotective agents and new treatments?

INTRODUCTION

It should come as no surprise that loss of neurons can couple to loss of function. Significant neuronal loss may occur suddenly, for example in traumatic injury experienced in a road accident, or may occur progressively over many years due to an underlying disease process. This latter situation is known as neurodegeneration and, irrespective of the actual mechanism responsible for the neuronal death, is responsible for a significant number of human diseases. As we saw in Chapter 1, there appears to be some degree of anatomical localisation within the brain for some functions. Consequently, if the neuronal loss occurs in one of these areas we may expect to see selective functional loss. However, where loss is diffuse the functional consequences may be diverse. Either way, the consequences for the individual are not insignificant; as we saw in Chapter 3, the ability of the human brain to repair itself is rather limited, so once an individual begins to show characteristic signs of a neurodegenerative disease there is no possibility for spontaneous reversal. Hence, the individual faces long-term disability and heavy reliance on health and social care systems which in turn place significant financial burdens on governments. Our current ability to support individuals with a neurodegenerative disease is largely limited to symptomatic relief which can only delay the requirement for significant care, and even this approach is far from ideal. A clear goal, therefore, is to understand the mechanisms by which neurodegeneration occurs, a necessity if we are to ever prevent these diseases occurring. Furthermore, this may help us to generate interventions to halt or reverse the neurodegeneration, or at least, develop drug therapies to better treat the symptoms.

In this spotlight the two most prevalent neurodegenerative disorders will be discussed in depth: Parkinson's disease and Alzheimer's disease. The current state of knowledge on the pathological processes and the resultant functional disruptions, particularly to behaviours, will be discussed. Whilst traditionally, Parkinson's has been considered a neurological disorder and Alzheimer's a psychiatric one, this distinction is becoming blurred such that both could be classed as neuropsychiatric. An understanding of the neurobiology underlying these disorders is not just of scientific interest but could also be useful for enabling us to develop new rational treatment approaches.

PARKINSON'S DISEASE

Parkinson's disease (PD) was first fully described by James Parkinson in 1817 in his essay on 'the shaking palsy'. We can still recognise his description of the major clinical features of what we now term Parkinson's disease, although we now have a more refined picture of the clinical manifestations (Goetz, 2011).

Prevalence

PD is the second most common form of neurodegenerative disease. The Parkinson's Society of the UK estimates that approximately 1 person in 500 has PD and the majority will be idiopathic, i.e. with no identifiable cause; patients with parkinsonian symptoms of known cause include drug-induced cases due to use of **antipsychotic** medication (see Chapter 9). In rare cases (<5%) there is an identifiable genetic cause. Most individuals receive their diagnosis when aged 50 or over, although around 1 in 20 patients are under 40 years old, and these tend to be those with a strong genetic component. Whilst a diagnosis of PD shortens the lifespan, the slow progressive nature of the disease still means that younger patients may survive for many decades and thus interventions are desirable. The disease is reported across all populations worldwide although it is difficult to definitively ascertain whether incident rates are constant across nations due to differences in diagnosis, treatment and lifespan.

Clinical characteristics

The initial recognition of PD as a medical condition by James Parkinson was based on a number of consistent functional deficits. The most prominent were associated with motor activity and so for many years Parkinson's disease was considered a pure movement disorder. What is now universally recognised is that functional deficits go beyond movement control and result in a range of behavioural changes.

Motor function

A diagnosis of PD is suspected in individuals who usually present with a combination of, sometimes quite subtle, motor deficits encompassing tremor, muscular rigidity and bradykinesia (slowness of movement) or hypokinesia (absence of movement) (Lees et al., 2009). Initially the tremor may be restricted to just the hands, involving the alternating movement of the thumb and fingers, when they are not otherwise being consciously moved, to produce the classic sign of resting pill-rolling. As the neurodegeneration progresses these signs become more profound such that, whilst a reduction in facial expression may be an early sign of hypokinesia only recognised by a clinician, patients themselves are more likely to become aware of the movement reduction as time passes. Signs and symptoms are often uneven between the sides of the body, although even if they are only present unilaterally initially, they usually progress to both sides, reflecting the bilateral pathological process described below. The balance of the signs and symptoms, rates of progression and response to therapy is highly variable between individuals, suggesting that there may be subtypes of PD with differences in the underlying pathology. For example, whilst a pill-rolling tremor may be the earliest recognised sign in some, it may never occur in others (Helmich et al., 2012).

Non-motor functions

In addition to the well-recognised motor control problems, it has been increasingly recognised that many Parkinson's patients show other changes including those affecting a range of cognitive functions (Elgh et al., 2009) and other behaviours such as sleep deficits or depression (Reichmann et al., 2009). Whilst it may be tempting to conclude that these are reactions to having PD, evidence suggests that they are actually related to the pathological processes that cause it, since they occur at a higher rate than for matched controls (Becker et al., 2011) and show improvement when individuals are treated with the standard dopaminergic therapy discussed below (reviewed in Chaudhuri and Schapira, 2009).

Although these non-motor changes may be present prior to, or simultaneously with, the onset of the motor deficits, the latter tend to have a much greater effect on the quality of life of the patient, so these are more likely to induce an individual to seek medical help. However, as the condition progresses the non-motor deficits may begin to significantly impinge on the functioning of the person. It is even relatively common for the late stages of the disease to include significant loss of cognitive function, i.e. **dementia**.

Cause of PD

It makes logical sense that if our goal is to reverse, halt or even just treat PD symptoms, then we need to have a sound understanding of its cause. One of the difficulties here is that studying the brains of PD patients post-mortem may reveal certain differences to normal brains, but it is difficult to know whether these changes are the cause or a consequence of the critical pathological process or even an effect of therapies. Nonetheless, as long ago as the end of the 19th century it was recognised that Parkinson's patients all shared a particular pathological feature (Parent and Parent, 2010).

Pathology

Loss of dopaminergic neurotransmission

All brains of PD patients studied exhibit a loss of dark staining in a small region of the midbrain known as the substantia nigra pars compacta (SNpc). This nucleus is a component of the **basal ganglia**, a group of interconnected structures found in various parts of the brain (Figure 3b.1). The basal ganglia mediate a variety of functions, including contributing to motor control, as we shall see in Chapter 6. The neurons of the SNpc appear dark in humans because they contain the pigment melanin which is a by-product of the synthesis of the neurotransmitter dopamine. As we saw in Chapter 1, dopamine is a catecholamine neurotransmitter and it is synthesised by a small number of nuclei in the mammalian brain. Pathological analysis also reveals the gradual accumulation of cellular inclusions known as Lewy bodies, which are composed of aggregates of a number of proteins including alpha-synuclein (Braak et al., 2003).

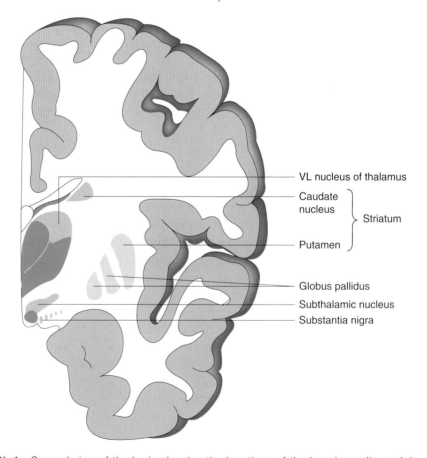

Figure 3b.1   Coronal view of the brain showing the locations of the basal ganglia nuclei

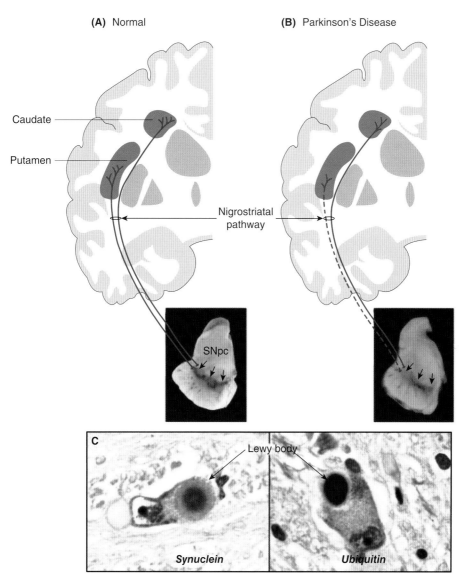

(A) Normal

(B) Parkinson's Disease

Caudate

Putamen

Nigrostriatal
pathway

SNpc

C

Lewy body

Synuclein

Ubiquitin

Figure 3b.2   Neuropathology of Parkinson's disease. (A) Schematic representation of the normal nigrostriatal pathway (in red). It is composed of dopaminergic neurons whose cell bodies are located in the substantia nigra pars compacta (SNpc; see arrows). These neurons project (thick solid red lines) to the basal ganglia and synapse in the striatum(i.e., putamen and caudate nucleus). The photograph demonstrates the normal pigmentation of the SNpc, produced by neuromelanin within the dopaminergic neurons. (B) Schematic representation of the diseased nigrostriatal pathway (in red). In Parkinson's disease, the nigrostriatal pathway degenerates. There is a marked loss of dopaminergic neurons that project to the putamen (dashed line) and a much more modest loss of those that project to the caudate (thin red solid line). The photograph demonstrates depigmentation (i.e., loss of dark-brown pigment neuromelanin; arrows) of the SNpc due to the marked loss of dopaminergic neurons. (C) Immunohistochemical labelling of intraneuronal inclusions, termed Lewy bodies, in an SNpc dopaminergic neuron. Immunostaining with an antibody against alpha-synuclein reveals a Lewy body (black arrow) with an intensely immunoreactive central zone surrounded by a faintly immunoreactive peripheral zone (left photograph). Conversely, immunostaining with an antibody against ubiquitin yields more diffuse immunoreactivity within the Lewy body (right photograph)

Source: Dauer and Przedborski (2003)

The progressive accumulation of Lewy bodies throughout the brain and the loss of the dopaminergic neurons ultimately results in the suite of signs and symptoms that form the basis of an initial premortem diagnosis of PD (Figure 3b.2). Interestingly, the evidence suggests that behavioural changes are not seen until at least 80% of the nigral dopamine is lost, implying that the system either has considerable redundancy or is able to adapt to the slow decline in dopaminergic transmission.

Recent advances in imaging techniques can now be used to provide a diagnosis during life. By labelling the dopamine transporters which would normally be found on healthy presynaptic terminals of dopaminergic neurons we can assess whether an individual showing the cardinal signs of PD also has signs of degeneration of nigral neuron terminals. Figure 3b.3 shows radio-labelled 18F-dopa uptake in a normal subject and early hemi-PD patient. The PD patient shows bilateral posterior putamen loss of signal.

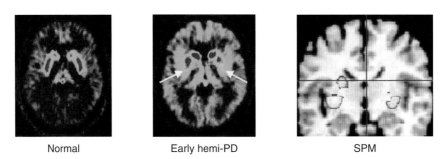

Normal   Early hemi-PD   SPM

Figure 3b.3 PET image showing reduction in striatal dopamine transmission in PD patient. Statistical parametric mapping (SPM) localises significant reductions in 18F-dopa uptake in the caudate and putamen contralateral and the posterior putamen ipsilateral to the affected limb in a group of hemi-PD cases. (Picture courtesy of J. Rakshi, MRC Clinical Sciences Centre and Division of Neuroscience, Faculty of Medicine, Imperial College London, UK)

Other pathological and neurotransmitter changes

Whilst the key pathological change is considered to be dopaminergic neuronal loss in the SNpc, there is evidence to suggest that pathological changes can also be detected in other brain regions. In some cases this appears to precede the nigral degeneration whereas in others it follows on and perhaps reflects the progressive and changing nature of the functional loss (Braak et al., 2003).

A number of studies have found evidence for depletion of the other monoaminergic neurotransmitters in PD. Hence, there is considerable evidence for altered serotonin (Fox et al., 2009) and noradrenaline (Delaville et al., 2011). Some studies also suggest that cholinergic transmission via the basal nucleus of Meynert may be affected, particularly in the latter stages of the disease when cognitive impairment is more apparent. As we shall see later in this spotlight, this is an interesting finding in the light of the pathological changes that we can see in Alzheimer's disease. It has been suggested that these non-dopaminergic changes may be responsible for the non-motor symptoms of PD (Grinberg et al., 2010).

Etiology of neurodegeneration in Parkinson's disease

Whilst there is universal agreement for the clear role for neuronal death in a limited number of anatomical locations in producing PD, the actual mechanisms causing these subsets of neurons to die has remained somewhat elusive. As we met in Chapter 3, the characteristics of biological systems are determined by the interplay between environmental and genetic influences and both of these have been implicated in PD. Indeed, in some cases, study of the dysfunctional proteins in rare monogenetic inherited forms has identified possible environmental factors that may be involved in sporadic forms (Corti et al., 2011).

Environmental factors

Over the course of many years, a number of chance observations and planned epidemiological studies have suggested particular environmental factors which may promote the selective neurodegeneration observed in PD. These include exposure to environmental toxins, such as pesticides or heavy metals, and infection, e.g. by influenza. A particularly striking global event occurred in the early 20th century when a large number of people developed a parkinsonian-like syndrome following brain inflammation – it is assumed due to a viral infection. It is proposed that these seemingly diverse insults produce the same pathogenic response via alterations in components of the cellular respiration processes mediated by mitochondria which may result in increased oxidative stress (Martin and Teismann, 2009). However, what remains unknown is why the neurons of the SNpc are so highly susceptible, compared to other neuron populations.

We should also note that some environmental factors have been shown to be protective. These include some factors which are usually considered to be deleterious to health such as alcohol, smoking and caffeine, although, again, the mechanisms are not well understood.

INSIGHT: SERENDIPITOUS ADVANCES IN UNDERSTANDING PD PATHOLOGY

A major advance in our understanding of pathology in PD came serendipitously from a botched attempt to make money from drug users. In the 1980s, a chemist in California was illicitly synthesising opioids to sell to drug users but an error in the process for one batch resulted in the production of a substance which had a profound and irreversible effect on those who used it. Almost literally overnight they developed symptoms which mimicked those of PD patients. Subsequent analysis revealed that the batch contained a high proportion of 1-methyl-4-phenyl-1,2,3,6-tetrahydropyridine (MPTP) (Langston et al., 1983). This observation had a number of consequences. First, MPTP has chemical structural similarities to some pesticide constituents and so epidemiological studies were conducted to see if there was a link between pesticide exposure and development of PD. Some studies have indicated this to be the case although this does not appear to be able to explain all cases (Lock et al., 2013). Second, the consequence of MPTP toxicity was demonstrated to be alterations in respiratory chain function in the mitochondria which led to the theory that all PD may be due to mitochondrial dysfunction. Finally, MPTP could be used in the laboratory to induce a parkinsonian-like state in experimental animals. Use of MPTP and related agents in non-human primates and rodents was key in enabling scientists to elucidate the complex neuroanatomical connectivity of the basal ganglia, and MPTP is still used today to provide an animal model of PD (Duty and Jenner, 2011).

Genetics of Parkinson's disease

Historically, PD was considered to be a purely sporadic condition. As we met in Spotlight 3a, studying genetic influence in brain function disorders has progressed through twin and family studies to sophisticated statistical analyses of large numbers of unrelated individuals, e.g. genome-wide association studies. Although rare, possibly accounting for no more than 5–10% of all cases, a number of monogenetic forms of PD have been identified often using familial linkage studies, and some progress has been made towards identifying the genes and the functions of the proteins that are produced from them. However, more recently, genome-wide association studies have identified a large number of genes which appear to confer susceptibility and so may be involved in the more common sporadic situation. Many of the genes identified have tended to be part of common pathways involved in either mitochondrial function or in processing of unwanted cellular proteins. This has suggested that all forms of PD, whatever the cause, may involve dysfunction of either of these two processes. A comprehensive review of all of the genes so far linked to PD is beyond the scope of this spotlight (reviewed in Corti et al., 2011). However, as an example of what this work is so far revealing, the first gene to be found (SNCA) is now known to encode the protein alpha-synuclein. Cell biology studies subsequently revealed that this protein was the major constituent of the Lewy bodies that are also seen in idiopathic cases.

TREATMENT FOR PARKINSON'S DISEASE

The ultimate therapy would involve identification of those likely to develop PD and intervention to prevent subsequent neurodegeneration. In the absence of this, being able to reverse, or at the very least, halt the neurodegeneration would be useful. However, currently none of this is possible and the only generally licensed therapies are aimed at achieving symptomatic relief by replacing the lost dopamine or the function it performs in the neuroanatomical circuitry.

Drug therapies

The most commonly used drug for PD is levodopa and the rationale behind its use is logical and simple to understand. As the disease is characterised by the specific loss of dopaminergic neurons from the SNpc, then clearly there will be a reduction in dopaminergic signalling between the presynaptic terminals of these cells and their postsynaptic targets. Hence, if the dopamine can be replaced exogenously this should, at least in part, reverse the problems seen in patients. The obvious substance to use is dopamine itself but in practice this doesn't work for a number of reasons. The preferred route of administration for therapeutic drugs is always oral, since this is the easiest and most acceptable for the patient. The problem in this case is that dopamine, being an active signalling molecule at various places in the body, would be extensively metabolised en route from the gut and in any case it only poorly penetrates the **blood brain barrier**. In neurons, dopamine is produced from the precursor levodopa which does not appear to have any biological activity itself but can cross the blood brain barrier. So, an alternative approach is to administer levodopa which can be metabolised in selected neurons which contain the necessary enzymes to produce dopamine (Figure 3b.4). Consequently, levodopa became and has remained a mainstay therapy for Parkinson's disease since the 1960s (Nagatsu and Sawada, 2009).

As with all drugs, levodopa use is associated with adverse effects and some can be rather severe. However, improvements have been made by combining it with an extracerebral dopa-decarboxylase inhibitor which prevents the conversion of levodopa to dopamine outside

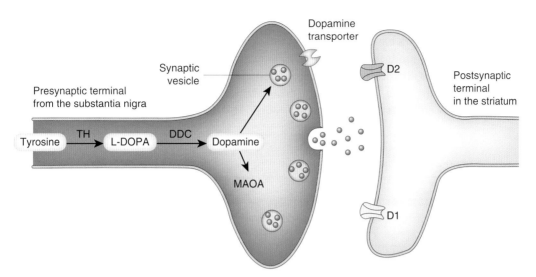

Figure 3b.4   Synthesis pathway of dopamine; levodopa (L–DOPA) is metabolised to dopamine by the enzyme dopa-decarboxylase (DDC). The dopamine is then packaged into vesicles or metabolised by the enzyme monoamine oxidase A (MAOA)

Source: Youdim et al. (2006)

of the brain thus reducing peripheral side effects and increasing the availability of the levodopa for neurons of the brain.

Unfortunately, after some years of use, patients report unwanted motor effects of taking the drug. These unwanted effects include: decreased effectiveness with prolonged use; development of unwanted movements (dyskinesias); and the so-called 'on–off' phenomenon. The mechanisms underlying these issues are poorly understood; declining effectiveness has been attributed, at least in part, to the continued degeneration of the dopaminergic neurons since it is their synaptic terminals that contain the enzymes necessary for conversion of levodopa to dopamine. In patients who experience a significant reduction in beneficial effect between doses, a third drug may be added to the levodopa/dopa-decarboxylase inhibitor combination. This drug is a catechol-O-methyltransferase inhibitor (COMT) which inhibits the actions of the enzyme responsible for degrading dopamine and levodopa and thus dopamine can be maintained at a therapeutic level for longer between doses (Fox et al., 2011).

Dyskinesias take the form of involuntary writhing movements and the evidence suggests that these are due to changes in neurotransmission via a range of transmitters, including dopamine. The on–off phenomenon is where, following a dose, the patient experiences periods when the symptoms are well controlled then rapidly changes to periods where they are not and then periods when they are better controlled again etc., and all before the next dose is due to be taken. It is believed that this may come about because the levels of extracellular dopamine fluctuate and can sometimes be present in excess, thus, in effect, over-stimulating the dopamine receptors.

Although levodopa use is clearly effective, at least for a while, these longer-term problems led to the search for new alternatives. Since dopaminergic neurotransmission replacement is clearly successful in symptom management, some form of dopaminergic therapy remains the most likely to have therapeutic benefit. Clearly, the loss of dopamine producing neurons as part of the disease process has its effect because the postsynaptic neurons expressing dopamine receptors, and which would normally have received the dopamine signal, are no longer being influenced by dopamine to the same degree. So, one solution would be to just target the receptors directly, in effect 'fooling' these neurons into behaving as if dopamine is present. Hence, another wave of research has focused on finding agents that can act as agonists at the dopamine receptors. The results of this work have suggested that this is a feasible goal and many dopamine receptor agonists have been produced and trialled in humans. When compared to using levodopa, the effectiveness of this approach is not so good. However, some of the known motor problems with levodopa do not appear to be so serious with dopaminergic agonists and so the balance between the relative pros and cons of these approaches needs to be made for individual patients.

INSIGHT: DOPAMINE AGONISM

With the advent of the dopamine agonists and the gradual increase in their use we have been able to observe the consequence of direct dopamine receptor agonism in the human brain. One of the more unexpected findings of these observations, backed up by recent detailed studies, is that some PD patients who gain symptomatic relief when treated with dopamine agonists also show other changes to their behavioural profiles. In particular they have an increased tendency to exhibit problems with impulse control, for example compulsively gambling or shopping (Voon and Fox, 2007). The recognition of this as a potential problem for the therapeutic use of dopamine agonists has led to warnings on their use from the official agencies that monitor drug use in humans, such as the Medicines Regulation Agency of the UK.

The underlying mechanisms for these behaviours are as yet unclear; the prominent role of dopamine in reward-related behaviours is supported by considerable evidence and may suggest that impulse control disorders in medicated parkinsonian patients may simply be occurring as a result of excessive stimulation of dopamine receptors, possibly in regions of the brain not directly affected by the neurodegenerative pathology. Furthermore, there are still a number of unanswered questions; for example, why is it not seen in all Parkinson's patients treated with dopaminergic agonists and why is it more prevalent in patients treated with dopamine receptor agonists compared to levodopa? The answer to the first question may well be linked to the underlying genetic make-up of the dopaminergic components in the individual, although evidence for involvement of particular alleles is not yet convincing. Nonetheless, this observation has given us some insight into the neurobiological mechanisms that may underpin impulse control disorders observed in humans without Parkinson's disease.

Non-drug therapies

Cell transplantation

A logical suggestion for neurodegenerative diseases may be that therapy could involve replacement of the lost neurons. For PD this is particularly attractive, as the neuropathology appears to be confined to distinct anatomical locations. In the 1970s, transplantation of cells from the developing substantia nigra region of foetuses were transplanted into the brains of PD patients. Unfortunately, this approach had limited therapeutic benefit and raised a number of logistical and ethical issues which resulted in the search for alternative sources of cells. Identification of stem cells, which retain the ability to produce a range of cell types including neurons, initially human embryonic stem cells, but more recently adult stem cells produced from the patient themselves, has meant that, as is covered later in the spotlight, this approach continues to be an active area of research.

Deep brain stimulation

Before PD was associated with reduced dopaminergic neurotransmission, surgical ablation of parts of the basal ganglia had been shown to produce symptomatic relief. This approach was abandoned upon discovery of levodopa but as the limitations of long-term levodopa therapy started to emerge, these approaches were revisited. Ablation of brain tissue is an extreme approach as it is, of course, irreversible. So, a less permanent approach was developed, known as deep brain stimulation. The mechanism underpinning this approach is poorly understood, but can be summarised – the stimulation delivered affects the neurons of the basal ganglia structure into which the electrode is implanted, causing a cascade of changes to the firing characteristics of the structures of the basal ganglia circuitry which mean they are closer to those seen in the normal brain. The relative lack of experience with this technique means that currently it is generally patients who are no longer deriving sufficient benefit from levodopa who are considered for this therapeutic approach (McIntyre and Hahn, 2010).

Implications: Cutting-edge research

Current research related to PD spans from understanding the underlying pathological processes and finding means of neuroprotection to improving symptomatic management.

Early markers of impending disease

The recognition that the degree of neurodegeneration before symptoms of PD emerge is extensive means that for any neuroprotective approach to be effective then it will be essential to be able to identify those at risk of PD before the symptoms become too bad. Clearly, for the monogenetic familial forms, genetic testing is possible. However, for idiopathic cases, looking for the very earliest behavioural signs or other presymptomatic markers will be beneficial for early intervention. Evidence from a diverse range of studies suggests that non-motor symptoms may be evident before the motor ones; for example, reduced olfaction, increased incidence of depression and sleep disorders (Braak et al., 2003; Postuma et al., 2010). However, the predictive power of these signs/symptoms is low; most individuals who show them will not go on to develop PD.

Understanding the pathophysiological processes

Although most undergraduate neuroscience textbooks will contain complex-looking diagrams of basal ganglia circuitry, it is clear that we do not have a complete understanding of the characteristics of the connectivity of all of the structures involved. Evidence is accumulating for subtypes of PD, and studies of these are beginning to suggest that there may be pathophysiological differences between them. This has two potential implications: first, we may need to employ different approaches to prevent development and progression of each subtype; and second, the most effective treatment for the subtypes may be different. A recent series of studies has investigated the possible underlying differences in PD patients with different degrees of tremor, who appear to show different rates of symptom progression as well as differential sensitivity to dopaminergic therapies (Helmich et al., 2012).

As discussed above, the accumulated evidence from studies of the pathological mechanisms is implicating two processes – mitochondrial dysfunction and mis-folded protein handling – and it is possible that these two processes are linked. So, if a goal is to identify neuroprotective strategies, then the potential for targets for therapeutic intervention is extensive (reviewed in Dauer and Przedborski, 2003)

Neuroprotective agents

There has been a significant amount of research activity devoted to identification of neuroprotective agents for use in neurodegenerative conditions, including PD. Many studies at experimental laboratory level have indicated the potential of many agents although as yet none has translated into the clinic. The recognition that, whatever the initiator of the pathological process, the ultimate consequence may be inappropriate activation of the immune system, has led to the proposal that modification of inflammation processes may be effective (Hirsch and Hunot, 2009). An alternative approach is to enable the dopaminergic cells to better resist the pathological insults; an accepted concept in neuroscience is that, during development and in maturity, neurons require trophic support. The most important trophic factor for nigral dopaminergic neurons has been identified as GDNF (glial-cell derived neurotrophic factor) and studies investigating the possibilities of increasing GDNF levels in the brain to produce pathological processes are being undertaken (Manfredsson et al., 2009).

Neuronal manipulation to increase dopamine production

In the absence of effective neuroprotective agents or an inability to identify those at risk of developing PD, one possibility is to replace neurons with the ability to produce dopamine in the right areas of the brain. Two approaches have been suggested: gene therapy to increase dopamine production by cells that would not normally do so and cell transplantation. Gene therapy using the gene for the dopamine synthesis enzyme has shown some promise but long-term efficacy is currently unclear (Mittermeyer et al., 2012).

The use of stem cells which have been induced in the laboratory to have the features of dopamine-producing neurons is a major area of current research (Allan et al., 2010). Our current understanding of how to support transplanted stem cells to allow them to form neurons that can make functional connections is currently insufficiently advanced for this to be considered a therapeutic option. There are also concerns that the transplanted cells may divide uncontrollably to produce tumours. One controversial issue is the source of the stem cells; initial work used cells from aborted foetuses, which brings about ethical concerns as well as them being in limited supply. Another source would be a patient's own cells, which appears attractive since the patient would be less likely to produce an immune response which would result in rejection. However, in the absence of a sound understanding of the cause of the PD in that patient, there is a potential that their transplanted stem-cell derived neurons could be genetically susceptible to the same pathology-inducing processes as caused the initial degeneration (Lindvall and Kokaia, 2010).

ALZHEIMER'S DISEASE

The dementias are a group of disorders characterised by the progressive decline in cognitive capability through a variety of pathological processes. Of the many forms, the most common is Alzheimer's disease (AD) which means it is the most common human neurodegenerative disorder.

Prevalence

Recent estimates suggest that approximately 5% of the global population has AD. Most individuals will be diagnosed when aged 65 or over; over the age of 80, 1 in 6 people will have AD. Since the incidence of AD increases with age, it is rapidly becoming a significant social and economic burden for governments worldwide faced with the prospect of dealing with ever-ageing populations; it has been estimated that there may be over 100 million diagnosed cases worldwide by 2050 (World Alzheimer report, 2009).

Clinical characteristics

In the very early stages, AD is often hard to diagnose, as the primary symptom is poor memory for recent events, which is rather subtle as it is hard to dissociate this from normal age-related memory decline. However, over time this simple forgetting spreads to include an inability to perform normal everyday tasks, such as shopping, because the individual may forget how to navigate from their home to the shops even though they may have been doing so for decades. Also, they show progressive changes in behaviour, often described by family members as changes in personality, including becoming aggressive or apathetic and showing some of the hallmarks of depression (Chapter 9). The later stages of the disease involve severe cognitive impairment where the individual may be unable to follow written instructions or recognise very close family members and at this stage are entirely reliant on carers even for basic needs.

Cause of Alzheimer's disease

As we saw with Parkinson's disease above, any attempt to understand how the deficits seen in the disease reflect disorder of the normal functioning of the brain requires us to know what processes underpin the disease. Historically this involved simple observation of the gross appearance of the brain coupled with microscopic study of the histology of the brain tissue.

Pathology

Neuronal loss

Like PD, a definitive diagnosis of AD can only be made at post-mortem. The pathological changes observed at post-mortem for an AD brain contrast to PD, where, as described above, the pathological changes are localised to subsets of neurons and the gross whole brain appears approximately normal. In the later stages of AD, the gross appearance is of widespread atrophy of the neocortex (Figure 3b.5). However, one of the difficulties for early diagnosis, for example with imaging techniques, is that the gross appearance of the AD brain does not appear markedly different from a brain of a normal individual of the same age. Interestingly, cortical loss does not appear to be uniform but is most severe in the temporal lobe with almost no sign of degeneration in the occipital lobe and hence the deficits match the regions most affected.

Histological examination of the atrophied regions reveals a number of features, many of which are also found in the elderly brain and in association with other neurodegenerative disorders. However, two of these features are considered diagnostic hallmarks of AD: intracellular

Healthy brain   Severe AD

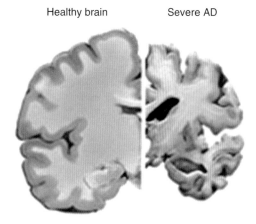

Figure 3b.5 Post-mortem appearance of the brain in advanced AD, showing significant loss of tissue

Source: National Institute on Aging, National Institutes of Health, http://www.nia.nih.gov/alzheimers/publication/part-2-what-happens-brain-ad/changing-brain-ad

neurofibrillary tangles and amyloid-containing **plaques** which are generally extracellular, both of which were described by Alois Alzheimer in the early 1900s (Perl, 2010).

Neurofibrillary tangles are produced by aberrant aggregation of a normal neuronal protein, tau. Tau is normally associated with the microtubules that form the intracellular scaffolding that neurons use for structural integrity and transport mechanisms. However, in AD tau is modified, becoming hyperphosphorylated, resulting in disruption to the microtubules as well as formation of the insoluble tangles which can persist in the brain even after the neurons in which they formed have died. Neurofibrillary tangles appear first in the temporal lobe and then progress to other brain regions in a characteristic progression. This pattern maps onto the progressive worsening and appearance of the symptoms, thus suggesting that the functional disruption caused by the presence of the tangles is responsible for neuronal death and the associated symptoms.

Biochemical analysis has revealed that the amyloid plaques are composed of aggregates of beta-amyloid (Aβ) peptide which is derived from a precursor protein (APP; amyloid precursor protein). The evidence suggests that APP is required for normal neuronal functioning, although its precise role is not fully understood. In the brain, APP can be processed in a number of ways by a suite of enzymes; in the normal brain, it is broken down into soluble, harmless fragments. However, APP can also be broken down by an alternative process, which generates Aβ of varying lengths which aggregate to form the plaques that gradually accumulate in the brain. However, in contrast to the situation for the tangles, location of the plaques does not map well to the progression of symptoms, suggesting that these form secondarily to the neuronal loss caused by the accumulation of the tangles.

Changes in neurotransmission

In addition to these two characteristic features, in-depth histological analysis indicates that there is extensive synaptic loss in many brain regions and that the degree of loss appears to correlate with cognitive impairment (Terry et al., 1991). As we might expect, reduced synapses results in the decline in level of neurotransmission. Two neurotransmitters in particular have been implicated in AD: acetylcholine and glutamate.

Acetylcholine has long been associated with human learning and memory processes. At post-mortem, one of the brain regions where neurofibrillary tangles are pronounced is in the basal forebrain which is a subcortical region that contains the cell bodies of acetylcholine-producing neurons which provide considerable cholinergic input across the cortex. Subsequent studies have indicated that a number of markers of cholinergic transmission, including synaptic density, are aberrant in AD brains, suggesting that changes in cognitive function in AD, as well as in cognitive changes associated with increasing age, may be at least partly attributable to reduced cholinergic transmission (Grothe et al., 2010). It is worth us remembering here that, in the section on PD above, neurodegeneration in this area can be seen in the later stages when patients show significant cognitive decline. The concept of reduced cholinergic transmission has been exploited to produce therapies for improving cognitive function as discussed below.

Glutamate is the major excitatory transmitter in the brain and as we saw in Chapter 1 has its action at a number of receptors. A large number of studies have indicated changes to many aspects of glutamatergic transmission in AD brains. Like acetylcholine, it too has been linked to the synaptic processes which underpin learning and memory (see Chapter 4).

The accumulating evidence is suggesting that Aβ production and synaptic activity are inter-linked such that the one can control the other. So we can see that where Aβ levels are elevated pathologically we might expect to see aberrant synaptic activity. Indeed one model proposes that Aβ can act presynaptically to alter signalling via acetylcholine receptors to influence the release of glutamate, thus linking cholinergic and glutamatergic neurotransmission (Palop and Mukke, 2010).

Aetiology

Our studies of the brains of AD patients have clearly shown that there is a correlation between specific pathological changes and functional changes. Whilst a description of the macro- and microscopic pathological changes can give us insight into how the normal brain functions, if our goal is to use our knowledge to prevent or reverse the consequences of the disease then we need to know something about how observed changes arise and whether they are the cause of the disease or just a consequence. The reason for the degeneration of the subsets of neurons that die in AD is still unknown. However, since the most dominant risk factor for developing AD is age, it may be tempting to assume that the neurodegeneration observed is simply associated with increasing age and that everyone might develop it if they lived long enough. However, the evidence suggests that it is entirely possible to live into extreme old age and not develop AD and, conversely, some individuals develop it much earlier in life. So, if AD is not just an inevitable consequence of the aging brain, then there is some merit in trying to find out what *does* cause the neurodegeneration in order to attempt to intervene and increase the period of normal brain function we might be able to experience.

If we take into account the concepts we met in Chapter 3 and the evidence for the etiology of PD above, it will be no surprise that individuals appear to get AD due to a combination of genetic and environmental factors.

Environmental factors

In addition to age, epidemiological studies have identified other situations which seem to increase the chances of someone developing AD. Some risk factors appear logical; for example AD is more prevalent in those who have had significant head injuries. Over the years a large number of studies have investigated the possibility that exposure to a range of substances from heavy metals to fungicides or hypothermia may increase the chances of developing AD. However, no single factor has emerged as a key candidate, suggesting that it might be that these diverse insults all converge on the same intracellular process which then results in neuronal death. The best candidates for this common intracellular process are those related to cellular meta-bolism and, in particular, those that act to protect neurons from oxidative stress. Furthermore, the possibility exists that these insults affect these pathways as a consequence of the epigen-etic phenomena that we met in Chapter 3. So, early life experience may result in epigenetic changes to the compliment of genes that produce the proteins involved in the common pathway. The gradual accumulation of these changes and the resultant changes in cellular function may explain why increasing age is such a strong risk factor for AD (Mastroeni et al., 2011).

What these epidemiological studies have also shown is that certain factors appear to reduce the chances of developing AD. Hence, high levels of mental activity, physical activity, and adequate sleep seem to postpone the onset of AD, but the precise reasons for this relationship here is unknown. One potential biological explanation for the relationship with mental activity may be that this stimulates the formation of a higher number of synapses and therefore when the degenerative process starts there is more capacity to lose connections and cells before this becomes noticeable functionally. This does though raise the intriguing possibility that my writing and you reading this spotlight may have staved off dementia in both of us for just that little bit longer!

Genetics

Amongst those with an AD diagnosis, the vast majority appear to be sporadic with little in their family history to suggest a strong genetic component. However, investigation of the genetic make-up of these individuals has revealed that many share a genetic component related to one of the apolipoprotein genes called the ApoE gene. Apolipoproteins are a large family of proteins encoded by multiple genes that generally function to bind lipids and aid their uptake and transport around the body. In the brain, ApoE is produced by glia, and the cell-surface receptors for it are found on neurons. In the human population, the ApoE gene exists as a number of variants and research has demonstrated that the ApoE variant which an individual expresses can influence their chance of developing AD. The ApoE4 variant is associated with an increased risk of developing AD, yet many AD patients do not express ApoE4 and many who have this variant do not develop the disease. This suggests that either ApoE4 predisposes the individual to environmental insult or the individual must also express a particular version of another gene or genes.

A small proportion of AD cases (<10%) fall outside of the pattern discussed above, primarily by showing signs of the disease at an unusually young age. More often than not these cases are not sporadic but appear to run in families which have therefore been studied to identify the genes involved (see Spotlight 3a). The results of this work have implicated mutations in three genes where the resultant defective proteins lead to AD: APP, presenillin 1 and presenillin 2. The involvement of APP is of obvious interest since, as we saw above, one of its potential products, Aβ, is the major protein constituent of plaques and so this implies that the accumulation of beta-amyloid in plaques is a key pathological process leading to AD. This has been reinforced following biochemical studies which demonstrate that the presenillins are involved in the processing of the APP. However, there are two issues with this simple view; first, as noted above, the correlation between symptoms and plaque location is poor; and second and rather frustratingly, mutations in these genes are rarely seen in sporadic cases. Our ability to now screen large numbers of individuals to assess even the smallest variation in their genetic make-up using a GWAS approach has indicated that, perhaps not unexpectedly, Alzheimer's disease is going to be a member of the group of human brain disorders with complex genetic influences (Avrampoulos, 2009).

Of note is that those who have the genetic make-up which makes it almost a certainty that they will develop AD show little in the way of signs and symptoms until well into their adulthood. This implies that their mutated gene(s) have little consequence for normal brain development and that there is still a requirement for other changes to occur in the neurons to precipitate the neurodegeneration. One possibility is that this is the same set of accumulated epigenetic changes that can be induced by environmental exposure as we discussed above.

Treatments for Alzheimer's disease

Our investigations of AD so far have been notable because, whilst we can give detailed descriptions of the signs and symptoms we might expect an AD patient to show and the likely histological features of their brain tissue, the cause of the disease remains elusive. So, it should be no surprise that therapeutic options for AD are currently limited and primarily focus on symptom management.

Drug therapies

Cholinergic therapies   As we met above, one of the consistent observations that we can see in the AD brain are alterations in components of the cholinergic neurotransmission systems and this therefore provides a rationale to use agents that adjust cholinergic transmission therapeutically. Consequently, a number of clinical trials have examined the effects of giving inhibitors of acetylcholinesterases which are enzymes that normally metabolise extracellular acetylcholine; the theory being that the longer active life of acetylcholine molecules increases their chances of interacting with postsynaptic receptors and thus maintaining pre- to postsynaptic cell signalling. The results of most of these trials, however, have been extremely disappointing since they suggest that these drugs are only effective in the early stages of the disease. Clearly, drugs of this type can only ever offer symptomatic relief and are not affecting the cause, namely neurodegeneration.

Pathological modification   The central role attributed to beta-amyloid in the pathogenesis of AD has attracted interest as a therapeutic target. It has been proposed that agents which promote a processing pathway of APP which does not produce beta-amyloid could be of benefit. Interestingly a number of agents already in therapeutic use for a diverse range of situations do this; for example the non-steroidal anti-inflammatory drugs and statins. Although epidemiological studies have shown promise for these agents, clinical trials have been less convincing, possibly because these agents are only effective in delaying or preventing onset but not at reversing the pathology once it has started (Bullock, 2004).

Non-drug therapies

Earlier we met the concept that epidemiological studies have told us that those who have had higher than average mental stimulation during their lives appear to be relatively spared from AD. This leads us to think that we may be able to use mental activity as a means to reduce the impact on mental function that AD patients show, in effect operating the 'use it or lose it' principle. A number of so-called cognitive interventions have been proposed and tried and, overall, the evidence suggests that, especially when used in combination with pharmacological therapies, this appears to offer the best solution for patients, although again, it cannot ultimately prevent decline (Buschert et al., 2010)

Implications: Cutting-edge research

Current research related to AD spans from understanding the underlying pathological processes and finding means of neuroprotection to improving symptomatic management.

Early markers of impending disease

As discussed above for PD, finding presymptomatic markers for AD is also a major goal in current research. One of the hurdles here is that normal ageing is associated with cognitive change and since the incidence of AD increases with age, then a way of separating these effects out is required. Studies using imaging techniques of families with inherited forms of AD show that signs of neurodegeneration can be detected presymptomatically. Furthermore, imaging studies on individuals who have a mild cognitive impairment associated with age show changes in cholinergic functioning. Since mild cognitive impairment is a risk factor for developing full-blown AD, then an imaging approach may form the basis of our ability to identify those at risk from developing AD in the future (Grothe et al., 2010).

Improving animal models

Human diseases are studied both to understand the science behind the disease process but also to attempt to prevent them or treat individuals. Whilst insights can be gained from studying people with the disease, to investigate anything happening at the cellular level, such as the synaptic loss and neuronal death of AD, we need to produce models of the disease. This is a particular challenge when we are dealing with disorders of brain function because the work that can be carried out *in vitro* is very limited and so there is a need for animal models. For neurodegenerative disorders, these models often take the form of reproducing the pathological situation. So, where that pathology is limited in location, for example stroke, or to particular subsets of neurons, such as the dopaminergic neurons lost in PD, this can be reproduced in an appropriate species. The validity of the animal model can then be determined by checking whether impairments observed in the animals match those of the humans with the disorder. However, for AD the situation is somewhat more difficult for a number of reasons. First, the pathology is rather non-specific, occurring at the level of individual synapses and across large areas of the brain. Second, as we met above, the pathology is not particular to AD, but degrees of it are seen in the aged brain where there is little loss of function. Finally, the functions that are disrupted in humans with AD are often of high level cognitive function and human specific behaviours, which, obviously, are rather hard to reproduce, particularly in lower species, such as the standard laboratory rat. Consequently many of the current animal models for AD tend to have the same genetic mutations as we see in humans, but as we now know, the proportion of AD patients with these mutations is very low. So, whilst we may have some confidence in these models as representing the situation for the genetic forms of AD, it is something of an over-interpretation to conclude that we are modelling AD in general. As such there is a clear need for us to develop a model which has as many of the hallmarks of the sporadic form as possible.

Preventing neurodegeneration

Accumulating evidence suggests that, although the neurodegenerative diseases like AD and PD have disease-specific features, there are some common features too. For example, it appears that neurodegenerative diseases are characterised by the accumulation of misfolded proteins which triggers a defensive response in the neurons that means that they indiscriminately stop all protein production, including of proteins critical for synaptic neurotransmission. Whilst a short period of reduced protein-production (translation) to enable the cell to deal with the misfolded proteins would be appropriate, if this is prolonged, as it appears to be in neurodegenerative disease, then this can result in death of the neurons and the subsequent behavioural changes observed. Most of the current work in this area is focused on prion diseases but the early indications are that interrupting the protein production shutdown will translate to AD too (Moreno et al., 2012).

The linking of cellular pathology to oxidative stress is a focus of a number of lines of research. Clearly, if oxidative stress precipitates processes, including epigenetic changes, that lead to the death of neurons, then this approach has therapeutic merit. However, one of the issues here will be whether we can find appropriate early markers of the disease since these agents are likely to be of little use in restoring function once neurodegeneration has occurred (Sultana and Butterfield, 2010).

Gamma secretase activity

The central role of Aβ in sporadic and genetic AD would naturally lead us to consider whether we can either prevent the formation of it or somehow break it down after formation. We know that APP is processed to Aβ by the enzyme gamma secretase and so one attractive possibility would be to reduce the activity of this enzyme, thus promoting processing of APP by less toxic routes. However, a problem with this is that the enzyme is involved in a number of other cellular processes and so indiscriminate gamma secretase inhibition could result in significant cellular dysfunction. So, some means of targeting the specific processing of APP by gamma secretase is required. Some experimental studies have indicated that this may be possible by targeting an activating protein which selectively allows gamma secretase to process APP. This work has shown much promise in the laboratory, including in mouse models, but has yet to be tried in humans (He et al., 2010).

Implications

The diagnostic descriptions of pathological changes in the brains of PD and AD are sufficiently distinct to allow a definitive diagnosis of one or the other condition to be given. However, there are a significant number of individuals who express symptomatic elements of both of these or indeed one of them with another neurodegenerative disorder altogether; it may be concluded that this is coincidental and that, perhaps, the individual was unlucky. However, histopathological reports often suggest that features of other neurodegenerative disorders are found in the brains of those given a diagnosis of PD or AD. Clearly then, it is possible that if the individual had lived longer they may have begun to show symptoms of disorders other than that for which they were given a preliminary diagnosis whilst alive. This may lead us to think that the difference between these neurodegenerative disorders is more minor than the diagnostic criteria may suggest. An attractive proposal, therefore, is that there are two elements to take into account in determining the risk that an individual expresses a neurodegenerative disorder: first, whether the individual is genetically predisposed to neurodegeneration in general; and then second, the actual disorder expressed may be influenced by a combination of their genetics and their particular exposure to environmental factors. Therapeutically this is very attractive; it suggests that if we can understand the basic mechanisms underlying neurodegeneration then we should be able to intervene and influence outcomes for a large number of individuals who would otherwise go on to show one of the many neurodegenerative diseases.

FURTHER READING

http://www.parkinsons.org.uk; and http://www.alzheimers.org.uk/
These are the websites of the UK national charitable societies for Parkinson's and Alzheimer's disease in the UK. They have some general information on the disorder and the current areas of research interest as well as pieces by patients and their carers about their experiences.

Corti, O., Lesage, S., & Brice, A., (2011). What genetics tells us about the causes and mechanisms of Parkinson's disease. *Physiological Review, 91*, 1161–218.
A comprehensive review of some of the recently identified mutations and how the dysfunction of their protein products may give us clues about how environmental insults may produce sporadic cases of PD.

Lindvall, O., & Kokaia, Z. (2010). Stem cells in human neurodegenerative disorders – Time for clinical translation? *Journal of Clinical Investigation, 120*(1), 29–40.
An overview of what stem cells are, where they come from and what the prospects are for using them in neurodegenerative diseases like Parkinson's and Alzheimer's disease.

Parent, M., & Parent, A. (2010). Substantia nigra and Parkinson's disease: A brief history of their long and intimate relationship. *Canadian Journal of Neurological Science, 37*(3), 313–9.
This is an excellent review of the history of the identification and long association of the substantia nigra with PD.

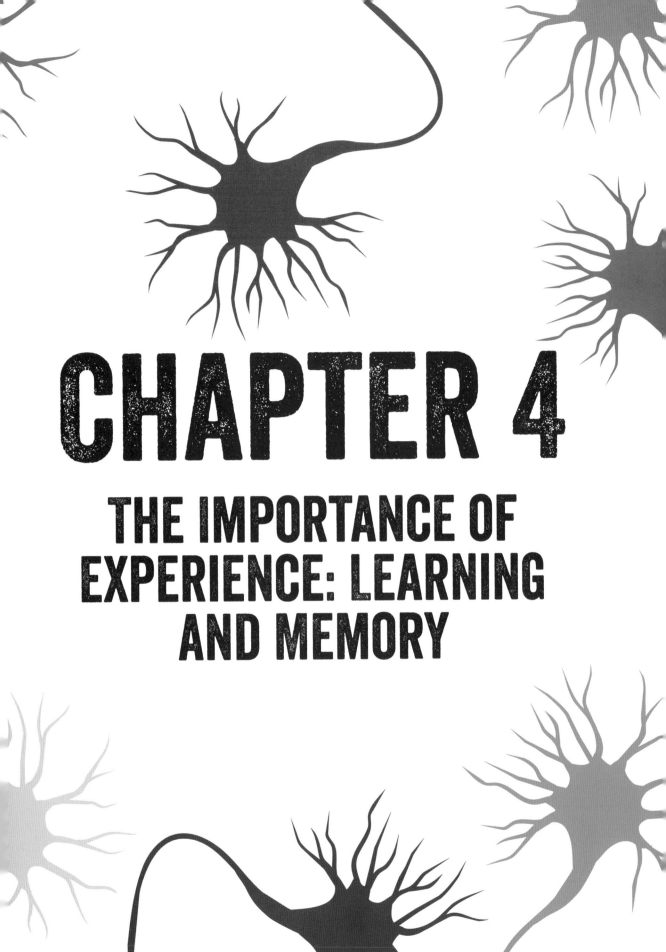

CHAPTER 4

THE IMPORTANCE OF EXPERIENCE: LEARNING AND MEMORY

CHAPTER BREAKDOWN

- What governs how much is learned from a given experience.
- Memories exist on different timescales.
- There are different forms of memories.
- Memories consolidate into a long-term form over time.
- Synaptic plasticity may underlie long-term memory.
- There are different forms of synaptic plasticity.
- Conscious memories are transiently dependent upon the hippocampus.

ROADMAP

In this chapter, we will be considering the biological mechanisms that support learning and memory. First, we need to understand how it is determined what needs to be learned by the brain. Next, we will see how there are different temporal spans of memory, ranging from the very transient (less than a second) to the long-lasting (up to a lifetime), and that these are supported by different biological mechanisms in the brain. A central question in learning and memory, which has dominated research for many years, is how memories are stored for long periods of time. We will see that there are numerous biological mechanisms that have been implicated, and these may all be involved in a general process of synaptic plasticity. Another theme that underlies this chapter is the fact that there are different types of memory, which are mediated by different regions of the brain. The chapter is therefore organised in a bottom-up fashion, starting with the simpler forms of memory and working up to end by considering complex and personal conscious memories.

In the course of this chapter, the content will rely partially upon concepts from previous chapters. These include the neuroanatomy of the brain to locate the various learning and memory processes (Chapter 1), the physiological properties of neurons that lead to synaptic plasticity (Chapter 1), and the notion that we can interfere with normal neurochemical processes with pharmacological tools (Chapter 2). Moreover, the importance of learning and memory will be noted in future chapters, in relation to perceptual and motor learning (Chapters 5 and 6), emotional learning and memory (Chapter 7) and the learning that underlies motivated behaviour (Chapter 8). Disorders in learning and memory processes may also contribute towards, or result from, a variety of psychological disorders.

WHAT IS LEARNING AND MEMORY?

Why are experience, learning and memory important in biological psychology? It seems obvious that memories are important to our sense of self, but from an evolutionary perspective, this cannot have been a driving force for the development of complex and sensitive memory systems. Therefore, memories must serve a more basic function. That function is one of survival. Memories impact profoundly upon an individual's behaviour, enabling both the avoidance of danger and the acquisition of food/water based upon prior experience and acquired knowledge. In avoiding danger, we can use both any previous bad experience we have had, and knowledge gleaned from others, to predict the occurrence of the threat. The better we can do this, and the earlier we can reliably predict the threat, the greater the chance of avoiding the danger. This may involve a variety of predictive stimuli, which might interact in a complex manner. Take for example the relatively simple act of crossing the road. We often use visual and auditory signals of approaching vehicles, but the use of these signals may differ whether or not we are waiting at a designated crossing point. How many of you have also almost walked out in front of a cyclist on the mistaken assumption that the lack of any engine noise signals that the road is clear? (You will probably have heard this argument in relation to silent electric cars.) So the predictive value of signals is learned through experience, in order to increase the chances of adaptive behaviour that helps survival.

We can think of the importance of learning and memory from a different perspective. Human and animal behaviour cannot be explained simply through the description and understanding of the circumstances immediately surrounding the act. We also need to know how the individual has been shaped by prior experience to respond in the manner that he does. This is the basis for the importance of learning and memory in psychology and in everyday life. To take a trivial example, compare your behaviour at lunchtime next time you are on campus, relative to your first day. The knowledge you have acquired concerning different food outlets, such as their location, quality and popularity, not to mention what you have recently eaten, all have an influence on your precise behaviour. Another way of thinking about it is that the information gathered from previous experiences leaves its mark on the brain, changing the way in which the brain responds in future situations, ultimately affecting behaviour. This applies not only to eating-related behaviours, but also to all aspects of psychology, from sensory perception to emotion and motivation.

So if learning and memory is so important, what happens when it goes wrong? We know that memory failure can be extremely debilitating (e.g. Alzheimer's disease). What may be less obvious is the impact of learning and memory being 'too good'. In post-traumatic stress disorder, the memory for the traumatic event is overly strong and too easily retrieved, causing great anxiety for the sufferer. Similarly, a major challenge for drug addicts is to resist the cravings induced by stimuli that are predictive of the drug. So the overly strong memories linking the stimuli to the drug perpetuate the condition. This means that an adaptive memory system has to be flexible, enabling the long-term storage of useful information, but also allowing that information to be modified if necessary.

Accepting that learning and memory are important, we need to take a step back to ask the more fundamental question: what is learning and memory? Learning and memory can be simply defined as the acquisition and retention of information, respectively. Under such a definition, memories are not limited to biological systems. Clearly, computer systems contain memories of different sorts, but we can also conceive of physical materials with mnemonic (memory-retaining) properties, from foam mattresses to the ground that retains our footprints.

From a psychological viewpoint, however, learning and memory are defined by the acquisition and retention of changes in behaviour.

The analogy between animal memories and physical memories is particularly useful. Just as we can find different objects with mnemonic properties, different areas of the brain mediate different types of memories. Any good cognitive psychology/neuroscience text on memory will note that human memories can be divided into classes (e.g. conscious vs. unconscious) that depend upon different areas of the brain, on the basis of evidence from patients with brain damage. Another similarity is in relation to the temporal duration of the memory. If we consider a footprint, it can persist for different lengths of time, depending upon the conditions. A footprint in dust may be blown or washed away rapidly. One in mud may dry and last until the next rainfall, and those left by the Apollo missions to the moon will persist much, much longer. Similarly, there are different stages of biological memory that depend upon separable mechanisms in the brain, and one focus of this chapter is to understand the temporal dynamics of memory. Given the different types and scales of memory, this chapter will be organised in a bottom-up fashion, starting with the simpler, unconscious forms of learning and memory. The most commonly investigated form of learning, due to its simplicity and the speed of learning, is **pavlovian (classical) conditioning**. Inspired by the work of Ivan Pavlov, this describes the learning of predictive relationships (or associative memory) between stimuli and outcomes. The principles derived from studies of pavlovian conditioning can then be applied to more complex, higher order memories.

A key principle of this chapter is the benefit of combining the study of experimental animals and human subjects. Our main goal is to understand human behaviour, but in many areas, this can only be achieved through the use of experimental animals. For example, experimentally-induced brain lesions are more localised than the effects of trauma or stroke, and the biological mechanisms within particular brain regions at the molecular level can only be studied in animals. Finally, an analysis of brain activity at the level of single neurons, currently impossible in all but a handful of humans (some of those undergoing brain surgery), is sometimes incredibly useful for the understanding of learning and memory, as in the following section.

KEY POINTS

- In biological psychology, we focus on behavioural learning and memory.
- Memories enable the prediction of future events, such that behaviour can be modified accordingly.
- Memories can exist on differing timescales.

PRINCIPLES OF LEARNING: THE ROLE OF SURPRISE

Before we get on to memory, we have to consider again when and why information is learned. If learning and memory is to be adaptively beneficial for behaviour, then it is not simply a matter of encoding everything that we experience and perceive. That would just lead to a problem of how to keep all the memories separate, intact, and easily retrievable.

There are, however, some people with 'highly superior autobiographical memory', who can remember as much detail from a day years in the past as you could remember from yesterday. For the rest of us, it appears that the information to be learned should only be that which is useful and improves the accuracy and relevance of the memory. Think of what you remember from many years ago. Most likely they are events that have lasting meaning for you, rather than simply banal and ordinary occurrences. In this way, it is quite easy to accept the principle of selective encoding of memory in relation to our conscious autobiographical memories. Importantly, though, it also applies to the non-conscious associative memories.

Studying non-conscious associative memories is important, as it allows us to study the process of learning in both humans and non-human animals. There is also an easier link to draw between the underlying memory and expressed behaviour. For example, a pavlovian memory associating a dark alley with danger has a more obvious impact upon our behaviour than does a detailed autobiographical memory of your 7th birthday.

The specific question that has been asked over many years is: how can we explain what is learned and how much is learned from a given experience? From this relatively simple question, we can then speculate as to how the brain allows us to remember events selectively. There are many theories of learning, but we will focus on just one, as it has received the most investigation and we are beginning to understand its biological underpinnings. This theory derives from the **Rescorla–Wagner rule** of learning and emphasises the importance of *surprise* in learning.

If we take a simple learning situation, such as pavlovian conditioning, we can start with two basic points. Before anything is learned, there is no knowledge and memory concerning the association, and so the initial presentation of the outcome is completely surprising. In contrast, when the memory is well-learned, the stimulus is known fully to predict the outcome, and so its delivery is not surprising at all. In other words, there is a clear need for learning at the start to increase the predictive strength of the stimulus, and no need at the end. If we assume that learning must be at least an energy- and resource-consuming process, a principle that restricts the extent of learning to the amount that is needed would be energy- and resource-efficient. So what happens in the middle? The amount of learning must be related both to how much has already been learned, and how much there is left to learn. We can see this in the shape of a behavioural learning curve (see the orange line in Figure 4.1). Initially, there is a lot of learning that greatly increases the memory strength. Subsequently, as the memory reaches its maximal level, there is less room for improvement and the gains are reduced. Essentially, learning obeys the law of diminishing returns, as you will also have experienced in revising for exams.

The Rescorla–Wagner rule of learning can account for the shape of the learning curve, and reduces the computation of the amount learned to a single term that denotes the level of surprise: the **prediction error**. When learning is incomplete, the degree to which we can predict the future occurrence of the outcome based upon the next stimulus presentation (i.e. the predictive strength of the stimulus) is sub-optimal, leading to an error in the prediction of the outcome. The presence and size of this prediction error influences the amount of learning that takes place on that given occasion. In Figure 4.1, when memory strength is low, the prediction error is high, leading to learning. Later on in the learning curve, the prediction error is low, and hence only a small amount is learned. So *learning only takes place when there is a prediction error*. Moreover, the equation that describes the Rescorla–Wagner rule states that the amount learned is proportional to the magnitude of the prediction error.

Behaviourally, there is substantial evidence implicating the need for a prediction error in driving learning. Perhaps the clearest demonstration is also one of the oldest, and predates the formal theory. *Blocking* is a phenomenon originally described by Leon Kamin in 1969, showing that surprise is critical in learning. In a concrete example, you might learn first that our first exposure to a new taste is followed some time later by illness, suggesting that the new food caused the illness. If you encounter the same food, but mixed with another new taste, and again become ill, you would not learn that the new taste predicts illness as the illness is not surprising. This seems obvious at a

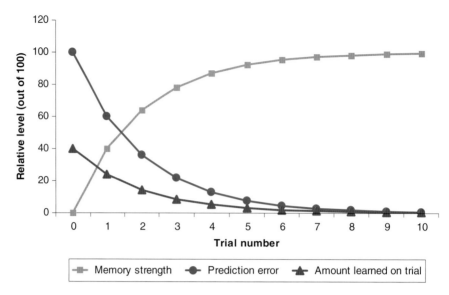

Figure 4.1   Graphical representation of how memory strength and prediction error progress with learning. Without any pre-existing memory, the memory strength is zero and the prediction error is at maximum. Other factors, such as the salience of the cues and outcome, determine the rate of learning, and hence when the prediction error is factored in, the amount learned. As learning progresses, the memory strength increases and so the prediction error decreases, thereby reducing the resultant amount of learning. Eventually, the memory approaches the asymptotic maximum possible, while the prediction error becomes negligible and no further learning is required

conscious level, but it is also a principle that applies to unconscious forms of learning in humans and other animals. In conceptual terms, because the outcome is already predicted fully by the first stimulus, the subsequent addition of the second stimulus is irrelevant to the prediction of the outcome, and so there is no prediction error and no learning takes place.

It is only relatively recently, since the first expression of the Rescorla–Wagner rule in 1972, that the biological substrates of the prediction error signal have been studied (Rescorla and Wagner, 1972). This has been aided by the development of correlative imaging methods in both humans and non-human primates. The first detailed analysis of prediction error signals was in the midbrain of macaque monkeys (see the Key Study below).

KEY STUDY

Mirenowicz, J., & Schultz, W. (1994). Importance of unpredictability for reward responses in primate dopamine neurons. *Journal of Neurophysiology, 72(2),* 1024–7.

Wolfram Schultz and his colleagues have carried out numerous studies investigating the neural mechanisms of prediction error signalling in macaque monkeys. In perhaps their most original and important experiment, they showed that *dopamine neurons in the midbrain* show exactly the activity that is expected of a prediction error signal.

The monkeys were trained on a pavlovian conditioning task, in which a stimulus predicted the delivery of a drop of juice reward, and electrophysiological recordings were taken from *dopaminergic cells in the substantia nigra and ventral tegmental area.* Schultz and colleagues found that the dopaminergic cells had a low but consistent rate of baseline firing in the absence of any stimulus input (Figure 4.2).

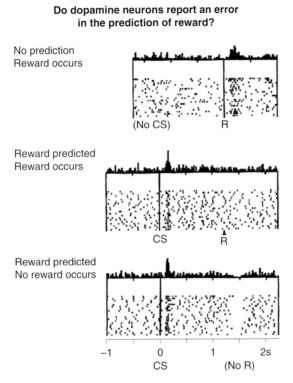

**Do dopamine neurons report an error
in the prediction of reward?**

No prediction
Reward occurs

(No CS)   R

Reward predicted
Reward occurs

CS   R

Reward predicted
No reward occurs

−1   0   1   2s
CS   (No R)

Figure 4.2 Midbrain dopamine neurons encode a prediction error signal. Monkeys learn that a CS predicts the delivery of reward. The raster plots show with a dot each action potential fired by an individual dopamine neuron, with timings relative to the presentation of the CS and/or reward (R). In the top panel, when the reward is not predicted by the CS (no CS), there is an increase in dopamine cell firing upon delivery of the reward (after the vertical line at R; high prediction error). In the middle panel, when the reward is predicted by the CS, there is no increase in firing in response to the reward (low prediction error). In the bottom panel, when the reward is expected due to the prediction of the CS, but does not occur (no R), there is a suppression of baseline firing levels (see the temporary decrease in dots at the time of no R; negative prediction error). Taken from Schultz et al. (1997).

Source: Schultz et al. (1997)

Early on in learning, the cells fire intensely when the juice reward is delivered. Given that the reward is surprising, this increase in firing is as expected from the hypothetical prediction error signal. However, as learning progresses and the outcome is better predicted, the cells fire much less upon juice delivery, as would be expected from a reduced prediction error. Instead, they start firing more when the stimulus is presented, indicative of a level of *expectation* of reward.

Moreover, when the juice is unexpectedly not delivered, dopaminergic cell firing is suppressed at the time the juice is expected. This can be thought of as a *negative* prediction error, because the

(Continued)

(Continued)

prediction was of a reward that did not occur, and so the prediction is too great and needs to be lowered. In this way, prediction error allows for both increases and decreases in predictive strength, leading to a flexible memory system.

While the data from this study are relatively straightforward to interpret, there are questions that arise when we consider the functional relevance of these findings to behavioural learning and memory.

- First, just because there are neurons in the brain that signal in a manner expected of a theoretical account of learning, this is not evidence that the signal is functionally *necessary* for learning. This is a critical caveat with all *correlational* methods of experimentation. In order to demonstrate necessity, we would need to show that the activity of these neurons is required in order for learning to take place.
- These data show strong evidence for the existence of a prediction error signal that can alter in its valence (positive or negative). However, the Rescorla–Wagner rule states that the magnitude of the prediction error determines the extent of learning on that trial. We have yet to observe such gradations in the intensity of the prediction error signal that would correlate with behavioural predictions.

These findings have since been corroborated in humans. In the most similar study, human subjects were scanned using **fMRI** while a juice reward was delivered (Berns et al., 2001). When juice delivery was unpredicted, there was greater activity in the nucleus accumbens, consistent with the expected activity of a prediction error signal. Importantly, the nucleus accumbens is one of the major targets for the dopaminergic cells in the midbrain, and hence increased accumbens activity measured by fMRI most likely reflects elevated firing of midbrain dopaminergic cells.

The dopaminergic midbrain is not the only area involved in prediction error signalling. There is converging evidence from both monkeys and rats, implicating the *orbitofrontal cortex* in outcome expectation and error signalling (Takahashi et al., 2009; Tremblay and Schultz, 2000). So why is it that more than one brain area seems to produce prediction error signals? It could be that, because different brain areas mediate separable memory types (see later), the prediction error-producing regions are also distinct. However, orbitofrontal signalling can be observed concurrently with midbrain/striatal activity. For example, the orbitofrontal cortex was also active in the above juice fMRI study by Berns et al. Therefore, it actually seems that the midbrain and orbitofrontal cortex work together to regulate learning as a result of surprise. The exact functional relationship has been analysed using human functional imaging. In quite a complex study, Hare et al. (2008) were able to distinguish between true prediction error signals, and activity that signalled the value of expected outcomes. They showed that it was activity in the ventral striatum alone that followed the pattern expected of a prediction error signal, whereas the orbitofrontal cortex appeared to be representing values.

UNCONSCIOUS FORMS OF MEMORY

There are many forms of unconscious (or **non-declarative**) memory that encompass not only the pavlovian conditioning that we have already encountered, but also perceptual and procedural learning. Perceptual learning involves the learning of perceptual information. The easiest to think about is visual memory (e.g. remembering a relative's face). Procedural memory is the memory for procedures or skills. One good example is learning to write or to play an instrument.

We will be covering visual memory, pavlovian fear memories and procedural motor learning. The reason for selecting these specific types of memories is to illustrate three particular aspects of memory:

1. Memories can persist for different lengths of time depending on the underlying mechanisms (visual memories).

2. Memories can be localised to specific areas in the brain, take time to stabilise, and are likely to be supported by synaptic plasticity (pavlovian fear memories in the **amygdala**).

3. Memories can be supported by decreases in synaptic strength (motor memories in the cerebellum).

PERCEPTUAL MEMORY

The biological basis of perception will be covered in greater detail in Chapter 5. However, an integral aspect of perception is the learning and memory associated with stimulus exposure, leading to recognition of that stimulus at a later time. Ultimately, this is fundamental to all aspects of learning and, more widely, to behaviour in general. It is only once a stimulus has been determined to be novel or familiar, and in the latter case identified, that appropriate behaviour can be executed. This can take place within any of the sensory domains (visual, auditory, olfactory or somatosensory). This section will focus on visual perceptual memory, as it is generally more easily accessible for the understanding of the guiding principles.

Temporal stages of perceptual memory

Visual memory can be separated into three stages, persisting for varying lengths of time. The presentation of a visual stimulus results in an immediate sensory *iconic memory*, a *short-term memory*, and a *long-term memory*. These are supported by differing mechanisms within visual areas of the brain.

Iconic memory is a very short-lasting memory for the visual stimulus that persists for around a single second, at most. It has been illustrated most famously by George Sperling (1960) using a simple task involving the visual perception of an array of 12 letters.

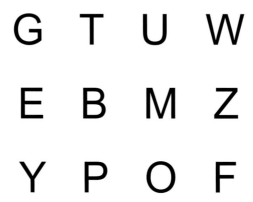

Figure 4.3 Sperling array

Sperling allowed participants a very brief glance (~50ms) at such an array, and then asked them immediately to recall as many as they could. If you do this yourself, you will likely be able to recall 4–5 of the letters (about 35–40% accuracy). However, when the participants were prompted, immediately after the array was removed, in a *partial report* procedure to recall just one of the three lines, they could recall on average 3 out of the 4 letters (75% accuracy). So it seems that upon presentation of the 12 letters, at least 9 must be initially held in the iconic memory store. This corresponds to the feeling that we have that there were more letters, just that we cannot remember them.

The explanation that Sperling proposed was that the iconic memory store is so transient that it decays while we are trying to retrieve the letters from it. The iconic memory is actually a representation of the entire visual image, but one that decays very quickly. So, when given a free recall of any item, 4–5 letters are retrieved before the memory disappears. In contrast, in the partial report procedure, the retrieval process can be focused on the selected line, allowing most of the letters to be reported before the memory decays. However, if the prompt is delayed by only 1 second, the advantage of the partial report procedure is lost, with participants only able to report 35–40% of the selected line. This indicates that the participants were only able to recall the letters that were retrieved in the second after the array presentation and before the prompt. Therefore, the iconic memory had already decayed in the 1 second after stimulus presentation.

Iconic memory is likely to result from brief after-images in the sensory neurons of the retinal surface in the eye. This is similar to the after-image you see when you close your eyes after a bright flash of light. The primary visual sensory area is the retina in the eye, in which there are complex cellular mechanisms that transduce the visual stimulus into a neuronal signal. The biochemical nature of this process means that it takes some time for the mechanism to return completely to its baseline state. Support for this account comes from the finding that the brighter the image, the longer the iconic memory persists (just as the brighter a camera's flash, the longer the after-effect). The brighter image affects the cellular machinery more, resulting in a longer duration of recovery to the normal baseline state. In other words, the visual stimulus leaves a transient imprint on the retinal machinery that is thought to be the basis for iconic memory.

So, does iconic memory serve any meaningful function, or is it simply a by-product of the sensory perception system? The answer is not clear, but some visual information does make it into longer-lasting memory stores, and perhaps even the very short-lasting iconic memory helps the selection of what information to store.

Visual **short-term memory** is a more long-lasting form of memory than iconic memory, persisting for several seconds. It allows you to keep images active for further processing. One example is the spot-the-difference puzzle, in which you have to compare the two pictures. Our understanding of visual physiology tells us that we can only focus on one location at a time within the visual world. Therefore, it is not possible to focus upon both pictures simultaneously in order to detect the differences. Instead, the image of one picture has to be held online for comparison with the second picture. It is this active online representation of the first picture that is supported by visual short-term memory.

Short-term memory is generally a quite poorly defined concept, as in different domains it can be used to describe memories that last on the order of a few seconds, through to several hours, and overlaps considerably with the concept of **working memory**. However, it is also generally thought that the biological mechanisms of short-term memory commonly include *sustained neural activity*. For example in monkeys, electrophysiological recordings showed that the activity of neurons in the visual association *inferior temporal cortex* (*IT*) that were sensitive to a particular complex visual stimulus actually outlasted the presentation of the stimulus (Miller and Desimone, 1994). Thus activity in IT is sustained for some time after the visual stimulus disappears, providing a neural substrate for a short-term visual memory that lasts several seconds. Indeed, if we trace the ventral visual pathway that is responsible for object identification (Figure 4.4) through the brain, neurons with memory-related (**mnemonic**) properties

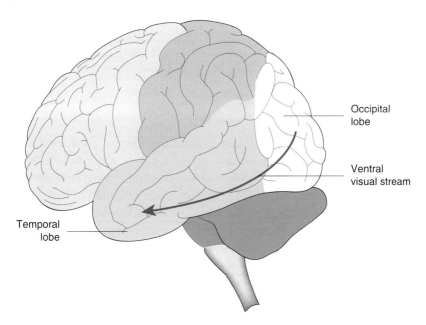

Figure 4.4 Visual information is processed in a hierarchical manner through the ventral visual stream, starting from the occipital lobe and progressing to the temporal lobe

become more frequently observed as we get 'higher' (i.e. further progressed) in the pathway. IT is considered to be near the end of the object identification visual pathway. In contrast, neurons in the 'lower' primary visual cortex have much simpler properties, responding to simple visual features only while they are present, and to an equivalent level each time a stimulus is presented. Complementary observations have also been demonstrated in humans, using non-invasive forms of brain imaging. fMRI scans show activity in the temporal visual association cortex that is sustained beyond visual stimulus presentation. Also the activity in higher temporal areas is more persistent than in occipital areas earlier on in the visual pathway (Courtney et al., 1997).

This sustained activity is important for behavioural function. A common behavioural test of visual short-term memory in humans involves presenting a series of visual stimuli, with the subject having to remember the stimulus that was presented two items previously. This is representative of everyday situations in which you have to hold on to and remember certain items for future use, whilst being subjected to a constant stream of information. When neural activity in the human visual association cortex was disrupted by **transcranial magnetic stimulation (TMS)**, performance on the short-term memory task was impaired. Importantly, this could be achieved only when TMS was applied 300ms *after* the presentation of each stimulus (Oliveri et al., 2001). Thus disruption of the sustained neural activity following stimulus presentation functionally impaired short-term memory function.

FOCUS ON METHODS: TMS

Transcranial magnetic stimulation (TMS) is a non-invasive method of altering brain activity in humans. TMS uses an electromagnet to induce small electrical currents. These electric currents can be focused on a region of the brain. The effect is to depolarise neurons in the region. This can achieve either an activation of the target region or an inhibition (depending on the stimulation of excitatory or inhibitory neurons). However, while the magnetic field penetrates through the skull to stimulate the brain, it can only do so to a depth of a few centimeters, and so beep brain structures remain inaccessible to modulation.

Visual **long-term memory** can last for up to an entire lifetime. Such memories allow us to recognise stimuli that have been previously encountered, in order to behave optimally in response to those stimuli. What kind of mechanisms might support long-term memory, and how could we unveil them? Take a simple task of long-term *object recognition*. We could present the novel object to a subject, and then some time later (typically a day or more), present the object again, perhaps among other items in a choice test. We might observe, using electrophysiological recordings or functional MRI, that certain areas of the brain are activated during the test, but how can we be certain that this activity is not simply related to perceptual functions, elicited by the presentation of the stimuli regardless of any prior learning?

One way is to look for differential responding between the initial presentation and test. We might observe a decrease in responding, which is termed *repetition suppression* and reflects the fact that the stimulus is no longer novel. Alternatively we might see an increase in responding, especially if the stimulus has previously been deemed to be salient and important, thus requiring more robust detection of future presentations. In fact, the former repetition suppression of activity is much more commonly observed. Although short-term effects are frequently reported, there is also evidence for long-term suppression of neuronal activity with repeated stimulus presentation. For example, electrophysiological recordings from the IT in monkeys have shown a reduced response to a complex visual stimulus compared to when it was presented initially over 24 hours previously (Fahy et al., 1993). Moreover, repetition suppression effects were observed in visual association cortical areas (as well as prefrontal areas) spanning up to three days using fMRI scanning in humans exposed to pictures (Meister et al., 2005; van Turennout et al., 2000).

The necessity for these activity effects in the long-term memory for visual stimuli can only be inferred indirectly. It is not possible selectively to interfere with the repetition suppression effect, especially as the underlying mechanisms are yet to be uncovered. However, the functional requirement for the brain areas in long-term visual memory can be substantiated using experimental lesions in animals, and by making use of patients with brain damage to the areas of interest. The latter are somewhat limited by the limited spatial precision of any neurological damage. However, it is a common finding that patients with large lesions to the temporal lobe suffer from amnesia (see later) that is characterised in part by an impairment in visual recognition memory. It appears that the critical focus of damage might be the perirhinal and parahippocampal cortices. These are areas to which inferotemporal cortex projects and they also provide the input to the hippocampus (more about this later on). Monkeys with lesions to the perirhinal and parahippocampal cortices were severely disrupted in a task that required them to retain a memory of a visual discrimination over 24 hours (Zola-Morgan et al., 1989). Therefore long-term visual memory recruits an area that can be considered to be further up the visual pathway than the areas implicated in short-term memory (IT) and iconic memory (retina).

As a final comment on perceptual learning, there appears to be a continuum between perceptual and **mnemonic** function in the ventral visual pathway. As mentioned earlier, the mnemonic properties of neurons become more pronounced the higher up the pathway you record, and information is eventually passed to areas which have traditionally been linked to memory (e.g. the hippocampus and perirhinal cortex). Inferotemporal cortex and perirhinal cortex stand at the interface of the perceptual-mnemonic system, with IT showing memory-related properties, and perirhinal cortex seemingly having a role to play in complex visual discriminations (see Barense et al., 2005). Therefore, there is no clear distinction between perception and memory, at least from a biological standpoint, which serves to reinforce the notion that memory is a fundamental process that underlies other functions in the brain.

KEY POINTS

- There are three different types of visual perceptual memory that differ in their timecourse.
- Iconic memory lasts for about 1 second and is explained by mechanisms in the eye.
- Visual short-term memory lasts for a few seconds, and is supported by visual cortical neurons that carry on firing even after the visual stimulus disappears.
- Visual long-term memory depends upon specific areas within the temporal lobe.

ASSOCIATIVE LEARNING

Associative learning encompasses forms of learning that involve the formation of predictive links between events. Such events can be broken down into stimuli (sounds, sights, smells) and responses (actions, behaviours). Associations involving just stimuli mostly result from pavlovian conditioning: learning the relationship between predictive stimuli and outcomes. Those incorporating responses arise from **instrumental conditioning**, whereby a behaviour is performed in order to produce a desired effect (e.g. the laboratory rat pressing a lever for some food). We will concentrate on pavlovian conditioning, as there is currently a clearer understanding of both the neuroanatomical substrates and the cellular mechanisms underlying this form of learning.

Pavlovian conditioning

Also termed classical conditioning, this takes its name from the original work of Ivan Pavlov, who observed that a stimulus that was consistently predictive of food elicited food-related responses in dogs. In formal terms, the previously insignificant stimulus is associated with the outcome (the **unconditioned stimulus**; US), and as a result becomes a **conditioned stimulus** (CS). Subsequent presentation of the CS triggers the retrieval of the CS–US association, and so the delivery of the US is predicted. This results in an anticipatory response; in the case of food this is salivation, which promotes digestion and hence nutrient acquisition. Two main questions arise when we consider the biological basis of pavlovian memories. Where in the brain are these memories stored, and how does the brain encode a long-lasting memory?

One of the most commonly studied forms of pavlovian conditioning is **fear conditioning**. This involves the formation of an association between a previously-meaningless stimulus and an aversive outcome. Subsequent exposure to the now-fear-conditioned stimulus results in fearful behaviour – you might stop in your tracks ('freeze') or jump out of your skin (increased startle), and your palms might start sweating (leading to increased skin conductance).

WHERE IN THE BRAIN? RESEARCH STRATEGIES

The main brain structure implicated in pavlovian fear conditioning in mammals is the amygdala. The amygdala is covered in greater detail in Chapter 7, in the context of emotional learning. However, it is not enough simply to know that the amygdala is important for fear conditioning. Instead, it is important to understand how we know the amygdala's involvement in, and necessity for, pavlovian fear memories. Therefore, in this section we will concentrate on the principles that have determined the role of the amygdala in fear conditioning, which are also applicable to other forms of memory in different brain areas. There are numerous strategies that can be used, but they can be reduced to two classes: correlational and causational approaches.

Causation

Historically, causational approaches have been more prevalent. These have classically capitalised upon neurological patients with brain damage, combined with experimental lesions in animals. Human patients may have suffered trauma in an accident resulting in brain damage, or a stroke that deprived a certain region of the brain with oxygen, causing neuronal cell death in that area. Some patients have had surgical resection of the brain to remove a particular area (e.g. for the last course treatment of epilepsy), though these tend not to have targeted the amygdala in any specific manner. In one example, epileptic patients who had a portion of the temporal lobe removed on one side of the brain were impaired in their ability to associate a picture of a face with a painful electric shock to their forearm (Weike et al., 2005). The impairment in this pavlovian fear conditioning was evident both during conditioning and in a memory test immediately after. However, the area of the brain removed, while consistently including the amygdala, also always extended to the hippocampus and often other temporal lobe structures. Therefore, patient studies rarely have sufficient spatial resolution to implicate a specific brain area (one exception being when there are very many patients, and behavioural performance can be correlated to the relative extent of damage across different areas).

Fortunately for researchers interested in the human amygdala, there is a condition that results in rather selective degeneration to the amygdala on both sides of the brain. This condition is called **Urbach-Wiethe disease**, and it is incredibly rare; first described in 1929, only about 250 cases have been recorded. It is a genetic disorder with a variety of symptoms, including a selective accumulation of calcium deposits in the amygdala. This results in neuronal cell death and hence a selective lesion to the amygdala. One such patient has been tested and found to have impairments in pavlovian fear conditioning (Bechara et al., 1995).

Apart from the difficulty in drawing conclusions from a single case study, human patient studies often suffer from a lack of temporal resolution that compromises our ability to isolate specific phases of memory. First, focus tends to be on the acquisition and immediate retention of memories, as it can be impractical to bring subjects back on subsequent days for retesting. Moreover, the neurological damage usually predates learning, and so conclusions are again limited to the understanding of the brain areas that are required for the acquisition of memories. There is no logical reason why the same brain areas need to be necessary for acquisition vs. storage and retention of memories. For example, activity in one area might be important for a memory to be stored in another region (see the emotion chapter for details concerning the role of the amygdala in the storage of emotionally-related memories in the hippocampal system). Equally, apparently normal learning and memory following damage to a certain region of the brain does not necessarily mean that that region isn't normally involved in mnemonic processing. There may well be a level of redundancy in the biological system, such that other regions can support memory processing in the absence of the primary functional area. A trivial, but useful analogy is the loss of sight in one eye. At one level, vision is not greatly impaired, because of the ability of the remaining functional eye to support visual function by itself. It doesn't mean that the dysfunctional eye was never important for seeing.

In experimental animals, the experimental damage to the brain can be induced at any time, giving a much greater control over the memory process being studied. It is also possible to carry out experimental lesions to spatially-restricted regions of the brain in rodents and monkeys. **Lesions** can be achieved by sucking out a part of the brain (**aspiration**), by causing electrical current-induced damage (**electrolytic lesions**), or by using chemicals to over-stimulate neurons to death (**excitotoxic lesions**). Each of these approaches can be used to make lesions either before learning, or between learning and testing, thereby distinguishing between those areas that might be involved in acquisition vs. retention and expression of memories.

Using such strategies, numerous studies have found that lesions to the amygdala in rats impair pavlovian fear conditioning regardless of whether they are made before or after learning (Gale et al., 2004; Maren, 1999; Nader et al., 2001; Sananes and Davis, 1992), although amygdala lesions in monkeys only impair fear conditioning when made before learning (Antoniadis et al., 2007).

Because of the long-lasting nature of lesions, both in humans and experimental animals, reversible manipulations are of particular use when investigating the neuroanatomical basis of learning. In humans, the only method of reversibly inactivating areas of the brain is **TMS**. However, this has limitations in its ability to target structures deep in the brain, and has yet to be optimised for amygdala inactivation. In experimental animals, two different strategies are used effectively to silence specific brain areas. The first employs the chemical **tetrodotoxin** (TTX), which is a toxin isolated from pufferfish that blocks sodium channels and hence prevents action potentials from firing. The second uses the chemicals baclofen and/or **muscimol** that are agonists for GABAergic receptor subtypes. As the activation of GABA receptors results in neuronal inhibition, increasing GABAergic neurotransmission results in a heightened level of inhibition within the targeted area, and so is believed to cause a functional silencing.

In one experiment, muscimol alone was infused into the rat amygdala either before fear conditioning or before fear testing. In both cases, the fear memory at test was greatly impaired, suggesting that the amygdala is required at the time of both learning and memory retrieval (Muller et al., 1997).

FOCUS ON METHODS: INACTIVATION

Brain regions can be reversibly inhibited, rather than permanently damaged. This brain inactivation allows the role of a brain area to be determined in a time-specific manner. There are several methods for inactivating the brain. Early methods included cooling the brain, which makes it less likely to fire action potentials. Regional cooling is possible, but is quite slow and not very localised. More recent methods involve the injection of specific drugs into the brain. This is achieved via a cannula that is implanted into the brain, and through which the drug can be injected at the appropriate time. Depending on the location of the injection and the amount of drug that is injected, very specific inactivation can be achieved. The most common drugs are tetrodotoxin, which blocks sodium channels and so prevents neuronal depolarisation, and the GABA receptor agonists baclofen and/or muscimol, which increase inhibitory GABAergic firing, thereby inhibiting the target region as a whole. The same practical methodology can be used to achieve inhibition of specific mechanisms (e.g. protein synthesis or NMDA receptors).

Correlation

Correlational strategies use various forms of imaging techniques in humans and other animals, which have already been covered earlier in this chapter. An increase in brain activity, measured through functional brain imaging or electrophysiological recording, reflects recruitment of the given region during that aspect of behaviour. An additional way of assessing brain activation is to measure the expression of so-called activity-related genes in the regions of interest. Brain activity robustly induces the expression of many genes, but the most commonly measured is *c-fos*. As predicted from the lesion studies, *c-fos* is engaged in the amygdala of rats and mice both after conditioning and following fear memory retrieval (Hall et al., 2001; Radulovic et al., 1998). The relevance of gene activation studies in rodents is supported by concurrent observations of increased amygdala activity during fear conditioning using fMRI (LaBar et al., 1998).

ENCODING LONG-LASTING MEMORIES

Although there is extensive anatomical evidence implicating the amygdala in pavlovian fear conditioning, the studies described above do not provide any insight into how the amygdala encodes memories that last for long periods of time. One of the major questions that has faced the psychobiology of learning and memory is how memories are stabilised into a long-term form. We have already seen how persistent neural activity can support a short-term memory that may last minutes or hours. However, eventually this activity dissipates, yet the memory remains intact for much longer. So how is the short-term memory converted into a long-term form?

The first point to make is that the notion that short-term memory (STM) is stabilised into a long-term memory (LTM) may be inaccurate. The assumption would be that a memory passes sequentially through the phases of acquisition, STM and LTM. However, it is not clear that the formation of LTM requires the existence of STM. For example, certain studies have shown that if STM is impaired, LTM still forms (Izquierdo et al., 2002). Therefore, perhaps the mechanisms of LTM are triggered directly by the learning event, and in parallel with the sustained neural activity that is thought to support STM (see Figure 4.5). That the two processes are largely independent is supported by numerous demonstrations that LTM for pavlovian conditioning can be disrupted, while leaving initial STM intact. Despite this evidence for a **double dissociation** (see 'Focus on Methods' box below) between STM and LTM, the process of long-term memory stabilisation is still commonly referred to as the *consolidation* of STM into LTM. In fact, the precise name is **cellular consolidation** (as opposed to the systems-level consolidation that we will encounter later in the chapter), reflecting the recruitment of a multitude of cellular processes.

FOCUS ON METHODS: DOUBLE DISSOCIATIONS

Double dissociations are highly valuable sources of evidence for revealing that functions/processes are separable and independent in the brain. As an analogy, we might consider the power supplies to a computer and its monitor as two processes. To show that they are independent, it is necessary to show that each can be specifically disrupted. This can be done for a desktop PC and monitor, as each has its independent power supply. However, for a laptop, the situation is different. There is a single dissociation, in that it is often possible to switch off the monitor, leaving the computer itself running. However, it is not usually possible to turn off the computer while leaving the monitor powered up. In such a situation, one process (monitor power) is dependent upon the other (computer power). Therefore, a single dissociation is not sufficient evidence to demonstrate independent processes.

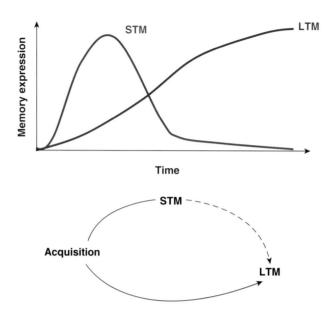

Figure 4.5   Conversion of short-term memory into long-term memory. Top panel: the STM system is fast, but transient. The LTM system is more gradual, but long-lasting. Therefore, soon after learning, STM supports the expression of the memory (red line), whereas at later timepoints LTM is crucial for memory expression (blue line). Bottom panel: the differing timecourses of STM and LTM lead to the illusion that STM is converted into LTM (dotted line), whereas both processes may be directly triggered in parallel by learning (solid lines)

The number of cellular mechanisms that have been implicated in memory consolidation is too extensive to summarise here. Instead, it is useful just to concentrate on certain principles of consolidation. One of the key distinguishing features between STM and LTM is their differing dependence upon the synthesis of new proteins. There are several compounds that have been isolated from bacteria, which have the effect of preventing the process of protein synthesis in multicellular organisms. The most commonly used of these is *anisomycin*, which can be infused directly into the brain of rats at levels that almost completely prevent the synthesis of any new proteins for several hours. Intra-amygdala infusion of anisomycin before or soon after pavlovian conditioning selectively disrupts LTM, while leaving STM intact, as shown in fear conditioning (Maren et al., 2003; Schafe & LeDoux, 2000).

Now, given that protein synthesis is necessary for memory consolidation, and that there is increased gene expression triggered by learning, it is reasonable to suggest that specific proteins encoded by those upregulated genes might be required for consolidation. Indeed this does appear to be the case (though not necessarily for *c-fos*). The **a**ctivity-**r**elated **c**ytoskeletal-associated protein (*Arc*) is similarly upregulated in the amygdala following pavlovian fear conditioning. Moreover, when the synthesis of *Arc* is selectively inhibited in the amygdala, the consolidation of the fear memory is impaired (Ploski et al., 2008).

Given that the synthesis of new proteins is a critical step in the consolidation of long-term memory, it is important to understand the mechanisms that translate behaviourally-induced electrical signals in the brain into gene expression. There are very many components, but we will zoom in on a single primary pathway, starting from the cell surface, through intracellular signals and to the cell's nucleus where gene expression begins.

One of the direct regulators of *Arc* expression is the so-called ERK/MAPK signalling pathway. This pathway consists of a series of *kinases* (the full names being **e**xtracellular signal-**r**elated **k**inase/**m**itogen-**a**ctivated **p**rotein **k**inase). These are protein enzymes that function to phosphorylate other proteins. The phosphorylation of proteins (adding a phosphate group to the protein), in many cases, causes their enzymatic function to be activated, leading to the activation of further downstream mechanisms in the pathway. The same study that demonstrated the upregulation of *Arc* following fear conditioning also showed that this upregulation was dependent upon ERK/MAPK signalling (Ploski et al., 2008), and, as expected, the inhibition of ERK/MAPK signalling also impairs the consolidation of fear memories in the amygdala (impaired LTM with intact STM; Schafe et al., 2000).

Upstream of the ERK/MAPK pathway, the primary cell-surface receptor involved in learning is the NMDA receptor. This is a subtype of glutamatergic receptor that has been heavily implicated in learning, with links to ERK/MAPK activation. Direct infusion of the NMDA receptor **antagonist** AP-5 into the amygdala blocks the acquisition of fear conditioning (Lee and Kim, 1998; Miserendino et al., 1990). Interestingly, NMDA receptor antagonism not only blocks LTM, but also impairs STM (Bauer et al., 2002), suggesting that the NMDA receptor may be critically involved in the process of memory *acquisition*, with divergent downstream mechanisms mediating STM and LTM. For example, it might be that NMDA receptor-mediated neuronal depolarisation is important for maintaining activity for STM, whereas its activation of ERK/MAPK is necessary for LTM.

The question that now remains is, what does this neurobiological pathway from the NMDAR to new protein synthesis do (in conjunction with other mechanisms not covered here) in order to form the long-term memory? The current consensus is that memories are encoded in the brain through changes in **synaptic plasticity**. The origin of this view lies with the writings of Donald Hebb (1949), who suggested at the neurophysiological level that if neuron A repeatedly causes neuron B to fire, 'some growth process or metabolic change takes place in one or both cells' such that A becomes more efficient at causing B to fire. In other words, the synaptic connection between the two neurons is strengthened by learning. This has the value of explaining the longevity of memories, as such synaptic plasticity, especially if it has a structural nature, has the potential to last much longer than sustained neural activity.

SYNAPTIC PLASTICITY AND LTP

When talking about synaptic plasticity, it is inevitably interlinked with the neurophysiological phenomenon of **long-term potentiation** (**LTP**). While Hebb's idea of synaptic plasticity was highly influential, until 1973 there was little or no evidence to support it. LTP was originally demonstrated by Terje Lømo in the hippocampus of anaesthetised rabbits earlier in 1966, but was not fully published until seven years later in collaboration with Tim Bliss. The basic observation was that if one of the pathways into the hippocampus (the perforant pathway terminating in the dentate gyrus) was stimulated at a high frequency, the subsequent response to a test stimulation was increased. Importantly, this potentiation lasted up to ten hours after stimulation, much longer than any sustained activity in studies of visual STM.

There is a significant leap from the work of Bliss and Lømo to the synaptic understanding of pavlovian conditioning in the amygdala. There are three main differences between the behaviour that we seek to understand and the original physiological approach: species, area and associative nature. While there has been substantial behavioural work done on the rabbit, the vast majority of experimental research carried out on pavlovian conditioning (and many other types of behaviour and memory) has been conducted in rodents. The study of LTP also progressed rapidly into rodents, and there have now been over 10,000 papers published on the subject of LTP, the majority in rats and mice. However, most of these have concentrated on hippocampal LTP. While this is important and relevant to hippocampal-dependent memories (more of which to come later in the chapter), it is not easy to explain how synaptic potentiation between two hippocampal neurons gives rise to the complex spatial and conscious memories that are thought to depend upon hippocampal processing. Instead, it is conceptually more straightforward to accept that a connection between two neurons may support the association between a stimulus and outcome that characterises pavlovian conditioning. This final point brings us onto the last difference; the original LTP observed was non-associative in nature, which contrasts with the **associative LTP** that is thought to underpin associative learning. In non-associative LTP, the stimulation of a single pathway at high intensity leads to an increased response to subsequent stimulation of the same pathway (Figure 4.6). In relation to fear memories, which are usually conditioned using an electric shock (to the feet in rodents and to the wrist in humans), this might be akin to a prior shock leading to a greater response to a subsequent shock exposure. This is very different to pavlovian fear conditioning, in which a stimulus comes to be feared

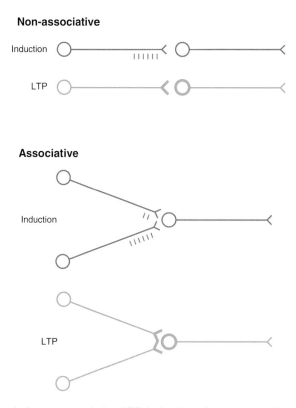

Figure 4.6 Non-associative vs. associative LTP. Induction of non-associative LTP requires only the high-frequency stimulation of a single afferent connection to the post-synaptic neuron (depicted by a train of six vertical dashes representing action potentials). The LTP is reflected by an increased response to a test stimulation of the same afferent fibre (shown as a darker synaptic connection). Associative LTP is induced by the coincident activation of two afferent fibres converging on a single post-synaptic neuron. As long as one of these afferents fires at a high frequency, both synapses will be potentiated

because of its association with the shock. Associative LTP may be able to explain pavlovian conditioning, because it involves two neural pathways. Intense stimulation of one of these pathways may represent the shock, and when it is paired with weak stimulation of a second pathway (the stimulus), subsequent responses to activation of the second pathway are increased. It is not too much of a stretch of the imagination to suggest that the fear of the shock is accrued to the stimulus through such associative LTP.

We do know that there is synaptic plasticity in the amygdala of rats and mice. Rogan, Stäubli and LeDoux (1997) conditioned rats to associate a tone with an aversive footshock, and then measured both the behavioural fear and the electrical activity in the amygdala elicited by the tone. The electrophysiological response in the lateral amygdala was substantially potentiated after conditioning, and only if the conditioning parameters induced a behavioural memory. Explicitly unpairing the presentations of the tone and footshock resulted in no fear memory and no synaptic plasticity. The study by Rogan et al. had the advantage of showing synaptic potentiation in the freely-behaving rat, and hence in the fully intact, living brain. This **in vivo** electrophysiology demonstrates that any effects are not an artefact of extracting the brain and preparing it for **in vitro** study.

While the demonstration of behaviourally-induced synaptic potentiation strongly suggests that synaptic plasticity mediates long-term memory, it does not necessarily follow that associative LTP in the amygdala is the underlying mechanism. Returning to our associative LTP model of fear conditioning, the neural pathways carrying the tone and footshock information do converge in the amygdala. However, is it the case that high activity in the footshock pathway leads to a potentiation of the tone pathway?

It is only recently that technological advances have enabled us to demonstrate directly the associative nature of amygdala LTP. We can now experimentally activate specific neurons in the amygdala, and if this is done at the same time as the presentation of a tone, it is possible artificially to induce conditioned fear in a rat that has never been exposed to footshock (Johansen et al., 2010).

KEY POINTS

- Brain imaging provides correlative evidence for the amygdala being involved in fear conditioning.
- Lesions and other inactivations provide causational evidence for the amygdala being necessary for fear conditioning.
- Memories take time to stabilise into a long-term form; this is known as cellular memory consolidation.
- Cellular consolidation involves many cellular mechanisms, including the synthesis of new proteins.
- Consolidation is linked to synaptic plasticity, the change in the strength of a connection between neurons.

PROCEDURAL MEMORY

Procedural memory involves the acquisition of skills. This takes place at a subconscious level and so is often also referred to as **implicit learning**. Perhaps the most easily accessible form of procedural learning is *motor learning*. A common example used to illustrate motor learning is the learning of a melody on the piano or touch-typing on a keyboard. Sequences of finger movements require fine control over the muscles in our arms and hands, and if we practise a given sequence we will eventually get faster and more accurate. This is actually the basis of many studies of human motor learning. For example, a subject might learn a sequence of five finger taps, and then have to recall that sequence some time later. An interesting feature of this motor learning is that it improves with sleep, independent of the amount of time that has elapsed since learning (Walker et al., 2003). However, we are more concerned here with the biological mechanisms of motor learning.

Many areas of the brain have been implicated in motor forms of procedural learning, from the prefrontal cortex, through motor cortical regions and subcortical areas. However, possibly the most celebrated brain area in relation to motor learning is the **cerebellum**. In humans, lesions to the cerebellum impair learning of an implicit motor sequence (Doyon et al., 1997). There are similar findings with experimental lesions in monkeys (Nixon and Passingham, 2000), and learning on the task activates the cerebellum in humans (Toni et al., 1998). This concordance of the correlational and causational data supports the conclusion that the cerebellum has a functional role to play in motor sequence learning (though the fine details of its specific role remain hotly debated).

The neurophysiological substrates of cerebellar-dependent procedural learning are likely to involve a conceptually different type of synaptic plasticity to the long-term potentiation covered earlier. Learning in the cerebellum, instead, appears to rely principally upon a process of **long-term depression** (**LTD**). LTD is a phenomenon whereby low frequency stimulation leads to a subsequent *decrease* in the response to a test stimulation. LTD has been linked to several forms of motor learning (see Ito, 2000). However, these are somewhat simpler than the sequence learning demonstrated in primates.

The neurophysiological analysis of cerebellar LTD has classically been carried out in rabbits, owing to their relatively large and hence more accessible cerebellum compared to rodents. In rabbits, there are two main forms of motor learning investigated. The first is eyeblink conditioning, which is actually a form of pavlovian conditioning where the rabbit has to learn that a tone predicts a puff of air to the eye and so it will blink in response to the tone. The second is the adaptation of the vestibulo-ocular reflex (VOR). The VOR is a reflex that maintains our focus of vision on a fixed point when we move our heads (i.e. if we move our heads to the right, our eyes have to move to the left in order to remain focused upon the words we are reading). However, if we introduce lenses that reverse left from right, we have to learn instead that when we move our heads to the right, we also have to move our eyes to the right to maintain a fixed gaze. This learning takes time and seems to involve the cerebellum, engaging similar mechanisms to cerebellar LTD.

However, whether LTD is actually the synaptic mechanism of motor learning in the cerebellum is as hotly contested a debate as the relationship between LTP and associative learning in the amygdala. Indeed, the debate extends to whether the cerebellum itself functionally supports motor learning. As noted by Mauk et al. (1998), a quotation that highlights the emotive nature of the debate is 'Every time I read a paper that says the cerebellum mediates motor learning, it makes me want to vomit.'

The mechanisms of LTD are as complicated as those of LTP. There are many forms of LTD, and the molecules involved overlap with those of LTP. To delve into them would likely result in confusion, so we will instead concentrate on one important issue concerning the relationship between LTP and LTD. It is, in fact, not true to think that only LTP occurs in the amygdala and hippocampus, and LTD alone is found in the cerebellum. There is LTD in the amygdala/hippocampus and equally, cerebellar LTP exists.

It is simply the current belief that the principle method of information storage is through relative elevations of synaptic activity in the primary information-storing neurons in the amygdala and decreases in the cerebellum. The reason that information is stored by means of synaptic depression in the cerebellum is that the neuronal connections that are altered are not those of the output neurons, but are rather inhibitory modulatory neurons. If LTD reduces the activity of these modulatory neurons, this has the effect of lowering the inhibition of the output neurons, and hence increasing their activity (Figure 4.7). So, in simplistic terms, the increased motor output with learning can be achieved through information stored as reduced synaptic responsiveness. A useful analogy is the control of a vehicle's speed by both the accelerator (the excitatory pathway) and brake (the inhibitory pathway). Increased speed can be achieved by increasing pressure on the accelerator or reducing pressure on the brake. So we could alter the 'behaviour' of the vehicle to be more prone to going faster either by increasing the power of the accelerator (equivalent to LTP in the excitatory pathway) or reducing the effectiveness of the brake (equivalent to LTD in the inhibitory pathway).

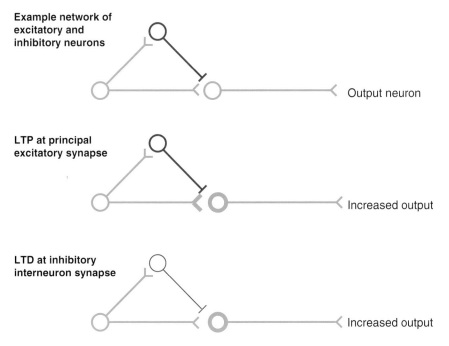

Figure 4.7 LTP and LTD can both lead to increased synaptic output. Neural networks are made up of both excitatory (green) and inhibitory (red) neurons. LTP at an excitatory synapse onto the output neuron (shown by an emboldended synaptic connection) increases the final output in this scheme. Similarly, LTD at an excitatory synapse onto an inhibitory interneuron (shown by a less bold synaptic connection) also results in increased final output. The difference is simply related to the location of information storage (i.e. principal output vs. inhibitory interneuron)

KEY POINTS

- Procedural memory is the memory for the learning of skills.
- Motor memory depends on the cerebellum.
- Cerebellar learning involves long-term depression.
- Long-term depression in inhibitory neurons can achieve increases in the firing of excitatory neurons.

CONSCIOUS FORMS OF LEARNING AND MEMORY

Conscious, or explicit/declarative, memories are those about which we are fully aware. They fall into two categories: **episodic** recollection and **semantic** knowledge. Episodic memory is the memory for events that we have experienced in the past, and which we can recall with details of time and place. Semantic memory, by contrast, incorporates acquired knowledge that has no particular root in time and space. A common illustration of the difference between episodic and semantic memory is when you bump into someone. You may well know who they are (semantic knowledge), for example if they are famous, even if you have not met before. Alternatively, they may be a friend and you can recollect the details of your last meeting (episodic memory).

Episodic vs. semantic memory

While it is obvious in descriptive terms that episodic and semantic memory are different, why should we believe that at the biological level they are separable, not only from each other, but also from unconscious forms of memory? The obligatory starting point for such a discussion is the single-case-study work on brain-damaged patients such as HM and KC, who suffered from amnesia.

Whether the damage to the brain is clinically induced (for the treatment of epilepsy; HM) or trauma-related (a motorcycle accident in the case of KC), the pattern of memory loss is of great interest to our understanding of the anatomical basis of conscious memory. HM had his entire medial temporal lobe removed on both sides of the brain, resulting in an inability to form new conscious memories. This definitely included episodic memory, and many also believe it stretched to semantic memory, though the latter is a bit more controversial. This tells us that the medial temporal lobe, an area that is relatively large and contains numerous subdivisions, is heavily implicated in conscious memory formation. Importantly, HM had completely intact unconscious memory. He was able to learn new motor skills, such as writing in mirror image, showed no perceptual memory deficits, and was able to acquire motor eyeblink conditioning. All of these occurred in the absence of any conscious memory of training having taken place.

This has similarity to the famous observation by Clarapede in 1911, who greeted an **amnesic** patient with a pin hidden in his hand. The patient subsequently avoided shaking hands with him, but could not explain why. We can interpret this behaviour as the intact fear conditioning, resulting in avoidance, but without the corresponding episodic memory for the event that caused the fear.

Research on KC progressed our understanding, because he had a specific loss of episodic memory, leaving even his ability to acquire semantic knowledge intact. The damage KC suffered was extensive, but researchers tend to concentrate on the fact that the hippocampus was completely lost. Therefore, there is a temptation to conclude that the hippocampus is selectively involved in episodic memory, whereas some other brain region mediates semantic memory.

The separability of episodic and semantic memory has now been given substantial support by the demonstration that a different class of neurological patient has a specific impairment in semantic memory, providing a **double dissociation** between the two memory types. Patients with *semantic dementia* have disrupted semantic knowledge, but are still able to lay down new episodic memories. In an experimental setting, Graham et al. (2000) showed that semantic dementia patients were unable to name a familiar object, such as a telephone, because of their impairment in semantic memory. In contrast, they were able to recognise a picture of a telephone previously shown to them; this is a measure of episodic memory as it requires the patient to remember a recent episode of seeing that particular picture. The brain damage suffered by patients with semantic dementia is varied, but seems to focus upon the *perirhinal cortex*, leading us to speculate that the hippocampus and perirhinal cortex form partially independent systems for episodic and semantic memory, respectively.

Given the complementary memory loss in patients like KC and in semantic dementia, there is strong evidence that episodic and semantic memory are separable at the biological and psychological levels of analysis. While the exact neuroanatomical substrates remain subject to debate, why should we be interested in whether they are separate or not? Well, there has been a long-standing debate on the relationship between the two, and the reality of the double dissociation leads to conclusions that might be surprising to some. First, there is no need for the brain to be able to record events (episodic memory) in order to extract knowledge (semantic memory). So some patients can acquire knowledge and understanding without having any recollection of how that knowledge came about. Indeed, patients amnesic from an early age are still usually able to progress through the education system up through to undergraduate degree level, perhaps even writing exams on memory without remembering learning about it. Second, there is no need for us to have semantic knowledge about the world in order to form meaningful episodic memories.

THE HIPPOCAMPUS AND MEMORY

Given the widespread interest in amnesics (generally focusing on episodic amnesics), and the personal nature of episodic memories, the hippocampus is often the area of the brain most readily associated with memory. We have already seen that this is an incomplete picture, with other areas being much more important for different memory types. However, it remains the case that the molecular and physiological basis of memory is best understood in the hippocampus. LTP was first discovered, and continues to be primarily investigated, in the hippocampus, and the hippocampus is also quite a large structure, making it well suited for experiments that use the processing of extracted brain tissue (e.g. the analysis of protein levels). As a result, there is a huge amount of data concerning the molecular basis of synaptic plasticity in the hippocampus (which happens to be largely similar to the process described in the amygdala). However, as noted earlier, there is a huge gap between understanding hippocampal synaptic plasticity and applying that understanding to the process of conscious rich episodic memories. This is further complicated by the debate over whether non-human animals actually possess episodic memory capabilities. There is a lot of theory (especially computational theory) concerning how synaptic plasticity in the hippocampus generates rich episodic memories, and some researchers now believe that classes of animals, such as corvid birds (jays and ravens) and non-human primates, do possess episodic-like memories. Out of such a complicated picture, we will focus on the specific role of the hippocampus in *spatial learning and memory*.

Patients with damage to the hippocampus, as well as suffering from episodic memory loss, exhibit an impairment in the spatial navigation of a previously-experienced environment. Therefore, as expected, when neurologically intact subjects perform a spatial navigation task in the PET scanner, the hippocampus is robustly activated.

Maguire and colleagues (1998) asked participants to explore a virtual town (within the computer game 'Duke Nukem 3D'). Immediately afterwards, in the scanner, the subjects were asked to navigate from a randomly assigned starting point to a specified destination. When compared to a control condition in which the subjects simply had to follow arrows laid out on the ground of the virtual town, the hippocampus was significantly activated. Moreover, the accuracy of the path adopted correlated with the level of activity in the hippocampus, supporting the conclusion that the hippocampus mediates experience-dependent spatial navigation. Maguire et al. suggested that while they navigate, the subjects may be consciously remembering prior episodes of being in the current position in the environment, and so spatial navigation may be a form of episodic memory recollection. As such, it should not be a surprise that the hippocampus is activated by, and necessary for, spatial navigation.

Given the assumption in humans that spatial navigation is closely linked to episodic memory, and both depend upon the hippocampus, it is tempting to reason that if spatial navigation can be shown to be hippocampal-dependent in experimental animals, we can use such a paradigm to investigate the neurophysiological and molecular mechanisms of episodic memory.

There are numerous ways of testing spatial memory in rats and mice. The most famous is the *spatial water maze*, used extensively by Richard Morris and many others. Rats are trained over multiple trials to learn the location of an escape platform that is submerged in a pool full of cloudy water. We can then test the navigational abilities of the rats by placing them back into the pool in a position from which they have not started, and record where they search for the platform. In order to navigate to the correct location, the rats have to use a combination of cues around the room. Experimental lesions to the hippocampus do disrupt performance in the water maze, and successful navigation to the platform location activates gene expression in the hippocampus, nicely matching the findings from the human studies. Nevertheless, does it necessarily follow that, similar to humans, rats solve the water maze by recollecting previous episodes from training? Clearly, they must be using some sort of acquired memory, but there is no clear way of knowing what the nature of that memory is, nor how they are using it. Given that there is a common involvement for the hippocampus, perhaps it is just the case that the kinds of neural computations required for spatial navigation in the rat are also useful in encoding and recollecting episodic memories in humans.

SYSTEMS-LEVEL CONSOLIDATION

The similarity between experimental hippocampal lesions in rats and neurological hippocampal damage in humans extends to the observation of a *temporally-graded retrograde amnesia*. Patients such as HM and KC not only failed to lay down new episodic memories (**anterograde amnesia**), but also appeared to lose the ability to retrieve some pre-existing memories. However, this **retrograde amnesia** for previously-learned memories followed a specific pattern; memories acquired more recently were more likely to be impaired, and more remote memories were preferentially spared. This temporal gradient spans many years in human amnesia (with memories around 20 years or so older being relatively spared), and has been replicated on a shorter timescale by hippocampal lesions in rats. A lesion on the day after training on the water maze produces a profound impairment, whereas delaying the lesion by two months renders it ineffective in disrupting spatial navigation (Clark et al., 2007). What happens to the memory to make it less dependent upon the hippocampus as time passes? And which area of the brain takes over responsibility for spatial/episodic memory storage and retrieval?

The first point to note is that the temporal gradient of retrograde amnesia for human episodic memory is, in fact, disputed. Cipolotti et al. (2001) describe a patient, VC, who had seizure-related damage to the hippocampus and subsequently displayed a loss of episodic memory that spanned at least 40 years, in contrast to the temporally-graded retrograde amnesia observed in other patients. How these discrepant findings can be reconciled is not clear, and the human imaging literature doesn't provide much help (see the Key Study below). Some studies appear to show that areas of the temporal lobe are more highly activated in the retrieval of recent memories than older memories, which would account for the more disruptive impact of temporal lobe damage on recent memories. However, this pattern of results has by no means been replicated universally.

A second problem is that there is little evidence in human amnesics for a retrograde amnesia for spatial memories. Amnesics don't appear to have a problem navigating through previously-familiar environments, which contrasts greatly both with their episodic memory deficits, and with the many studies in rodents showing a retrograde amnesia for spatial memories. This further questions the relevance both of rodent studies to the understanding of human memory in general, and of spatial memory and navigation to episodic memory in particular.

KEY STUDY

Haist, F., Bowden Gore, J., & Mao, H. (2001). Consolidation of human memory over decades revealed by functional magnetic resonance imaging. *Nature Neuroscience*, 4(11), 1139–45

If we want to use human brain imaging to inform retrograde amnesia, we have to be able to activate memories of different ages. One way is to present pictures of people who became famous at different times in the past. Photos taken of the faces of these people when they became famous can be presented to neurologically intact participants (who are necessarily of an appropriate age to be able to recall photos that are several decades old), who are asked to identify and name the individual.

Using functional magnetic resonance imaging (fMRI), Haist et al. showed that the identification of recent famous faces (up to 20 years old) triggers stronger activation of the brain than is the case for older faces (40–50 years old). However, given that identification was successful for both recent and older faces, the differential strength of activity is difficult to interpret. Instead we are interested in the location of activity, and it was the entorhinal cortex on the right-hand side of the brain that was more strongly activated, presumably reflecting a more crucial role in retrieving the memory.

Therefore, it appears that the hippocampal formation in the temporal lobe (of which the entorhinal cortex is a part) is more crucially involved in the retrieval of recent vs. remote memories, which is consistent with the observation of temporal gradients of retrograde amnesia after temporal lobe damage.

When critically analysing this study, there are some important considerations to make:

- How relevant is the behavioural task to the reality of human amnesia? Certainly, amnesics have poor recognition memory. However, the authors chose to validate their procedure by testing patients who were less able to identify the recent faces and hence showed a clear temporal gradient of retrograde amnesia.

(Continued)

(Continued)

- Why is it only the entorhinal cortex that shows the temporal gradient of activity? While the entorhinal cortex provides a major input to the hippocampus, there was no temporally-graded activation of the hippocampus itself. So does the entorhinal cortex play a different role to the hippocampus itself? And where does that leave our understanding of the role of the hippocampus in memory?
- And finally, as is important for all research, is it replicable? Well, unfortunately other studies using the recall of autobiographical memories have failed to replicate these findings (Ryan et al., 2001), meaning that functional imaging leaves us currently no closer to explaining the discrepancy between patients VC and HM.

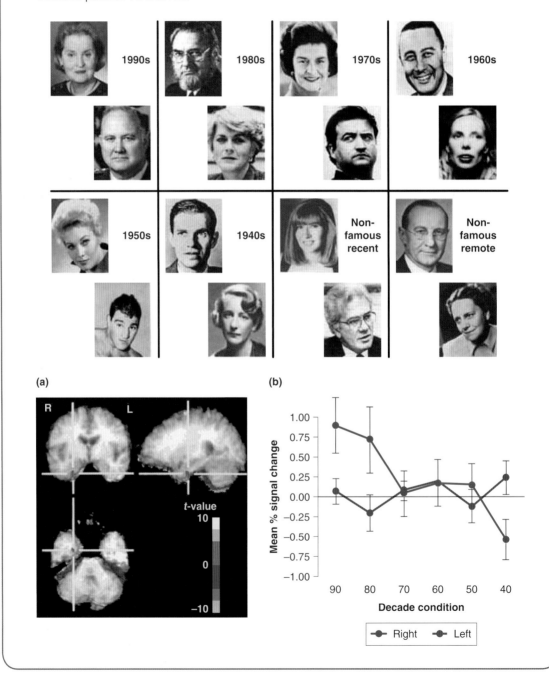

Despite these caveats, there are some conclusions we can make with some level of confidence. First, there is some degree of sparing of very remote memories in humans with hippocampal damage. This might be limited to semantic memory, or to the precise detail of episodic memory (Nadel and Moscovitch, 2001). Second, there are many demonstrations of temporally-graded retrograde amnesia in experimental animals (Squire et al., 2001).

The failure consistently to observe a temporal gradient in brain activation may reflect the fundamental difference between correlative and causational approaches. It is certainly possible that, even though the hippocampus is equally activated when retrieving recent and remote memories, it is actually only functionally necessary for the retrieval of recent memories. In other words, even though the hippocampus would normally be engaged by the process of remote memory retrieval, it is not absolutely necessary for that process to be achieved successfully. So we still need to explain the apparent progression of certain memories from being hippocampal-dependent to being more independent of hippocampal processing, and there are two main theories to consider.

Both theories suggest that the neocortex has an important role to play, but place different emphases on the relationship between the hippocampus and neocortex. The first and most commonly adopted theory is that of **systems consolidation**. Inherent in the name, and the use of the term *consolidation*, this theory accepts the temporally-graded nature of retrograde amnesia, with memories becoming more stable and resistant to (hippocampal) disruption over time. It suggests that episodic and/or semantic memories 'move' from the hippocampus to areas in the neocortex.

This would explain why hippocampal lesions soon after learning impair the memory, but once the memory has 'moved', lesions to the hippocampus have no obvious effect. In support of this theory, studies have found that the *anterior cingulate cortex* is activated by retrieval of spatial and contextual memories that are no longer hippocampal-dependent, and are necessary for the successful retrieval and expression of those memories (Frankland and Bontempi, 2005; Teixeira et al., 2006). However, the notion that the memory physically moves from the hippocampus to the neocortex may be flawed.

One of the proposed features of hippocampal processing is that it is optimally wired to encode information rapidly, as well as having strong connections with many other regions of the brain, including many cortical areas. As conscious memories are multimodal in nature, and probably involve information from many cortical areas, perhaps the hippocampus is able to encode an episode quickly, binding together the cortical elements of the memory. If the connections between the cortical elements themselves form more slowly, then the hippocampus will be required for successful memory retrieval until such time as the memory can be supported and retrieved independently of the hippocampus (see Figure 4.8).

In a strange way, it is similar to how you form lasting friendships with some of your university peers. If you think of the cortical units in Figure 4.8 being you and your friends, initially you are brought together only by the common enrolment at university (the links in the hippocampus). However, over time the friendships are strengthened such that they persist outside of the university environment. So if your university were for some reason to close down during your time studying, it would likely have a much greater impact on the friendships you are forming than if it closes down a long time in the future.

Returning to memories and the brain, what specific role the neocortex plays within the systems consolidation scheme remains unclear, given that the anterior cingulate cortex is only necessary for remote memory retrieval and is neither engaged by or required for *recent* memory retrieval.

As should by now be clear, there remains a great deal to be understood concerning the nature of remote memory storage and retrieval. Thus it should come as no surprise that there is an almost equally well-regarded theory that stands in direct contrast to the systems consolidation framework. *Multiple trace theory* (MTT) takes the complete retrograde amnesia of patient VC as a critical constraint. Hence, Lynn Nadel and Morris Moscovitch have suggested that the hippocampus,

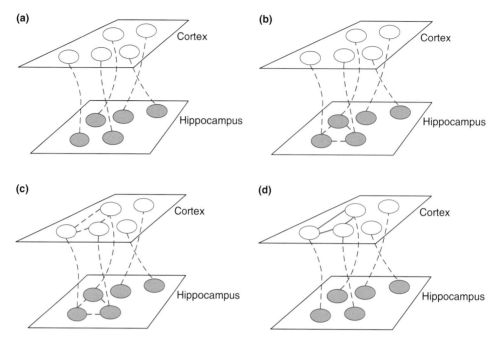

Figure 4.8   Systems consolidation. (a) Units (circles) in the hippocampus are intrinsically linked to units in the cortex (red dashed lines). (b) Learning results in rapid synaptic plasticity in the hippocampus, connecting together certain units (blue dashed lines). (c) Over time, with rehearsal and reactivation of the memory, the associated cortical units become linked together. (d) Finally, synaptic plasticity at the cortical level is stabilised, enabling the cortex to mediate memory retrieval and expression independent of the hippocampus (blue solid lines)

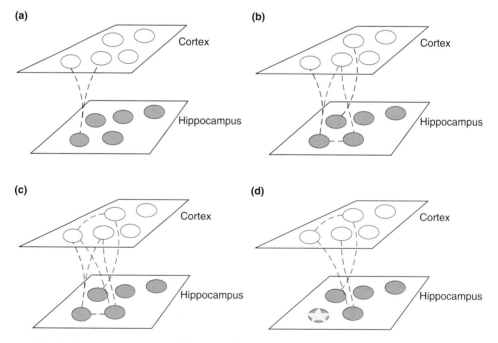

Figure 4.9   Multiple trace theory. (a) Units (circles) in the hippocampus are linked to units in the cortex (black dotted lines) by learning. (b) Retrieval/rehearsal of the memory results in the formation of a parallel, overlapping trace in the hippocampus and cortex (blue dotted lines). (c) With further retrieval and rehearsal of the memory, more traces are added (red dotted lines). (d) When the hippocampus is partially damaged (yellow star), this impairs any trace that the affected unit mediated. However, other traces are left intact, which may be sufficient still to retrieve the memory

in conjunction with the neocortex, is actually always necessary for episodic memory retrieval. However, the hippocampus is very rarely entirely damaged or removed. So if preserved memory is mediated by some spared hippocampal region, why should older memories be more likely to reside in that spared area? The suggestion is that each time an episodic memory is retrieved, a new trace is laid down in parallel with the existing trace(s). So the older a memory, the chances are that it will have been retrieved/rehearsed multiple times, leading to multiple memory traces distributed across the hippocampus and cortex. As the number of memory traces increases, their distribution makes it more likely that one or more of the traces will be unaffected by partial hippocampal damage, leading to intact retrieval of remote memories (Figure 4.9).

KEY POINTS

- Conscious memories include episodic and semantic memories.
- Episodic and semantic memories are separable biologically from each other and from non-conscious forms of memory.
- The hippocampus is strongly associated with conscious episodic memory.
- The hippocampus is also important for spatial memory.
- Hippocampal damage not only impairs the acquisition of new spatial/episodic memories, but also impairs some previously-acquired memories.
- The loss of pre-existing memories (retrograde amnesia) follows a temporal gradient (more recent memories are more likely to be impaired).
- Systems consolidation may account for the temporal gradient of retrograde amnesia.

CHAPTER SUMMARY

Memories not only enable us to remember the past, but allow appropriate preparation for future action. This can occur at subconscious and conscious levels. First, the amount that you learn appears to be regulated by the level of surprise at the occurrence of an event. The more surprising it is, the less able you were to predict it, and so the more you should update your memory. Learning does not result in an immediately-stable long-term memory trace; rather, the memory needs to be consolidated, which takes a period of several hours. This may allow for synaptic plasticity to take place, which strengthens or weakens synaptic connections in a persistent manner. Therefore, synaptic plasticity and memory consolidation require cellular processes, central among which is the synthesis of new proteins within the specific brain areas that support the memory. These principles of learning and memory have been derived from studies of unconscious associative memory, although it is possible that they apply equally to conscious declarative memories. When it comes to these declarative memories, however, we see that there is another process that takes place over a much longer time period. The memories initially require the hippocampus in order to be retrieved, but after many years they appear to become independent of the hippocampus. Therefore, amnesics who have suffered damage to the hippocampus not only lose the ability to form new declarative memories, but are seemingly stuck in the past some time before the brain damage actually occurred.

FURTHER READING

Dudai, Y. (2002). Molecular bases of long-term memories: A question of persistence. *Current Opinion in Neurobiology, 12(2),* 211–16.

Reviews the issues concerning how memories persist. It is quite molecular in places, but provides a readable overview of important concepts. It also provides a good link to the reconsolidation topic in Spotlight 4a.

Maren, S. (2005). Synaptic mechanisms of associative memory in the amygdala. *Neuron, 47(6),* 783–6.

Gives a concise review of the role of synaptic plasticity in amygdala-based learning, and provides additional information on synaptic mechanisms (especially AMPA receptors). It is relevant also to some aspects of Chapter 7.

Moscovitch et al. (2006). The cognitive neuroscience of remote episodic, semantic and spatial memory. *Current Opinion in Neurobiology, 16(2),* 179–90.

Gives a comparison of systems consolidation and multiple trace theories while also introducing the cognitive map theory of hippocampal function. It is relevant both to retrograde amnesia and the role of the hippocampus in memory.

Schultz, W. (2007). Behavioral dopamine signals. *Trends in Neurosciences, 30(5),* 203–10.

Provides a review of prediction error signals, covering both rewarding and aversive situations, and a variety of experimental approaches are discussed.

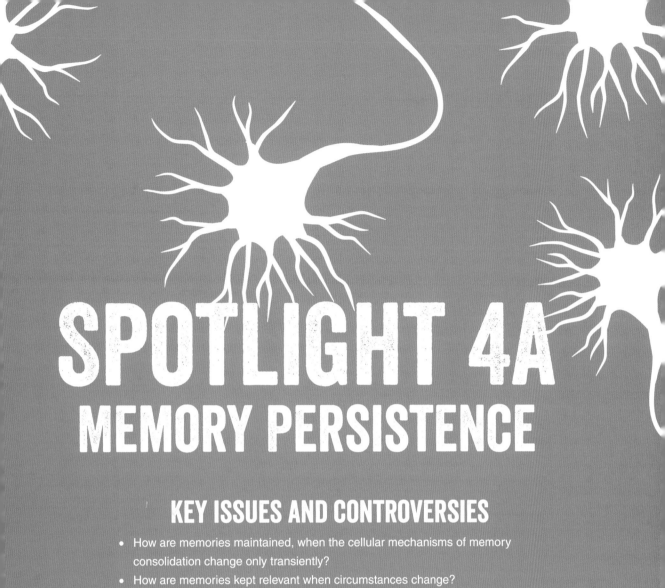

SPOTLIGHT 4A
MEMORY PERSISTENCE

KEY ISSUES AND CONTROVERSIES

- How are memories maintained, when the cellular mechanisms of memory consolidation change only transiently?
- How are memories kept relevant when circumstances change?
- Do new experiences result in the creation of new memories, or the modification of existing memories?

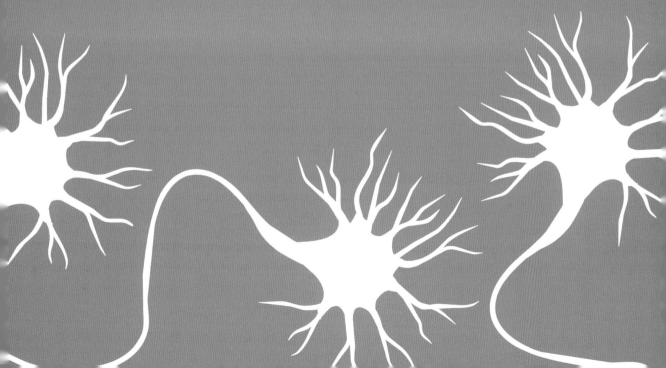

INTRODUCTION

In Chapter 4 we discovered that memories take time to stabilise in a process known as memory consolidation. We explored certain mechanisms of memory consolidation for fear memories in the amygdala. These included the requirement for NMDA receptors, the phosphorylation of kinases, and the synthesis of proteins such as Arc. Therefore, the focus was mainly on the question of how the brain goes from a state of no memory to one of a stable long-term memory. In this spotlight, our aim is to delve deeper into memory research, with a particular focus on what happens after this initial phase of memory consolidation. We will explore three issues in depth and along the way we will analyse some key research papers and critically appraise methods and findings. Memory consolidation at the cellular level is completed within a timeframe of hours to days. However, our memories (both conscious and unconscious) last for much longer. How are these memories maintained for such long periods of time? Moreover, sometimes previously acquired memories support behaviour that is no longer useful or relevant. So how are memories modified in order to maintain their relevance? This leads on to a final conceptual question of how we deal with a vast number of learning experiences. Is each one encoded discretely as its own independent memory, or are memories updated such that we have a more limited number of accurate memories?

HOW ARE MEMORIES MAINTAINED?

Memories are stabilised into a long-lasting form within a few hours after their acquisition. Critical to this process is the synthesis of new proteins such as Arc, controlled by the activation (phosphorylation) of intracellular kinases, as presented in Chapter 4. We can observe an activation of kinases and an upregulation of the synthesis of Arc and many other proteins soon after learning. However, this activation and upregulation is transient and usually dissipates within a few hours. This means that the levels of learning-induced proteins rapidly fall back to baseline. In this section, we will think about if and how such transient cellular changes can result in a persistent memory.

If a brief increase in the levels of some proteins is sufficient to support much longer-lasting memories, we would expect that there should be some other biological change that correlate with the longevity of the behavioural memory. One potential candidate is the concept of structural plasticity. In studies of LTP, synaptic potentiation changes the morphology (i.e. the shape) of neurons. One main method is through the production of more dendritic spines. These spines are protrusions on the dendrites of a neuron where synaptic contacts are made with the afferent axon. So the dendrites are the location of the synapses. Fear conditioning causes an increase in the size of spines in the amygdala (Ostroff et al., 2012). What this likely means is that activity in the afferent axon is more likely to depolarise the altered neuron, which is argued to underlie the synaptic potentiation observed. Given that the changes in neuronal structure are likely to be long-lasting, this provides both a target for the more transient cellular mechanisms of synaptic plasticity and a persistent trace for the memory.

However, we know that neuronal networks are dynamic; an individual neuron's synapses die off and are replaced by new ones, and neurons themselves may die with no obvious consequence for the behavioural memory. There appears to a natural rate of spine turnover, such that spines persist for several weeks to months, but then are likely to disappear and be replaced by newly formed spines (e.g. Holtmaat et al., 2005). This leads to the question of how the plastic changes are maintained in the face of synaptic turnover and neuronal cell death. The initial transient cellular change surely cannot continually ensure that synapses remain potentiated.

Suppose that there were a mechanism that truly determined whether a memory persisted or not. We might expect that mechanism to be induced by learning, perhaps along the same time-course as the emergence of the long-term memory trace. Importantly, it should remain active continuously for as long as the memory persists behaviourally, and disruption of the mechanism would be expected effectively to erase the memory. We could then suggest that it is this process that maintains synaptic plasticity in the face of the dynamic nature of the biological substrates that effect the synaptic changes. In fact, this is a hypothesis that was originally proposed by Francis Crick (of DNA fame), who suggested that some enzymes might fulfil such criteria if they were continuously active.

Now, while most learning-induced changes are indeed transient, there are a couple that appear to be more long-lasting, perhaps sufficiently so to fulfil the above criteria. In recent years, one of these (PKMζ) has been held to be a so-called 'memory maintenance molecule'.

PKMζ has special characteristics that make it possible to be constantly active. It is part of a family of protein kinases, the **p**rotein **k**inase **c** (PKC) family. There are many PKC subtypes, and PKMζ is not a typical member, being different from the conventional PKCζ form. Most PKC proteins act in a manner that ensures transient functionality (see Figure 4a.1). There is an active part of the protein (the catalytic domain), which is normally occupied by another part of the protein (the regulatory domain). Thus the protein, if we think of it in pharmacological terms, essentially antagonises itself, thereby remaining inactive. PKC proteins are activated by messenger molecules in neurons that themselves are activated by pharmacological processes. Thus synaptic activity translates into PKC activation. The way in which these messenger molecules operate is to bind to the regulatory domain, forcing it to detach from and free the active domain, which can then carry out its phosphorylating function. When the messengers degrade, the regulatory domain is released and re-occupies the active domain, inactivating the kinase.

Where PKMζ differs is that it lacks the regulatory domain of PKCζ, meaning that it is constantly active. While this fulfils our requirement for long-lasting enzymatic activity, it does not sit so easily with the additional requirement that the mechanism be activated by learning. If PKMζ is always active, surely it would be active both *before* learning, as well as during the course of the memory. Also, the removal of the regulatory domain appears to separate PKMζ activity from the messenger molecules that would translate learning-related synaptic activity into kinase activity. In fact, the activation of PKMζ does appear to be dependent upon plasticity-inducing synaptic activity in a very complex process. First, the PKMζ protein itself is not present in neurons that haven't been engaged by learning. It must be translated from the mRNA that is ready and present in the synaptic region of the neuron (this process requires, among other mechanisms, ERK, which we already know to be involved in memory consolidation: see Chapter 4). Even then, the initially-translated protein is not in its optimally-active conformation, needing to be phosphorylated before it becomes constantly active. As well as carrying out functions related to synaptic plasticity, this activated PKMζ also ensures that there is a sufficient pool of PKMζ protein, by assisting the translation of more mRNA into protein. This complex process seems to ensure that PKMζ is only persistently engaged by learning-related synaptic activity.

So, PKMζ has the molecular characteristics to be ideally-placed as a mechanism of memory maintenance. But what about evidence that PKMζ has a functional role in maintaining synaptic plasticity? Well, initially it was very strong and grew rapidly, but all is not as clear as we might have hoped.

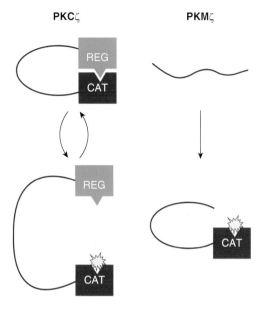

PKCζ **PKMζ**

Figure 4a.1 Persistent activity of PKMζ. Conventional PKC proteins have a regulatory domain (REG) of the protein that occupies the active catalytic domain (CAT). This means that the protein is normally inactive. The catalytic domain can be freed by synaptic activity to become active (star), but eventually the regulatory domain will re-attach and inactivate the kinase. In contrast, the atypical PKMζ protein does not have a regulatory domain. When the protein is initially synthesised, it is not in an active form. However, when activated by synaptic activity, the catalytic domain is revealed and because there is no regulatory domain, the protein remains active indefinitely, continually carrying out its phosphorylating function

Initial findings were generated in the context of LTP. PKMζ has been inhibited by two substances in experimental studies. The first is chelerythrine, which binds to and prevents the functioning of the active domain. However, as the conventional PKCζ protein shares exactly the same active domain as PKMζ, the effects of chelerythin cannot be attributed selectively to the inihibition of PKMζ. Therefore, Todd Sacktor and colleagues have developed an artificial small protein (a peptide) that replicates the function of the PKCζ regulatory domain. This **z**eta **i**nhibitory **p**eptide (ZIP; zeta being the anglicised form of the Greek letter ζ) can be added to hippocampal slices and infused directly into the brains of rats and mice. When ZIP was infused into the hippocampus of a rat, it completely reversed LTP that was induced 22 hours before (Pastalkova et al., 2006). This is a timepoint at which no other substance has been effective at disrupting established LTP. New protein synthesis is only needed for a few hours after LTP induction, and protein synthesis inhibition has no impact upon established LTM. Therefore, inhibition of PKMζ is sufficient to reverse the synaptic plasticity that maintains LTP. Given that PKMζ is known to be persistently active during LTP, it is reasonable to draw the conclusion that it is PKMζ that maintains LTP. If PKMζ is maintaining synaptic plasticity then, when it is inactivated, the downstream mechanisms will rapidly degrade or inactivate, resulting in the decay of plasticity and LTP.

The effect of ZIP to reverse LTP both *in vivo*, and in brain slices *in vitro*, has subsequently been extended to behavioural memories. The first demonstration, also in Pastalkova et al. (2006), used a hippocampal-dependent spatial memory to show that the same ZIP infusion into the hippocampus erased the previously-learned memory. This memory reversal was rapid and, as far as it is possible to tell, permanent. The theoretical account for this effect is essentially an extension to that of the reversal of LTP. Assuming the same kind of synaptic plasticity processes maintain hippocampal LTP and hippocampal-based memories, and these processes depend upon the persistent presence and activity of PKMζ, then ZIP will result in rapid deactivation of such processes, thereby causing the memory to be irretrievably lost.

In fact, many types of memory have now been shown to rely upon persistent PKMζ activity in a variety of brain areas. This includes the hippocampus, amygdala and areas of the cortex for memories that are up to one month old. Moreover, ZIP appears to erase all memories encoded in the target brain area. Shema et al. (2007) infused ZIP into the insular cortex of rats and showed that it erased two different conditioned taste aversion memories learned seven and nine days previously. So PKMζ can maintain different and independent memories within the same brain region. How does it do this? If a neuron is already involved in an existing memory, and then gets recruited to participate in a new memory, surely PKMζ is already active and functional, and so how does the new memory get encoded and persist in a way that does not produce confusion or interference? Of course, it might be the case that any single neuron cannot be involved in representing more than one piece of information (this is related to the so-called *grandmother cell* hypothesis), but the prevailing current view is that neural representations (and hence memory representations) in the brain overlap, with individual neurons participating in more than one ensemble of neurons. The answer to this problem comes in part from a deeper understanding of how PKMζ operates.

The mRNA that codes PKMζ protein is ready and waiting in close vicinity of each synapse. Moreover, the process of mRNA translation into protein, and the activation of the new PKMζ protein, is a highly localised process. Therefore, it is only in the synapse that is activated by learning that PKMζ becomes functional. As a result, PKMζ operates to maintain plasticity *at individual synapses*, and not at all the synapses of the activated neuron. In this way, different memories can be maintained by PKMζ in the same neuron. This also explains why ZIP erases all memories in the target brain region. Despite this, there is some indication that PKMζ may not be a universal mechanism. ZIP had no effect upon a contextual fear memory when infused into the hippocampus, but was effective when infused into the amygdala (Kwapis, Jarome, Lonergan, and Helmstetter, 2009). Moreover, there was subsequently some evidence that the memory impairment induced by ZIP might not be permanent, suggesting instead that inhibition of PKMζ could cause some transient deficit in memory retrieval, rather than true memory erasure (Parsons and Davis, 2011). Finally, it has now been suggested that ZIP itself is not as selective as previously assumed, casting doubt on whether its memory-impairing effects are actually due to an inhibition of PKMζ.

KEY STUDY

Lee, A.M. et al. (2013). Prkcz null mice show normal learning and memory. *Nature*, 493(7432), 416–19

Lee and colleagues took a different approach to the study of PKMζ in learning and memory, rather than relying upon the use of ZIP. Reliance upon only one experimental approach (e.g. ZIP) risks the possibility of false conclusions, even if the findings are replicated. In order to provide convergent evidence, Lee et al. used a genetic approach. They created mice that lacked a part of the *Prkcz* gene, such that those mice were unable to produce PKC or PKMζ.

If PKMζ is necessary for memory maintenance, we would expect the inability to synthesise the protein to result in substantial memory deficits. Moreover, given that ZIP impairs the maintenance of many memory types, memory deficits should be readily apparent. However, surprisingly, the Prkcz mutant mice appeared to be perfectly capable of forming long-lasting memories, with no observable impairments. Importantly, Lee et al. demonstrated that this was the case for a number of memory paradigms, not just relying on a single experimental observation.

So does this mean that the PKMz hypothesis is wrong? Not necessarily. One of the strengths of the study is that it makes a decent effort to explain the surprising findings and reconcile them with the previous literature. Perhaps the mutant mice somehow overcame the lack of PKMζ (and indeed PKC). Two of the interpretative problems with the use of standard genetically-modified mice are that

(Continued)

(Continued)

the protein is lost throughout the brain and body, and is also never expressed during the development and lifetime of the mouse. The first of these is probably not an issue for this particular study. The global loss of a protein may have non-specific effects that impair a mouse's ability to perform a task. However, given that the mice here were seemingly normal, that is not a concern. The developmental loss of PKMζ, though, may explain the lack of memory deficit. If the brain and body have developed in the absence of PKC and PKMζ, that may have resulted in compensatory processes such that memory persistence is no longer dependent upon PKMζ. Therefore the Prkcz mutant mice would not be an appropriate way to assess the requirement for PKMζ in memory maintenance in genetically-normal mice.

If the above criticism were correct, we would expect that the memories that formed in the Prkcz mutant mice would not be affected by ZIP. However, Lee and colleagues demonstrated that ZIP did impair a number of memories in the mutant mice. This posed a problem in that ZIP was believed to be a very selective inhibitor of PKMζ, and so should not have had any biological effect in the mice lacking PKMζ. Lee and colleagues used pharmacological assays to show that ZIP is not, in fact, selective for PKMζ, but also inhibits the related kinases PKCζ and PKCι (the expression of which was not affected by the genetic mutation). Therefore, perhaps these are the important mechanisms of memory maintenance.

While the effects of ZIP, combined with the normal memory in the mutant mice, are suggestive of PKMζ not being all-important for memory maintenance, we still cannot get fully around the criticism of developmental effects. It can still be argued that in normal wild-type mice, PKMζ is the principal, but perhaps not the only, mechanism of memory maintenance. The PKMζ hypothesis, however, does not need any exclusivity of PKMζ over the process of memory maintenance. Indeed the authors do not over-interpret their findings, limiting themselves to concluding that ZIP is not as selective as previously thought and that PKMζ is not required for long-term memory. Note that the lack of requirement is not the same as saying that PKMζ is not involved in long-term memory.

In isolation, the study by Lee and colleagues provides intriguing evidence against the PKMζ hypothesis of memory maintenance. It becomes a lot more convincing, however, when taken alongside another paper published at the same time (Volk et al., 2013). Volk and colleagues generated, completely independently, another line of mice that lacked PKC and PKMζ. In these mice, memory was again apparently normal, as was hippocampal LTP. Moreover, ZIP impaired the maintenance of LTP in the same mice. Finally, and perhaps most importantly, Volk and colleagues bred a separate line of mice, in which the loss of PKC/PKMζ could be controlled. In these so-called conditional knockout mice, PKC and PKMζ were 'deleted' only in the forebrain and only during a restricted period during adulthood. In these mice, LTP was also unimpaired. What this means is that the normal LTP is not due to some developmental compensation for the lack of PKC/PKMζ. Instead, it is much more likely that PKMζ is somewhat dispensable for memory maintenance.

Implications

Given that the studies by Lee et al. and Volk et al. are recent, their long-term implications remain to be seen. However, it appears clear that the involvement of PKMζ in the maintenance of long-term memories is not as clear-cut as the early literature indicated. Maybe this is to be expected, as memory maintenance surely cannot come down to a single member of a family of kinases. Therefore, our understanding of memory maintenance remains at an early stage. This also means that it remains unclear whether the potential targeting of PKMζ for improving memories in amnesia and cognitive decline (Shema et al., 2011) is viable.

HOW ARE MEMORIES KEPT RELEVANT WHEN CIRCUMSTANCES CHANGE?

While it is obviously an advantage to learn from experiences in order to predict their future occurrence, what happens when things change and the predictions are no longer valid? This is a simple yet powerful example that we can use to illustrate the dynamism of memories, and it leads us to consider the specific case of **memory extinction**.

The history of memory extinction is as old as that of associative conditioning. Ivan Pavlov noted soon after his original classical conditioning observations that the conditioned responses would diminish in strength if the CS no longer predicted the US. This makes perfect sense; there is no advantage for Pavlov's dogs to salivate to the CS if food is no longer likely to be presented soon after. Thus the conditioned response extinguishes. Given the nature of memory extinction, it is relevant specifically to associative learning, as it is the association that extinguishes (whether it is the association between a stimulus and outcome or a response and an outcome; pavlovian or instrumental conditioning, respectively). The question for us here concerns the biological mechanisms of the extinction process, and we will see that extinction necessitates a more complex network of brain regions than does initial learning. However, in order to answer the question, we must first consider the pure psychology of memory extinction.

The first point to note about extinction is that it is not the same as unlearning (at least not under most circumstances). Instead, extinction is most commonly described as new inhibitory learning. Extinction involves learning that the CS no longer predicts the US, and so a new memory for the association between the CS and the lack of a US (CS–no US) is formed, which inhibits the expression of the original CS–US association. Why do we need to resort to this rather complex notion, instead of simply saying that extinction involves the unlearning of the CS–US association? The answer comes from a set of incredibly consistent findings that the original memory survives extinction and can be expressed again if the conditions are right. If extinction erased the original memory, under no circumstances should we be able to express the original memory after extinction is complete. However, there are three simple manipulations that can be used to recover extinguished memories of all types, regardless of their nature and neural substrates (from amygdala-based fear memories to cortically-encoded taste aversion memories).

The three causes of recovery from extinction are simply waiting (spontaneous recovery; originally observed by Pavlov), reminding the subject of the outcome (reinstatement) and changing the context (renewal). We will concentrate on renewal as an illustrative example, which also tells us something more about the likely neural mechanisms of extinction. There are multiple subtle variations in how we can conduct an extinction experiment, depending upon the specific environmental context in which conditioning, extinction and final testing take place. Despite this, there is one universal finding from each variant; if the final test takes place in a different context to the extinction training, recovery will be observed (see Figure 4a.2). The explanation for this finding is that whereas the original memory generalises across

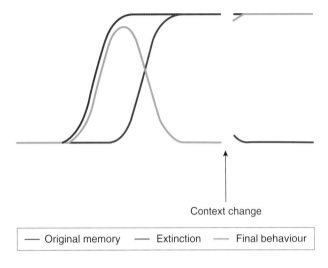

Context change

— Original memory   — Extinction   — Final behaviour

Figure 4a.2 The inhibitory effect of extinction is modulated by context. Conditioning forms the original memory, which is inhibited by the inhibitory extinction memory to reduce the final behaviour. However, upon a shift in context, the extinction memory is only weakly expressed, resulting in renewal of the final behaviour

contexts, the inhibitory extinction memory is much more context-specific. If we think about this in a fear conditioning setting, it again makes sense; while the conditioned stimulus has been learned to be safe in one particular environment, it is no guarantee that it is also safe in different contexts. Therefore, it would be adaptive sense to maintain a level of fear to the CS in any non-extinguished context. What this tells us from a biological perspective is that not only does extinction consist of inhibitory processes, but also contextual information must be incorporated into the inhibitory process.

We will consider the neural substrates of extinction by focusing on the simple model of pavlovian fear conditioning. We will see that the contextual modulation is mediated by the hippocampus, whereas the inhibitory process relies upon prefrontal cortical modulation of amygdala activity.

The hippocampus – contextual modulation

We have already seen in Chapter 4 that the hippocampus has been heavily implicated in spatial navigation. Part of this involves the formation of a spatial memory of the environmental context. Therefore, spatial and contextual processing are likely to overlap significantly. In order for a subject to display renewal of fear memory extinction, (s)he must have spatial representations of the extinction context and the test context in order to be able to distinguish between them. As such, the spatial processing that is characteristic of hippocampal function should contribute to the context-dependent renewal of extinction.

The evidence for a hippocampal role in renewal is somewhat mixed. Early studies failed to show that lesions to the hippocampus had a detrimental impact upon renewal. However, lesions to the hippocampus often do not have the effect expected, especially if the lesions are carried out before training; the mammalian brain appears to have a capacity to compensate for hippocampal damage, at least in the realm of contextual processing. This has led to the increased use of reversible lesion approaches being applied to investigate hippocampal function. Using the GABA receptor agonist muscimol functionally to inactivate the rat hippocampus, Corcoran and Maren (2001) showed that the hippocampus is necessary at the time of the post-extinction test in order for fear memory renewal to be observed. Importantly, the effect of hippocampal inactivation was to render the levels of conditioned freezing the same regardless of whether the test was conducted in the extinction context, or in an alternative context. Moreover, the levels of freezing were at the same low level as would be expected in control rats tested in the extinction context. Therefore, the hippocampus is not necessary for fear memory extinction *per se*; rather it is of critical importance in restricting the expression of the extinction memory to the extinction context alone.

The prefrontal cortex – source of the inhibition

One of the cardinal features of prefrontal cortical function is that of inhibition. Patients with lesions to the prefrontal cortex (PFC) exhibit impulsive behaviour characterised by poor inhibitory control. Therefore, it is reasonable to suggest that the PFC might be the source of the inhibition that is necessary for fear memory extinction. This is supported first by the observation that the ventromedial portion of the PFC (vmPFC) is active in functional brain imaging of human fear memory extinction. Importantly, the vmPFC is activated by the CS only when the post-extinction test is conducted in the extinction context (Kalisch et al., 2006). This would suggest that the vmPFC might be critical in the extinction-mediated inhibition of fear responses. Thus when vmPFC activity is high in the extinction context, fear memory expression is low. In contrast, when the memory renews in the conditioning context, vmPFC activity is low. Consistent with such a notion is a significant inverse correlation between vmPFC activity and fear memory expression (Milad, Wright et al., 2007).

Much of the research into the role of the PFC in extinction has been conducted in rodents. Therefore, it is first important to note that rodent brain imaging techniques equivalent to the human fMRI studies also implicate the vmPFC. In rats and mice we can use metabolic mapping techniques that, in a similar manner to fMRI, point to those brain areas that are consuming more energy at a particular time. With such an approach, it has been shown that the largest increase in metabolic activity following fear memory extinction occurred in the infralimbic (IL) region of the mouse vmPFC (Barrett et al., 2003). However, the nature of metabolic mapping means that the enhanced spatial resolution comes at the expense of temporal resolution. The IL activity is linked only to the post-extinction test in general, and cannot be attributed to IL responsiveness to the CS during the test, as has been established in human functional imaging. This shows the utility of multiple experimental approaches, and electrophysiological recording in rats can both show CS-related activity, and can demonstrate that the fMRI BOLD response and the metabolic activity are likely to be attributable to increased *neural activity* in the IL. Unlike during conditioning and extinction, the activity of IL neurons when extinction was expressed during the final test was significantly increased in response to the CS. Moreover, as was previously seen using fMRI, the greater the IL neuronal activity, the lower the level of fear memory expression.

So if IL activity inhibits fear memory expression, extinction should be impaired when the IL is not functional. This is exactly what has been shown in one study that lesioned the IL in rats (Quirk et al., 2000). However, these lesions were conducted before conditioning, and so even though there were no apparent effects of the lesion upon conditioning and the acquisition of extinction, we cannot rule out the possibility that the deficit in extinction expression was attributable to subtle changes in behaviour during conditioning and extinction training. The likelihood of such an account is perhaps increased by other studies that fail to show an effect of vmPFC lesions upon fear memory extinction. Attempts to clarify the situation using reversible brain inactivations have not proved hugely successful, with a similar level of confusion in the literature. Some studies show an increase in fear expression (and hence an impairment of extinction; e.g. Sierra-Mercado et al., 2011), but others either show no effect or even the opposite (lower levels of fear memory expression). Perhaps this reflects a complexity of the mechanisms of extinction that is not reflected by simply focusing on the IL. For example, returning to the metabolic mapping study, it was not only the IL that was activated, but also other cortical areas such as the dorsal, medial and lateral frontal cortex.

Even though the lesion and inactivation evidence is somewhat mixed, there are other methods of demonstrating a functional role for the IL in extinction. Principal among these would be to show that artificial stimulation of the IL, which would be expected to mimic the normally-induced IL activity present during the expression of extinction, reduces fear behaviour. Remarkably, when the IL was stimulated immediately after the CS was presented, conditioned freezing to the CS was greatly reduced (Milad et al., 2004). This behavioural effect was associated with a direct electrophysiological effect upon the amygdala, indicating that the amygdala, to which the IL strongly projects, is the target of the cortically-mediated inhibition during extinction.

The amygdala – target of fear inhibition

The inhibitory projection from the infralimbic cortex to the amygdala provides an obvious explanation for how extinction might suppress the fear responses that are controlled by the amygdala. It is interesting to note, though, that the amygdala is not a passive actor in this process. It would be tempting to think that the amygdala, in neurophysiological terms, remains unaffected by extinction, with the IL simply inhibiting the capacity of the amygdala to produce the fear response. However, there is a huge amount of evidence that there is synaptic plasticity taking place in the amygdala during extinction learning.

Why might amygdala plasticity be important for extinction? At a basic level, in order for the IL to inhibit the amygdala through extinction, stronger inhibitory connections would probably be required. These inhibitory connections are located in the amygdala, with the axons of IL neurons terminating upon the dendrites of amygdala neurons. Moreover, the synaptic plasticity required to strengthen the inhibitory connection will require molecular processes in both the presynaptic IL neuron *and* the postsynaptic amygdala neuron. Therefore, in a simplistic scheme, if the IL encodes the extinction memory, the expression of that memory needs plasticity in the amygdala in order for it to be able to inhibit the amygdala-based fear memory.

Now we have seen the contributions of the hippocampus, prefrontal cortex and amygdala to extinction, we can produce a description of what happens during conditioning, extinction and renewal of fear memories (Figure 4a.3). After conditioning, and before extinction, the conditioned stimulus activates the amygdala to produce the fear memory response. Extinction training recruits the IL, which then inhibits the amygdala to reduce the fear memory response when tested in the extinction context. However, when testing takes place in an alternative context (either back in the conditioning context, or in some new context), hippocampal processes modulate prefrontal processing, such that the inhibition of the amygdala is reduced and hence the fear memory response renews back to a high level. Now, the hippocampus might achieve this either by inhibiting IL when the CS is presented in the alternative context (as depicted in the figure), or by helping to activate the IL when the CS is presented in the extinction context. It is difficult to distinguish between these possibilities, but both come under the notion of hippocampal modulation of the inhibitory process. Regardless of the fine details, what should be clear is that extinction is a complex process, both psychologically and biologically.

Before extinction

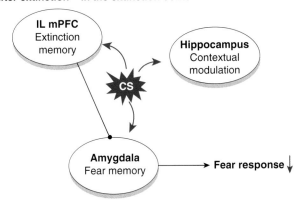

After extinction – in the extinction context

After extinction – in a different context

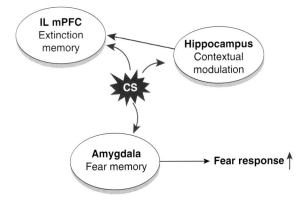

Figure 4a.3 Integration of infralimbic cortical, hippocampal and amygdala contributions to memory extinction. Initial conditioning results in an amygdala-based fear memory. Therefore, presentation of the CS results in activation of the amygdala and elicits the fear response. Extinction training forms an inhibitory extinction memory in the infralimbic (IL) region of the medial prefrontal cortex (mPFC). Therefore, CS presentation activates the amygdala, but also activates the IL, which in turn inhibits the amygdala. The overall result is an inhibition of the fear response. However, this is subject to contextual modulation. In the extinction context, the IL is allowed to inhibit the amygdala. In contrast, in any other context, the hippocampus exerts a modulatory effect upon the IL, releasing the amygdala from inhibition and thereby resulting in renewal (recovery) of the fear response

Implications

The abnormal strength and persistence of fear memories results in problems of phobias and post-traumatic stress disorder, and we know that extinction is often deficient in such patients (Milad et al., 2009). From our understanding of the neurobiology of fear memory extinction, it is apparent that such a deficit could stem from abnormalities in any of a number of critical components (hippocampus, prefrontal cortex and amygdala). Moreover, therapy could be targeted at different processes in order to enhance extinction and thereby reduce anxiety (Ressler et al., 2004).

DO NEW EXPERIENCES RESULT IN THE CREATION OF NEW MEMORIES OR THE MODIFICATION OF EXISTING ONES?

When considering the biological mechanisms of learning and memory, a great emphasis is placed upon understanding the stability and maintenance of memories. The concept of memory extinction as new inhibitory learning also assumes implicitly that the original memory remains stable and largely unchanged by extinction learning. So we seem to be working towards an understanding of a system that creates long-lasting, fixed memories, which can be inhibited if circumstances change. But the changes of circumstances for which extinction is useful are quite limited: simply a stimulus no longer being predictive of an outcome. How, then, can our memory systems cope with more complex cases of memory updating? This is not simply a difference between complex declarative memories, and simple non-declarative ones. Even pavlovian memories can change in nature. For example, a new stimulus may be added to an associative chain, meaning that we can predict the outcome more reliably or quickly. The question is how a rigid memory system can carry out subtle and complex changes in memory. There are two possibilities:

1. Pre-existing memories are modified to incorporate new information as appropriate in order to maintain their relevance and value.

2. Each new experience results in an independent memory; all relevant memories are retrieved and combined to control appropriate behaviour.

These possibilities are not necessarily mutually exclusive, and we will see examples where each appears to be true.

The case for memory modification – memory reconsolidation

Let's take a very simple example of a new experience that is similar to prior memories: the second of a series of days of learning. Each day's learning could be encoded separately, and then added together at test, or there could be a singular memory that is updated and strengthened. The difference can be conceptualised by looking at the learning curve (Figure 4a.4). Each increment could represent a different memory, or the modification of the single original memory. The problem here is how to distinguish the two.

For this example, our best guess is that the memory is truly modified, and this is achieved through a process of **memory reconsolidation**. We know this because, in contextual fear memories, we can distinguish between reconsolidation and initial learning, allowing us to dissociate the contribution of new learning from updating of a pre-existing memory.

When established and consolidated long-term memories are retrieved, it seems that they undergo some physiological and cellular process that is similar to initial cellular consolidation. That is, if the same kind of interventions that impair consolidation are applied to a recently-retrieved memory, that memory is often impaired. The most famous example is that of the protein synthesis inhibitor being infused into the amygdala of rats immediately after the retrieval of a pavlovian tone–footshock memory (Nader et al., 2000; Figure 4a.5). This impairment is critically dependent upon the recent retrieval of the memory; simply applying the intervention long after learning, as we have seen previously, has no effect. Given the biological similarity of the post-retrieval process to initial memory consolidation, it has come to be known as memory reconsolidation.

Ever since reconsolidation was discovered in the late 1960s, it has been suggested that this window of synaptic plasticity induced by the retrieval of a memory would be ideal to update the memory with new information. There have also been a number of findings that seem to fit with such an idea. For example, memories do not always undergo reconsolidation, but appear only to do so when there is some new information present at the time of retrieval (Lee, 2009; Morris et al., 2006). However, that reconsolidation actually serves to update memories could never be confirmed experimentally because by and large the cellular mechanisms that are necessary to reconsolidate a memory are the same as those required for initial consolidation.

Fortunately, for some reason, there is an exception in the hippocampus for contextual fear memories. Now, we don't know exactly why, but there are mechanisms (such as the synthesis of brain-derived neurotrophic factor; BDNF) that are only required for consolidation. On the other hand, a different protein (Zif268, which

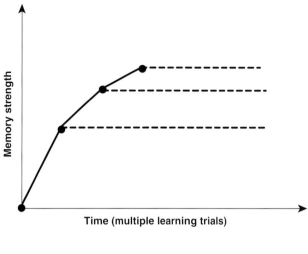

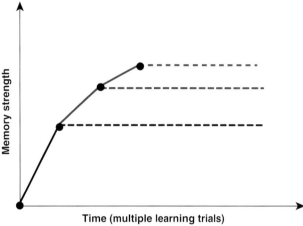

Figure 4a.4 Does additional learning strengthen the original memory or create an independent supplementary memory? Learning over multiple trials results in a traditional learning curve. The first trial forms a memory of a certain strength, and additional learning produces a larger behavioural memory. This might be due to the original memory being modified into a stronger state (top). The entire learning curve is the same colour, reflecting the single memory trace. Getting to the final memory strength is achieved by improving the strength of the original memory, just as more intense original learning might have resulted in a memory of that strength in the first place. Alternatively, each individual trial might produce an independent memory (bottom). Thus the stronger memory is made up of separable (different colour) memories that are summed together. Importantly, the magnitude of the additional learning with each trial may be regulated by the size of the prediction error, which would not differ between the cases, resulting in the same shape of the learning curve

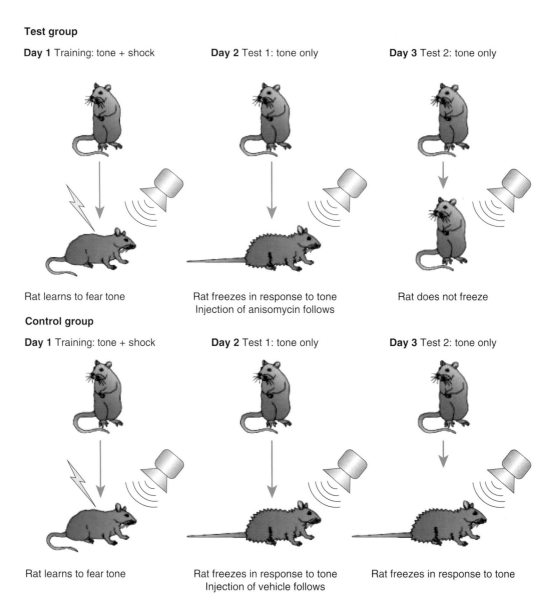

Test group

Day 1 Training: tone + shock

Rat learns to fear tone

Day 2 Test 1: tone only

Rat freezes in response to tone
Injection of anisomycin follows

Day 3 Test 2: tone only

Rat does not freeze

Control group

Day 1 Training: tone + shock

Rat learns to fear tone

Day 2 Test 1: tone only

Rat freezes in response to tone
Injection of vehicle follows

Day 3 Test 2: tone only

Rat freezes in response to tone

Figure 4a.5   Memory reconsolidation in rat pavlovian fear conditioning. Nadel et al. (2000) took rats and subjected them to simple pavlovian fear conditioning. Association between a tone and footshock results in a memory-dependent fearful freezing response to the tone. On the next day, in the test group (top), the rats had a protein synthesis inhibitor (anisomycin) infused directly into the amygdala immediately after memory retrieval. This resulted in a subsequent lack of freezing on day 3, reflecting a loss of the fear memory. Control rats (bottom), infused with vehicle instead of anisomycin on day 2, continued to freeze at high levels on day 3, showing the effect is caused by the protein synthesis inhibition. Finally, if the anisomycin is infused without retrieving the fear memory immediately beforehand, there is no effect, demonstrating that memory retrieval induces a state of protein synthesis-dependent plasticity. Figure taken from Nadel & Land (2000)

controls the synthesis of other proteins) is selectively required for reconsolidation. What this means is that it became possible selectively to impair consolidation or reconsolidation and assess its impact upon the strengthening of a contextual fear memory (Lee, 2008). Surprisingly, inhibition of the consolidation process had no detrimental effect of memory strengthening. Instead, when the synthesis of Zif268 was inhibited, the memory failed to be strengthened and was actually disrupted. The explanation is that additional learning reactivated the memory, and normally the memory would have reconsolidated in a strengthened form. However, interruption of the reconsolidation process by inhibiting Zif268 resulted in the reactivated memory failing to reconsolidate at all, leading to amnesia. Therefore, it is the reconsolidation process that allows new learning to strengthen an existing memory.

Remarkably, the role of reconsolidation in memory strengthening appears to extend to situations where there is no explicit additional behavioural learning. In a passive avoidance form of rat fear learning, Inda et al. (2011) have demonstrated that a brief retrieval of an existing memory strengthens that memory for future expression. This is not particularly surprising, as there is a long history of similar observations that retrieval aids future retrieval (that is why testing yourself during revision is such a good idea). However, what they also showed is that it is seemingly the reconsolidation process that mediates this retrieval-induced memory strengthening.

Now strengthening a memory remains a rather trivial form of memory updating. What about changing the content of a memory? Does this involve reconsolidation? Well, there is some evidence to suggest that it does. Lee (2010) used the same dissociable mechanisms of consolidation and reconsolidation to show that updating a memory for a spatial context to include emotional footshock information (i.e. going from a purely spatial memory to a contextual fear memory) uses reconsolidation processes, rather than new learning.

KEY STUDY

Hupbach et al. (2007). Reconsolidation of episodic memories: A subtle reminder triggers integration of new information. *Learning and Memory 14*(1–2), 47–53

Hupbach and colleagues tested human participants on an episodic memory task in order to study reconsolidation-based memory updating. The participants were brought into the testing laboratory on two or three occasions (Figure 4a.6). On the first of these, all participants were presented with a basket of 20 objects and asked to memorise them (List 1). Their memory was tested immediately in order to check that all participants achieved a similar level of initial learning. This was ensured by imposing a criterion of learning: any participant that failed to remember at least 17 of the 20 objects were given further time for learning.

The participants were then split into three groups. The reminder group were returned to the same testing room and met the same experimenter as on the first day. They were shown the basket (now empty) and asked 'Do you remember this basket and what we did with it?' This aimed to reactivate the memory for List 1 subtly without necessarily triggering full recollection of the objects. In the no-reminder group, the participants went to a different laboratory, and were met by a new experimenter. They were not shown the basket or reminded of the first day in any way. Both the reminder and no-reminder groups were then asked to learn a new list of objects that were presented simply on the table

(Continued)

(Continued)

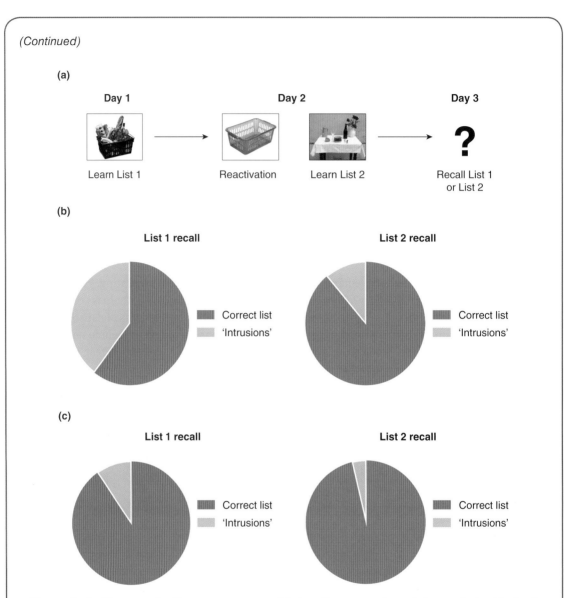

Figure 4a.6 Human episodic memory reconsolidation. Representation of the study by Hupbach et al. (2007). **(a)** experimental design showing the reactivation group. Participants learned a list of items in a basket on Day 1. On the experimental manipulation Day 2, the participants were presented with the empty basket to reactivate the Day 1 memory, and then were given a second list of items to learn. They were subsequently tested on their recall of List 1 or List 2 items on Day 3. **(b)** when recalling List 1, the reactivated participants mistakenly attributed many List 2 items as having been presented on Day 1 ('Intrusions'). This effect was directionally specific, as the same participants did not show as many intrusions of List 1 items when recalling List 2. **(c)** the non-reactivated control group was not shown the basket prior to learning List 2. This group showed low numbers of intrusions regardless of the list being recalled. The reactivation-dependence of the intrusion effect shows that it is related to memory reconsolidation

(List 2). Again, the same criterion of learning was applied to the second list. A final no-interference control group did not have any testing experience on Day 2. These groups were designed to target the reconsolidation process. The reminder should reactivate the memory, triggering reconsolidation, whereas the group in the no-reminder condition would just be subject to the direct effect of interference from List 2. To assess this impact of the second list, the no-interference group was used that was not exposed to the second list at all.

The key measure in the study was the recall exhibited at the final test on Day 3 (or Day 2 for the no-interference control). The participants were simply brought back into the lab (the same one as used on Day 1) and were met by the original experimenter. They were then simply asked to recall as many items as they could from the first list of objects that was presented in the basket. In order to maximise the reliability of the results, the participants were tested four times in succession, with a brief interlude between each recollection. The analysis consisted of the number of objects from Lists 1 and 2 that were recalled as being present on the first day. The rationale was that if reconsolidation mediates memory updating, the reminder group should be induced falsely to update their memory for List 1 with objects from List 2. This was exactly what was observed. While there was no difference between the groups in the recollection of List 1 objects, there were many more 'intrusions' of List 2 objects in the reminder group than the other groups; i.e. the reminder group mistakenly attributed a number of List 2 items as having been presented on Day 1. There was also no statistically-significant difference between the no-reminder group and the no-interference control, suggesting that the learning of List 2 by itself neither disrupts not updates the List 1 memory.

At face value, this set of results might be convincing both for human memory reconsolidation and the hypothesis that reconsolidation mediates memory updating. However, there is an interpretative problem. Participants in the no-reminder group learned the two lists in different contexts. Context is a very powerful cue for the retrieval of memories, and so it might be expected that this context differentiation helped the no-reminder group to distinguish between the two lists better than the reminder group, for which time was the only distinguishing factor. Therefore, the reminder group may have suffered from a 'source-monitoring' deficit, in which they could not effectively monitor the source of information, rather than there being any reconsolidation effect. Hupbach and colleagues readily accepted this potential explanation, and so carried out a further experiment, in which reminder and no-reminder groups were tested on their recall of List 2 objects. If the original results were due to source monitoring, the reminder group should have been equally impaired in the second experiment. However, there were very few intrusions from List 1 into recollection of List 2. This asymmetry of the impairment, therefore, provides stronger support for human memory reconsolidation and its link to memory updating.

Since Hupbach et al.'s original study, they have replicated the effect several times, further confirming that there is no source-monitoring deficit and that the context (i.e. experimental room) in which List 2 is learned is the critical trigger for reconsolidation (Hupbach et al., 2008). Similar effects have also been observed by other research groups (Forcato et al., 2010). However, a critical view of these studies may still be unconvinced of its link to reconsolidation. In the reminder group, the reminder process may establish a link between aspects of the memory for Day 1 and the experience on Day 2. Therefore, at test, recollection of the D1 experience could, by extension, lead to retrieval of Day 2 items. If we look at the actual level of recall, it was not particularly good. Even in the no-interference control, only 50% of objects from List 1 were, on average, accurately recalled. Perhaps in the reminder group, the participants were aware of the fact that they could remember only a fraction of the objects that were present, and so in an effort to recall more items, the memory for List 2 was activated. The asymmetry of the effect might be explained by suggestion that the reminder experience (and the fact that the participants were prevented from fully recalling the List 1 objects) would not be expected to result in the Day 2 experience being able to activate the memory for Day 1.

(Continued)

(Continued)

While the above is a speculative alternative explanation, we can argue that it cannot be ruled out. Moreover, it is not possible fully to conclude that the data from Hupbach et al. show definitively that reconsolidation mediates memory updating. Certainly, if we accept the reconsolidation interpretation, there is *correlative* evidence that reconsolidation occurs under conditions that seemingly update the episodic memory. But to go from that to concluding that reconsolidation is the mechanism by which the memory is updated is less clear. Perhaps this shows the respective value of different research approaches, with the aforementioned studies of contextual fear memory strengthening and updating providing more direct evidence for reconsolidation, albeit in arguably less convincing models of memory updating.

Implications

If very subtle reminders can trigger reconsolidation, leading to the opportunity for memory modification, this has implications for the reliability of memory. Hupbach et al. (2007) show that a simple procedure can induce participants falsely to remember the experience they had on the first day of testing. Perhaps, then, reconsolidation-mediated memory updating is one mechanism that underlies the false memory and misinformation effects that are widely studied in cognitive psychology and that may have important implications for eyewitness testimony (Loftus, 2005).

The case for new memories – second-order conditioning

Not all instances of memory updating need to involve reconsolidation. Rather they could engage new learning to link new information to existing memories. It is perhaps easiest to think of events associated with a particular place. Each new experience that we have in a given environment does not overwrite previous memories; nor do we end up with a single memory of all our experiences. Rather the common element of the location links together multiple memories, such that retrieval of one memory can easily trigger recollection of another. This is one conscious example where it appears obvious that it would be better simply to add a new memory that links to the existing one. But what about more simple memories?

We can make an associative analogy that involves the fear conditioning paradigm that we have seen repeatedly in this spotlight. For example, we might start with a tone predicting a footshock, but then a light might become associated with the tone. The tone is, therefore, the common element that is linked to both the light and the footshock. This also means that the light becomes predictive of both the tone and subsequently the footshock. Therefore, it is useful to learn the predictive value of the light in order to avoid the footshock. The question is whether the information concerning the light is integrated into a single memory containing the light, tone and footshock, or whether it is simply added on.

What we find is that in the case of *second-order conditioning*, the new information is added on as a separable memory. In second-order conditioning, there are two phases to the conditioning. The first-order conditioning is simple pavlovian conditioning between a stimulus (CS1) and an outcome (US). In the second phase, the second-order conditioning takes the form of associating a new stimulus (CS2) with the original CS1. This might result in one of two possibilities. First, the original CS1–US memory may be updated to incorporate CS2 (e.g. forming a CS2/CS1–US memory). Alternatively, CS2 might just be linked to the memory of CS1–US (creating something like CS2–[CS1–US]). Talking about it in these terms is pretty confusing, so it might be easier to think about an analogy involving toy train tracks and whether the addition of a new loop (the new memory) involves true modification of the original track/memory or simply addition of an extra link (Figure 4a.7).

These two possibilities have been disentangled again by using dissociable mechanisms of consolidation and reconsolidation to see which are required for the memory updating. However, it was not done in contextual fear conditioning, but rather in a model of fear avoidance learning. If rats experience an aversive outcome when they move out of a safe environment, they will subsequently show an avoidance response and will not move out again. Tronel et al. (2005) used a light CS1 to signal and predict the occurrence of the aversive outcome when the rats moved out of the safe chamber. They then added a second-order memory by presenting the light CS1 in a different context (CS2). The rats would then avoid leaving the CS2 context because of the second-order memory. The memory updating in this setting selectively required the new learning consolidation mechanism (gene expression in the hippocampus), as opposed to the reconsolidation process (gene expression in the amygdala). Therefore, when a complex memory system is updated to link new information to an existing retrieved memory, new learning can also be critically important.

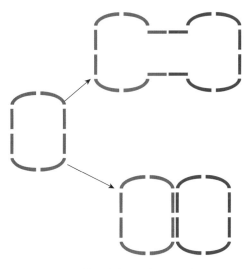

Figure 4a.7 New information can be integrated or appended. If we think of a memory as a network of neurons, a crude analogy would be a toy train track. The existing memory (left) needs to be updated with new information (the red pieces). This can either be done by creating a single new larger track (top), or appending the additional information to make two independent, but interacting tracks (bottom). The critical difference is that in the bottom case, the new information can be removed without impacting upon the integrity of the original memory. In the same way, a new predictive CS2 can either become fully integrated into a CS2/CS1 → US memory, or can be added in a more sequential fashion to make a CS2 → (CS1 → US) associative chain

Implications

Knowledge of how an individual memory relates to other memories will become incredibly important with the advent of memory-modifying cognitive treatments. If a problematic memory is a discrete entity, separate from previous similar memories, then erasing it may not have much of an adverse effect on other memories that we wish to retain. In contrast, if a problematic memory has arisen from the modification of previously-existing memories, its erasure may well result in the loss of adaptive information.

FURTHER READING

Lee, J. L. C. (2009). Reconsolidation: Maintaining memory relevance. *Trends in Neuroscience, 32*(8), 413–20.

> This work presents the opinion that the function of reconsolidation is to update memories. It provides more evidence in relation to the requirements for memories to be reactivated and compares other theories of memory reconsolidation.

Quirk, G. J., & Mueller, D. (2008). Neural mechanisms of extinction learning and retrieval. *Neuropsychopharmacology, 33*(1), 56–72.

> This provides a review of memory extinction mechanisms and focuses on the different temporal phases of extinction learning, consolidation and retrieval. It looks mostly at fear memories, but also has some coverage of appetitive reward-related memories.

Sacktor, T. C. (2011). How does PKMzeta maintain long-term memory? *Nature Reviews Neuroscience, 12*(1), 9–15.

> This provides a review of PKMζ and gives more detail on the activity-dependence of PKMζ activation. It also raises future avenues of research.

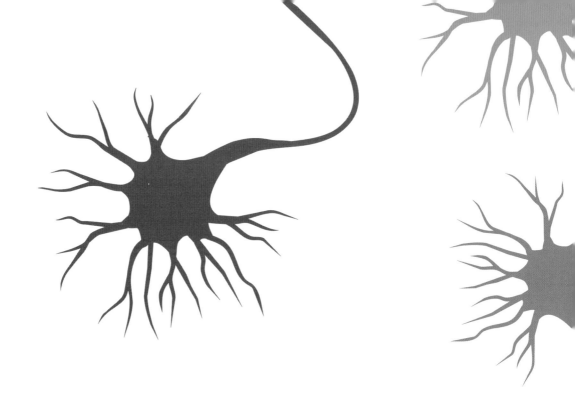

CHAPTER 5

SENSORY SYSTEMS

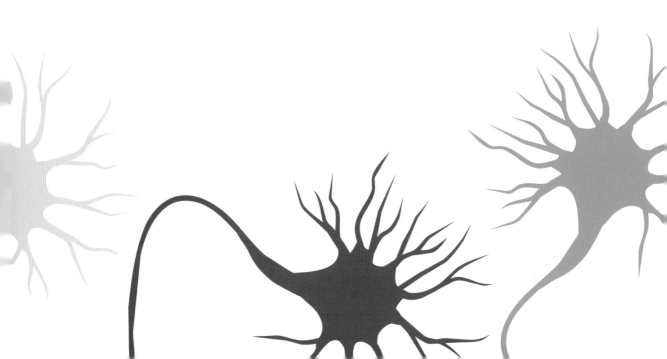

CHAPTER BREAKDOWN

- The difference between sensation and perception.
- Processing of light from the retina through to the visual cortex.
- How our ears and brains process and analyse sound waves.
- Balance and the vestibular system.
- Somatosensation: touch, pain and proprioception.
- Taste, smell and flavour.

ROADMAP

Each of our senses is equipped with specialised receptor cells that respond to a particular physical aspect of the environment. For example, in vision, **photoreceptors** respond to light; in hearing, balance, touch and proprioception, mechanoreceptors respond to physical distortion of the receptor cell; and in taste and smell, chemoreceptors respond in the presence of particular molecules.

Within each sensory modality, different receptors are selective for, or 'tuned' to, a different property of the stimulus. For example, in vision, different cone photoreceptors respond best to different wavelengths of light; in hearing, different hair cells respond best to different sound frequencies. In some cases, as for the cones in vision, this selectivity is a property of the receptor itself. In others, as for the hair cells in hearing, it arises from the properties of the sense organ itself. In some cases, the range is fairly narrow – in vision, for example, the wavelength of visible light varies only from about 400 to 700nm, so that each type of cone responds at least a little over almost the whole range. In others, the range is much broader – sound wavelengths vary from about 2cm right up to almost 7m, for example, and individual auditory hair cells respond to only a tiny fraction of the range.

But, whatever the details, the result is that each different pattern of physical stimulation produces a different pattern of response across the relevant receptors. And, in each sensory modality, this pattern of response is conveyed – usually via a synapse in the thalamus of the forebrain, and sometimes after considerable preliminary neural processing – to the cerebral cortex. Each sensory modality has its own specialised region of cortex. For example, the visual cortex is located at the back of the brain in the occipital lobe, whereas the auditory cortex is located at the side of the brain, in the temporal lobe. The initial stages of cortical processing seem to be concerned with disambiguating and further refining the pattern of sensory response provided by the recptors; different areas of the visual cortex are devoted to recovering information about the stimulus's wavelength and movement, for example. And here, presumably, the complex process of making sense of the physical stimulus really begins.

We have a good understanding of how the receptors work in each of the different senses. But our understanding of neural processing within the sensory cortices, and of how that processing ultimately results in our rich perceptual experience, is still far from complete. Vision is the most studied of our senses and, even though it is by far the most complex, is currently the best understood. As we shall see, our grasp of the other senses remains comparatively tenuous. But, before considering each of our different senses in more detail, we must put the fundamental problem faced by any sensory system into a more general context.

WHAT DO SENSORY SYSTEMS DO?

Our sensory systems provide our only contact with the world, so they have to provide us with descriptions that can reliably guide our behaviour. We need to know not only what and where things are but also what they are likely to do, how they might be useful, or whether they might be dangerous. Despite our conscious impression that our perception of the world is simple and direct, this turns out to be a rather difficult task.

Imagine the surface of a small lake, thrown into a complicated pattern of moving ripples by the activities of toy boats, ducks, rain and wind. Suppose that you can't see or hear the lake but have to make sense of what's going on just by dipping your index fingers into the water so that you can feel these ripples drifting by. Can you locate and recognise the objects on the lake using only this information? Although this might seem difficult, perhaps impossible, it's actually a simplification of what's involved in hearing. The auditory world is like a three-dimensional lake, filled with air rather than water. Moving things produce expanding, spherical ripples of air pressure and our ear drums vibrate as they drift past each ear. We have no direct contact with the objects in our auditory world but can only detect their effects upon the air around us. Yet we locate and identify sound sources without apparent effort. Hearing seems simple, not because it's easy, but because we're very, very good at it.

Describing the sensory world is difficult because the stimuli available to our senses are not the objects themselves but the effects they have upon some physical medium. This is true of all senses. Even when we touch something, for example, we sense the deformation of our skin rather than the object itself. It is also true of vision; even though images *seem* to provide us with direct contact with the world, they are just as indirect as the ripples on our lake. To convince yourself of this, try drawing a cube and then writing down a simple definition of a cube. The chances are that your definition contains words like 'square' and 'right angle' and that your sketch contains neither of these things. How can an image provide direct contact with the world if it doesn't preserve the defining features of the thing it represents?

Can this indirect information provided by our sensory systems really account for our rich conscious experience of the world? Ultimately, the answer must be no. It's certainly true that, though the representations provided by our sense organs are necessarily indirect, they do contain a wealth of information about the world – perhaps enough completely to account for some of our behaviour. But it's also clear that we must bring a great deal of previous knowledge to sophisticated tasks like visual recognition – we *know* that a cube has six sides, for example, even though we can see no more than three of them at the same time. Broadly speaking, we can think of sensation as the process of registering and representing physical effects upon our sense organs, and perception as the process of figuring out what caused them. This chapter deals primarily with the first of these aspects, which is itself an intriguing topic. But we should always bear in mind that it is only part of the story.

THE VISUAL SYSTEM

Electromagnetic radiation, varying over a very broad range of wavelengths, fills the universe. We detect only a tiny fraction of the available range, between about 400 and 700nm, as visible light. Ordinary sunlight contains all wavelengths in this visible range in roughly equal proportions, and is seen as white, uncoloured light. However, when a single wavelength is presented by itself, it evokes a strong sensation of colour; long wavelengths are seen as red and, as wavelength progressively shortens, we see orange, yellow, green, blue, indigo and, finally, violet.

Most objects don't emit light. Instead, a few light sources, such as the sun, bathe the world in light, and visible objects reflect some of it into our eyes. Different surfaces reflect different amounts of light and this surface reflectance, or **albedo**, determines how light a surface appears; reflective surfaces appear light, whilst unreflective surfaces appear dark.

Surfaces with the same overall reflectance may not reflect all wavelengths equally well. When white light strikes a surface, for example, the long and medium wavelengths may be absorbed; the reflected light would then contain mostly short wavelengths and the surface would appear blue. A second surface with the same overall reflectance might relect mainly long wavelengths, and would consequently be seen as red. Ironically, given its environmental associations, green is the colour that nature 'rejects' – a leaf absorbs and uses the high and low frequencies present in sunlight but simply reflects the medium frequencies that we perceive as green.

The eye captures some of the light reflected from surfaces and forms it into an image – an orderly map of the light reaching the eye from each visible direction. Each point in the map tells us about the light coming from one specific direction and, if there is an object in that direction, potentially about how reflective it is overall and whether it reflects some wavelengths more than others.

The retina

The first step in seeing is to measure the amount of light at each point in the image. This process of transduction takes place in the photoreceptors – rods and cones – which, as Figure 5.1 shows, are rather inconveniently located *behind* the network of interneurons and blood vessels making up the rest of the retina. Rods are much more sensitive than cones, dominate in the retinal periphery, and are most responsive in twilight conditions. There are three types of cone, responsive in daylight conditions and underpinning colour vision. Each type of cone contains a slightly different variant of the visual pigment **rhodopsin** that is most sensitive to a different frequency range, so that each wavelength produces a unique pattern of response across the three cone types. Light bleaches the pigment within the receptors, causing a change in its molecular shape and triggering a rapid series of chemical reactions culminating in a reduction in the flow of sodium and calcium ions into the photoreceptor. Unusually, the rod and cone receptor potential is a *hyper*polarization, causing a graded reduction in the steady release of the transmitter glutamate.

Each receptor thus produces a graded receptor potential, a tiny voltage that depends upon the intensity and wavelength of the light striking it. Since receptors are very small and densely packed, the overall result, across all the receptors, is a very fine-grained 'neural image'. As a comparison, a computer monitor typically presents an image using about one million separate points of light, or 'pixels'; the eye is very much smaller but its neural image contains about 100 times as many points.

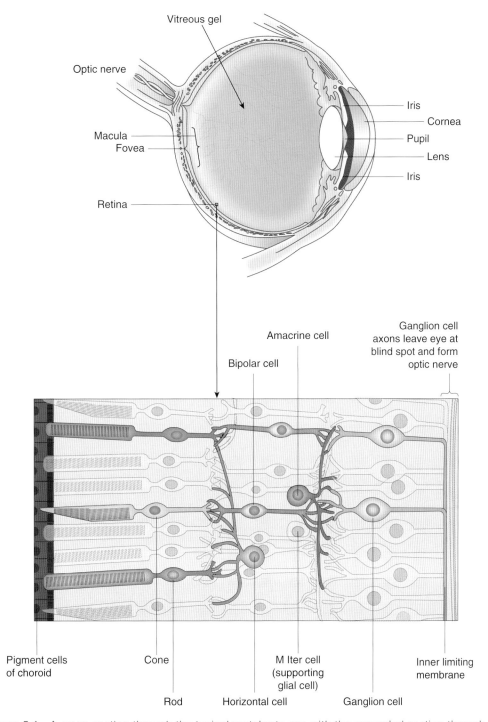

Figure 5.1   A cross-section through the typical vertebrate eye with the expanded section through the retina showing receptors, interneurons and retinal ganglion cells. Note that light has to pass through the layers of ganglion cells and interneurons before it reaches the rods and cones, which are the photoreceptors

Source: National Eye Institute, National Institutes of Health, www.nei.nih.gov/health/eyediagram/index.asp

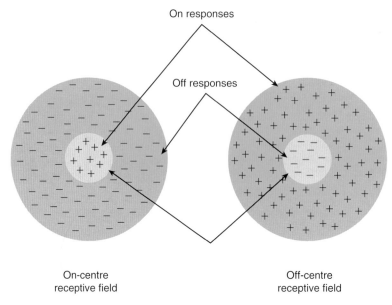

Figure 5.2 Retinal ganglion cell receptive fields showing the typical centre-surround arrangement. The + and − symbols represent each sub-region's reponse to light. In a + 'on' sub-region, light increases the gangion cell's response whilst darkness decreases it. In a − 'off' region, the reverse is true. There are roughly equal numbers of on-centre and off-centre cells

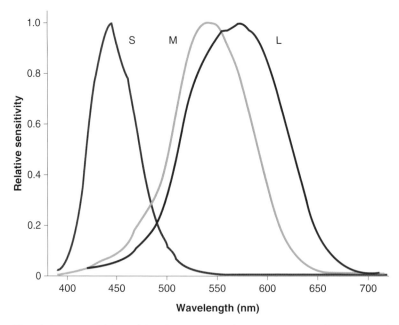

Figure 5.3 Plot of the sensitivities of the three types of retinal cone to different wavelengths of light. Note that each of the three types responds over a broad range of wavelengths. Conventionally the sensitivities are drawn with all three types having the same peak sensitivity but, in reality, the S cone is much less sensitive than the other two

A fine-grained neural image is a good place to start, but it contains a great deal of data, much of which isn't needed for the tasks of seeing. The next step is therefore to simplify it, preserving only the most important aspects of the image. These are the places where the light *changes* abruptly from one position to the next, which tend to signal the boundaries of objects or of surface markings. The network of retinal interneurons (horizontal, bipolar and amacrine cells) carries out this task, detecting changes by comparing the response at each point with the responses in its immediate neighbourhood through a process called lateral inhibition. The details of this process are explained in Spotlight 5a.

As explained in Spotlight 5a, retinal interneurons transmit the result of their processing to retinal ganglion cells and, as a result, each **retinal ganglion cell** responds to light in a small region of the retina, called the cell's **receptive field**. Ganglion cell receptive fields are typically circular and consist of two distinct sub-regions – one exciting the cell, the other inhibiting it, as shown in Figure 5.2. This 'centre-surround' arrangement ensures that retinal ganglion cells do not respond to the uniform regions that make up much of the image, so that the neural image provided by the photoreceptors is reduced to a kind of 'neural line-drawing' at the retinal ganglion cells, which carry the output from the retina.

The idea of a single neural line-drawing is an over-simplification because the retina actually produces several different line-drawings in parallel. We mentioned above that differently coloured surfaces reflect different patterns of wavelengths and that each pattern evokes a characteristically different pattern of response across three types of cone. As shown in Figure 5.3, each type responds over a wide range but is most sensitive either to long (L), medium (M), or

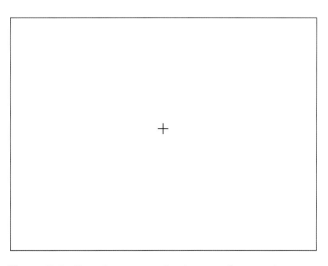

Figure 5.4 Complementary after images. Gaze at the fixation cross between the squares at the top of the figure for about 30 seconds. Then transfer your gaze to the fixation cross at the bottom of the figure. After a few seconds you should see ghostly coloured squares. Notice that the colours are the 'complements' of the squares at the top of the figure; the red square produces a green ghost, the green square produces a red ghost, the blue square produces a yellow ghost, and the yellow square produces a blue ghost

short (S) wavelengths. The retina simplifies this complex pattern by combining the cone outputs in varous ways. Some retinal ganglion cells, called M or parasol cells, receive input from all three cone types across the whole receptive field, so producing a conventional, 'black and white' line drawing. A second type, called P or midget cells, receives input only from L-cones in one sub-region (centre or surround) and M-cones in the other, so producing a sort of 'red and green' line-drawing. A third major type, called S cells, produces a 'blue and yellow' line-drawing by combining S-cones in one sub-region with a mixture of L- and M-cones in the other. In effect, our rich, colourful visual experience is based on the responses of relatively few retinal ganglion cells, capable of detecting changes and telling us that the light on one side of the change is brighter or darker, redder or greener, and bluer or yellower than the light on the other.

The process of comparing the responses of different cone types is called **opponency**. For example, a red-green opponent mechanism might receive excitation from L-cones and inhibition from M-cones. So a positive response would indicate that the L-cones are responding more than the M-cones (perceived as red), while a negative response would indicate a stronger M-cone response (perceived as green). You can demonstrate opponency to yourself using the complementary after images illustrated in Figure 5.4.

Normally, when we look at a white figure, our L- and M-cones are equally excited and the red-green opponent mechanism gives a neutral response, which we interpret as neither red nor green. When we stare at a red square, the L-cones will be more active than the M-cones and, assuming that the L-cone has an excitatory connection, the red-green opponent mechanism will respond positively, which we interpret as red. When we then transfer our gaze back to a white image, the L-cones will be fatigued for a few seconds and the normal L-M balance will be upset. Consequently, the M-cones will respond more than the L-cones and the red-green opponent mechanism will respond negatively, which we interpret as green.

INSIGHT: DEFECTIVE COLOUR VISION

There are three main types of defective colour vision, each resulting from a problem with one of the three types of cone. So-called colour blindness – really an inability to discriminate between certain wavelengths rather than blindess – is rare, but occurs if one of the cone types is missing. Colour anomaly is more common and occurs when all three types of cone are present but the pigment in one of them is altered. In protanomaly ('first' type), the peak sensitivity of the pigment in the L-cones is shifted toward medium wavelengths, so that reds become difficult to distinguish from greens. Deuteranomaly ('second' type) is the most common problem, occuring in about 5% of males, and has a similar perceptual effect, though here the peak sensitivity of the M-cones is shifted towards longer wavelengths. In the very rare tritanomaly ('third' type), blues are difficult to distinguish from yellows because the peak sensitivity of the S-cone pigment is shifted towards medium wavelengths. Genes coding for the L- and M-cone pigments are located on the X-chromosome, so both protanomaly and deuteranomaly are more common in males because they have only a single X-chromosome whereas females have two.

Spatial and temporal changes

As we have seen, the retina focuses upon spatial changes in the image by comparing responses across positions through lateral inhibition, and across cone types through opponency. It also focuses on the other important type of change – change over time – through delayed inhibition. The retinal ganglion cells that detect spatial changes are midget (or P) cells, and their responses are sustained throughout the stimulus. Parasol (or M) cells have a much more transient response – their firing rate changes only briefly at the onset and offset of the stimulus. The interneurons driving these cells seem to inhibit themselves after a short delay; in effect, they detect temporal change by comparing the current response with the response a moment ago, responding only if the two are different. Signalling these temporal 'events' seems crucial in drawing our attention to changes in the image, so that we do not notice quite profound changes in the image if they occur slowly or if they occur simultaneously with other events – a phenomenon called change blindness.

THE PATHWAY TO THE VISUAL CORTEX

The axons of all the retinal ganglion cells converge and leave the eye together as the optic nerve. There can be no photoreceptors at the point where the fibres leave so, although we are not usually aware of it, each eye has a 'blind spot' where there is no response to light.

The optic nerve projects to the optic chiasma, where half the fibres from each retina cross over in an arrangement that ensures that the two images of an object – one in each eye – are processed in the same place; objects to our left project to the right hemisphere, and *vice versa* (Figure 5.5). Most fibres synapse for the first time at the lateral geniculate nucleus (LGN) in the thalamus and project from there to the visual cortex via the optic radiation. There are smaller projections, for example, to the superior colliculus (concerned primarily with eye movements) and the suprachiasmatic nucleus (concerned with circadian rhythms).

LGN cells typically have circular receptive fields like those of retinal ganglion cells. The LGN has six layers, each receiving input from only one eye and each retinotopically mapped – adjacent regions of the retina project to adjacent regions in each layer so that the overall layout of the image is preserved. The two innermost layers form the magnocellular layers (containing large cells), whereas the other four layers form the parvocellular layers (containing small cells). This anatomical difference seems to reflect different functions; the magnocellular layers receive input from retinal parasol cells and are concerned with signalling movement, whereas the parvocellular layers receive input from retinal midget cells and are concerned with signalling colour and fine detail. Interspersed between the main layers are layers of konio cells, which are also concerned with signalling colour information; konio cells make comparisons between S- and M- or L-cones and are thus 'blue-yellow' opponent cells, whereas parvo cells make comparisons between L- and M-cones and are thus 'red-green' opponent cells.

The separation into parvo- and magnocellular layers is thought to form the early stages of two distinct processing 'streams', one (parvocellular) concerned with *what* things are, the other (magnocellular) with *where* things are and, perhaps, *how* to deal with them. The LGN also receives copious input from the visual cortex, providing ample opportunity for later ('top-down') processing to influence this earlier ('bottom-up') stage.

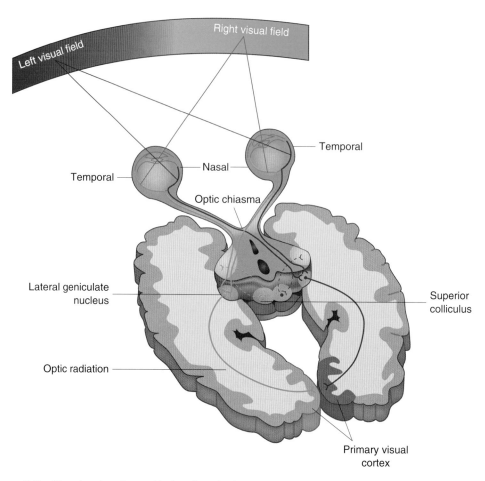

Figure 5.5   The visual pathway. Notice that the image of an object in the left visual field (represented in red) falls on the temporal half of the retina in the right eye and the nasal half of the retina in the left eye. Fibres from the temporal half of each retina do not cross over at the optic chiasma whereas fibres from the nasal half do. This arrangement ensures that the two images of the object are processed together in the visual cortex; the two images of the object in the left half of the visual field are both processed in the right visual cortex

THE VISUAL CORTEX

From the LGN, the geniculostriate pathway projects via the optic radiation to the primary visual cortex (also called the striate cortex, Area 17 or, in primates, V1), as shown in Figure 5.5. V1 is retinotopically mapped, though the map is distorted because the fovea projects to a dispro-portionately large region of the cortex. At each point in the map, many thousands of cells have receptive fields at roughly the same retinal position, providing the neural machinery needed to analyse one small region of the image.

Figure 5.6 shows typical receptive fields of one type of cortical cell, called a simple cell. Simple cells receive input from several retinal ganglion cells and, like them, have receptive fields divided into distinct, antagonistic sub-regions. Most strikingly, the receptive fields are elong-ated, so that each cell responds best to one particular orientation. Moreover, cells are organised

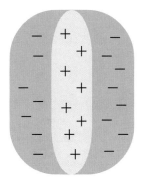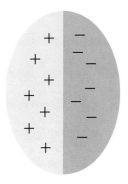

Figure 5.6 The receptive fields typical of cortical simple cells. On and off sub-regions are represented by + and − symbols and have the same meaning as in Figure 5.2. A cell with an on-centre receptive field like that on the left would respond well to a vertically oriented bar of light falling within the central sub-region. A cell with a receptive field like that on the right would respond well to a suitably positioned light-dark edge. As in the retina, there are equal numbers of on- and off-centre cells, and also of light-dark and dark-light cells

anatomically into columns projecting down through the six layers of the cortex. All the cells in a column have receptive fields with roughly the same orientation, and preferred orientation changes systematically from column to column across the cortical surface so that each patch of cortex contains cells covering the full range of orientations. The pattern of response across this set of orientation-selective cells is thought to encode the orientation of any spatial change falling within the corresponding small region of the retina.

Other aspects of the image are encoded by different populations of cells. For example, some cells respond best to rapid temporal changes and are selective for the direction of any image motion. Others are particularly selective for wavelength. V1 is also the first stage at which the images from the two eyes are combined; some cells are binocularly driven, responding to light in roughly the correponding position in each eye. These cells are thought to provide the neural basis for binocular stereopsis (literally, solid vision), one of the most important depth cues.

INSIGHT: BINOCULAR STEREOPSIS

The images in our two eyes are slightly different because they are taken from slightly different viewpoints. The differences, called binocular disparities, depend upon the different distances of objects in the world. Figure 5.7 shows this relationship. Objects at different distances along a line of sight from one of the eyes have images at the same position in that eye, but at systematic-ally different positions in the other. By comparing the relative positions of the two images using binocularly-driven cells, we can measure disparity and thus recover the relative distance of the object. Binocular stereopsis is used in 3D films and television to produce a compelling impression of depth. This is why special glasses are needed so that the slightly different images can be sep-arately presented to each eye.

(Continued)

(Continued)

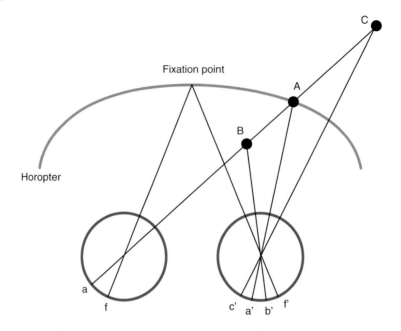

Figure 5.7 Binocular disparity. When we look at a fixation point with both eyes, all the objects that appear to be in the same direction from both eyes fall on an imaginary line called the horopter, represented by the solid curve. Images of objects on the horopter are said to fall on 'corresponding points' on the two retinae; for example f and f', and a and a'. When images fall on corresponding points, they have zero disparity. When an object moves off the horopter along a line of sight from one of the eyes, here the left eye, its image does not move in that eye. But, as the figure shows, the image does move in the other eye and therefore no longer falls on the corresponding point (a'). The distance between the image and the corresponding point is called **binocular disparity** (c'-a', and b'-a'). As can be seen from the figure, the direction and size of the disparity tells you the distance of the object relative to the horopter

V1 seems beautifully equipped to provide a rich description of the image, with different aspects being processed by separate populations of appropriately selective cells. This division of labour is further developed in the many different areas of the cortex to which V1 projects. For example, the 'what' stream originating in the parvocellular layers of the LGN projects ventrally to the temporal and inferotemporal cortex, whereas the magnocellular 'where' stream projects dorsally to the parietal lobes. And within these streams there is further specialisation into separate 'functional modules' processing specific aspects of the image. For example, motion information projects dorsally to V5. We are beginning to understand the neural processes underpinning the various functional modules, but several important and interrelated questions remain.

How do we put together the fragments?

The initial cortical description is very localised; the small receptive fields of neurons in V1 mean that they 'see' only fragments of the image, rather like the individual pieces of a jigsaw. How are the fragments put together to capture larger-scale aspects of the image like textures, or to separate out the parts of an object from its background? We know, from Gestalt psychologists, many of the rules by which local elements can be grouped together into coherent clusters – for example, we spontaneously group together elements that are close to each other, or that are the same colour, or that are moving in the same direction. We also know from cognitive psychologists working on visual attention that some features stand out from their background whereas others do not – for example, we can easily detect a horizontal line amongst a cluster of vertical lines, but not an inverted T amongst a cluster of upright Ts. And we know from neurophysiologists that receptive field sizes generally become larger as we ascend the visual pathway – for example, in the later stages of motion processing, individual cells respond to coherent motion covering as much as half the visual field. When all these diffferent sources of information are put together and tested in computer models, we can propose some general ideas about how cells looking at different regions of the image might influence each other – for example a cell responding to a particular property (e.g. vertical) might cooperate with (i.e. excite) cells sharing the same property at neighbouring positions but compete with (i.e. inhibit) cells with different properties (e.g oblique, horizontal) at the same position. So, ironically, we have fragmentary glimpses of different pieces of the visual grouping problem, but have not yet solved the complete jigsaw.

How do we put together information about different aspects of the stimulus?

The initial stages of visual processing are modular, with different cortical regions focusing on different aspects of the image. But often several aspects will provide information about the same thing; the boundary between an object and its background, for example, will probably produce a whole range of different image cues including abrupt changes in brightness, colour, retinal disparity, and perhaps motion. How does the visual system recombine all this different information so that we see a single feature? Again, we don't know the complete answer but we do have some important insights. Neural processes are inherently 'noisy' so that different modules are likely to produce slightly different estimates of, say, a feature's position. We can study this using features defined by multiple cues. We can independently vary the position, say, of each cue, and also its reliability – for example, by making each cue more or less blurred. When several cues are slightly misaligned, we still see a single feature, and we can indicate its perceived position, for example by adjusting a simple visual marker. Under these circumstances, it seems that we don't simply average together the various estimates of position but, much more sensibly, we take into account how reliable each estimate is – biasing the final estimate towards the more reliable cues. Large-screen televisions provide a familar cross-modality example of this phenomenon. Vision is much more reliable than hearing at providing information about the direction of a stimulus and we typically hear the voices of actors correctly as arising from their lips, even though the sounds often come from speakers located off the screen.

How do we interpret the sensory information?

The processes we've described provide a rich description of the image, rather than of the object that produced it; they describe only the ripples on our imaginary lake. A feature of the image, such as an abrupt change in brightness, might result, among other things, from a change in surface markings, or a change in depth, or merely a shadow. So how is the feature to be interpreted? Is it purely a bottom-up process; for example, are there simple rules that allow us to interpret changes appropriately – a shadow is a change in brightness without a change in colour or depth, for example? Can such bottom-up rules go beyond the merely physical (it's a surface marking) to provide more meaningful interpretations (it's part of an eye)? These intriguing and complex questions remain very active topics of research and debate.

KEY POINTS

- Photoreceptors (rods and cones) convert the retinal image into a neural image.
- Retinal interneurons (horizontal, bipolar and amacrine cells) compare responses at different positions and times to detect changes in the image and so produce a neural 'line-drawing'.
- Retinal interneurons compare reponses in three different types of cone to provide the basis of colour perception.
- Retinal ganglion cells transmit information via the LGN to the primary visual cortex.
- Cortical cells are selective for different aspects of the stimulus and separately encode the orientation, wavelength, movement, and relative distance of simple visual features such as lines and edges.

THE AUDITORY SYSTEM

Sounds are caused by movements in the external world creating waves of pressure variation in the air that are picked up by the tympanic membrane, or ear drum, in each of our ears. Figure 5.8 shows a typical auditory stimulus. Unlike visual images, which have obviously important features like abrupt changes in brightness, it's harder to identify obvious features in an auditory waveform. However, like vision, hearing starts by measuring basic properties of the stimulus and, to understand how the initial description works, we must first introduce an alternative way to think about waveforms.

Sounds as frequencies

Periodic, or repetitive, sounds consist of a series of harmonics. Harmonics are just a simple type of waveform, sometimes called a pure tone or sine wave, that can vary in frequency and amplitude but that always has the same 'sinusoidal' shape, shown in Figure 5.8. The first harmonic, or fundamental frequency, of a periodic waveform is a pure tone with the same frequency as the original waveform. The other harmonics have whole-number multiples of this fundamental frequency. So, if a waveform repeats 100 times per second, its first three harmonics will be at 100, 200, and 300 cycles per second, or **Hertz** (Hz).

As shown in Figure 5.8, an alternative way to describe a periodic waveform is to plot the amplitude of each of its harmonics in what is called a **frequency spectrum**. Each different waveform contains a different pattern of harmonics and so has a different frequency spectrum. Changes in the repetition rate of a periodic stimulus change the fundamental frequency of its spectrum and are heard as changes in pitch. Changes to the shape of the waveform change the amplitudes of its harmonics and are perceived as changes in sound quality, or timbre.

Less intuitively, *any* waveform – even non-repeating, or aperiodic, stimuli – can be decribed in this way. The only difference is that aperiodic waveforms potentially contain *all* frequencies rather than a series of discrete harmonics. The important point is that we can describe *any*

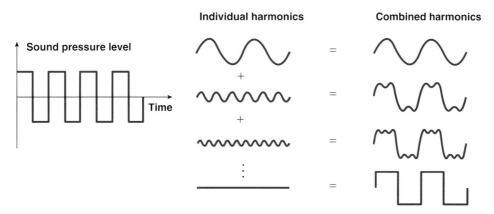

Figure 5.8   An auditory waveform and the harmonics making up its frequency spectrum. The left side of the figure shows a square-wave as a periodic (i.e. repeating) variation in sound pressure level over time. The middle section shows some of the harmonics which make up the square wave. Each harmonic is a pure tone (i.e. a sinewave) of a specific frequency and amplitude. The right side shows how, as each higher harmonic is added, the resulting waveform better resembles the squarewave. (Theoretically, we would have to add together an infinite number of harmonics to reproduce the perfect squarewave)

auditory stimulus either as a sound pressure waveform varying over time or as a set of sine waves of particular frequency and amplitude.

How the ear describes sounds

Periodic stimuli cause the ear drum to vibrate at the same frequency as the stimulus and these vibrations are transmitted by tiny bones, or ossicles, in the middle ear to the oval window of the **cochlea** (Figure 5.9). Each pulse of the oval window causes a pulse to travel along the **basilar membrane**. Each point on the basilar membrane moves up and down as the pulse travels past it and this mechanically distorts the cilia of the inner hair cells that are arrayed along the membrane and act as the auditory receptors. The distortion causes graded receptor potentials in the inner hair cells which in turn cause action potentials in the fibres of the auditory nerve innervating the basilar membrane. The stiffness of the basilar membrane varies along its length so that high frequency sounds produce pulses that start large and become gradually smaller as they travel along, whereas low frequencies produce pulses that start small and become gradually larger. Each frequency therefore causes a peak at a different position on the membrane and, consequently, produces action potentials in different fibres of the auditory nerve. Outer hair cells enhance this effect by actively contracting to fine tune the stiffness of the basilar membrane, and recordings from the auditory nerve show that each individual fibre responds to only a very narrow range of stimulus frequencies.

For periodic sounds, the distortion of the hair cells also occurs periodically as successive cycles travel down the basilar membrane. The activity in the auditory nerve fibres is therefore also periodic, with a burst of action potentials corresponding to each cycle of the stimulus. This is termed phase locking; the action potentials in a fibre occur at the same position, or phase, of each stimulus cycle.

The early stages of the auditory system thus represent stimulus frequency in two different ways. First, each frequency produces activity in different nerve fibres, so activity in a given nerve

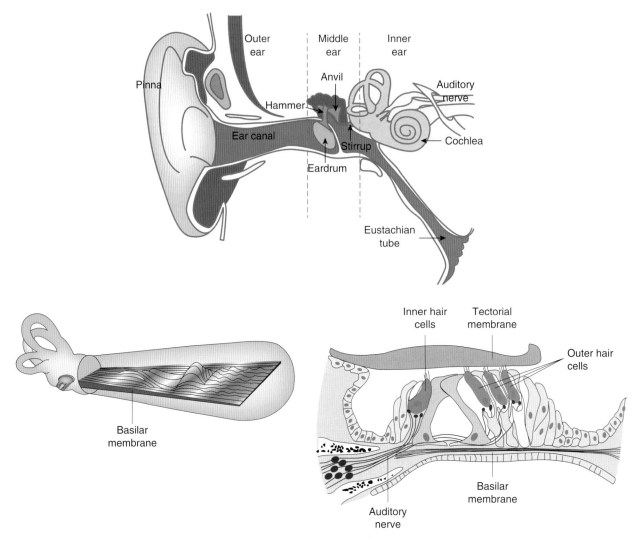

Figure 5.9   Diagram of the auditory system. The main organ is the cochlea, which forms part of the inner ear. The bottom left inset is the cochlea 'unrolled' to show the the movement of the basilar membrane in response to sound. The bottom right inset is a cross-section through one loop of the cochlea to show how auditory receptors (hair cells) are located on the basilar membrane

Source: Barnes (2013)

fibre should signal a specific stimulus frequency. This is called place coding. Second, bursts of action potentials are synchonised with the stimulus so that, irrespective of the identity of the nerve fibre, the interval between bursts should signal the duration of each cycle. This is called time coding.

The two codes are, to some extent, complementary. Place coding is poor at signalling low frequencies because the position of the peak displacement of the basilar membrane doesn't change much at these frequencies. Time coding is limited at high frequencies because an individual nerve can't respond more than 1,000 times per second and even the pattern of activity across a group of neighbouring nerve fibres can't keep track of the individual cycles above a few thousand Hz.

Nonetheless, the basilar membrane will, within these limitations, break down any waveform into its harmonic components – each frequency causing a peak of displacement at a different position. Moreover, at each peak, the basilar membrane moves up and down at the frequency of the corresponding component, so that the timing of the resulting action potentials also encodes its frequency. The resulting pattern of response in the auditory nerve is very like a spectrum. The identity of each harmonic is given by the identity of the responding fibre and/or by the temporal pattern of its response, whilst the amplitude of each component is given by the total amount of neural activity associated with that harmonic. This description, as explained above, captures not only the frequency of the stimulus but also the timbre of complex sounds.

Locating sounds

In vision, the image provides a directional map of the external world and, by comparing the two images for example, it is possible to estimate relative distances. In hearing, there is no directional map, so recovering the sound source's direction is difficult, and estimating its distance is very difficult indeed.

There are two ways to estimate auditory direction, both based on binaural comparisons of the stimulus to the two ears. First, sound travels relatively slowly, so a sound to the left, for example, will reach the left ear before the right. Interaural delay therefore provides information about direction and is useful where the sound source has recognisable 'landmarks', like onsets and offsets, that can be matched in each ear or, if the stimulus is periodic, where the interaural delay is small in relation to the repetition period. For continuous, high frequency stimuli, it is difficult to work out which cycle in one ear corresponds to which in the other, so timing cues are less reliable.

Second, the head blocks sounds, casting an acoustic shadow so that, if a sound source is to the left for example, the stimulus will be more intense in the left ear than the right. Interaural intensity differences therefore also provide information about direction, though they are ineffective at low frequencies because the head doesn't block these wavelengths well.

The auditory system uses both timing and intensity cues. A tone presented over headphones with the signal louder in, say, the left ear, seems to come from the left. If the stimulus to the left ear is then delayed slightly, to provide a conflicting timing cue, the sound shifts back to a central direction. When we measure the amount of one cue needed to balance the other at each frequency, it turns out that the two sources of information complement each other as you would expect; timing differences are more important at low frequencies and intensity cues are more important at high frequencies. Stereophonic recordings rely entirely upon intensity differences, which is why bass sounds don't have an identifiable direction.

Timing and intensity cues are encoded by different neurons in the superior olivary complex, the first stage in the pathway receiving input from both ears (Figure 5.10), and provide an example of how neurons can solve complex problems using the simple processes of inhibition and excitation. Timing differences are encoded by a system of delay lines and 'coincidence detectors' in the medial superior olive. Each cell receives an excitatory input from both ears and responds best when the two excitatory inputs arrive simultaneously. By varying the relative delay between the two inputs, each cell can be tuned to respond best to a different direction; a cell with a long delay from the right ear and a short delay from the left will, for example, respond best to stimuli on the right.

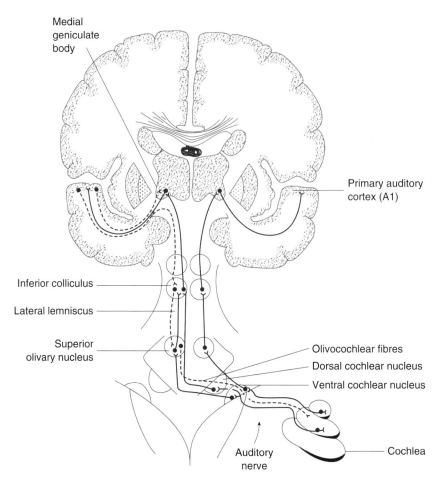

Figure 5.10   Diagram of the auditory pathway

Source: Barnes (2013)

Intensity differences are encoded in the lateral superior olive by cells that receive an excitatory input from one ear and an inhibitory input from the other. If the two inputs have similar properties (i.e. they respond identically to a stimulus of a given amplitude and frequency) then subtracting one response from the other is a simple way to remove all these common properties and produce a response that depends only upon the relevant cue – the difference in intensity. A small difference will signal targets close to the centre of the auditory field, while a large difference will signal targets off to one side.

The pattern of response across sets of neurons, each tuned to a slightly different delay or intensity difference, is thought to provide the information needed to estimate target direction. However, even both cues together don't *completely* solve the problem. A source with neither timing nor intensity differences, for example, could come from in front, behind, or, in fact, anywhere on a vertical plane through the centre of the head. We can rotate our head to resolve this type of ambiguity, but the shape of the external ear, the pinna, is also important. Its spiral-shaped fold of skin creates tiny echoes, and the delay between the sound and its echo varies systematically with direction. Although we do not hear these echoes consciously, we do use them because, when the spirals are temporarily modified with Plasticene, our ability to locate sounds is dramatically reduced.

THE AUDITORY CORTEX

The primary auditory cortex (A1) is much less well understood than the visual cortex. It is tonotopically organised, with the preferred frequency of cells changing gradually across its surface. At each frequency, there seem to be localised clusters of cells selective for particular types of binaural interaction or a particular range of intensities, for example. It is difficult to identify the auditory equivalent of a visual feature, such as a moving line, but many cells in the auditory cortex do respond to particular aspects of the stimulus, such as an abrupt change in frequency or intensity, and many also respond to natural sounds, such as speech. However, these responses to complex stimuli often cannot be predicted by the cell's response to simple individual frequencies, and it seems that cells can change their properties depending upon the stimulus context.

As in vision, the projection from A1 appears to be organised into distinct functional streams, with an anterior 'what' projection focusing on pitch and speech perception, and a posterior 'where' projection focusing on spatial processing.

How do we pick out individual sounds from the background?

In vision, objects in different directions project to different positions in the image and so can often be processed separately from each other. In hearing, however, stimuli from different directions are superimposed on each other, arriving at the ear in a single auditory stream. How does the auditory system disentangle this information to recover the separate sound sources? Prior knowledge about specific sounds is often needed for a complete, 'top-down' solution, but the problem can also be simplified in a 'bottom-up' way by making use of the fact that basilar membrane breaks down the stimulus into its separate frequency components. For example, sounds from different directions will have different interaural intensity and timing cues, so components that share a particular combination of cues can be grouped together into a separate 'auditory stream'. Similarly, different sounds may follow different time courses, so components can be streamed together on the basis of shared timing information. Unfortunately, the required ability to resolve different frequencies often deteriorates with age, so that older people often find it difficult to cope with noisy environments, where they are required to separate several sound sources, even though they can make sense of the individual sources when presented by themselves.

KEY POINTS

- Hair cells in the cochlea transduce the auditory stimulus.
- The basilar membrane encodes pitch and timbre by breaking down sounds into their constituent frequency components.
- Comparisons of the arrival time and intensity of sounds in the two ears are used to locate the direction of auditory stimuli.
- Cortical cells respond to different aspects of the stimulus, but the processing of auditory features is less well understood than in vision.

THE VESTIBULAR SYSTEM

The vestibular system is primarily concerned with maintaining balance by detecting movements of the head. As shown in Figure 5.11, it consists of three **semi-circular canals** and two small organs, the **utricle** and **saccule** that, together with the cochlea, form the inner ear; they use hair cells like those found in the cochlea as receptors.

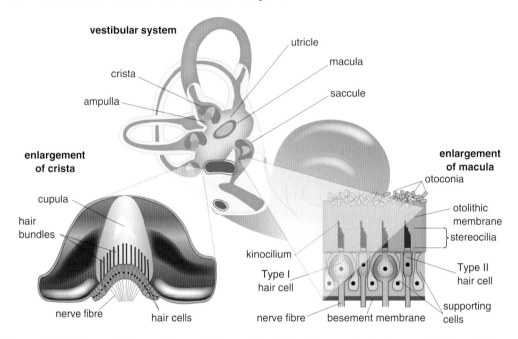

Figure 5.11   The vestibular system, which consists of the three semi-circular canals, the utricle, and the saccule. The insets show the arrangement of the hair cells, which are the receptor cells for the semi-circular canals (on the left) and the utricle and saccule (on the right)

Source: Barnes (2013)

The semi-circular canals lie at right angles to each other, and between them can signal rotational acceleration of the head about any axis. Each canal is filled with fluid and has a small swelling, the ampulla, containing hairs cells at one end. Bending of a hair cell's cilia causes a receptor potential, which may be either a depolarisation or a hyperpolarisation, depending on the direction in which the cilia are bent. When the head rotates, the fluid initally lags behind, causing the cilia to bend in one direction and producing a receptor potential, say a depolarisation. If the rotation continues, the fluid catches up so that the bending of the cilia and, consequently, the hair cells' response, stops. When the rotation stops or slows down, the fluid continues to rotate for a few moments, bending the cilia in the opposite direction and causing a graded response of the opposite polarity, in this case a hyperpolarisation.

In the utricle and saccule, hair cells project into a gelatinous membrane incorporating small, relatively heavy calcium carbonate crystals (otoliths). They work in a similar way to the semi-circular canals but signal linear acceleration; the heavy gelatinous membrane lags behind during acceleration and overshoots during deceleration, distorting the hairs cells and causing a graded response of the appropriate polarity. The cilia in the utricle and saccule are arranged in different directions so that, between them, they detect movement in any direction.

Rather like visual cells that respond only to *changes* in light, the hair cells in the vestibular system respond only to changes in the motion of the head. In the vestibular system, this depends upon the mechanical arrangement of the receptors, whereas in vision it arises from neural interactions (lateral inhibition), but both examples illustrate the general importance of improving the efficiency of coding by recording changes, which are generally informative, while ignoring unchanging stimulation, which is generally uninformative.

VESTIBULAR INTERACTIONS WITH VISION

The vestibular system makes an important contribution to vision through the vestibulo-ocular reflex. When you rotate your head in one direction, the resulting signal from the semi-circular canals is used to rotate the eyes in the opposite direction. This means, as you can easily demonstrate to yourself using a looking glass, that you automatically maintain visual fixation on a given target despite large, active or passive, movements of your head. Such a system is important, given the relatively small region of the retina capable of detailed vision.

Perhaps less obviously, vision also contributes to balance. This is convincingly demonstrated by a study in which young children stand on a movable trolley inside a small 'room' that can also be moved backward or forward relative to the observer. When the trolley moves by itself, the child experiences normal movement signals from the vestibular and visual systems and easily maintains balance. But when the trolley and room move together (producing a vestibular signal without a visual signal) or when the room moves but the trolley does not (producing a visual signal without a vestibular signal) they sway or fall over (Lee and Lishman, 1975). This last condition, particularly, indicates that vision by itself is sufficient to produce balancing movements.

As the above examples imply, vestibular and visual signals are normally tightly coupled; movement of the head usually produces both a vestibular and a corresponding visual response. Motion sickness and the discomfort sometimes associated with heights may arise, at least in part, from a temporary conflict between these responses. For example, travelling in a car or boat reliably produces a vestibular response but the visual world may be deceptively stable because the car or boat moves with the observer so that there is little visual motion. Similarly, when standing on a high building, the normal visual signals associated with the tiny swaying movements needed to maintain balance are reduced because we are typically looking at a distant visual world, and distant objects produce negligible visual motion.

KEY POINTS

- Three semi-circular canals, sensitive to rotational acceleration, and the saccule and utricle, sensitive to linear acceleration, together detect changes in the movement of the head.
- The vestibular system interacts with the visual system to stabilise vision and to maintain balance during movements.

SOMATOSENSATION

Touch

Unlike vision and hearing, which have separate receptor cells, touch receptors are simply the modified ends of myelinated (Aβ) sensory nerves. They are specialised to detect different aspects of the stimulus, such as pressure or stretching of the skin, by different mechanical structures surrounding the nerve ending. As shown in Figure 5.12 and Table 5.1, in addition to unmodified nerve endings, there are four distinct types of touch receptor differing mainly in the depth at which they are found in the skin, receptive field size, sensitivity, and the rate at which they adapt to continuous stimulation. The number of receptors varies across the body, with much higher densities in the most sensitive areas (e.g. the fingertips or lips) than in less sensitive areas (e.g. the shoulders).

Table 5.1   Properties of touch receptors

	Merkel's disc	Meissner's corpuscle	Ruffini ending	Pacinian corpuscle
Location	Shallow	Shallow	Deep	Deep
RF size	Small	Small	Large	Large
Sensitivity	Medium	High	Low	Very high
Adapt	Slowly	Fast	Slowly	Fast
Stimulus	Pressure	Pressure	Stretch	Vibration

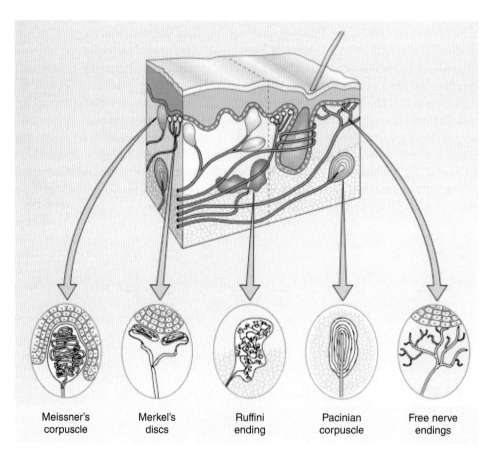

| Meissner's corpuscle | Merkel's discs | Ruffini ending | Pacinian corpuscle | Free nerve endings |

Figure 5.12   The main types of touch receptor in the skin

Source: Open University Course SD329: *Sensation and Perception* (2003)

The dorsal column-medial lemniscal (DCML) pathway

As shown in Figure 5.13, touch-sensitive fibres enter the spinal cord and ascend directly in the dorsal columns through the medulla. Medullary neurons cross the midline and project in the medial lemniscus to the ventral posterior nucleus (VPN) of the thalamus. Like visual cells in the LGN, somatosensory cells in the VPN have circular receptive fields with antagonistic centre-surround sub-regions, further illustrating the general principle of using **lateral inhibition** to pick out the informative spatial changes in stimulation.

VPN cells project to the primary somatosensory cortex (S1) on the post-central gyrus. S1 is somatotopically mapped, with adjacent regions of the body projecting to adjacent regions of the cortex. Like the retinotopic map of the retina in V1, the somatotopic map in S1 is distorted, with more sensitive regions (e.g. the finger tips) taking up more cortical space than less sensitive areas (e.g. the shoulder). Again like V1, S1 is organised into columns, with each column of cells responding to just one of the four types of sensory receptor. And again like V1, S1 cells respond selectively to more complex properties of the stimulus, such as the orientation of an edge pressed onto the skin or its direction of movement.

S1 projects first to the secondary somatosensory cortex (S2), which is just behind S1 and which is also somatotopically mapped, and from there to many sensory and motor cortical areas. As in vision and hearing, later cortical processing may be divided into a ventral 'what' stream concerned primarily with recognition, and a dorsal 'where' stream concerned primarily with location.

Passive and active touch

When an object is pressed against the skin, the pattern of response across the different types of receptors will encode the position, intensity and something of the nature of the stimulus – for example its shape and orientation. The detail available will vary according to the position on the body; those areas with a richer innervation and larger cortical representation will provide more accurate information. If the object is moved, other aspects, such as the direction of motion, will emerge and the pattern of response over time, especially in the rapidly adapting receptors, may signal something about the texture of the object. For most areas of the body, the information provided by this kind of *passive* touch is all that is available and all that is needed. But for the hands, which are often used to explore objects, much richer information is available from *active* touch.

Active touch, or haptic perception, involves exploring an object with our hands using a series of coordinated movements, termed exploratory procedures. For example, we may trace round the countours of the object to gauge its shape, probe it with a fingertip to check its temperature and consistency, or gently stroke its surface to determine its texture. In this way, we can rapidly recognise familiar objects when blindfolded and, with practice, can learn to read the tiny raised dot patterns of the Braille alphabet at up to 100 words per minute. These abilities require careful correlation of very complex patterns of sensory and motor activity, and functional imaging suggests that a specific area of the posterior parietal cortex may be particularly concerned with this task.

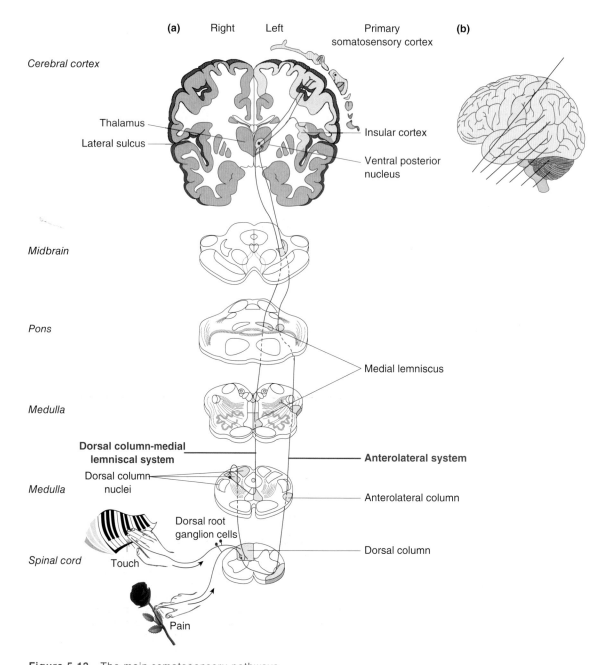

Figure 5.13   The main somatosensory pathways

Adapted from Open University Course SD226: *Biological Psychology* (2006)

Temperature and Pain

Extreme temperature and pain are both signalled by free nerve endings in the skin and project together in a separate spinothalamic pathway to the somatosensory cortex. Both serve to warn of actual or potentially damaging stimulation and are, appropriately, perceived as unpleasant.

Temperature

The receptor sites on the temperature-sensitive thermoreceptors consist of transient receptor proteins (TRPs). There are at least six different types of TRP, each sensitive to a different range of temperatures and together covering a wide range from cold (i.e. below normal skin temperature) to extremely hot. Thermoreceptors are important in regulating body temperature, for example by provoking shivering or sweating, as well as in signalling the temperature of objects in contact with our skin. Some TRPs also respond to particular chemicals, such as capsaicin (the active ingredient of pepper) and menthol (the active ingredient of mint), which may explain why these ingredients evoke an impression of heat or coldness.

Pain

Receptors sensitive to tissue damage are called nociceptors and form the first stage of the process that leads to the subjective experience of pain. Like thermoreceptors, nociceptors rely on TRPs, and some polymodal free nerve endings respond to either extreme temperature or tissue damage – hot things hurt. Sodium channels are also important in nociception.

In addition to causing a direct neural response, tissue damage typically releases a cocktail of chemicals, including 5HT and prostaglandins, that sensitises and stimulates the nociceptors and produces the painful inflamation that outlasts the damaging stimulus. This longer-term painful aspect of the swelling is important in encouraging you to rest and protect the damaged area while it heals.

Ascending and descending pathways

Thermoreceptors and nociceptors project via Aδ and C fibres to the spinal cord, and make their first synapses in the dorsal horn. Aδ fibres transmit more quickly and are responsible for the sharp pricking component of pain, while the slower, unmyelinated C fibres produce the subsequent throbbing or aching. The dorsal horn synapse is the proposed site of a spinal 'gate' that controls the onward transmission of the pain signal (Melzack and Wall, 1996). Interneurons in the substantia gelatinosa (SG) region of the spinal cord can inhibit the dorsal horn synapse and thus 'close the gate'. These SG neurons receive inhibitory input from the nociceptors (preventing the gate from closing), and excitatory input, tending to close the gate, from peripheral touch fibres and from fibres descending from higher centres. Activation of the ascending pain pathway beyond the first spinal synapse thus depends on the balance of activity between nociceptors and other peripheral and central inputs.

Ascending fibres from the spinal gate cross to the other side of the spinal cord and project upwards in the spinothalamic tract to the ventral posterior nucleus (VPN) and other thalamic nuclei, either directly or via the reticulothalamic tract and the periaqueductal grey (PAG) in the midbrain. From the thalamus, fibres project first to the somatosensory cortex (S1) and the anterior cingulate cortex (ACC), and from there to several structures including the insular cortex, the amygdala and the prefrontal cortex.

Fibres concerned with pain also project downwards from the prefrontal cortex and hypothalamus, via the PAG and the raphe nucleus in the midbrain, to the 'gates' in the spinal cord. This tract makes use of endogenous opioids, or *endorphins*, which are neuromodulators acting upon specific opioid receptors, and which are known to be involved in pain relief and in the pleasurable sensations associated with reaching motivational goals.

The subjective experience of pain   Much work on pain focuses on its subjective nature, emphasising the tenuous link between objective tissue damage and the experience of pain. For example, tissue damage often occurs without pain, most dramatically in soldiers who sometimes do not notice severe injuries until the battle is over. Conversely, pain can occur without tissue damage, as in phantom limbs where some doubly unfortunate individuals experience pain in a limb that has long-since been amputated. None of this is unique to pain, since *all* conscious experience is by definition subjective – and there are many examples of visual illusions, for example, where we perceive things that aren't there or miss things that are. But the phenomena are often particularly dramatic in pain and serve to remind us that our conscious experience of the physical world is mediated by neural activity.

Pain researchers also often stress three different aspects of pain:

- A sensory component – the actual conscious experience, which seems to be mediated primarily by activity in the somatosensory cortex.

- An affective component – pain is unpleasant, and this is thought to be important in teaching us to avoid painful situations. Hypnosis can independently manipulate the unpleasantness of pain, and brain imaging suggests that activity in the ACC and amygdala is crucially involved.

- A cognitive component through which our expectations can profoundly influence the perceived intensity – for example, an inert placebo can reduce pain. This effect seems to involve the prefrontal cortex and the descending pathways and it can be reduced by naloxone, which blocks the effects of endorphins.

Of course, other modalities also involve not only the more obvious sensory (bottom-up) and cognitive (top-down) aspects, but also important affective components. The other senses also have projections to the amygdala that are presumably involved in 'gruesome sights' and 'disgusting smells', for example, and it is certainly more useful to find a lion's roar frightening than to find its bite excruciating. But pain is a relatively basic sense that offers a promisingly simpler way to study these different general factors.

Pain relief

Pain relief, or analgesia, relies on interrupting the transmission of pain signals, which can be achieved at several stages in the pain pathway. Non-steroidal anti-inflammatory drugs (**NSAIDs**) and local anaesthetics work at the periphery. NSAIDs, such as aspirin and ibuprofen, block the production of prostaglandins and so reduce both local swelling and the activation of nociceptors. Local anaesthetics, such as lidocaine, inhibit sodium channels in the peripheral nerve and so block the transmission of action potentials. Epidural anaesthesia, commonly used in childbirth, applies the same blocking technique at the spinal level. Other techniques also affect the spinal 'gate'. Simply rubbing an injured part can alter the balance of touch and pain signals arriving from the periphery, closing the gate and bringing temporary relief. Transcutaneous electrical nerve stimulation (**TENS**) applies electrical pulses to the skin, which stimulate the underlying nerves, and is thought to act, at least in part, by closing the spinal gate. Direct electrical stimulation, using electrodes implanted into the PAG or thalamus, is thought to activate the pathway descending to the spine which closes the spinal gates. Powerful morphine-based analgesics mimic the effects of endorphins and are thought to act, at least in part, at the spinal level. Finally, acupuncture seems to achieve the same effect, without the use of drugs, by stimulating the release of endorphins.

FOCUS ON METHODS: ELECTRICAL STIMULATION

Stimulating electrodes can be permanently implanted into the brain of experimental animals. An electrical current can be delivered through the electrode to activate the neurons in the target region. This can allow the effects of activity in a region to be determined. Alternatively, the stimulation can be used to induce synaptic plasticity (LTP or LTD). Finally, in human beings, electrical stimulation using temporarily inserted electrodes can map regions of the brain, which is useful in brain surgery to determine the precise area that needs to be operated upon.

Though this battery of techniques is generally effective in treating acute (i.e. short-lasting) pain, chronic pain – defined as persisting for six months or more – is sometimes resistant to any treatment. For example, **neuropathic pain** arises from damage and subsequent re-wiring of the pain pathway, for example following limb amputation. Because the re-wiring of the peripheral nerves often leads in turn to changes in the spinal connections, the spinal 'gate', upon which many treatments ultimately rely, may become more difficult to close.

PROPRIOCEPTION

Golgi tendon organs detect tension in the tendons that join muscles to bones, while muscle spindles detect stretch in the muscles themselves. Together, they signal both the position and movement (kinesthesis) of the limbs. They project both to the somatosensory cortex and directly to the cerebellum, which is crucially involved in motor control and which allows us to perform complex learned movements with a minimum of conscious intervention (see Chapter 6).

Proprioception works together with touch receptors, vision, and the vestibular system to provide us with a **body schema** – a remarkably sophisticated awareness of where our body is in relation to nearby objects that allows us, for example, to 'feel' a hammer that we are holding, or even the corners of a car that we are driving, as a temporary extension of our own body. The body schema relies on input from several modalities and seems continuously to monitor and adjust itself to keep everything in synchrony. For example, we rapidly change the felt position of our limbs to coincide with the incorrectly seen position produced by visual displacing prisms, and will even come to accept a rubber hand as our own if we see it being stroked while feeling equivalent stroking of our real (hidden) hand.

KEY POINTS

- Specialised nerve endings in the skin respond to different aspects of touch, such as pressure.
- Exploratory movements of the hands allow a rich description of the stimulus through active touch.
- Nociceptors respond to harmful or potentially harmful stimuli.
- Neural 'gates' in the spinal cord receive input from the periphery and from higher centres, and regulate the flow of information from nociceptors.
- Pain relief can normally be achieved by interrupting the flow of information at an appropriate stage of the nociceptor pathway.
- Proprioceptors in the muscles and joints provide information about the position and movement of the limbs.
- Proprioception is integrated with visual and tactile information to form a sohisticated body schema.

TASTE AND SMELL

Taste and smell together make up the chemical senses, respectively detecting molecules dissolved in our saliva or in the air. Despite their relative simplicity, our understanding of the chemical senses is far from complete – not least because it is technically difficult to produce well controlled tastes and smells as stimuli.

Taste

What we commonly think of as taste is technically called 'flavour' and results from the combination of inputs from taste, smell and texture receptors. Taste itself is currently thought to be based on just five basic qualities, though umami has only recently become generally accepted and other unique tastes may yet emerge. The five accepted tastes seem well suited to distinguishing between nutritious and unnutritious or potentially dangerous foods.

Sour – based on detecting the hydrogen ions associated with the acids that are common in unripe fruits or 'spoilt' dairy foods.

Bitter – based on detecting molecules typically found in poisons.

Salty – based on detecting the sodium and chloride ions essential for, amongst many other things, neural function.

Sweet – based on detecting the sugars associated with nutritious foods.

Umami – based on detecting glutamate and possibly other amino acids, useful as a signal
of protein-rich foods.

Each of these basic tastes is associated with a specific type of receptor or family of receptors distributed across the roof of the mouth and the tongue. Those on the tongue are found in distinct physical structures called papillae. Different types of papillae are found in different regions of the tongue and it was originally believed that taste receptors were also unevenly distributed to form a taste map with bitter receptors, for example, predominant at the back of the tongue. It's now accepted though that all types of receptor are roughly evenly distributed around the edges of the tongue, though there are no receptors in the centre of the tongue.

As shown in Figure 5.14, receptor cells are clustered together in taste buds, which are also equipped with temperature/pain receptors accounting for the hot feeling provoked by peppers. A given taste bud may contain more than one type of taste receptor. Receptors for salt and bitter are fairly simple, relying on more or less direct activation of membrane channels by the relevant ions, but the other three types involve G-proteins and sites to which the relevant molecules bind in a 'lock and key' fashion. Several keys may fit the same lock, so each receptor may be activated to some extent by a range of similar molecules. There are also variants of each type of receptor, especially for bitter, which further increases the range of molecules that elicit the same taste.

The receptors project in three different cranial nerves (the facial, glossopharyngeal, and vagus) via the solitary nucleus to the ventral posterior medial nucleus of the thalamus, thence to the insular cortex, which is part of the somatosensory cortex, and finally to the orbitofrontal cortex, where the taste, smell, texture, and sight of food are integrated. Taste fibres also project to the amygdala, giving taste a direct affective component like that for pain, and to the hypothalamus, which is important in feeding motivation.

Individual taste fibres in the early stages of the pathway typically respond best to just one of the basic tastes (e.g. 'salt best' or 'sweet best') and the perception of taste seems to preserve these separate components. For example, tonic water tastes both bitter and sweet. This contrasts with colour vision, where the pattern of activity across a small number of receptor types (cones) typically produces a new colour in which the components may not be readily discernible.

It seems sensible to keep basic tastes separate if they serve to signal important properties of food, but the story is not quite that simple. First, we can adapt to a particular taste – eating something sweet can make something that's less sweet taste sour, for example, so a crisp Chablis is not a good accompaniment to a sweet pudding. Second, mixtures do not always preserve the components' tastes. Many people use sugar to mask the bitterness of the caffeine in their tea or coffee, for example, and some mixtures can even produce an unexpected new taste – a dab of salt followed immediately by lemon or lime juice can taste strangely sweet. It seems foolhardy to suppress or modify a signal that might warn us of potential poisons, but we may be flexible enough to learn that particular patterns of taste activity do not cause lasting damage. Certainly, though newborn babies are predisposed to like sweet things and dislike bitter things, we subsequently learn to like many things that we dislike on first exposure and it is surprising how many of our favourite foods are 'acquired tastes'. More important, such learning need rarely rely on taste alone, but on the much richer gamut of flavours available when taste is combined with smell.

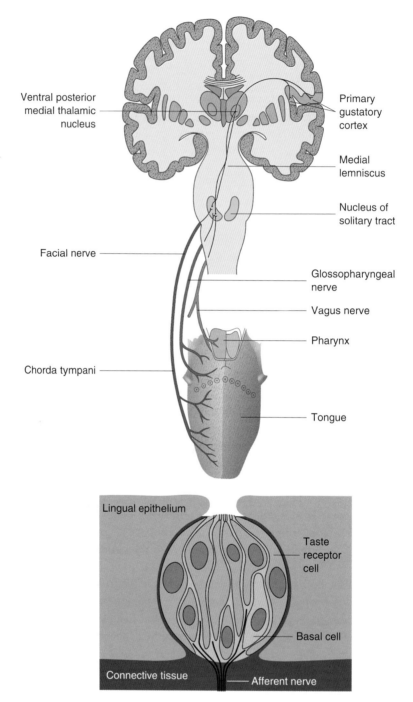

Figure 5.14   A map of the tongue, including an image of a taste bud, and the main neural projection to the thalamus and cortex

Source: Barnes (2013) and NEUROtiker, Wikimedia Commons

Smell

Smell serves two functions which depend on different routes. Stimuli arriving through the nose, via the orthonasal route (directly through the nose), can alert us to dangerous (e.g. the smoke from a fire) or desirable (e.g. the smell of cooking) stimuli in the external world, while stimuli arising in the mouth and arriving via the retronasal route (from the back of the mouth) can richly enhance the information available about foods in our mouths.

We have about 10 million olfactory receptor neurons (ORNs) embedded in the olfactory epithelium, an inch square patch located at the back of the nose above the hard palate. Each ORN contains a number of olfactory receptors which, like the taste receptors for bitter, sweet and umami, operate a 'lock and key' mechanism involving G-proteins. Each receptor binds with and responds to a narrow range of odorants depending on how well the odorant molecule's 'key' fits the receptor's 'lock'.

Unlike colour and taste, which are based on a small number of receptor types, we have about three to four hundred different types of olfactory receptor, each responsive to a narrow range of molecules. Interestingly, there is a universal set of about 1,000 receptors, and different patterns of them are functional in different species. Animals that rely heavily upon smell typically have both more ORNs and more functional types of receptor, so that they have both better sensitivity and better discrimination.

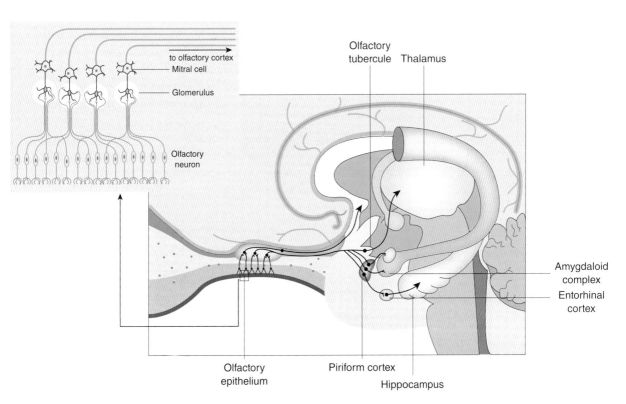

Figure 5.15   The main olfactory pathway from the olfactory epithelium via the olfactory bulb to the olfactory cortex. The inset shows how receptor cells project to mitral cells

Source: Adapted from Open University Course SD329: *Sensation and Perception* (2003)

As shown in Figure 5.15, olfactory receptors project in the olfactory nerve to the olfactory bulb where they synapse with mitral cells in distinct spherical structures called glomeruli. Each ORN possesses just one type of receptor and all the receptors of one type project to just a few mitral cells. Unlike other senses, mitral cells project directly to the piriform cortex (the primary olfactory cortex) without a synapse in the thalamus. Mitral cells also project directly to the amygdala and entorhinal cortex. From the piriform cortex, smell information passes to the orbitofrontal cortex, where it is integrated with taste and visual information. The nose also contains temperature and pain receptors, projecting separately to the somatosensory cortex, which helps explain why menthol (the basis of mint) 'smells' cold and pungent smells sting.

We can experience many more different smells than the three to four hundred types of receptor available so, rather than each smell being associated with a particular receptor, our perceptual experience depends upon the pattern of activity across the different types of receptor. Monitoring Ca^{++} concentration or oxygen uptake as markers of neural response in the olfactory epithelium or olfactory bulb reveals that each contains an organised smell map. Each odorant typically activates about ten receptor types, and odorants with similar molecular structures usually produce activity in neighbouring regions of the olfactory bulb. More important, odorants producing similar patterns of response generally smell alike, while those producing different patterns typically smell different.

Though individual molecules often have characteristic smells, the majority of our smell, and hence flavour, experience is based on mixtures. The smell of coffee alone depends upon hundreds of different chemicals, and the stimulus becomes almost unimaginably complex when coffee is combined with bacon, eggs and other breakfast ingredients. Clearly, our perception of these complex stimuli must involve a pattern of response across many receptor types and must depend to a large extent on learning. Reassuringly, functional imaging and single-cell recordings from the olfactory regions suggest that cortical cells respond to a broader range of molecules than do mitral cells, and that they can modify their responses when repeatedly exposed to new mixtures.

Though it is commonly believed that smells can evoke particularly vivid memories, research shows that memories triggered by smells are no more accurate than those triggered by sights and sounds. However, memories triggered by smells do typically have more emotional content, which may reflect the direct connections from mitral cells to the amygdala as well as the olfactory cortex.

KEY POINTS

- The perception of flavour depends on the combination of taste with smell.
- Taste is encoded by the pattern of response across just four or five different types of receptor.
- Smell is encoded by the pattern of response across three to four hundred diferent types of receptor.

CHAPTER SUMMARY

Vision, hearing and smell provide information about distant objects and therefore about potential near-future events, whilst balance, touch, temperature, pain, proprioception and taste provide information about our current state. These senses do not directly detect objects in the world but, rather, they detect the effects these objects have upon some aspect of the world. Nonetheless, by describing these effects they allow us to work out – to perceive – something about the objects that caused them. For example, from vision, we might work out how reflective a surface is or, from hearing, we might work out how rapidly something is vibrating.

Sensory systems thus provide only indirect contact with the world and their task is to pick out useful information from the vast array of stimulation that bombards us. In vision, the focus is upon detecting changes in the pattern of light across space and over time. These changes are detected by simple networks of neurons in the retina and passed on to the visual cortex via the optic nerve. In the visual cortex, different aspects of the changes are captured by the patterns of response across different sub-populations of cells, each tuned to a different aspect of the stimulus. For example, different patterns describe the orientation of the change, or how fast it is moving. The same general principle seems to apply in all our senses – emphasis shifts from an initial pattern of response at the receptors, to multiple patterns of response across sub-populations of more specialised cells in the sensory cortex.

We currently have a good understanding of our sensory receptors and some useful insights into the early stages of processing within the sensory cortex. To develop this understanding, we first need to understand what useful information is available in the physical stimulus, and then whether and how this information is represented in the patterns of response observable within the sensory cortex. We can then hope to tease apart how these patterns arise by carefully analysing the properties of the cells involved, the neurotransmitters that they use, and the interconnections between them. And, by systematically varying the stimulus and monitoring how this affects not only the pattern of response but, importantly, our perception of the stimulus, we can begin to unravel the final mystery of how patterns of neural response are related to our rich, conscious experience of the perceptual world.

FURTHER READING

Bregman, A. S. (1990). *Auditory Scene Analysis: The Perceptual Organization of Sound*. Cambridge, MA: MIT Press.
> The original and definitive account of how the auditory system makes sense of the auditory world.

Goldstein, E. B. (2010). *Sensation and Perception*, 8th edition. Wadsworth Cengage Learning.
> Provides a more detailed overview of the main sensory systems.

Snowden, R. J., Thompson, P., & Troscianko, T. (2012). *Basic Vision: An Introduction to Visual Perception*. Revised edition. Oxford: Oxford University Press.
> A very readable, often amusing, account of human vision.

SPOTLIGHT 5A
RETINAL SPATIAL PROCESSING

KEY ISSUES AND CONTROVERSIES

- Retinal ganglion cells respond only when a luminance edge is present within the receptive field.
- Luminance edges are detected by spatial comparisons, using lateral inhibition.
- Spatial comparisons are made in all directions, so receptive fields are circular.
- Comparisons are made using ratios, so retinal cells signal the relative reflectance of neighbouring surfaces.
- Comparisons are made at a range of spatial scales, so receptive fields vary in size.
- Before making comparisons, receptive fields average the responses of more than one photoreceptor to produce a more reliable estimate of the amount of light at each point in the image.

INTRODUCTION

All the cells in the visual system, even those deep within the brain, have receptive fields; they respond to light in some limited region of the retina. Almost all of these cells are not, themselves, directly sensitive to light – cells in the visual cortex, for example, would not respond if you could shine a light directly upon them. They nonetheless respond to light because they receive input from cells that, ultimately, are connected to light-sensitive photoreceptors in the retina. Sometimes the chain of connections is very long, involving many synapses. But, no matter how long the chain, if it leads from a photoreceptor at a given position on the retina to a given cell, then that position on the retina will fall within the cell's receptive field.

The cells described here – retinal ganglion cells – are just a few synapses back from the photoreceptors. Nonetheless, those few synapses are still enough to accomplish a great deal of processing. The receptive fields of retinal ganglion cells have evolved so that the cells respond only to luminance edges – places in the image where the amount of light changes fairly abruptly from one position to the next. To understand why they do this, imagine yourself drawing a visual scene. You would most likely start by sketching in the outlines of things, rather than by filling in solid regions of colour. The outlines are particularly important because they define the shape of things, so a good line-drawing is just about as recognisable as the scene on which it is based. The outlines of objects in a scene will tend to show up in images as luminance edges, so retinal ganglion cells have evolved to pick out the most useful features of images and to ignore the solid regions. In effect, ganglion cells reduce the retinal image to a retinal line-drawing.

To understand how retinal ganglion cells work, and to appreciate how much can be achieved just by connecting together a few cells so that they excite or inhibit each other to different degrees, we need to consider some of the problems retinal processing has to overcome.

Although we focus upon vision, similar problems are encountered in other sensory systems and the solutions that have evolved are remarkably similar. For example, some touch-sensitive cells in the early stages of the somatosensory system have receptive fields for touch just like those of retinal ganglion cells for light.

THE RETINAL GANGLION CELL RECEPTIVE FIELD

Retinal ganglion cells carry the output of the retina, their axons forming the individual fibres of the optic nerve, which projects from the eye via a synapse in the lateral geniculate nucleus to the visual cortex. Unlike photoreceptors and most other retinal interneurons, which generate only graded potentials, retinal ganglion cells generate action potentials, so they are well suited to transmitting information rapidly over relatively long distances.

Recordings from individual retinal ganglion cells show that they are spontaneously active, firing at a steady background rate even when unstimulated by light. This means that they can respond to an appropriate stimulus either by increasing or by decreasing their firing rate.

Retinal ganglion cells respond when a spot of light falls anywhere within a circular region of the retina, called the cell's receptive field. These receptive fields are typically divided into two concentric, antagonistic sub-regions, as shown in Figure 5a.1. Light falling anywhere within an 'on-region' causes the cell to increase its response above the background rate. Light falling within an 'off-region' causes a decrease in response rate. The converse is also true; a dark spot

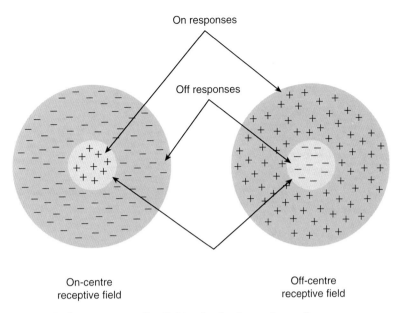

Figure 5a.1   On-centre and off-centre receptive fields of retinal ganglion cells

falling within an on-region causes a decrease in response rate, whilst a dark spot falling within an off-region causes an increase in response rate.

Cells with a receptive field consisting of a central on-region and surrounding off-region, as on the left in Figure 5a.1, are called on-centre cells. An increase in light makes these cells respond more quickly, whilst a decrease in light makes them respond more slowly. Their response rate therefore directly signals how light it is in the relevant region of the retina; an increase in their response is interpreted as an increase in light, whilst a decrease in response is interpreted as a decrease in light. Cells with receptive fields showing the reverse arrangement, as on the right of Figure 5a.1, are called off-centre cells. Their response rate complements that of on-centre cells by signalling how dark it is in the relevant region of the retina; an increase in their response is interpreted as a decrease in light, whilst a decrease in response is interpreted as an increase in light.

There are roughly equal numbers of on- and off-centre cells but we will focus only upon on-centre cells. We just need to remember that, if an on-centre cell with its receptive field at a given position fires more quickly than the background rate, then an off-centre cell with its receptive field at the same position will fire more slowly than the background rate; an increase in lightness is equivalent to a decrease in darkness.

Retinal Interneurons Form the Receptive Field

Figure 5a.2 illustrates how the receptive fields of retinal ganglion cells, like those in Figure 5a.1, might arise from photoreceptors. This picture does not represent the true complexity of the retinal wiring, but simply shows how interneurons could, in principle, be used to create the excitatory and inhibitory sub-regions that cause the ganglion cell to respond. Light falling on any of the photoreceptors numbered 2–9 will cause a response in retinal ganglion cell 1, because

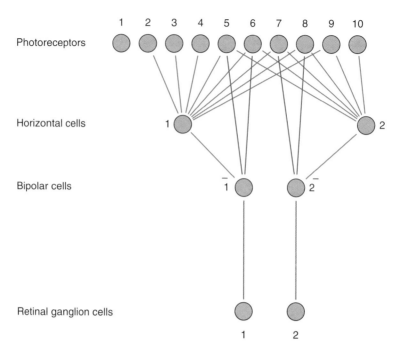

Red connections carry the receptive field centre
Blue connections carry the surround

Figure 5a.2   A simplified schematic view of how the receptive fields of retinal ganglion cells arise by wiring together outputs from neighbouring photoreceptors

all these receptor are connected to the cell, by horizontal cell 1, bipolar cell 1, or both. These receptors therefore define the cell's receptive field. Light falling on photoreceptor 1 has no effect on ganglion cell 1, because it is not connected to it and is therefore outside its receptive field.

Light falling on photoreceptor 2, which lies in the off-surround, causes a decrease in ganglion cell 1's firing rate, because they are connected to each other via horizontal cell 1, which is inhibitory. Light falling on photoreceptor 5, which lies in the on-centre, will cause both an inhibitory response, via horizontal cell 1, and an excitatory response, via bipolar cell 1. This nonetheless causes an increase in firing rate because its connection via the bipolar cell is stronger than that via the horizontal cell.

Note that a given photoreceptor may be connected by different interneurons to the same retinal ganglion cell, and by still other interneurons to more than one retinal ganglion cell. For example, photoreceptor 5 contributes both to the centre and surround of ganglion cell 1 and, via horizontal cell 2, to the surround of ganglion cell 2. This last connection shows how the receptive fields of neighbouring ganglion cells typically overlap.

As suggested above, for on-centre cells, the individual excitatory connections are stronger than the individual inhibitory connections. Consequently, when the whole receptive field is evenly illuminated (i.e. photoreceptors 2–9 are all stimulated), the total excitatory influence of the small central sub-region balances the total inhibitory influence of the larger surround, and the retinal ganglion cell shows, at best, only a small change in response rate. This example of lateral inhibition, where stimulation at one position inhibits the response at a neighbouring position, underpins the main role of retinal processing – to suppress uniform regions and to respond only to luminance edges in the image.

Retinal ganglion cells respond to luminance edges

Figure 5a.3 shows how a row of ganglion cells, each with its receptive field centred at a slightly different position, responds to a luminance edge. Cell A does not respond at all (i.e. it maintains its background firing rate) because its receptive field is uniformly illuminated so that its excitatory and inhibitory inputs cancel each other out. Cell B responds above the background rate because the whole of the excitatory sub-region is illuminated but only part of the inhibitory surround, which is insufficient to cancel the excitatory input. In addition, part of the inhibitory surround is in darkness, which will also tend to increase the ganglion cell's firing rate (remember that darkness in an off-region increases response). Cell C, which has its receptive field directly beneath the edge, does not respond because exactly half of both the excitatory and inhibitory sub-regions are illuminated, again cancelling each other out. Cell D is just the complement of cell B; it responds below the background rate because the whole of the excitatory centre is in darkness (dark in an on-region reduces response) but only part of the inhibitory surround is in darkness, which is insufficient to cancel the effect. In addition, part of the inhibitory surround is illuminated, which will also decrease the ganglion cell's response (light in an off-region decreases response). Finally, cell E does not respond because, like cell A, its receptive field is uniformly illuminated.

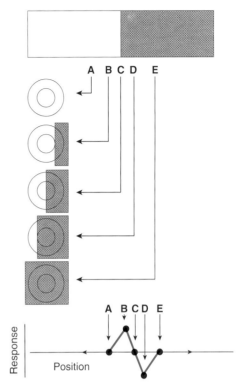

Figure 5a.3 Schematic representation showing how an array of retinal ganglion cells, with adjacent receptive fields, responds to a luminance edge. The characteristic peak-trough response is centred under the edge

Retinal ganglion cell response efficiently describes the image

The on-centre ganglion cell response shown in Figure 5a.3 is very efficient; just a few ganglion cells responding above or below the background level are needed to signal the presence of a luminance edge in the image. Consequently, there are about 100 times fewer retinal ganglion cells than there are photoreceptors in each eye. The characteristic 'peak-trough' pattern of response signals not only where the edge is, but also its polarity – the peak always falls on the light side of the edge, and the trough always on the dark side. Moreover, this characteristic retinal pattern does seem to be all that's needed for us actually to perceive an edge, as indicated by the Craik–O'Brien–Cornsweet illusion shown in Figure 5a.4.

The top section of Figure 5a.4 looks like an edge, with the region on the left appearing darker than that on the right. In fact, both regions are exactly the same, as you can demonstrate by covering the centre of the picture with your finger or a pencil. The trick is revealed in the lower section of Figure 5a.4, which shows the actual luminance profile of the top section and

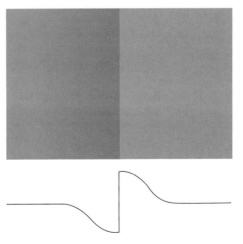

Figure 5a.4 The Craik–O'Brien–Cornsweet illusion

confirms that, except near the centre, the left and right sides are identical. The central region of the image is designed to produce the same 'peak-trough' pattern of retinal response as a real edge. It does this because the sharp change in the centre is easily detected by retinal ganglion cells, but the ramps to either side are too shallow to be detected. The visual system simply interprets this pattern of response as it normally does – 'There's a change from dark to light in the middle and, since there aren't any other changes, the left side must be darker than the right.'

Lateral inhibition works by making spatial comparisons

If you knew nothing about receptive fields or lateral inhibition and were given the task of detecting luminance edges, you would sooner or later almost certainly adopt the solution of comparing the response of each photoreceptor with that of its immediate neighbour; where there's a difference, there's a luminance edge. This simple strategy is shown schematically in Figure 5a.5(a).

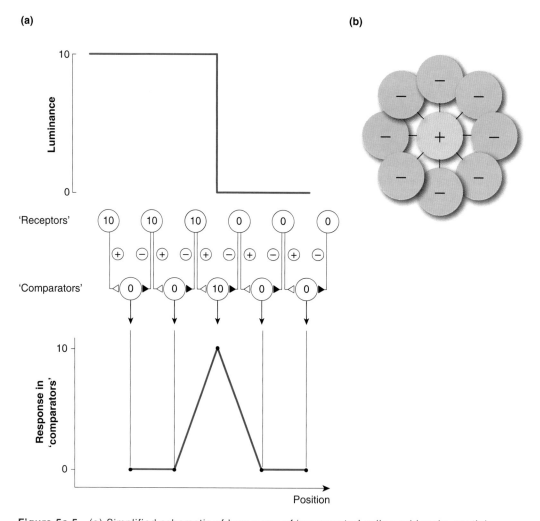

Figure 5a.5 (a) Simplified schematic of how a row of 'comparator' cells could make spatial comparisons between the outputs of neighbouring receptors. The numbers in the 'cell bodies' represent the response of each cell. (b) How a retinal receptive field can be regarded as a way to make spatial comparisons at all orientations

A layer of cells compares the responses of adjacent photoreceptors by summing an excitatory input from one photoreceptor with an inhibitory input from its immediate neighbour. In almost all cases, this results in no response because most photoreceptors have the same response as their neighbours. But, directly under the edge, there is a large response. This again emphasises the efficiency of focusing on changes; all the useful information is captured in this single response. And it gives us a better insight into what lateral inhibition is actually doing – providing a way for neurons to make spatial comparisons.

Receptive fields are circular because they make spatial comparisons in all directions

We can relate the simple scheme shown in Figure 5a.5(a) to retinal ganglion cell receptive fields with just one extra step. Comparing the responses of neighbouring photoreceptors along a horizontal line is fine for detecting vertical edges, but it will not detect horizontal edges. To do that, we need to make comparisons along a vertical line. In fact, since luminance edges can occur at any orientation, we really need to make the comparisons in all directions. We can do that by using a cell that connects each photoreceptor to *all* of its neighbours, in all directions instead of just to the right or left. The result, shown in Figure 5a.5(b), is a simplified version of the circular receptive fields familiar from Figure 5a.1. Receptive fields are just a way to detect edges at any orientation by making spatial comparisons in all directions.

Lightness constancy: ratios are more useful than differences

Making spatial comparisons by calculating differences, as in Figure 5a.5, will certainly detect luminance edges, but there is a simple refinement that will help to solve the additional problem outlined in Figure 5a.6. A given surface will reflect different amounts of light as the illumination varies throughout the day. In fact, a brightly lit, unreflective surface may reflect exactly the same amount of light as a dimly lit, reflective surface; compare the surface at the top right with that at the bottom left in Figure 5a.6. Yet we don't normally see surfaces varying in lightness as the sun goes behind a cloud, or as it gets dark; relatively light surfaces always look relatively light irrespective of how well they are lit.

The basis of this ability, called lightness constancy, is also apparent in Figure 5a.6. Irrespective of the lighting, a surface that is ten times as reflective as its neighbour will always reflect ten times more light than its neighbour. Making spatial comparisons by subtracting neighbouring values would return a difference of 90 units under the edge at the top of Figure 5a.6, but of only 9 under the same edge at the bottom. However, making the comparisons by *dividing* neighbouring values would reveal the underlying consistency by returning a value of 10 in both situations. But how might lateral inhibition, which is inherently a subtraction, be used to do division?

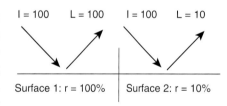

(a) Bright illumination

I = 100   L = 100   I = 100   L = 10

Surface 1: r = 100%   Surface 2: r = 10%

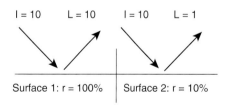

(b) Dim illumination

I = 10   L = 10   I = 10   L = 1

Surface 1: r = 100%   Surface 2: r = 10%

Figure 5a.6 Surfaces reflect a different amount of light in different illuminations. Hence the brightly lit unreflective surface at the top right reflects exactly the same amount of light as the dimly lit reflective surface at the bottom left. We nonetheless always see reflective surfaces as light and unreflective surfaces as dark – an ability called lightness constancy

Figure 5a.7   The horizontal strip at the top of the figure appears roughly evenly light, while the one at the bottom appears lighter on the left than the right. In fact, the reflectance (and therefore the lightness) of the top strip varies from low to high whilst that of the bottom strip is uniform. The illusion arises because the background varies from light to dark. For the top strip, the reflectance ratio of the strip to its background is always the same and this results in lightness constancy. For the bottom strip, this ratio varies from high on the left to low on the right and this results in **lightness contrast**

Recordings from photoreceptors show that their response is not directly proportional to the amount of light in the image. Rather, as the light increases, their response increases progressively less and less, so that increasing the light from 10 to 100 units produces only the same increase in response as increasing it from 1 to 10 units. Technically, this means that photoreceptors do not signal the amount of light in the image but, instead, the logarithm of the amount of light in the image. One useful property of logarithms is that subtracting the logarithms of two numbers is the same as dividing the original numbers. So using lateral inhibition to subtract the logarithmic responses of the photoreceptors on either side of an edge is the same as dividing the amount of light on either side of the edge. And, in effect, retinal ganglion cells signal the relative reflectance of two neighbouring surfaces so that we always know that a given surface is, say, ten times as reflective as its neighbour, irrespective of the lighting conditions.

Figure 5a.7 confirms this very useful property and demonstrates both **lightness constancy** and lightness contrast. The top bar varies physically in luminance from left to right but appears uniform (lightness constancy) because it maintains a constant ratio with the changing background. Retinal ganglion cells give a constant response along the top and bottom edges. The bottom bar is physically uniform but appears to vary (lightness contrast) because its ratio with the background varies. Retinal ganglion cell response decreases from left to right along its top and bottom edges. This figure is a typical visual illusion but we should remember that although this title emphasises a visual 'mistake', it reveals a generally sensible visual strategy that makes the mistake only when applied to an artificial, laboratory stimulus.

At each retinal location, cells with different sized receptive fields make spatial comparisons at different scales

Comparing the responses of nearby photoreceptors would certainly detect sharp edges, but it would be less suitable if the edge were shallow, like that shown in Figure 5a.8(a) because, here, luminance does not change much over such a small distance. Making the comparisons over a larger distance, as in Figure 5a.8(b), would solve this problem but it would create another, as shown in Figure 5a.8(c); if several edges were close together, a large-scale comparison would give a misleading result because it would no longer compare adjacent regions of the image. Unfortunately, there is no single 'correct' scale; if the comparisons are close together, they will miss shallow edges, but if they are far apart they will miss fine detail. The solution adopted by the retina is to make comparisons at a range of different scales using receptive fields of different sizes.

At each position on the retina, there are retinal ganglion cells with a range of different receptive field sizes. Small receptive fields make small-scale comparisons, while large receptive fields make large-scale comparisons. Between them they detect edges at a range of spatial scales and thus signal fine detail as well as more gradual changes. In addition, the average receptive field size varies gradually from very small in the fovea to much larger in the retinal periphery. This not only further increases the range of scales detectable, but also further reduces the data transmitted to the visual cortex. Only large-scale, relatively coarse features are picked up by the retinal periphery but, if necessary, the eyes can be moved to explore them in the finer detail provided by the smaller, more densely packed receptive fields in the fovea.

Receptive fields use weighted averages to reduce noise

In reality, images are always corrupted by 'noise' because the amount of light arriving at any point varies quite widely from moment to moment. So the instantaneous

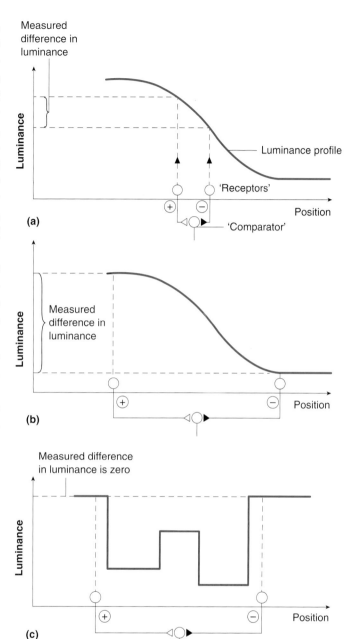

Figure 5a.8 Detecting edges at different scales. (a) Spatial comparisons would be insensitive to large-scale (blurred) edges because there is little difference in luminance between the two points. (b) Doing the comparisons at a larger spatial scale would solve this problem. (c) But large-scale comparisons would give misleading results when several edges are close together

profile of a light–dark edge might look more like that shown at the top of Figure 5a.9 than the idealised representations shown in previous figures. A system that focuses on changes will inevitably pick up these spurious fluctuations.

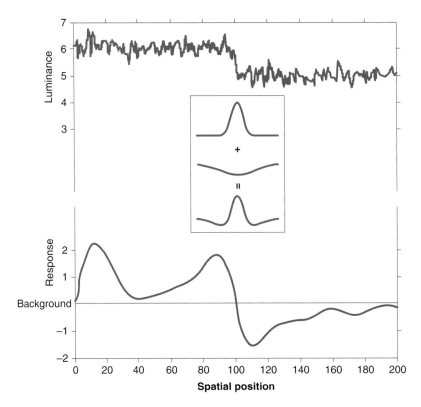

Figure 5a.9 Spatial averaging

One strategy to avoid this problem would be to 'clean up' the image before making the comparisons, by averaging together the responses of several neighbouring receptors. But averaging over a few receptors would not reduce the noise enough, whilst averaging over many receptors would inevitably lose fine detail. So a sensible compromise would be to take a *weighted* average – one in which the responses close to the point you're interested in contribute a good deal to the average whilst those further away contribute less. The normal distribution, shown at the top of the inset in Figure 5a.9, and probably familiar from statistics, provides an ideal weighting function because it falls off fairly rapidly as you move away from the centre, so that only a few responses make a major contribution, but its tails stretch over a very large area, so that even distant responses make a small contribution.

The bottom of the inset in Figure 5a.9 shows the receptive field response profile of a typical on-centre retinal ganglion cell – a plot of the response of the cell to a spot of light at each position across the field. This profile can be modelled by adding together two normal distributions – one representing the excitatory centre (at the top of the inset), and one representing the broader, negative inhibitory surround (in the middle of the inset). In effect, it seems that the responses of many photoreceptors are first averaged by retinal interneurons to reduce 'noise', using a normal distribution as the weighting function. Then retinal cells make spatial comparisons by combining a small-scale excitatory average with a large-scale inhibitory average centred on the same position. The result of this process is shown in the bottom line of Figure 5a.9 – the response to a 'noisy' edge (Figure 5a.9 top line) across a set of retinal ganglion cells, each with a receptive field profile like that shown at the bottom of the inset. These cells do not respond very much to the random fluctuations evident in the image, but nonetheless give a strong, characteristic 'peak-trough' response centred upon the original edge.

SOME THINGS THE RETINA CANNOT DO

All of the above discussion is based on the assumption that luminance edges in the image correspond to changes in reflectance in the external world. This is very often true – for example, at the boundaries of surface markings, like a leopard's spots, and at the boundary between an object and its background. But it's not *always* true. Sometimes a luminance edge is produced by a change in lighting rather than a change in reflectance – for example, at the edge between two surfaces of an object with one surface angled more toward the light and therefore better lit, or at the edge of a shadow cast upon a flat surface. Both these cases are potentially useful in telling us about how surfaces are arranged in 3D and about the direction and type of light source. But they emphasise that we cannot simply 'read off' the output of retinal ganglion cells as always telling us about reflectance. Instead, each feature in the retinal 'line-drawing' that retinal ganglion cells convey needs to be carefully interpreted. No matter how clever the eyeball, we also need a brain.

IMPLICATIONS

The network of cells making up the retina 'compress' the raw image data so that retinal ganglion cells signal only its luminance edges. Interneurons first clean up the image using weighted averages and then make spatial comparisons in all directions and at a range of spatial scales.

By considering some of the problems that have to be overcome in detecting luminance edges in the image, we gain some insight into just how elegant these processes are. Indeed, computer systems designed to process and enhance images make use of very similar techniques and, although different approaches are often based upon very different and sometimes complex mathematics, all end up with 'receptive fields' just like those of retinal ganglion cells. By gradually forming and shaping the network of cells that make up the retina, using only simple excitatory and inhibitory connections, evolution has proved an excellent engineer.

FURTHER READING

Bruce V., Green P. R., & Georgeson, M. A. (2003). *Visual Perception: Physiology, Psychology and Ecology*, 4th edition. Hove & London: Psychology Press.
Chapter 5, in particular, provides a more detailed and technical but eminently readable account of retinal processing, as well as developing the approach to include cortical processing and to include the description of other aspects of the image, such as motion.

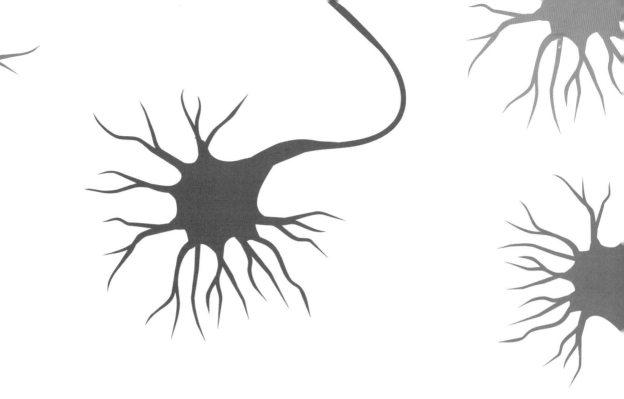

CHAPTER 6

MOTOR CONTROL

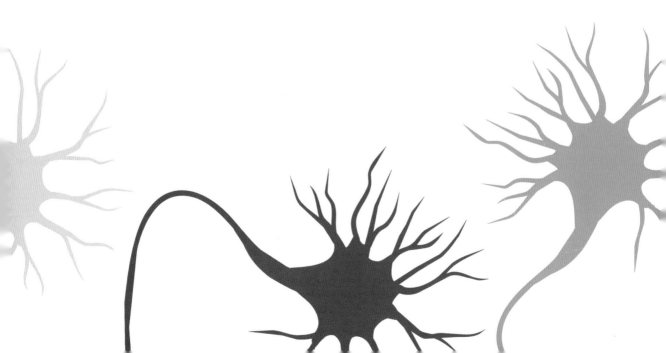

> # CHAPTER BREAKDOWN
>
> - How muscles contract and how they are controlled by nerves.
> - From simple reflex circuits to complex interactions in the spinal cord.
> - The primary motor cortex and its connections to spinal circuits.
> - Building complex actions from simple movements in the secondary motor cortex.
> - Selecting movements in the basal ganglia.
> - Planning movements in the parietal cortex.
> - Learning and refining movements in the cerebellum.

ROADMAP

Place this book on a flat surface in front of you, then reach out and grasp a corner of the page as if to turn it. You almost certainly managed this without much thinking beyond simply deciding to do it. So, without conscious effort, you moved your arm smoothly and accurately from wherever it was to wherever you wanted it to be. It arrived with your hand already in the right position to grip the page and you picked it up with just the right amount of pressure. And, still without even being aware of it, you probably shifted your body slightly to remain balanced as your arm extended in front of you. How is all this achieved so effortlessly and with a minimum of conscious intrusion?

In an attempt to answer these questions, this chapter starts by describing how muscles contract and how their control is organised within the spinal cord to produce simple movements. We next consider the primary motor cortex and the spinal pathways through which it can control these simple movements. We go on to discuss how simple movements are combined within the secondary motor cortex to achieve coherent actions, how actions are selected within the basal ganglia, and how they are planned within the parietal cortex. Finally, we outline the role of the cerebellum in improving these plans through trial and error, so that actions become smooth, accurate, and largely automatic.

MUSCLES AND THEIR INNERVATION

Muscles are attached to the skeleton by tendons and can pull, by actively shortening, but not push. Nor do they need to, for they are arranged in opposition to each other around joints so that active contraction of one muscle passively stretches the other. Often, several muscles work together as **agonists** and are opposed by several **antagonists**. For example, the biceps acts with the brachialis and coracobrachialis as **flexors** to bend the elbow, while the triceps acts with the anconeus as **extensors** to straighten it.

Each muscle is made up of many bundles of **extrafusal muscle fibres**, arranged in parallel along the muscle and individually capable of contracting. There are two main types of extrafusal fibre: slow fibres are relatively sluggish but can maintain their contraction over long periods and are suited to tasks like keeping us standing up, whereas fast fibres are more dynamic but fatigue more easily and are suited to more strenuous activities like running.

These different properties arise from a difference in the enzymes releasing the energy needed for contraction. Each muscle contains the appropriate mixture of slow and fast fibres to suit a particular range of tasks. Muscles can adjust this mixture over time to reflect changes in behaviour because each muscle fibre's type depends on the pattern of neural activity it receives; intermittent, high frequency bursts of neural activity produce fast fibres whereas sustained, low frequency activity produces slow fibres.

The arrival of a single action potential at a **neuromuscular junction** is sufficient to cause a brief contraction of the muscle fibre, called a twitch. Acetylcholine released at the junction causes an excitatory potential that opens voltage-gated Na^+ channels in the muscle membrane and, much as in an axon, produces an action potential in the muscle fibre. This releases Ca^{++} which, in turn, causes interleaved filaments of two proteins, **actin** and **myosin**, to slide over each other, shortening the muscle fibre. In the presence of Ca^{++}, the ends of individual myosin filaments form links that move like tiny oars, 'rowing' myosin along the actin, as shown in Figure 6.1. Unlike a

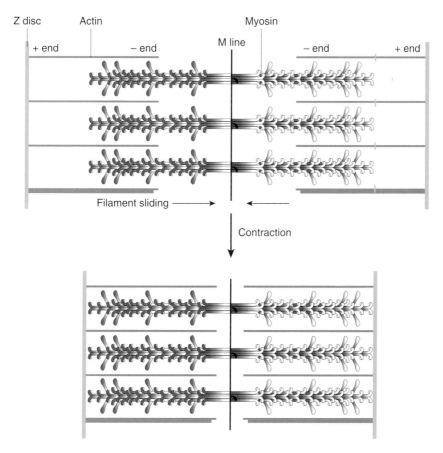

Figure 6.1 Muscle fibre contraction. The tips of the myosin fibrils 'row' themselves along the actin filaments, causing the muscle to shorten

well-drilled rowing eight, the filaments move in waves rather than all together, so that there are always some links between the actin and myosin. After the action potential, the Ca^{++} is mopped up, all the links are broken, and the muscle fibre relaxes.

Extrafusal muscle fibres are innervated by alpha motoneurons that have their cell bodies in the ventral horn of the spinal cord (see Figure 6.2). Each motoneuron typically forms many neuromuscular junctions with a given fibre, so that it contracts throughout its length at the same time. Each motoneuron also innervates several different muscle fibres, and the neuron and its associated muscle fibres are together called a **motor unit**. All the muscle fibres in a motor unit are of the same type because they all receive the same pattern of neural activity. Motor units vary considerably in size; those in the muscles of the eyelid, which makes only relatively weak movements, involve only a few muscle fibres, whereas those in the more powerful thigh muscles typically involve many hundreds. Each muscle involves many motor units, with their cell bodies close together in the spinal cord, forming a **motor pool**.

Since activity in a motoneuron causes all its innervated muscle fibres to contract, motor units provide the smallest functional elements with which to control the strength of contraction. At moderate firing rates of the motoneuron, the individual twitches in the muscle fibres merge together over time to produce a smooth, **tetanic contraction**. As the firing rate increases further, the strength of this smooth contraction increases. However, this increase is rather limited in range and the main means of controlling tension is by recruitment of additional motor units. At low levels of excitation of the motor pool, just a few motor units will be active. As excitation increases, these motor units quickly saturate and additional motor units are recruited. Recruitment follows a strict order determined by size, with the smallest motor units (those with fewest muscle fibres) responding first, and the largest responding last. Consequently, we have finer control of movement when we are relaxed than when our muscles are tensed and therefore using large motor units.

KEY POINTS

- Each **alpha motoneuron** innervates several extrafusal muscle fibres within a muscle. The nerve and its associated muscle fibres together form a motor unit.
- Activity within an alpha motoneuron releases Acetylcholine at neuromuscular junctions, causing an action potential in each muscle fibre, which produces a contractile twitch as actin and myosin molecules slide over each other to shorten the fibre.
- Smooth contraction is achieved by the fusion of a rapid series of twitches within each muscle fibre, and by simultaneous activity in several motor units.

THE SPINAL CORD

Figure 6.2 shows the circuitry of the spinal stretch reflex, an example of the simplest functional sensorimotor system capable of producing an appropriate movement to an external stimulus. First, consider the part of the circuit shown in red. Muscle spindles, located throughout the muscle, in parallel with the extrafusal fibres, are innervated by sensory nerves with their cell bodies in the dorsal root ganglia, close to the spinal cord. Stretching the spindle, for example by exerting some force on the relevant joint, causes a response in the sensory nerve and this directly excites the alpha motoneuron via a synapse in the spinal cord, causing the muscle to

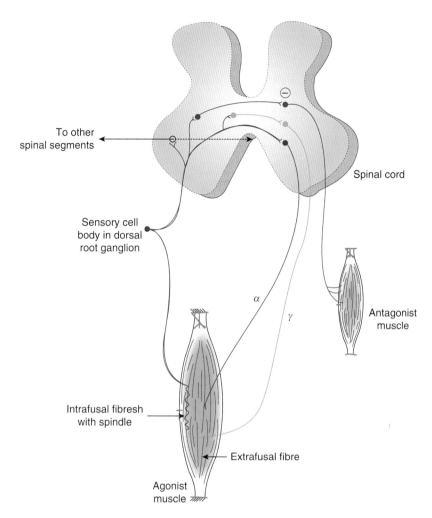

Figure 6.2   Spinal circuitry. The spinal stretch reflex, involving muscle spindles, alpha motoneurons, and extrafusal muscle fibres, is shown in red. The innervation of the intrafusal muscle fibres by gamma motoneurons is shown in green. The inhibitory loop to relax the antagonistic muscle is shown in blue. The connections to (and from) other spinal segments are indicated in black.

contract. This is an example of a negative feedback loop, a general method of keeping a system at some required level by automatically opposing any departure from it. In this case, the attempt to *increase* muscle length produces a response tending to *decrease* it. Note that there is no need to detect attempts to shorten a muscle because they will always be accompanied by attempts to stretch the antagonistic muscle. Nor is there any point, because muscles cannot actively lengthen.

Feedback loops need a method of setting the required level, and this is shown in green in Figure 6.2. Muscle spindles are associated with **intrafusal muscle fibres** which are innervated by gamma motoneurons. These fibres can contract but are much weaker than extrafusal fibres, while gamma motoneurons conduct more slowly than alpha motoneurons. When a muscle contracts, alpha and gamma motoneurons generally fire together, the former acting to contract the muscle and the latter shortening the intrafusal fibres so that the spindles remain under tension and can detect the slightest stretch. In effect, the gamma motoneurons and intrafusal muscle fibres set the required length of the muscle, whilst the alpha motoneurons and extrafusal fibres achieve it and then, with the help of the spindles, maintain it. This elegant system allows you, for example, automatically to vary the force needed to keep your elbow at a fixed angle despite varying loads on your hand.

A further aspect of the stretch reflex is shown in blue in Figure 6.2. Activity in spindle fibres not only causes agonistic muscles to contract but also, via spinal interneurons, inhibits the contraction of antagonistic muscles. This type of inhibitory link facilitates the required withdrawal movement associated with the stretch reflex and, more generally, provides the basis of a simple pathway through which to balance the tension in opposing muscles.

One final, important refinement is not shown in detail in Figure 6.2. The movement of one part of the body generally requires compensatory changes in other parts in order to maintain balance; lifting one foot from the ground, for example, requires an increase in tension in both the agonists and antagonists of the other leg to take the additional load. To a large extent, these compensatory movements can be accomplished automatically, within the spinal cord, by interneurons running between segments and connecting circuits like the one illustrated in Figure 6.2. The expression 'running around like a headless chicken' has its origins in the disconcerting phenomenon, well known to farmers, in which headless chickens continue to run around. In other words, the spinal cord contains the circuitry underpinning sophisticated motor programmes and is quite capable, by itself, not only of producing complex, multi-limbed movements, but also of generating repetitive sequences like those involved in locomotion.

KEY POINTS

- Muscle spindles detect stretching within a muscle and activate alpha motoneurons via a synapse in the spinal cord to produce a compensatory contraction in a simple negative feedback system.
- Muscle spindles are wrapped around intrafusal muscle fibres, which are innervated by gamma motoneurons. Activity in a gamma motoneuron causes the intrafusal fibres to contract so that they maintain the same length as the extrafusal fibres and can detect any stretch away from this required length.
- Connections to antagonistic muscles within the same spinal region and to similar circuits in other spinal regions allow more complex movements to be built from these simple reflexes.

CORTICAL CONTROL OF MOVEMENTS AND ACTIONS

The main cortical areas involved in motor control are shown anatomically and schematically in Figure 6.3. The primary and secondary motor cortex, occupying neighbouring areas of the frontal lobe, form the final stages of central motor processing. They receive direct sensory input from the somatosensory and parietal cortex, involved in planning movements, and influence the motor circuits in the spinal cord through two descending tracts. The pyramidal tract descends laterally in the spinal column to connect directly with spinal motoneurons. It is concerned with finely controlled voluntary movements and when it is lesioned all such movements are abolished. The extra-pyramidal tract descends ventromedially in the

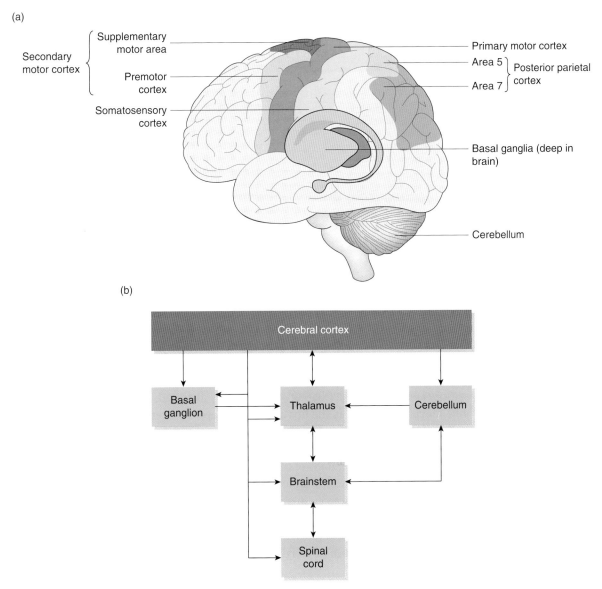

Figure 6.3   (a) Cortical anatomy showing the main areas involved in motor control. (b) Schematic diagram of the major pathways connecting the main regions

spinal column and does not connect directly with motoneurons. It is largely concerned with involuntary movements including the maintenance of posture and control of locomotion and posture. Almost all descending motor fibres cross over in the midbrain so that each cerebral hemisphere controls the movement of the opposite side of the body.

Through its two direct pathways to the spinal cord, the motor cortex can therefore initiate conscious movements, such as pointing, and can also command the largely unconscious postural adjustments that these voluntary movements may demand. In addition, the motor cortex also has two indirect outputs forming loops through the basal ganglia, involved in the selection of appropriate movements, and through the cerebellum, involved in learning and refining complex sequences of actions.

FOCUS ON METHODS: LESIONS

Lesions involve experimentally-induced damage to the brain. This allows studies to determine whether a brain area is necessary to carry out a given function. Lesions can be induced in three main ways. First, a region of the brain can be cut out, sucked out or simply destroyed (ablation). It is difficult to achieve selective damage to deep brain areas (leaving the overlying tissue intact) with this method. Electrolytic lesions involve the insertion of a stimulating electrode into the target region and then passing a high current through the electrode. The current causes death to nerve tissue in the area (both cell bodies and axons). Finally, selective damage to cell bodies in the target region can be achieved by excitotoxic lesions. This method involves the injection of a neurotoxin into the brain that overexcites the neurons to death. One example of such a neurotoxin is actually NMDA, which activates NMDA receptors.

PRIMARY MOTOR CORTEX

The primary motor cortex forms a strip across the top of the frontal lobe, immediately in front of the central sulcus (Figure 6.3a). It is somatotopically mapped into a motor homunculus so that stimulation of a given region of the cortex causes movement of a specific part of the body. Like its somatosensory counterpart (see Chapter 5), the map is distorted; parts of the body that are capable of fine movements, such as the lips and tongue, are represented by a correspondingly larger cortical area.

Just as different columns of cells within the visual cortex encode different orientations of simple visual features, different columns of cells within the primary motor cortex encode movements in different directions. Activity in a particular column might cause the right arm to move to the left, for example, whereas activity in a nearby column might cause it to move downward. And just as the overall visual code for feature orientation appears to depend upon the pattern of activity across a set of neighbouring orientation columns, the code for movement direction appears to depend upon the pattern of activity across a set of neighbouring columns tuned to different directions.

Although the motor homunculus and the underlying columnar organisation suggest a simple and direct linkage between cortical cells and specific muscles, the relationship is actually rather complex and indirect. Some cortical cells do appear to be active only when a specific muscle contracts, but others code for a particular movement irrespective of the pattern of muscular contraction involved – for example, a cell may respond during a leftward movement of the forearm, both when the movement is made with the palm of the hand facing upward (in which case a particular muscle might relax), or downward (in which case the same muscle might contract). Moreover, whereas some cells appear to be concerned with specifying the trajectory of a movement (i.e. its direction, speed or extent), others appear to encode the force necessary to achieve it. Cells in the monkey cortex, for example, fire more rapidly when a movement is made against a load than when the identical movement is made without resistance. These findings suggest that the primary motor cortex is equipped to command specific movements under a variety of circumstances, rather than simply controlling the contractions of individual muscles.

SECONDARY MOTOR CORTEX

The secondary motor cortex forms a strip across the frontal lobe immediately in front of the primary motor cortex. It consists of two areas: the supplementary motor area (SMA) forming the medial part of the strip, and the premotor cortex (PMC), forming the lateral part (Figure 6.3a). Both areas receive sensory input from the parietal cortex and both output directly to the spinal motor tracts and indirectly via the primary motor cortex. The secondary motor cortex is thus ideally equipped to select the individual movements encoded by the primary motor cortex (e.g. move the right forearm to the left) and to build them into the more complex sequences and patterns that make up more meaningful actions (e.g. reach out and grasp a visual target with the right arm).

fMRI studies support the idea that the secondary motor cortex plays a role in both planning and executing a movement, whereas the primary motor cortex is concerned only with execution. When we point at a target, for example, both primary and secondary motor cortex are active but, when we think about the same movement without actually making it, only the secondary motor cortex continues to respond. One particular type of cell found within the secondary motor cortex responds both when we make a particular movement and when we see or hear another person make the same movement. These **mirror neurons** are discussed in detail in Spotlight 6a.

The SMA is particularly important in controlling movements requiring coordination of the two arms, such as opening a bottle or clapping. More generally, it is responsible for intentional movements, i.e. those initiated *internally*, and with learning complex sequences. The PMC, on the other hand, is particularly important in postural control, ensuring that the rest of the body adopts an appropriate pose for a particular movement. More generally, in contrast to the SMA, it is involved in the planning and coordination of *externally* initiated movements, such as pointing at a visual target. If the PMC is lesioned to remove a tumour, patients no longer make the appropriate responses to a visual stimulus, even though they can still recognise the stimulus and can make the required movement in a different context.

KEY POINTS

- The pattern of activity across columns of cells in the primary motor cortex can encode a simple movement, such as an arm extension.
- The secondary motor cortex is important in planning and executing more meaningful actions, such as reaching for a visual target, building upon the simple movements controlled by the primary motor cortex.

INSIGHT: INTERNALLY AND EXTERNALLY GUIDED MOVEMENTS

The finding that internally and externally guided actions are coded in separate cortical regions merits an interesting aside. Niels Bohr, the influential theoretical physicist, was a fan of Westerns and frequently challenged his colleagues to quick-draw contests, which he apparently always won. Bohr

(Continued)

(Continued)

believed that the secret of his success was that he never drew until his opponent made the first move. This approach is somewhat vindicated by recent work by Welchman and colleagues (2010), who confirmed that a given movement is faster when made in reaction to an external stimulus than when intentionally initiated. This makes sense, given that a change in the external world is potentially dangerous and may require an immediate reaction, whereas intentional movements can generally afford the luxury of a slower but more accurate approach. It only partly accounts for Bohr's success, however, because the reaction time between the onset of the stimulus and starting to move far outweighs the slightly faster movement. So it seems likely that Bohr, who at one time kept goal in professional football, was simply an accomplished athlete as well as a Nobel Prize-winning scientist.

SELECTING THE APPROPRIATE MOVEMENT: THE ROLE OF THE BASAL GANGLIA

We are bombarded by sensory information about the world and we have at our disposal a wide range of possible actions for dealing with it. However, by and large, we can only attend to one thing at a time, and we can only do one thing at a time. Deciding what to attend to and what to do are clearly crucial to our survival and require a great deal of largely unconscious processing, much of which is carried out in the association regions of the frontal cortex. The basal ganglia play some role in making these decisions but, more importantly, they provide the neural machinery for implementing them, ensuring that the appropriate stimulus is attended to and that the appropriate response is properly selected once a decision has been made.

The striatum, consisting of the caudate nucleus and the putamen in primates, forms the main input stage of the basal ganglia, receiving information from all areas of the cortex and from the limbic system. It projects via two separate pathways to the output stage, which consists of the globus pallidus and the substantia nigra, and thence to the thalamus, which loops back to the cortex (see Figure 6.3b).

A *direct* pathway, as its name suggests, projects straight from the input to the output stage. It has a predominantly excitatory influence and is thought to 'enable' the required set of movements within the secondary motor cortex. An *indirect* pathway projects from the input to the output stage via the subthalamic nucleus. It has a predominantly inhibitory influence and is thought to 'veto' all the other, potentially incompatible, movements. More generally, this need to suppress inappropriate movements, which inevitably outnumber appropriate movements, accounts for the otherwise surprising finding that central motor pathways are predominantly inhibitory. Finally, the substantia nigra seems to play an important role in learning, modulating the balance of responses in the two pathways so that successful responses are more likely to be selected in future and unsuccessful responses are more likely to be suppressed.

This basic model is complicated by a network of additional excitatory and inhibitory loops between the various bodies of the basal ganglia – kept functionally separate by the use of different neurotransmitters. But whatever the details, it's clear that the selection function of the basal ganglia depends crucially upon the balance between excitatory and inhibitory influences. This is unfortunately illustrated by the profound effects on movement that emerge when the system goes wrong. For example, in Huntington's disease a lack of inhibitory GABAergic neurons in the indirect pathway weakens the suppression of inappropriate movements and results in spontaneous, jerky, dance-like movements. In contrast, in Parkinson's disease, a lack of dopaminergic neurons in the pathway from the substantia nigra weakens the excitatory effect of the direct pathway so that responses become slow and hesitant because of difficulties in selecting the appropriate action.

KEY POINTS

- The basal ganglia are important in selecting the movements required for a particular action. An excitatory pathway to the secondary motor cortex 'enables' the required movements, whilst an inhibitory pathway suppresses incompatible movements.
- Correct function depends upon a proper balance between excitatory and inhibitory neurotransmitters. Upsetting this balance leads to profound movement disorders, such as Parkinson's and Huntington's disease.

PLANNING: THE ROLE OF THE POSTERIOR PARIETAL CORTEX

Suppose that you have decided to point at a visual target and that the basal ganglia have accordingly selected the required movements of the shoulder, elbow, wrist and hand. How do you then go about deciding exactly how to coordinate these movements and how do you ensure that the movements are as you intend? One way to tackle this problem would be simply to start moving your arm in roughly the right direction and then gradually to home in by watching your hand in relation to the target. This type of feedback system, using visual information to correct any error in the initial trajectory, does play an important role in pointing but, though it is accurate, it has the major disadvantage of being relatively slow. To have enough time to register the visual information and to use it to make large corrections would limit us to rather slow movements – far too slow, for example, to accomplish a more demanding, interceptive task, such as catching a ball.

The motor system minimises the delays inherent in a feedback system and so can make rapid, accurate movements by also making use of feedforward information. It avoids the need for large corrections by developing not only an accurate plan of the required movement but also a prediction of its sensory consequences, which can rapidly be compared with the subsequent sensory feedback. Most of us are unfortunately familiar, for example, with the momentary feeling of horror when this planning goes wrong while descending a staircase and the 'final' step fails to produce the expected sensory confirmation of a firm surface beneath our feet.

The system for ensuring that the visual world remains stable despite movements of our eyes provides a simple example of this forward modelling. Eye movements often produce rapid and large shifts in the position of the image. We are not aware of these shifts and the visual world appears stable because the motor system produces not only a command to move the eyes but also a prediction of the resulting shift in the image. If this prediction matches the resulting shift, the visual world does not appear to move. You can demonstrate this to yourself, and confirm that the system does not rely on feedback alone, by closing one eye and very carefully moving the other eye with your finger. As your eye moves, the visual world appears to move in the opposite direction because in this situation there is no motor command to the eye muscles and therefore no predicted shift in the image to 'cancel' the actual shift in the image that your retina detects. It is also possible to do the complementary experiment, gently fixing your eye with your finger so that it remains stationary when you try to move it. Under these circumstances the visual world again appears to move because now the predicted shift is not 'cancelled' by an actual shift in the image.

It is relatively easy to plan and predict the sensory consequences of an eye movement because the eyes can move only by rotating in their sockets and they always present the same load, so that a given contraction of the muscles produces the same rotation of the eye and consequently the same shift in the image. Planning and predicting the sensory consequences of an arm movement is a much more formidable task. For example, the starting position of the arm will vary: there are many possible combinations of shoulder, elbow, and wrist angles that can achieve the same final position of the hand; and the load and thus the force required may change dramatically if you are carrying something or holding a tool. Moreover, the task has to be accomplished very quickly since the point of using a feedforward system is to allow more rapid responses than would be possible using feedback alone. All this is managed primarily within the posterior parietal cortex, though with important contributions from the cerebellum.

The posterior parietal cortex is well placed to plan movements, receiving input from all areas of the cortex and from the cerebellum, and outputting directly to the secondary motor cortex where coherent movements are coded. It is organised into a functional mosaic with different areas concerned with the movement of different parts of the body, such as the eyes or limbs. One area, sometimes termed the parietal reach region (PRR), is particularly concerned with arm movements. Its role is thought to be to devise a motor plan that includes the changes in the angles of the joints needed to achieve a particular arm position, and a prediction of the sensory feedback that the movement will produce. To achieve this, it must integrate proprioceptive information from the somatosensory cortex about the current positions of the limbs into a sophisticated body schema that can incorporate tools so that they feel like parts of our body, allowing us to adjust our movements accordingly (see Chapter 5).

As an important destination of the visual dorsal stream, the PRR receives information about the spatial layout of the visual world, and must use this to code the relative positions of the arm and the target. It must also take into account knowledge about the relevant properties and functions of objects, for example that eggs are fragile and need to be gripped gently or that a pencil should be picked up so that it can be used for writing rather than with the pointy bit upward or with fingers firmly clasping it to your palm. And finally, of course, it must convert all this sensory and cognitive information into an appropriate set of motor commands.

Cells within the PRR do possess some of the properties needed to solve these complex problems. Recordings from monkeys show that some cells' responses correlate with the current visual directions of the hand and of the target, while others seem to encode the distance and direction of the target relative to the hand – perhaps providing a suitable signal on which to base a motor command. Moreover, processing seems to be appropriately flexible. For example, imaging studies show that responses within the same region reflect the visual directions of the arm and target during visually-guided pointing, but reflect the position of the arm relative to the body when the same movement is made with eyes closed. Even though we do not yet know the details of the neural processing involved, signals within the PRR do seem to provide the working basis of a motor plan. Simultaneous recordings from groups of cells within the monkey parietal cortex, made while the monkey makes directed movements of a cursor around a screen using a computer mouse, can be processed externally to reproduce the same movements of the cursor. Even though the movements involved are only two-dimensional and therefore relatively simple, this clearly raises the tantalising prospect of harnessing sophisticated neural processes to the control of artificial limbs.

No matter how sophisticated the plan devised within the posterior parietal cortex, it can only be as good as the information on which it is based. Some of that information is immediately available, such as the current visual direction of a target. But other crucial information, such as how a moving arm is likely to react when a particular muscle exerts a given force, can only be learned by trial and error. Such learning takes place within the cerebellum, which is also concerned with the fine control of movements by correcting any immediate deviations from the current plan.

KEY POINTS

- The posterior parietal cortex integrates signals from the sensory cortices to produce a 'forward plan' of any intended movement. This includes a prediction of the sensory feedback that the movement will produce, allowing any small deviations to be rapidly corrected.
- Eye movements provide a simple example of forward planning. The visual world remains stable because the actual movement of the image matches the predicted movement.
- The parietal reach region (PRR) is specialised to produce the forward plans needed for complex reaching movements of the arm.

LEARNING AND CONTROL: THE ROLE OF THE CEREBELLUM

Think back to your first attempts to acquire a new motor skill – perhaps changing gear when learning to drive, or playing a scale on a musical instrument. Despite focusing all your conscious attention, your efforts were probably embarrassingly primitive, consisting of a series of discrete and sometimes inappropriate movements – for example, moving your hand toward the gear lever, grasping it firmly, and then attempting to move it tentatively in the wrong direction followed by a convulsive, corrective lunge as your foot prematurely released the clutch. Yet, with practice, your hand, arm and feet came to move smoothly and simultaneously in what feels like a single fluid movement requiring no conscious attention.

When the cerebellum is lesioned, this improvement with practice is abolished, and movements are typically rather inaccurate and can only be accomplished as a series of discrete stages. But normally, given an initial crude plan requiring continuous and sometimes drastic modification through feedback, the cerebellum can not only make the necessary corrections but can gradually learn, through repeated trial and error, the proper timings, the forces required, and the sensory feedback associated with an efficient movement. Feeding this information back to the parietal cortex produces a forward plan that normally requires little or no modification through feedback, so that we come to change gear or play a musical scale almost automatically, or to be able to reach out and grasp a visual target with our eyes closed. Through diligent practice, the forward plans of professional athletes become so accurate that basketball players, for example, can make accurate shots even when the lights are turned out just as they begin their throw.

The cerebellum is also important in monitoring and, if necessary correcting, the relationship between the different sensory modalities. For example, we normally have both proprioceptive and visual information about the current position of the arms, and it is important that they agree – when you *see* your arm straight in front of you, for example, it should also *feel* straight in front of you. When people wear a displacing prism that shifts their visual world to one side, they, not surprisingly, lose the ability to point accurately at a visual target. But if they repeatedly try to point and can see their errors, they learn within a few minutes to point accurately again, despite the distortion of the prism. When they subsequently remove the prism, they again make errors – this time in the opposite direction – and, if asked to close their eyes and hold their arm straight ahead of them, they hold it at an angle. Fortunately, this effect is temporary and with a little practice, they rapidly return to normal. Lesions of the cerebellum completely abolish the ability to learn to adapt to the prism. This suggests that the cerebellum constantly monitors proprioceptive and visual information and, if there is any consistent disagreement, modifies felt position to bring it in line with vision, which (prisms notwithstanding) normally provides the more reliable information about direction.

The cerebellum is part of the hindbrain and contains more than half of the total number of cells in the entire brain. Like the forebrain, it consists mainly of a highly folded cortex although, in this case, the folds are very regular like those of an accordion (see Figure 6.3). Also like the forebrain, the surface of the cerebellar cortex contains a distorted somatotopic map with different patches, or microzones, concerned with different parts of the body. However, unlike the cerebral cortex where there is a great deal of connectivity between adjacent regions, each microzone of the cerebellum appears to function largely independently of its neighbours. And, because the cerebellum is located after fibres from the cortex cross over, each half of the cerebellum controls the *same* side of the body.

The cerebellar cortex has an unusually regular structure consisting of three layers, shown diagrammatically in Figure 6.4. The deepest layer contains the tiny cell bodies of granule cells, which are by far the most common type of cell within the cerebellum and thus the brain. The axons of each granule cell project up through the cortex to the surface layer, where they split into two 'parallel fibres' running in opposite directions parallel to the cortical surface. The middle layer contains the cell bodies of Purkinje cells. The dendrites of the Purkinje cells

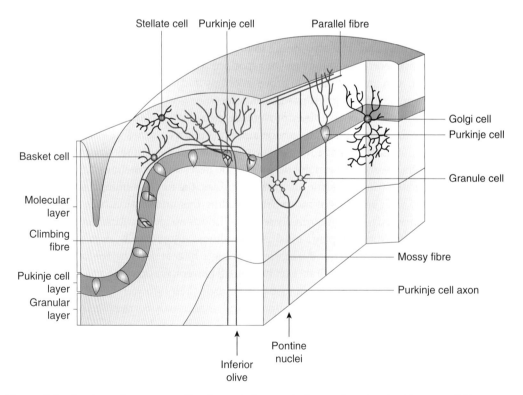

Figure 6.4   A schematic cross-section through the cerebellar cortex showing the overall three-layered structure and some of the main cell and fibre types

Source: Ramnani (2006)

project up into the surface layer where they form very flat dendritic trees at right angles to the parallel fibres. Each parallel fibre runs through and synapses with the dendrites of several Purkinje cells, while each Purkinje cell receives input from many parallel fibres. Inhibitory axons from the Purkinje cells form the outputs of the cerebellar cortex, each projecting to one of several deep cerebellar nuclei which, in turn, provide the output of the cerebellum.

The cerebellum receives input from two types of cell. Mossy fibres carry sensory input from the cortex and spinal cord and form excitatory synapses with granule cells and with the output cells in the deep cerebellar nuclei. Each granule cell receives input from several mossy fibres. Climbing fibres, originating in the inferior olive and carrying information from the cortex, form excitatory synapses with the cell bodies of Purkinje cells and with the deep cerebellar output cells. Each Purkinje cell receives input from just one climbing fibre, but the connection is so strong that a single spike in a climbing fibre causes a train of spikes in the Purkinje cell. In contrast, inputs from many parallel fibres are needed before the Purkinje cells responds.

Cells in the deep cerebellar nuclei thus receive excitation from mossy fibres and climbing fibres, and inhibition from Purkinje cells. They provide excitatory output to cells in the sensory and motor areas and an inhibitory output to the same cells in the inferior olive that provided their excitatory input via climbing fibres.

All of this detail might seem unnecessarily complex but we are, after all, dealing with the brain, and the cerebellum actually also contains several other types of cell. In fact, it is the relative simplicity and regularity of the cerebellar anatomy that has led to a great deal of research into how it functions. So far, no clear answer has emerged, but there are many tantalising possibilities. For example, cerebellar output cells receive both a direct excitatory input from mossy and climbing fibres and an indirect inhibitory input, based on the same information, from Purkinje cells. This suggests a mechanism for comparing the current sensory state with whatever transformation of it that Purkinje cells are providing, before relaying the signal to the spinal cord and back to the sensory and motor cortex. Similarly, there are a huge number granule cells and thus of parallel fibres and, if each responds only when several of its sensory inputs are active, this might provide a way to represent different combinations of sensory activity. The fact that many parallel fibres themselves need to be active before a Purkinje cell responds might represent a further necessary stage in catering for all the myriad possible combinations. On the other hand, the fact that a single spike in a climbing fibre can cause a response in a Purkinje cell suggests a mechanism for modifying its particular set of input connections and thus favouring or discouraging the particular combination that they represent. Most theories of cerebellar function do regard climbing fibres as crucial in learning, and some hold that their response might strengthen the connections from simultaneously active parallel fibres, thus helping Purkinje cells to represent the particular combinations of input that are particularly relevant. Others hold that the response of a climbing fibre signals an error, i.e. some deviation from expectation. This would obviously be particularly attractive if the error were between current feedback and a predetermined plan, since such a signal would be useful both in learning and in immediate control.

KEY POINTS

- The cerebellum is responsible for the learning and 'automation' of complex movements. It works with the posterior parietal cortex to develop and monitor forward plans, and it ensures that directional information from different sensory systems is correctly aligned.
- The cerebellum has a very regular cellular architecture, which appears well suited to the tasks of comparing predicted with actual sensory feedback and of detecting and correcting any errors.

CHAPTER SUMMARY

Look back at the opening sentences of this chapter and consider what is involved in the apparently simple act of reaching out and turning the page. Your basal ganglia select the appropriate movements of your arm and temporarily suppress any incompatible movements. Your posterior parietal cortex formulates a sophisticated forward plan specifying the sequence of movements required and predicting the type of sensory feedback to expect. This plan includes information about how and how hard to grasp the page, and relies upon knowledge gained through repeated trial and error by the cerebellum. Since this is an externally guided movement the pre-motor cortex becomes active in anticipation of your movement, and your primary motor cortex responds to initiate the movement. At the same time, the pre-motor cortex also automatically organises any postural changes that are needed to maintain your balance. The outputs from the motor cortex recruit the appropriate motor circuits in the spinal cord and set in train a series of events leading to coordinated changes in the shape of billions of molecules, causing tiny filaments to slide over each other as the appropriate sets of muscles contract and relax. Information from sensors in the muscles and joints is fed back to the cerebellum, which detects and corrects any deviations from the plan and, if necessary, informs the parietal cortex of any changes needed for future plans. All of this happens with a minimum of conscious awareness, which fortunately leaves you free to concentrate on the task of reading about how it's done.

FURTHER READING

Graziano, M. (2008). *The Intelligent Movement Machine: An Ethological Perspective on the Primate Motor System.* **USA: Oxford University Press.**

  An interesting, and controversial, alternative view of how movement is organised in the cortex.

Heuer, H. & Keele, S. W. (eds) (1995). *Handbook of Perception and Action: Motor Skills, Volume 2.* **New York: Academic Press.**

  Still an excellent source, providing detailed reviews of many aspects of motor control.

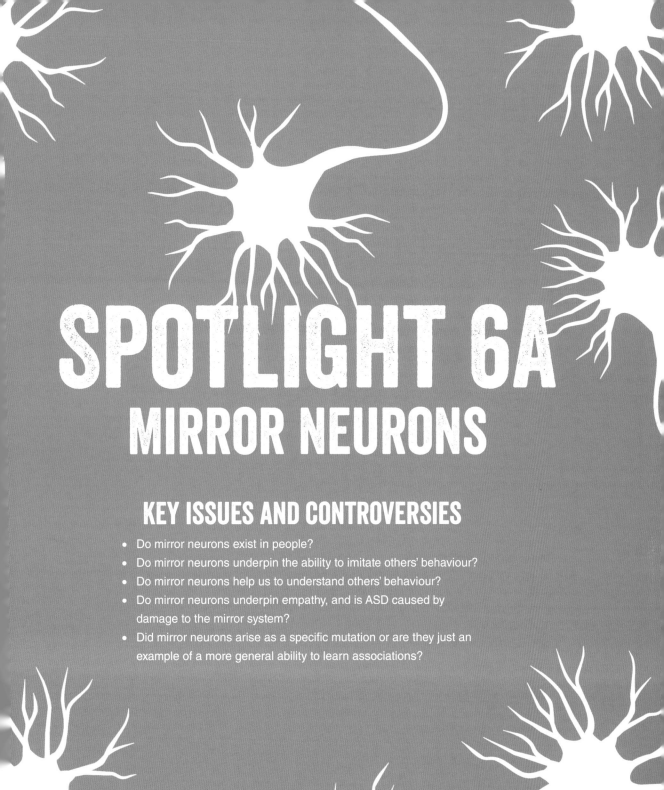

SPOTLIGHT 6A
MIRROR NEURONS

KEY ISSUES AND CONTROVERSIES

- Do mirror neurons exist in people?
- Do mirror neurons underpin the ability to imitate others' behaviour?
- Do mirror neurons help us to understand others' behaviour?
- Do mirror neurons underpin empathy, and is ASD caused by damage to the mirror system?
- Did mirror neurons arise as a specific mutation or are they just an example of a more general ability to learn associations?

INTRODUCTION

Mirror neurons are cells that respond not only when a monkey performs an action, such as cracking a peanut or exploring it with the lips, but also when the monkey sees or hears another monkey, or an experimenter, performing the same action. First described in the early 1980s (Perrett et al., 1982; 1985), they did not arouse particular interest or acquire their name until the early 1990s, when a team led by Giacomo Rizzolatti reported them in part of the premotor cortex (Di Pellegrino et al., 1992) and later also in part of the parietal cortex (Fogassi et al., 1998) of macaque monkeys. Since then, they have provoked a great deal of controversy. Even their very existence in human beings was uncertain until very recently. Nonetheless, much of the discussion has assumed that human mirror neurons do exist and has centred instead upon what they are for. One suggestion is that they enable imitation and learning by observation. Another is that they play a crucial role in understanding others' behaviour, from making sense of simple actions, to providing the neural basis of empathy and social cognition – and consequently explaining autistic spectrum disorder (ASD) if their function is impaired.

This discussion is further complicated by the fact that mirror neurons are often linked to a fundamental theory of brain function called, in its most general form, 'situated cognition'. The relevant aspect of this holds that thinking is not just the abstract manipulation of meaningful symbols, but actually depends on the same neural machinery that we use when we actually perceive or do something – imagining a movement makes use of our motor systems, and imagining what something looks like makes use of our visual systems, and so forth.

Mirror neurons fit neatly with this theory by suggesting an ideal link between our sensory and other systems. In the simplest case, they might allow us to bring knowledge about how and why we perform certain actions to the process of making sense of those actions in others. Consequently, evidence for situated cognition is often taken as evidence for mirror neurons, and evidence for mirror neurons is often taken as evidence for situated cognition, even when neither conclusion is fully justified.

Many theories of mirror neuron function imply that they arose as a specific evolutionary advance that made possible some new advantageous behaviour – the ability to learn by imitation, for example. The alternative holds that mirror neurons are not 'special' in this way but simply arise from a more general ability to learn associations between things that frequently occur together – a motor act and its sensory consequences, for example. This view holds that mirror neurons might contribute to a wide range of activities, rather than being crucial to the evolution of just one specific ability.

As we review each of these areas, bear in mind that, though they are often credited with very sophisticated abilities, mirror neurons do not act alone. They presumably form part of a much more extensive network connected to, on the one hand, neural systems concerned with the complex analysis of sensory data and, on the other, to neural systems concerned with the complex programming of actions. The properties of mirror neurons therefore reflect the results of processing within other complex systems rather than the processing carried out by the mirror neurons themselves.

MIRROR NEURONS IN MONKEYS AND PEOPLE

Mirror neurons make up 10–25% of recorded units in the relevant areas of the monkey premotor and parietal cortex. They do not require a specific, stereotyped movement, but instead respond

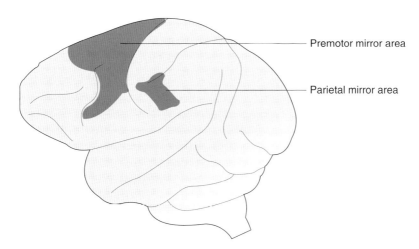

Premotor mirror area

Parietal mirror area

Figure 6a.1 Schematic diagram showing the cortical areas containing mirror neurons in the monkey

Source: Adapted from Pineda, 2008

to a particular goal-directed action, such as grasping or sucking, no matter how it is performed. They respond only when both an action and its target are involved, and not to either the target or the action by itself. However, the nature of the target does not matter – grasping a toy block or a peanut produces the same response. For some 'strictly congruent' cells, the observed and executed actions are the same. For other 'broadly congruent' cells, the observed action need only be roughly the same as the executed action – for example a cell that responds only when the monkey grasps an object might respond whenever the monkey sees any goal-directed arm movement.

Until recently, there has been only indirect evidence that mirror neurons exist in human beings. For example, EEG recordings show the same changes when an observer observes and performs the same action. In addition, when the motor cortex is weakly activated using TMS, small motor evoked potentials (MEPs) can be detected in the corresponding muscles when an observer passively watches an action. And fMRI recordings show that some areas, including the human equivalents of monkey mirror regions in the premotor and parietal cortices, are active both when observing and performing the same action (see Molenberghs et al., 2012 for a review). Taken together, this evidence shows that sensory and motor information is tightly coupled together, sometimes in the same cortical areas, and suggests that some sort of 'mirror system' exists within the human brain. But it does not prove that the *same* cells are involved in the sensory and motor aspects of the tasks and so it does not confirm the existence of human mirror neurons.

One indirect technique to address this problem uses cross-modal adaptation, relying on the fact that neurons temporarily reduce their response when they are repeatedly activated. If mirror neurons are activated by repeating a goal-directed action, then the ability to perceive the same action should subsequently be affected. Conversely, repeated observation of a goal-directed action should affect the ability to perform the same action. Cells that respond only to motor or only to sensory stimulation should not show this cross-modal effect. Results using this technique have so far been equivocal. Using fMRI, Dinstein et al. (2007) reported several areas of the human brain that reduced their activity to both motor and sensory stimulation, but none that exhibited the required cross-modal reduction. However, more recently, by monitoring performance rather than brain activity, Glenberg et al. (2010) showed that participants who repeatedly moved beans away from or towards themselves (a task that should activate mirror neurons since it involves both a movement and a target) were subsequently biassed in judging whether a computer-simulated hand holding a bean was moving towards or away from them.

The most direct and ultimately convincing evidence of human mirror neurons did not emerge until 2010. Using electrodes that had been implanted as part of the long-term treatment for epilepsy, Fried and his co-workers (Mukamel et al., 2010) were able to record the activity of individual cells in 21 patients as they observed or made grasping movements and facial expressions. They found cells with mirror properties in the expected prefrontal and parietal areas, but also in other areas, including the supplementary motor area (SMA) and the hippocampus. Interestingly, some of these cells were excited during action but inhibited during observation. These findings demonstrate that human mirror neurons do exist, and also suggest that they may be more extensive and complex than those found in monkeys.

THE POSSIBLE FUNCTIONS OF HUMAN MIRROR NEURONS

Imitation

Perhaps the most obvious potential function of mirror neurons would be to support imitation and learning by observation, both of which require an observer to repeat an action after observing it. Early work did not emphasise this potential role because of a general belief that macaques do not imitate or learn by observation. Nonetheless, recent reports that infant macaques do in fact imitate (Ferrari et al., 2006), and that adults are capable of learning behaviours that they see others performing (Subiaul et al., 2004), have reawakened interest in this topic. For example, imitation is rather rare amongst animals and so it is particularly intriguing that audio-vocal mirror neurons have been reported in birds that do imitate and learn the local song dialects of their peers (Keller and Hahnloser, 2009). It remains possible, though, that there are other animals that possess mirror neurons but do not imitate.

It is difficult to establish a role for mirror neurons in human imitation because imitation necessarily involves both observation and action so that it is difficult to isolate these separate components. However, Catmur et al. (2008) avoided this problem by asking participants to move either their index or little finger depending on the colour of a visual cue. In imitation trials, each cue was accompanied by an irrelevant image of the correct finger making the required response, whilst control trial cues were paired with the wrong finger. Performance was better in imitation trials and, crucially, this advantage was abolished by rTMS to the inferior frontal gyrus, an area believed to contain mirror neurons. This result provides indirect evidence that mirror neurons might at least facilitate imitative behaviour even if they are not essential for imitation.

Despite these somewhat equivocal and circumstantial findings, the notion that mirror neurons are crucially involved in imitation is fundamental to two much more general speculations. First, Ramachandran (2000) has suggested that human mirror neurons might have driven the sudden and dramatic range of advances, including the development of increasingly sophisticated tools and the mastery of fire, that appeared more or less simultaneously about 40,000 years ago. He argues that the ability to learn by copying would have allowed new developments to spread quickly through a population rather than remaining confined to those who first stumbled upon them.

Second, Arbib & Rizzolatti (1997; see also Arbib, 2005) have speculated that our capacity for language has its origins in the ability to communicate through gesture, and that mirror neurons played two essential roles in its evolution. Not only would they have underpinned the imitative behaviour needed for gestures to spread and become established, but they would also have allowed the understanding of another's gestures, as described in the next section.

Given their historical nature, neither of these interesting speculations is directly testable, but the second at least is not supported by circumstantial evidence; sign language is a contemporary, gesture-based language but fMRI suggests that the mirror system is not active during sign perception (Emmorey et al., 2010).

Understanding actions

The idea that the motor system might be involved in perception may seem strange, but it has a long history. When planning an action, we generate not only the required motor commands but also a 'forward model' of the sensory consequences of that action (see Chapter 6). If we could recruit this same sensorimotor representation when we observe someone else's behaviour, then it might be useful in making sense of that behaviour (see, for example, Prinz, 1990). Making sense of speech illustrates this type of theory and the potential role that mirror neurons might play in it.

Speech perception

The auditory stimuli associated with individual speech sounds depend a great deal upon their immediate context. For example, the sound waveform corresponding to the sound /b/ is very different when it is followed by /e/ from when it is followed by /o/ because the mouth needs to adopt a different shape in each situation. Sub-vocalising when listening to speech might give us an idea of what the mouth and tongue need to do to produce a particular sound in a particular context, and so might help us to understand the sounds we hear (e.g. Liberman et al., 1967).

There does appear to be a context-sensitive link between speech production and forward planning. For example, if you imagine saying the word 'bubble' whilst pursing your lips ready to whistle, you'll probably find yourself imagining something like 'wuh-wul'. Moreover, watching a speaker's mouth can certainly affect what we hear. In the McGurk effect (McGurk and MacDonald, 1976), when the speech sound /ba/ is synchronised with a video of the speaker saying /ga/, it is consistently heard as /da/ because it is not possible to say /b/ without closing the lips.

Mirror neurons seem ideally placed to provide the necessary link between observing the speaker's mouth movements and our own motor system, allowing us to generate a forward model of the expected speech sound that we can compare with the incoming auditory waveform. Moreover, the location of mirror neurons in monkeys coincides with Broca's area in humans, which is known to be important in speech production, and several fMRI analyses (e.g. Fadiga et al., 2002; Pulvermüller et al., 2006) have reported that this area is active during speech perception. Finally, using TMS to stimulate the part of the motor cortex concerned with lip and tongue movement does produce a small (10%) improvement in the speed of speech recognition (D'Ausilio et al., 2009). However, temporarily disrupting these regions with rTMS seems to have no effect on speech perception (Mottonen & Watkins, 2009; Sato et al., 2009). In general, rTMS has an effect only when the speech stimulus is degraded, for example by embedding it in noise. All this suggests that the motor system, and thus probably mirror neurons, are not essential for speech perception, though they may contribute to it under some conditions.

Perceiving simple actions

A similar story emerges when considering the possible role of mirror neurons in perceiving simple actions, such as reaching or grasping. Common sense tells us that the motor system is not essential for perceiving actions because we can understand things that we are unable to do, such as flying. Nonetheless, the motor system, and possibly mirror neurons, may play some role in action perception.

For example, performing an action, or watching someone else performing an action, can affect a related percept. Repp & Knoblich (2009) showed that, when pianists moved their hands either leftward or rightward on a keyboard, they tended to hear an ambiguous pitch change to be compatible with their movement – rising when they moved the hand rightward and falling when they moved leftward. More directly relevantly to mirror neurons, pianists, but not non-pianists, showed a similar bias when they watched someone else's hand moving on the keyboard.

In addition, neuropsychological patients who have difficulty in making sense of action photographs often have lesions in the regions of the premotor and parietal cortex associated with mirror neurons (Tranel et al., 2003). And, finally, rTMS to the premotor cortex seems selectively to disrupt action perception, since it impairs participants' ability to judge the weight of a box lifted by an actor but not the weight of a bouncing ball (Pobric & Hamilton, 2006).

Supporters of the idea that the motor system is involved in action perception argue that, though not essential, access to one's own motor representations – presumably via mirror neurons – provides a better understanding of others' behaviour. This implies that the better you are at doing something, the better you should be at perceiving it. There is some evidence that this is true. For example, expert basketball players are better than expert watchers (sports journalists) at judging whether a free throw will hit or miss the target when shown a brief video clip of the beginning of the throwing movement (Aglioti et al., 2008). These behavioural effects may reflect changes at the neural level, possibly involving mirror neurons. Calvo-Merino et al. (2005) used fMRI to show increased activation of parts of the premotor and parietal cortex when dancers watched video clips of dancing, but only when the dance movements were ones that they normally performed. Importantly, to rule out the possibility that the dancers had watched a great deal of dancing and so had simply become better at making use of purely sensory data, they also showed that the increased activation was gender specific – even though they had reportedly watched men and women equally often, increased activation was found only when dancers watched their own gender, whose repertoire matched their own motor expertise (Calvo-Merino et al., 2006).

Inferring intention

One of the more controversial claims about the role of mirror neurons suggests that they might provide a limited form of mind reading. By activating our own motor representations when we see somebody performing an action, mirror neurons might not only help us to recognise the action but might also place us, in a limited sense at least, in the same state as the actor, thus allowing insight not only into what the actor is doing, but also into why he or she is doing it. As with many theories about their function, mirror neurons are certainly not essential for judging an actor's intentions. For example, in a famous study, Heider & Simmel (1944) devised a simple cartoon of simple geometric shapes (circles and triangles) moving around and interacting with each other. Even though the movements were necessarily very different from their own repertoire, viewers spontaneously and consistently described the shapes' 'intentions' and even assigned them characters. Moreover, as Hickok points out (in Gallese et al., 2011), if the ability to understand intention were confined to an animal's own behavioural repertoire, it would be of little evolutionary advantage to animals that need to avoid predators with very different behaviours; how could a mongoose and a snake make sense of each other's behaviour, for example?

Despite these reservations, mirror neurons do display some of the sophisticated properties needed for this role. They are sensitive to a concept, such as grasping, rather than to a stereo-typed movement, and are capable of some degree of abstraction. For example, mirror neurons selective for 'grasping' in monkeys respond even if the actual act of grasping takes place behind a screen, provided the monkey observes a suitable arm movement and has been shown that there is a target behind the screen (Umilta et al., 2001). They may also be selective for a partic-ular, meaningful action. For example, a mirror neuron may respond when a peanut is grasped and raised to the lips, but not when the peanut is grasped and placed in a container close to the mouth (Fogassi et al., 1998). Such a neuron therefore seems selective not just for grasping a target (e.g. a peanut), but for grasping it with a particular intent (i.e. to eat it). And, finally, mirror neurons are sensitive, not only to an action, but also to the context in which it takes place. Iacobomi et al. (2005) used fMRI to demonstrate that there was more activation in the frontal cortex to a film of a hand grasping a cup in a relevant scene (a table laid with other mealtime items) than to the hand movement or to the scene alone. Moreover there was greater activation when the film depicted the more familiar and practised 'grasping to drink' than 'grasping to clear away'.

Social behaviour and autistic spectrum disorder (ASD)

If one accepts that mirror neurons might be involved in understanding an actor's intention, then it is natural to speculate that they might be more generally involved in the social beha-viour. Keysers and Gazzola (2006) outline a general model for the neural basis of social cogni-tion, centred on the notion of empathy mediated by 'shared circuits'. Mirror neurons provide an example of a shared circuit linking perception with action, and Keysers and Gizzola suggest that there may be similar links between perception and other aspects of our conscious experience including touch, pain, and emotion. For example, fMRI studies show regions of the secondary somatosensory cortex that are active both when the subject's leg is touched and when the sub-ject observes someone else's leg being touched (Keysers et al., 2004). Similarly, parts of the anterior cingulate and insular cortex are active both when subjects experience a small electric shock and when they see someone else being shocked (Singer et al., 2004). And, finally, the anterior insular cortex responds both when subjects experience a disgusting smell and when they see the disgusted facial expressions that the smell evokes in others (Wicker et al., 2003). Like the original, indirect evidence for a human mirror system, these studies suggest that there may well be a more general neural linkage between perception and experience, but they do not confirm the existence of shared circuits based upon mirror-like neurons. Nor do they tell us what the proposed linkages might be for.

However, if mirror neurons, or shared circuits, are indeed important in social cognition, then any impairment of their function should lead to difficulties in social engagement and might, particularly, be important in explaining autistic spectrum disorder. But, although this is a very active area of research and speculation, there is currently no undisputed evidence to support it. For example, there are conflicting anatomical claims that the cortex in mirror neuron areas is either thicker or thinner in ASD. Some studies have reported abnormal cortical activity in those diagnosed with ASD but these have not been replicated, have often highlighted areas not thought to be mirror areas, and have sometimes lacked the essential controls needed to ensure that the abnormalities do not arise simply from some more general symptom such as abnormal eye movements. Similarly, though some studies report that ASD sufferers have difficulties in understanding the intentions of others' actions, a greater number suggest that they don't (see, for example, Gernsbacher in Gallese et al. (2011) for a review) and, given the communication problems associated with ASD, apparently specific behavioural deficits may have a more general cause, such as the misinterpretation of the experimenter's instructions.

It seems unlikely that a problem with conventional mirror neurons – those linking the perception and execution of goal-directed actions – could lead to all the symptoms associated with ASD which, as well as social and communication problems, typically include a tendency to focus on the local features of visual displays, and generally greater sensitivity to sensory stimulation. Rather, this approach seems more plausible if one also accepts Keysers and Gazzola's (2006) speculation that the human mirror system is much more extensive, forming a more general neural basis for empathy. The finding that the cortical abnormalities associated with ASD are not confined to established mirror areas is certainly compatible with this view, although it obviously cannot be taken as evidence directly for it. More investigations of human mirror neurons, like those provided by Fried's team, are clearly needed.

THE ORIGIN OF MIRROR NEURONS

Most theories about the possible function of mirror neurons suggest that they enable some specific ability, such as learning by imitation or understanding others' actions. These theories typically hold that mirror neurons arose as a genetic mutation that was selected for because of the advantage that the new ability conferred. However, Keysers and Gazzola (2006), who suggest a more general role for mirror neurons in social cognition, argue that mirror neurons arose not as a specific mutation but from the nervous system's well established ability to learn associations between events by Hebbian learning. The basic idea is that connections to a neuron that are simultaneously active will be strengthened so that the linkage can come to dominate the input to the neuron. Neurons that respond both when we command a movement and when we see and feel ourselves making that movement could easily arise by this means, because a motor command will almost always be accompanied by visual and proprioceptive feedback about its consequences. Moreover, neurons that respond to the sight of a particular movement are often 'viewpoint independent', responding when the movement is seen from a range of different perspectives, so that it is also possible that mirror neurons could arise by the generalisaton of the visual information to include other people making the same movement.

The innate and learned accounts are not mutually exclusive, of course, and even proponents of the former approach acknowledge that mirror neurons can be modified by experience. Nonetheless, Heyes (2009) has recently championed the advantages of emphasising the learning aspect. She argues, for example, that there is little evidence in human neonates of innate behaviour that could reasonably be attributed to mirror neurons. Even tongue protrusion, the only apparent imitation reliably shown by newborns, may in fact be a non-specific arousal response. Moreover, mirror neurons clearly need to be flexible to account for their proposed role, described above, in pianists and dancers. And direct studies of learning confirm their plasticity. For example, there is normally greater mirror activity to hand than to foot movements, but this relationship can be reversed by repeatedly pairing foot movements with images of hand movements and *vice versa* (Catmur et al., 2008).

The suggestion that mirror neurons provide an example of a general neural flexibility, rather than a specific adaptation, is more compatible with the bulk of the evidence reviewed above, which suggests that they play some role in a range of processes – including those involved in imitation, the understanding of others' behaviour and, possibly, empathy – rather than providing the essential neural base that enables one particular ability.

IMPLICATIONS

Recordings from human brains provide direct evidence of mirror neurons in people, and suggest that they are both more widespread and more sophisticated than those originally found in monkeys. However, despite much research and discussion, we do not yet have clear ideas about what they might be doing or how they might have evolved. Theories about their function are both interesting and important, promising a different way to think about how the brain works, for example, or explaining how ASD might arise. And each theory is supported by some of the evidence. But this is not enough – there is, after all, much evidence that the earth is flat. More tellingly, no theory is supported by *all* of the evidence. Instead, the picture that emerges is that mirror neurons *may* play in a variety of behaviours but that they are not crucial to any one. Consequently, they seem more likely to have evolved through the accumulation of marginal gains rather than through some spectacular behavioural breakthrough.

The debate about mirror neurons is important and interesting not only because mirror neurons are possibly important and certainly interesting. It also provides excellent insights into how scientific ideas really become, or fail to become, established. The *Mirror Neuron Forum*, mentioned under Further Reading below, illustrates how evidence is rarely clear-cut but can often be interpreted in more than one way – that those holding one view often cling to that view by accepting one particular interpretation, and that, consequently, a coherent view can often emerge only after many years of argument and research.

FURTHER READING

Gallese, V., Gernsbacher, M. A., Heyes, C., Hickok, G. & Iacoboni, M. (2011). Mirror Neuron Forum. *Perspectives on Psychological Science*, 6(4), 369–407.
  Summary of a detailed, and sometimes heated, discussion amongst leading supporters and critics of current ideas about mirror neurons.

Hickok, G. (2009). Eight problems for the mirror neuron theory of action understanding in monkeys and humans. *Journal of Cognitive Neuroscience*, 21(7), 1229–43.
  A well argued plea for caution in interpreting the evidence about mirror neurons.

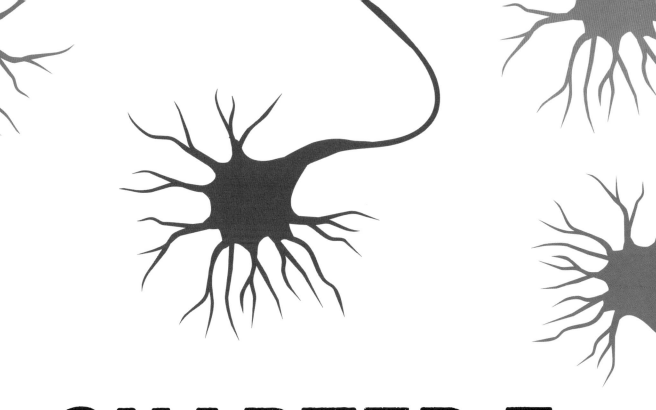

CHAPTER 7
EMOTIONAL BEHAVIOURS

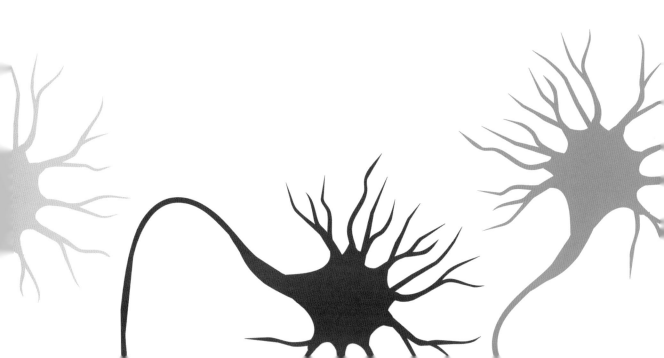

CHAPTER BREAKDOWN

- Emotions comprise biological responses as well as subjective feelings.
- The biological responses may be important in triggering subjective emotions.
- Emotional behaviour is supported by multiple brain areas.
- The amygdala is associated primarily with fear, but also plays a role in other emotions.
- The amygdala plays a specific role in emotional pavlovian memories.
- The prefrontal cortex regulates emotional expression.
- Emotional facial expressions appear to be conserved across cultures and are biologically determined.

ROADMAP

In this chapter, we will be considering the biological mechanisms that support emotional behaviour. First, we need to understand what emotion is and how it can be measured. Next, we will consider the central question of how the biological components of the emotional response relate to our subjective feelings of emotion. It is within this context that we can then ask which brain areas are important for emotion and what their functions are. We will focus in particular on the amygdala, with some consideration of 'higher' and 'lower' structures. Finally, we will look at the case of emotional facial expressions and show that, perhaps contrary to one's assumptions, these are not unique to humans, and in fact have developed through evolution with a strong biological basis. One important theme in this chapter is a focus on the emotion of fear. This is principally due to the fact that fear is the most-researched emotion. However, it is important to appreciate that the principles covered in this chapter will likely apply to all emotions.

In the course of this chapter, the content will rely partially upon concepts from previous chapters. These include the neuroanatomy of the brain to locate the various emotional processes (Chapter 1). Moreover, we will highlight the importance of learning and memory (Chapter 4) in emotional processes.

When we think of emotions, our minds turn immediately to the very real feelings of joy, love, fear, anger and other types of emotion. Why, though, do we have these feelings? Of course, without our emotions we would probably consider ourselves to be at least a little less human, but what purpose do they serve? From an evolutionary perspective, the existence of emotions must have some function to help survival. We can see this most easily with fear, which can help us avoid danger. Anger and rage may assert dominance, thereby avoiding confrontation. Perhaps love helps ensure procreation and the passing on of our genes. What of happiness? Does it help foster social communities that will work together? So maybe they do serve a useful function.

From the perspective of biological psychology, we want to understand the biological under-pinnings of emotional behaviour. Rooted in materialism, rather than dualism, we would like to make the assumption that our emotions can be explained from a biological perspective. This is not simply a focus on the brain. Of course the brain is important for emotional behaviour and feelings. However, we will see that the peripheral body also has a strong role to play. Moreover, an understanding of normal emotional function enables us to begin to account for conditions in which this breaks down. For example, anxiety results from excessive fear, and the mechanisms that mediate positive emotional behaviour may become subverted to produce the compulsive reward-seeking that is characteristic of drug addiction and even obesity.

WHAT IS EMOTION?

We have all experienced emotions. The feelings of happiness, sadness, anger and other emotions are almost a constant experience in our lives, and they undoubtedly impact upon our behaviour. Sometimes this can be to the detriment of normal behaviour. For example, the mood disorders, such as depression, are characterised by abnormal control of mood, and hence abnormal emotional behaviour. This emphasis on emotional behaviour presents an insight into the fact that emotions are more than simply the subjective feeling that we experience. While such conscious feelings are perhaps the most prominent manifestation of emotion, they are accompanied by a multitude of other bodily responses. This includes psychological changes, in both behavioural and cognitive domains, as well as more biological responses.

There are argued to be six core emotions that are experienced and expressed in humans across all cultures. These are happiness, sadness, anger, fear, surprise and disgust. These are defined in relation to the facial expressions that characterise each emotion (see later for the evidence supporting the supposed universality of the core emotions across cultures), and they make up part of the repertoire of emotional responses.

Of these, we will concentrate most upon the emotion of fear. The reason for this is quite simple. The responses that characterise fear are well understood and, more importantly, in contrast to the subjective feeling, they can be measured and studied in experimental animals. This enables us to use experimental techniques to research the brain mechanisms of fear. Of course, it is by no means certain that understanding fear should give us an insight into the other emotions. However, we will see that the processes that underlie fear responses may also mediate other emotions as well.

When we are in a state of fear, there are many characteristic bodily responses that accompany the subjective feeling (see Table 7.1). To focus on a salient few, there are **autonomic** (organ-controlling) changes in heart rate, blood pressure and breathing rate. There are also other **physiological** responses, such as the release of the stress hormone corticosterone into the blood stream. Finally, at the behavioural and cognitive level, there are characteristic behavioural responses, including the well-known fight-or-flight response, and we will often have a more detailed memory of fearful experiences than of more mundane events. Similar repertoires of bodily responses can also be associated with the other core emotions.

KEY POINTS

- There are six core emotions.
- Emotional responses comprise biological responses in the body as well as the subjective feeling.

Table 7.1   Bodily characteristics that accompany fear

Heart pounding

Dry mouth

Upset stomach

Increased respiration (i.e. shallow, faster breathing pattern)

Scanning and vigilance

Jumpiness, easy startle

Frequent urination

Diarrhoea

Fidgeting

Apprehensive expectation – something bad is going to happen

Release of stress hormones into the bloodstream

WHAT IS THE FUNCTION OF EMOTIONS?

The importance and function of subjective emotional feelings is a discussion that is best left to a different setting. However, we can say something meaningful in terms of the biological function of emotions, and essentially it all boils down to aiding survival. The classic fight-or-flight behaviour response in fearful situations improves the prospect of surviving. In evolutionary terms, it increases the chances of the gene pool being passed on to the next generation. The decision is either to flee (in order to escape the imminent danger), or to stay and fight (in order to overcome the danger). Moreover, the biological fear responses of increased heart rate, muscle tension and stress hormone release can all be related to adaptive preparatory responses for both actions.

In a similar manner, emotional responses associated with positive outcomes, such as food, may assist with localising and digesting those foods and hence improve nutrition and survival. However, one concept that emerges is that if these emotional responses do have adaptive survival value, they would be even further enhanced if they were activated as early as possible.

To put it in concrete terms, it would be better to initiate an escape response to a snake if we could predict when we will encounter the snake. Therefore, stimuli that are predictive of an emotion-inducing event should become able to elicit the emotional responses (and possibly feelings?) themselves. What this means is that *learning* is an integral part of emotion. We will see later that this is manifested in our understanding of the biological mechanisms of emotion.

KEY POINTS

- Emotional responses ultimately aid survival and procreation.
- As a salient example, fear responses help avoid danger.

WHAT IS THE RELATIONSHIP BETWEEN EMOTIONAL RESPONSES AND FEELINGS?

If we are to understand the biological mechanisms of emotion, we can capitalise upon the information that can be obtained from studying emotional responses in both experimental animals and humans. However, there is clearly great interest also in the biological processes that underlie subjective emotional feelings. Much of the current research into fear and other emotions is based upon the premise that studying emotional responses must inform our understanding of emotional feelings. However, there is a long history, much of it laden with controversy, concerning the question of how emotional responses and feelings relate to one another.

James–Lange theory

It was William James who began the debate surrounding the relationship between emotion responses and feelings. In his *Principles of Psychology*, William James (1890) posed the very simple question in relation to fear of how we should interpret the situation of a man meeting a bear, being frightened and running away (he also used the example of losing a fortune, being sorry and weeping in the case of sadness, as well as being insulted by a rival, being angry and striking out in the case of anger). The natural assumption is that the man becomes frightened upon seeing the bear (the emotional feeling) and hence runs away (the emotional response). James, and also Carl Lange seemingly independently in Denmark, argued that this order of sequence is, in fact, incorrect. Instead, they argued that 'the bodily manifestations must first be interposed', such that we should describe the event as the man running away upon seeing the bear, and hence being frightened. So in order to *feel* an emotion, we must first experience these 'bodily manifestations', which are the aforementioned biological responses (Figure 7.1).

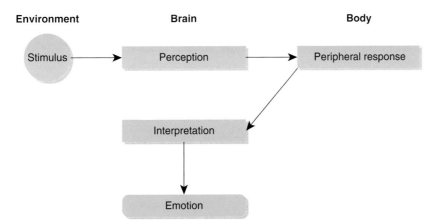

Figure 7.1 Schematic representation of **James–Lange theory**. An emotionally-salient stimulus in the environment is perceived in the visual system of the brain. The perception of the emotional stimulus directly activates an appropriate repertoire of peripheral responses in the body, the exact pattern of which is detected by the brain and interpreted as a specific emotion

Most people, when faced with the James–Lange theory, find it difficult to accept at first. The assumption that the emotional feeling is central to, and activating of, the bodily responses is embedded even within language (e.g. 'My heart was pounding *because* I was afraid'). However, there are two initial arguments that James makes to persuade the unconvinced. First, and easily accepted, is the fact that we can feel the bodily changes. A racing heart is an overt manifestation of anxiety. Think back to your last exam or presentation and you will readily remember the feeling of being nervous and all the associated symptoms (heart beating, sweaty palms, etc.). So if the subjective emotional depends upon feeling the bodily responses, it certainly appears possible.

Second, and more importantly, James poses the theoretical question of what is emotion if it is stripped of its bodily responses? As he states, 'What kind of an emotion of fear would be left if the feeling neither of quickened heart-beats nor of shallow breathing, neither of trembling lips nor of weakened limbs, neither of goose-flesh nor of visceral stirrings, were present, it is quite impossible for me to think.' If the subjective feeling precedes and triggers the bodily responses, the bodily responses should be unimportant to the nature of the emotional feeling. Yet, in common with James, most would think it strange and artificial to have fear stripped of the bodily feelings, i.e. 'a purely disembodied emotion is a nonentity'.

Further support for the James–Lange theory can be found by taking an evolutionary perspective. If we accept the survival value of emotional responses, it would make sense that such a value would be optimal if the responses are triggered as quickly as possible. Why, then, should the mechanism that enables us to escape a threat require first that the feeling of fear be experienced? Indeed, our own experiences will tell us that our bodily responses can take place almost instantaneously and often before any feeling of emotion. Similarly, many would accept that at some point lower down the evolutionary ladder there are species that show defensive responses but we would find it hard to attribute subjective feelings to those same species. For example, a worm will recoil upon a tap to its body. This is a defensive response in the same way as running away from a bear. So if we can assume that there exist species that show emotional responses *but not* emotional feelings, surely their bodily responses must be triggered directly upon exposure to the emotional stimulus. Why, then, in humans and other species, should we think that a stage of subjective experience be interposed in order to elicit the bodily response? Is it not more parsimonious to suggest that the subjective feeling, instead, is an addition to the process, interpreting the situation and the bodily responses in order to give cognitive meaning to them? This latter account is exactly in line with the theory suggested by James and Lange.

When thinking about an individual emotion, such as fear, it might now be easier to accept that the feeling of being afraid depends upon the bodily fear responses. However, this leaves us with the question of how our bodies give rise to different emotions. Even if we set aside the long list of emotions that humans experience and concentrate on the six core emotions, how can we explain the fact that we experience the appropriate emotion with little or no confusion?

James–Lange theory answers this question by pointing towards the *differences* in the bodily responses between emotional states. For example, fear is associated with the release of adrenaline, whereas anger is characterised by a greater release of noradrenaline (Henry, 1986). Therefore, upon encountering an emotional stimulus, a repertoire of bodily responses is engaged as appropriate for that stimulus. This repertoire has a pattern that is characteristic of a specific emotion, and so is followed by the subjective feeling of that emotion. So the different specific patterns of bodily responses give rise to the different and relevant emotions.

Cannon–Bard theory

The theory of James and Lange became very rapidly entrenched in scientific thought, such that by 1927, dissenting voices were almost completely absent. However, it was then that Walter Cannon published his now-acclaimed critique of James and Lange. Cannon (1927) attributed this progress to an accumulation of previously unknown physiological information (in conjunction with Philip Bard) in the intervening years. We will come on to the physiological points for critical consideration. However, first it is again helpful to consider some broader questions.

If it is a requirement that the bodily responses be produced and then monitored in order to feel an emotion, how can we reconcile this with the speed with which we feel the subjective emotion? Going back to the man and the bear, what James and Lange are suggesting is that the bear is seen by the visual system, and that this information is somehow translated into bodily responses (changes in heart rate and breathing). Those bodily responses are then detected, and the pattern interpreted as a specific emotion. This seems to be quite a long and complex process for situations where we feel emotions very rapidly. So the same problem of temporal sequence that contributed to James–Lange theory suggesting a direct activation of biological responses by the emotional stimulus also argues that the subjective feeling might need to be directly activated too.

Cannon–Bard theory takes the view that 'the bodily changes occur almost simultaneously with the emotional experience'. In other words, perception of the emotional stimulus triggers *in parallel* both the bodily responses and the subjective feeling. It does not advocate a return to pre-James thinking that the subjective feeling triggers the biological response. However, it does place an emphasis on the ability of the subjective feeling to modulate the bodily response. For example, if we consciously decide to be in a state of fear, the bodily responses associated with fear will be more intense should a fearful stimulus be encountered.

In some ways, this is the basis of one of the behavioural measures of fear. We have a natural startle response to a loud noise, which helps us localise the source of the noise and prepare for escape if necessary. If we are afraid at the time, the magnitude of the startle response is increased. This fear-potentiated startle demonstrates that the state of fear, which encompasses the subjective feeling, modulates the biological emotional startle response. Most importantly, however, the subjective experience of emotion does not depend at all upon the peripheral bodily responses (Figure 7.2).

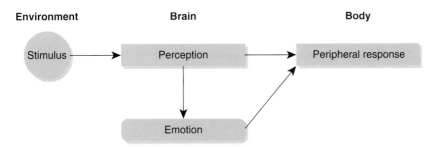

Figure 7.2 Schematic representation of Cannon–Bard theory. An emotionally-salient stimulus in the environment is perceived in the visual system of the brain. The perception of the emotional stimulus directly activates both the peripheral responses in the body and the subjective emotion. The process of subjective feeling can then modulate the intensity of the peripheral response, but there is no complementary impact of the peripheral response upon the subjective feeling

So far, we have considered the merits of the James–Lange and Cannon–Bard theories in general terms. What about the specific points of critical comparison? We will focus on three main questions that Cannon posed.

Are bodily changes different enough to account for specific emotional feelings?

Many of the bodily responses to emotional stimuli are co-ordinated by activation of the **sympathetic nervous system**. The sympathetic nervous system controls the internal organs, such that its activation results in a wide range of effects, including an increase in heart rate, blood vessel contraction (raising blood pressure) and sweating. Importantly, the sympathetic nervous system is stimulated not only in times of fear, but also for anger and even in non-emotional conditions such as fever.

How, then, does our body distinguish between fever-induced heart acceleration, and that related to fear? Perhaps a focus on individual responses is misleading, as James emphasised specific *patterns* that are associated with particular emotions. Ekman et al. (1983) induced emotions using instructions to produce distinct emotional facial expressions (see later section on facial expressions). The six emotions investigated (fear, anger, sadness, happiness, disgust and surprise) could be partially distinguished on the basis of heart rate and skin temperature information alone (Figure 7.3). However, skin conductance (i.e. sweating) and muscle tension did not provide any discriminatory value. Therefore, it remains possible that distinct emotions are characterised by specific patterns of many biological responses.

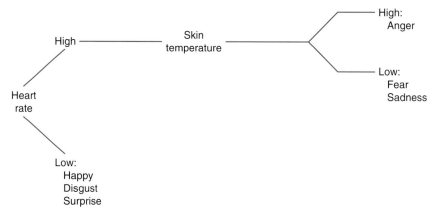

Figure 7.3   Decision tree hypothesised to determine the selection of an appropriate subjective emotion. On the basis of measuring just two bodily responses (heart rate and skin temperature), it was possible to distinguish between three sets of emotions. Low heart rate was associated with happiness, disgust and surprise. High heart rate predicted anger, fear and sadness. Moreover, skin temperature discriminated between anger (high temperature) and fear/sadness (low temperature). Therefore, the addition of further responses may be able to discriminate fully between the six core emotions

Source: Ekman et al. (1983)

Even if emotions are characterised by individual patterns of bodily responses this leads us back to the issue of time. Some bodily responses are undoubtedly rather rapid in onset. However, many others are much slower. For example, the release of the stress hormone corticosterone into the bloodstream peaks many minutes after the induction of stress. If it is the integration of all these responses that defines an emotion, how is it that our subjective experience can begin within one second of stimulus presentation, while many of the bodily responses lag behind?

Does prevention of peripheral feedback abolish emotional feelings?

According to James–Lange theory, if we were able to prevent any information about the bodily responses from being detected by the area of the brain responsible for producing emotional feelings, there should be an absence of subjective experience. Cognitively, such an individual might think that the situation is fearful, for example, but would not have the emotional sensation of fear.

Cannon cited evidence from Sherrington showing that when the spinal cord of dogs was severed (thereby preventing bodily information from returning to the brain) emotional *behaviour* remained relatively intact. However, such emotional behaviour may be part of the pattern of bodily responses, rather than an indirect measure of subjective feelings in experimental animals.

The most relevant evidence to this question remains a study by George Hohmann in 1966. Hohmann was a paraplegic, and interviewed other patients with spinal cord damage to determine whether there were any changes in emotional feelings as a result of their injuries. When evaluating sexual excitement, fear and anger, it was clear that there was a decrease in emotional feeling. This was especially so when the spinal cord had been damaged at a higher level, thereby depriving the patient of sensory feedback from a greater portion of the body. For example, one patient with damage at neck-level reported 'I say I am afraid, like when I'm going into a real stiff exam at school, but I don't really feel afraid, not all tense and shaky, with that hollow feeling in my stomach, like I used to.' In contrast, grief was often enhanced, and almost all patients reported increased episodes of weeping and getting 'choked up', for example when saying goodbye to a loved one.

Ultimately, the evidence is mixed, and we are unable to conclude one way or the other. Why should deprivation of peripheral feedback impair some emotions, but enhance others? Moreover, the patients report being conscious of the absence (or lessening) of the bodily symptoms. Therefore, it cannot be determined whether the decreased emotional feeling is a result of disruption of the James–Lange process, or whether it is simply a cognitive appreciation that the emotional experience has changed as a result of the spinal injury.

Does artificial stimulation of bodily responses induce emotional feelings?

If James–Lange theory is true, we might expect an emotional feeling to be triggered if the correct pattern of bodily responses were stimulated artificially. Early attempts to do this involved giving human volunteers a dose of adrenaline. Adrenaline activates the sympathetic nervous system, and so causes many of the bodily responses associated with emotion. However, as noted by Marañon (1924), the effects were not clearly in favour of James–Lange theory. While the subjects became consciously aware of the cardiac and pulmonary effects of adrenaline, there was no real experience of subjective emotion. Sometimes, the subjects reported feeling 'as if' they were afraid, but without the true emotional feeling.

It might well be that a single administration of adrenaline is insufficient to create an appropriate specific pattern of bodily responses, and hence does not trigger emotional feeling. However, also within Marañon's study was an intriguing observation that does support a role for peripheral responses enhancing emotional experience. In a subset of cases, adrenaline induced a real emotion of grief/sorrow, coupled with tears and sighs. This was seen only when those subjects had shortly before been talking about their sick children or dead parents. So when an emotion pre-exists, stimulation of the periphery strengthens the intensity of the feeling. To some extent, this goes against the main thrust of Cannon–Bard theory, which instead emphasises the effect of subjective feelings to modulate the bodily response. Nevertheless, what these findings indicate is that there is a complex interrelationship between the cognitive and peripheral aspects of emotion that leads to the rich emotional experience.

Schachter–Singer theory

The more recent theory from Schachter and Singer (1962; often referred to as the cognitive labelling or two-factor theory) represents one approach to reconciling the interaction between cognition and the periphery in emotional experience. At its core is an acceptance of certain aspects of both James–Lange and Cannon–Bard theories.

Principally, it is argued that there is no real distinction between the bodily responses of different emotions (Cannon–Bard). However, the bodily responses that are common to all emotions do trigger the subjective feeling (James–Lange). So how then is it possible that a common bodily response can elicit different emotional states? Schachter and Singer argue that this is the role of cognition (Figure 7.4). To put it crudely, the stimulation of the bodily response (the first factor) tells us that we should be experiencing some emotion. However, it is a process of cognitive labelling (the second factor), dependent upon the particular situation in which we find ourselves at the time, that determines which emotion should be felt.

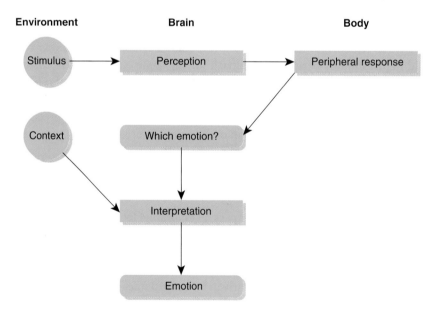

Figure 7.4   Schematic representation of Schachter–Singer theory. An emotionally-salient stimulus in the environment is perceived in the visual system of the brain. The perception of the emotional stimulus directly activates the peripheral responses in the body, which is detected by the brain to trigger a subjective feeling. In parallel, the context in which the emotionally-salient stimulus was presented is evaluated, leading to an interpretation of the cognitive context, which determines the actual emotion experienced

In their now-classic study, Schachter and Singer (1962) gave subjects adrenaline (just like Marañon did). However, the subjects were told instead that they were receiving a novel vitamin supplement 'Suproxin'. Half of the subjects were prepared cognitively for the physiological effect of adrenaline ('What will probably happen is that your hand will start to shake, your heart will start to pound, and your face may get warm and flushed'), whereas the other half were not given any cognitive explanation for the effects they would feel. As a second manipulation, after being given adrenaline half of the subjects were placed in a room with another person who was acting euphorically, whereas the actor was angry for the other half. The subjects who had been informed of the effects of adrenaline displayed no emotional behaviour, nor did they report feeling emotion. In contrast, those subjects who had no prior cognitive explanation for the physiological effects began to behave in the same manner as the actors, and reported feeling the appropriate emotion of happiness or anger. This pattern of results supports the notion that the adrenaline triggered emotion, but the precise subjective feeling experienced was determined by the cognitive context (resulting in euphoria, anger or no emotion when the physiological effects were expected).

Schachter and Singer's cognitive labelling theory has remained influential to the present day, though there is cause to modify certain assumptions. In reality, it appears that the truth about the nature of the physiological emotional response lies somewhere in between the views held by James and Cannon. Clearly the patterns associated with different emotions overlap substantially. Nevertheless, there are reliably observed differences as well. For example, whereas fear is associated with adrenaline release, anger is actually linked to the release of noradrenaline. Therefore, the pattern of bodily responses may place some constraint upon the range of emotions than can be experienced. However, remember that Schachter and Singer's subjects were successfully induced into a state of anger, despite the fact that they had adrenaline, and not noradrenaline, in their bodies.

KEY POINTS

- The biological responses in the body and the subjective feeling both emerge very rapidly.
- It has been vigorously debated whether and how each depends on the other.
- James–Lange theory suggests that the pattern of responses activate and determine the feeling.
- Cannon–Bard theory suggests the responses and feelings occur in parallel, with the feeling influencing the responses.
- There are several points of contention in the debate between the James–Lange and Cannon–Bard theories.
- **Schachter–Singer theory** suggests that the biological responses trigger the subjective emotion, but the nature of the emotion is determined by cognitive interpretation of the environment.

WHAT BRAIN AREAS MEDIATE EMOTIONS?

Given that there is some relationship between biological/behavioural emotional responses and the subjective emotional experience, an understanding of the brain mechanisms of emotional behaviour is also informative to the process of subjective experience. In fact, we will see that the same areas that are important for physiological and behavioural emotional responses in animals and humans are also necessary for normal subjective human experience. First, however, we need to be convinced that emotional responses and feelings are really the domain of the brain.

The first convincing evidence that emotion is a product of the brain comes from clinical observations of patients with neurological damage. In some cases, the consequences of brain damage include an alteration in emotional behaviour and feelings. One of the most famous of such patients is Phineas Gage (Damasio et al., 1994). Documented by Harlow, Gage's fame stems not so much from the consequence of his brain damage, but rather from its cause and the fact that he lived to exhibit a change in emotional behaviour. A construction foreman on the New England railroads, Gage suffered a bizarre accident in 1848 that destroyed part of his prefrontal cortex. A tamping iron (3cm in diameter and 109cm long; used to trigger rock blasts in order to clear the way for the railroad) was propelled up through Gage's skull on its way into the sky. Remarkably, he was only temporarily stunned, regaining consciousness straight away and proceeded to walk away talking to other workers. The damage has recently been reconstructed from his recovered skull, showing a specific removal of tissue in the ventral region of the prefrontal cortex (Damasio et al., 1994; Figure 7.5).

In many ways, Gage was unaffected, with normal speech, intelligence and memory surviving the accident. However, he was completely transformed by the brain damage, seemingly acquiring a different personality. These changes were described by Harlow as reflecting a dominance of animal propensities. Nowadays, we view this complex change in behaviour as a consequence of the dysregulation of emotional behaviour. As one example, a study of Vietnam war veterans who had suffered traumatic damage to their ventral prefrontal cortex revealed a greater propensity for aggressive and violent behaviour (Grafman et al., 1996).

The other major brain system that has been implicated in emotion is the temporal lobe. In 1939, Klüver and Bucy conducted bilateral temporal lobectomies in 15 rhesus monkeys and one cebus monkey, and subsequently conducted an extensive behavioural analysis of the surgical consequences. Among the many effects observed (collectively named Klüver–Bucy syndrome; a rare condition subsequently described in humans, resulting also from bilateral temporal damage) were a number of emotional changes. The monkeys seemed to become tame, with an absence or great reduction in fear- and anger-related behavioural and vocal responses, even though these were previously wild and aggressive monkeys. This was most clearly manifested through temporal lobectomised monkeys showing no hesitation in approaching new objects, animals and people. Normally, monkeys display substantial **neophobia**, which protects against potential harm from new objects. However, this adaptive fear of new objects was absent when the temporal lobe was excised.

Now, a superficial conclusion that one might draw from the above descriptions of Phineas Gage and **Klüver–Bucy syndrome** is that the temporal lobe and ventral prefrontal cortex

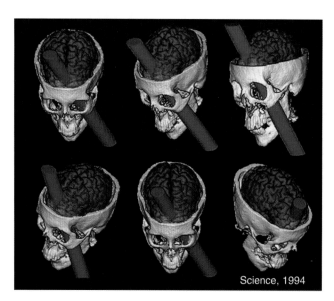

Figure 7.5 Representation of the damage suffered by Phineas Gage. The position of the tamping iron as it passed through the ventral prefrontal cortex is reconstructed from the skull of Phineas Gage

Source: Damasio et al. (1994)

mediate negative emotions (fear and anger). This might suggest that other brain areas support different emotions. However, it is clear from other observations of Klüver and Bucy's monkeys that the changes in emotional behaviour were not limited to the negative domain.

To give a specific example, the temporal lobectomised monkeys showed a marked increase in the frequency and duration of sexual activity. Moreover, there is evidence implicating the human **ventromedial prefrontal cortex** in social reward. Human participants showed activation of the ventromedial prefrontal cortex when they were led to believe that they were liked by people whom they admired (Davey, Allen, Harrison, Dwyer, & Yucel, 2010). This leads to two possible interpretations: (i) different areas within the regions of interest (the temporal lobe, for example, comprises many distinct areas) mediate the different emotions; or (ii) individual brain areas serve common functions for different emotions. Therefore, while we will focus mainly upon the emotion of fear, we will be asking the question of whether those regions implicated in fear are also involved in other emotions.

The limbic system

A trivial answer to the question 'Which brain areas mediate emotion?' is the limbic system. Why this is a trivial answer lies in a problem of definition. The limbic system is a concept that has existed from the 19th century, being named by Broca (he of Broca's language area) as a group of brain regions that, common to all mammals, are found on the border (Latin *limbus*) of the corpus callosum and other structures in the middle of the brain (Figure 7.6). Paul Broca originally hypothesised that the limbic system had an olfactory function, though this is now largely discredited, and the link between the limbic system and emotion was initially proposed by James Papez well into the 20th century. Papez proposed a circuit within the limbic system that was important for emotional behaviours and their conscious sensation. Importantly, however, Papez's circuit does not include the whole of the anatomically-defined limbic system. While Papez himself did not suggest altering the anatomical definition of the limbic system, it has been modified repeatedly in order to accommodate brain areas that have emerged as being important in emotional function (e.g. the shell of the nucleus accumbens in relation to reward,

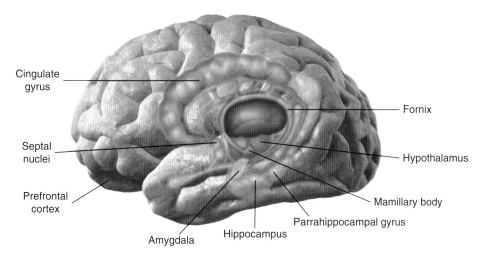

Figure 7.6 Representation of the limbic system. Major components of the limbic system are located around the corpus callosum

and cortical areas beyond the cingulate cortex). These moves have attempted to ensure the concordance between the limbic system and emotion, but have simply ensured that the limbic system remains an appropriate answer to our opening question. Therefore, to say that emotion is mediated by the limbic system is a truth that is ensured by its definition as the system that comprises areas involved in emotion.

THE AMYGDALA

While the concept of a limbic system may be useful as a term to summarise the complexity of emotional processing within the brain, we are left with the question of how we can determine the specific involvement of individual brain structures in emotion. Perhaps the most-researched area within the limbic system is the amygdala, which has been strongly implicated in fearful behaviour.

Anatomy of the amygdala

The amygdala is an almond-shaped structure (amygdala is the Latin for almond), located deep within the temporal lobe. It has traditionally been a principal component of the limbic system, and does actually have some olfactory functions in support of Broca's original hypothesis. Most importantly, however, it appears anatomically to be ideally situated in order to perform a function of coordinating emotional responses to salient stimuli. First, the amygdala receives sensory input from all modalities. This information arrives both directly from the sensory thalamus, and also from sensory cortical areas. Therefore, to return to William James' hypothetical situation, the visual information in relation to the sight of the bear can easily be transmitted to the amygdala.

Downstream, the amygdala projects to a number of regions, all of which have functions that are related to emotional biological responses (Figure 7.7). For example, in relation to fear, the lateral hypothalamus regulates heart rate and blood pressure; the paraventricular nucleus coordinates the release of stress hormones; and the periaqueductal grey matter is important for the behavioural freezing response. Thus the amygdala is in a position to coordinate the characteristic patterns of bodily responses that are associated with emotional experience.

FOCUS ON METHODS: ANATOMICAL TRACING

In order to determine the targets to which a particular brain area projects, it is possible to carry out anatomical tracing. A tracing agent is injected into the given brain area. This tracer is taken up by neurons and transported down their axons to the target region. The brain can then be extracted, sliced into thin sections and processed so that the tracer can be visualised under a microscope. This is known as anterograde tracing, as it traces the pathways from the injected region. The alternative is to use a retrograde tracer that is taken up by axon terminals and transported back to the cell body. In this way, it is possible to determine the source of a pathway that terminates in the region of interest.

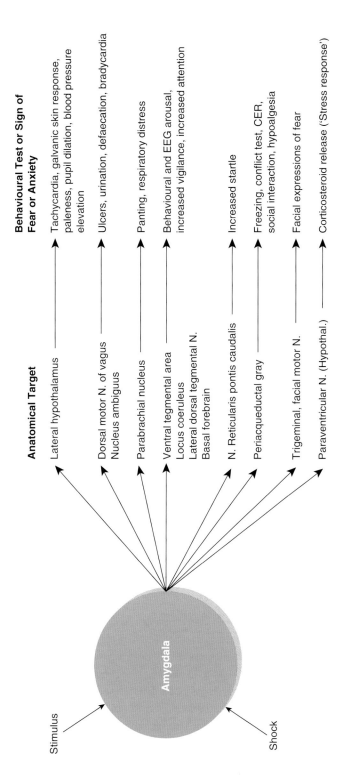

Figure 7.7 The amygdala connects to areas of the brain responsible for coordinating fear responses

Adapted from Davis (1992)

Stimulation of the amygdala elicits emotional responses

If the amygdala is directly connected to brain areas responsible for producing emotional responses, it follows that if we stimulate the amygdala, this should produce activity in the downstream regions that results in an apparently emotional state. In monkeys, there is some evidence that this is the case, with amygdala stimulation resulting in increased heart rate (Reis and Oliphant, 1964). This has been replicated in rats, along with both raised blood pressure (Iwata et al., 1987) and corticosterone release into the bloodstream (Dunn and Whitener, 1986). Moreover, amygdala stimulation in the rat actually produces fear-like behaviour, potentiating the acoustic startle reflex in the same way that stimulus-induced fear does (Rosen and Davis, 1988).

In humans, the amygdala has been stimulated in epileptic patients undergoing exploration of the epileptic focus. Halgren et al. (1978) described comprehensively the mental phenomena resulting from stimulation of the amygdala. Some patients reported feeling that their heart was beating faster, and some (it is not reported whether they were the same patients at the same time) reported feelings of fear or anxiety. We might interpret these findings positively, as they appear both to match the animal observations of increased heart rate, and link these to actual subjective feelings of fear. However, there remains the question of why it was only a subset of the patients that experienced these feelings. Other studies found that the reports of fear were pronounced when the patients appear to be anxious of the experimental procedure itself. Moreover, stimulating the amygdala in aggressive patients led to aggressive behaviour. So it might be that the cognitive context affects the subjective impact of amygdala stimulation. These studies did not take physiological measurements of cardiovascular responses, and so we cannot make any links between these subjective feelings and any biological responses.

Damage to the amygdala impairs normal emotional responses

while human stimulation provides only rather weak evidence for a role of the amygdala in subjective fear, studies of amygdala damage are much more convincing. The amygdala is, in relative terms, a very small region in the human brain, occupying only about 2cm³ deep within the temporal lobe. What this means is that damage resulting from stroke, trauma or surgical resection would never be limited to the amygdala, but would also impact upon the overlying cortex and also the hippocampus.

Fortunately for amygdala researchers, there is a clinical condition that results in selective amygdala degeneration (Urbach–Wiethe disease; see Chapter 4). One such patient, SM, has been extensively investigated, and appears to show little or no experience of fear. Interviews with clinical psychologists revealed that SM was dispassionate when relating emotional experiences. More recently, a comprehensive analysis of SM's fear experience was conducted (Feinstein et al., 2011). Despite stating that she hates snakes and spiders, SM showed no hesitation in approaching and touching them, saying that she was overcome with curiosity. This showed a distinct lack of fear and avoidance. She also reported absolutely no fear when visiting one of the most haunted places in the world on Halloween. Finally, when repeatedly tested on standard questionnaires of fear and anxiety over a period of three years, SM scored consistently at a much lower level than controls. The authors state that SM cannot be described as 'emotionless', as she reported high levels of excitement in the haunted house, therefore suggesting that the amygdala has a particular role to play in subjective fear.

In comparison to the recent work on Urbach–Wiethe patients, the first explicit implication of the amygdala in emotion, and fear in particular, came from the work of Lawrence Weiskrantz in the mid-20th century. Subsequent to Klüver and Bucy's original temporal lobectomies, the critical loci of some of the non-emotional consequences had been determined using more selective lesions. In a continuation of this tradition, Weiskrantz (1956) carried out bilateral lesions to the amygdala, which replicated the emotional aspects of Klüver–Bucy syndrome. The monkeys were tame, and showed little or no neophobia. Moreover, they showed impairments in experimental fear memory paradigms. Weiskrantz tested his amygdala-lesioned monkeys on both conditioned avoidance and conditioned suppression tasks. These assess the acquired fear properties of a light or sound stimulus that is classically conditioned to an aversive outcome (mild electric footshock). The conditioned stimulus then has the capacity both to trigger an avoidance response (moving away from the stimulus) and a suppression response (decreasing or stopping ongoing behaviour). The amygdala-lesioned monkeys showed marked reductions in both avoidance and suppression compared to controls. This initial demonstration was then explored systematically in rats by Joseph LeDoux and colleagues, who carried out a series of experiments lesioning different areas of the brain. These targeted the areas involved in the detection of the stimulus (in this case, an auditory tone). LeDoux found that lesions to the auditory midbrain and the auditory thalamus impaired fear conditioning, but that damage to the auditory cortex had no disruptive impact. Therefore, the auditory information must be sent from the thalamus to some other region, the primary candidate being the amygdala. LeDoux and many others have since demonstrated that damage to, or other methods of disruption of, the amygdala does indeed impair fear conditioning in rodents.

This link between the amygdala and emotional *memory* is further substantiated by another study of SM, which also looked at her capacity to acquire conditioned fear responses. Rather than the behavioural responses studied by Weiskrantz in monkeys, Bechara et al. (1995) looked at SM's physiological galvanic skin response (a sweating response to fear and anxiety that increases electrical conductance across the skin) to colours associated with an aversive startling sound. While controls showed a large skin conductance response, SM showed no evidence of a physiological emotional response.

The amygdala and emotional memory

One of the main concepts to emerge from the study of the amygdala is that it has particular importance for emotional learning and memory. There is a huge amount of evidence showing that impairment of normal amygdala function in experimental animals disrupts fear learning and memory. This complements the findings from patients with Urbach–Wiethe disease or more widespread temporal lobe damage including the amygdala. Unfortunately, there is no current way to disrupt reversibly the amygdala in humans, as transcranial magnetic stimulation is not reliably effective for structures located deep in the brain. Therefore, we will concentrate instead upon the contribution of imaging approaches to the understanding of emotional learning and memory.

Some of the initial human functional imaging studies focused not on fear learning, but on direct fear processes such as recognition. The amygdala is activated by exposure to fearful facial expressions, and this activation is thought to be a necessary mechanism in the processing of fearful stimuli as Urbach–Wiethe patients are impaired in the recognition of fear in facial expressions. However, while the recognition of fearful expressions may be supported by prior experience and learning, it is not obvious from such studies that the human amygdala necessarily plays an important role in fear learning and memory.

In order to answer this question, two groups of researchers simultaneously adapted pavlovian conditioning procedures for use in the scanner. Büchel et al. (1998) also used faces as stimuli, but these faces had neutral expressions, and conditioned them such that the conditioned faces were paired half the time with an unpleasant tone. The control faces were never paired with the aversive outcome. The amygdala was activated on both sides of the brain during learning of the conditioned faces, and this activation correlated with the magnitude of the skin conductance response on each individual trial. While this provides strong evidence that the amygdala is critically involved in fear learning *in relation to facial stimuli*, it does not rule out the possibility that the human amygdala is somehow specialised for emotional (or even specifically fear-related) faces. However, such a specialised account is not consistent with the work of LaBar et al. (1998), which used coloured squares as the conditioned stimuli. Moreover, the aversive outcome was an electric shock to the wrist, yet the same pattern of amygdala activation correlated with skin conductance was observed. This means that the involvement of the amygdala in fear learning and memory is not limited to specific stimuli and outcomes. The assumption is, therefore, that some synaptic plasticity is taking place in the amygdala (see Chapter 4) that mediates the learned fear, and this plasticity process is reflected in the enhanced amygdala activity.

While studies of human fear conditioning seem merely to corroborate what is known from animal research, there are aspects of human emotional learning and memory that can only be studied in our species. We can simply be instructed to fear a stimulus. In an experimental situation subjects are told that one stimulus might be associated with delivery of a shock, whereas the other stimulus was completely safe. Despite there never being any shock delivery, presentation of the 'shocked' stimulus elicited activity in the left amygdala, correlated with the emergence of a skin conductance response (Phelps et al., 2001). The significance of the amygdala activation being unilateral in this setting, compared to bilateral in standard fear conditioning, is not clear. However, the existence of an apparently normal fear response (both the amygdala activation and the skin conductance response) after simple instruction may explain how fears can be acquired in a purely social manner.

Beyond fear

If one important role for the amygdala is in the pavlovian conditioning of neutral stimuli to aversive outcomes, why should this not be extended to non-aversive outcomes? From certain perspectives, it would seem simplest if the amygdala mediated all forms of pavlovian conditioning, regardless of the valence of the outcome, rather than being specifically the brain's fear area, as it is often depicted. There is actually a very large literature on the amygdala and its involvement in positive reward-related pavlovian conditioning. To give a specific example, pavlovian conditioning in the setting of cue-induced addictive drug seeking is very much associated with amygdala function.

The behaviour of drug addicts to seek out and take drugs is profoundly under the control of stimuli that have previously been associated with the drug. In rodent models, exposure to drug-associated stimuli activates the amygdala, and lesions to the amygdala disrupt cue-induced drug seeking. Perhaps most interestingly, functional imaging in humans has shown that when abstinent cocaine addicts are show videos of cocaine-related stimuli (the simulated purchase, preparation and smoking of crack cocaine), the amygdala was significantly activated compared to a neutral video condition (Childress et al., 1999). This has even been replicated using **subliminal** presentations of drug-related stimuli (see Key Study box below), showing that the pavlovian control of drug seeking behaviour occurs at a subconscious level.

KEY STUDY

Childress, A. -R., Mozley, P. D., McElgin, W., Fitzgerald, J., Reivich, M., & O'Brien, C. P. (1999). Limbic activation during cue-induced cocaine craving. *American Journal of Psychiatry, 156*(1), 11–18.

Anna-Rose Childress and colleagues have carried out a series of functional imaging studies focusing on the brain activation induced by drug-associated stimuli. This study is of particular interest as it makes use of subliminal stimulus presentation. Very brief visual presentations of pictures are not accessible to the conscious brain. This is especially the case when the image is 'masked'. The presentation of a random image (scrambled noisy pictures) prevents any after-image of the target picture, ensuring that it is not consciously seen. This can be verified by asking subjects to make a forced choice between the target image and an unpresented one; they are unable to select the one that had been presented.

By subliminally presenting various stimuli, Childress and colleagues were able to see the 'unconscious' brain activation. Given that much of the impact of emotional stimuli upon our behaviour occurs at a subconscious level, this provides evidence that the brain processes these stimuli in a meaningful manner. The stimuli that were used were drug-related, sexual, neutral or aversive.

What is interesting is that the amygdala was activated (as part of a wider neural circuitry) for each of the motivationally-relevant stimuli compared to the neutral control. This was regardless of the emotional valence of the stimuli (aversive fear vs. appetitive sexual or drug-related). Therefore the amygdala is important not only for fear, but other positive emotions as well.

An important further question is whether the amygdala's role in learning and memory is limited to non-declarative pavlovian memories. Returning to the patient work by Bechara et al., SM was actually compared to another patient, WC, who suffered from damage to the hippocampus, but not the amygdala. WC performed perfectly normally when tested on the galvanic skin response. However, he had no conscious memory for which colours were associated with the aversive noise. In contrast, SM, who showed no galvanic skin response, could remember which colours were followed by the noise, along with other factual aspects of the task. This might suggest to us that the amygdala has no role to play in conscious memories.

However, this appears not to be completely true, with the amygdala seeming to play an important part in memories for real-life emotional events. SM herself exhibited a dispassionate recollection of traumatic life episodes, and a study of Japanese Alzheimer's disease patients provides strong evidence that deficits in real-life emotional memory result from a disruption of amygdala, rather than hippocampal, function.

Mori et al. (1999) questioned 36 patients with Alzheimer's disease 6–10 weeks after they had experienced the devastating Kobe earthquake of 1995. In particular, factual memories for events surrounding the earthquake were assessed. The accuracy of these memories was then correlated with the damage to different regions of the brain as a result of the Alzheimer's-related neurodegeneration. Focusing on the amygdala and hippocampus, Mori et al. showed that degeneration in the amygdala was strongly predictive of poor declarative emotional memory. In contrast, damage to the hippocampus seemed to bear no obvious relation to the accuracy of those same memories. Therefore, the amygdala is important for declarative as well as pavlovian memories. However, clearly it does not operate in isolation. Rather, it is the interaction between the amygdala and other brain areas that forms emotional memories and determines their impact upon behaviour.

DOWNSTREAM FROM THE AMYGDALA: THE PERIAQUEDUCTAL GREY (PAG)

The amygdala projects to a number of brain areas (see Figure 7.7). Each of these may be associated with a particular emotional response, given their natural function. To go through each in turn would comprise a chapter in itself, so we will use one in particular as an exemplar. The periaqueductal grey (PAG) region in the midbrain receives strong projections from the amygdala, and is specifically involved in the *behavioural* emotional response of freezing in fearful situations.

Given that the amygdala sends projections to the PAG, we would expect that stimulation of the amygdala would lead to downstream activation of the PAG. This can be done electrophysiologically, showing that amygdala stimulation leads to electrical activity in the PAG, or even cellularly, using the activation of gene expression as a marker. However, most relevant is the behavioural evidence. We have already seen that amygdala stimulation leads to fearful responses in humans and non-human animals. This includes the induction of freezing behaviour in rats and other animals (Davis, 1997). Presumably, therefore, this elicitation of freezing is mediated by the PAG. However, when the PAG is stimulated, the picture is not so clear. PAG stimulation can be achieved either through direct electrical stimulation or by application of chemicals that elicit neuronal activity. While such approaches do sometimes produce freezing behaviour, they also tend to elicit active responses such as running and jumping (in order to escape the threat).

So why does the response to PAG stimulation vary? It is not a context effect, depending on which response is of most relevance at any given time. Instead, the main reason is that the PAG is not a homogeneous structure. Like many other areas of the brain (the amygdala included; see Spotlight 7a), the PAG can be broken down into subdivisions. Of particular interest here is the separation between the ventral (or ventrolateral) portion, the vlPAG, and the dorsal/dorsolateral dlPAG (Figure 7.8).

Electrical stimulation of the vlPAG in rats produces the expected effect of a direct activation of freezing behaviour (Vianna et al., 2001). In contrast, dlPAG stimulation sometimes produces active responses and at other times, freezing, on a seemingly random basis. The mechanism by which the dlPAG activates active or freezing responses remains unclear; however, as it is the vlPAG to which the amygdala primarily projects, we can conclude that the behavioural freezing response to fear that is triggered in the amygdala is mediated downstream by the vlPAG. Such a conclusion is supported even more by lesion studies to the vlPAG, which show a selective loss of the freezing response to innate and learned fearful stimuli, without affecting other classes of fear responses.

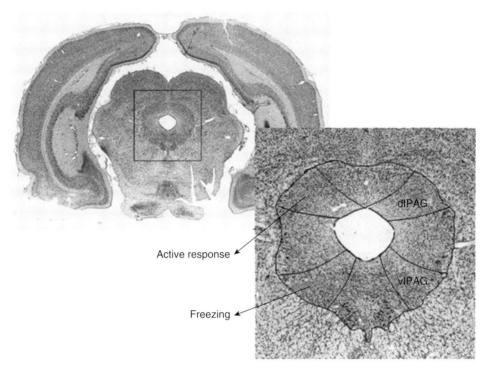

Figure 7.8   The periaqueductal grey (PAG) has subdivisions that mediate different fear responses. The PAG is located around the central aqueduct of the brain (here a histological photo of a rat brain). The PAG can be divided into several regions, including the dlPAG and vlPAG. Stimulation of the dlPAG elicits an active escape response, whereas stimulation of the vlPAG leads to freezing

UPSTREAM FROM THE AMYGDALA: THE PREFRONTAL CORTEX (PFC)

If we have an exemplar pathway from the amygdala to the vlPAG, this appears to be sufficient to regulate basic emotional responses. The amygdala receives sensory information and can mediate emotional learning, and downstream targets such as the vlPAG can produce the relevant emotional responses themselves. However, emotional behaviour is more complex than this simple scheme, and importantly requires top-down regulation. As the prefrontal cortex is commonly recognised as being important for top-down inhibitory processes, it is an obvious candidate for the control of subcortical emotional processes.

The prefrontal cortex is the source of many inhibitory projections to subcortical brain areas. In particular, there is a connection between the ventral prefrontal cortex (vPFC; equivalent to the medial prefrontal cortex (mPFC) in rodents) and the amygdala. Therefore, we would expect that if this inhibitory influence were to be removed, amygdala-mediated emotional processes would run unhindered. This is essentially what is believed to be an important problem in post-traumatic stress disorder (see Spotlight 7b), with the failure to regulate and inhibit fear processing leading to clinical anxiety. But what is the evidence that this is actually the case?

There is a whole field that looks into the role of the prefrontal cortex in fear **memory extinction** (see also Spotlight 4a). We can view this as a form of emotional inhibition. The fear extinction memory results in the suppression of fear expression, in a process that depends critically upon the mPFC in rodents. Thus the mPFC has a functional role to play in regulating fear expression.

Importantly, this principle can be extended to non-fear memories. For example, lesions to the mPFC result in impaired memory extinction in a procedure in which rats learn that a tone predicts the delivery of food, and hence they approach the food hopper when the tone comes on. Normally, this behaviour can be extinguished and only recovers in the normal manner (see Spotlight 4a). However, rats with mPFC lesions recovered the food-related response more readily, indicating an impairment in the inhibition of the original pavlovian memory (Rhodes and Killcross, 2007). The reason that this generalisation across memory types is important, as is also seen for the amygdala, is that we cannot, therefore, conclude that the mPFC is involved in specific emotions. This is especially important when it comes to looking at the evidence from humans.

Much of the most compelling evidence implicating the prefrontal cortex in human emotional regulation comes from the study of aggressive subjects (Brower and Price, 2001). Antisocial behaviour traits were identified as a problematic consequence of prefrontal cortical damage as far back as 1835 (see Benson and Blumer, 1975). However, the link between the prefrontal cortex and aggression is not limited to cases of brain damage. Natural variation in the structure and function of the prefrontal cortex may underlie differences in aggressive behaviour with clinical and other serious consequences. Patients with antisocial personality disorder have a reduced volume of grey matter in the prefrontal cortex (Raine et al., 2000). This structural abnormality has a functional consequence, as evidenced by the fact that perpetrators of violent murders have lower functional activity in the prefrontal cortex compared to controls, as assessed by PET scans (Raine et al., 1997). Therefore, the prefrontal cortex appears to act in an inhibitory manner, suppressing aggressive behaviour. A reduction in the capacity of the prefrontal cortex to carry out this function, either due to damage or through other variations, results in an increase in aggression.

Despite this heavy implication of the prefrontal cortex in aggressive behaviour, we cannot simply conclude that the human prefrontal cortex is selectively involved in aggression. First, this is inconsistent with the animal literature suggesting a more generalised role in emotional regulation. Second, there is also extensive evidence in humans to indicate an important role in fear inhibition. Functional imaging of fear memory extinction implicates the human vPFC, as well as the amygdala. Moreover, the strength of the connection between the vPFC and amygdala appears to be important for normal function. Magnetic resonance imaging can be used not only to identify increased blood flow to infer localised brain activation, but also to establish the strength of functional connectivity between two brain areas (diffusion tensor imaging). Kim and Whalen (2009) used these approaches to show that the strength of the vPFC–amygdala pathway was inversely correlated with an assessment of trait anxiety. Hence the stronger the connection between the vPFC and the amygdala, presumably resulting in a greater capacity of prefrontal inhibition of amygdala function, the lower the likelihood of anxiety.

The prefrontal cortex is much more than simple inhibition, however. With an established link to executive functions, it would seem logical that the prefrontal cortex might use emotional information in order to influence decision-making. The first evidence to support such an idea comes again from the case of Phineas Gage. The damage to vPFC that Gage suffered did not result simply in a loss of behavioural inhibition and capacity for extinction learning, but seemed to impact upon his behaviour more widely. This has been characterised as a state of risky decision-making in the absence of normal vPFC function (the somatic marker hypothesis; see Insight box opposite). Hence the vPFC serves a complex higher-order function in relation to emotional processing.

INSIGHT: THE SOMATIC MARKER HYPOTHESIS

A major hypothesis of emotion has been proposed by Antonio Damasio. This is not to be confused as an alternative hypothesis to those considered earlier in the chapter, as it concerns two main questions:

- What is the contribution of emotional responses to cognitive decision-making?
- What is the contribution of the prefrontal cortex to emotional processing?

Damasio takes as his starting point the observations of Phineas Gage. While the neurological trauma that Gage suffered was extensive and therefore likely had a number of consequences, Damasio concentrates on the apparent change in decision-making behaviour. Gage was previously a law-abiding citizen, who quietly held down his construction job. Following his injury, focused on the ventral prefrontal cortex, he seemed no longer to be himself, engaging in risky behaviours that betrayed a failure of good decision-making.

So what helps us make decisions? Damasio argues that unconscious emotional responses guide our behaviour. When we are about to perform a behaviour, the emotional physiological and autonomic responses that have been associated with a prior erroneous decision (these are the somatic markers) unconsciously 'warn' us against taking that course of action. Similarly, somatic markers associated with a good decision will encourage that response. Therefore, emotional responses ensure adaptive behaviour. Without them, we will make risky decisions like those of Phineas Gage. Moreover, given the focus on the ventral PFC, it must be this area of the brain that has the important role of processing these somatic markers to guide behaviour.

Is there evidence to support the specifics of this hypothesis? The best support comes from studies using the Iowa Gambling Task (see also Figure 7b.3). This is a card-based game (that can be computerised), in which subjects have to win money simply by selecting cards from one of four decks. Two 'good' decks give small wins, intermixed with small losses, but over time they give a profit. The other two 'bad' decks give larger payouts, but much larger losses, thus losing the participant money over time. Therefore, good decision-making will lead subjects to select cards from the good decks only. When neurologically-intact participants perform the task, they show an emotional galvanic skin response (sweating) when hovering over the bad decks, which guides them away and towards the good decks. Therefore, they perform the task well. In contrast, patients with ventral prefrontal cortex damage do not show this emotional response, and hence perform poorly on the task (Bechara et al., 1997).

KEY POINTS

- The brain is essential for emotional responses and feelings.
- The ventral prefrontal cortex and temporal lobe have been broadly implicated in emotion.
- The limbic system has been historically associated with emotion, but there is a problem with its definition.
- The amygdala, within the temporal lobe and limbic system, is critical for fear and, in particular, fear memories.
- The amygdala also plays a role beyond fear.
- Subdivisions of the periaqueductal grey region downstream from the amygdala mediate the freezing response.

(Continued)

(Continued)

- The prefrontal cortex is involved in the regulation and inhibition of amygdala-based fear and aggression.
- The prefrontal cortex also regulates non-fearful/aggressive behaviours, and appears to play a role in decision-making based upon emotional cues.

HOW DO WE COMMUNICATE EMOTIONS?

From multiple perspectives, it is important that emotional states are communicated in a consistent and rapidly-detectable manner. Socially in humans, it tells us how others feel and so how they might react to certain situations. For example, we would be much less likely to challenge someone who appears to be in an aggressive state than one who is in a fearful state. In this way, we can avoid confrontation and potential danger. Similarly, we might avoid conflict by displaying our own state; either by showing fear in order to 'submit' to an aggressor, or showing aggression in order to deter others. Therefore, there is an advantage both to *recognising* emotions and *expressing* them.

There are a number of ways in which we can express our emotional state. These consist of changes in our posture, sounds that we make (e.g. growls), and facial expressions. We will concentrate on facial expressions, as they are the most easily recognisable and distinct across emotions. There are a number of core emotions that are defined by their distinct facial expressions

| ANGER | FEAR | SURPRISE |
| SADNESS | JOY | DISGUST |

Figure 7.9 Core emotional facial expressions. There are six core expressions that are consistently produced and easily recognised

Photographs by Andrei State

(Figure 7.9). There is agreement on six of these (anger, sadness, happiness, fear, disgust and surprise), though others are sometimes included (e.g. contempt, embarrassment, affection and expectation). We will not concern ourselves with the merits of including individual emotions among the core set. Instead, we will concentrate on some fundamental questions concerning the biological psychology of emotional facial expressions.

If emotional facial expressions are to serve a useful purpose, they must be consistent. What is the use of making a facial expression when you are in a state of fear, if others do not recognise that it denotes fear? So the expression of fear must be similar across individuals, such that it can be easily and quickly recognised. How can this be achieved? First, the development of these specific facial expressions, as argued above, serves a functional purpose, and so would have emerged through evolutionary processes. This is the domain of evolutionary psychology, whereby not just biology, but also behaviour, is shaped by evolution. So we would expect that emotional facial expressions have an evolutionary basis.

Second, as a consequence, if facial expressions have an evolutionary basis, then they are determined by genetic and biological processes. Hence, emotional facial expressions should have a biological underpinning. We will see the evidence for the evolutionary and biological bases of facial expressions, thereby supporting the assertion that facial expressions serve an adaptive function.

Emotional expressions have an evolutionary basis

What kind of evidence would support an evolutionary basis for emotional facial expressions? If facial expressions are useful in humans, perhaps they are also useful in other animals. So human use of emotional expressions may be based upon their prior development in 'evolutionarily older' animals. This has two implications. First, facial expressions are likely to be similar across all cultures of humans, regardless of environmental influence. Second, similar facial expressions might be seen also in non-human animals.

The relationship between human and animal facial expressions has a long history. Darwin noted the similarity in his book *The Expression of the Emotions in Man and Animals*. While his book considered the whole range of emotional responses, Darwin also drew on the work of others to highlight the fact that different emotional facial expressions use distinct patterns of facial muscle contraction. He then noted certain similarities between human expressions and those of animals. The first parallel he drew was in the context of pain, which is characterised in part by clenched teeth. Another comparison was that of rage, in which the teeth are bared in dogs, cats, horses and various species of monkeys (Figure 7.10). This is also evident in humans, with Darwin aptly quoting Shakespeare:

> In peace there's nothing so becomes a man,
>
> As modest stillness and humility;
>
> But when the blast of war blows in our ears,
>
> Then imitate the action of a tiger:
>
> Stiffen the sinews, summon up the blood,
>
> Then lend the eye a terrible aspect;

Now set the teeth, and stretch the nostril wide,

Hold hard the breath, and bend up every spirit

To his full height! On, on, you noblest English

Henry V, iii, 1

Figure 7.10   Facial expressions of rage in a dog, child and adult
Source: Darwin (1872)

Finally, limiting ourselves to the comparison between monkeys and humans, we can see notable similarities in the expressions of happiness, with the corners of the mouth being raised (Figure 7.11).

Figure 7.11   Facial expressions of happiness in monkeys and humans
Source: Darwin (1872)

Facial expressions are also similar in their production across cultures. The evidence is limited, and the focus has usually been of the *recognition* of facial expressions. However, Darwin himself attempted a study, by distributing a questionnaire in 1867 to various people, including missionaries and those working with aboriginal cultures. He described the Western/British characteristics of various emotional facial expressions and asked if these were similar in the local cultures. Upon receiving 36 responses (covering Australia, China, Borneo, Malaysia, India, regions of Africa and the Americas), Darwin noted that there appeared to be a remarkable uniformity in 'all the races of mankind'. In a more recent seminal study, Ekman and Friesen (1971) observed that members of an isolated New Guinea tribe that were not literate (and so had not been exposed to influences from other cultures) produced emotional facial expressions that were easily recognisable and matched those observed in other mainstream cultures.

Emotional expressions have a biological basis

These observations by Darwin and subsequent researchers suggest that facial expressions have a hereditary basis (i.e. they are inherited by our descendants through biological/genetic means). So they seem not to be determined by us learning from our parents how to make the expressions, but may be truly innate. The classic way to investigate whether a behaviour is innate is to study newborn babies.

While newborns do not appear to show the full range of adult facial expressions, they do display characteristic expressions from very early on, perhaps even before they have opened their eyes. One prime example is their reaction to different tastes. A sweet taste elicits in all babies a characteristic expression of sticking the tongue out that might be classed as happiness or pleasure, and a bitter taste results in an open-mouthed 'gaping' response. Moreover, supporting the evolutionary basis of these expressions, responses with incredibly similar characteristics are seen in other mammals, from different species of monkeys to rats.

Even if basic facial expressions are present from birth, are the diverse expressions in adults innate and biologically determined, or do they depend upon learning from others? The similarity seen across cultures in adults might reflect biological underpinnings, or simply that the cultures themselves operate similarly to shape the different expressions as we grow up.

One class of individuals that fall outside of this potential environmental influence is those who have been blind from birth. Given that they have not had any visual experience of seeing the facial expressions of others, they cannot model (i.e. practise and copy) those expressions as they grow up. So if they show a similar range and specificity of facial expressions at adulthood, this would be strong evidence for the biological basis of facial expressions.

The evidence in this area is somewhat mixed, with some studies showing that congenitally blind individuals produce the same range of emotional facial expressions as fully-sighted people, and others showing that the facial expressions in blind subjects were less recognisable. An important distinction that appears to account for these differences is the manner in which the facial expressions were generated. When they were spontaneous, they appeared not to differ from fully-sighted expression. For example, in a study of congenitally and non-congenitally (i.e. not from birth) blind judo contestants in the 2004 Paralympic Games, compared with fully-sighted Judo contestants in the Olympic Games, it was observed that there was no discernible difference in the facial expressions displayed at the end of the gold and bronze medal matches (Matsumoto and Willingham, 2009). The expression of disappointment in the losers and enjoyment in the winners were similar in nature, indicating that at least these facial expressions are innate and do not require a modelling process.

In contrast to the similarity of spontaneous facial expressions in congenitally-blind individuals to those of fully-sighted subjects, voluntarily-produced facial expressions do appear to differ. People blind from birth do produce facial expressions when instructed to do so (e.g. 'smile as if you are happy'). However, these expressions are much more poorly recognised by observers than those voluntarily produced by control subjects. What this means is that the congenitally blind produce 'normal' emotional facial expressions unconsciously/spontaneously, but not voluntarily/consciously.

This distinction between conscious and unconscious production of emotional facial expressions also occurs at the level of the underpinning brain mechanisms. This is shown by the description of two separate conditions, resulting from different brain lesions (Hopf et al., 1992), both of which impair emotional facial expressions.

The condition of **emotional facial paresis** is characterised by an impairment in unconscious spontaneous facial expressions. For example, such patients would not smile when winning a competition. However, they can move their facial muscles upon instruction in order to mimic a smile. In contrast, there is a different condition, **volitional facial paresis**, in which patients have precisely the opposite problem. They cannot voluntarily move their facial muscles, but will spontaneously smile when happy. Therefore, in congenitally blind individuals, the brain mechanisms that mediate spontaneous facial expressions are intact and can generate the appropriate characteristic expressions. However, try and imagine that you have never seen a smile or a frown before. If we are unaware of the movements that we are producing when we smile or frown unconsciously, how would we be able to generate them on demand? So it is not really surprising that the congenitally blind cannot voluntarily produce recognisable emotional facial expressions.

The final, and perhaps conclusive, evidence that emotional facial expressions have a biological basis is the demonstration that they are inherited. Despite the fact that the core emotions have characteristic recognisable expressions, it is possible to discern differences in the exact nature of the facial expression across individuals (we will term these specific 'expression structures'). If facial expressions are biological and ultimately genetically determined, these subtle differences in expression structures should be inherited from generation to generation.

Of course, standard family studies would be hampered by the fact that children do mimic their parents, and so any 'inheritance' of facial expression structure might have both a genetic and a modelling factor. However we can, again, draw upon the study of congenitally blind individuals. Since they are not susceptible to modelling factors, if they inherit their parents' expression structures, this would be strong evidence for facial expressions being genetically heritable. Peleg et al. (2006) conducted such a study, analysing the whole range of core emotions, and observed that there was a high correlation between the expression structures of the blind subjects and those of their parents. Therefore, facial expressions, just like the other classes of emotional responses, are truly biological responses.

KEY POINTS

- Facial expressions are a component of the emotional response.
- Facial expressions are similar across human cultures and even non-human animals, and so likely have an evolutionary basis.
- Facial expressions are similar in newborn babies and in people blind from birth, and so likely have a biological/genetic basis.

CHAPTER SUMMARY

Emotions are not simply the subjective feelings that you experience. They are associated with characteristic patterns of biological responses. These include physiological and behavioural changes, which serve to provide an appropriate response to the emotional stimulus. Ultimately, this leads to increased chances of survival and procreation. Some believe that the biological responses activate and determine the subjective feeling that is experienced. Other hypotheses suggest a more nuanced interaction between the two processes. Regardless, the study of the mechanisms of the biological responses will ultimately aid our understanding of subjective feelings as well. The amygdala is a critical node in the brain circuits that underlie emotion. It is strongly linked to fear, and in particular fear learning and memory. However, it also plays a role in positive emotional responses, and so is not just a fear brain area. Similarly, while studies of the prefrontal cortex implicate it strongly in the inhibition of aggressive behaviour, the prefrontal cortex may play a more general inhibitory role in regulating all emotions. Finally, facial expressions are another important component of the emotional response. These emotional facial expressions are not under conscious control, and have a strong biological/genetic component, being conserved across human cultures and even across non-human species. Therefore, the study of emotional responses in non-human animals is relevant to the understanding of human emotion.

FURTHER READING

Dalgleish, T. (2004). The emotional brain. *Nature Reviews Neuroscience, 5*(7), 583–9.
Historical review of the biological psychology of emotion. Covers the major theories and provides detail on the amygdala and prefrontal cortex (as well as the hypothalamus).

Davis, M. (1992). The role of the amygdala in fear and anxiety. *Annual Review of Neuroscience, 15*, 353–75.
Review of the amygdala and fear, focusing on rodent studies. Ignores the subdivisions (see Spotlight 7a) and concentrates on viewing the amygdala as a whole.

Ekman, P. (1993). Facial expression and emotion. *American Psychologist, 48*(4), 384–92.
Broad but concise review of emotional facial expressions. It focuses particularly on the contribution of Paul Ekman, and considers the concept of universal facial expressions.

Phelps, E. A. (2006). Emotion and cognition: Insights from studies of the human amygdala. *Annual Review of Psychology, 57*, 27–53.
Provides a review of studies on the human amygdala. Its main focus is on functional imaging, principally focused on fear.

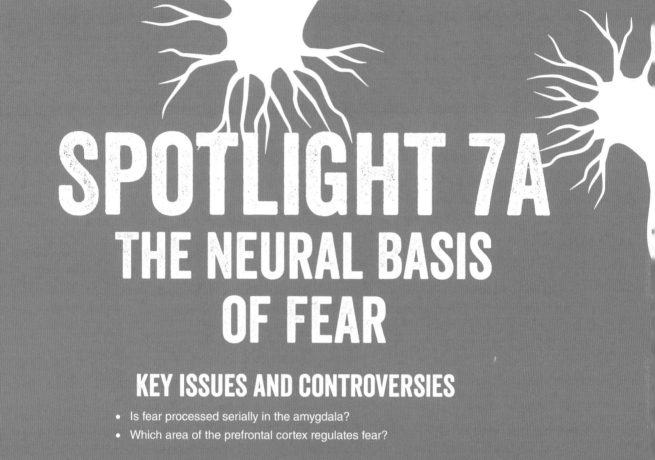

SPOTLIGHT 7A
THE NEURAL BASIS OF FEAR

KEY ISSUES AND CONTROVERSIES

- Is fear processed serially in the amygdala?
- Which area of the prefrontal cortex regulates fear?

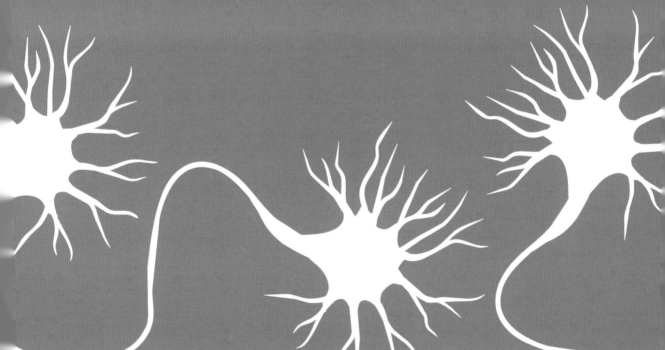

INTRODUCTION

In Chapter 7 we discovered that the amygdala and ventral prefrontal cortex are both involved in the regulation of emotion. We saw that damage to either region resulted in abnormal emotional behaviour. However, we considered the amygdala and ventral prefrontal cortex as uniform areas, without paying consideration to the anatomical variations within each structure. In this Spotlight, our aim is to revisit the neural basis of emotion, with a focus on fear. We will explore two issues in depth and along the way we will analyse some key research papers and critically appraise methods and findings. The amygdala is a complex structure, with many subdivisions serving potentially-different functions. Is information processed serially through these subdivisions, following a standard route from one area to another? The ventral prefrontal cortex can also be divided into at least two distinct regions. Which of these areas serves the function of regulating (inhibiting) fear expression?

IS FEAR PROCESSED SERIALLY IN THE AMYGDALA?

In previous sections, we have referred to the amygdala as a single structure that is implicated in emotion, and in particular in emotional learning and memory. However, this is a gross over-simplification. While the principles outlined previously are correct, there is an additional level of complexity introduced when we consider the true anatomical nature of the amygdala. In this section, we will look at the actual anatomical nature of the amygdala and focus in on specific subregions that play important roles in fear. Therefore, there will be quite a lot of material first introducing the critical subregions, with the evidence that they play a functional role in fear, before going on to the central question of how information passes between them.

The amygdala

The amygdala is actually an incredibly heterogeneous structure. It consists of many subdivisions or 'nuclei'. These nuclei can be distinguished on the basis of their **cytoarchitecture**. This refers to the structure of the neurons that are located in each area, as well as their relative connectivity. On this basis, there are at least 11 nuclei that have been defined in the rat brain (see Figure 7a.1), and arguably more in the primate (including human) brains. Not all of these are directly relevant to this discussion of fear. For example, the cortical nuclei appear to have functions that are largely associated with olfaction (the sense of smell), especially given that they receive their strongest input from olfactory sensory areas of the brain.

The fact that the amygdala has different subdivisions with differential connectivity means that they likely serve different functions. This level of specificity is obscured by studies that treat the amygdala as a unitary structure. Sometimes this is unavoidable, for example in the case of Urbach–Wiethe disease and other forms of human brain damage. Moreover, human brain imaging has not historically had the spatial resolution to distinguish between subdivisions of the amygdala. However, experimental studies in animals are well-placed to answer questions about the relative functions of the small amygdala nuclei. We can create very selective lesions to individual nuclei, and gene/protein imaging techniques have a resolution not only to very small spatial areas, but also to different neuronal subtypes (e.g. inhibitory vs. excitatory) within an area. Therefore, much of the available information comes from research carried out in experimental animals, and in rats in particular.

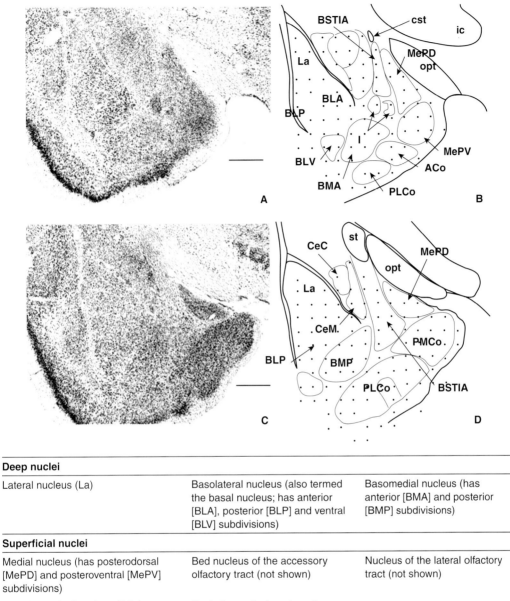

Deep nuclei		
Lateral nucleus (La)	Basolateral nucleus (also termed the basal nucleus; has anterior [BLA], posterior [BLP] and ventral [BLV] subdivisions)	Basomedial nucleus (has anterior [BMA] and posterior [BMP] subdivisions)
Superficial nuclei		
Medial nucleus (has posterodorsal [MePD] and posteroventral [MePV] subdivisions)	Bed nucleus of the accessory olfactory tract (not shown)	Nucleus of the lateral olfactory tract (not shown)
Anterior cortical nucleus (ACo)	Posterior cortical nucleus (has lateral [PLCo] and medial [PMCo] subdivisions)	
Other amygdaloid areas		
Central nucleus (has capsular [CeC] and medial [CeM]) subdivisions)	Amygdalo-hippocampal area (not shown)	Intercalated cell masses (I)

Figure 7a.1 Subdivisions of the amygdala. A & C, two sections through the amygdala of the rat. B & D, schematic representation of the subdivisions of the amygdala represented on the sections. Acronyms are presented in the table, which groups the subregions into cytoarchitectonic groups

Source: King et al. (2003)

Which nuclei of the amygdala are important for fear?

The nuclei that have received the most attention in relation to fear are the lateral nucleus (LA), the basal nucleus (B) and the central nucleus (CeN). We will consider these in turn, as it is generally considered that information flows through the amygdala from the LA to the B and then out of the CeN.

The lateral nucleus

The LA, together with the B, forms the basolateral complex of the amygdala (BLA). This complex bears certain similarities to the overlying temporal cortex, leading some to term it a pseudo-cortical area. The LA itself is the area of the amygdala that receives the greatest input from outside of the amygdala (Amaral et al., 1992). The sources of these inputs include all cortical areas, as well as the thalamus and the striatum. What this means is that the LA receives all manner of sensory information, which has led LeDoux to term it the 'sensory interface' of the amygdala (LeDoux et al., 1990).

Given that the LA receives sensory information, it is ideally placed to be the site of the associative convergence of the information that underlies pavlovian fear conditioning. However, just because there are anatomical pathways that have been traced in the brain that could send conditioning-related information to the LA, is this sufficient evidence to conclude that such information is, in reality, conveyed to the LA through these pathways? The best support comes from electrophysiological recordings in the LA. Recording in anaesthetised rats showed that the LA does respond to the presentation of a variety of auditory stimuli (Rogan and LeDoux, 1995). Similarly, presentation of the standard footshock outcome also elicits neuronal activity in the LA (Romanski et al., 1993). Most importantly, Romanski et al. identified single neurons that responded to both auditory (CS) and somatosensory (footshock US) stimulation, thereby making them ideal candidates for the associative locus of fear conditioning. Interestingly, these neurons were not distributed throughout the LA, but were concentrated in the dorsal region of the LA, suggesting that there may be further anatomical localisation within amygdala subnuclei.

The assumption is, therefore, that these dorsal LA neurons that receive convergent CS and US information should be the ones that form the fear conditioning memory. With the predominant theory of memory being that it is mediated by *synaptic plasticity* (see Chapter 4), we would expect these same neurons to undergo synaptic potentiation following fear conditioning. This is exactly what has been found. Quirk et al. (1995) recorded from the dorsal LA prior to and following fear conditioning, and showed that the response to the tone CS was significantly potentiated by conditioning. Therefore, the LA is both anatomically and functionally well-placed to mediate fear learning and memory.

So, finally, is the LA necessary for pavlovian fear conditioning? We will concentrate on lesion evidence, though the picture from other, reversible, treatment methods is largely consistent. The earliest evidence came from LeDoux and colleagues (1990), who were the first to attempt selectively to lesion the LA, while leaving the other amygdala nuclei intact (especially the central nucleus). They did this by electrolytic means, by passing an electric current through an electrode lowered into the LA. This has the advantage of creating a very localised lesion in quite a replicable manner, and LeDoux et al. observed that the lesion greatly disrupted fear conditioning to a tone stimulus. However, electrolytic lesions suffer in our ability to interpret their effects, as they also cause damage to axons passing through the lesioned area. Therefore, we might erroneously attribute the behavioural function to the amygdala, when the function is really supported by the passage of information between two completely unrelated structures via an axonal tract that just happens to pass through the amygdala. However, excitotoxic lesions to the LA, which damage only the cell bodies and not the axons in the target area, replicate the deficit in fear conditioning (e.g. Goosens and Maren, 2001). Therefore, anatomical, electrophysiological and functional evidence strongly implicates the LA in the associative element of pavlovian fear conditioning.

The basal nucleus

As mentioned previously, the B is linked to the LA, being structurally similar. The B also receives much the same innervation as the LA, though it is significantly less dense. There are important differences, however, in that the B receives input from the hippocampus (McDonald, 1998) and also from the LA itself (Pitkänen et al., 1997). What this means is that there is anatomical evidence for serial processing from the LA to the B; however, there is also the potential for parallel information processing, as the B is innervated independently of any contribution from the LA.

A number of studies have investigated the role of the B in pavlovian fear conditioning. These have mostly used lesion techniques, in order reliably to dissociate the B from the LA. However, the picture remains a little complicated. Two groups have found that electrolytic lesions of the B do not impair fear conditioning to a tone (Anglada-Figueroa and Quirk, 2005; Nader et al., 2001). However, this appears only to be the case when the lesion is made prior to conditioning, as, when the B is lesioned after conditioning and before the test, tone conditioned freezing is impaired (Anglada-Figueroa and Quirk, 2005). Therefore, the B may be involved in the expression of conditioned fear, without having a critical role to play in the acquisition and memory for fear conditioning. This would be consistent with the LA playing the associative role, and the B acting to relay information to downstream structures (perhaps via the central nucleus).

The issues with electrolytic lesions are not so problematic here. A negative effect of electrolytic lesions simply implies that neither the target area, nor any potential axons passing through, are important for fear conditioning. Nevertheless, it is reassuring to find that the effect of excitotoxic lesions is the same. Onishi and Xavier (2010) carried out selective excitotoxic lesions of the B, and similarly observed a lack of effect on the acquisition of fear conditioning to a tone.

At this stage, we are again treating the B as a homogeneous structure within the amygdala. However, as we have previously seen for the LA, there is also sub-structural variation in the B that lends an added level of complexity. One study that goes against the pattern of results is from Goosens and Maren (2001). They carried out a large amygdala lesion on one side of the brain, and small excitotoxic lesions of selective nuclei on the other side. This effectively created a bilateral lesion only of the selective area, and enabled them to do this while minimising the number of rats that they had to use (the small lesions being quite difficult to create). What Goosens and Maren found was an impairment of both discrete tone and contextual fear conditioning when the lesions were made before conditioning. However, they explain this discrepancy by noting that these effects were only observed when the anterior portion of the B was damaged. Therefore, there appears to be regional variations within the B in terms of its involvement in fear conditioning.

The central nucleus

The CeN has traditionally been viewed as the output structure of the amygdala. It is the source of the strongest efferent connections to subcortical targets (Davis, 1992). Indeed, when we talk of the amygdala being ideally located to coordinate fear responses (see Chapter 7, particularly Figure 7.7), it is in fact the CeN that appears to serve this function. Thus it is stimulation of the CeN that elicits fearful responses, such as increased heart rate, blood pressure and startle behaviour. The input to the CeN largely arises from the LA and B. Therefore, the CeN receives, indirectly, all the sensory information that reaches the BLA. Given the anatomical position of the CeN in relation to its inputs and outputs, it is therefore not surprising that selective lesions to the CeN impair the production of fear responses.

Lesions to the CeN impair fear conditioning to both discrete and contextual stimuli. This is the case whether they are created electrolytically or excitotoxically, and whether they are created before or after conditioning (Campeau and Davis, 1995; Goosens and Maren, 2001; Zimmerman et al., 2007). This is quite conclusive evidence that the CeN is important in the expression of conditioned fear memories, likely through its downstream targets. The slight problem with CeN damage always impairing fear conditioning is that it leaves open the possibility that the fear *response* cannot be performed in the absence of the CeN. Thus is the CeN merely important for producing fear responses, regardless of the cause, or does it have a specific role to play in *learned fear*? The answer is the latter, and has been demonstrated elegantly in a number of studies that have looked at unconditioned, or innate, fear. Rats show fear responses automatically to a number of situations, without having first had to learn that they are fearful. Examples of these are bright light and exposure to fox urine. Therefore, rats will display behavioural indices of fear (e.g. freezing and potentiated startle) in such situations. This unconditioned fear is not affected by CeN lesions (Walker and Davis, 1997), showing that rats can produce the fear response in the absence of the CeN; instead, they are incapable of coordinating *conditioned* fear responses.

Serial or parallel processing in the amygdala?

From the anatomical evidence outlined above, there appears to be a strong serial pathway through the amygdala, with sensory information primarily entering through the LA, and then passing to the CeN either directly or via the B. Moreover, it is the CeN that projects to downstream target structures that are implicated in the production of fear responses. This view of serial processing within the amygdala is further supported by the associative plasticity in the LA, as well as the functional necessity of the LA, B and CeN in fear conditioning (Figure 7a.2).

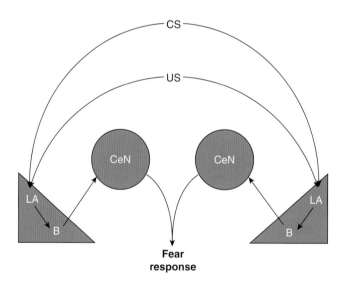

Figure 7a.2 Serial processing within the amygdala. On each side of the brain, afferent fibres carrying CS and US information converge in the lateral amygdala (LA), from where the information is passed serially through the basal amygdala (B) to the central nucleus (CeN). From the CeN, efferents to downstream structures coordinate the fear response

The fact that independent lesions to the LA, B and CeN all impair fear conditioning does not, however, tell us that the information processing in the amygdala is truly serial in nature. Despite the anatomical evidence for a pathway through the amygdala from the LA to the CeN, this does not necessarily mean that this is how the amygdala functionally operates. Take an alternative explanation. Simplifying the picture by considering the BLA as a whole, serial processing suggests that damage to the BLA prevents sensory information from reaching the CeN, and similarly damage to the CeN prevents information from the BLA accessing downstream structures (Figure 7a.3).

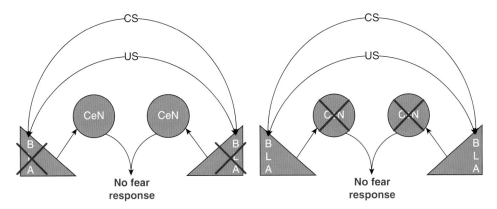

Figure 7a.3 Impact of lesions upon serial processing. Bilateral lesions to the basolateral amygdala (BLA; left) or central nucleus (CeN; right). Lesions to the BLA prevent CS (and US) information from being passed to the CeN, and so no fear response is produced to the CS. Lesions to the CeN leave the BLA unable to coordinate the fear response as the CeN is required to innervate downstream structures

However, it might instead be that the information from the BLA is sent directly to the downstream areas that the CeN innervates. Also, the CeN might receive direct sensory input independently of the BLA. If the downstream targets require input from both the BLA and CeN, damage to either structure would result in the kind of deficits that have been described above, despite the information processing through the amygdala being parallel (Figure 7a.4). Therefore, independent lesions to individual brain areas tell us nothing about the functional connections between those areas.

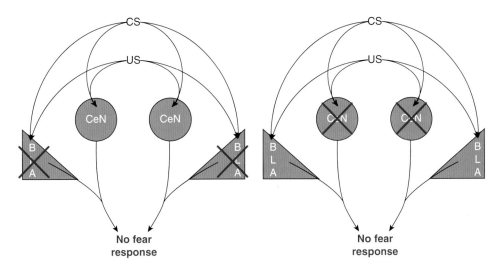

Figure 7a.4 Impact of lesions upon parallel processing. Bilateral lesions to the basolateral amygdala (BLA; left) or central nucleus (CeN; right). Lesions to the BLA do not prevent CS and US information from converging on the CeN. However, as the information from the CeN needs to be combined with BLA output (and the latter is impaired), no fear response can be produced. Similarly, with lesions to the CeN, the intact BLA and its output is unable to coordinate the fear response

We might try to stop the hypothesised information flow by cutting the axons that project from one area to another (e.g. the BLA to the CeN), although this is rarely technically feasible. There is, however, a way of determining serial neural processing using lesions. This is known as a disconnection technique, and makes use of the fact that the mammalian brain operates mainly in an ipsi-hemispheric fashion. What this means is that a brain structure in the left hemisphere communicates almost exclusively with other areas on the same side of the brain, but not meaningfully with areas on the opposite side of the brain. Therefore, if we lesion the BLA on one side, the CeN would be expected not to receive the necessary input *if there is serial processing in the amygdala*. Similarly, if the CeN were lesioned on the opposite side, we would expect the BLA not to be able to access output structures (Figure 7a.5). Therefore, this asymmetrical lesion approach impairs serial processing on both sides of the brain without creating a bilateral lesion in any area. In contrast, if the amygdala operates in a parallel manner, it should be able to cope with the unilateral damage to the BLA and CeN, as the intact CeN should receive sensory input directly, and the intact BLA should be able to activate downstream output structures. This is exactly what Jimenez and Maren (2009) did, and they found that fear conditioning in rats was severely disrupted by the disconnection technique. This provides strong evidence that the amygdala does function in a serial manner for fear learning and memory.

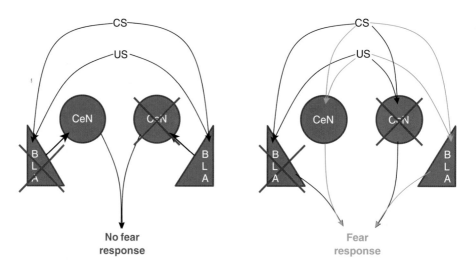

Figure 7a.5 Impact of neural disconnection upon serial (left) and parallel (right) processing. Neural disconnections consist of unilateral lesions to the basolateral amygdala (BLA) and central nucleus (CeN) in opposite hemispheres of the brain. Under a serial processing scheme, each unilateral lesion prevents the flow of information through the amygdala on the respective side of the brain, leaving both sides unable to produce a fear response. Under the parallel processing scheme, there remain operational routes of fear information processing via the intact CeN and BLA. The BLA and CeN outputs (even though there is just one of each) can be combined to coordinate the fear response. Therefore, neural disconnections distinguish between serial and parallel processing hypotheses

KEY STUDY

Killcross, S., Everitt, B. J., & Robbins, T. W. (1997). Different types of fear-conditioned behaviour mediated by separate nuclei within amygdala. *Nature, 388(6640),* 377–80

Killcross and colleagues used excitotoxic lesions of the BLA and the CeN to re-assess their contribution to fear responses. Importantly, what set this study apart was its choice of fear memory measures. It did not use the more standard freezing or potentiation of startle, but embedded the fear assessment in an instrumental reward-seeking setting. This is actually reminiscent of the original way in which researchers used to study fear in the 1960s and 1970s, and goes by the name of a **conditioned emotional response**. The procedure takes as its basis the fact that rats (and indeed humans) will not engage in reward-seeking behaviour as much if they are in a state of fear. So we initially train rats to press a lever for food. Then, the rats undergo fear conditioning to a discrete stimulus (e.g. a light). Subsequently, the presentation of the fearful stimulus should suppress instrumental responding. When the fear-conditioned stimulus is presented by the experimenter, this results in *conditioned suppression*. In contrast, if the stimulus is presented contingent upon the lever press response it *punishes* the response, also causing it to be emitted less frequently.

Killcross et al. (1997) showed that lesions to the BLA impaired conditioned punishment selectively, whereas CeN lesions only disrupted conditioned suppression. Given that the BLA lesion involved bilateral damage to both the LA and B, this means that neither of these areas is necessary for certain forms of fear (in this case conditioned suppression). The conclusion we have to draw, then, is that the CeN can operate independently of the BLA, and can support some forms of fear without input from the LA or B. We know that the CeN does receive direct sensory input from cortical, thalamic and hippocampal areas, though it is certainly less dense that that going to the LA (McDonald et al., 1999). Therefore, the CeN appears to have parallel input to the BLA, which might support its independent role. Moreover, it has been known for many years, even longer than for the LA, that there is synaptic plasticity in the CeN. Back in the 1980s, Bruce Kapp and colleagues demonstrated repeatedly that there was synaptic plasticity in the CeN of rabbits subjected to fear conditioning (e.g. Pascoe and Kapp, 1985). Why the CeN was then relegated to a simple output structure for many years is a bit of a mystery, but it has recently re-emerged as a potentially important site of associative plasticity (Wilensky et al., 2006).

A parallel conclusion can be drawn for the BLA, in that it appears to operate independently of the CeN in order to support conditioned punishment. Again, we know that the LA and B do project directly to areas outside the amygdala (Pitkänen, 2000). These include the hypothalamus, which coordinates **autonomic** and **endocrine** responses, as well as targets in the cortex, striatum and thalamus, any of which might coordinate the conditioned punishment response. What this means is there may be no serial processing within the amygdala *in the settings studied by Killcross et al.* It is important to

(Continued)

(Continued)

provide this caveat, as there is no doubting that for situations such as conditioned freezing, there is a huge amount of evidence supporting serial amygdala processing.

If we take a critical view of the study by Killcross and colleagues (e.g. Nader and LeDoux, 1997): first, the excitotoxic BLA lesions might not have damaged sufficiently the dorsal LA neurons that have been shown to be of prime importance in fear memory acquisition. We cannot provide a definitive answer to this question at present, and it remains a matter of opinion (see Killcross et al., 1997b). The second criticism is that Killcross et al. may have over-conditioned their rats. The standard procedure for fear conditioning involves one or only very few pairings of the CS with the footshock US. In contrast, Killcross et al. exposed their rats to over 100 pairings. Perhaps then, the CeN operates independently of the LA only after such over-training. This is supported by the demonstration that BLA lesions impair conditioned suppression after a few CS–US pairings, but not after over 30 pairings (Lee et al., 2005). Moreover, even conditioned freezing becomes independent of the BLA with over-training, but this recovery relies upon CeN function (Zimmerman et al., 2007).

So where does this leave us? Serial processing in the amygdala from the LA to the CeN certainly does take place, and appears to be particularly important for rapidly-acquired conditioned fear. This makes use of plasticity in the LA, but possibly also in the CeN. However, some fear responses do not require the downstream structures innervated by the CeN, and instead make use of outputs from the B (Amorapanth et al., 2000). Furthermore, with more extensive conditioning, the CeN can operate independently of the LA, relying exclusively on its own plasticity. As such, there seems to be both serial and parallel processing in the amygdala.

Implications

The distinction between serial and parallel processing is potentially important, not only for the basic understanding of fear processing in the brain. Given that fear comprises different responses, and the problematic nature of some fear responses, it is possible that certain classes of fear response might be selectively targeted for intervention, based upon their specific neural underpinnings. This may allow for more adaptive treatment strategies, rather than simply reducing fear responses across the board.

WHICH AREA OF THE PREFRONTAL CORTEX REGULATES FEAR?

We have already seen that there is a particular sub-area of the prefrontal cortex (PFC) that is implicated in emotional function. The evidence from neuropsychology (e.g. Phineas Gage) points towards the ventral region of the PFC, which is architecturally linked to the medial PFC (mPFC) in rodents. The overall picture from human and animal studies is that the PFC operates, at least in part, as a controlling brake upon subcortical function. Thus the PFC inhibits many areas, including the amygdala, thereby controlling the expression of fear responses. The ventral PFC in humans and the mPFC in rodents are simply regional designations, and actually both comprise relatively large areas of the brain. They also have subdivisions that are distinguished both cytoarchitecturally and in terms of their connectivity. In this section, we will concentrate on the rat mPFC, as the most informative studies have been carried out in rodent models. Moreover, the function of the mPFC to inhibit fear is most evident in the setting of fear memory extinction. So the question we will be asking is whether the whole of the mPFC mediates the extinction of fear memories, thereby reducing fear memory expression.

Lesions to the mPFC initially appeared to provide good support for a role in fear extinction. Electrolytic lesions did not affect the ability of rats to acquire the fear memory in the first place, but substantially impaired their ability to extinguish it (Morgan et al., 1993). Even when the fear memory was acquired with an intact brain, mPFC lesions did not impair the expression of fear, but did disrupt its extinction (Morgan et al., 2003). However, several other research groups failed to replicate these findings, showing normal extinction even with mPFC lesions (e.g. Gewirtz et al., 1997). There is the possibility that there was some

difference between the lesions that explains the conflicting results. For example, in the cases of apparently unimpaired extinction, the lesions may have been less extensive, or there may have been more recovery of function. To address these shortcomings, the mPFC has been reversibly inactivated during the recall of extinction. Unfortunately, however, the results remain conflicting, with all manner of findings having been observed. Sometimes mPFC inactivation impairs extinction to increase fear expression, or has no effect on extinction, leaving fear expression inhibited. The inactivations can even reduce fear expression compared to normal extinction, suggesting some other mechanism is also at work in the mPFC (Sierra-Mercado et al., 2006).

Subdivisions of the mPFC

Much of the confusion arising from lesion and inactivation studies of the mPFC might be explained by the fact that there are multiple subdivisions within the mPFC (Figure 7a.6). The mPFC comprises several areas. These are the anterior cingulate (CG), prelimbic (PL), infralimbic (IL) and dorsal peduncular (DP) cortices. These are located adjacent to each other in a dorsal-to-ventral direction and comprise a volume of about 1–2mm³ each in the rat. What this means is that lesions and inactivation infusions targeted to the mPFC are likely to have affected each of these areas

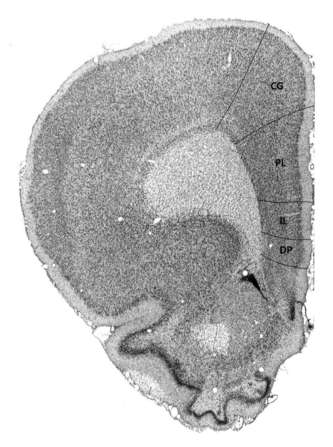

Figure 7a.6 Subdivisions of the rat medial prefrontal cortex. The medial prefrontal cortex consists of the medial wall of the prefrontal cortex (i.e. down the middle of the brain). Only the left hemisphere is shown in a photo of a histological section. The medial prefrontal cortex can be divided into the anterior cingulate cortex (CG), the prelimbic cortex (PL), the infralimbic cortex (IL) and the dorsal peduncular cortex (DP). The PL and IL are located adjacent to each other and are key areas in the regulation of fear responses.

to differing degrees, which may explain the varying results across studies. We will concentrate on the IL and PL in particular, as these equate more closely to the ventral prefrontal cortex of humans. Accordingly, they have received the most attention in relation to fear. Most of the evidence that is known about the IL and PL in fear memory comes from the work of a single laboratory. Greg Quirk has conducted an extensive programme of research, using electrophysiological, microstimulation, lesion and inactivation methods in order to study the precise functional roles of these small brain areas (Sotres-Bayon and Quirk, 2010).

The infralimbic cortex inhibits fear

Careful placement of lesions can lead to fairly selective damage to the IL. Such lesions do disrupt the expression of fear extinction, but there is still significant damage to the ventral portion of the PL (Quirk et al., 2000). Therefore, it has not been easy to distinguish the functional roles of the IL and PL to fear memory extinction. One way is to compare directly the effects of treatments targeted at the IL, and those focused on the PL. Sierra-Mercado et al. (2011) have done this using the GABA agonist muscimol to inactivate target regions. By minimising the dose and volume of muscimol infused into the brain, we can be fairly confident that the main area affected by the infusion is the targeted region. Moreover, if inactivation of the target region produces an effect, we can check whether this is mediated by diffusion into adjacent structures by targeting those areas directly. Accordingly, infusion of muscimol into the IL during extinction training impaired the long-term extinction memory, leaving subsequent fear responding higher than in controls. In contrast, PL infusions had no impact on long-term extinction memory. Therefore, the effect of infusions into the IL cannot have been due to diffusion of muscimol into the PL. Similarly, infusions into the PL cannot have diffused into the IL, or else we would have seen an effect on extinction. So the conclusion of this careful study is that it is the IL in particular that supports the extinction of fear memories.

Muscimol is hypothesised to inhibit neurons in the IL by stimulating inhibitory interneurons. Therefore, the IL must be active during the extinction of fear in order that its inhibition removes the effect of extinction. This is exactly the case, as shown by Milad and Quirk (2002). The recall of the fear extinction memory was correlated with increased neuronal activity in the IL in response to the fear-conditioned and extinguished tone (Figure 7a.7). Moreover, fear extinction could be facilitated by stimulating the IL upon each tone presentation (Milad et al., 2004).

If extinction involves the strengthening of the tone input to the IL, thereby resulting in greater inhibition of the amygdala, this explains why greater IL tone responsiveness correlates with fear extinction. Pairing tone presentation with IL stimulation would likely also result in potentiated IL tone responses. This is because IL stimulation probably depolarises post-synaptic neurons, leading to synaptic plasticity that is associated to the tone presentation. As a result, subsequent tone presentations will also depolarise IL neurons, leading to increased activity. This plasticity-related account is further supported by the fact that infusions of brain-derived neurotrophic factor (BDNF) directly into the IL *in the absence of any tone presentations* results in extinguished tone fear responses when tested the next day (Peters et al., 2010). When infused into the hippocampus, BDNF induces long-lasting LTP, and so is known to 'create' synaptic plasticity in the absence of any stimulation or behavioural experience. Presumably, then, when BDNF is delivered into the IL, it stimulates synaptic plasticity such that subsequent tone presentations activate the IL and hence inhibit fear.

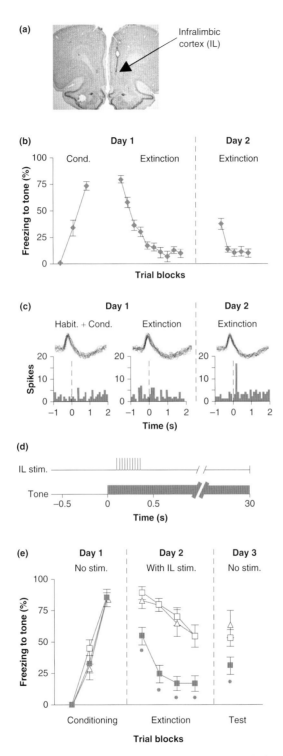

Figure 7a.7 Electrophysiological evidence that the infralimbic cortex (IL) mediates fear extinction. The IL is activated in correlation with the extinction fear responses. Recording electrodes were implanted into the IL (a). Fear was conditioned to a CS and then extinguished (b). The IL was not activated by the CS during conditioning or extinction training, but was activated during the recall of the extinction memory on day 2 (c). Stimulation of the IL enhances extinction. After fear conditioning to a tone CS, some rats had their IL stimulated upon presentation of the tone (d). These rats (filled squares) extinguished their fear response to a greater degree than did groups that received IL stimulation less tightly coupled with the tone presentation (e; open symbols)

Source: Milad and Quirk (2002)

The prelimbic cortex activates fear

If there is now such strong evidence for the IL in fear memory extinction, how can we explain the variation in the effects of less selective manipulations? Some of the first suggestions came from an exploration of the effects of stimulating the mPFC. We have already seen that IL stimulation, when combined with tone presentation, facilitates extinction of tone fear. However, stimulation of the PL has a completely different outcome. Pairing PL stimulation with tone presentation actually retarded extinction. Moreover, it increased the acute conditioned freezing response to the tone (Vidal-Gonzalez et al., 2006). So while the IL acts to inhibit fear memory expression, the PL appears to have the opposing role of facilitating fear.

Electrophysiological data do support the notion that the PL activates fear responses. Activity in PL neurons is elicited by exposure to fear-conditioned stimuli. Moreover, that activity is sustained and matches the duration of expression of the fear response, which is consistent with the hypothesis that PL activity is required to produce fear responses (Burgos-Robles et al., 2009). So, if the PL is required to express fear, its absence should result in an impairment in fear responses. Selective lesions of the PL do not appear to have had any reported effect, given that there are no findings in the literature. This may be due either to the difficulty in creating selective lesions, or perhaps because there is recovery of function that masks any deficit. The latter problem is circumvented by the use of reversible inactivations. In the same study by Sierra-Mercado et al. that inactivated the IL, the authors also inactivated the PL in different rats. What they found was that infusions of muscimol into the PL prior to extinction training reduced the expression of fear acutely during the extinction session, with no impact upon the later retention of the extinction memory. Therefore, the PL does have a functional role to play in the production of fear responses, in complete contrast to the function of the IL in inhibiting fear.

KEY STUDY

Milad, M. R., Wright, C. I., Orr, S. P., Pitman, R. K., Quirk, G. J., & Rauch, S. L. (2007). Recall of fear extinction in humans activates the ventromedial prefrontal cortex and hippocampus in concert. *Biological Psychiatry*, 62(5), 446–54

and

Milad, M. R., Quirk, G. J., Pitman, R. K., Orr, S. P., Fischl, B., & Rauch, S. L. (2007). A role for the human dorsal anterior cingulate cortex in fear expression. *Biological Psychiatry*, 62(10), 1191–4

Milad and colleagues conducted two parallel studies looking at the human equivalents of the IL and PL. The IL corresponds to the human ventromedial prefrontal cortex (vmPFC), whereas the human dorsal anterior cingulate cortex (dACC) is thought to be equivalent to the rodent prelimbic cortex.

In the first study, Milad, Wright et al. (2007) fear conditioned participants and then extinguished that acquired fear memory. They then used functional MRI to record brain activity during the recall of the fear extinction. The critical comparison was the activity induced by presentation of the extinguished stimulus as opposed to that induced by another fear-conditioned stimulus that had not been extinguished. For this comparison, activity was revealed in two areas: the vmPFC and hippocampus. The hippocampal activation is likely associated with the contextual control of memory extinction (see Spotlight 4a). The activity in the vmPFC mirrors that observed in the IL in the rodent electrophysiological studies. This similarity is strong evidence that the human vmPFC operates in a highly similar manner to the rodent IL. However, it remains only correlational evidence, and it has yet to be determined that the vmPFC alone is responsible for fear extinction in humans. Given the lack of spatial resolution afforded by neuropsychological patients or transcranial magnetic stimulation, it remains to be seen whether any such causational evidence will be observed.

In their second study, Milad, Quirk et al. (2007) looked at brain activity (again using fMRI) correlated with the expression of conditioned fear in humans. They had two stimuli,

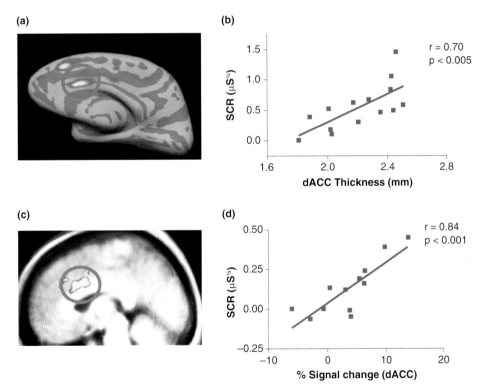

Figure 7a.8 Activity and thickness of the dACC is correlated with fear expression in humans. The dACC is the area circled in red. (a) representation of the areas of the brain in which the thickness of the cortex was correlated with fear expression. (b) correlation of dACC cortical thickness with fear expression (skin conductance response; SCR). (c) activity in the dACC when the contrast between the fearful CS⁺ and a non-feared CS⁻ was analysed. (d) the activation of the dACC correlated with the magnitude of the fear response

Source: Milad et al. (2007a)

(Continued)

(Continued)

only one of which was fear conditioned. As a result, they could look at differential fear conditioning to the CS⁺, as measured by the skin conductance responses to the two stimuli. This contrast was then used to identify brain regions that were more active to the CS⁺ than to the CS⁻. This analysis revealed significant activation of the dACC. However, this alone does not tell us about its function – remember that the IL/vmPFC is also activated by fear stimuli. The evidence that the dACC has a similar fear-activating role as the PL is twofold (Figure 7a.8). Structurally, there was a correlation between dACC cortical thickness and the magnitude of expressed fear. Therefore, the bigger the dACC, the stronger the fear response. Second, and functionally, the activity in the dACC was correlated with the magnitude of the fear response.

One important point to note about the second study on the dACC (Milad, Quirk et al., 2007) is that it involved reanalysis/further analysis of data from studies that had already been published, including from the first study (Milad, Wright et al., 2007). While this is not a problem in itself, and is a fairly routine occurrence in functional imaging studies, it does raise certain questions. The first is whether the experiments were optimally designed in order to answer the research question. Functional imaging studies, like many other research approaches, depend critically upon appropriate experimental design and control groups. It does appear that the design, as outlined above, was perfectly reasonable to assess the neural mechanisms of fear expression. However, there were slight differences between the functional and structural studies. This can be viewed as a strength or a weakness. If could be argued that the differences limit the extent to which the two studies can be compared. Nevertheless, the conceptual concordance of the findings is a strength in itself, and the minor differences in experimental procedures indicates further that the link between the dACC and fear expression is not limited to certain experimental parameters.

At a conceptual level, it is surprising that no attempt was made to relate the activity in the dACC to the amygdala. There is reference in the introduction of the paper to the interconnectivity between the dACC and the amygdala, which is presented as a rationale for the hypothesis that the dACC served an analogous function to the rodent prelimbic cortex. It cannot be that only the prefrontal cortex was imaged; you can clearly see in Figure 7a.8 that there are mild hotspots of correlation of cortical thickness with fear expression throughout the brain. While the functional imaging analysis used the dACC as a specific region of interest (and therefore would not have automatically analysed activity in other brain areas), no rationale is given for not also targeting the amygdala, which seems to be an obvious region of interest. Therefore, it would have been particularly interesting to have seen an analysis of amygdala volume and activity, and even correlation of dACC activity against activity in the amygdala.

Implications

Given its involvement in fear expression, the dACC may be an important target for the treatment of anxiety. Reducing the activity of the dACC, for example through deep brain stimulation, might be able to inhibit the expression of anxiety in various psychiatric disorders. Indeed there is already some convergent evidence supporting such a hypothesis. Patients with obsessive compulsive disorder (OCD) sometimes undergo surgical treatment to lesion the anterior portion of the ACC as a last resort. Milad et al. note that the typical region lesioned is very similar to the locus of activation that they observed. Interestingly, these patients displayed significantly reduced clinical symptoms of OCD (Dougherty et al., 2002).

FURTHER READING

Balleine, B. W., & Killcross, S. (2006). Parallel incentive processing: An integrated view of amygdala function. *Trends in Neuroscience*, 29(5), 272–9.
> Provides a review of parallel processing in the amygdala and considers evidence from both appetitive and fear settings. It also draws on motivational concepts (see Chapter 8).

Sotres-Bayon, F., & Quirk, G. J. (2010). Prefrontal control of fear: More than just extinction. *Current Opinion in Neurobiology*, 20(2), 231–5.
> Provides a review of IL and PL. Gives more detail on the evidence supporting dissociable functions, and considers the central role of the amygdala basal nucleus.

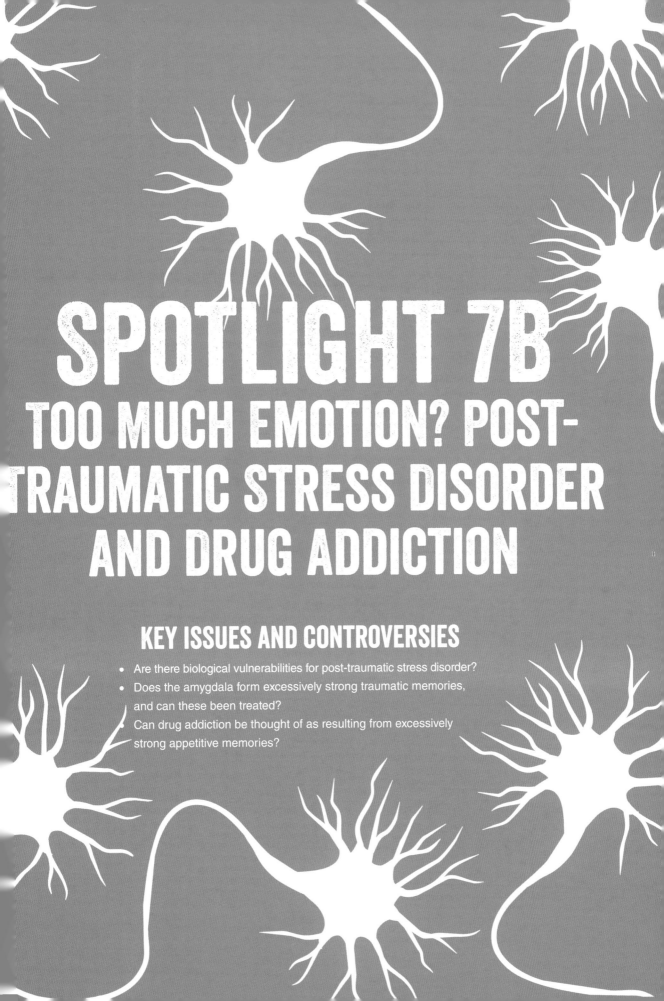

SPOTLIGHT 7B
TOO MUCH EMOTION? POST-TRAUMATIC STRESS DISORDER AND DRUG ADDICTION

KEY ISSUES AND CONTROVERSIES

- Are there biological vulnerabilities for post-traumatic stress disorder?
- Does the amygdala form excessively strong traumatic memories, and can these been treated?
- Can drug addiction be thought of as resulting from excessively strong appetitive memories?

INTRODUCTION

In Chapter 7 we discovered that learned emotional responses exist to aid survival. Cues that are predictive of aversive outcomes help us to avoid danger, and equally stimuli that are associated with positive outcomes promote adaptive behaviour in relation to food and other rewards (e.g. water, sex, social interaction). We have seen that the normal regulation of emotional responses is supported by a relatively complex network of brain areas, including at least the amygdala, prefrontal cortex and midbrain structures.

Patients with damage to the amygdala show a paucity of fear responses. While it is clear that a failure to produce emotional responses is maladaptive, potentially leading to consequences such as a greater chance of encountering danger and poorer social interactions, it may be less obvious that too much emotion may be equally disruptive to normal behaviour. We have already seen the case of damage to the prefrontal cortex, leading to increased aggressive behaviour and impaired inhibition of other emotional responses. In this Spotlight, our aim is to explore two neuropsychiatric conditions that appear to stem, at least in part, from abnormal emotional memory processing. These are post-traumatic stress disorder (PTSD) and drug addiction. We will explore three issues in depth and along the way we will analyse some key research papers and critically appraise methods and findings. First, we have to acknowledge that not all victims of trauma go on to develop PTSD. Therefore, what biological processes render individuals vulnerable to PTSD, and can these be linked to emotional memory processing? PTSD patients suffer intrusive recollections of the traumatic experience. Is this reflective of an overly strong traumatic memory, and if so, can such memories be inhibited or erased? Finally, and conceptually related, can drug addiction truly be considered to result from overly-strong appetitive memories?

POST-TRAUMATIC STRESS DISORDER

Post-traumatic stress disorder (PTSD) is one member of the family of anxiety disorders. This family also includes specific phobias, social phobia, panic disorder, obsessive compulsive disorder and generalised anxiety disorder. The distinguishing feature of PTSD is that its origin can be traced to an identifiable traumatic event. The traumatic episode is required to be of a sufficiently serious nature, involving actual or threatened death or serious injury, or a threat to the physical integrity of self or others (American Psychiatric Association [*DSM-IV-TR*], 2000). The severity of the trauma means that it induces acute feelings of fear, helplessness and horror at the time, and in PTSD sufferers, the episode is subsequently re-experienced both in dreams and when awake. The triggers are often apparently meaningless stimuli that appear capable of reactivating the emotional memory. As a consequence, patients with PTSD exhibit so-called avoidance symptoms, which involve attempts to avoid, both behaviourally and cognitively, the traumatic memory. For example, patients will avoid talking about the traumatic episode, or will avoid people or places that they have learned tend to reactivate the aversive memory. Finally, PTSD patients also suffer from the more general hyperarousal symptoms of anxiety, including sleep disturbance and increased startle responsivity.

From an epidemiological perspective, PTSD is a relatively common disorder, with a lifetime prevalence of around 5–6% in men, and 10–14% in women in the USA (see Yehuda, 2004, for a review). However, these broad statistics mask substantial variation depending on the exact situation. First, we have to distinguish prevalence from incidence. Prevalence simply describes the proportion of the population suffering from the condition at a given time. By contrast, the incidence rate concerns the number of individuals that develop PTSD out of the total number exposed to the traumatic event, and it is the incidence that varies dramatically. For example, accidents and disasters give rise to an incidence of around 4%, whereas rape leads to PTSD in around 55% of victims. Clearly, PTSD is not an inevitable consequence of trauma. In the short-term aftermath of trauma (<1 month), victims may display the symptoms of PTSD described above. However, at this early stage, it would be diagnosed as acute stress disorder (for PTSD to be diagnosed, symptoms must be present for at least one month; when they persist for over three months, this becomes classified as chronic PTSD). While the presence of acute stress disorder is associated with the subsequent development of PTSD, this is by no means a definite progression of events. Therefore, acute reactions are only mildly predictive of the long-term outcome.

What makes individuals vulnerable to PTSD?

The question of vulnerability to psychiatric disorders, including PTSD, is complex and not easily answered. Ultimately, we are seeking to define some difference that is observable prior to trauma, which explains why some individuals go on to develop PTSD and others do not. Without screening large populations for multiple variables and then following up on those that have traumatic incidents, we are left with more indirect approaches. Principal among these is the notion that the atypical responses observed in clinical patients are likely to be somehow related to the underlying vulnerability factors. Given the central role of stress in PTSD, therefore, much focus has been placed on the stress response.

Is the stress response abnormal in PTSD?

First, what is stress? Perhaps the most relevant dictionary definition is that of 'bodily suffering or injury'. But then how do we define suffering and injury? At one level, the only objective measure of an event causing suffering/injury is to isolate a relevant bodily response to that event, and the one that is most commonly used is the release of the hormone *cortisol* (although this is usually also accompanied by adrenaline and noradrenaline release). So we might simply say that stress consists of an event that results in the release of cortisol and adrenaline/noradrenaline. Given that the noradrenergic system is chronically overactive in PTSD, this seems to fit with PTSD involving a persistent and abnormal stress response. However, when we come to look at cortisol, the picture is not quite so clear. We know that cortisol is released after fear conditioning in humans (Zorawski et al., 2005) and rats (Swenson and Vogel, 1983), and subsequent re-exposure to a fear-conditioned stimulus also increases the levels of cortisol in the blood (Vandekar et al., 1991). Therefore, we might expect that following severe trauma, cortisol levels would be greatly increased, and perhaps remain elevated persistently, thereby perpetuating the stressed state. However, whether this is actually the case is controversial.

   In patients with PTSD, a number of studies have shown that basal cortisol levels (i.e. the levels that naturally occur in the individual without exposure to a stressor) appear actually to be lower than normal. For example, in a study of Holocaust survivors, those that suffered from PTSD had lower basal levels of cortisol in their urine than did non-sufferers (Yehuda et al., 1995). Moreover, the same authors conducted a subsequent follow-up ten years later, with much the same findings (Yehuda et al., 2007). Interestingly, there was also a further supportive pattern of results showing that in the handful of subjects who had remitted from the condition, their cortisol levels had apparently normalised. Conversely, some individuals had suffered a delayed-onset PTSD in the intervening period, and they were characterised by a drop in basal urinary cortisol levels. Therefore, low basal cortisol levels appear to correlate with PTSD. This may appear to be counter-intuitive, as why would a condition characterised by extreme stress be associated with low levels of our marker of stress? However, this pattern of reduced cortisol is by no means universal. Indeed there have been many studies of cortisol levels in patients with PTSD, with findings ranging from a replication of the patterns observed by Yehuda – no difference between patients and controls – to an increase in basal cortisol with PTSD. Merwisse and colleagues (2007) have analysed all such studies and argue that, overall, there is no difference in basal cortisol levels between PTSD patients and controls. The decrease observed in certain studies may simply reflect some factor that has yet to be identified (e.g. female-specific or also being victims of abuse).

So where does this leave the importance of the stress response? Even if we can explain why, under certain circumstances, cortisol is decreased in PTSD patients, this does not provide a compelling argument that low basal cortisol is important for PTSD, given that many sufferers do not appear to have low cortisol. Perhaps, however, the focus on basal cortisol is not of most importance. Instead, the more relevant question might be whether cortisol *responses* are altered in PTSD. While this might not explain why the traumatic memory is so easily reactivated, it would explain the physiological and avoidance consequences of re-experiencing the traumatic episode. While studies of cortisol responses have observed an exaggerated increase following cognitive stress manipulations (e.g. exposure to trauma-related stimuli or psychosocial stress), these have always been accompanied by elevated basal cortisol (de Kloet et al., 2006). Therefore, it is not clear whether there is a genuine alteration in cortisol response.

Perhaps, then, measures of cortisol activity are not particularly informative, and we should look, instead, to a wider consideration of the stress response. Cortisol forms one part of the hypothalamic–pituitary–adrenal (HPA) axis that regulates stress responses. Put simply, in the hypothalamus, the hormone corticotrophin-releasing factor (CRF) is released and acts on the pituitary gland, which synthesises and releases adrenocorticotrophic hormone (ACTH) into the bloodstream. ACTH acts at the adrenal glands to stimulate the release of cortisol and adrenaline/noradrenaline (Figure 7b.1a). Therefore, the regulation of basal cortisol levels and cortisol responses is achieved through CRF and ACTH in an apparently simple and linear manner (if CRF goes up, ACTH goes up and then so does cortisol). Hence, it is interesting to note that even when basal cortisol levels are low, CRF levels are elevated (Baker et al., 1999). So how can high CRF co-exist with low cortisol? The answer lies in the feedback effect that cortisol has on its own production and that of the other stress hormones. When cortisol is released into the bloodstream, it reaches the hypothalamus and pituitary, where it acts to suppress the release of CRF and ACTH (Figure 7b.1b). Moreover, in PTSD patients, the sensitivity of this negative feedback system is enhanced (as evidenced by the results of a dexamethasone suppression test; see de Kloet et al., 2006 for review), thereby allowing the high CRF levels to be less effective in promoting ACTH and cortisol release. By analogy, imagine that a central heating system worked in a way that as the temperature rises (mirroring cortisol rises), it affects the thermostat (CRF) as usual, but also directly turns off the boiler (ACTH). If this feedback to the boiler is enhanced, the boiler is persistently switched off, even if the thermostat is detecting that the temperature is too low. In this way, the thermostat could be highly activated (high CRF) but not raising the temperature (low cortisol). This is a complex explanation, which again only really applies to the situation of low basal cortisol (although the heightened sensitivity of the feedback loop is more widely observed). Nevertheless, overall there is compelling evidence that the brain's stress system is dysregulated in some manner in PTSD.

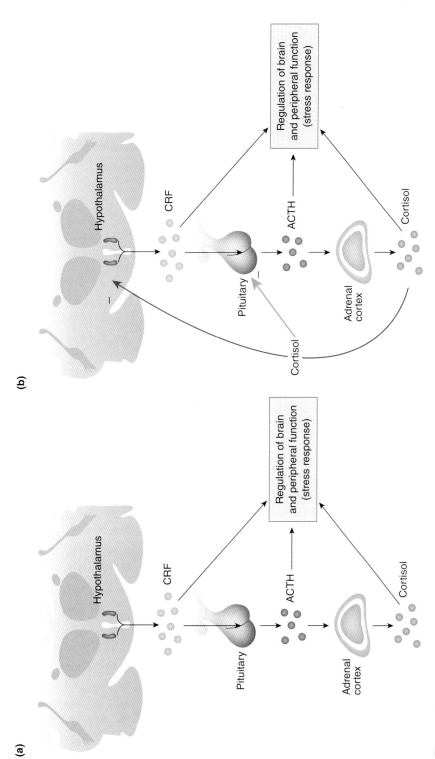

Figure 7b.1 The hypothalamic–pituitary–adrenal axis. (a) The hypothalamus releases CRF (corticotrophin-releasing factor), which acts on the pituitary gland to release ACTH (adrenocorticotrophic hormone). ACTH then stimulates the adrenal cortex to release cortisol. The combined release of CRF, ACTH and cortisol comprises the stress response. (b) Cortisol inhibits the release of CRF from the hypothalamus and ACTH from the pituitary. Cortisol thus inhibits its own release, and so low basal cortisol can lead to high levels of CRF and ACTH

Adapted from Hyman (2009)

Are stress response abnormalities pre-existing or induced?

If we accept that there is some dysregulation of the HPA axis in PTSD, an important question to consider is whether that dysregulation existed at the time of trauma, and so contributed to the development of acute and subsequent post-traumatic stress disorder, or whether it only emerged after the traumatic episode. Of course, there must be some mechanism of vulnerability that explains why some, but not other, victims of trauma go on to develop PTSD. However, the question is whether this involves the HPA stress response.

There is some evidence to suggest that HPA dysregulation pre-dates the traumatic episode. In particular, in certain groups, low basal cortisol appears to pre-date the traumatic episode. The strongest evidence comes from the study of Holocaust survivors with PTSD, and their children. We have already seen that the survivors with PTSD had low basal cortisol. Interestingly, their children also had lower than normal basal cortisol levels in the absence of any evidence of traumatic experience (Yehuda et al., 2000). This means that the causes of low cortisol may be primarily inherited, and hence would have pre-existed in the Holocaust survivors themselves. Moreover, the children had a much higher rate of developing PTSD (31%) than matched controls (9%), suggesting that their innate low basal cortisol confers a genuine risk factor for PTSD (Yehuda, Schmeidler et al., 1998). However, it is becoming increasingly recognised that acquired alterations in gene expression can be inherited through **epigenetic** processes. So it remains possible that the PTSD survivors could have developed low cortisol levels that were then epigenetically passed on to their children.

In other groups of PTSD patients, the observation of low basal cortisol seems to have been dependent in certain cases upon the patients having suffered abuse previously. Moreover, early life stress is increasingly recognised as an important factor in PTSD (Heim and Nemeroff, 2001). Thus prior abuse and stress itself may have altered HPA function, with an altered state at the time of subsequent trauma being important for the development of PTSD. In support of this hypothesis, studies of victims of trauma suggest that those individuals who have a lower than normal cortisol response in the immediate aftermath of the event are more likely to go on to develop PTSD (McFarlane et al., 1997). Moreover, evidence from animals confirms that prior stress alters the response to later stressful events (Antelman et al., 1992). Therefore, it is possible that PTSD results, at least partially, from an abnormal acute stress response to trauma that may depend upon pre-existing dysregulation of the HPA axis.

Are there neural vulnerability factors for PTSD?

Dysregulation of the HPA axis is not the only change that has been observed in PTSD patients. Changes in neural reactivity are also observed in functional imaging studies. For example, the amygdala becomes hyper-reactive. In a study of war veterans, those with PTSD showed an exaggerated fMRI amygdala response to subliminally-presented fearful facial expressions compared to veterans without PTSD (Rauch et al., 2000). This may well reflect atypical amygdala processing. However, it may also be a consequence of the increased fear and anxiety present in PTSD, rather than a cause of the disorder. Perhaps, then, the more recent observation that the amygdala is smaller in volume in PTSD sufferers than in matched controls (Morey et al., 2012) suggests a pre-existing amygdala deficit?

Anatomical differences in PTSD patients extend also to the hippocampus. It is relatively well established that the hippocampus is smaller in PTSD (Bremner et al., 1995; Gurvits et al., 1996).

We might, therefore, assume that the smaller hippocampal volume pre-dated the traumatic episode, and hence is a vulnerability factor for PTSD. However, we also know that cortisol is **neurotoxic** at high levels, resulting in damage particularly to the hippocampus (Hoschl and Hajek, 2001). This means that the smaller hippocampus in PTSD may actually be a consequence of the trauma and the dysregulated stress response.

KEY STUDY

Gilbertson, M. W., Shenton, M. E., Ciszewski, A., Kasai, K., Lasko, N. B., Orr, S. P., & Pitman, R. K. (2002). Smaller hippocampal volume predicts pathologic vulnerability to psychological trauma. *Nature Neuroscience, 5*(11), 1242–7

Gilbertson and colleagues took a novel approach to the question of whether hippocampal volume reductions are a cause or consequence of trauma. They used a twin study in order to obtain as reliable information as possible on the pre-existing hippocampus volumes of PTSD patients.

Gilbertson et al. recruited **monozygotic** twins. These are genetically-identical twins, meaning that they could look at trauma-induced neural changes. It is the closest we can get to a comparison before and after trauma. One of the twins was a Vietnam war veteran who had since been diagnosed with PTSD that was still present at the time of the study. The other twin had not had any exposure to combat in any wars.

First, it was confirmed using structural MRI scans that the volume of the hippocampus was negatively correlated with PTSD symptom severity in the PTSD sufferers. This means that the smaller the hippocampus, the worse the PTSD. Moreover, when compared to a separate group of twins who had combat experience but did not suffer from PTSD, there was an overall group difference in hippocampal volume; the PTSD group had smaller hippocampi than the non-PTSD group.

The critical comparison of interest was the hippocampal volume in the PTSD-diagnosed combat veterans vs. their identical twin. Here, Gilbertson et al. found that there was no difference in the size of the hippocampus. This lack of difference also manifested itself in a significant negative correlation between the severity of the PTSD and the size of the hippocampus in the patient's twin. Both of these pieces of evidence strongly suggest that variations in hippocampal volume that correlate with PTSD predate the traumatic episode. This is further supported by observations that the twin pairs that included a PTSD sufferer had smaller hippocampi than the twin pairs without PTSD (Figure 7b.2). Put together, all of this evidence strongly suggests that a smaller hippocampus may contribute to the development of PTSD, rather than being a consequence of trauma.

Within the Gilbertson et al. study, there were companion control analyses. These were to rule out the possibility that the PTSD twin pairs had smaller brains overall, thereby focusing the interpretation on the hippocampus. The control analyses involved looking at the total brain volume and the volume of the amygdala. For neither of these measures were any group differences or correlations observed. While this supported the authors' interpretation that the only major neurological difference is in the hippocampus, it contrasts somewhat with the Morey et al. (2012) study mentioned previously. At

(Continued)

(Continued)

present, it is difficult to reconcile the two studies, other than noting the larger sample size used by Morey et al. (2012), and so we have to bear this conflict in mind when interpreting the strength of each individual study's evidence.

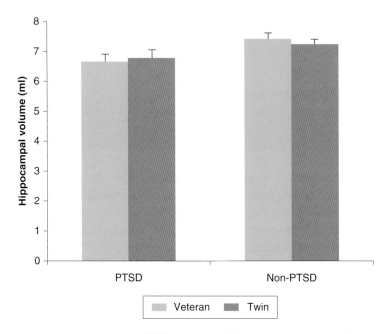

Figure 7b.2 Hippocampal volumes in PTSD and non-PTSD twin pairs. The PTSD-sufferers had smaller hippocampi than the non-PTSD-suffering war veterans. However, within each group of twin pairs, there was no difference in hippocampal volumes between the combat veterans and their twins. This indicates that the smaller hippocampi are likely genetically determined and hence pre-dated the combat and trauma experience. Data adapted from Gilbertson et al. (2002).

IMPLICATIONS

The finding that the hippocampus is already small before trauma is experienced, and that PTSD develops, suggests that hippocampal volume may be a useful predictive factor in identifying those individuals vulnerable to PTSD. However, it does not exclude a role of stress-induced damage to the hippocampus, and may not even extend to the conclusion that the smaller hippocampus is a causal factor in PTSD. In a rat model of PTSD, symptoms of enhanced anxiety correlated with induced hippocampal atrophy (Conrad et al., 1999). However, prevention of the hippocampal atrophy did not alleviate the enhanced anxiety, suggesting that variations in hippocampal volume are not causal in increasing anxiety.

Are there overly strong fear memories in PTSD?

The evidence that PTSD patients may have pre-existing differences in hippocampal anatomy suggests that hippocampal dysfunction may contribute towards the development of PTSD. As the hippocampus is associated with memory, and PTSD clearly involves an exaggerated aversive memory, this raises the question of whether memory processing is dysregulated in PTSD, leading to overly strong and persistent traumatic memories.

Are brain areas associated with traumatic memory processing abnormal in PTSD?

As explained in Spotlight 4a, the hippocampus is strongly implicated in fear memory extinction. The hippocampus provides the source of the contextual modulation of extinction, ensuring that the extinction memory is only expressed in situations that have been learned to be safe. An impairment in hippocampal function, therefore, would actually be expected to enhance the suppression of fear memories, by reducing the propensity of the fear memory to renew in new contexts. Clearly this is not compatible with the nature of PTSD and so it remains unclear to what extent and how the pre-existing reduction in hippocampal function contributes to the development of PTSD. However, hippocampal dysfunction in PTSD patients, whether it is purely pre-existing or perhaps exacerbated by stress-induced damage, may well be a factor in some of the cognitive deficits that they display.

Outside of the hippocampus, we have seen previously (Chapter 7) that two important brain regions in emotional processing are the amygdala and ventral prefrontal cortex. The standard model of fear regulation in the mammalian brain (but see Spotlight 7a) is that the amygdala subserves the principal CS–US association (i.e. the memory that a stimulus is associated with the traumatic outcome), and that the ventral prefrontal cortex provides an inhibitory constraint upon amygdala-mediated fear responses. Therefore the excessive anxiety that emerges in PTSD might result from either or both of enhanced amygdala function and impaired prefrontal function. Both of these would be expected to cause increased fear responses. Indeed animal studies, from which the understanding of the neurobiology of PTSD largely arises, clearly show that enhancing memory formation in the amygdala (e.g. LaLumiere et al., 2003) and impairing neural activity in the infralimbic cortex (e.g. Sierra-Mercado et al., 2011) both result in higher than normal conditioned fear behaviour.

A number of studies, using both PET imaging and functional MRI, have observed that the amygdala is hyper-responsive to emotional stimuli in PTSD patients. For example, Rauch and colleagues (2000) used subliminally-presented images of fearful and happy facial expressions to provoke a response in the amygdala. Fearful faces generally induce greater amygdala activity than happy faces as assessed with fMRI. This differential activity (specifically in the right dorsal amygdala) was greater in PTSD patients than in control subjects. This suggests that PTSD patients have enhanced amygdala reactivity to fear-related stimuli. Moreover, the magnitude of the right amygdala response to the fearful faces correlated with the clinical severity of PTSD in both the study by Rauch et al. and in an independent replication (Armony et al., 2005), indicating that there is a real functional link between the two measures.

When we turn to the ventral prefrontal cortex, a different picture is seen. When patients with PTSD were prompted to recall their traumatic episode, this triggered both physiological symptoms of PTSD and a pattern of brain activity that was different from comparison subjects that were also victims of trauma, but who did not go on to develop PTSD (Lanius et al., 2001). In particular, the PTSD patients showed a decreased activation of the ventral PFC (among other areas). Given that one of the functions of the ventral PFC is to inhibit the amygdala, this apparent negative relationship between amygdala and prefrontal activity in PTSD is not unexpected. Indeed other investigators have gone on to show that in PTSD, there is a negative correlation between activity in the amygdala and prefrontal cortex (Shin et al., 2005). What this correlation does not tell us, however, is where the source of the deficit lies. We might suggest a number of different hypotheses. First, it might be that there is a causal deficit in the prefrontal cortex that allows amygdala activity to run unchecked, resulting in heightened fear memories. Alternatively, the amygdala may be predisposed to forming excessively strong fear memories in the absence of any prefrontal impairment. Finally, PTSD may rely upon dysfunction in both areas, or the altered brain activity may simply be a consequence, rather than a cause, of the disorder.

What mechanisms underlie the abnormally strong amygdala memory?

Earlier in this Spotlight, we saw that there was evidence for a reduced amygdala volume in PTSD (Morey et al., 2012). However, it is not clear how we can reconcile reduced volume with enhanced activity. Therefore, if anatomical changes are not the cause of enhanced traumatic memory, where does that leave us in terms of understanding the **mnemonic** basis of PTSD?

Rachel Yehuda argues that the low basal cortisol characteristic of PTSD does have a biological impact upon memory processing, due to a competition between cortisol and noradrenaline (Yehuda, 2002). If cortisol levels are low, then this may result in an enhanced effect of noradrenaline. Victims of trauma who go on to develop PTSD appear to display higher than normal heart rate both immediately after the traumatic episode, and one week later (Shalev et al., 1998). Given that heart rate is under noradrenergic control, the elevated rate is symptomatic of an increased effect of endogenous noradrenaline. Noradrenaline has an important role to play in memory consolidation, and so enhancing noradrenergic efficacy at the time of trauma might lead to the formation of an enhanced traumatic memory. The converse is certainly true. We are generally better at remembering emotionally-laden information than neutral information. Larry Cahill and colleagues (1994) exploited this to show that participants' memory for an emotional narrative was enhanced relative to a neutral narrative. However, if beta-adrenergic receptors were blocked (using the beta blocker propranolol; commonly prescribed for hypertension), this advantage for the emotional narrative disappeared. Therefore, the emotional aspect of the memory was dependent upon noradrenergic function.

If excessive noradrenergic signalling at the time of the traumatic episode is an important cause of PTSD, then couldn't we simply inhibit this biological process to prevent PTSD from developing? While this might sound far-fetched, there is, in fact, evidence that this is a clinical possibility. Studies have been conducted in which the researchers were based in the emergency room of hospitals (Pitman et al., 2002). When victims of trauma were brought into the emergency room, some were given a dose of propranolol within six hours in order to block the beta-adrenergic receptors and hopefully attenuate the consolidation of the trauma memory. The propranolol treatment continued for ten days and the patients were tested for clinical symptoms of PTSD one month after trauma (i.e. when PTSD is usually expected to emerge). The clinical score of PTSD was significantly lower in the patients given propranolol, compared to a placebo control group. Therefore, noradrenergic activity in the period after a traumatic episode is important for the development of PTSD, presumably through its amnesic effects in the traumatic memory.

Noradrenaline levels are enhanced not only in the immediate aftermath of trauma, but also more persistently. For example, a study of combat veterans with PTSD showed that they had increased levels of noradrenaline in their bloodstream (Yehuda, Siever et al., 1998). So does this chronic noradrenaline elevation have implications for the persistence of the disorder? We know from animal studies that noradrenaline is important for fear memory retrieval and expression. Giving rats propranolol before testing a conditioned fear memory resulted in lower levels of fear responding (Rodriguez-Romaguera et al., 2009). Therefore, it is conceivable that increased noradrenaline levels facilitate the retrieval of the traumatic memory, leading to the intrusive recollections and physiological symptoms.

High noradrenaline activity at memory retrieval does not just have an effect acutely on the expression of the memory. It also increases the subsequent strength of the memory through the process of reconsolidation. In Spotlight 4a the phenomenon of **memory reconsolidation** is described more fully. For the current purposes it is sufficient to understand that when a memory is reactivated, it often undergoes a phase of synaptic plasticity that is similar to initial memory consolidation (hence the name 'reconsolidation'). From what we know about the reconsolidation process, it largely depends upon the same biological mechanisms as consolidation. Hence, given that noradrenaline is important for fear memory consolidation, it is not surprising that it also has a role to play in fear memory reconsolidation. Therefore, if noradrenaline levels are high during the retrieval of a traumatic memory, this might be predicted not only to facilitate the retrieval of the memory, but also to enhance its reconsolidation, thereby further strengthening the memory. Given that noradrenaline levels are persistently high, and PTSD is characterised by frequent intrusive recollections, this would lead to a progressive strengthening of the memory and potential worsening of the condition. The evidence to support such a scheme is a little indirect, but it provides some intriguing possibilities for the treatment of PTSD.

Much of the reconsolidation literature has been carried out in rodents, using pavlovian fear conditioning as a simple model of anxiety. Initially, it was discovered that the reconsolidation of pavlovian fear memories could be disrupted by propranolol, leading to the impairment of a previously-strong fear response (Debiec and LeDoux, 2004). More recently, the converse has been shown. The drug isoproterenol is a beta-adrenergic receptor agonist, and when it was given to rats immediately after fear memory retrieval, the memory was strengthened, leading to heightened fear responses (Debiec et al., 2011). Moreover, the strengthened fear memory became resistant to **memory extinction**, which mirrors the unresponsiveness of PTSD to cue exposure therapy. However, giving the rats propranolol instead of isoproterenol resulted in disruption of memory reconsolidation, and hence an impairment in the fear memory. Therefore, it would be predicted that giving PTSD patients propranolol when their traumatic memory is retrieved should also disrupt the reconsolidation of the traumatic memory, potentially leading to a reduction in the severity of the clinical symptoms.

KEY STUDY

Brunet, A., Orr, S. P., Tremblay, J., Robertson, K., Nader, K., & Pitman, R. K. (2008). Effect of post-retrieval propranolol on psychophysiologic responding during subsequent script-driven traumatic imagery in post-traumatic stress disorder. *Journal of Psychiatric Research, 42(6), 503–06*

and

Brunet, A., Poundja, J., Tremblay, J., Bui, E., Thomas, E., Orr, S. P., ... Pitman, R. K. (2011). Trauma reactivation under the influence of propranolol decreases posttraumatic stress symptoms and disorder: 3 open-label trials. *Journal of Clinical Psychopharmacology, 31(4), 547–50*

Brunet and colleagues have conducted two studies looking at the potential for impairing traumatic memory reconsolidation as a treatment for PTSD. Capitalising upon the rodent research, they tested the hypothesis that propranolol would impair traumatic memory reconsolidation and thereby improve measures of PTSD.

In the initial study, Brunet et al. (2008) looked at the effect of propranolol upon the physiological anxiety responses characteristic of PTSD. They measured heart rate, skin conductance and the contraction of the left 'facial frowning' muscle. They did not measure these responses during the reactivation session itself, but only at a test session seven days later. The traumatic memory was reactivated by asking the participants to describe the event that caused their PTSD. They then received a standard medical dose of propranolol, or a placebo control. For the test, a script was written, based upon the participants' description of their traumatic event. This script was designed to drive mental images of the episode and physiological responses. In the test, the participants that had received propranolol showed a reduced change in heart rate and skin conductance, but no alteration of the facial muscle contraction.

These physiological alterations were certainly encouraging, but were of no clear relevance to the question of whether such an approach could ultimately enable remission from PTSD. Therefore, Brunet, Poundja et al. (2011) went on to conduct open-label trials in Montreal, Boston and Toulouse. Propranolol was given to patients with chronic PTSD (i.e. persisting more than six months after the traumatic event) on six occasions prior to reactivating the traumatic memory through recounting the event. When tested six months later, 31 out of the 42 patients no longer displayed clinical PTSD as assessed using a standard psychiatric scale. This was not simply a natural recovery over time unrelated to the propranolol treatment, as, in a control group given placebo, only two out of the 25 patients showed clinical evidence of remission.

These two studies suggest that using beta-blockers to disrupt the reconsolidation of traumatic memories may provide genuine clinical benefits. We should be careful, however, not to draw overly strong conclusions. While the two studies do seem to be mutually supportive, it is worth noting that there are some salient differences in the treatment procedure that demand further exploration. In the physiological study, only one treatment session was used, whereas there were six in the clinical study. This raises the question of whether multiple sessions are necessary to maximise the beneficial effect. So, would there have been a greater reduction in the physiological changes (including, perhaps the facial muscle contraction) with repeated treatment sessions? Or conversely, were the six sessions in the clinical study excessive, and similarly beneficial results might have been observed with a single session?

A second difference was the timing of the propranolol administration. It was after memory react-ivation in the physiological study, but beforehand in the clinical study. The latter was selected on the basis of maximising the pharmacological action of the drug (Brunet, Ashbaugh et al., 2011). However, pre-reactivation drug administration does present some interpretative difficulties (Schiller & Phelps, 2011), as it is not clear whether the effect observed at the final test is due to a modification of behaviour during the memory reactivation session itself, rather than truly due to reconsolidation impairments. Indeed, there is actually a more fundamental problem with the design of both studies (Brunet et al., 2008; Brunet, Poundja et al., 2011), in that they failed to include a critical non-reactivation control con-dition. Non-reactivation controls are necessary to rule out the possibility that the drug administration simply causes a long-lasting memory impairment unrelated to the reactivation and reconsolidation of the memory. Without such a control, it is not possible to link the effect of propranolol to an impairment of memory reconsolidation. Nevertheless, regardless of the mechanism of action, what cannot be denied is the potential therapeutic utility of propranolol in the treatment of PTSD.

DO EXCESSIVELY STRONG APPETITIVE MEMORIES UNDERLIE DRUG ADDICTION?

We have seen that PTSD appears to be characterised by abnormally strong memories for the traumatic episode. We might equally argue that positive memories can be too strong and per-sistent, leading potentially to conditions such as drug addiction. Key within this hypothesis is the observation that a central acute problem that faces addicts is relapse, which is often precipit-ated by exposure to drug-associated cues. Indeed, this has been highlighted by the World Health Organisation in their description of drug addiction:

> a syndrome in which the use of a drug is given a much higher priority than other behaviours that once had a greater value. In its extreme form it is associated with compulsive drug taking behaviour and has the characteristics of a chronic relapsing disorder.

WHO, 1981

What memories are formed when drugs are taken?

the reasons why addictive drugs are taken in the first place are varied. Most illicit drugs have pleasurable or euphoric effects that individuals find rewarding. However, this is not so obvi-ous in the case of legal drugs such as alcohol and tobacco, for which the initial experience can be aversive. Nevertheless, in general it can be accepted that drugs are taken because of their rewarding effects. As such the drug itself can be considered to be a **reinforcer**, which has implications for associative conditioning.

First, the actual action to take a drug can be considered associatively to be an example of **operant conditioning**. Individuals seek and take drugs operantly in order to receive its rewarding effects. This seems obvious in the human setting, but can also be replicated in experimental animals that will hold no socially-acquired preconceptions of addictive drugs. Monkeys, rats and mice will self-administer drugs. For example, they will perform operant responses (such as a lever press) in order to receive an intravenous infusion of drugs such as cocaine, heroin or nicotine (Koob, 1992), and rodents can also be trained to drink and seek highly alcoholic liquids (Samson et al., 1988).

The taking of drugs is not, however, a purely operant process. Drug self-administration occurs in the presence of stimuli and places to which **pavlovian conditioning** will take place. For example, the preparation and self-administration of each drug is associated with particular paraphernalia (e.g. syringes or the sight of a cigarette or alcoholic drink; even within advertisements) or places. These paraphernalia and places act as pavlovian **conditioned stimuli** that become associated with the rewarding effects of the drug. The pavlovian stimuli do not just predict the occurrence or availability of the drug, but have very important psychological and biological effects. Drug-associated stimuli activate the brain and trigger intense cravings for the drug (Childress et al., 1999). Moreover, they can be sufficiently rewarding in themselves to elicit drug rituals, and enhance the sensation of reward. This explains first why nicotine patches are only of limited efficacy in stopping smoking; the ritual of smoking and its associated stimuli become intrinsically linked to the rewarding effects of nicotine, such that nicotine administration in the absence of such stimuli, as is achieved using a patch, is somewhat less effective. This has led to the promotion of electronic cigarette replacements that both supply nicotine and attempt to replicate many of the sensations of smoking. Moreover, the acquired properties of drug-associated stimuli can be so powerful that they can even be of some comfort in the absence of the drug itself. This is the explanation for why some addicts (so-called needle-freaks) resort to injecting themselves with saline, as the small reward elicited by the conditioned stimulus of the injection can partially substitute for the absence of the drug. Levine (1974) describes a 27-year-old woman who used to inject herself with tap water. She pushed in the needle slowly in order to maximise the pain, stating 'I kept remembering what it was like when I shot up'.

Is the amygdala abnormal in addiction?

We have seen in Chapter 7 that the amygdala is an important area for pavlovian emotional memory formation. Importantly, this is not limited to fear memories, but also extends to appetitive (i.e. positive emotional) CS–US associations. We can see this by looking at the effect of lesions to the amygdala in experimental rats. Pairing a stimulus such as a light with a drug reward leads to a light–drug association that has a powerful impact upon behaviour. Of most relevance to the current discussion is the use of a cue-induced relapse-type task. In this paradigm, rats learn to press a lever for the reward, and each time the reward is delivered, the light is illuminated. This leads to the pavlovian light–reward association being learned. The rats are then trained that pressing the lever does nothing, and so their responding falls to very low levels. At test, we simply see how much the rat will start pressing the lever again for *the light alone*. The rats still no longer receive the reward and so the relapse-like behaviour of pressing the lever again is reinforced only by the acquired motivational properties of the light through its pavlovian association with the reward. Lesions to the basolateral portion of the amygdala disrupt cue-induced relapse in such a task when cocaine was used as the reward (Meil and See, 1997). Moreover, the same impairment was observed when rats were self-administering heroin (Fuchs and See, 2002).

If impaired amygdala function disrupts cue-induced relapse to drug seeking, perhaps the amygdala is hyperfunctional, or over-reactive, in addiction? We know from rodent studies that exposure to drug-related cues activates the amygdala. The approach that is usually taken to assess brain activation in rats is an analysis of gene expression. There are a class of genes, called the immediate-early genes (IEGs), which are rapidly expressed after patterns of brain activity. One of these IEGs is called c-fos, and appears to be expressed under the broadest of conditions, making it a good marker for recent brain activity. By quantifying the amount of c-fos expressed in different areas of the rat brain, Kufahl et al. (2009) showed that a number of areas were activated by the cue-induced relapse to the cocaine seeking test. The basolateral amygdala was one of the areas, and the magnitude of its activation correlated with the cue-induced cocaine seeking behaviour. Given the disruptive effect of amygdala lesions, this finding is not particularly surprising. However, it leads to a strong hypothesis that the amygdala should be responsive to drug-related stimuli in humans.

There are many functional imaging studies purporting to show that the amygdala is one of the areas that are activated in human drug addicts when exposed to drug-related stimuli. In one such study, Childress and colleagues (Childress et al., 1999) exposed abstinent cocaine addicts to a cocaine video that showed a simulation of the purchase, preparation and smoking of crack cocaine. Compared to a control video of a nature story, the exposure to cocaine-related stimuli induced activation in the amygdala, as well as in the anterior cingulate cortex. This cocaine response was not seen in non-addicts. While this might suggest that the amygdala was somewhat abnormal in the addicts, the difference may simply reflect the fact that the cocaine stimuli had not been associated with the rewarding effects of cocaine in the non-addicts, and so had no pavlovian meaning that would have activated the amygdala. Therefore, while amygdala function is certainly implicated in drug addiction, this is not the same as saying that amygdala dysfunction is contributory to an individual descending into clinical addiction.

There is, in fact, very little evidence on which to base a conclusion on whether amygdala dysfunction contributes to drug addiction. Instead, one study by Bechara and Damasio (2002) suggests that drug addicts display cognitive deficits that are not characteristic of a dysfunctional amygdala, but rather point towards the ventral prefrontal cortex as an important locus.

Is the prefrontal cortex abnormal in addiction?

The aforementioned study by Bechara and Damasio (2002) was predicated upon previous consistent observations that drug addicts perform poorly on tests of executive function. One particular impairment that addicts show is in emotional decision-making (see box on the somatic marker hypothesis in Chapter 7). In the Iowa Gambling Task, subjects simply have to make as much money as possible by selecting cards from any of four decks. Two of the decks produce a net gain, and the other two produce a net loss. However, the bad decks have bigger individual gains than the good decks. Therefore, optimal behaviour would involve selecting cards preferentially from the good decks. However, addicts that were regular users of either opiates (e.g. heroin) or stimulants (e.g. cocaine) performed poorly, although they were still slightly biased towards the good decks (Grant et al., 2000). This impairment in emotional decision making was similar to, though not as great as, that observed in patients with damage to the

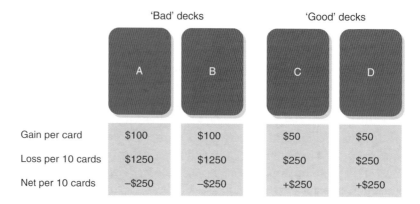

Figure 7b.3 Iowa Gambling Task. Participants select repeatedly from four decks of cards. The good decks yield a net gain, whereas the bad decks yield a net loss, despite intermittent high gains. Drug addicts and patients with ventral prefrontal damage perform poorly on this task, selecting from the bad deck more frequently than control participants

Source: Bechara et al. (2005)

ventral prefrontal cortex (Bechara et al., 1994), suggesting that drug addiction is associated with a degree of ventral prefrontal cortical dysfunction. Moreover, the dysfunction may be regionally specific, as the same addicts were unimpaired on a different test of executive function (the Wisconsin Card Sorting Test) that relies primarily upon the dorsolateral prefrontal cortex.

The ventral prefrontal cortex, however, does not operate in isolation in order to support adaptive decision-making in the Iowa Gambling Task. As highlighted by the somatic marker hypothesis, adaptive behaviour is guided and influenced by bodily signals. One of these is the skin conductance response (SCR; an increase in sweating). The SCR occurs when a subject hovers over the bad decks; this is an emotional response learned from prior selections from these decks that have led to large monetary losses. Once this SCR emerges, behaviour starts to be directed away from the bad decks and towards the good decks. In patients with ventral prefrontal cortex lesions, not only is adaptive behaviour disrupted, but the SCR is also absent (Bechara et al., 1999). In the same study, Bechara et al. (1999) tested patients with amygdala lesions, who showed similar but more extended deficits. Unlike ventral prefrontal patients, amygdala patients were unable to generate SCRs under any circumstances. When Bechara and Damasio (2002) tested drug addicts, they showed a profile of behavioural and SCR deficits that resembled those of ventral prefrontal, rather than amygdala, patients, indicating that addiction is truly associated with ventral prefrontal dysfunction.

The apparent dysfunction of the ventral prefrontal cortex might emerge from structural and/ or functional deficits, and both appear to be present in addicts. An analysis of prefrontal cortical volume in abstinent cocaine/amphetamine/alcohol addicts showed a reduction in ventral prefrontal grey matter (Franklin et al., 2002; Tanabe et al., 2009). Moreover, the smaller the volume of ventral prefrontal grey matter, the poorer the addict's performance on the Iowa Gambling Task (Tanabe et al., 2009). Given that the ventral prefrontal cortex is activated during performance on the Iowa Gambling Task in control subjects (Li et al., 2010), and such activity correlates with behavioural performance (Northoff et al., 2006), we might expect that addicts would show altered ventral prefrontal activity that explains poor behavioural performance. While this has been shown in one study of abstinent addicts (the drugs in question not being specified; Tanabe et al., 2007), another study of cocaine addicts in particular revealed an increase in ventral prefrontal activity compared to controls (Bolla et al., 2003). While the difference between these two studies remains to be resolved, they both point towards altered, and hence potentially dysfunctional, ventral prefrontal activity in drug addiction.

One further question that remains is whether the prefrontal dysfunction is caused by the taking of drugs of abuse, or whether there might have been a pre-existing deficit in decision-making that contributed to the initial taking of drugs and the subsequent descent into clinical addiction. Drugs of abuse are certainly toxic. In cell cultures of rat cortical neurons, the application of cocaine, amphetamine or heroin induces neuronal cell death (Cunha-Oliveira et al., 2006; Cunha-Oliveira et al., 2007). Therefore, it is certainly feasible that an addict's chronic intake of drugs will cause the death of cortical neurons, leading to the decreased grey matter volume and dysfunctional activity described above. However, this does not preclude the possibility that addicts suffer from a pre-existing ventral prefrontal cortical deficit that is exacerbated by drug use. However, there is currently no longitudinal, heritability or twin study data with which to assess such a hypothesis.

IMPLICATIONS

We have seen that the amygdala and ventral prefrontal cortex are both implicated in drug addiction. Perhaps, then, they might be targets of treatment strategies to promote abstinence and reduce relapse? From a theoretical perspective, if we could diminish or erase the amygdala-supported cue–drug association, this might beneficially reduce cue-induced drug seeking and relapse. Moreover, an enhancement of ventral prefrontal cortical function may improve decision-making and thereby reduce addictive behaviours. While these might sound like fanciful ideas, there is emerging evidence in rodents that at least the former is actually possible (Lee et al., 2006; Milton et al., 2008; Xue et al., 2012).

FURTHER READING

Rauch, S. L., Shin, L. M., & Phelps, E. A. (2006). Neurocircuitry models of posttraumatic stress disorder and extinction: Human neuroimaging research – past, present, and future. *Biological Psychiatry, 60*(4), 376–82.
Provides a review of neuroimaging of PTSD, making explicit links to neuroimaging of fear learning and memory in non-patients. It links to underlying knowledge from animal studies.

Robbins, T. W., Ersche, K. D., & Everitt, B. J. (2008). Drug addiction and the memory systems of the brain. *Annals of the New York Academy of Sciences, 1141*, 1–21.
Gives a review of drug addiction and focuses on underlying associative memories. Covers the neural bases of those memories (including amygdala and prefrontal cortex).

Yehuda, R. (2002). Post-traumatic stress disorder. *New England Journal of Medicine, 346*(2), 108–14.
Provides a review of epidemiology, psychology and biology of PTSD, with a focus on cortisol. Details implications for treatment.

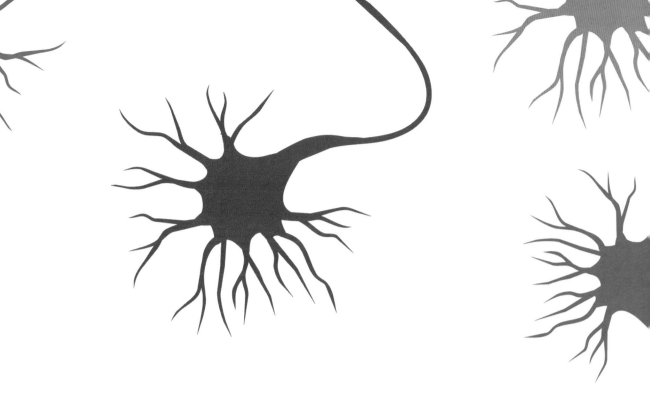

CHAPTER 8
MOTIVATED BEHAVIOURS

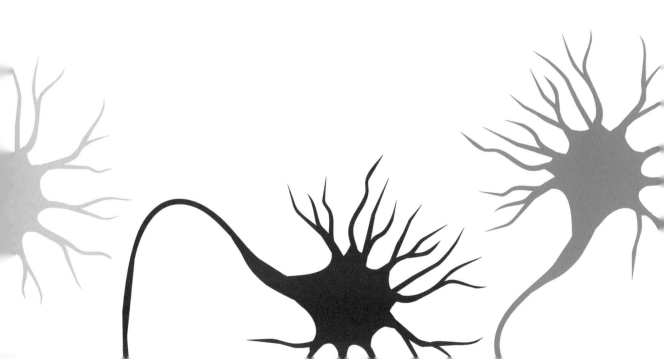

CHAPTER BREAKDOWN

- Motivated behaviours defined.
- Homeostatic and incentive theories of motivation.
- The biological bases of eating.
- Eating disorders.
- The biological bases of sleep.
- Sleep disorders.

ROADMAP

In this chapter we will be considering the biological bases of motivated behaviours. But before we delve into this topic we will need to consider what we mean by motivated behaviour. We will also need to understand the concepts that have been developed to try to explain motivation. After this, we will consider how these motivation concepts help us understand the control of two specific motivated behaviours: eating and sleeping. Within this context we will ask about the important biological mechanisms and critical brain areas. Finally, we will consider disorders of eating and sleep and relate these back to the biological processes that support eating and sleep.

Motivation is at the heart of most behaviour. Motivation gives behaviour direction and intensity and explains why we do certain things at certain times. It is important to understand these fundamental processes not only for their own sake (aren't you interested in finding out what drives your behaviour?) but also to understand what happens when motivation gets out of control or when someone lacks motivation.

The themes and issues discussed in this chapter link to ideas from previous chapters and feed forward to subsequent chapters. There are close links between emotion (Chapter 7) and motivation and we will be referring back to emotion concepts a lot in this chapter. Associative learning and memory processes are important for understanding motivated behaviour so we will need to be familiar with the underlying principles described in Chapter 4. We will also use our understanding of brain anatomy to locate motivational processes. Our understanding of how neurons communicate will also be essential for understanding the central control of motivation (Chapter 1). Finally, concepts of motivation and the biological bases of motivation help us understand psychological disorders such as depression, schizophrenia and anxiety that all involve altered motivation (Chapter 9).

WHAT ARE MOTIVATED BEHAVIOURS?

If you were forced to think about what constitutes a motivated behaviour then you might come up with something along the lines of 'a behaviour that has purpose and leads to a desired outcome'. You might also consider that motivation is something which waxes and wanes. Sometimes behaviour is highly motivated but other times it isn't. But what is it exactly that defines motivated behaviours and makes them different from, say, reflexes that most people would agree are not 'motivated'? If we look at the ways in which scientists have conceptualised motivated behaviour then we find that their criteria really just refine the ideas outlined above.

The first thing to note is that most people would agree that motivated behaviours are associated with emotion. In Chapter 7, we learned that emotions are usually accompanied by behaviours that are directed towards specific goals. For example, fear is associated with an avoidance response, such as moving away from what is perceived to be a dangerous situation. This is a motivated behaviour. Specifically, it is a behaviour associated with an emotional response (e.g. fear) that is directed towards a specific outcome (e.g. removing oneself from danger). But perhaps if these were the only criteria for defining motivated behaviour then might a simple reflex qualify?

The application of a painful stimulus to the foot results in a reflex withdrawal of the foot from the stimulus. This reaction might be associated with an emotional response and is certainly associated with a specific outcome. But it is also a predictable reaction that is very rigid. That is to say, it is performed in the same way whenever the relevant stimulus is encountered. Motivated behaviours on the other hand are the opposite of rigid; they are very flexible. The reaction to a fearful stimulus is not always to run away; it might be to hide. Therefore, motivated behaviours are distinct from simple reflexes because they are flexible in their expression.

Something else that marks out motivated behaviours is that even if a motivational stimulus is present, the relevant behaviour may not be displayed. The thing about motivated behaviours is that they vary over time as well as in how they are expressed. So even if we found ourselves in a fear-provoking situation, we might not run or hide but instead stand our ground. Our reaction will also depend upon other features of the context such as the perceived level of danger and whether there are other competing demands on behaviour. We might run away from a large spider we have never encountered before even if we were in the middle of eating but if the spider is small and we know it is not poisonous then we may carry on eating, especially if we are really hungry. So, another point of note is that motivated behaviours compete with each other, and sometimes one motivation will win out over another.

Finally, it should be obvious from the above examples that learning is an essential part of motivated behaviour. We learn that goals can be achieved in different ways and we are sensitive to the consequences of achieving those goals. This allows us to adjust our behaviour in the future and maintain flexibility in responding. If our experience teaches us that one fear avoidance strategy is very effective then we would be more likely to use that strategy in the future in a similar situation.

In summary, motivated behaviours are strongly linked with emotion. They are behaviours directed towards specific outcomes but there is variability in how the outcome is obtained and so motivated behaviours are more than simple reflexes. Motivated behaviours also vary in their expression over time and place and there is competition between motives to direct behaviour, explaining why different people do different things at different times.

Motivated behaviours may be directed towards outcomes that are important for survival such as avoiding danger. They are also important for maintaining basic physiological needs such as eating, drinking, sleeping and keeping warm. We are motivated to seek out food and drink, obtain enough sleep and maintain our body temperature. But people are also motivated by other types of goals such as doing well in exams or in a job. These motivations may seem worlds apart but the mechanisms underlying them are likely to be very similar. Much work on the psychobiology of motivation has focused on behaviours such as eating and sleep and these behaviours will be specifically discussed later in this chapter. But first, we will think about some basic concepts in motivation that can be applied to an analysis of any kind of motivated behaviour.

MOTIVATIONAL CONCEPTS

Homeostasis and motivational drives

The physiologist Claude Bernard noted that in order to survive we must maintain a stable internal physiological environment in the face of changes in the environment that pose a threat to this stability. Our body tissues require a certain temperature to function, as well as adequate supplies of oxygen and energy. If the external temperature changes then we would eventually die unless something is done to counter the effect of this change on body temperature. Hence, one factor that motivates behaviour is the need to ensure an adequate internal environment for vital physiological functions. We change our behaviour to counter disturbances to the body that threaten life. This principle was termed the 'wisdom of the body' by another physiologist, Walter Cannon, who was also responsible for introducing the idea of **homeostasis**.

Homeostasis is the idea that we are able to detect when a critical variable like body temperature is deviating from its stable point and put in train reactions that serve to bring the variable back in line (Cannon, 1932). Homeostatic systems have been suggested to comprise a set-point detector and a mechanism for correcting deviations from the set point. Once the correcting mechanism is activated then this provides a signal that feeds back into the system to eventually shut off the response. This is known as a negative feedback signal. In the case of temperature regulation, a deviation from our usual temperature of 37 degrees results in physiological and behavioural reactions that have the effect of increasing body temperature. These effects can range from shivering (which generates heat) to reduced blood flow to the skin (which reduces heat loss from the skin), to putting on more clothes (which traps heat). These reactions raise the body temperature, which then signals back to stop the heat generating response before it gets out of control.

A broader view of homeostasis suggests that behaviour does not just occur in response to an actual serious deviation from set points but that corrective mechanisms come into play before there is the possibility of extreme perturbations that threaten survival. This is known as anticipatory responding. This might occur because 'early warning' systems kick start corrective mechanisms. For example, a drop in skin temperature is an early warning of a decrease in core body temperature. This drop in skin temperature, which is not in and of itself life threatening, can trigger a shivering response. In addition, cues that are predictive of a change to a cold environment can trigger anticipatory increases in body temperature, even in the absence of any deviation from a set point. The rise in temperature then mitigates the effects on the body of the change to the environment (Woods and Ramsay, 2007).

Homeostatic mechanisms are important in explaining some behaviours, but homeostasis does not seem to encapsulate all of the features of motivated behaviours. Emotion does not feature in homeostasis. Linking the concept of homeostasis with the idea of drives was one way in which some theories put the emotion back into motivation. It was suggested that deviations from the ideal state are associated with an aversive psychological state, usually referred to as a drive state, which activates and directs the behaviour (Miller, 1973). For example, the detection of water loss from the body is associated with feelings of thirst, and the detection of low blood sugar is associated with hunger. The drive state is aversive, so its removal is rewarding. This means that if removal of the drive state is associated with a particular behaviour (e.g. eating or drinking) then this behaviour is reinforced and the behaviour is likely to occur again when the drive state is encountered.

The problem with homeostatic drive theory is that mere removal of hunger states does not always stop eating. A prediction of the theory is that reduction of the drive should be associated with cessation of the drive-reducing behaviour. However, humans and other animals that are fed intravenously will carry on eating even though physiological drive has been reduced and nutrient levels are restored (Wolf and Wolf, 1943). Given the opportunity, they will eat food normally to the point of gaining weight (Turner et al., 1975). Also difficult to explain in terms of drive reduction are behaviours such as drinking saccharin-sweetened drinks that provide no calories and so cannot be reducing drives. Moreover, removal of drive states is not actually rewarding. Electrical stimulation of certain brain sites reduces eating behaviour. Drive theory would predict that stimulation of these sites should also be rewarding, but this is not the case (Valenstein et al., 1969). These data suggest that something else is going on with motivation that is not about homeostatic drives.

In fact, some theorists suggest that the idea of a homeostatic set point is not actually needed to explain how we achieve the internal physiological stability that is important for survival. Apparent internal stability could be achieved simply as a natural consequence of the balance between a number of factors, resulting in a 'settling-point' rather than a set point (Berridge, 2004). Clearly, the original concept of homeostasis was developed with more reflexive physiological processes in mind and so the question arises as to how well it accounts for all kinds of flexible and goal-directed behaviour. More recently, effort has gone into thinking about how motivated behaviour might be pulled towards goals rather than pushed by drives.

INSIGHT: THE APPEAL OF CHEWING

Wolf and Wolf (1943) reported the case of a man named Tom who permanently damaged his oesophagus by accidentally drinking hot soup. From then onwards he could no longer eat normally because the scalding soup had sealed his oesophagus. He had to eat by passing food directly into his stomach via a tube. Although there was no need to taste the food, Tom continued to chew his food and then spit it out before placing it in his stomach. It seems he was not satisfied unless he was able to chew the food, which supports the idea that reducing physiological drive via intravenous feeding is not sufficient to reduce appetite.

INCENTIVE MOTIVATION

Incentive motivation theories emphasise that behaviours are directed towards stimuli that evoke a positive emotional state, for example food and drink. These stimuli are rewarding, and people and animals will act to maintain contact with them or consume then. They are referred to as **incentives** because they are attractive and act as a 'pull' on behaviour. Learning is important in incentive motivation because the idea is that from experience we associate the pleasurable response gained from consuming the reward with some of its features. For example, we may be drawn towards eating a particular food because we learn its flavour is associated with a positive **hedonic** response. Even the thought of a food might come to be associated with its rewarding properties through pavlovian conditioning and so act as an incentive stimulus. This explains why being reminded of a tasty meal can make one feel hungry.

Now, of course we know that we do not always seek out food even if we are reminded of it and we might decline even a favourite food if we have just eaten. So, behaviour cannot be solely motivated by incentive stimuli. If it were, then seeing a food would always elicit eating in a rather habitual fashion. Incentive motivation theories account for this by stating that the incentive value of a stimulus (the extent to which it attracts behaviour) is modulated by internal factors such as nutritional state. The sensory pleasure we gain from a reward is relative in that it depends on the state we are in. Sweet solutions taste better when we are food deprived than when we have just stuffed ourselves. This is a phenomenon known as 'alliesthesia' (Cabanac, 1971). In the same way, stimuli associated with rewards are also modulated by internal states so that we are attracted to a drink in the fridge when we have just come in from the sweltering heat but the same drink lacks appeal if we are freezing cold (Toates, 1986). Therefore, disruption to homeostatic processes can motivate behaviour but indirectly via modulation of incentive processes.

KEY POINTS

- Motivated behaviours are flexible and goal directed.
- Motivated behaviours are governed by incentive processes.
- The incentive processes are modulated by internal states.

In the next sections we will consider two specific motivated behaviours: eating and sleeping. We will focus on these behaviours because quite a bit is known about their biological bases and many people are motivated to find out more about them!

EATING

Over the course of your lifetime you will probably consume about 80,000 meals. That is a lot of eating. It is obvious to say that we need food to survive and we should not forget that many people in the world today still die due to starvation. But have you thought about why it is that, given a choice, you tend to select certain food over others? Why do you decide to eat in the first place and why stop a meal once it has started? All of these questions have been asked by researchers interested in the psychobiology of eating, as we will find out. But before we do, let us take a step back and think about why it is that we need to eat at all and what we get from food. Understanding what happens to food once we eat it is helpful in answering questions about eating motivation because ultimately these motivations are tied to the reason why we eat, which is to get food inside the body. However, the importance of food to us is also reflected in our culture so it is important to remember that our behaviour towards food is also a reflection of our identity and values.

Why do we need food?

We eat food because it provides the energy that our bodies need to function. Nutrients from food power the processes that keep our cells alive. They allow us to grow and build body tissue and to move about and keep warm. The purpose of eating is therefore to provide a flow of energy through the body. We survive by ensuring that we have stores of nutrients that we can draw on when circulating levels are low and food is not immediately available. As we will discover, the coordination of these processes is a complex feat.

How does the body deal with food?

To use the energy from food we have to get it inside the body in a useable form. When we eat, food is broken down into its constituent parts so that the useful bits (nutrients) can be absorbed from the gut and the bits that cannot be used by the body are excreted. The nutrients enter the blood stream where they are transported all around the body and their energy harnessed in the biological processes that sustain life. This is made possible by chemical reactions that break down molecules to release energy (known as catabolic processes) coupled with reactions that require energy (known as anabolic processes). Collectively these reactions are known as metabolism.

The main sources of food energy used by the body are glucose from carbohydrates and fatty acids from triglycerides, which are fats in food. Amino acids from proteins can be used but this is a last resort under conditions of starvation. We need a current supply of circulating energy and stores of energy so that the circulating energy flow can be maintained by drawing on these stores. When the amount of food energy we consume exceeds that which is being used, which is known as positive energy balance, then the excess energy is stored. When the amount of energy that is being used exceeds that which is being taken in, which is known as negative energy balance, then energy is taken from the storage sites.

The main energy storage sites in the human body are the liver and the fat cells that are found under the skin, around internal organs and in muscle. Collectively these fat cells make up white fat. There is another type of fat, called brown fat. Brown fat is different from white fat because it generates heat energy and so is important for temperature regulation, especially in animals that live in cold environments. Newborn humans have some brown fat and so do adult humans but the amount is small (Nedergaard et al., 2007).

The liver stores glycogen, which is made from glucose. Glycogen is also stored in smaller amounts in muscle. The conversion of glucose to glycogen requires the hormone **insulin**. Glycogen stores are limited because of the relatively fixed size of the storage organs but an advantage of storing energy this way is that glycogen can be readily converted to the body's preferred source of useable energy: glucose.

Most energy in the body if not used is stored in white fat as triglycerides. Fatty acids from food are taken up into white fat adipose tissue and this process is facilitated by insulin. More energy can be stored as fat than glycogen for a given weight. Storing glycogen requires water and so if we had to store all our energy as glycogen then we would find it very difficult to move about because large glycogen stores would add a lot of weight. In fact, humans are very good at storing fat. The average-weight person probably has enough fat to maintain basic metabolic processes for about a month without food. The hormone glucagon enables glycogen and triglycerides to be converted back to glucose and fatty acids and used as fuels.

To eat or not to eat? Understanding eating patterns

The purpose of eating seems simple enough but human eating behaviour is a complex motivated behaviour. We do not eat all the time and even though food might be available we might not necessarily eat it. Many people eat about three times a day and would be likely to refuse food if it is offered just after eating. Why is that? Eating in discrete bouts that we call meals is an efficient way of acquiring energy and allows eating to be coordinated with other behaviours. We could eat intermittently throughout the day but eating a small number of meals means we spend less time procuring food, thus freeing up time to engage in other activities important for survival. Meal eating probably evolved as a response to adaptive pressures on our ancestors and has become a culturally transmitted eating pattern. However, we are also flexible in our eating patterns and can adapt eating behaviour according to circumstance. If there is uncertainty about when food will be available next, or food is scarce, we might eat fewer but larger meals to take advantage of eating opportunities as they come along. This is quite an achievement if one considers that consuming, digesting and metabolising food puts a strain on our physiology (Woods, 1991).

When we eat, the stable internal physiological environment is severely perturbed by incoming levels of glucose. Although we need food to live, dealing with it presents a considerable challenge to the body. Ultimately, eating patterns are a reflection of strategies that maximise the costs and benefits associated with eating (Collier, 1985). We also have anticipatory physiological mechanisms that prepare the body for incoming food (Woods, 1991). In understanding eating behaviour we must consider how we are able to ensure that we eat enough to maintain metabolic processes but at the same time consume food in amounts that can be dealt with by our physiology.

The biological bases of eating

It is generally agreed that we have evolved mechanisms that promote eating, as well as mechanisms that inhibit eating. What we actually experience is a disposition to eat, which is expressed as appetite. Appetite may be associated with bodily sensations that are experienced when we are food deprived, such as the feeling of an empty stomach. But appetite is not just about bodily sensations since appetite can be expressed in the presence of a full stomach, for example eating pudding after a main meal. It is also generally agreed that there are many different mechanisms that underlie appetite. This is to be expected given that eating behaviour is too important for our survival to be trusted to one system. However, there are differences in how researchers conceptualise these mechanisms and the importance they place on the different influences.

Time to eat: what factors affect when we start and stop eating?

We seek out foods and then decide to consume them because they act as a 'pull' on behaviour, drawing us towards them. In other words, foods are incentives that direct our behaviour (Berridge, 2004). Food-seeking behaviour can be initiated for various reasons. A state of food deprivation may act on the mechanisms underlying incentive systems in the brain to focus our attention on thoughts of food and eating. Alternatively, the sight or smell of food may be attractive in and of itself, even in the absence of food deprivation. So the mere whiff of baking bread in the supermarket may have us taking a loaf home to eat.

Why are foods such powerful incentives? As we learned earlier, some experiences elicit pleasurable reactions that can be described as 'liking' reactions. Stimuli that are associated with these reactions become attractive or 'wanted'. For example, we might learn that a particular food flavour is associated with a sweet taste. Most people find tasting something sweet a naturally pleasant experience and so as a result of learning that a flavour is associated with sweetness the flavour itself becomes highly attractive to us and the thought of it or sight of it tempts us to eat, especially if we have not eaten for a while. We only have to think about how attractive chocolate is to most people to understand how this works!

We should also note that, for many people, eating is governed by strong habits. Often the time of day is the strongest influence on when eating occurs. In this case, the stimulus that triggers eating might be the sight of a clock showing a time usually associated with eating in the past. All of this underscores the important role of learning in appetite. We learn that certain stimuli (flavours, smells, food logos, places or reminders of the time) predict positive experiences and these stimuli can prompt eating.

Quite a bit is known about the biological bases of incentive learning as we will find out below. Researchers have also mapped out the systems that monitor nutrient levels and provide information about food deprivation. More recently, there has been great progress in uncovering how incentive learning systems and nutrient monitoring systems interact to explain why food is so much more attractive when we are hungry but also conversely why a strong motivation to eat when food deprived can be consciously suppressed.

Decisions to stop eating are also influenced by many factors and are subject to change based on previous experience or with foods (learning). Feelings of fullness are associated with the release of peptides from the gastrointestinal tract. These peptides act as signals to the brain about the nutrient content of foods and are associated with changes in food intake. Their effects are influenced by the presence of hormones that are secreted in relation to the amount of energy stored by a person in fat. In turn, these nutrient and fat-related signals interact with incentive reward systems to tone down the attractiveness of foods.

Eat this not that: understanding food choice

Decisions about what foods to eat are equally as complicated as decisions about when to eat and when to stop eating. We are omnivores, which means we are able to digest many different types of food. But this brings with it the challenge of selecting a nutritional balance of foods from a vast array of potentially edible items. We express preferences for some foods over others and usually manage to avoid eating toxic or nutritionally inadequate foods. But as well as providing nutrients, food also plays an important role in human social relations and culture. A look at the rich cuisines of the world confirms that food also serves an aesthetic function. Cleary, it is not necessary to have high quality restaurant food to fulfil our energy requirements. Food marks important social occasions; it distinguishes ethnic groups and takes on symbolic meanings in human culture (Rozin, 1996). What we eat is therefore influenced by many different factors and is underpinned by learning.

Figure 8.1 Cultures differ in what they find acceptable as foodstuffs. In Western cultures eating insects is usually thought to be disgusting but not so in non-Western cultures where insects are more commonly consumed. The thought of eating insects for people who have never considered this as a food item can cause a disgust reaction. Yet, as global food demands grow, insects offer a cost effective means of feeding people as they are efficient at converting feed to body mass. Disgust responses will have to be modified if insects are to be on the menu in the future for most Westerners

© iStock.com/macky_ch

One way to think about the psychobiology of eating is to consider what is known about the mechanisms that underlie an eating episode. Given concerns about the rising incidence of different types of eating disorders, understanding of these mechanisms is important because it could help in developing new approaches to the prevention and treatment of such disorders.

Let us consider the following scenario. It is getting close to midday and your thoughts turn to lunch. As you make your way to the kitchen, you remember the bread you bought for your sandwich and you start to feel really hungry, especially as you had to skip breakfast. You look inside the fridge and select some filling for the sandwich. You make the sandwich and then sit down and take the first bite of the sandwich. The sandwich is tasty and you eat most of it, just leaving a little because you feel satisfied. But then you remember the cake that is also in the fridge and so you decide to get that and eat it too. Now, let us think about what psychobiological processes might underlie the behaviour in this scenario.

Food recognition and sensory responses

First, let us consider your memory of the bread for the sandwich. Most of us will recognise bread as an edible item that provides nutrition. We are able to do this because we store representations of foods in the brain that can be recalled from memory. When we eat a food we have a range of sensory experiences related to its look, taste, texture, and smell (see Chapter 5). These experiences combine to form a multimodal representation generated in the orbitofrontal cortex (OFC) of the brain (Rolls et al., 1998). Interestingly, how this representation is constructed is influenced by conditions both internal and external to the taster. Zampini and Spence (2004) asked participants to eat crisps while listening to the sounds they made when eating through headphones. An increase in sound level was associated with crisps being rated as fresher whereas a decrease in sound level was associated with crisps being rated as staler. In another study, participants rated some unusual bacon and egg ice-cream while listening to two soundtracks: one was bacon sizzling in a frying pan and the other was the clucking sounds of farmyard chickens. The ice-cream was rated as having a stronger bacon flavour when eating was accompanied by sounds of frying bacon but a stronger egg flavour when accompanied by the chickens clucking! This is likely because the sounds influenced the way in which the sensory experiences were combined to form the whole representation of the ice-cream in the brain (Spence et al., 2009).

In a similar vein, expectations of the taster can influence flavour perception. When a smoked salmon ice-cream was labelled as an ice-cream it was rated as more salty than when it was labelled as a savoury mousse, presumably because the ice-cream was not expected to have a salty flavour whereas the savoury mousse being salty did not violate expectations (Yeomans et al., 2008). So the perception of our sandwich will depend on the context it is eaten in and the expectations we have about it and this will be in part mediated by the presentation of similar sandwiches we have eaten in the OFC (Plassman et al., 2008).

Cephalic responses

As you think about the sandwich and anticipate eating it, this will trigger anticipatory physiological reactions that serve to prepare your body for incoming food. These are known as cephalic phase responses and they counteract the impending increase in blood glucose that will occur once the food is digested and absorbed. Insulin will be released (Teff et al., 1991) and you might start to salivate as well, to prepare your mouth for chewing the food as did Pavlov's dogs! These reactions may be associated with an increase in feelings of hunger and a willingness to eat.

Affective responses and incentive learning

Once you actually get round to tasting the sandwich, the experience will involve an emotional response such as liking or disliking. Responses to some basic tastes have an unlearned or innate component. So, human babies and other animals have a positive affective reaction to sweet taste and a negative affective reaction to bitter tastes (Steiner et al., 2001). This is probably because these reactions serve to ensure the acceptance of milk and the rejection of poisons and so are adaptive. Most of the foods we eat are not terribly sweet or bitter but are more complex, such as our sandwich. We do not have innate positive or negative reactions to these foods. Instead we learn about the consequences of eating new foods and adjust our behaviour accordingly based on our experience.

Our initial predispositions towards foods and flavours can be readily modified via experience, such that we can come to like some bitter tasting foods if we learn that they are not actually dangerous (Kalat and Rozin, 1973). Some of this learning occurs socially as we observe the eating patterns of others (Baeyens et al., 1996; Birch, 1990) allowing for social and cultural influences on food choice. But we also learn in other ways, for example, by repeated exposure to small amounts of food (Pliner, 1982). If a new food flavour is associated with positive consequences, such as the delivery of nutrients or an already-liked taste, then via the process of associative conditioning we may come to like it and accept it (Sclafani, 1995; Zellner et al., 1983). Conversely, if a novel food leads to undesirable consequences such as sickness then we would learn to dislike it and avoid it in future (Garcia et al., 1955). Also, it is not just flavours that can come to be associated with the consequences of eating. Smells and even the sight or thought of foods can act as conditioned stimuli and we learn to like them too.

Figure 8.2 Babies are born with an innate reaction to reject bitter and sour tasting foods, but with learning, bitter foods such as olives can come to be liked. Social learning is an important part of developing food preferences. If we see someone else enjoying a food then we are more likely to try it and enjoy it

© iStock.com/alexdans

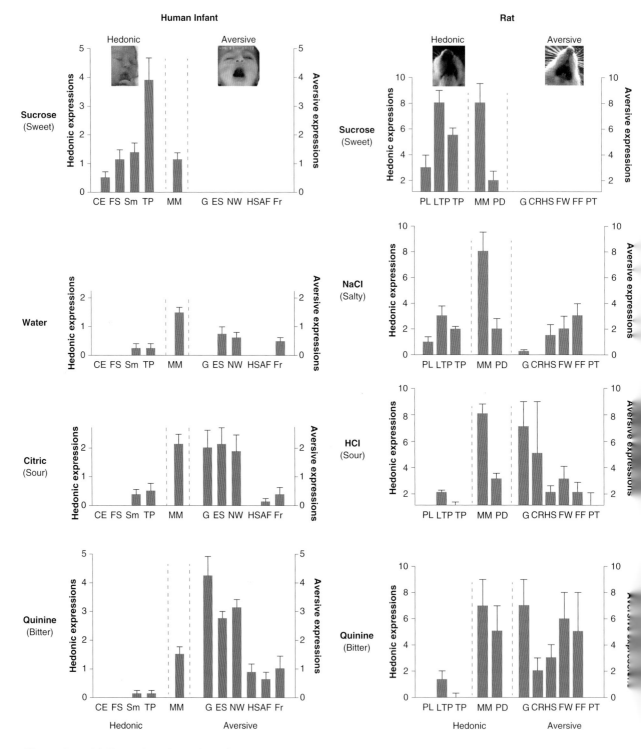

Figure 8.3   (a) Examples of emotional facial expressions to taste by human infants, apes, monkeys, and rats. (b) Similar reactions are seen across species. Taken from Berridge (2004)

As well as learning to like flavours we also learn to 'want' them. This is the process of incentive learning whereby conditioned stimuli also become attractive to us and so we will seek them out (Weingarten, 1983). The brain mechanisms that underlie hedonic responses to food are separate from those that govern their incentive properties. In other words, the systems that mediate 'liking' for foods are not the same as those that mediate food 'wanting'.

It is important to note here that researchers use the term 'liking' and 'wanting' in rather specific ways that do not equate to the way in which we might use these terms in normal conversation. In the context of incentive motivation, 'liking' and 'wanting' are basic emotions that are not necessarily available for conscious reflection (Winkielman and Berridge, 2004). In other words 'liking' is not the same as explicit feelings of pleasure, and 'wanting' is not the same as an expressed desire. This is reflected in the fact that the brain structures that mediate these processes are sub-cortical areas such as the nucleus accumbens and brainstem (Berridge, 2003) that are not thought to be involved in conscious emotional feelings. Liking reactions are often measured by analysis of facial expressions that are elicited by tastes. These are basic emotional reactions that are somewhat similar in human babies, other primate species and rats, as shown in Figure 8.3.

Brain systems for food 'liking'

Opioid signalling in the brain is important for 'liking' reactions. Opioids are released in the brain when a sweet taste is encountered (Levine et al., 2003), which explains why sugar can have pain relieving properties and is sometimes used as an analgesic when babies undergo mild medical procedures such as a vaccination. If people are given an opioid receptor blocker (antagonist) before tasting food then the food is rated as less pleasant than after a placebo (Yeomans and Gray, 1997). Endogenous cannabinoids are probably also important for liking reactions (Higgs et al., 2003).

The brainstem is an area that plays an important role in liking reactions. Babies with congenital problems, such that they are born without a forebrain, show the same affective reactions to sweet tastes as babies with an intact brain (Steiner et al., 2001). Similarly rats that have undergone a procedure that disconnects the forebrain from the brainstem (known as decerebration) also show positive reactions to sugar solutions (Grill and Norgren, 1978). This suggests that the brainstem is sufficient for 'liking' reactions to occur.

In the intact brain, brainstem liking reactions are modulated by activity in forebrain areas. Specific brain areas that are important include the parabrachial nucleus of the brainstem (Higgs and Cooper, 1996; Söderpalm and Berridge, 2000) and parts of the nucleus accumbens (Peciña and Berridge, 2000).

Brain systems for food 'wanting'

Dopamine signalling in the brain is important for mediating 'wanting' reactions; in particular, the mesolimbic dopamine system. Although dopamine is often associated with feelings of pleasure in popular media, dopamine signalling is not related to 'liking'. In studies where dopamine levels are measured in the human brain, dopamine levels are associated more with 'wanting' than 'liking' reactions (Leyton et al., 2002; Volkow et al., 2002). In addition, experimental manipulations that alter dopamine signalling in the brain alter 'wanting' responses but do not affect 'liking' reactions. This supports the idea that there are separate systems for 'wanting' and 'liking' (Berridge, 1996).

Mice bred to have extra dopamine in their synapses run faster to obtain a sweet reward in a runway than mice with normal dopamine levels, but they actually have reduced affective reactions to sweet taste (Peciña et al., 2003). The reward is more attractive to them than the normal mice and so they run faster to obtain it but they do not like it as much.

It might seem odd that something could be 'wanted' much more than it is 'liked'. One would think that these emotions should go together; we want the things we like. In everyday situations this is true, but under some circumstances, because the neural substrates are independent, they can become detached from each other. This might be the case for some pathological conditions in which reward responding goes awry. One possible reason for over-eating might be that people are attracted to eating some foods because they have an exaggerated 'wanting' response, even though they may not like the food that much (Berridge et al., 2010).

Bringing this all back to our scenario, we can say that dopamine-dependent incentive learning underlies your motivation to seek out the sandwich ingredients, and opioid signalling in the brain underlies the hedonic response to the sandwich taste. Now, once you start to eat the sandwich, your response to it will change as you eat and this will influence how much you eat. The change in responding will depend on the sensory experience as well as the effects of assimilating the nutrient in the food.

Sensory specific satiety

As we eat, our liking and desire to eat a food declines relative to other foods that have not been eaten. This is known as **sensory specific satiety** because the decline in rated pleasantness is specific to the properties of the food (Rolls et al., 1981). This is a basic mechanism that encourages us to eat a diversity of foods to ensure we obtain adequate nutrition. Think of our scenario in which we stop eating our sandwich but then are tempted to eat the chocolate cake. There is a decline in motivation for the sandwich but the chocolate cake is still attractive. Sensory specific satiety may relate to changes in the presentation of foods in the OFC with repeated presentations (Kringelbach et al., 2000).

As eating continues any food will become less attractive and appetite wanes (alliesthesisa). Also, hormonal signals that tell us about the types and amounts of foods that have been eaten are released. These signals can then provide us with important information that can be used to predict the effects on the body of eating foods in the future. We can learn to avoid the aversive effects of feeling too full. This is known as learned satiety (Booth et al., 1976). Based on learning about how filling different foods tend to be, we tend to pre-empt satiety by serving ourselves amounts that we expect to be satiating (Brunstrom et al., 2008). In other words we learn about the satiating effects of food that we have eaten and this affects our future choices about how much of that food will fill us up.

So what are the important mechanisms that underlie alliesthesia and our ability to make predictions about the effects of food on the body? Obviously, we need to be able to monitor the amounts and types of nutrients that are being processed and then integrate this with brain reward signals. In the next section we will consider these nutrient monitoring systems and how they interact with brain incentive systems.

MECHANISMS OF NUTRIENT MONITORING

Signals from the gastrointestinal system

The brain receives information continuously about food that is being eaten and absorbed and nutrient levels that are circulating and being stored. The important point to remember here is that we are able to sense nutrients at various stages of digestion, absorption and metabolism and send information about these nutrients via signalling pathways to the brain.

When we eat, nutrients enter the stomach and then pass into the intestines to be absorbed into blood circulation. This causes the release of specific hormones such as cholecystokinin (CCK), which is released when nutrients, especially fat and protein, are detected in the gastrointestinal system (Liddle et al., 1985). CCK binds to receptors that are located on the vagus nerve that connects the gastrointestinal system to the brain. This provides information that fat/protein is being processed and will soon be absorbed (Moran et al., 1997). CCK release is associated with reductions in the size of meals (Gibbs et al., 1973), which is consistent with its role in providing information about meals with a high fat content. Another peptide that provides information about processing of nutrients is GLP-1, which is produced by cells further down the gastrointestinal system in the ileum and colon (Abbott et al., 2005). Similarly, in between meals there are changes in release of gut hormones that are related to depletion of energy stores. **Ghrelin** is a hormone secreted by the stomach, and levels of ghrelin are highest after fasting (Ariyasu et al., 2001; Cummings et al., 2001). Ghrelin increases food intake (Asakawa et al., 2001) and is associated with over-eating in people with Prader–Willi syndrome (Cummings et al., 2002). Ghrelin may function as a signal for low circulating nutrient levels.

Signals from fat

Some hormones are secreted in proportion to the amount of fat stored in adipose tissue and so provide a signal about nutrient storage. The amount of insulin in circulation tracks changes in body fat (Baskin et al., 1999). The hormone **leptin** is also secreted in direct proportion to body fat and levels fall after weight loss (Maffei et al., 1995). Insulin and leptin enter the blood stream and are able to cross the blood brain barrier and act on specific receptors in the brain. Reductions in insulin and leptin signalling in the brain result in over-eating and weight gain which is consistent with the idea that these signals about body fat stores contribute to appetite control (Benoit et al., 2004).

Figure 8.4 The ob/ob mouse has a genetic mutation which means that it does not produce the hormone leptin (Halaas et al., 1995). The word leptin comes from the Greek word *leptos*, which means slender. Leptin is released from fat tissue and when it gets into the brain it binds to receptors in the hypothalamus. It acts as a signal for the amount of stored fat. The absence of leptin signals that there are no fat stores. This promotes over-eating behaviour, which is why the ob/ob mouse becomes obese and diabetic. A similar but rare mutation has been observed in some severely over-weight children (Montague et al., 1997)

Photo courtesy of The Jackson Laboratory, Bar Harbor, ME USA, www.jax.org

Processing of metabolic signals in the brain

Information from the gastrointestinal tract and fat stores reaches the brain and then undergoes further processing and integration with other inputs relevant to eating so that eventually motor outputs (eating behaviours) are generated. One thing to bear in mind is that although research in this area has generally focused on a few brain areas, it is more appropriate to think of neural systems for eating behaviour rather than thinking about single brain areas involved in appetite control (Grill and Hayes, 2012). The hypothalamus has been in the spotlight for many years and as a consequence a lot is known about the signalling in this brain area as it relates to eating behaviour, but there is now growing interest in how the hypothalamus interacts with areas in the brainstem and cortex to influence eating.

Brainstem circuits

Nuclei in the brainstem such as the nucleus of the solitary tract (NTS) and parabrachial nucleus (PBN) receive information from the gastrointestinal tract and the mouth relating to food being consumed. The brainstem is the first point of integration of different types of nutrient-related signal. The brainstem also contains motor circuits that are responsible for producing ingestive responses such as chewing (Grill, 2010). Neurons in the NTS respond to leptin, and leptin acting on receptors in the NTS modulates the response of rats to nutrients in the gastrointestinal tract (Kanoski et al., 2012).

Hypothalamic circuits

Pioneering studies in the 1940s and 50s demonstrated that lesions to the ventromedial hypo-thalamus cause over-eating and obesity (Anand and Brobeck, 1951; Hetherington and Ranson, 1942), whereas lesions to the lateral hypothalamus result in loss of appetite (Anand and Brobeck, 1951). These studies had the limitation that the lesions were not very specific, but later studies that employed more precise chemical lesions supported in broad terms the suggestion that the hypothalamus is important for appetite control (Dunnett et al., 1985; Stricker et al., 1978).

We now know a lot about the specific signalling in the hypothalamus and how this relates to appetite. A particularly important area that has been pinpointed is the **arcuate nucleus** of the hypothalamus. The arcuate nucleus receives information from the NTS in the brainstem and contains receptors for leptin and insulin (Ricardo and Koh, 1978), which suggests it plays a role as a centre of convergence for nutrient-related signals. In addition, the arcuate nucleus is located very near to the third ventricle in the brain in an area where the blood brain barrier is rather leaky. This means nutrient-related factors from the periphery borne in the blood will have greater access to the arcuate nucleus relative to other regions (Cone et al., 2001). Cells in the arcuate nucleus are also able to monitor local levels of glucose (Levin, 2002), suggesting that decreased availability of glucose might also be a trigger for eating but this is probably under severe deprivation (Smith and Epstein, 1969).

Two important populations of arcuate neurons have been identified: neurons that express Agouti-related peptide and neuropeptideY (AgRP/NPY) and neurons that express pro-opiomelanocortin (POMC) and cocaine–amphetamine (CART)-expressing neurons. Activation of AgRP/NPY neurons is associated with increases in eating, whereas activation of POMC and CART neurons is associated with decreases in food intake. This is in part due to effects on neurons in other areas of the hypothalamus, such as the lateral hypothalamus and paraventricular hypothalamus. For example, orexin neurons in the lateral hypothalamus are activated by NPY (Horvath et al., 1999). In addition, the activity of the arcuate nucleus is mod-ulated by insulin and leptin, providing a link to stored energy, and by serotonin which has long been known to reduce appetite (Blundell and Latham, 1979).

Interactions between nutrient monitoring and incentive systems

Leptin acts as a signal for the amount of stored fat and it modulates the activity of neurons in the hypothalamus and brainstem that receive information about short-term changes in energy availability. In this way, leptin can tune up or down these short-term satiety signals (Kanoski et al., 2012). Leptin has also been shown to modulate the activity of dopamine neurons that are important for incentive learning (Fulton et al., 2006). This may be to a direct effect of leptin on dopamine signalling or via an effect on orexin neurons that project from the lateral hypothalamus to the mesolimbic dopamine system (Leinninger et al., 2009). Insulin has also been shown to act in a similar way (Figlewicz et al., 2003). These mechanisms provide the means whereby nutritional state affects food liking and wanting, and why food is more attractive in states of energy depletion and less attractive in states in energy repletion. On the other hand, presentation of a conditioned incentive stimulus may affect signalling in hypothalamic areas to facilitate eating even when satiated (Petrovich et al., 2012).

Socio-cognitive processes in appetite

If we return to our original scenario we can observe that the eating situation described is rather sparse and may not be representative of usual meals. Most people do not eat alone but in social groups, whether with family at home or out with friends. Many people eat in a busy environment with many things going on. Do you eat in front of the TV or while working or playing on a computer? Lots of people do. Also, we have not considered the attitudes you may bring to an eating situation. Some people avoid certain foods for religious reasons or are actively trying to restrict their intake to lose or maintain weight. All of these factors affect our eating.

Evidence suggest that people often eat more when they dine in large groups of people they know (de Castro and Brewer, 1992), but might eat less if they are with a potential partner they are trying to impress (Pliner and Chaiken, 1990). Meals eaten in the presence of distractions, such as the TV, are larger than meals eaten alone (Bellisle et al., 2004). A dieter may have intentions to cut back on their intake at lunch, but their good intention might be derailed if they perceive the diet has already been broken that day (Herman and Mack, 1975). At present we know very little about the

Figure 8.5 Eating while distracted, for example while watching TV, can increase the amounts of food consumed (Bellisle et al., 2004). This may be because our attention is drawn away from what we are eating. This might make it harder to monitor how much is being consumed and inhibit attention to satiety signals. TV watching while eating may also impair our memory for what we have eaten which could result in a greater tendency to snack later on (Higgs and Woodward, 2009)

© runzelkorn/Shutterstock.com

biological bases of social and higher-level cognitive control of food intake or how they interact with metabolic and incentive systems, although areas of the brain, such as the prefrontal cortex, associated with behavioural control are likely to play a role (Batterink et al., 2010).

One mechanism that might explain increased food intake due to distractors while eating is impaired encoding of food memories by the hippocampus. Amnesic patients who have damage to the hippocampus over-eat when they are provided with one meal after another (Higgs et al., 2008; Rozin et al., 1998). Similarly, specific lesions to the hippocampus produce disruption to appetite control in rats (Davidson et al., 2009). Also, TV watching during a lunch meal is associated with greater afternoon snacking and poorer meal memory (Higgs and Woodward, 2009). These data suggest that episodic food memories are factored into decisions about eating.

KEY POINTS

- Food is a powerful reward that directs eating behaviour.
- We learn about the rewarding effects of foods.
- Brain opioid and dopamine signalling is important for food 'liking' and 'wanting' respectively.
- The brainstem and hypothalamus are important brain areas for integrating metabolic signals relating to foods eaten and stored nutrients.
- There is close communication between brain reward pathways, nutrient sensing pathways and learning and memory circuits in the control of food intake.

OBESITY AND EATING DISORDERS

When eating behaviour becomes disturbed there are serious consequences for individuals and society. Obesity levels have been rising worldwide for a number of years now and many people with obesity suffer from a range of health problems, including diabetes and heart disease (Wang et al., 2011). **Anorexia** is a very serious condition that involves weight loss and is associated with a very high mortality rate (Keel and Brown, 2010). To develop effective treatments for these disorders it is important to understand more about their biological bases.

Defining obesity

To say that someone is overweight or underweight we need to define a healthy weight, but this is not so straightforward as one would imagine (Flegal et al., 2013). There is some agreement that a key factor linking health and weight is the amount of body fat someone has. Overall body weight will not tell us specifically about body fat. A tall or muscled person will obviously have a higher body weight than a small person, but might actually have less body fat.

It is possible to measure body fat accurately but the techniques used are expensive so health professionals tend to use a measure which takes into account both height and weight; this is called the body mass index (BMI). This is your weight divided by the square of your height. According to the BMI system, a BMI under 18.5 is underweight; between 18.5 and 24.9 is a healthy weight; between 25 and 29.9 is overweight; and over 30 is obese.

Obesity

The accumulation of body fat leading to **obesity** is due to someone expending fewer calories than they consume as food. We burn off energy as we fuel the body (this is our basic metabolic rate) and we expend energy when we move about and exercise. If this is not balanced against the number of calories we eat then the extra energy is stored mainly as fat, as we learned previously. But this simple fact does not tell us about the complex causes of obesity. One way of looking at this issue is to ask the question of why so many more people these days are obese compared to, say, 30 years ago. What has changed over this period?

We can first ask whether excess food intake or too little energy expenditure is the issue. One way of approaching this question is to find out if energy expended on physical activity has changed over the time that levels of obesity have been increasing. Westerterp and Speakman (2008) looked at accurate measures of energy expenditure from studies carried out over a number of years and found that it had remained constant despite increasing levels of obesity, suggesting that increased food intake probably explains why more people are obese these days compared with 20 or 30 years ago.

But why are people eating more nowadays? Studies suggest that about 65% of variation in obesity is due to genetics (Segal and Allison, 2002). A likely scenario is that some people have a genetic predisposition to over-eat and become obese, which is expressed under certain environmental conditions. One theory is that the ability to deposit fat stores may have been selected for in our evolutionary history, because it confers an advantage during times of famine. However, in the modern food environment, where food is plentiful, this trait in no longer adaptive and promotes obesity (Neel, 1962). This is known as the 'thrifty' gene hypothesis. But, if the thrifty gene idea is correct we should all have inherited advantageous mutations in thrifty genes and should all be obese.

An alternative idea is the 'drifty gene' hypothesis (Speakman, 2008), which suggests that obesity genes have not been selected for during evolution, but are the result of random mutation and drift. The idea goes that early humans were under selection pressure to avoid starvation, but were also under pressure to avoid predation. Therefore, we evolved behaviours that ensure body weight does not go too high or too low. However, with the development of social behaviour and tool use, the selective pressure from predators was effectively removed. In this scenario, behaviours resulting in excess body fat accumulation would not have been removed by natural selection, and allowed to drift. In today's environment the extent of this variation is revealed.

Naturally the question arises as to which genes are involved. Mutations in the gene that codes for leptin leads to severe obesity, but these mutations are rare (Montague et al., 1997). Mutations in melanocortin genes that code for receptors in the hypothalamus also are associated with obesity, but these are also quite rare in the general population (Farooqi and O'Rahilly, 2008). Having a variant of the fat mass and obesity associated gene (FTO gene) is associated with increased risk of obesity due to increased energy intake, and this gene variant is relatively common (Frayling et al., 2007; Wardle et al., 2008). The number of genes that contribute to variation in body weight is probably very large. Advances in genetic technologies are likely to shed more light on these genes and how they interact with the environment in the near future.

Many environmental factors that could contribute to levels of obesity have been highlighted. Much emphasis is placed on what has been termed the 'toxic' food environment in which a large variety of high calorie foods are readily available and aggressively marketed (Swinburn et al., 2011). Portion sizes have also increased and there is evidence that people eat more over a sustained period when they are served larger portions (Rolls et al., 2007). Stress might also play a role. Many people report feeling stressed in today's society and stress is associated with increased consumption of high calories for many people (Dallman, 2010). Stress is associated too with lack of sleep, which has also been associated with increased eating and obesity (Taheri, 2006). Another idea is that contamination of the environment by plastics may have led to increases in obesity because these compounds may affect appetite hormones (Newbold et al., 2009).

ANOREXIA AND BULIMIA

Anorexia has been present in Western civilisation for millennia. There are numerous historical accounts of women in the Middle Ages engaging in starvation to obtain sainthood. In terms of the clinical diagnosis today, anorexia is defined as a syndrome in which the individual maintains a body weight at least 15% below that expected for their height and age. There is a disturbance of eating habits that are associated with clinically significant impairment of physical health or psychosocial functioning. The disturbance should not be secondary to any other general disorder such as that associated with loss of appetite due to cancer or other illnesses (Fairburn and Harrison, 2003). Anorexia is more common in women than men.

One difficulty that researchers encounter when trying to uncover the cause of anorexia is dissociating symptoms that arise from starvation from those that might be linked to its cause. There are changes that occur in the body as a result of lack of food for a prolonged period and these effects may maintain the anorexia, but may not trigger the disorder in the first place. Concentrations of neuropeptide Y (NPY) leptin, corticotrophin-releasing hormone (CRH) and cholecystokinin are altered in anorexia. These changes may be compensatory responses to conserve energy or promote eating. Anorexia is also associated with reduced brain volume and altered metabolism in frontal, cingulate, temporal and parietal regions (Katzman et al., 1996). The starvation-related changes are likely to sustain anorexia behaviours by driving a desire for more weight loss. Although starvation increases the incentive value of food to prompt eating, it has been suggested that the associated release of opioids might actually serve to reinforce the starvation for some people. In other words, they become 'addicted' to the endogenous opioid release (Marrazzi and Luby, 1986).

Ideally, longitudinal studies are needed to be able to find out the factors that predict whether someone will develop anorexia. However, this is difficult because of the young age of sufferers (the onset is usually in adolescence) and its rarity (around 0.5% of 15-year-old girls). Another approach is to study patients who have recovered from anorexia, because this removes the effects of current starvation. However, it is possible that people who have recovered from the disorder still show some scarring effects of previous malnutrition. For these reasons studying anorexia is very challenging.

Early research focused on sociocultural explanations of the cause of anorexia such as the portrayal of very thin models as the desirable body shape for women (Garner and Garfinkel, 1980). But an issue here is that not everyone exposed to these influences develops anorexia. More recent theories focus on predisposing genetic factors that interact with sociocultural factors and early life events to explain the onset of anorexia (Kaye et al., 2009).

There is a genetic component to anorexia (Bulik and Tozzi, 2004) although there is a lot of uncertainty about the specific genes involved owing to difficulties in conducting large-scale studies with small numbers of patients. Some insight has been gained into the biological bases of anorexia by characterising endophenotypes. These are measurable behavioural features that are linked to the underlying cause. They can be used to help diagnose and search for causative mechanisms and genes. The rigid thoughts that anorexic patients have are also found in unaffected sisters of anorexia patients, suggesting it is a family trait (Holliday et al., 2005). Such rigid thinking could relate to the obsessiveness and perfectionism that might predispose some people to develop the disorder (Lilenfeld et al., 2006) and may be underpinned by disturbed serotonin function in the brain (Kaye et al., 2005). Another endophenotype might be an impaired sense of the body which is also known as a lack of interoceptive awareness. Body awareness has long been recognised to be impaired in anorexia (Bruch, 1962) and could relate to the distorted sense of body image that sufferers experience. Interoceptive awareness has been linked to the insula which has been shown to be less responsive to taste stimuli in recovered anorexics versus controls (Wagner et al., 2007).

Bulimia involves repeated binge eating, followed by behaviours to counteract the binging such as laxative use or vomiting. It has been noted that anorexia and bulimia are not totally separate disorders because it is often the case that they co-occur – some anorexics engage in binging behaviours, or the patient moves from one diagnosis to another. This is likely because there is some shared genetic vulnerability (Strober et al., 2000). The trans-diagnostic model of eating disorders suggests that there are common mechanisms and core psychopathologies for anorexia and bulimia (Fairburn and Harrison, 2003). However, bulimia is associated with high levels of impulsiveness and risk taking especially in the context of negative affect (Vitousek and Manke, 1994). Bulimia patients also show heightened reward responses to food and other cues which could relate to disturbances in brain serotonin and dopamine function. The binging and purging cycle in bulimia might cause changes in brain reward circuitry that maintain the cycle, as has been modelled in rats (Colantuoni et al., 2001).

KEY POINTS

- High levels of obesity today are likely due to over-eating relative to energy needs.
- Genetic predispositions combined with aspects of the modern food environment and other features of modern lifestyles are important in explaining obesity.
- Anorexia and bulimia are also the result of complex gene–environment interactions.
- Individuals with anorexia have perfectionist traits and an impaired sense of the body that may relate to altered serotonin and insula function respectively.

SLEEP

Sleep is a subject that fascinates most students. How much sleep do you need? Many people today report that they do not get enough sleep and yet there is still controversy over the function of sleep and how much sleep is 'enough'. Sleep qualifies as a motivated behaviour in that it is directed towards a specific goal, but there is flexibility, since sleep is adapted depending on the current environment and other competing motivations. A number of species, us included, invest time and effort in finding safe sleep sites. The onset of sleep varies according to levels of sleepiness, and the period of sleep can be extended or shortened according to circumstance. You might delay sleep even if you feel tired to make sure you get an assignment in on time. However, there are consequences of sleep deprivation such as increased likelihood of having an accident while driving. Disorders of sleep such as insomnia and **narcolepsy** can be very debilitating. So what is exactly is sleep? Why do we sleep at all and what are the biological mechanisms that orchestrate sleep-waking cycles?

What is sleep?

If I were to ask you to say what sleep is you would probably be reasonably confident of providing an answer. Yet when one starts to unpick this question it becomes a little more complicated. You might say that sleep is a period of reduced activity during which a person has their eyes closed and is not aware of their immediate environment. But how is this different from someone under an anaesthetic or in a coma? Perhaps then you would add that sleep is a period of reduced activity that can be reversed rapidly since we know that it is possible to wake someone from slumber, but not from a coma or anaesthetic. How is this different from someone who is merely resting with their eyes closed? One way of distinguishing these states is to measure cortical brain activity using electroencephalography (EEG).

FOCUS ON METHODS: EEG

EEG (electroencephalography) provides a measure of overall brain activity. In EEG, electrodes are attached to the scalp with a special paste. These electrodes measure the activity of large populations of neurons that are recordable on the head surface. The electrical signals detected by the scalp electrodes are amplified, and then passed to a computer and the resultant 'brain waves' can be displayed. EEG can record spontaneous activity and activity in responses to a specific stimulus. The latter are called evoked potentials. EEG has been around for a long time.

In 1924 Hans Berger, a German neurologist,

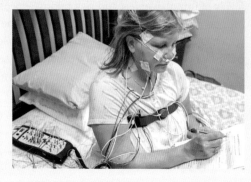

Figure 8.6   Recording of EEG during sleep
© iStock.com/Jodi Jacobson

used ordinary radio equipment to amplify the brain's electrical activity and depict it graphically on a strip of paper. He observed that the activity changed in certain neural diseases, such as in epilepsy. EEG recording procedures are non-invasive, safe and painless. The figure shows a woman who has electrodes placed on her scalp to allow recording of EEG during sleep.

EEG shows us that different levels of responsiveness to external stimuli are associated with specific patterns of brain activity. Therefore, in humans, sleep is usually defined according to electrophysiological criteria. Different states of waking and sleep are also associated with changes in the patterns of muscle activity and eye movements that can be measured by electromyography (EMG) and electro-oculography (EOG). Collectively, these measures provide what is known as a polysomnograph. More recently other brain imaging techniques such as fMRI and PET have also been applied to the study of sleep and waking states, and techniques such as optogenetics are revealing more about the biological bases of sleep.

Defining sleep stages: the polysomnograph

It used to be thought that the brain is active during waking and inactive during sleep. However, it is now clear that the brain is active during both waking and sleep, but in different ways. Indeed, there are some areas of the brain that are more active during sleep than waking. In addition, only small reductions in cerebral blood flow have been observed during sleep (Kety, 1956), suggesting that the brain is quite active and capable of a large amount of information processing during sleep. Sleep involves specific patterns of brain activity as we will discover. But first, to be able to understand the activity of the brain during sleep it is necessary to be familiar with some terminology.

Electrical activity in the brain and in muscles and the eyes that can be measured by EEG, EMG and EOG is characterised by oscillating activity represented by wave forms that vary in their frequency (the rhythm of the waves), amplitude (the wave intensity or height) and shape. When the peaks and the troughs of the waves are close together the frequency is fast, and when they are spaced far apart the frequency is slow. When the peaks are high and the troughs low this is a high amplitude wave and when they are more compact this is a low amplitude wave. When the pattern repeats, this is a regular or synchronised waveform and when there is no discernible repeating pattern this is an irregular waveform. We will first describe the activity associated with the waking state and then define sleep according to changes in this pattern.

The waking state

During the alert waking state, the EEG consists of what is called **beta activity**. Beta waves are irregular, high frequency waves of around 13–30Hz (Hz is a measure of frequency and is defined as the number of wave cycles per second; the higher the number the more frequent the waves). The beta waves also have low amplitude. When a person is relaxed, but still awake, the EEG consists of lower frequency waves of around 8–13Hz that have a more regular pattern than beta waves. These waves are called **alpha activity**. More alpha wave activity is usually observed when a person is resting with their eyes closed. During waking there is also evidence of muscle and eye movement activity in the EMG and EOG.

The transition to sleep and light sleep

The transition from waking to sleep is defined by the presence of a different kind of EEG activity: **theta waves**. Theta waves occur at a frequency of 3–7Hz and they have slightly higher amplitude than alpha waves. The transitional stage is known as Stage 1 sleep and it usually lasts for a short period. A person may open and close their eyes and the eyes may roll upward and downwards during this period. After about 10 minutes of theta wave activity, the EEG changes again and very distinctive patterns interrupt the theta rhythms. These patterns take the form of sleep spindles, which are a burst of high frequency activity lasting between 0.5 and 1.0 second, and K-complexes, which consist of a sharp negative deflection in the waves followed immediately by slower positive deflection. The presence of sleep spindles and K-complexes defines Stage 2 of sleep. This is still a light phase of sleep when a person may still be woken easily by noises and changes in the environment and they may deny being asleep if roused.

Deep sleep

As a person continues to sleep, it becomes more difficult to wake them and this coincides with another change to the EEG pattern. When someone goes into deep sleep, regular, high amplitude and low frequency waveforms of about 1–4Hz begin to be seen. Hence, this type of sleep is known as **slow wave sleep**. The large, slow waveforms are called **delta waves** and when they become apparent in the EEG this defines Stage 3 of sleep. When the proportion of the EEG taken up with delta waves is more than 50% then this defines Stage 4 sleep. You might recall an occasion when you have been woken in the middle of the night and felt extremely groggy and confused. You were probably woken from Stage 3 or 4 sleep. Muscles are relaxed and EOG activity is reduced during Stages 1–4 of sleep, but a sleeper will usually show some movement during these phases.

Look at Figure 8.7 and you can see the different patterns of EEG activity that have been mapped onto different stages of wakefulness and sleep.

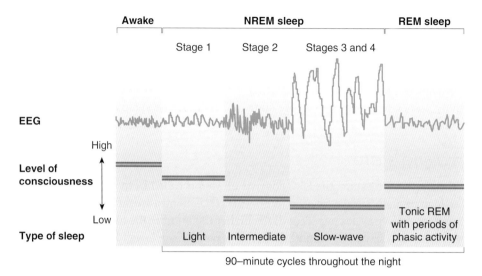

Figure 8.7   Different EEG patterns are observed during waking and sleep. As the depth of sleep increases, the EEG recordings are progressively dominated by more regular waveforms that are slower and of higher amplitude

Source: Bryant et al. (2004)

Rapid eye movement (REM) sleep

After a person has fallen asleep they progress through Stages 1–4 of sleep and this takes about an hour. They then cycle back up to Stage 2 sleep and something strange happens. The EEG shows patterns of activity that are very similar to the beta waves that are characteristic of the waking state, but the person will still look as if they are asleep. The French researcher Michel Jouvet termed this stage 'paradoxical' sleep for this reason. You may know it better as **rapid eye movement sleep** or REM sleep because it is a stage of sleep in which the eyes are also seen to dart quickly back and forth (Aserinsky and Kleitman, 1953). At the same time however, most major muscles in the body lose their tone and so the sleeper effectively becomes paralysed.

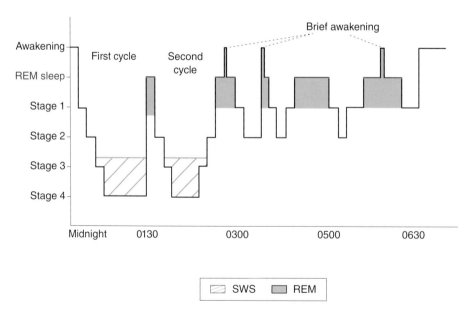

Figure 8.8   Sleep stages during one night (after Dement and Kleitman, 1957)

Source: Barnes (2013)

After the first period of REM sleep, which lasts about 20 minutes, there is a cycling back down through the stages of non-REM sleep and back up again to another period of REM. As sleep continues, the cycling continues, but there is more Stage 2 sleep and less of Stage 3 and Stage 4 sleep and the bouts of REM become longer (see Figure 8.8). Hence, during sleep there is alternation between periods of REM and non-REM taking about 90 minutes. This kind of rhythm, which lasts less than 24 hours, is known as an **ultradian rhythm**.

KEY POINTS

- Sleep is a state of altered brain activity associated with reduced responsiveness to external cues.
- There are different stages of sleep: Stages 1, 2, 3 and 4 and REM sleep.
- Each stage is associated with different brain activity as measured by EEG.
- We cycle through the different stages of sleep during a typical night.

THE BIOLOGICAL BASES OF WAKING AND SLEEP STATES

Now we have defined sleep in terms of its electrophysiological and behavioural characteristics, we can consider the biological bases of sleep. What are the neurobiological mechanisms that underlie the timing and duration of sleep? Understanding these mechanisms can shed light on what might be happening when the controls of sleep go awry, as in sleep disorders, and provide clues as to why we sleep at all.

An important observation is that people usually sleep every 24 hours, which suggests that sleep is in part controlled by mechanisms underlying **circadian rhythms**. As daylight recedes and night approaches, increasing feelings of drowsiness result in the desire to sleep. But there are other influences on sleep because we do not immediately fall asleep as soon as night falls. Sleep is a motivated behaviour and the timing and duration of sleep can vary according to competing demands. If someone is deprived of sleep for a period there is some extra compensatory sleep to make up for the loss. This suggests that there are also homeostatic controls of sleep (Borbely and Achermann, 1999). However, even if the desire for sleep is high due to homeostatic influences, sleep can be overcome if the situation requires it. Imagine encountering a dangerous situation late at night. The stress of this encounter would override sleep controls to maintain vigilance and the ability to react to the situation. Finally, there must also be systems that are responsible for the cyclical alternation of REM and non-REM sleep within a sleep episode (ultradian mechanisms).

It has been proposed that several different neurobiological mechanisms underlie sleep onset and offset: circadian mechanisms, homeostatic mechanisms, and emotional and cognitive influences (Saper et al., 2005). The next section will describe what is known about these systems and how they interact to coordinate sleep-waking episodes. Our first task is to think about the systems in the brain that are responsible for maintaining the waking state, then we will consider the sleep-promoting brain mechanisms and finally the mechanisms that control the transition between sleep and waking.

Wake-promoting brain systems

Early studies that employed electrical stimulation techniques identified an area of the brain stem that produced a cortical pattern consistent with a waking aroused state when it was activated (Moruzzi and Magoun, 1949). Since then, more detailed studies have pinpointed the specific neurotransmitter systems that were activated by electrical stimulation in these early studies. Researchers have identified an ascending arousal system in the brain consisting of two main pathways. These pathways project from areas in the brain stem, hypothalamus and basal forebrain to provide wide stimulation of the cortex that produces the waking desynchronised EEG.

The first pathway projects from the brainstem to the thalamus and is a major relay of sensory information from the external world to the cortex. The source of this pathway is a group of acetylcholine-containing neurons in the brainstem: the pedunculopontine and laterodorsal tegmental nuclei (PPT/LDT). These acetylcholine neurons are active during waking and REM sleep, but less active during non-REM sleep (El Mansari et al., 1989). They promote waking and arousal at least in part by altering activity in the thalamus. Modulation of specific types of neuronal firing patterns in the thalamus by acetylcholine affects information transfer from the thalamus to the cortex and produces a desynchronised cortical EEG (McCormick, 1989).

The second pathway originates from monoaminergic neurons in the brainstem to the lateral hypothalamic area, basal forebrain (BF) and cortex (Jones, 2003). The important neurons are noradrenergic (originating from the locus coeruleus), serotonergic (from the raphe nucleus), dopaminergic (from the ventral tegmental area) and histaminergic (from the tuberomammillary nucleus). These neurons fire most during wakefulness and are silent during REM sleep (Aston-Jones and Bloom, 1981).

Much of the evidence pointing to the involvement of acetylcholine and monoamine pathways in wakefulness comes from studying the effects of agonist and antagonist drugs on arousal. For example, acetylcholine receptor agonists produce the desynchronised cortical activity seen in wakefulness, and agents that reduce acetylcholine transmission, such as the antagonist atropine, produce the EEG slow waves found in sleep (Vanderwolf, 1992). The noradrenergic agonist isoproterenol acts in the BF to increase wakefulness (Berridge and Waterhouse, 2003).

There are also forebrain neuronal systems that maintain wakefulness. The lateral hypothalamus contains melanin-concentrating hormone (MCH) and orexin neurons that are involved in wakefulness (Mileykovskiy et al., 2005; Verret et al., 2003). Orexin neurons connect with other arousal systems such as the PPT /LDT and raphe nucleus to promote wakefulness (Bayer et al., 2001; Brown et al., 2002). Orexin neurons also connect with basal forebrain neurons that contain acetylcholine and GABA (Eggermann et al., 2001). These BF neurons then project to the cortex and their activation contributes to cortical activation and EEG desynchronisation (Jones, 2004). Using optogenetic technology that enables the selective activation of specific neurons, it has been shown that activation of orexin neurons also contributes to waking from sleep (Adamantidis et al., 2007; Carter et al., 2009).

FOCUS ON METHODS: OPTOGENETICS

Optogenetics is the use of genetics and optics to alter the responses of specific cells or groups of cells within living tissue. The technique involves inserting genes that confer light responsiveness into cells. 'Opsin' proteins are photosensitive. The genes coding for these proteins can be inserted into neurons using harmless viruses. When the opsins are exposed to light they can either activate or inhibit neuronal activity. Light can be delivered to just the right spots by threading thin optical fibres through layers of nervous tissue. Optogenetic tools are a big methodological breakthrough because they allow scientists to obtain very precise control over the function of specific types of neurons.

Each wake-promoting system is likely to be involved in specific aspects of arousal that guide behaviour such as sensory arousal and alertness (acetylcholine), vigilance (noradrenaline) and emotional reactivity (serotonin) (Pfaff and Banavar, 2007), but there are also interactions between the systems and a lot of redundancy, so that if a system fails there is another to take over. Nevertheless, damage at the junction of the midbrain and forebrain that disrupts the ascending arousal pathways has profound effects (See figure 8.9). This was first noted by Baron Constantin von Economo, a Viennese neurologist, who documented the effects of a form of encephalitis that resulted in extreme sleepiness; it was named after him (encephalitis lethargica or von Economo's sleeping sickness). The encephalitis patients, who could sleep up to 20 hours a day, had lesions at the junction of the midbrain and forebrain (von Economo, 1930).

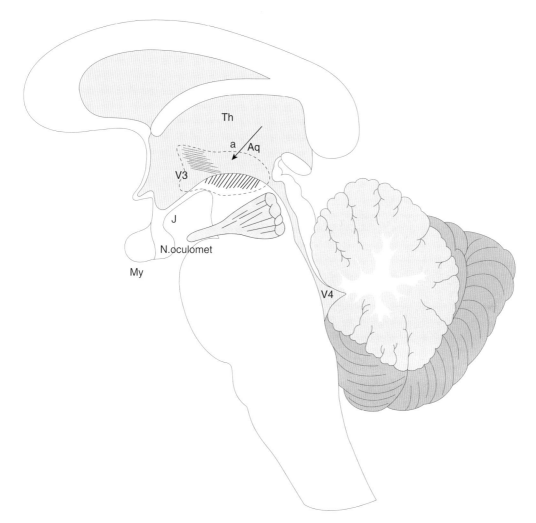

Figure 8.9   A drawing of the human brainstem, taken from von Economo's original work. It illustrates the site of the lesion (diagonal hatching) at the junction of the brainstem and forebrain that caused prolonged sleepiness, and the site of the lesion (horizontal hatching) in the anterior hypothalamus that caused prolonged insomnia. The arrow points to a region between the two, including the posterior lateral hypothalamus. Von Economo suggested that narcolepsy was caused by lesions at this site

Adapted from Saper et al. (2005)

Sleep-promoting brain systems

Non-REM sleep

One area of the brain that is more active during sleep than wakefulness is the ventrolateral preoptic nucleus (VLPO) (Sherin et al., 1996; Szymusiak et al., 1998). Neurons in this region of the hypothalamus contain the inhibitory neurotransmitters GABA and galanin (Gaus et al., 2002; Sherin et al., 1998) and they connect with the monoaminergic arousal systems in the hypothalamus and brainstem (Sherin et al., 1998) (See Figure 8.10). When the VLPO is damaged this causes insomnia (Lu et al., 2000). This evidence suggests that projections from the VLPO form a sleep-promoting pathway that inhibits arousal systems (Saper et al., 2010). A consequence of inhibition of arousal systems is that transfer of information from the thalamus to the cortex is shut off which effectively puts the brain into an 'offline' state in which activity in the cortex is not influenced by sensory inputs. This helps us to understand the reduced consciousness that occurs during sleep. Consistent with this, imaging studies have shown that sleep is associated with reduced activity in the thalamus and prefrontal cortex (Maquet, 2000).

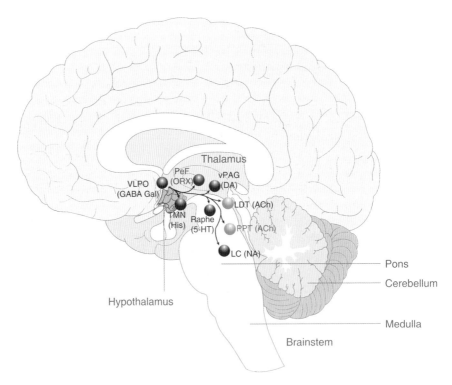

Figure 8.10   A schematic drawing to show the key projections of the ventrolateral preoptic nucleus (VLPO) to the main components of the ascending arousal system. It includes the monoaminergic cell groups (red) such as the tuberomammillary nucleus (TMN), the A10 cell group, the raphe cell groups and the locus coeruleus (LC). It also innervates neurons in the lateral hypothalamus (LHA; green), including the perifornical (PeF) orexin (ORX) neurons, and interneurons in the cholinergic (ACh) cell groups (yellow), the pedunculopontine (PPT) and laterodorsal tegmental nuclei (LDT). Note that the VLPO neurons lie within the region outlined by von Economo for the anterior hypothalamic lesion that caused insomnia

Source: Saper et al. (2005)

REM sleep

Early studies of the controls of REM sleep by Jouvet and others showed that large lesions made in the pons disrupted REM sleep, suggesting that this brainstem area is important for REM sleep (Jouvet, 1962; Webster and Jones, 1988). A subset of cholinergic neurons in the PPT /LDT in the pons are active not only during waking, but also during REM sleep (Boissard et al., 2002) and may help generate the cortical activation of REM sleep via effects on the thalamus (Boissard et al., 2002). At the same time, monoaminergic pathways remain supressed in REM and so the REM brain is selectively reactivated (Maquet et al., 2005) which may explain the type of dreams reports in REM (Hobson and Pace-Schott, 2002). Models of REM initiation generally suggest that there are REM 'off' and REM 'on' neurons in the brainstem that inhibit each other and that transitions from REM to non-REM are brought about by modulatory neurotransmitters that flip the on-off switch (Fuller et al., 2007; McCarley and Hobson, 1975).

Transitions between waking and sleep

The shift from waking state to sleep state is also thought to be controlled by a switching mechanism that depends upon groups of neurons that inhibit each other (Saper et al., 2001). The idea is based on electronic switches called 'flip-flops' that enable fast and complete transitions between different states. When applied to waking and sleep this kind of mechanism would explain why transitional sleep-waking states are short lived. This kind of system might have been selected for during evolution because of the vulnerability associated with a mixed sleep-waking state of reduced alertness. Because each side of the flip-flop mechanism inhibits the other side, when activity in one side increases it turns off activity on the other side and there is a switch into the alternative state. In this way, sleep is either switched 'on' or 'off' and in-between states are avoided.

The biological basis of the flip-flop is thought to be, on the one side, the sleep-promoting cells in the VLPO, and on the other side, the monoaminergic cells that form the ascending arousal pathways. Evidence in favour of this comes from the effects of lesions and recordings of the firing rates of neurons in these areas. For example, lesions of the VLPO affect the duration of sleep and increase the frequency of transitions between sleep and waking (Lu et al., 2000). Interestingly, there is a reduction in the number of VLPO cells with age and this coincides with greater waking during sleep (Ancoli-Israel and Kripke, 1991). In addition, firing patterns in VLPO and arousal neurons increase just before transitions (Aston-Jones and Bloom, 1981; Szymusiak et al., 1998).

Flip-flop switches avoid ambiguous in-between states, but there can be unwanted transitions if one side gains a slight advantage over the other. Therefore, there are ways of stabilising the switch, and this is thought to involve the orexin system. Because orexins promote activity in monoamine arousal pathways, this stabilises the waking state in the 'on' position to prevent unwanted switching between states (Saper et al., 2005) (Figure 8.11). Various physiological and external factors also affect the switching mechanism and these determine the timing and duration of sleep as we will find out next.

KEY POINTS

- Wake-promoting brain systems include acetylcholine, monoamine and histaminergic neurons that project from the brainstem to modulate cortical activity.
- Sleep occurs when the VLPO becomes active.
- The VLPO is inhibited by wakefulness-promoting regions.
- A flip-flop mechanism controls shifts between sleeping and waking and is stabilised by orexins.

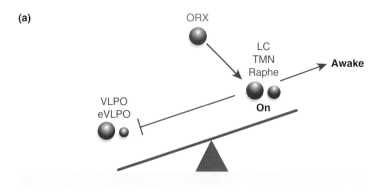

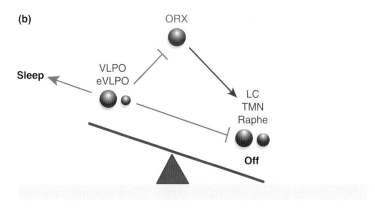

Figure 8.11 A schematic diagram of the flip-flop switch model. During wakefulness (a), the monoaminergic nuclei (red) inhibit the ventrolateral preoptic nucleus (VLPO; purple), thereby relieving the inhibition of the monoaminergic cells and that of the orexin (ORX) neurons (green), the cholinergic pedunculopontine (PPT) and laterodorsal tegmental nuclei (LDT; yellow). Because the VLPO neurons do not have orexin receptors, the orexin neurons serve primarily to reinforce the monoaminergic tone, rather than directly inhibiting the VLPO on their own. During sleep (b), the firing of the VLPO neurons inhibits the monoaminergic cell groups, thereby relieving their own inhibition. This also allows it to inhibit the orexin neurons, further preventing monoaminergic activation that might interrupt sleep. The direct mutual inhibition between the VLPO and the monoaminergic cell groups forms a classic flip-flop switch, which produces sharp transitions in state, but is relatively unstable. The addition of the orexin neurons stabilises the switch

Source: Saper et al. (2005)

CIRCADIAN INFLUENCES ON SLEEP

Think about how your levels of sleepiness vary over a day. Regardless of how much sleep you have had the night before you would probably agree that tiredness does not increase in a linear fashion throughout the day. Rather, there are ups and downs in levels of tiredness that coincide with specific points in the day. Let us say you've stayed up all night – you are likely to feel tired during the night, but when morning comes you are likely to feel more alert and less like sleeping. However, by the late evening you will be feeling more tired again and wanting to sleep (Åkerstedt, 1979). This is because the propensity to sleep is influenced by multiple factors. One factor is the time you have spent awake. Another factor is a circadian rhythmic influence that waxes and wanes throughout the day.

Humans are adapted to a diurnal pattern of behaviour. Our physiology is different at night than during the day time. Effectively we have a biological day time and a biological night time. For example, our body temperature rises during the day and then decreases overnight. This pattern is not just due to our being more active during the day than the night, because studies have shown that even when activity and eating is kept constant over the day, the temperature rhythm is still there (Mills et al., 1978). It is also not just related to changes in light over the day, because other studies in which people have lived in constant dim light have found that the rhythm does not go away. The reason for this is that we have an internal biological clock that keeps track of time.

So how do we know that the sleep-waking cycle is influenced by circadian rhythms generated by a biological clock? After all, daily rhythms could be generated by both internal (clock) and external components (light and time cues). This is not an easy question to answer because it is difficult to study circadian rhythms. We can observe that people tend to fall asleep more easily at night. However, this could be for all sorts of reasons. Early studies of sleep circadian rhythms involved people living for a time in the absence of time cues and on a constant schedule of activities, e.g. regular small meals and bed rest. In this set-up, the effect of environmental cues and sleep-wake activity on sleep cycles is removed. The problem here though is that the sleep-waking is still influenced by time spent awake (which can vary) as well as body clock influences. However, the results of other studies, in which the time spent awake was controlled alongside other factors, suggest that the propensity to sleep does vary according to a circadian rhythm and that sleep is optimal when aligned with the biological 'night' (Czeisler et al., 1999).

The role of the master body clock

So what is the basis for circadian effects on sleep? The master body clock that is responsible for orchestrating biological rhythms consists of a pair of nuclei, one nucleus on either side of the brain, in the hypothalamus called the suprachiasmatic nuclei (SCN) (Ralph et al., 1990). The SCN do not make direct connections with sleep centres in the brain. They communicate indirectly, via other hypothalamic nuclei to the VLPO sleep-promoting centre. These connections are inhibitory, suggesting that the circadian system mainly promotes wakefulness. This is supported by the finding that lesions to the SCN result in a loss in circadian rhythms and reduce time spent awake (Chou et al., 2003).

Setting the biological clock

Light is not required for circadian influences on sleep, but light cues are important for keeping the biological clock in check and keeping it synchronised to the solar day. This is because, in the absence of external cues to time of day, the biological clock runs slightly longer than 24 hours and so without resetting our internal cycles would get out of sync with the environment. Other cues may also reset the clock, but the evidence here is less clear (Mistlberger and Skene, 2005).

Collectively, cues that reset the clock are called **Zeitgebers** which means 'time-giver' in German. When the sleep-wake cycle and biological clock are uncoupled this can have consequences for health as discussed in detail in Spotlight 8a. The mechanism for light entrainment of circadian rhythms is that light is detected by rods and cones and another type of cell in the retina, the retinal ganglion cells that contain the photopigment melanopsin, and this signal is passed on to the SCN via the retino-hypothalamic tract (Gooley et al., 2001; Hattar et al., 2002; Moore et al., 1995). The involvement of retinal ganglion cells in resetting circadian rhythms explains why some blind people who lack rods and cones, but have intact retinal ganglion cells, nevertheless show entrainment of circadian rhythms (Czeisler et al., 1995)

HOMEOSTATIC INFLUENCES ON SLEEP

Sleep may be easier at some times of day than others, but we do not just sleep at set times based on a circadian cycle. If sleep is disturbed for some reason, then catch-up sleep occurs (Agnew and Webb, 1964). We experience greater tiredness after sleep deprivation and sleep time is extended. Models of the influences on sleep therefore accommodate both a circadian component and a homeostatic component (Borbely and Tobler, 1985). Homeostatic theories suggest that there is an optimal level of sleep that we require and so if we do not get enough sleep there are mechanisms that work to compensate for this by increasing sleep. Quite some time ago it was proposed that there are sleep-promoting substances that accumulate in the body during prolonged wakefulness. This idea was based on reports that injections of CSF from sleep-deprived dogs induces sleep in recipient dogs (see Kubota, 1989). At the time it was not known what these sleep factors or 'somnogens' might be, but now we know about some likely candidates.

The main candidate for a sleep factor is adenosine. Production of adenosine in the brain is linked to energy utilisation by cells. Since energy stores in astrocytes get used up during prolonged waking it seems plausible that adenosine could be a sleep factor. In support, there is evidence that a genetic mutation that prevents the production of adenosine by astrocytes reduces compensatory sleep (Halassa et al., 2009). Adenosine receptors are located throughout the brain and activation of adenosine receptors is thought to promote sleep via inhibiting arousal pathways and possibly also by biasing the flip-flop mechanism in favour of sleep. Injection of an adenosine agonist into the BF wake-promoting area or near the VLPO sleep-promoting area causes sleep (Scammell et al., 2001). Interestingly, caffeine is an adenosine antagonist and this mechanism could explain why it is not a good idea to drink a cup of coffee before bed time.

There are likely to be other sleep factors, and additional candidates are cytokines and prostaglandins that are associated with immune function and which may be responsible for the increased sleep that is observed during illness (Krueger and Majde, 1994). More recently it has been hypothesised that sleep factors may exert their effects via cortical interneurons that express neuronal nitric oxide synthase (nNOS) and are active during sleep in proportion to the amount of SWS (Gerashchenko et al., 2008).

EMOTIONAL AND COGNITIVE INFLUENCES ON SLEEP

Even if homeostatic and circadian influences combine to promote sleep at certain times, sleep can be resisted in response to external factors. Sleep can be put off to deal with an emergency. The ability to stay awake even when other factors are pushing us towards sleep probably involves activation of prefrontal cortical areas perhaps driven by emotional responses generated in the amygdala (Nofzinger et al., 2004). Sleep can also be promoted by the presence of cues previously associated with sleep. In other words we learn that some environments are good for sleep and these cues (bed) can make one feel sleepy.

Stressful situations reduce the propensity to sleep and increase levels of arousal. The stress neurotransmitter corticotrophin-releasing hormone (CRH) has been found to stimulate orexin neurons and it has been proposed that arousal associated with the stress response is mediated by release of orexins (Paneda et al., 2005). Hunger is also associated with increased arousal and reduced sleep and this is probably also due to increased levels of orexins during food deprivation

(Sakurai et al., 1998). Mice lacking orexin neurons do not show an increased arousal response to food deprivation (Yamanaka et al., 2003).

Stress-induced insomnia has been modelled in rats and cFos staining has been used to measure activity in sleep-waking areas of the brain. Rats were stressed by putting them in an unclean cage that had been occupied by another rat. The stressed rats took longer to fall asleep and then had disturbed sleep. An unusual pattern was observed whereby both wake-related and sleep-related areas showed activation after sleep (Cano et al., 2008). These results might suggest that the stress was activating arousal areas whereas homeostatic and circadian mechanisms were promoting activity in sleep areas, and the result was that neither system could win out, leading to disrupted sleep.

KEY POINTS

- There are circadian influences on sleep that are orchestrated by the master body clock in the suprachiasmatic nuclei of the hypothalamus.
- Homeostatic influences on sleep are mediated by the build-up of adenosine.
- Arousal due to stress or emotion can disrupt sleep and this depends on orexins.

THE FUNCTION OF SLEEP

All mammals and birds sleep. Many theories have been proposed to account for sleep. In reality sleep probably serves more than one function. Some of these functions are probably essential for us to stay healthy and require a certain amount of core sleep while other functions are optional and serve an adaptive function (Horne, 1988).

One idea is that sleep is a behaviour that evolved to keep animals out of danger during times they may be vulnerable to predators (Meddis, 1977). This might be why we humans sleep at night because we would not be able to avoid predators very well in the dark.

There has been some debate about whether sleep is required for the building and restoration of material used during wakefulness. Biochemicals and tissue may be depleted dur-

Figure 8.12   The bottlenose dolphin goes to extraordinary lengths to sleep. One hemisphere sleeps at a time to make sure it can continue swimming! The other half of the brain stays awake at a low level of alertness (Mukhametov et al., 1977)

© Anna segeren/Shutterstock.com

ing waking and these are restored by sleep. In support of this idea, growth hormone is released during sleep. Evidence from sleep deprivation studies might also support a recuperation model of sleep. Studies in rats have shown that sleep deprivation can be fatal (Rechtschaffen et al., 1983). The severely sleep-deprived rats develop sores and infections before eventually dying. However, these experiments involved forced sleep deprivation which is stressful. This makes their interpretation difficult. It could be the stress, not the sleep deprivation, that is fatal. In addition, in humans, physiological changes following moderate sleep deprivation are not easy to demonstrate. The main effect of deprivation is to impair cognitive performance and decrease mood rather than prevent tissue restoration. Indeed, general bodily repair does not require sleep and could occur during periods of relaxed wakefulness. According to the recuperation model, if people exercise a lot they would be expected to sleep more, but this is not the case. People may fall asleep quicker following exercise, but they do not sleep for longer. Also Ryback and Lewis (1971) found no change in sleep in healthy subjects who spent six weeks in bed.

More recent evidence from genetic studies suggests that sleep may be important for more subtle restorative effects on cellular function. Genes that are unregulated in sleep produce agents that are involved in combating the stress associated with waking metabolism, and are important for neurotransmitter signalling and may be involved in stabilising synapses (Bushey et al., 2011; Mackiewicz et al., 2009). Overall these studies are consistent with the idea that wakefulness exerts some stress on the body and brain and that the sleeping state restores optimal functioning.

Another core function of sleep seems to be in facilitating learning and memory. Compared with a wake interval of equal length, a period of post-learning sleep enhances memory retention and improves performance in procedural skills (Plihal and Born, 1997). There is evidence that both slow wave sleep and rapid eye movement sleep support memory consolidation (Diekelmann and Born, 2010).

SLEEP DISORDERS

Insomnia is the most common form of sleep disorder. It is a difficulty initiating or maintaining sleep that is associated with the feeling that sleep has not been refreshing. A person with insomnia may have a problem falling asleep or they may wake up often during the night and have trouble going back to sleep. Some people with insomnia wake up too early in the morning. However, insomnia is difficult to define because whether or not someone has had enough sleep needs to be defined in relation to sleep needs. For some people, waking up early may be the norm. The cause of insomnia is usually secondary to other problems such as mental health problems or illness and pain. Also, ironically, insomnia can be caused by withdrawal from some sleeping medications.

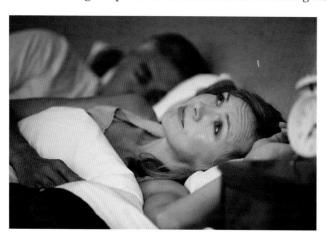

Figure 8.13 Insomnia affects approximately 25% of the population occasionally, and 9% regularly

© Monkey Business Images/Shutterstock.com

Another disorder, narcolepsy, is characterised by sleep at inappropriate times rather than too little sleep. Narcolepsy is a neurological disorder that has its onset usually in the teens or 20s. There are four main features of narcolepsy. Sleep attacks are an irresistible urge to sleep during the day, usually under conditions of monotony. The attacks last about 2–5 minutes. Cataplexy is the second major feature of narcolepsy. It involves complete paralysis during waking and is usually triggered by strong emotions or physical effort. The person with narcolepsy will collapse while fully conscious and will be unable to move for a few seconds to several minutes. Cataplexy is a component of REM sleep (loss of muscle tone) occurring at an inappropriate time. **Sleep paralysis** is another symptom that occurs just before or after normal sleep. It can usually be terminated by the person being touched. Finally, hypnagogic hallucinations are the experience of dreaming while awake. The cause of narcolepsy is a specific mutation in the gene that codes for orexin. Studies have shown absence of orexin in the cerebrospinal fluid of patients with narcolepsy and a reduction in the number of orexin cells (Thannickal et al., 2000). There is no cure for narcolepsy, but the drug Modadfinil helps control some of the symptoms. In the future it may be possible to implant orexin-secreting cells into the brains of people with narcolepsy although that is a long way off right now.

Some sleep disorders involve problems that occur during normal sleep and are referred to as parasomnias. One such disorder is **REM behaviour disorder**, in which the usual loss of muscle tone during REM does not occur. Patients with REM behaviour disorder can act out violent dreams during REM or they may experience limb twitching, yelling, and jerking. REM behaviour disorder is uncommon and usually occurs in men over 50. It is probably a neurodegenerative disorder with some genetic component. Other parasomnias such as sleep walking (**somnambulism**) and sleep talking are associated with slow wave sleep. They are not pathological and usually something that children grow out of.

Figure 8.14 Sleep attacks are a feature of narcolepsy. They usually last only a few minutes but can greatly affect daily activities. People may unwillingly fall asleep while at work or at school, when having a conversation, after eating a meal, or, most dangerously, when driving

© iStock.com/RyanJLane

KEY POINTS

- The function of sleep may involve a combination of restoration, predator avoidance, energy conservation and memory consolidation.
- Although many people can get by with small amounts of sleep, we all sleep, suggesting that sleep has some essential function.
- There may be core sleep (essential for brain/body functioning) and optional sleep which is a means of keeping inactive.
- Sleep disorders include insomnia, narcolepsy, and parasomnias such as REM behaviour disorder.

CHAPTER SUMMARY

In this chapter we have found out that motivated behaviours are fundamental yet complex behaviours that are governed by homeostatic and incentive processes. The biological bases of motivated behaviours involve close communication between the body and brain and there is some overlap in the underlying brain circuits across motivations. The hypothalamus is important for both eating and sleep, and orexins play an important role in both behaviours. Learning is an important feature of motivated behaviour and allows us to adapt to our environment.

FURTHER READING

Berridge, K. C. (2004). Motivation concepts in behavioural neuroscience. *Physiology & Behavior, 81*(2), 179–209.
Detailed but accessible review of the development of theories of motivation.

Berthoud, H. R. (2011). Metabolic and hedonic drives in the neural control of appetite: Who is the boss? *Current Opinion in Neurobiology, 21*(6), 888–96.
A concise and clear overview of the interactions between metabolic and hedonic neural circuits that control eating.

Saper, C. B., Fuller, P. M., Pedersen, N. P., Lu, J., & Scammell, T. E. (2010). Sleep state switching. *Neuron, 68*(6), 1023–42.
Discusses the neural circuitry underlying the regulation of sleep and provides a framework for understanding homeostatic, circadian, and hedonic influences on sleep. Also covers breakdown of sleep switching mechanisms in narcolepsy.

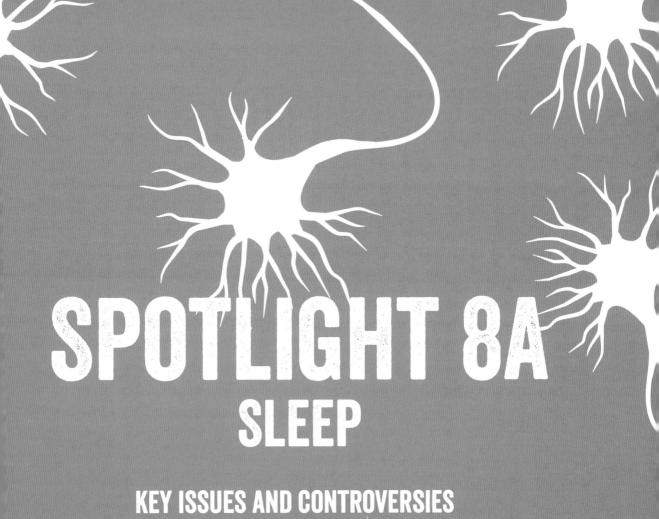

SPOTLIGHT 8A
SLEEP

KEY ISSUES AND CONTROVERSIES

- How much sleep is 'enough'?
- What is the relationship between sleep and health?
- How does sleep improve memory?

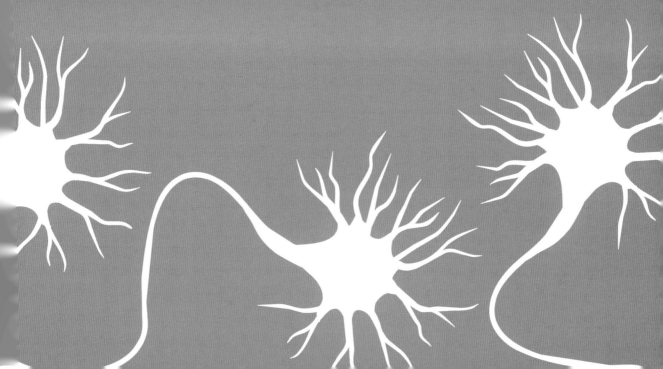

INTRODUCTION

In Chapter 8 we learnt that sleep is essential for brain functioning and that sleep deprivation is associated with impaired cognitive performance and reduced mood. This begs the question, how much sleep does an individual need to avoid these detrimental effects? What is the optimum amount of sleep? Concerns that we do not get enough sleep have been around for a long time. Even back in 1894, scientists worried that the 'hurry and excitement' of modern life was causing insomnia. Similar concerns abound today, especially in relation to the amount of sleep that children get. In this Spotlight we will ask questions about how much sleep we need. The answers to these questions are important not only because they will guide practical advice on sleep but also because they might reveal something about the function of sleep. We will also investigate the relationships between sleep and mental and physical health and find out about the complex links between sleep and emotional processes. Do sleep disturbances trigger emotional problems or do mood and anxiety disorders lead to difficulty sleeping? The causal relationship between sleep and emotional processing have yet to be fully worked out but an implication of this work is that sleep therapy could be a novel way of tackling emotional disorders. Finally, we will examine memory function of sleep. It has been known for some time that sleep improves memory but recently scientists have been uncovering the specific mechanisms through which sleep establishes memories. This research is important because it gives us insights into the biological processes underlying memory formation. There are also implications for understanding the relationship between aging, memory and sleep. An exciting idea emerging is that treatment to improve sleep in older adults could reduce the cognitive decline experienced in later life.

SLEEP DEPRIVATION: A MODERN PROBLEM?

Do you think you get enough sleep? What if I asked you if you need more sleep? What would you say? Many people today complain that they are sleep deprived and a common refrain is that the hectic lifestyles we all tend to lead nowadays means we can't possibly be getting enough sleep. Surely the game playing and TV watching that children get up to before bedtime must mean they are not getting enough sleep? But how much sleep do we get on average? How does this compare with the amount of sleep our grandparents or great-grandparents got?

According to large surveys of sleep habits, adults in the UK and USA sleep for about seven hours a night on average (Groeger et al., 2004; Krueger and Friedman, 2009). Of course there is quite a bit of variation: a small percentage of the population report sleeping less than six hours a night and a similarly small proportion say that they habitually sleep for more than nine hours. If we take a snapshot of sleep times in the UK and USA then it seems that there is a relationship between working hours and sleep time such that as people work longer they accommodate this by sleeping less (Basner et al., 2007; Chatzitheochari and Arber, 2009). This supports the idea that the current culture of long work hours and commuting are leading to people sleeping less today than they used to (Van Cauter et al., 2008; Webb and Agnew, 1975). However, the results of studies that have looked at measures of sleep duration over time suggest that there has been no consistent change in the average night's sleep over the last 50 years. These data challenge the notion that people today are living a 24-hour lifestyle that minimises sleep (Bin et al., 2012).

Children and adolescents sleep for longer on average than adults, with the average being about 11 hours for 6-year-olds and 10 hours for 10-year-olds. In general, the average amount of sleep declines steadily from infancy to the age of 11. There is also a striking variability in the

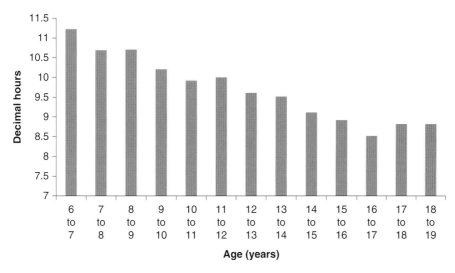

Figure 8a.1   The amount that children sleep declines as they reach adulthood

Source: Horne (2011)

amount of sleep that young children (especially) get, with values ranging from about 10 to 17 hours for infants (Blair et al., 2012). A recent analysis of changes in children's sleeping times suggest that over time children in some countries (e.g. in the USA) are sleeping about one hour less nowadays than they did 100 years ago, mainly due to later bedtimes rather than earlier waking times (Matricciani et al., 2012). However, in other countries, children are sleeping for slightly longer than their grandparents did as children (e.g. in the UK).

It seems that there is no convincing evidence for a consistent and large decline in sleeping duration over the past 100 years. Of course it is difficult to compare data over time, particularly when the data are on self-reported sleeping times rather than actual measured sleep duration by activity monitors, so some caution is needed when thinking about these results. In addition, even if we accept that children in some countries may be sleeping an hour or so less than children did in the past, it is not really known what the consequences of this amount of sleep reduction might be. It could be that children used to sleep more than they needed in the past and not that children are sleep deprived today.

In actual fact you might be surprised to learn that there is no real consensus about how much sleep children should get. We do not really know what constitutes 'normal' sleep for children. The same is true for adults. Six hours sleep a night may leave some people feeling perfectly refreshed and able to concentrate during the day. Margaret Thatcher, the first woman Prime Minister in the UK, famously said that she only needed four hours' sleep a night to function. Other people may experience day-time sleepiness if they do not get nine hours' sleep a night. To say six hours is not enough and nine hours is too much does not take into account individual differences in the amounts of sleep required to avoid sleepiness during the day (Van Dongen et al., 2004).

The tendency to be a short or long sleeper is partly down to genetics (He et al., 2009). But there is also evidence that some people can adapt to shorter sleeping times without much trouble (Horne and Wilkinson, 1985). Individuals who are able to adapt their sleep to amounts below the daily norm are unlikely to be experiencing sleep 'deprivation'. However, some people have a genotype that makes them more vulnerable to the effects of sleep loss, especially in the early morning (Viola et al., 2007). In addition, reductions in sleep to amounts less than five hours a night are probably outside the limits of adaptation for most people and may result in adverse consequences (Horne, 2011).

IMPLICATIONS

Altogether the evidence suggests that most people sleep for about the same amount as their grandparents did on average. Despite perennial worries about sleep deprivation, most people also seem to get sufficient sleep to avoid problems with day-time sleepiness. Exactly how much sleep a person requires varies quite a bit and is influenced by both genetic predisposition and adaptation to environmental demands. However, some people are in a state of sleep deprivation and accumulating a sleep debt, which means that they are getting less sleep than they need to function optimally. This may be because they are sleeping for very few hours or they are very sensitive to moderate sleep loss. Getting less sleep than you need is associated with feelings of tiredness but also with other physical and mental problems as we will discover next.

SLEEP AND HEALTH

It has been suggested that both very short (less than six hours a night) and long sleeping times (more than nine hours a night) may be associated with greater risk of dying than sleeping for around six to nine hours a night (Ferrie et al., 2007; Gallicchio and Kalesan, 2009). The potential underlying reasons for this relationship are complex and the direction of the relationship is unclear.

There is evidence from laboratory studies that extreme sleeping times are associated with changes in metabolism and immune function that could contribute to serious health conditions such as heart disease, diabetes and obesity (Spiegel et al., 1999). For example, experimentally reducing the amount of sleep of healthy volunteers to about four hours a night leads to signs of insulin resistance, which may be a risk factor for the development of diabetes (Spiegel et al., 2004). There are also effects of very short sleep times on the release of the appetite hormones leptin and ghrelin, which have been linked to obesity (Spiegel et al., 2004). Large population-wide studies have also linked short sleep time with increased risk of diabetes and obesity (Ayas et al., 2003; Taheri, et al., 2004). These data support the idea that short sleep may cause metabolic problems and weight gain that increase mortality, and are consistent with the idea that sleep serves some kind of restorative function because severe lack of sleep is associated with physiological problems.

CRITICAL ANALYSIS

In thinking about the impact of sleep on health there are a few issues that we should cast a critical eye over. One point is that very few people actually habitually sleep for as little as four hours over a sustained period, which may limit the conclusions we can drawn from lab studies using this level of sleep reduction (Horne, 2008). It is not known whether smaller reductions in sleep over longer periods would have the same kinds of effects. Such studies may be difficult to justify ethically because the prediction would be that in the long term, people's health would suffer. Lab studies are important in revealing the biological mechanisms that could explain why short sleep may result in health problems but they do not necessarily mimic conditions in the real world.

There have been many studies that have looked on a population level at the association between sleep time and health outcomes but not all of these studies have found a significant relationship (Magee et al., 2008). In other words, the relationship is not reported consistently. This might be explained by the different methods used to assess sleep across studies and the fact that some of these methods are more reliable than others. Some studies only measure self-reports of sleep duration rather than actual measures of sleep using activity monitors or EEG (Kurina et al., 2013). It is possible that the important relationship is between perceived sleep duration and health and not between actual sleep duration and health. A person who is stressed may think that they get very little sleep and may also be at more risk of adverse health outcomes, even though they actually sleep a normal amount.

Lack of consistency in reporting on the relationship between sleep and health is probably due in part to the fact that there are differences between studies in how they control for potential confounding variables (Nielsen et al., 2011). A confounding variable is something that is associated with one of the variables of interest and may explain all or part of an observed relationship between the variables of interest. For example, a study may show that shorter sleep is associated with obesity but it is possible that this relationship is actually explained by the confounding variable of alcohol use. It could be that people who use alcohol a lot are more likely to be obese and alcohol use just so happens also to be associated with short sleeping. Controlling for alcohol use would then mean that the relationship between short sleeping obesity disappears but not controlling for it in the analysis would give a spurious result.

Short sleeping time is a likely consequence of having a health condition. For example, obesity is associated with sleep apnoea, which is linked to sleep problems. If we just take a snapshot of the association between sleep duration and obesity then this does not tell us whether short sleep duration causes obesity. Tracking people over time can tell us more about whether short sleep leads to later health problems or increased risk of death. Researchers can separate people out at a baseline assessment point and determine their health status to see if this is related to later outcomes. More studies are needed that examine in a prospective fashion whether short sleeping results in later obesity. The current state of play here is that studies in children appear to support the idea that short sleeping contributes to later increases in body mass index (BMI) but the evidence is much less clear for adults (Magee and Hale, 2012). One recent study found that short sleeping was only associated with greater risk of mortality for adults who had existing health problems at baseline. This suggests that the relationship between short sleeping and mortality may be explained by pre-existing disease, at least for adults (Magee et al., 2013).

Another possibility is that it is not just sleep duration that is important for health outcomes but also the quality of sleep. A person might sleep for a long time but this sleep might be interrupted leading to reductions in the amount of REM sleep. Poor sleep has been associated with cardiovascular disease and metabolic problems (Hoevenaar-Blom et al., 2011; Spiegel et al., 2009). A disrupted pattern of sleeping has been associated with increases in hunger and tendencies towards uncontrolled or binge-like patterns of eating, which might relate to weight gain in the longer term (Chaput et al., 2011; Gonnissen et al., 2012; Kilkus et al., 2012).

It should be clear that in evaluating the evidence we need to take into account the methods used and take care in how we extend conclusions from carefully controlled lab studies and apply them to the population at large. It is possible that there is some risk associated with sleeping around five hours a night over a long period for physiological function (St-Onge, 2013). This would suggest that increasing the sleep of short sleepers should be beneficial for health. It will be important to examine in randomised controlled trials whether extending the sleeping of short sleepers has a positive impact on health markers and conditions such as obesity. Ultimately, there may be other reasons for suggesting that people get a good night's sleep other than trying to avoid weight gain and it is these reasons we will consider next.

SLEEP AND MENTAL HEALTH

Ever felt grumpy and moody after a bad night's sleep? The links between sleep and emotional well-being are probably well known to many of us and supported by scientific studies (Dinges et al., 1997; Kim and Dimsdale, 2007). Intriguing new research into what underlies the complex relationship between sleep and mental health is providing new ways of thinking about how to help people with serious psychological disorders such as post-traumatic stress disorder and depression.

Sleep disturbances are commonly associated with psychological disorders such as depression. It has been suggested that as many as 90% of people suffering from depression also report insomnia (Riemann et al., 2001). Depression is further associated with changes to the structure of sleep such that people with depression enter REM more quickly than non-depressed people and experience more REM sleep (Gottesmann and Gottesman, 2007). These sleep disturbances are likely due in part to the depressed state, given that there is overlap between the biological mechanisms that underlie both sleep and depression (Wulff et al., 2010). But recently, scientists have been asking whether sleep problems may play a role in maintaining or even causing depression.

One of the ways in which sleep disturbances may exacerbate depression is by altering emotional memories (Walker and van der Helm, 2009). Evidence suggests that sleep is important for memory consolidation (Rasch and Born, 2013). The effect of sleep on memory processing is particularly marked for emotional memories (Wagner et al., 2006) and this has been linked to the amount of REM sleep in particular. One hypothesis is that increased REM sleep results in very strong memories for emotional events. If this is coupled with an existing bias for processing negative information in depression (Mogg et al., 1993) then one can see that increased processing of negative emotional memories in REM sleep might perpetuate or produce an unhealthy emphasis on negative thoughts which could trigger or maintain a depressive state. This idea is supported by the observation that some therapies for depression also reduce REM sleep (Buysse et al., 1997).

In a similar vein, sleep has also been shown to enhance the learning of fearful memories (Menz et al., 2013), which has implications for the treatment of post-traumatic stress disorder. A prediction from this research is that after a fearful event, sleep should be avoided to reduce the consolidation of the fearful memory. Therefore sleep deprivation might be a useful way of reducing the power of memory for

Figure 8a.2 A recent study found that patients who underwent exposure therapy for spider-phobia were less scared of a live spider the following week if they were allowed to sleep after being exposed under controlled conditions to a virtual-reality spider (the exposure therapy). Presumably, this was because sleeping strengthened new non-fearful memory traces established during therapy (Kleim et al., 2013)

© Oksana Savchyn/Shutterstock.com

traumatic events such as natural disasters. In support of this idea, participants who saw emotionally negative pictures had poorer memory for them and reacted to them less if they stayed awake than if they slept (Baran et al., 2012). This kind of approach might also be useful for treatment of phobias (see Figure 8a.2).

In summary, there are likely complex, bidirectional relationships between sleep and mental health. Common underlying mechanisms predispose individuals towards mental health and sleep problems and these sleep problems contribute to maintaining the condition probably through effects on emotional processing. Having raised the idea of the importance of sleep for learning and memory, let us now turn in detail to current ideas about sleep and cognitive function.

SLEEP AND COGNITIVE FUNCTION

We have discussed the idea that a certain amount of core sleep may be important for optimal metabolism and release of hormones and that severe disruption to sleep can have detrimental effects on these processes. However, the effects of sleep deprivation have been found to be particularly profound on the brain, leading some researchers to claim that sleep is 'of the brain, by the brain, and for the brain' (Hobson, 2005).

The importance of sleep for cognition is underlined by reports that accidents, for example the Chernobyl nuclear disaster and the loss of the space shuttle 'Challenger', were due to lapses in cognitive performance induced by sleep deprivation. Furthermore, sleep-related car crashes have been found to account for about 16–23% of road accidents (Horne and Reyner, 1995). Sleep deprivation has been shown to produce impairments on a hand–eye coordination task equivalent to those induced by alcohol consumption at or above the legal limit (Dawson and Reid, 1997). Cleary, driving when sleep deprived can be very dangerous.

Sleep deprivation affects the ability to maintain attention on monotonous but demanding tasks (Lim and Dinges, 2008) but it has less of an effect on well-practised skills (Killgore, 2010) suggesting that not all cognitive functions are impaired equally by sleep deprivation. Various higher-level processes such as working memory and the ability to inhibit inappropriate responses are affected, which can lead to risky decision-making and poor judgement (Chee and Chuah, 2008). This obviously has implications for the ability of people to function effectively in a work environment, especially when they are required to deal with unexpected or crisis events (Horne, 2012).

Exactly why sleep deprivation impairs complex cognitive functions is unclear but one underlying factor might be the adenosine. As we learned in Chapter 8, adenosine builds up during the day and promotes sleep by inhibiting acetylcholine systems that are important for maintaining the waking state. Acetylcholine systems are also important for attention and working memory and so the effects of sleep deprivation on these processes could be underpinned by the build-up of sleep-promoting factors, such as adenosine, after prolonged wakefulness (McCoy and Strecker, 2011). In other words they might be due to 'sleepiness'. Alternatively, it could be that parts of the brain that are important for decision-making, such as the prefrontal cortex, are vulnerable to the effects of prolonged metabolic activity and hence they become disproportionally 'tired' with sleep deprivation (Cirelli and Tononi, 2008).

Another effect of sleep deprivation is on the ability to acquire new information. Sleep-deprived participants in a study were less able to recognise pictures that they had viewed previously than participants who had a usual night's sleep and this effect was related to reduction of processing in the hippocampus (Yoo et al., 2007). Taken together, the results of studies on the effects of sleep deprivation on cognition suggest that 'pulling an all-nighter' before an exam may not be the way to get good grades! But could getting a good night's sleep or taking a day-time nap after learning actually improve memory? Evidence has now accumulated that a period of sleep after learning consolidates this learning and that this is an important function of sleep.

SLEEP AND LEARNING AND MEMORY

Unfortunately, the idea that one might be able to learn a new skill, such as speaking a new language, during sleep has no scientific support, but the notion that memories for already-learned information can be reinforced during sleep is supported by a large body of experimental evidence.

The first studies on benefits of sleep on memory were conducted nearly 100 years ago. Recall of nonsense syllables was reported to be better after sleep than after an equivalent amount of wakefulness (Jenkins and Dallenbach, 1924). Many other studies since have found similar results. In a typical experiment, some participants are trained on a task in the morning and then tested several hours later in the evening whereas other participants are trained in the evening and then tested in the morning after a night of sleep. A consistent finding is that the participants who get the chance to sleep after the learning perform much better when they repeat the task than the participants who stay awake between training and testing. This holds true for many different types of training task, from learning lists of words to learning how to type a sequence of letters or trace a figure in a mirror (Rasch and Born, 2013).

Early theories about the benefits of sleep for performance on these memory tasks related to the idea that sleep provides an opportunity to consolidate the memory representations that underlie the learning, in the absence of encoding of new information that would disturb this process. More recent evidence suggests that sleep not only protects memories from being interfered with by new encoding, but also facilitates processes that boost specific memories. The theory here is that memories are 'replayed' during sleep and this helps transfer them from a temporary short-term store in the hippocampus to a more stable long-term store in the cortex (Rasch and Born, 2013). This idea is supported by the finding that the specific neuronal firing patterns of rats that explored a novel environment were replayed in the same pattern during subsequent sleep (Wilson and McNaughton, 1994). These neuronal firing patterns are possibly mimicked by applying low-level electrical stimulation to people during sleep to enhance slow waves during sleep and increase memory (Ngo et al., 2013).

KEY STUDY

Rasch, B., Büchel, C., Gais, S., & Born, J. (2007). Odor cues during slow-wave sleep prompt declarative memory consolidation. *Science*, *315*(5817), 1426–9

An important study in humans found that experimental reactivation of memories during sleep improved memory. The task in this study was to learn the location of 15 objects in a two-dimensional array that was presented on a computer screen. The task is basically the same as the card game 'concentration' in which the aim is to flip over matching card pairs. In the learning part of the task, the first card of each card pair was presented alone followed by the presentation of the matching card in the array and so on for all the 15 card pairs. This was done twice in a different order each time. The participants were then tested on their memory for the card locations. The first card of each pair was presented and the participants had to indicate with the mouse where the second card was located in the array.

The researchers were interested in finding out if reactivation of the memory for the object locations during sleep would improve their ability to remember the object locations the next day. To reactivate the memory they used an odour cue; the odour was the scent of a rose. The authors chose an olfactory cue because smells are well known to evoke memories. The odour was present when the learning took place and was then represented during sleep. The idea was that when the participants learned the location of the objects this memory was associated with the rose smell. When this smell was presented again during sleep it would reactivate the previous memory and boost the consolidation of that memory, so in theory the object recall would be better than if the memory had not been boosted by the odour during sleep.

The researchers performed four studies that involved presenting the odour or an odourless control sample at different times during the study. In the first study, participants performed the learning task with the odour and then on the subsequent two nights were re-exposed to either the odour or the control sample during slow wave sleep (SWS). The participants attended two overnight conditions; half had the odour during sleep first and the other half had the odourless control sample during sleep first, so that the order of the conditions was counterbalanced. Even though the participants said they were not aware of the presentation of the odour during sleep, they later recalled significantly more

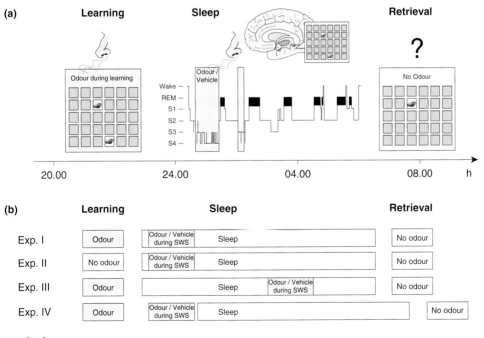

Figure 8a.3

Source: Rasch et al. (2007)

(Continued)

(Continued)

correct object locations when the odour was presented during SWS compared with when the odour-less control sample was presented during SWS.

The researchers then wanted to rule out the possibility that improved memory for the object locations was merely due to the presentation of the odour during sleep, rather than due to a specific effect of presenting the odour on memory consolidation. For example, it could be that odour presentation during sleep affects sleeping some way that improves cognitive performance the next day irrespective of whether the odour was presented during learning and so was acting as a memory cue. So the researchers did another very similar study in which the odour was not presented during learning and was only presented during sleep. In this way the odour could not act as a cue for the memory of task learning and so would not be predicted to have an effect. In line with the prediction there was no effect on recall the next day of having been exposed to the odour during sleep only.

Another control study examined the effect of odour presentation during a different stage of sleep: REM sleep. This study was identical to the first study apart from the timing of the odour presentation, which was in the first two major periods of REM sleep rather than during SWS. No effect of odour presentation during REM sleep on recall was found. Finally, the researchers also tested whether presentation of the odour would enhance memory consolidation during waking by presenting the odour during the learning task and again after learning but when the participants were awake and performing a different computer task. In this case there was also no effect of odour presentation after learning on memory performance the next day.

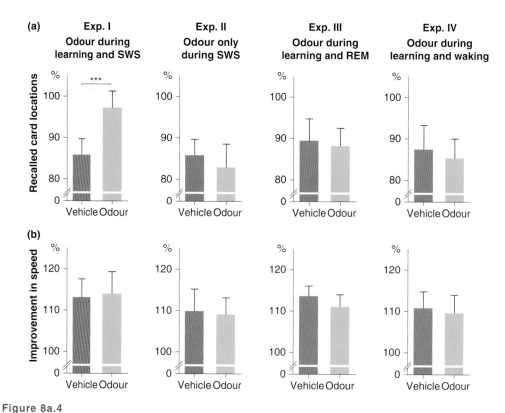

Figure 8a.4

Source: Rasch et al. (2007)

The researchers also checked that the effect of odour presentation during learning and SWS was not due to there being a difference in the baseline responding on the two test days (there was not). They further checked whether the odour affected the structure of sleep and reported that the EEG patterns were not altered by the odour. Finally, the researchers examined whether the presentation of the odour during SWS was associated with activation of the hippocampus, which is hypothesised to the critical structure for replay of memories. This study was identical to the first study apart from the fact that the participants had been somewhat sleep deprived so that they would be able to sleep in the brain scanner! This functional magnetic imaging confirmed that odour presentation during SWS caused much greater activation of the hippocampus than odour presentation during waking. Overall the results suggest that experimentally induced reactivation of memories enhance later recall of the memories and provide evidence for a causal role of such reactivations for memory consolidation.

Sleep and selective memory consolidation

More recent studies on memory consolidation and sleep have found that not all memories are consolidated equally and that sleep preferentially enhances some memories over others. There is now evidence that emotional memories are more likely to be consolidated during sleep (Hu et al., 2006). Knowledge that some items will later be tested, or knowledge that remembering some items over others will result in monetary rewards, also leads to selective consolidation of memories during sleep (Fischer and Born, 2009; Wilhelm et al., 2011). These results suggest that during sleep new information is selected for assimilation in memory in a discriminatory fashion with more important or salient items being selected preferentially.

Sleep memory and the lifespan

Sleep patterns change as we get older. Unfortunately, the way in which our sleep patterns change is not good for our memory. In the over-60s, 70% experience a loss of deep sleep and this has been linked to memory impairments (Mander et al., 2013). An implication of these results is that improving sleep for older people would be a way of preventing memory decline.

Children also experience sleep-dependent memory consolidation in a similar manner to adults but children have more SWS and so one might expect that their memory consolidation during sleep is better (Wilhelm et al., 2012). In line with this idea, in one study, children and adults were trained on a task that involved pressing a button according to a repeating pattern. As training progressed the participants got faster at pressing the button in the right sequence. What was striking in this study was that after sleep, more children than adults could report the correct button sequence, suggesting that the children showed greater consolidation of the learning than the adults. Interestingly, even napping may be good for children's memory. Naps at nursery may be important – midday naps in preschool children enhances memories acquired earlier in the day (Hupbach et al., 2009; Kurdziel et al., 2013).

IMPLICATIONS

Sleep is important for consolidating memories. Sleep after learning something new helps cement that new information into the brain, so it is more likely to be remembered, and this may be especially so for young children.

FURTHER READING

Horne, J. (2011). The end of sleep: 'Sleep debt' versus biological adaptation of human sleep to waking needs. *Biological Psychology, 87*, 1–14.
> Critical review of evidence on the relationship between sleep duration and mortality and morbidity.

Rasch, B., & Born, J. (2013). About sleep's role in memory. *Physiological Reviews, 93*(2), 681–766.
> A detailed and comprehensive review of research on sleep and memory. It provides a historical perspective on concepts and a discussion of recent key findings.

St-Onge, M.-P. (2013). The role of sleep duration in the regulation of energy balance: Effects on energy intakes and expenditure. *Journal of Clinical Sleep Medicine, 9*(1), 73–80.
> Recent evaluation of studies that have assessed food intake, energy expenditure, and leptin and ghrelin levels after periods of restricted and normal sleep.

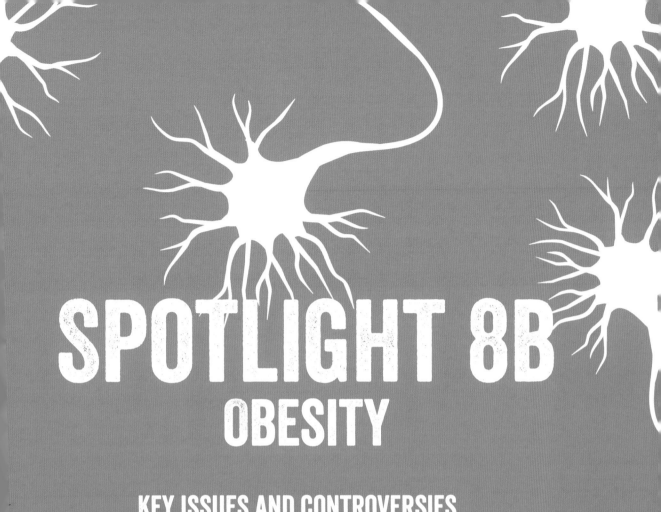

SPOTLIGHT 8B
OBESITY

KEY ISSUES AND CONTROVERSIES

- How do we define obesity?
- What are the consequences of obesity?
- Can people be 'addicted' to food?

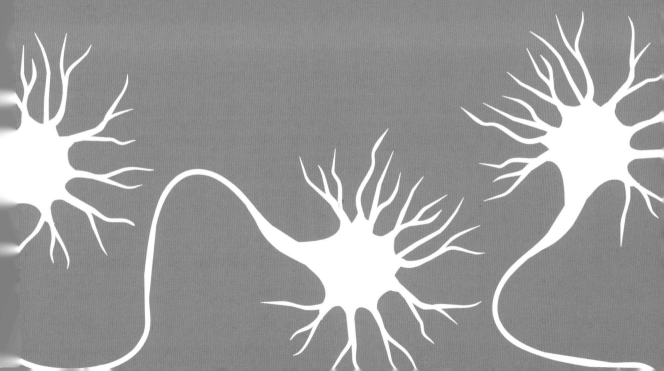

INTRODUCTION

In Chapter 8 we examined some of the factors that influence the development of obesity. Many countries are seeing obesity levels rising year on year. The International Obesity Task Force reported in 2010 that 1.0 billion adults are currently overweight and a further 475 million are obese. There is concern about these rising levels of obesity because of the reported association between obesity and adverse health outcomes such as diabetes, cardiovascular disease and cancer. Given the potentially huge cost of dealing with an obese population it is important to understand how obesity is defined and what the causes might be. One factor that has gained attention is the idea that certain foods have addictive properties that promote their over-consumption, leading to obesity. In this Spotlight we will go deeper into some controversial research on obesity by examining the consequences of obesity and the research on food addiction.

DEFINING OBESITY

As we learned in Chapter 8, BMI is a crude but practical way to define obesity. Measuring someone's height and weight to calculate BMI is easy, but BMI does not tell us about how much body fat someone has or where it is distributed. This is important because fat that accumulates around internal organs is associated with worse health outcomes than if it accumulates under the skin (Després and Lemieux, 2006; Janssen et al., 2004). BMI is reasonably good at accounting for differences in body fat between individuals (Keys et al., 1972), but it is not a perfect indicator of metabolic health and the risk of developing diseases such as diabetes.

Some people who are obese can have a healthy metabolic profile whereas some people who have a normal BMI can be in poor metabolic health and have high blood pressure, high blood lipid levels and high fasting blood glucose levels (Wildman et al., 2008). In addition, some studies have reported that there is not a straightforward relationship between BMI and death rates (Flegal et al., 2013). While a BMI over 35 was associated with higher mortality than normal BMI, being overweight with a BMI of 25–50 was associated with a lower mortality rate than having a normal BMI. This may be because fat reserves provide energy reserves to meet metabolic demands during chronic illness, hence increasing the chances of survival. Another study found that for patients with coronary heart disease, high fitness levels predicted a good outcome regardless of levels of body fatness

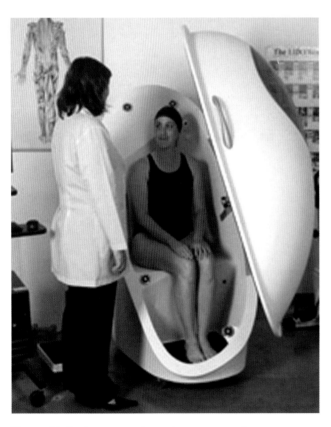

Figure 8b.1   Image courtesy of www.cosmed.com

(McAuley et al., 2012). If we are concerned about obesity because of the health consequences, this suggests that we need to think more about how we define obesity in relation to treatment.

A measure of waist circumference in addition to BMI has been suggested to be useful in deciding whether or not someone might need a referral to have an assessment for markers of metabolic health (Klein et al., 2007). Other methods that provide an accurate measure of body composition are magnetic resonance imaging and dual-energy X-ray absorptiometry (DEXA) scanning. These scans show the amount of fat in the body and where it is distributed, but the equipment is costly.

All of this suggests that although BMI may be an indicator of potential health problems, in deciding whether someone is at risk of poor health outcomes related to body fat accumulation, one needs to take into account many other factors. These include body fat distribution and other factors that impact health more generally such as sex, age and fitness levels.

PSYCHOLOGICAL CONSEQUENCES OF OBESITY

There is evidence that fat accumulation is associated with increased risk of various diseases, although there is a debate about the optimal weight for health (Ahima and Lazar, 2013). But obesity is associated too with adverse psychological outcomes that can also contribute to poorer health generally in obesity. Obesity is associated with increased rates of depression (Stunkard et al., 2003) and this may in part be due to the stigmatisation of obesity in many societies (Puhl and Heuer, 2009).

Negative treatment of an obese individual begins in childhood and has been linked to body dissatisfaction (Wardle and Cooke, 2005). Even 6–11-year-olds assign negative characteristics (e.g. lazy, dirty, mean, stupid) to pictures of overweight children (Latner and Schwartz, 2005) and 30% of all adolescent girls report weight-related teasing by peers or family members (Neumark-Sztainer et al., 2002). These experiences have been suggested to hinder the social, emotional, and academic development of children (Puhl and Latner, 2007).

It has been argued that considering obesity as a disease might have positive consequences if it means that there are increased efforts in trying to understand the causes and more funds are put towards prevention and treatment programmes. There may also be an effect to reduce the stigma and discrimination experienced by many obese people.

One idea about why levels of obesity have increased in recent times that has gained a considerable amount of attention is that the environment is laden with artificial foodstuffs that we are consuming in unhealthy quantities because they are addictive. This is a controversial area and one that has serious implications for how we think about obesity. In the next section we will examine the science behind food addiction so that you will be equipped to think about this problem in an informed way.

FOOD ADDICTION

The idea that some foods are addictive and that addiction drives over eating, possibly leading to obesity, is a pervasive concept in modern society. Popular books and websites promote the notion that food addiction, like addiction to drugs abuse, is a very serious problem. There has also been lively debate among scientists about the usefulness of the concept of food addiction in explaining why some people overeat and whether or not it is a valid concept at all (Blundell and Finlayson, 2011; Gearhardt et al., 2011a; Stice et al., 2012; Ziauddeen et al., 2012).

One thing for sure is that there are significant implications that flow from accepting that people can be addicted to foods. We might want to control access to addictive foods in the same way that access to drugs is regulated. We might also want to impose taxes and restriction on advertising since these approaches are thought to be effective in reducing the harm from using legal drugs like alcohol and tobacco (Brownell and Frieden, 2009; Frieden and Bloomberg, 2007). Indeed some of these approaches have already been tried. Advertising of certain food products is regulated during children's television programming (Adams et al., 2009). We might also want to rethink the way in which treatment programmes aimed at helping people reduce their overeating are targeted. Maybe treatment approaches that have had some success in treating drug addiction might be useful for people who have problems with diet control. It is therefore important to be able to evaluate the evidence on food addiction and assess what the gaps in our knowledge are so we can come to an informed conclusion on policy issues relating to health and diet.

TYPES OF EVIDENCE

Three different scientific approaches have provided the bulk of the evidence on food addiction. The first approach has been to compare the behavioural features of drug addiction with problems around food. Parallels have been drawn between the diagnostic features of drug addiction and problems that can be experienced with food, leading to the conclusion that there is a clinical syndrome of food addiction that is very similar to drug addiction. It is just that the addictive substance is food rather than a drug of abuse such as heroin.

The second approach has been to examine the neural substrates that underpin responses to both palatable foods and drugs of abuse. Studies have been conducted on laboratory animals and humans and it has been noted that there are common brain mechanisms that underlie the rewarding effects of food and drugs. It has been suggested that some foods may have such a powerful effect on these reward systems that they are acting in a similar way to drugs of abuse and may be changing the brain in ways that promote dependence.

Finally, several animal models have been developed in which rats show behavioural features of addiction when exposed to certain dietary regimes. The suggestion here is that these models may mimic the situation that some people experience in relation to food and that if the rats can become addicted to food then so might people.

Critical analysis

In thinking about whether food addiction is something that really exists we need to think carefully about the evidence and the conclusions we can draw from the evidence. Next, we will look in turn at the different lines of evidence on food addiction and ask some critical questions about the approaches and where possible make some suggestions about the further research that might help clarify what is a complex picture.

Overlapping clinical features

One way of diagnosing drug addiction is to use the *Diagnostic and Statistical Manual IV* (*DSM-IV*) criteria, which states that if someone presents with any three of the criteria presented in Table 8b.1 then they have a problem with drug dependence. It has been suggested that the *DSM-IV* criteria can be translated across to problems with overeating so that, for example, a person who experiences a loss of control of eating (eating more than intended), has tried unsuccessfully to cut down on their eating (failed dieting attempts), and continues to eat regardless of negative health consequences might be diagnosed as having food addiction.

Table 8b.1

Substance dependence criteria	Corresponding behaviours for obesity
Tolerance: increasing amounts of drug to reach intoxication	Tolerance: increasing amounts of food to maintain satiety
Withdrawal symptoms	Distress and dysphoria during dieting
Larger amounts of drug taken than intended	Larger amounts of food eaten than intended
Persistent desire and unsuccessful attempts to cut drug use	Persistent desire for food and unsuccessful attempts to curtail the amount of food eaten
Great deal of time spent on getting the drug, using the substance	Great deal of time is spent eating
Important activities given up because of substance abuse	Activities given up from fear of rejection because of obesity
Substance use continued despite knowledge of problems caused by the drug	Overeating despite knowledge of problems caused by excessive food consumption

Source: Volkow and O'Brien (2007)

The *DSM-IV* criteria have been used to develop a scale to try to quantify food addiction (the Yale Food Addiction Scale; Gearhardt et al., 2009). A group of obese patients completed the scale and a small subset of them was found to score highly. These participants were more likely to report binge eating tendencies and experience more food cravings than obese participants who did not qualify as being food addicted (Davis et al., 2011). Another study found that participants scoring highly on the Yale Food Addiction scale showed greater activation in reward areas of the brain when viewing pictures of food (Gearhardt et al., 2011c). More recently, a small sample of food addicts was identified in a community sample and these food addicts scored higher on a measure of dopamine signalling and showed higher binge eating and emotional eating tendencies compared with the non-food addicts (Davis et al., 2013). These results suggest that it is possible to identify people who endorse the food addiction criteria and these individuals differ from control participants in their neurobehavioural responses.

A question that has been raised about these types of studies is whether the Yale Food Addiction questionnaire is specifically measuring a food addiction syndrome, or if it identifies people who have a range of problems with eating behaviour that include binge eating and loss of control over eating. It might be that people who score highly on food addiction have a very severe form of binge eating disorder (BED). Further investigation of the links between eating disorders like BED and addictive-like behaviours would be helpful in figuring out whether BED and food addiction are separate entities that might require different treatment approaches.

It has also been noted that some of the *DSM-IV* criteria are more important than others when thinking about food addiction. Tolerance to drugs is the phenomenon whereby a user has to take more and more of a drug in order to experience the same pharmacological effects. The extent to which this applies to problems with foods is not easy to discern because, unlike drugs, food does not have a specific pharmacological action. Others have pointed to evidence of reduced reward responses of obese people to the actual consumption of food, which might imply a kind of tolerance (Kenny, 2013). Withdrawal symptoms are experienced for some drugs of abuse and may be a factor that motivates consumption. An addict may be motivated to take a drug to avoid the negative state that is experienced when someone stops taking a drug. But how does this translate to food addiction? One possibility is that the depressed mood state that sometimes accompanies food restriction or avoidance of certain foods in dieting is a kind of withdrawal state that may trigger overconsumption of food (Volkow et al., 2013) but is this recognised as 'withdrawal' by people? Everyone has to eat and so what is the withdrawal from?

Cravings are associated with drug taking (Robinson and Berridge, 1993) and many people also report strong desires for certain foods, which is suggestive of another behavioural overlap between the consequences of drug taking and consumption of tasty foods (Weingarten and Elston, 1991). Indeed there is evidence from fMRI that there is a common underlying neural circuit including the hippocampus, amygdala and caudate, that mediates drug and food cravings (Pelchat et al., 2004). But in and of itself, this does not provide evidence for food addiction, because food cravings could be a normal response to the sight of foods that encourage consumption. Or, they could be a way of explaining the difficulty people experience when trying to resist consuming foods that they think are 'naughty but nice' (Rogers and Smit, 2000).

Another important point for consideration is what foods might actually be addictive. Can we identify specific foods that are more likely to engender addiction? Is there a specific food component that drives addiction? Clearly this would be important to have a handle on if addictive foods were to be regulated in some way. There is no answer to this question at present but some have suggested that foods with very high fat/sugar or their combination might provide a hyper-palatable stimulus that is sufficient to mimic the effects of some drugs of abuse (Gearhardt et al., 2011b).

In summary, a proportion of individuals with obesity identify with statements about their relationship with food that imply food addiction. However, there has been debate about whether food addiction as defined by questionnaires such as the Yale Food Addiction Scale is sufficient to accept that food addiction is a real phenomenon that is more than a severe form of binge eating disorder. Other research points towards overlaps between the neural changes that accompany drug addiction and those observed in obesity and binge eating. It is this neurobiological evidence that we turn to next.

Overlapping neurobiological features

There are similarities between the effects of drugs of abuse and consumption of food on neural processes. For example, both the acute administration of drugs of abuse and food consumption result in an increase in dopamine signalling in the striatum (Di Chiara and Imperato, 1988; Hernandez and Hoebel, 1988). This response can become sensitised (increase over repeated experience), which leads to an enhanced motivational response (increased 'wanting') to the sight of cues associated with the drug use or food consumption (Robinson and Berridge, 1993). This sensitisation has been suggested to underlie the development of addiction to drugs and so could be a mechanism that underpins food addiction (Berridge et al., 2010). However, although there are similarities between the effects of food and drugs on the brain there are also important differences. For example, distinct subpopulations of neurons in the nucleus accumbens are activated selectively by food versus cocaine (Carelli et al., 2000). In addition, the dopamine response to food stimuli habituates more rapidly than the response to cocaine (Di Chiara, 1999). It is likely that reward circuits for food and drugs use similar mechanisms yet operate slightly differently, and so it may not be automatic that drugs and food will have the same behavioural consequences in relation to addiction. This might explain why the motivation to consume food may rarely, if ever, attain the intensity of the motivational pull or 'wanting' for drugs of abuse. It is not often reported that people will commit serious crimes to obtain chocolate bars whereas drug addicts will go to severe lengths to obtain their next fix.

Brain imaging studies have given some insight into similarities between the response to food and drug cues. When lean people view tasty food pictures in an fMRI scanner increased activation in reward-related brain areas such as the striatum, orbitofrontal cortex, insula and amygdala has been observed when compared with viewing non-food images (van der Laan et al., 2011). Similar circuitry is activated when viewing pictures of drug-related paraphernalia (Tang et al., 2012). Other studies have attempted to test the prediction that drug use and overeating leading to obesity are associated with similar responses to the relevant motivational cues.

There is evidence that obese versus lean participants show greater activity to food cues in areas of the prefrontal cortex areas that are associated with the anticipation of eating, but reduced activity in areas of the brain that have been linked with bodily awareness and cognitive control of behaviour (Brooks et al., 2013). Some studies have found that reward response to food-related cues are related to future weight gain (e.g. Yokum, Ng and Stice, 2011) other have not found such a relationship (Stice et al., 2013). Due to the relatively small number of studies that have been conducted to date and the variability of the methods employed, the general picture is one of inconsistent results across studies. Furthermore, there is no firm evidence that areas of the brain that are important for the rewarding effects of drugs of abuse, such as the striatum, show differential activity in response to food cues in lean versus obese participants (Brooks et al., 2013; Ziauddeen et al., 2012).

Another method for examining overlap between the addicted and obese brain is to use positron emission tomography to measure levels of dopamine receptors in key reward areas. A classic study conducted in 2001 found that, like drug addicted individuals, obese people have reduced levels of dopamine D2 receptors when compared with control participants.

KEY STUDY
Wang, G. J. et al. (2001). Brain dopamine and obesity. *The Lancet*, 357(9253), 354–7

The participants in this study were ten severely obese people with a BMI of greater than 40 and ten lean participants of a similar age. The obese and lean groups were also matched for education level and socio-economic background. The participants agreed to undergo a PET scan that involved them being placed in the scanner and receiving an intravenous injection of the dopamine D2 antagonist raclopride.

The raclopride had been tagged with a radioactive label so that it could be detected by the PET scanner. These kinds of radioactive tracers are short-lived and the amount of radiation emitted is very small, no more than that experienced during an X-ray. As the tracer decays, it emits positrons. When the positrons come into contact with electrons in neighbouring atoms they generate gamma rays. The PET scanner detects the gamma rays and then it is possible to build up a picture of the location of the molecule attached to the tracer. Because raclopride binds to dopamine D2 receptors, it is possible with this method to figure out the levels of dopamine D2 receptors that are available for binding in the striatum in the obese versus lean participants. This is done by assessing the concentration of the tracer in the blood versus the concentration in different parts of the brain over time. The researchers compare the concentration in the striatum with the concentration in another

(Continued)

(Continued)

area of brain (the cerebellum) which is known to be devoid of dopamine D2 receptors. This provides a measure of the specific binding to D2 receptors versus the amount of tracer in tissue that is not bound to receptors. The researchers can calculate an estimate of the available receptors for binding in the area of interest.

Some of the participants were also scanned with a radioactive marker of blood glucose usage in the brain. This provides a measure of the levels of metabolic activity in different brain regions that relate to neuronal activity.

The researchers found that there was a negative correlation between BMI and dopamine D2 receptor availability, such that within the obese group, greater BMI was associated with less dopamine D2 receptor availability. Within the control group there was no relationship between BMI and dopamine D2 receptor availability, and age was the best predictor of receptor availability in this group. No differences were found between the obese and lean groups in terms of brain metabolism in the striatum or several other brain areas examined.

The researchers interpret their data as suggesting that like drug addiction, obesity is characterised by low numbers of D2 receptors and that low dopamine D2 receptor number may increase vulnerability to addictive behaviours, including compulsive food intake. They further suggest that reduced numbers of dopamine D2 receptors may be associated with a reduced capacity to experience reward from food, and that this results in compensatory overconsumption. In other words, they argue that obesity is a reward deficiency syndrome in which obese people consume more food than lean people to experience similar levels of reward.

The researchers further argue that because there was no difference between the groups in terms of brain metabolism in the striatum, it is unlikely that the observed effects are explained by differences in uptake of the tracer in the lean versus obese participants. However, they also acknowledge that because the study was cross-sectional in design and tested participants were already obese, it is impossible to rule out that the down-regulation of dopamine receptors was a result of prior overstimulation of dopamine D2 receptors by overeating.

Another point of evaluation is that because of the nature of the study design, it is also possible that the reduced dopamine D2 receptor availability reflects increased levels of endogenous dopamine at the time of the scan in the obese versus lean participants. This is because raclopride and dopamine compete for occupancy of the dopamine D2 receptor, and more dopamine at the synapse binding to the receptor would decrease the number of receptors binding raclopride.

Since the original study by Wang and colleagues, the results have been replicated in some studies (de Weijer et al., 2011; Volkow et al., 2008) but there are other reports of failures to find a similar relationship between BMI and dopamine D2 receptor availability (Haltia et al., 2007). This may be because of differences in the participant characteristics (morbidly obese in some studies versus obese in other studies), reflecting that the complex nature of obesity is unlikely to be fully captured by a crude measure of BMI. A more recent study of rats found that levels of D2 receptors in the ventral striatum predicted weight gain over one, but not two, months (Michaelides et al., 2012). This study is a start on addressing the issue of cause and effect in the role of dopamine D2 receptors in obesity because the rats can be observed over time before the onset of overfeeding and obesity. Rodent models have also been used by other researchers to assess the possibility of food addiction and it is to this literature that we now turn.

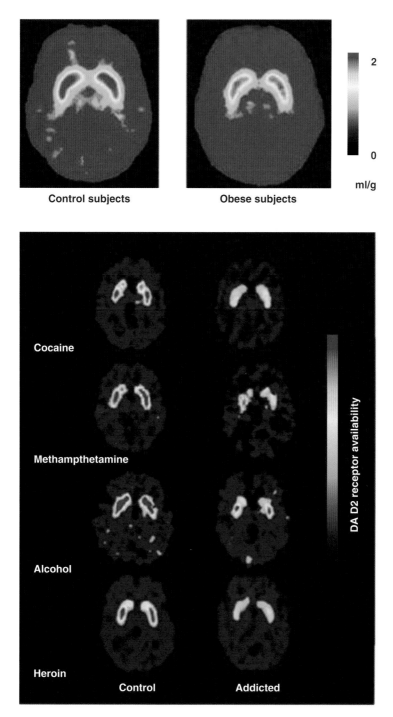

Figure 8b.2

Source: Wang et al. (2001)

Animal Models of Food Addiction

When rats are given limited access to sugar solutions, over time they develop a binge-like pattern of eating behaviour that has been suggested to resemble the escalating pattern of intake seen in drug addicts (see Avena et al., 2008a). In the model, the rats increase their intake of the sugar solution and this is correlated with various changes in brain chemistry. They are usually food-deprived for half the day and then have access to a glucose solution alongside their normal rat diet (called chow). The behaviour of these deprived rats is compared to a control group of rats that have access to glucose and chow all the time. After a few days of the experimental regime, the deprived rats take larger amounts of glucose. If food is removed totally for 24 hours they exhibit what might be thought of as withdrawal-like symptoms that include teeth chattering and anxiety (Avena et al., 2008b). The withdrawal symptoms can also be induced if the rats are given an opioid antagonist, much the same as a heroin addict experiences opiate withdrawal when given an opioid antagonist (Colantuoni et al., 2002). The 'addicted' rats have also been found to have lower striatal D2 receptors, similar to reports of lowered dopamine D2 receptors in obesity (Colantuoni et al., 2001), although the rats do not actually gain weight in the model.

In other similar models, access to fat is similarly limited to a few days a week or there is limited access to palatable foods combined with exposure to a stressor (Boggiano and Chandler, 2006; Corwin and Buda-Levin, 2004; Hagan et al., 2002). The outcome is that the rats show binge-like behaviours that are accompanied with changes to the brain that are similar to those observed in rats that are addicted to drugs (Corwin et al., 2011).

In another model, rats are exposed to what is called a 'cafeteria' diet in which they access a range of palatable foods such as bacon and cheesecake. These rats gain a lot of weight and are prepared to endure mild foot shocks in order to gain access to the foods, which suggests that they are prepared to endure negative consequences such is their compulsion to eat the tasty food (Johnson and Kenny, 2010). They also show a decreased response to brain stimulation reward (Johnson and Kenny, 2010). The changes observed in this model may be similar to the decrease in reward that is a response to increases in fat accumulation (Berthoud, 2011).

Taken together, the results from these animal models are consistent with the idea that under certain circumstances, palatable food can lead to neural adaptations that produce an addiction-like syndrome. However, it has been argued that the specific conditions required to produce these effects may not be easily translated to human eating behaviour (Ziauddeen and Fletcher, 2013). We would want to ask how similar the very controlled conditions that the laboratory rats experience are to real human eating situations. It may be that very specific patterns of binging are more like food addiction rather than food addiction being relevant to many people with obesity.

IMPLICATIONS

Evidence suggests that there are common underlying neural mechanisms that underlie the compulsive pattern of drug taking and consumption of palatable foods. There are also changes in brain reward mechanisms that occur when continued drug taking and the development of obesity are compared. Some people argue that this evidence should inform the development of approaches to tackle obesity that borrow from the field of drug addiction. Others are more cautious in their interpretation of the evidence and argue that while certain patterns of disordered binge eating may be usefully labelled as food addiction, further research is required before large-scale policies are built on the notion that food addiction is a major cause of the recent rise in obesity levels. There are also suggestions that too strong a focus on the contribution of food addiction to obesity will detract from a fuller perspective on the factors that contribute to over-eating, which are many and varied as we found out in Chapter 8.

There may be both positive and negative consequences of describing some people as being addicted to food and this being therefore out of their control. On the one hand, a food addiction explanation of obesity might help reduce what is experienced by obese people (Sikorski et al., 2011). More empathy is shown towards people who suffer from mental illnesses for which they are not thought to be responsible than for conditions such as alcohol addiction in which the person is thought to be personally responsible (Schomerus et al., 2011). Neurobiological explanations of drug addiction seem to have done little to remove the stigma of addiction for those individuals (Pescosolido et al., 2010). However, ratings of an obese peer were more positive when participants in a study were told that the obese person in the video they were watching was overweight because of a hormonal disorder than when they were told there was no explanation for the obesity (DeJong, 1980). In addition, there is evidence that people might be more likely to support public funding for obesity treatment if individuals are not seen as being personally responsible (Lund et al., 2011).

It has been suggested that a diagnosis of food addiction may become a convenient way for people to explain their overeating tendencies regardless of whether they are food addicted or not (Rogers and Smit, 2000). Some have cautioned that food addiction might be seen as an excuse for unhealthy eating behaviour (Epstein and Shaham, 2010). Indeed, an adverse effect of a label of 'food addiction' could be the undermining of motivation for changing dietary habits due to a belief that change is not under personal control (Ogden and Wardle,1990).

The research reviewed above opens up very important questions about our relationship with food and how we respond to the so-called 'obesity crisis'. The debate on food addiction will no doubt stimulate new lines of research that will help clarify the usefulness of the concept and may lead to insights as to how we might better help people to control what they eat.

FURTHER READING

Puhl, R. M., & Latner, J. D. (2007). Stigma, obesity, and the health of the nation's children. *Psychological Bulletin, 133*(4), 557.
  A very detailed and comprehensive review of the evidence of the stigmatisation of obese children and the many and varied serious consequences of this stigma.

Ziauddeen, H., Farooqi, I. S., & Fletcher, P. C. (2012). Obesity and the brain: How convincing is the addiction model? *Nature Reviews Neuroscience, 13*(4), 279–86.

Avena, N. M., Gearhardt, A. N., Gold, M. S., Wang, G. J., & Potenza, M. N. (2012). Tossing the baby out with the bathwater after a brief rinse? The potential downside of dismissing food addiction based on limited data. *Nature Reviews Neuroscience, 13*(7), 514.
  A series of papers debating the core issues around food addiction from different perspectives.

Ziauddeen, H., Farooqi, I. S., & Fletcher, P. C. (2012). Food addiction: Is there a baby in the bathwater? *Nature Reviews Neuroscience, 13*(7), 514.
  A follow-up to the above paper.

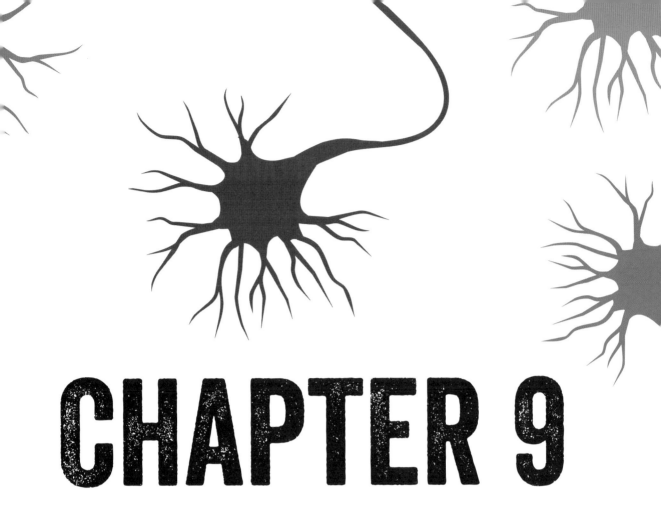

CHAPTER 9

PSYCHOLOGICAL DISORDERS

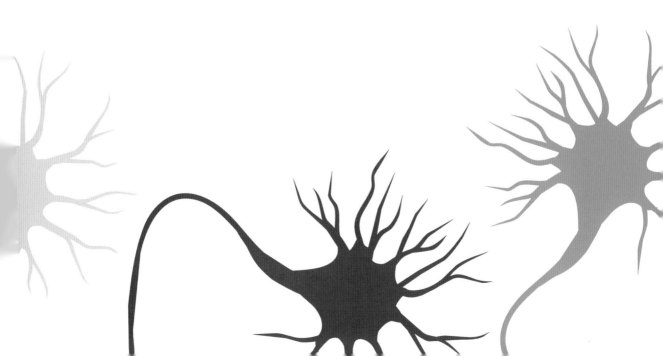

CHAPTER BREAKDOWN

- The nature of psychological disorders focusing on schizophrenia, depression and anxiety.
- Clinical symptoms, prevalence and progression of psychological disorders.
- The importance of gene–environment interactions in the cause of psychological disorders.
- The biological bases of psychological disorders.
- Drug treatments for psychological disorders.

ROADMAP

In this chapter we will be considering the biological bases of psychological disorders. Psychological disorders can have a profound impact on the quality of life of individuals, and there are major costs for governments both in terms of direct costs associated with healthcare and indirect costs associated with loss of income for people with psychological disorders who are unable to work. For these reasons it is important that we improve our understanding of the cause of psychological disorders and how best to treat or even prevent them. First we will consider the classification of psychological disorders and how the major psychological disorders of schizophrenia, depression and anxiety are diagnosed, along with their clinical symptoms, onset and course. We will be focusing on these disorders because they are the most common and debilitating. We will consider the evidence that schizophrenia, depression and anxiety are caused by dysfunction in brain circuits that result from complex interactions between genetic predispositions and environmental influences. We will discover that while much progress has been made in understanding the biological underpinnings of psychological disorders, and this has contributed to development of treatments, there is still much to be learned and this is in part due to the challenge of studying the organisation and function of an organ as complex as the brain. Along the way we will consider some of the methods that have been developed to uncover the neurobiology of psychological disorders, and their limitations.

The themes and issues discussed in this chapter link to ideas from previous chapters. Knowledge of the biological bases of perception, learning and memory, emotion and motivation will enhance understanding of how aberrant brain circuitry in psychological disorders might relate to specific behavioural characteristics (Chapters 4, 5, 7 and 8). We will use our understanding of how neurons communicate (Chapter 1) and how these processes may be modified by pharmacological tools, to understand how drug treatments for psychological disorders might be effective in offering symptom relief by correcting deficits in neuronal signalling (Chapter 2). Concepts of neural plasticity will be important for understanding the development of psychological disorders, and understanding behavioural genetics will illuminate gene–environment interactions in the cause of psychological disorders (Chapter 3).

WHAT ARE PSYCHOLOGICAL DISORDERS?

From time to time we all experience disturbances in our emotions and thought processes that affect our ability to cope with daily life. Problems in relationships or at work can trigger changes in mood that most people recover from. Sometimes psychological disturbances are experienced when there are no triggers or persist as intense or unusual responses to a trigger. When this happens a person might be diagnosed as having a psychological disorder. Psychological disorders are quite common and it is likely that you either will know someone who has a psychological disorder or may be diagnosed yourself.

Living with these disorders can have severe effects on a person's health and wellbeing, disrupting their ability to maintain relationships and function day to day, sometimes leading to self-harm and suicide. Psychological disorders affect populations around the world and account for a high proportion of long-term medical and social care costs.

Although historical descriptions of the symptoms of psychological disorders are recognisable today, how we think about these disorders is very different from the view not so long ago. The term schizophrenia was not even part of the vocabulary until 1911. Before then, in the mid-1800s, psychological disorders were thought to have either a physical or moral cause, but otherwise were not differentiated. Further back, all people with psychological disorders were treated the same because it was generally thought that they were possessed by devils and that this could be treated by blood letting or releasing evil spirits through holes drilled in the skull. The modern idea that psychological disorders are disorders of the brain was important for developing appropriate treatments but it also contributed to the categorisation of different types of psychological disorders thought to be caused by specific underlying problems in brain functioning.

CLASSIFICATION OF PSYCHOLOGICAL DISORDERS

Various different classification systems have been used to advance understanding of psychological disorders. The most commonly used system today is the *Diagnostic and Statistical Manual of Mental Disorders* (*DSM*, APA), which has been revised several times since it was published in the 1950s. The manual sets out criteria, based on behavioural symptoms, for diagnosing disorders like depression and schizophrenia. It has been helpful in standardising diagnoses and providing more accurate information on the prevalence of psychological disorders, but it has also come in for a lot of criticism along the way.

The number of psychological disorders listed in the *DSM* has increased dramatically as it has been revised over the years and some argue this is because behaviours that were considered part of the normal spectrum are now classified as pathological. The *DSM*, and other manuals like it, define a psychological disorder as 'a collection of behavioural symptoms associated with distress and dysfunction'. Some critics argue that this means that a behaviour could be judged distressing just because it is socially unacceptable, opening up the system for misuse. Others point out that a behaviour might be distressing and might appear dysfunctional but could actually just be an eccentric expression of normal behaviour or a normal response to an abnormal situation.

Even if agreement can be reached as to what constitutes distressing and dysfunctional behaviour there are other issues with classification schemes based on descriptive criteria like symptoms. Many symptoms cut across disorders meaning that one person can satisfy the criteria for several disorders and two people with different symptoms can be classified with the same disorder. Some of these issues might be resolved by adding knowledge about the biological bases of psychological symptoms to classification schemes. Better knowledge about the relationship between biological dysfunctions and the symptoms of psychological disorders could contribute to refining diagnoses and explaining why people present with clusters of symptoms. This chapter will discuss three of the most commonly experienced and debilitating psychological disorders: schizophrenia, major depression, and anxiety.

SCHIZOPHRENIA

Schizophrenia is a complex psychological disorder that can have severe effects on a person's health and wellbeing. People with schizophrenia usually seek help from medical professionals because they find aspects of their disorder disturbing, but they can also experience stigma due to misunderstandings about the disorder. A person diagnosed with schizophrenia may find it difficult to express their thoughts and may behave in ways that are difficult for others to understand. With support, most people with schizophrenia can lead ordinary lives but this is not made easy by the prejudices they sometimes encounter. It is sometimes assumed that people with schizophrenia are more likely to commit violent acts than people without a diagnosis of schizophrenia. Statistical associations between violent offending and schizophrenia have been reported but when interpreting such findings it is important to account for other factors that might predispose a person to violent acts. Drug abuse is associated with increased likelihood of violence and when this is taken into account, someone with schizophrenia is no more likely to commit violent acts than anyone else (Fazel et al., 2009). Schizophrenia affects fundamental processes of perception, emotion and cognition.

Clinical symptoms of schizophrenia

Schizophrenia is characterised by three broad categories of symptoms: positive or psychotic symptoms, negative symptoms, and cognitive disturbances. Psychotic symptoms include **delusions** and **hallucinations**. Hallucinations are perceptual experiences that occur in the absence of a sensory stimulus and can occur in different sensory systems. Hearing voices is common, but also are smelling, feeling or seeing things that are not there. A delusion is a fixed and false belief that a person is unwilling to change even when confronted with evidence that it cannot be true. Delusions can lead people to read special meanings into things that other people find innocuous. Someone might believe that their thoughts are being controlled by their neighbours or they might believe that their partner is being unfaithful, even though there is no actual evidence to suggest this.

Negative symptoms are changes in emotional state involving the loss of usual motivations and feelings. Common negative symptoms are reduced expression of emotion, diminished ability to experience pleasure (anhedonia) and problems initiating and completing plans. Cognitive symptoms are seen as especially problematic because the more cognitive problems someone has the worse they tend to do on quality-of-life measures such as the ability to function at work and live independently (Green, 1996). Patients with schizophrenia perform significantly worse than people without schizophrenia on many different types of cognitive test and some deficits are apparent well before other symptoms emerge, suggesting that they are a core feature of the disorder (Gunnell et al., 2002). Memory is usually impaired along with difficulties thinking ahead, sustaining attention, thinking critically and problem solving; see the Insight box below (Goldman-Rakic et al., 2004).

INSIGHT: COGNITION IN SCHIZOPHRENIA

Performance on cognitive tasks that depend on the frontal lobes is particularly impaired in schizophrenia (Goldberg et al., 1987). These deficits are likely to be related to impaired function in dorsolateral prefrontal areas and manifest as problems with executive functions such as memory, attention and flexible thinking.

The ability to do well on tests that measure executive functions, for example the Wisconsin Card Sorting Test and delayed word recall, predicts the ability to carry out everyday activities, whereas positive symptoms are not predictive. Negative symptoms can affect outcome owing to the effect of reduced motivation on engagement with social activities.

Significant relationships have been found between performance on specific executive functions and real world outcomes, as indicated below. Addressing cognitive symptoms in schizophrenia is therefore crucial for improving treatment outcomes.

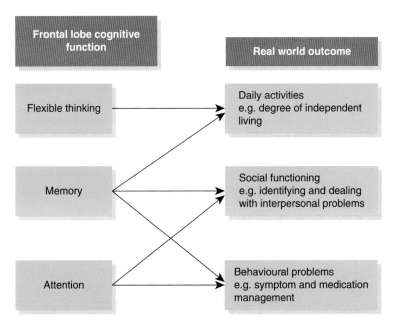

Figure 9.1 Cognitive prediction of real world outcomes in schizophrenia. Arrows indicate significant relationships across a number of studies. Adapted from Green et al., 2005

Other conditions can co-occur with schizophrenia and many patients additionally show symptoms of depression and anxiety and have substance abuse problems. Smoking rates are particularly high in people with schizophrenia (Masterson and O'Shea, 1984). Sadly, suicide is a leading cause of death among people with schizophrenia (Schwartz and Cohen, 2001). A combination of lifestyle factors, difficulties accessing healthcare and the side effects of some medications contribute to a generally higher incidence of disease among people with schizophrenia than in the population at large (Allebeck, 1989).

Each person's experience of living with schizophrenia is different. Some experience symptoms for a short time, others may have longer and repeated episodes, and a few will have very troublesome symptoms for long periods.

The symptoms of schizophrenia typically appear in the late teens and early twenties. The onset can be abrupt or gradual but there is usually a preceding period, known as the prodromal phase, in which symptoms are apparent, but not at clinical levels (Lieberman et al., 1991). The prodromal phase can last from months to years. Some signs of schizophrenia can also be present a long time before diagnosis. Subtle disturbances in social and cognitive function have been identified in children at risk of schizophrenia.

There is wide variation in the progression of schizophrenia. Some people recover completely but others will continue to experience recurring episodes over their lifetime. Many people with schizophrenia experience recurring periods of positive symptoms with some ongoing negative and cognitive symptoms (Harrow and Jobe, 2007). Treatments help around 80% of patients who are experiencing their first phase of positive symptoms and increase the likelihood and length of recovery in between episodes (Robinson et al., 1999). Factors such as early age of onset, longer duration of untreated psychosis, stress and living with family members who express negative attitudes can worsen the outcome (Jobe and Harrow, 2010).

Prevalence of schizophrenia

Estimates of the prevalence of schizophrenia suggest that around seven out of 1,000 people are affected (McGrath et al., 2008). Schizophrenia occurs in all countries but the incidence varies according to a number of risk factors. Living in an urban area is associated with increased risk of schizophrenia (Pedersen and Mortensen, 2001) and there is a link between migration and schizophrenia (Cantor-Graae and Selten, 2005). Men are more at risk than women (Aleman et al., 2003) and the risk increases if a person has a family member with schizophrenia (Kendler and Diehl, 1993). The degree of genetic relatedness between family members is important. The lifetime risk of developing schizophrenia in the general population is around 0.5% but this increases to about 9% if you have a brother or sister with schizophrenia, to just under 50% if you have two parents with schizophrenia and to 50–70% if you have an identical twin with schizophrenia. The **concordance rate** for identical or **monozygotic twins** is much higher than the concordance rate for non-identical or **dizygotic twins**. This means that the likelihood of one twin having the disorder, given that the other twin has, is much higher for identical than non-identical twins.

A higher concordance rate for identical twins than for non-identical twins is an indication that genetics play a causal role in the disorder; there is something about the disorder that is heritable which explains why it runs in families. Comparing adopted children with their biological and adoptive parents can tell us something about the role of genetics in schizophrenia. What happens if the children of parents with schizophrenia are raised by parents without schizophrenia? On the other hand, what happens if adopted children of parents without schizophrenia are adopted into families of parents with schizophrenia? The risk of schizophrenia appears to be related to the presence of schizophrenia in the biological parents not the adoptive parents, confirming that genes are important (Heston, 1966; Kety et al., 1968). See the Focus on Methods box on genetic studies for information on twin and adoption studies.

But it is not the case that schizophrenia is under complete genetic control. If it were, then we would expect the concordance rate between identical twins to be 100%. The fact that it isn't suggests that non-genetic factors are also important. Neither is it likely that schizophrenia is inherited via a single gene because if that were the case then we would expect the likelihood of having schizophrenia if you have two parents with the disorder to be much higher than it actually is. All of this goes to suggest that whether someone has schizophrenia is dependent upon the interaction between genetic and environmental factors and that there are likely to be multiple genes that increase the risk of developing the disorder.

FOCUS ON METHODS: GENETIC STUDIES

TWIN STUDIES

Twin studies can identify genetic contributions to psychological and other types of disorders by comparing the occurrence of the disorder in identical (monozygotic) and non-identical (dyzygotic) twins. Monozygotic twins share the same genotype whereas dyzygotic twins share on average half their genes so if a disorder has a genetic component then the percentage of twins who both have the disorder (the concordance rate) should be higher for monozygotic than dyzygotic twins, as is the case for schizophrenia.

One limitation of the twin method is that it assumes that both types of twins experience similar environments. But it could be that monozygotic twins have a more similar environment than dyzygotic twins because people around them treat them similarly owing to them looking identical. Questionnaire measures can be taken to assess the contribution of shared environment to concordance rates, for example asking whether twins were dressed the same as children or had shared friends. Another option is to study twins who have been misinformed about whether they are identical. In this way the perception of similarity, which could increase shared environmental influences, can be accounted for. Finally, it is possible to study identical twins who have been raised in different environments, but there are few sets of twins that are reared apart and so the samples may not be representative.

It can also be difficult to study twin pairs in a controlled way because monozygotic twins who share traits may be more likely than those who do not share traits to volunteer to take part in studies. This can be addressed by studies that recruit all twins in a geographical area. For example, in some countries, there are large national registers of all twins born, which makes unbiased recruitment easier. Whether twins are identical cannot always be identified using reliable genotyping methods, either practically speaking or because of the expense, and so in many large-scale studies zygosity is determined using questionnaires that have about a 95% accuracy. More recently, studies have also examined rates of occurrence of a disorder in people who are unrelated, and compared these rates with the rates in people who are related but to varying degrees, for example half-siblings, uncles or aunts.

(Continued)

(Continued)

ADOPTION STUDIES

The occurrence of a disorder can be assessed in people who have been adopted and compared with the rates of occurrence in the biological and adopted relatives of the adoptee. It is assumed that genetic and environmental influences are separated if a child is adopted soon after birth. One approach is to examine the occurrence of a disorder in adoptees who have a parent who is affected, and compare this with the rate of occurrence in adoptees who do not have an affected parent. Alternatively, the occurrence of the disorders is assessed in the biological and adopted parents of individuals who have the disorder. A more complex design involves crossfostering in which the rate of the disorder in adoptees who have a non-affected biological parent and an affected adopted parent are examined and vice versa. Adoption studies have the drawback that adoption is rare, and so the samples may be small. Also the influence of the prenatal environment has to be dissociated from the genetic influence of the biological mother by taking into account information about the prenatal experience such as birth trauma.

INTERACTIONS BETWEEN GENES AND ENVIRONMENT IN SCHIZOPHRENIA

We have discovered that schizophrenia is not under complete genetic control. Even if a person has risk genes for schizophrenia it is not certain that they will develop the disorder. The environment that a person grows up in is also important. Some events and environments appear to tip the balance and increase the likelihood that someone with risk genes will develop the disorder. It is important to remember therefore that both the environment and genes influence whether or not someone will develop schizophrenia. In other words, there is not a simple relationship between having a particular gene variant and developing schizophrenia. Similarly, not everyone exposed to a particular environmental factor will develop schizophrenia. It is how they interact that is critical. Understanding these gene–environment interactions can help predict who will develop schizophrenia and shed light on what might be happening in the brain to cause schizophrenia.

Genetic risk factors

Initial studies of the genetics of schizophrenia focused on finding locations on the chromosome that were linked to having a diagnosis of schizophrenia. Further studies then attempted to identify specific risk genes located in those areas of the chromosome. This is a difficult task because it is possible that schizophrenia is caused by the combined effects of many gene variants, perhaps thousands, each accounting for a very small effect and interacting with environmental factors. Gene variants are copies of the same gene that differ slightly in their DNA sequence usually by a single nucleotide. Some variants, or **alleles**, as they are known, are common in the population which means that researchers can see if they are more likely to be found in people who have schizophrenia than in people who don't have schizophrenia. Some potential risk genes that exist in different forms have been identified: Regulator of G Protein Signaling 4 (*RGS4*, on chromosome 1), Disrupted in Schizophrenia 1 (*DISC1*, on chromosome 1),

Dystrobrevin-Binding Protein 1 (*DTNBP1*/Dysbindin, on chromosome 6), and Neuregulin 1 (*NRG1*, on chromosome 8) (Williams, Owen and O'Donovan, 2009).

An issue to consider is that all of the candidate risk genes so far identified only account for a very small amount of the genetic component of schizophrenia so there is still a lot that is unexplained. It may be that a number of relatively common genes, each having a small effect, act together to increase the risk of schizophrenia (Allen et al., 2008). Alternatively, it is possible that there are some rare single genes that each have a large effect but are specific to an individual or family, making them difficult to identify. Such rare variants may be due to sub-microscopic variations in DNA structure, so-called copy number variants or CNVs. It has been reported that the rate of rare CNVs are much greater in patients with schizophrenia than healthy controls and the rare CNVs identified in patients contribute to functions critical to neuronal development (Walsh et al., 2008). Perhaps more likely is that schizophrenia risk is conferred by a combination or common and rare variants (Owen et al., 2010).

To complicate matters further, it has been suggested that inherited differences in the expression of genes due to reversible chemical changes to DNA, as opposed to changes in the sequence of DNA, might explain susceptibility to schizophrenia (Tsankova et al., 2007). This idea is supported by the finding that there is different gene expression in an identical twin who has schizophrenia compared with their twin who does not have schizophrenia (remember schizophrenia does not always co-occur in identical twins) (Tsang, Huang, Holmes and Bahn, 2006). These epigenetic effects could provide a link between genetic and environmental influences because factors like stress and diet can cause epigenetic changes.

INSIGHT: EPIGENETICS

Epigenetics refers to chemical changes to DNA, and the proteins that package DNA, that are associated with the regulation of gene expression. Epigenetic events are important for determining the development of different cell types. For example whether cells with the same DNA will turn into liver cells versus brain cells is determined by the turning-on of different genes by epigenetics. This has been known about for a long time, but more recently evidence has emerged that environmental events such as changes in diet can affect epigenetics and more intriguingly that these changes can be passed on to subsequent generations. Clues about the influences of epigenetics came from the study of people who had undergone transitions from famine to feast in Sweden in the 1800s. Careful scrutiny of agricultural records to assess the likely diet of people at the time showed that the grandsons of men who had experienced a glut of food and lived through a feast year were more likely to die younger than men whose grandfathers had lived through famine. The conclusion was that the environment left its mark on the epigenome and this was passed on to the children and grandchildren. Evidence from studies of laboratory animals suggests that epigenetic changes, which unlike inherited mutations, do not change the structure of DNA, can explain how environmental influences interact with the genome to produce particular phenotypes.

ENVIRONMENTAL RISK FACTORS

There is some evidence that complication during pregnancy or birth increases the risk of schizophrenia. Complications during labour and delivery that cause oxygen deprivation (hypoxia) are associated with later schizophrenia (Clarke et al., 2006). A likely explanation is that the birth complications result in brain damage and this is associated with later schizophrenia (Murray, Jones and O'Callaghan, 1991). A study by Jones and colleagues found that in a group of 11,017 Finnish subjects, 76 people developed schizophrenia by age 28 and they were seven times more likely to have had brain damage at birth than the rest of the group (Jones et al., 1998).

Another environmental factor that has been identified is viral infection during pregnancy. This might explain why babies born in winter have a slightly increased risk of developing schizophrenia than babies born at other times of the year (Torrey et al., 1997). The flu virus is more common in the autumn and it is possible that some mothers who contract the flu virus experience an abnormal immune response that affects development of the foetus (Zuckerman et al., 2003). This idea is supported by the finding that the incidence of schizophrenia increases after a flu epidemic (Adams et al., 1993). Stress may have a similar effect on the immune system during pregnancy: higher rates of schizophrenia are found for children of women whose husbands died during their pregnancies than for children of women whose husbands died after birth (Huttunen, 1989). Adverse events after birth might also play a part. Having a head injury before the age of 10 is associated with developing schizophrenia later in life (AbdelMalik et al., 2003).

There have been various reports that living in a city rather than in a rural environment is associated with increased risk of schizophrenia and that there is a greater risk in populations that have migrated from one country to another. The rate of schizophrenia is much higher in Norwegian migrants to the USA than in the Norwegian population (Odegaard, 1932). Similar findings have been noted for African-Caribbean migrants to the UK (Harrison et al., 1997). The reasons for these findings are unclear and could relate to other risk factors such as stress.

Life events are likely to act in conjunction with genetic susceptibility such that people with a genetic predisposition are perhaps more sensitive to the effects of prenatal and post-natal complications. Interestingly, one of the genes linked to schizophrenia, the Disrupted in Schizophrenia 1 (DISC1) gene codes for a protein that is required for normal growth of neurons (Schurov et al., 2004). This raises the possibility that the genetic risk for schizophrenia relates to the effect of genes on the complex process of brain development.

A factor that has received much attention, especially in media reports, is adolescent cannabis use (Andréasson et al., 1987). The relationship between cannabis use and schizophrenia appears to be related to the level of cannabis use and is more pronounced for individuals with other risk factors (van Os et al., 2002; Zammit et al., 2002). It is difficult to establish a causal link between cannabis use and schizophrenia. One has to be careful to control for the effects of other factors that might explain any association such as other illegal drug use. Also, it could be that schizophrenia causes cannabis use rather than the other way round. Some people could be using cannabis to alleviate early symptoms of schizophrenia. Against this, it has been reported that an increase in symptoms is not positively associated with increased use of cannabis (Fergusson et al., 2005).

It remains to be seen whether recent changes in the levels of cannabis use by young people will be related to increased rates of schizophrenia as would be predicted if there is a causal relationship between cannabis use and schizophrenia (Hickman et al., 2007). It is possible that genes moderate the link between adolescent cannabis use and the risk of developing schizophrenia. Researchers found that cannabis users with one particular variant of a gene called COMT were more likely to develop schizophrenia than users with a different variant (Caspi et al., 2005).

Of course genetic and environmental influences can only bring about their effects by acting to change the brain in some way, which then results in the manifestation of the clinical symptoms of schizophrenia. An important question concerns the relationship between clinical symptoms

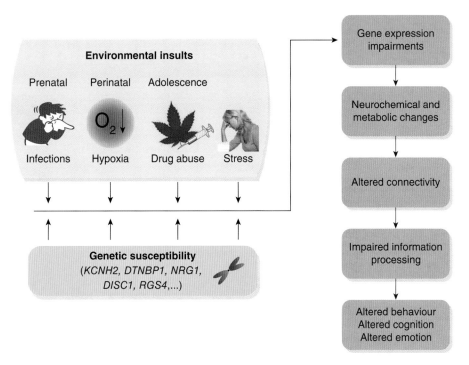

Figure 9.2   Genetic factors interact with the environment to affect whether someone will develop schizophrenia. Changes in gene expression will result in neurochemical disturbances that affect information processing in the brain of affected individuals. These changes ultimately lead to behavioural, cognitive and emotional deficits that characterise schizophrenia

Source: Horváth and Mirnics (2009)

and changes in underlying biological processes. At present there is no easy answer to this. There has been progress in refining knowledge about which aspects of behaviour are altered in schizophrenia and in identifying dysfunction in neurochemical systems in the brains of people with schizophrenia, but there is still some way to go before joining up the dots. Next, we will discuss research that has told us about the biological changes associated with schizophrenia.

Biological bases of schizophrenia

What is the evidence that brain structure and function are altered in schizophrenia? Researchers have used different approaches to try to answer this question. Here we will examine the main evidence from neuroanatomical studies and pharmacological studies.

Neuroanatomical and imaging studies

Post-mortem examination of the brains of people with schizophrenia shows that they look different to the brains of people without schizophrenia. These studies can be difficult to interpret though because brain structure can be affected by drug treatment. It could be that any differences in brain structure between people with and without schizophrenia is not due to the disorder but related to having taken medication for a long time. However, data from brain imaging studies confirm that there are differences in brain structure between schizophrenic and non-schizophrenic participants even before drug treatment has begun (Velakoulis et al., 1999).

FOCUS ON METHODS: STRUCTURAL IMAGING

The human brain varies not only in its activity but also in its structure from person to person. The structure of the brain can be imaged accurately using MRI scanners (or CT scanners) and the images compared across individuals or groups. Importantly, grey matter (cell bodies) can be distinguished from white matter (axons). In this way it is possible to correlate grey or white matter volume in particular areas of the brain to alterations in specific functions.

Some of the differences in brain structure have also been detected in the brain scans of people at high risk of schizophrenia. The scans of individuals who later develop schizophrenia are very similar to those of patients with full symptoms, indicating that structural changes associated with schizophrenia are evident before the onset of symptoms in early life (Lawrie et al., 1999; Sun et al., 2009). One explanation is that early life events alter brain development, which then later predisposes towards schizophrenia. An implication here is that it might be possible to use brain scans to predict who is likely to develop schizophrenia (see Figure 9.3).

So how do early structural changes in the brain account for the emergence of positive symptoms much later in adolescence? Here it is important to remember that our brains change throughout life, and during adolescence there are some particularly dramatic changes that are important

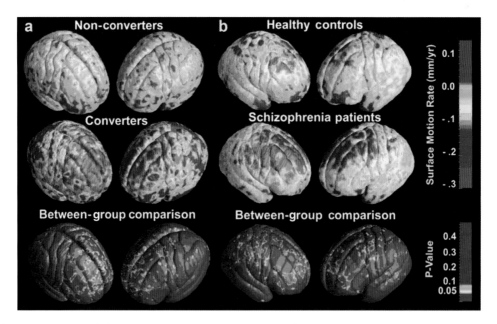

Figure 9.3 Maps of the average annual rates of brain surface contraction in: (a) individuals at ultra-high risk for developing psychosis who converted to psychosis (converters) versus those who did not convert (nonconverters), and (b) schizophrenia patients versus healthy controls. Converters and schizophrenia patients showed significantly greater brain-contraction rates compared with nonconverters and healthy individuals, respectively. A similar pattern of prominent prefrontal surface contraction was shared across groups. For the top two rows, bluer areas indicate regions of higher surface motion (in mm/year), while red and pink areas indicate areas of negative motion, or contraction; in the bottom row, red indicates regions that show statistically significant differences in the rate of contraction between groups

Based on data in Sun, Stuart, Phillips, et al. (2009) and Sun, Stuart, Jenkinson, et al. (2009)

for development. It is possible that these brain changes during adolescence are compromised if someone has suffered a brain injury early in life. A result then might be the emergence of the symptoms of schizophrenia.

The most consistent changes in brain structure seen in schizophrenia are increases in the size of ventricles and associated decreases in grey and white matter volumes (Shenton et al., 2001). Some areas of the brain are particularly affected. The hippocampus, thalamus, and frontal lobes are involved in emotional and cognitive functioning and are all smaller in patients with schizophrenia than in healthy controls. These changes could be related to some the symptoms of schizophrenia.

In addition to changes to the structure of the brain, there are also alterations in brain function associated with schizophrenia and these have been studied using positron emission tomography (PET) and functional magnetic resonance imaging (fMRI). Abnormalities in brain blood flow have been found in the frontal lobes of patients with schizophrenia when performing tasks involving memory and attention (Buchsbaum and Hazlett, 1998). Impaired memory function in schizophrenia is associated with altered function in the dorsolateral prefrontal cortex (DLPFC) as measured by fMRI (Barch et al., 2001). Similar impairments have also been reported for participants at high risk for schizophrenia (Seidman et al., 2006). This indicates that like the structural changes, functional impairments in frontal lobe function are not the result of living with the disorder or due to the effects of medication.

FOCUS ON METHODS: PET AND fMRI

fMRI and PET scanning have been used to investigate the differences in brain function between people who have schizophrenia and people without a diagnosis of schizophrenia. PET scanning involves injecting a person with a radioactive tracer. As the tracer decays, it emits positrons. When the positrons come into contact with electrons in neighbouring atoms they generate gamma rays. These gamma rays can be detected by a gamma ray detector and a computer can work out how many gamma rays are coming from specific areas of the brain. Areas with high blood flow are associated with high gamma rays and these are likely to be areas of the brain that are most active. fMRI works by detecting the changes in blood oxygenation and flow that occur in response to neural activity. When a brain area is more active it consumes more oxygen and to meet this increased demand blood flow increases to the active area. fMRI can be used to produce maps of changes in blood flow in the brain that are linked to neural activity.

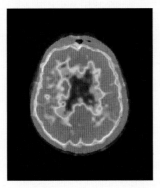

Figure 9.4   A PET scan of a healthy patient

© iStock.com/BanksPhotos

Findings from neuroanatomical and imaging studies help to explain how neurodevelopmental challenges might cause changes in brain structure and function that mediate some of the cognitive and emotional symptoms of schizophrenia. But an issue here is that most of the structural and functional differences observed are not specific to people with schizophrenia. Alterations in the size of the hippocampus and reduced frontal lobe function are also seen in other psychiatric disorders like depression. So, analysis of gross anatomy or general brain function does not tell us what the specific brain changes are that mean someone will develop schizophrenia as opposed to, say, depression. Studies of brain neurochemistry can highlight changes occurring at the level of the synapse that are specific to schizophrenia.

PHARMACOLOGICAL STUDIES

A lot of what we know about how neurochemical transmission is altered in schizophrenia comes from studying the drugs that have been used to treat the disorder. This might seem strange. Surely one would need to know what the underlying neurochemical problem is in schizophrenia before developing treatments to correct the problem. The fact is that early drug treatments for schizophrenia were discovered accidentally and it was only after they had been prescribed for some time that knowledge about how they worked influenced theories about the biological bases of schizophrenia.

The first drug for schizophrenia was a chemical called chlorpromazine. It was originally used as a pre-medication for surgery. By chance, it was noted that chlorpromazine had a calming effect on patients and so in 1951, Henri Laborit, a French military surgeon, began experimenting with it as a treatment for various psychiatric disorders.

Chlorpromazine proved effective in reducing the positive symptoms of schizophrenia and it was soon prescribed throughout France and more widely in the UK and US. This was a significant event in the history of psychiatric treatments because before the 1950s treatments acted by completely subduing or sedating the patient. Chlorpromazine is a sedative-type drug but its effects go beyond simple sedation. Before drug treatments were available, in the 1930s and 1940s, patients with schizophrenia were subjected to procedures like frontal leucotomy, which involved using a blunt knife to destroy part of the frontal lobe. These procedures were not only ineffective but had a high death rate.

Because of the initial success of chlorpromazine, other similar drugs, such as haloperidol, were developed. They were known collectively as antipsychotics because of their effectiveness in treating the positive symptoms of schizophrenia. The widespread use of antipsychotic drugs contributed to the transfer of many patients out of mental asylums into the community for treatment. Studies of the pharmacological action of these drugs also led to the development of a theory about the neurochemical dysfunction in schizophrenia called the dopamine theory.

The dopamine theory of schizophrenia

A common feature of the first generation of antipsychotic drugs is that they are all antagonists at the dopamine D2 receptor. This information led to the development of the dopamine theory of schizophrenia (Carlsson, 1977). The logic behind the dopamine theory is that if the symptoms can be treated by dampening dopamine neurotransmission via a blockade of dopamine receptors then schizophrenia probably involves overactivity of dopamine systems in the brain. This seems very reasonable, but evidence from the action of antipsychotic drugs is not sufficient to support the hypothesis. We also need to know whether increased dopamine neurotransmission is associated with schizophrenia. We can ask two questions. First, does experimentally increasing dopamine neurotransmission elicit the symptoms of schizophrenia as the theory would predict? Second, is there evidence that dopamine neurotransmission is enhanced in schizophrenia?

The drug amphetamine releases dopamine in the brain and it can induce psychosis in people without schizophrenia when taken in large, repeated doses. Other drugs like cocaine, which prolong the action of dopamine at the synapse, can have a similar effect and can also exacerbate existing symptoms of schizophrenia. Interestingly, cannabis also increases dopamine release in the brain and has been linked with schizophrenia. These findings suggest that the psychotic symptoms of schizophrenia can be mimicked by drugs that act in the brain to increase dopamine neurotransmission.

The amount of dopamine that is released by neurons can be measured indirectly in people by injecting a radioactive tracer that binds to dopamine D2 receptors. It is possible to see the location of the tracer using a technique called single photon emission computed tomography (SPECT). Because the tracer competes with dopamine to bind to the D2 receptor, more dopamine in the synapse will mean reduced binding of the tracer because it is being displaced by the dopamine at the receptor site. Abi-Dargham and colleagues found that after taking amphetamine, patients with schizophrenia showed a greater reduction in binding of the tracer than matched controls and there was a slight worsening of symptoms after amphetamine (Abi-Dargham et al., 1998; Laruelle et al., 1996). These data suggest that more dopamine is released from the pre-synaptic neurons of patients with schizophrenia than controls after amphetamine. Other similar studies indicate that more dopamine is synthesised in the brains of people with schizophrenia and as a consequence they have greater release of dopamine (Abi-Dargham et al., 2000; Laruelle et al., 1996) (see Figure 9.5).

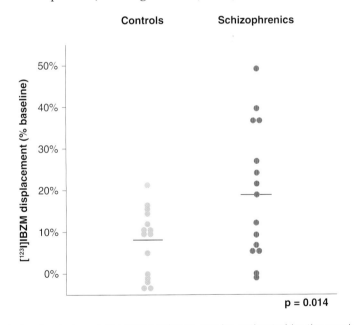

Figure 9.5 Amphetamine-induced dopamine release can be estimated by the amphetamine-induced reduction in dopamine D2 receptor availability, measured as the binding potential of the specific D2 receptor radiotracer [123I]IBZM. The amphetamine-induced decrease in [123I]IBZM binding potential is significantly greater in the schizophrenic group compared with the control group. These data are consistent with the idea that dopamine neurons are more responsive in schizophrenia

Source: Laruelle et al., 1996)

EVALUATION OF THE DOPAMINE HYPOTHESIS

The dopamine hypothesis is supported by various lines of evidence as we have seen and it has endured over time, but it has also been criticised on a number of counts. Some have argued that overactivity in the dopamine system cannot provide a full account of the pathology of schizophrenia because antipsychotic drugs block dopamine D2 receptors as soon as the patient starts taking them, but there is a lag between the starting treatment and experiencing relief from symptoms. This would suggest the therapeutic effects arise from some other effect of the drugs that develop over time. However, this argument has been countered more recently by data suggesting that there is an early but subtle response to antipsychotic treatment that strengthens as it is taken (Kapur et al., 2005).

Another issue is that antipsychotic drug treatments are not good at helping with the negative and cognitive symptoms of schizophrenia, suggesting that the cause of these symptoms does not lie with overactivity of dopamine neurotransmission. Even the newer drug treatments for schizophrenia are no more effective at treating the cognitive and negative symptoms than the earlier drugs. The newer types of drugs are an improvement on the older generation because they do not induce the side effects associated with those drugs.

Haloperidol and similar drugs are problematic because they have severe side effects such as the development of problems with movement that resemble Parkinson's disease. The newer drugs are better because are less likely to induce these side effects, although they do have side effects of their own. All antipsychotic drugs have effects to stabilise or dampen down dopamine neurotransmission but they differ in the side effects they produce owing to their differing action at other receptor sites. So overactivity in dopamine transmission may explain the positive symptoms of schizophrenia but its role in the other symptoms is less clear.

Another criticism of early formulations of the dopamine hypothesis was that it did not explain how overactivity in dopamine transmission is related to psychotic symptoms. It has been suggested that overactivity in dopamine transmission in specific areas of the brain might be related to the experience of the positive symptoms of schizophrenia. Remember from Chapter 8 that the mesocorticolimbic dopamine system is thought to be important for assigning incentive salience to stimuli or events that are linked with reward. There is evidence to suggest that dopamine plays a critical role in the ability of motivationally significant objects like food or drugs to grab attention and direct behaviour. It is possible that a consequence of dopamine overactivity in this system is to be very willing to assign significance to things (Gray et al., 1991). Certainly, there are reports that people experiencing the onset of schizophrenic symptoms report changes in how they see the world that are confusing. Delusions might be one way of coping with such changes.

Another idea is that the symptoms of schizophrenia are due to a more general problem with the learning that underlies the beliefs we have about the world. Humans are generally very good at learning that some events are highly predictable and that the relationship between stimuli are predictable. This learning is thought to depend on the fact that when novel or unexpected events occur they generate an error that signals the event was not predicted. The error signal then facilitates new learning about the novel stimuli such that the error signal is then reduced (Murray et al., 2007).

The midbrain dopamine system is thought to be important for prediction error signalling and it has been suggested that delusions and hallucinations may be explained by aberrant prediction error signalling (Corlett et al., 2009). Imagine a situation in which someone experiences excessive prediction error signalling due to an overactive dopamine system. This might result in that person feeling that everyday events are unusual or strange and therefore diffi-cult to understand. A consequence might be that the person develops a new set of beliefs to explain the uncertainty. They might also begin to readily associate events and stimuli due to facilitation of learning by a large error prediction signal. This might result in the idea that they are experiencing lots of coincidences (Fletcher and Frith, 2008). Importantly, both the incentive salience and prediction error accounts are beginning to link brain and behaviour in understanding schizophrenia.

We have observed that there is clear evidence of overactivity of dopamine neurotransmis-sion in schizophrenia that can be plausibly linked to psychotic symptoms. However, there are other changes in neurotransmission that accompany schizophrenia, such as alterations in GABA and glutamate systems. It is less clear how changes in these neurotransmitter systems account for the cognitive and negative symptoms, partly because they have been less well studied than dopamine. Another question is whether an overactive dopamine system is the primary dysfunction in schizophrenia. It is possible that increased dopamine release is the primary dysfunction in schizophrenia and this has knock-on effects for neurotransmission in other systems to cause the negative and cognitive symptoms. Or, it could be that the positive, negative and cognitive symptoms are mediated by completely independent biological path-ways. Another alternative is that there is a common underlying biological disturbance that leads to increased dopamine transmission. An interesting suggestion is that altered glutamate transmission might be this common underlying disturbance.

The role of glutamate in schizophrenia

An observation that links schizophrenia with problems in glutamatergic neurotransmis-sion is that drugs such as PCP and ketamine which are antagonists at a subtype of glutam-ate receptor, the NMDA receptor, can induce symptoms that are similar to those seen in schizophrenia (Krystal et al., 1994). Interestingly, ketamine is much less likely to induce psychotic symptoms in children compared to adults (Reich and Silvay, 1989), which is in line with the idea that brain abnormalities conferring vulnerability to schizophrenia arise early in development, but are only revealed during adolescence when later brain changes occur (Weinberger, 1987). There is also evidence that various aspects of glutamate function are impaired in schizophrenia such as changes in receptor numbers (Ibrahim et al., 2000). These data suggest that hypofunction of NMDA receptors may be a causal factor in schizo-phrenia. There are possible links to risk genes for schizophrenia because neuregulin modu-lates aspects of NMDA receptor function (Hahn et al., 2006). Perhaps early developmental challenges interact with genetic risk to result in an NMDA receptor hypofunctional state (Olney et al., 1999).

KEY POINTS

- Schizophrenia is characterised by altered perception, emotion and cognition.
- The likelihood of developing schizophrenia is related to a genetic predisposition that interacts with environmental conditions.
- Some of the symptoms of schizophrenia are related to overactivity in brain dopamine systems, and they can be treated by medications that act to dampen down dopamine neurotransmission.
- Disturbance in glutamate neurotransmission may be a causal factor in schizophrenia.

DEPRESSION

Overview

Depression is a widespread psychological disorder characterised by lengthy periods of low mood and other associated symptoms. The line between depressive illness and usual variations in mood can be difficult to draw. Depression is related to the feelings of unhappiness that we all experience at times, but clinical depression may be diagnosed if the feelings do not subside in the usual way after a distressing event or if they are experienced when there is no obvious cause. Either way, the symptoms are long-lasting and can severely disrupt a person's ability to carry on with their life. Because it is a common disorder, the costs associated with depression, both personal and societal, are huge. The ability to work productively may be reduced, leading to losses in income. Social skills are often impaired resulting in a reduced ability to maintain relationships. Depression is often misunderstood and this can lead to stigma and failure to seek help. Common misperceptions are that people with depression are unsociable and that depression is a sign of personal weakness (Barney et al., 2009).

Different types of depressive disorder are diagnosed depending upon the severity of the disorder and the co-occurrence of other symptoms. The *DSM-IV* includes categories of major depression, dysthymic disorder and bipolar disorder. Major depression is characterised by a combination of symptoms, the key features being depressed mood or a loss of interest in daily activities for at least two weeks. Dysthymic disorder is characterised by milder symptoms of depression that are experienced for long periods of about two years. People with dysthymia may experience one or more episodes of major depression at some point. Bipolar disorder is characterised by alternating periods of low mood and mania. The focus of this section will be on major depression, as the most commonly occurring depressive disorder.

Clinical symptoms of major depression

Depressed mood and negative thinking are core features of major depression. People with depression do not differ much from people without depression in their initial reactions to a negative event but they may have difficulties switching from a negative focus back to a more positive outlook. When someone has depression they pay more attention to negative things and they have a tendency to remember more negative than positive things (Mathews and MacLeod, 2005). Another cognitive characteristic is that depressed people tend to ruminate more than people without depression. This means they experience persistent negative thinking that is difficult to shake off (Lyubomirsky, Caldwell and Nolen-Hoeksema, 1998). A focus on negative information contributes to the maintenance of a depressed mood state due to increased accessibility of negative information in memory and reduced ability to access positive information that could distract from the current state and lift mood (Joormann, 2010). Depressed patients also respond differently to positive emotional pictures such as those of happy faces (Harmer et al., 2009).

Another hallmark of major depression is the diminished experience of pleasure, which is known as anhedonia. People with depression react much less than non-depressed people to emotional stimuli, including attractive pictures and funny films (Rottenberg et al., 2002). Depressed people may also experience less motivation to engage in enjoyable activities and derive less enjoyment from those activities than people without depression.

In addition to the core features of depression, a diagnosis usually requires the presence of other symptoms such as changes in appetite and sleep, low energy and tiredness, reduced ability to concentrate, loss of self-esteem and thoughts of suicide. People with depression often also have problems with long term memory. The *DSM-IV* definition requires the presence of five out of nine possible symptoms, highlighting the varied nature of depression. It is possible for two individuals to both be diagnosed with major depression while only sharing one symptom.

Major depression often co-occurs with anxiety and substance use disorders and other physical illnesses. The seriousness of depression is underlined by the fact that having depression is associated with a four-times higher risk of suicide compared with the general population (Bostwick and Pankratz, 2000). Major depression is also associated with increased rates of death from coronary heart disease, and depressive symptoms increase the risk of incident coronary heart disease (Musselman et al., 1998).

Depression can occur throughout life but the average age of onset is usually around 20–30 years. Depression is not commonly diagnosed in childhood but some people who go on to be diagnosed with depression in adulthood experience milder symptoms such as extreme mood swings when they are young (Fava and Kendler, 2000). For some, these symptoms develop rapidly into an early onset form of the disorder.

Depression is usually experienced in episodes that last a few months but some people experience a chronic form of the disorder that can last for years (Weissman and Klerman, 1977). Many people recover fully from a first episode of depression but about half of people with depression will go on to have at least one more episode (Kupfer, 1991). Recurrence of the disorder is more likely in patients with early onset depression (Lewinsohn et al., 1999). Recovery from depression can occur in a seasonal pattern whereby depression occurs at the same time of year, usually in the winter, and there is recovery in between episodes. This pattern has been termed 'seasonal affective disorder' (SAD; Rosenthal et al., 1984)

Prevalence of depression

Estimates of the occurrence of depression vary according to country and from one study to another. Estimates may vary because of real differences between countries but also because of differences in the diagnostic tools that are used and the willingness of respondents to report particular problems. The same systems are not always used to diagnose depression and in some countries people may not be willing to admit that they have suffered from depression.

Most studies involve interviewing adults and asking them to recall previous episodes of depression and so the measure is also influenced by memory accuracy. Nevertheless, recent surveys suggest that severe psychological disorders such as depression are common worldwide with a reasonable estimate of the numbers of people affected in their lifetime being about 10% (Kessler et al., 2009). Some evidence suggests that the prevalence of depression has increased in the last few decades, especially among young people in countries like the US and UK (Lewinsohn et al., 1993; Collishaw et al., 2010), raising concerns about the potential over-diagnosis of depression (Parker, 2007). To address this issue, studies that track the occurence of depression in different age groups over time are required.

Across different countries and cultures women are twice as likely to develop depression than men (Nolen-Hoeksema, 1990). There are a number of possible explanations for why depression occurs more commonly in women than men. It has been argued that because of their position in society many women are exposed to more of the risks that predispose towards depression such as stressful experiences (Nolen-Hoeksema et al., 1999). Another possible reason is that women have an enhanced reaction to stress that makes it more likely that they will develop depression, perhaps due to the influence of female sex hormones on the physiological responses to stress (Young and Korszun, 2009). This might explain why some people experience depression at times when they also experience dramatic changes in sex hormones after pregnancy. However, little is known about the underlying mechanisms partly because studies in laboratory animals have mainly been conducted using males. Differences in coping styles between men and women might also contribute since there is some evidence that women are more likely than men to ruminate on a problem (Nolen-Hoeksema et al., 1999).

Surveys in the UK and US find that depression is also more common among people with lower educational attainment, people who are unemployed and people who have had marriage breakdown, suggesting a link to socioeconomic factors and stressful life events (Kendler et al., 1999; Lorant et al., 2003).

Like schizophrenia, depression runs in families. A person has a greater risk of developing depression if they have a first degree relative with depression (Birmaher et al., 1996). The children of depressed parents are three times more likely to have a lifetime episode of depression than children of parents without a diagnosis of depression (Weissman et al., 1997). Adoption and twin studies suggest that depression is partly heritable and that about 30–40% of the variability in the occurrence of depression is due to genetics.

INTERACTIONS BETWEEN GENES AND ENVIRONMENT IN DEPRESSION

The focus of current research into the causes of depression is on how genetic susceptibility interacts with environmental influences to increase the risk of developing the disorder. The idea is that people differ in their genetic make-up and this affects how they respond to external triggers such as stressful events. Some people will show resilience to depression and others vulnerability depending on their DNA. It is not nature or nurture but how nature modifies the effects of nurture.

We now know that the environment plays an important role in psychiatric disorders like schizophrenia and the same is true for depression. But not everyone who experiences a particular environment develops a disorder: gene–environment interactions explain why this is so. Thinking about genetic and environmental influences in this way helps us to understand how the things that happen in our lives impact our nervous system to bring about changes in behaviour. An important discovery in understanding gene–environment interactions and depression was that a person's genetic makeup affects the likelihood that they will develop depression, but this is dependent upon the experience of stressful life events. In particular, there is evidence that inherited variations in serotonin neurotransmission interact with stressful life events to affect the likelihood of someone developing depression (Caspi et al., 2003).

KEY STUDY
Caspi, A. et al. (2003). Influence of life stress on depression: Moderation by a polymorphism in the 5-HTT gene. *Science Signaling,* *301*(5631), 386

Serotonin transporters remove serotonin from the synapse and the gene that codes for these proteins can exist as two alleles, either long or short. Caspi and colleagues asked a group of 847 people to report on the stressful life events they had experienced in their early twenties and then looked at whether the number of stressful life events was related to whether or not someone had depression. They found that the likelihood of having an episode of depression increased in line with the number of stressful events but only for people who had two copies of the short allele of the serotonin transporter gene. In other words, people with two forms of the short allele are vulnerable to depression when under stress.

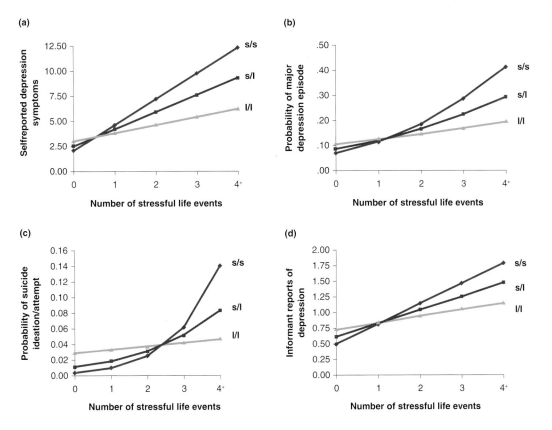

Figure 9.6   An increase in various measures of depression as a function of the number of stressful life events was stronger for individuals with two copies of the short allele of the 5-HTT promoter polymorphism (s/s) compared to individuals with two copies of the long form (l/l) or one copy of the short and long form (s/l)

Source: Caspi et al. (2003)

(Continued)

(Continued)

There has been controversy though because other researchers have reported that stress predicts the likelihood of depression but this is not dependent on genotype (Gillespie et al., 2005). Different results could be explained by researchers studying different types of stresses and different age groups. It will be important to find out more about the specific kinds of stresses that interact with genotype to increase the risk of depression. Another important step in verifying the serotonin–stress sensitivity hypothesis will be to explain how the expression of the serotonin transporter in people with the long and short forms of the gene modifies stress responses in a way that triggers depression.

Biological bases of depression

Early ideas about the biological bases of depression came from the study of antidepressant medications. At the same time that drug treatments were beginning to be prescribed for schizophrenia in the early 1950s, the first medications for depression were introduced. The discovery of antidepressants, like antipsychotic drugs, was a serendipitous event. The first drug to be used as an antidepressant, Isoniazid, was actually used for the treatment of tuberculosis (TB) but it was noted that the drug had an effect of improving mood in the TB patients and so it was promoted as a treatment of depression. A little later, the drug imipramine, which had been synthesised as part of a programme to improve antipsychotic drug treatment, was also found to enhance mood in patients with depression. Knowledge about the mechanism of action of these first antidepressant drugs sparked ideas about the possible cause of depression.

Isoniazid and imipramine have something in common, which is their ability to increase the level of monoamine neurotransmitters in the brain. The mechanism of action of the two drugs is different but a common outcome is that levels of serotonin, noradrenaline and to a lesser extent dopamine are increased at the synapse. Isoniazid is a monoamine oxidase inhibitor, which means that it blocks the action of the enzyme monoamine oxidase. Monoamine oxidase is present in the presynaptic neuron and its function is to break down serotonin, noradrenaline and dopamine. Inhibition of the breakdown of monoamines increases release of these neurotransmitters. Imipramine blocks the reuptake of monoamines from the synapse, which also increases availability of monoamines at the synapse. Because these early drugs that helped with the symptoms of depression had this common mechanism of action, it was hypothesised that they were acting to correct an underlying problem in the brains of depressed people, namely that there are low levels of monoamines. Particular attention was given to levels of serotonin because later antidepressant drugs had a more specific action to reduce reuptake of serotonin selectively. These are drugs like Prozac which are known as the selective serotonin **reuptake inhibitors** or SSRIs.

The monoamine-deficiency theory of depression

the idea that depression is related to reduced levels of monoamines in the brain, particularly serotonin, is based on an understanding of how antidepressants bring about their therapeutic effects. But aside from the action of antidepressant drugs is there additional evidence that depression results from a deficit in monoamine neurotransmission and perhaps more specifically serotonin neurotransmission? We might expect to be able to detect differences in markers of serotonin transmission between depressed and non-depressed people. A marker of reduced brain serotonin is the amount of serotonin metabolites in cerebrospinal fluid. If people with depression have reduced brain levels of serotonin they should have reduced levels of serotonin metabolites in CSF. However, the results of these types of studies have been mixed, most probably because of the technical challenges associated with obtaining the measures accurately.

More recent investigations using brain imaging techniques have reported over activity of monoamine oxidase in some patients with depression (Meyer et al., 2006). More breakdown of serotonin by monoamine oxidase might implicate lowered serotonin levels in depression. An issue with these studies is that the data can be difficult to interpret because differences in serotonin metabolism could be a cause or effect of depression. Also, not all people with a diagnosis of depression present with abnormal serotonin function. So what other evidence is there?

An alternative experimental approach to investigating the role of serotonin in depression is to actually manipulate levels of serotonin in the brain of participants. Serotonin is made from an amino acid called tryptophan and so serotonin in the brain can be reduced by depleting the amount of available tryptophan. A reduction in the levels of tryptophan can be achieved by asking participants to consume a drink that contains all other amino acids apart from tryptophan. This treatment works because it stimulates the production of proteins, which uses up tryptophan in the blood plasma (proteins are made from amino acids). The amino acids in the drink also compete with tryptophan to cross the blood brain barrier, thus reducing the entry of tryptophan into the brain (Bell et al., 2001). Tryptophan depletion can induce relapse into depression in patients who are in remission, although it does not affect mood in healthy volunteers (Ruhé et al., 2007).

The reason why not everyone responds to a decrease in serotonin levels by experiencing depressed mood may be because there are other factors that confer vulnerability to changes in serotonin levels. One possibility is that differences in the type of serotonin transporter (long or short allele) affect the response to tryptophan depletion (Neumeister et al., 2004). There may be other factors such as differences in serotonin receptor number and sensitivity or the function of receptor second messenger systems.

It seems that a simple version of the monoamine hypothesis does not hold up. It has not been possible to highlight a specific deficit in serotonin transmission in all cases of depression, and depletion of serotonin levels does not produce depressive symptoms in all people. Moreover, not all people with depression respond to treatment with drugs that increase serotonin levels, and some newer drugs that are effective in treating depression do not have a major effect on serotonin neurotransmission. But should we discount the role of serotonin in depression? The modern version of the monoamine hypothesis takes these issues into account. The suggestion is that there is variability in serotonin function across individuals and that people with low serotonin function may be more susceptible to developing depression given the presence of other contributing factors. Variability of serotonin function could be due to individual differences in 5-HT synthesis, release, reuptake or metabolism, or could be due to differences in pre- or post-synaptic receptors and their responses.

Another reason why a simple explanation of depression relating to monoamine deficiency is not sufficient to account for all the data is that different types of depression exist and these types may have different causes. Depression takes varied forms and the mechanisms that underlie stress-induced depression may differ from the mechanisms the underlie depression that occurs in the absence of an external stressor.

The hypothalamic–pituitary–adrenal axis, stress and depression

When we experience a stressful event various physiological responses occur that help us deal with the stress. We might experience a quick burst of energy or improved memory function as a result of the release of stress hormones. Not everybody responds in the same way to stress though and there is some evidence that some people have dysfunctional responses to stress which contribute to the development of depression. This is consistent with the evidence that periods of depression often coincide with a stressful event.

One of the physiological responses to stress is release of corticotrophin-releasing factor (CRF) by the hypothalamus. CRF acts on receptors in the pituitary gland to produce adreno-corticotropin (ACTH). Stimulation of receptors in the adrenal cortex by ACTH then causes release of the glucocorticoid cortisol into the blood, which helps the body deal with the stress. Normally, cortisol then exerts a feedback effect to shut down the stress response: when cortisol binds to receptors in the hypothalamus this provides a signal to reduce levels of CRF. There is evidence that in depression this hypothalamic–pituitary–adrenal (HPA) axis response to stress is dysfunctional. Depression is associated with excess plasma cortisol levels and about half of people with depression do not show the normal feedback response to reduce cortisol levels (Carroll et al., 2007).

Excess cortisol is problematic because it can damage the brain. This is known because Cushing's syndrome, which is a disorder in which a person produces too much cortisol, is associated with shrinking of the hippocampus (McEwen, 2007). Although the levels of cortisol in depression are not as high as in Cushing's syndrome, similar reductions in the size of the hippocampus have been noted in brain imaging and post-mortem studies of depressed patients (Harrison, 2002). People with Cushing's syndrome also suffer depressive symptoms. Linking these findings together we can hypothesise that damage to the hippocampus due to overactivation of the HPA axis in response to stress may explain some of the symptoms of depression. Given the role of the hippocampus in learning and memory function it may be that reduced hippocampal volume explains the cognitive problems in depression.

We should remember though that not all people with depression show signs of overactivity of the HPA axis. Also, not everyone responds to severe stress by developing depression so we need to find out more about why some people experience an excessive HPA axis response to stress. Gene–environment interactions are likely to be important here because there is some evidence that the impact of childhood abuse on subsequent responses to stress and vulnerability to depression is dependent upon the type of CRF gene that a person has (Bradley et al., 2008).

An overactive HPA axis has also been linked with a persistent inflammatory response in the immune system that leads to overproduction of substances called cytokines that orchestrate the response to infections. Cytokines are also linked with the progression of coronary heart disease and so a chronic inflammatory response could provide the link between depression and coronary heart disease noted previously (Miller and Blackwell, 2006).

An important question to ask is, how does stress damage the brain? There is evidence that excess cortisol can affect brain structure by suppressing nerve growth and **neurogenesis** (the birth of new neurons) in the hippocampus (McEwen, 2001). In some parts of the adult human brain, the structure and number of neurons is not fixed and can change in response to stimuli like stressful events (Gage, 2000). The hippocampus is one of the areas in which neuroplastic changes can take place (Eriksson et al., 1998). A normal response to an acute stress is to increase levels of peptides, like brain-derived neurotrophic factor (BDNF), that promote neural growth and neurogenesis to combat the stress. When there is chronic stress, or an excessive response to stress, levels of BDNF are reduced (Duman and Monteggia, 2006). Reduced BDNF can contribute to loss of neurons because BDNF is important for supporting the survival of existing neurons and encouraging neurogenesis (Kirschenbaum and Goldman, 1995).

Understanding how the brain responds to stress has contributed to the development of another hypothesis about the cause of depression. The neurogenic hypothesis suggests that depression is related to a problem with the factors in the brain that support neural plasticity.

The neurogenic theory of depression

The observation that antidepressant treatments take several weeks to bring about their therapeutic effects suggests that there are actions of these drugs which are secondary to their immediate ability to increase monoamine levels that explain their clinical usefulness. In thinking about what these mechanisms might be, researchers have drawn on knowledge of depression pathology, in particular the reduced size of the hippocampus, and suggested that the cause of depression might lie in deficits in the factors that regulate the survival of neurons in the adult brain. These factors are called neurotrophins and most research so far has focused on the most prominent neurotrophin which is BDNF. The suggestion is that depression arises when there is a deficit in neurotrophins. This leads to the neuronal damage underlying depression, for example in the hippocampus. The idea then is that antidepressants are effective in treating depression because they reverse the neurotrophin deficit.

The evidence in favour of this hypothesis comes from studies of people with depression and animal models. There is post-mortem evidence that the brains of people who suffered from depression have reduced levels of BDNF in the hippocampus compared to healthy brains (Karege et al., 2005). These data can be difficult to interpret because the sample sizes are small and include individuals with very different clinical histories but they are consistent with the idea that depression involves neurotrophic deficits. Of course, if reduced levels of

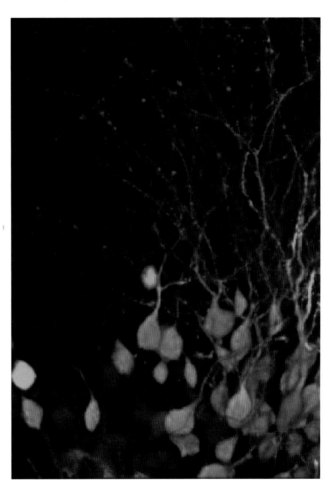

Figure 9.7 Neurogenesis is the process by which new neurons are created. The finding that neurogenesis takes place in the adult human brain throughout the life cycle was a major change in thinking, which reversed the prevailing belief that adults could not generate new neurons. Neurogenesis can occur in the dentate gyrus within the hippocampus as shown in this figure. Dentate granule cells generated in the developing and adult hippocampus have been retrovirally labeled with green and red fluorescent proteins. Adult-born cells are coloured red

Source: Schinder et al., PLoS Biology

neurotrophins are related to depression then we would expect that antidepressant treatments should reverse the deficit.

Many studies have been conducted on the effects of antidepressant drugs on levels of BDNF in the brain, in particular in the hippocampus, and it has been reported that these levels increase after chronic administration (Altar et al., 2003; Nibuya et al., 1995; Russo-Neustadt et al., 2000). Different types of antidepressant drugs share this common action to increase BDNF levels. In addition, electroconvulsive therapy, which is an effective treatment for depression, also stimulates neurogenesis in the hippocampus (Perera et al., 2007). Furthermore, the most effective drugs appear to have the biggest effect on BDNF, whereas non-antidepressant drugs do not affect BDNF levels, suggesting specificity. However, the effect of antidepressant drugs and ECT on BDNF could be correlated with their clinical effects but are not causal. To address this issue it is necessary to examine the effects of directly manipulating levels of BDNF and in animal models of depression.

Features of the depressed state such as behavioural despair are thought to be modelled in rats when they are placed in a mildly stressful situation that is difficult to escape. Direct infusion of BDNF into the hippocampus of rats in these tests has an antidepressant effect (Shirayama et al., 2002). A question that arises here is, what is the effect of BNDF in the hippocampus? It is possible that increasing levels of BDNF plays a role in ameliorating depression by increasing neurogenesis in the hippocampus because blocking neurogenesis here blocks the effects of antidepressants in animal models (Santarelli et al., 2003).

Evidence is also now accumulating that stress may alter the functioning of brain reward circuits too, due to plastic changes in glutamatergic, GABAergic and dopaminergic signalling. However, this research emphasises that the relationship between the brain's reward circuitry and depression is complex, and much remains to be investigated (Russo and Nestler, 2013).

KEY POINTS

- Major depression is associated with biased negative thought patterns and rumination alongside a decreased ability to experience pleasure.
- Low serotonin function is a risk factor that combines with other contributing environmental factors to increase the likelihood of developing depression.
- Stress can trigger depression and this may be related to brain damaging effects of excess stress hormones.
- Medications that act to increase serotonin neurotransmission are helpful in alleviating the symptoms of depression for some people. This may be related to drug effects on neurogenesis.

ANXIETY

Anxiety represents the most common psychological disorder and although many different types of anxiety disorder have been classified they all share the common feature of fear and avoidance in situations that are not associated with actual danger or risk. Everyone experiences anxiety at some time or other when faced with a stressful situation, but when the anxiety persists and there is excessive worry that leads to difficulties in dealing with everyday events, an anxiety disorder is likely to be diagnosed. The specific diagnosis will depend on the type of worry and the situations that provoke the anxiety. For example, someone with social anxiety disorder might dread eating in public or they might have a fear that people are watching them and that they will do something embarrassing. In obsessive-compulsive disorder (OCD) the experience is of persistent upsetting thoughts and the development of rituals to try to control the anxiety associated with these thoughts. For example, if someone has obsessive thoughts about contamination by germs then they may deal with this by compulsive hand washing. Post-traumatic stress disorder (PTSD) is triggered by a terrifying event, usually one which is life threatening. After the event, a person suffering from PTSD may re-experience the anxiety associated with the traumatic event even though they are no longer in danger. In panic disorder, people experience sudden and intense attacks of fear that are usually accompanied by physical symptoms such as a racing heart beat, chest pain and shortness of breath. When someone has a fear of having a panic attack in a social situation they may also be diagnosed with agoraphobia, which is anxiety associated with being in situations where it might be difficult to leave. Finally, generalised anxiety disorder is when a person experiences excessive concerns and worries about a range of everyday situations for a prolonged period.

Anxiety disorders can be very disabling and like the other psychological disorders discussed in this chapter they have significant implications in terms of economic and social costs (Greenberg et al., 1999). This is partly because many people do not seek help for their condition and so do not access treatment. Chapter 7 has discussed PTSD and phobias as emotional memory disorders. We will focus here on generalised anxiety disorder as an example of a common anxiety disorder although as we will see there is considerable overlap in the biological bases of anxiety disorders.

Clinical symptoms of generalised anxiety disorder (GAD)

GAD is associated with free-floating, disproportionate worry about a broad range of everyday life events and situations. These thoughts are difficult to control, which also contributes to the anxiety. GAD is also associated with symptoms such as feeling tense, having problems concentrating, irritability, difficulty sleeping, sore muscles, sweating and diarrhoea. A problem for diagnosis of GAD is that it often co-occurs with other anxiety disorders and with depression or other psychiatric disorders (Wittchen et al., 1994). This can worsen the outcome (Kessler et al., 1999). Patients with anxiety disorders are also at increased risk for chronic pain, asthma, cardiovascular disease, hypertension, migraine, and gastrointestinal disorders (Härter et al., 2003; Roy-Byrne et al., 2008). The effects of living with GAD are estimated to be similar to the disability associated with depression (Wittchen et al., 2000). People with anxiety pay more attention to stimuli in the environment that they find anxiety provoking or threatening (Mogg and Bradley, 1998). That is, they appear to be very quick to detect and react to information or situations that are anxiety provoking, which could maintain an anxious state.

The onset of GAD varies but occurs most often in the mid-twenties. The course is usually chronic with patients experiencing a coming and going of symptom severity over a number of years (Wittchen et al., 2000). The likelihood of recovering from GAD is significantly less than that of recovering from major depression (Yonkers et al., 2000).

Prevalence of GAD

Anxiety disorders overall are the most common of psychological disorders with estimates suggesting that at some point in their lives 29% of the population will suffer with an anxiety-related condition (Kessler et al., 2005). It is difficult to estimate the prevalence of GAD because recognition of the symptoms by medical practitioners is variable, partly because many people with GAD often seek help for physical symptoms rather than their anxiety (Kennedy and Schwab, 1997) and because criteria for a diagnosis of GAD has changed over the years. Nevertheless, a UK survey indicates an incidence of 44 people in 1000 and suggests that after anxiety with depression, GAD is the second most prevalent form of anxiety (O'Brien et al., 2001). The same survey found that prevalence rates were higher among women than men for all anxiety disorders except panic, and that people with anxiety were more likely to be aged between 35 and 54 and to be divorced or separated (O'Brien et al., 2000).

Biological bases of GAD

Twin studies suggest that anxiety disorders run in families, which is consistent with a genetic contribution, but the heritable component of anxiety is thought to be less than for schizophrenia (Hettema et al., 2001). Studies so far have not identified any specific genetic risk factors associated with anxiety disorders and it is likely to be caused by complex gene–environment interactions.

Given the importance of the amygdala in the processing of fear-related stimuli it is not surprising that much focus of research into the biological bases of anxiety has been on this brain structure (Chapter 7). Imaging studies have found increased activation of the amygdala in response to fearful facial expression in patients with a range of anxiety disorders including GAD (Rauch et al., 2003; McClure et al., 2007). Activation of the amygdala was also associated with severity of GAD symptoms in a study of adolescents (Monk et al., 2008) and in adolescents with high trait anxiety but subthreshold clinical symptoms (Stein et al., 2007). The results of these studies are consistent with the idea that anxiety is associated with biased attention to threat-related cues, perhaps mediated by hyper-activation of the amygdala, which is known to play a key role in processing of emotional stimuli and fear conditioning. However, not all studies have found hyperactivity in the amygdala in adults.

More recent research suggests that in GAD, hyperactivity in the amygdala is observed robustly in tasks where there is anticipation of potentially threatening stimuli. There is also a suggestion based on imaging studies that GAD is characterised by dysfunction in emotional regulation circuitry that includes the amygdala and areas of the prefrontal cortex (Etkin et al., 2011). In particular, anxiety may result from an inability of cortical areas to regulate emotional responses mediated by the amygdala.

People with high levels of anxiety also show greater activation in the insular cortex in response to fearful faces or when asked to attend to internal sensations such as listening to heartbeats (Critchley et al., 2004; Stein et al., 2007). This might suggest that anxiety is associated with sensitivity to monitoring and interpretation of physical sensations. One idea is that people with anxiety make exaggerated predictions about experiencing aversive bodily sensations due to heightened insular responses and this results in cognitive strategies such as avoidance in an attempt to control these feelings (Paulus and Stein, 2006).

The GABAergic System and Anxiety

Interest in the GABAergic system in anxiety stemmed from knowledge of the mechanism of action of the drugs used to treat the disorder. Of course, alcohol has been used to calm nerves for centuries and is known to increase GABAergic transmission, but the first drugs that were medically prescribed for the treatment of anxiety disorders were the barbiturates.

The barbiturates were first synthesised in the early 1900s and although they were effective in reducing anxiety, they proved problematic in many ways. First, there is little separation between the clinically effective dose and a dose that can prove fatal, because it depresses neuronal activity in the brain regions that control breathing. Second, barbiturates are sedating at doses that provide anxiety relief which means they are dangerous to take while driving or doing other complex tasks. Third, they interact synergistically with drugs like alcohol and this can contribute to accidental overdose. A combination of alcohol and barbiturates is thought to have been the cause of death of the film actress Marilyn Monroe. There are also numerous side effects associated with barbiturates such as disruption of REM sleep and dependence.

The second class of drugs that was developed to treat anxiety was the benzodiazepines (BZs). The archetypal BZ is the drug valium. BZs were much safer than the barbiturates and were effective as both anti-anxiety treatments and sleeping pills. They were widely prescribed, some would say over-prescribed, as life-style drugs and were referred to in popular culture, for example, their mention in a track by the Rolling Stones as 'mother's little helper'. Now we know that the BZs are not without problems because of their side effects; they cause sedation and impair memory. The fact that BZs induce amnesia can be a benefit when the drugs are used as a pre-treatment for dental procedures because patients do not acquire painful memories of the encounter that might put them off going back to the dentist ever again! However, the amnesic effects of BZs have also been used for criminal purposes as it is the drug of choice for date rape (Woods and Winger, 1997). There is also evidence that BZs can induce dependence and so they are usually only prescribed nowadays for a limited period.

Both barbiturates and BZs act in the brain to alter GABAergic transmission, although in slightly different ways. The BZs enhance inhibitory GABAergic transmission by acting as allosteric

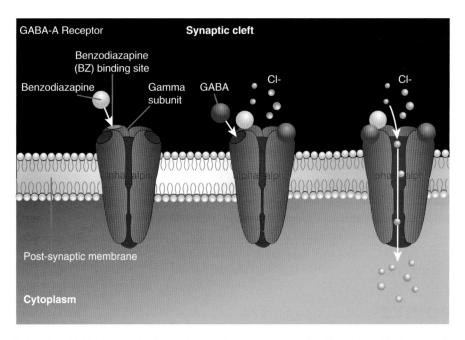

Figure 9.8 The GABA-A receptor is made up of different subunits. There is a binding site for benzodiazepine drugs on the GABA-A receptor. When a benzodiazepine agonist binds to the site this increases the frequency of opening of the integral Cl-channel, which potentiates GABA transmission

Source: www.cnsforum.com

modulators. This means that they augment the response to GABA, and the mechanism involves the GABA-A receptor. The receptor for BZ drugs is located on the GABA-A receptor and when BZs bind to the receptor the responsiveness of the GABA-A receptor to GABA is increased. The fact that BZs are limited to enhancing normal GABAergic transmission explains why they are safer in overdose than the barbiturates. Barbiturates alter GABA-A receptor function directly and so are not reliant on the presence of endogenous GABA for their effects. Therefore they can achieve inhibitory effects over and above that achieved by the natural effects of GABA.

The demonstration that drugs that increase GABAergic transmission have anti-anxiety or anxiolytic effects suggests that the GABA system has a role to play in anxiety. Interestingly there are drugs that act to reduce GABAergic transmission and these drugs are called BZ inverse agonists. As one might predict, inverse agonists have the opposite effect to BZ agonist drugs like valium and induce an anxiety-like state (Nutt and Malizia, 2001).

The effects of BZs on GABA-A function are dependent upon the particular type of GABA-A receptor that has the BZ receptor. GABA-A receptors are built from five protein subunits that can exist in slightly different forms known as isoforms. This means that many different sub-types of GABA-A receptor exist in the brain because they are made from different combinations of subunits. New, selective drugs have been synthesised that bind to BZs receptors on some GABA-A receptor types and not others. Interestingly, these drugs have different effects on behaviour, suggesting that the effects of BZs can be dissociated. For example, the sedative effects are mediated by binding to one kind of GABA receptor and the amnesic effects are mediated by a different kind. More importantly for the treatment of anxiety disorders there is the potential for drugs that have anti-anxiety effects without causing sedation or other undesirable effects of BZs (Atack, 2010).

Other evidence that disturbances in GABAergic function underlie anxiety comes from imaging studies of GABA-A receptors. It has been reported that there is a reduction in benzodiazepine receptor sites throughout the brain in patients with panic disorder, especially in the insula (Malizia et al., 1998). A similar reduction in GABA-A binding sites has been observed in the temporal lobe of patients with GAD (Tiihonen et al., 1997).

Other neurotransmitter systems and anxiety

Although BZs have been the drug of choice historically for the treatment of anxiety, the drugs that are used now are selective serotonin reuptake inhibitors (SSRIs). However, exactly how SSRIs bring about their anyxiolytic effects is still a matter for debate and so the role of serotonin in anxiety is unclear, but may involve the 5-HT1A receptor (Akimova et al., 2009). Drugs like buspirone which are 5-HT1A agonists are effective in treating anxiety. Problems with inhibitory neurotransmission that underlie anxiety could result from reduced inhibitory GABAergic neurotransmission but also from increase in excitatory glutamatergic transmission. Accordingly, inhibitors of the NMDA glutamate receptor have been shown to be anxiolytic in animal models (Plaznik et al., 1994).

KEY POINTS

- GAD involves disproportionate worry about a broad range of everyday life events and situations.
- GAD has been linked to increased fear responses due to overactivity in brain circuits involving the amygdala and frontal cortex, perhaps due to reduced inhibitory GABAergic neurotransmission.
- Drugs that increase inhibitory neurotransmission in the brain are useful in treating anxiety.

CHAPTER SUMMARY

Knowledge about the biological bases of psychological disorders is progressing and has led to the development of medications and other treatments that alleviate some symptoms. However, all medications are associated with problematic side effects and many people do not respond to them. In addition, none provide a cure for the disorders. There is still some way to go to link complex symptoms that characterise schizophrenia, depression and anxiety to specific underlying causes. Studying the relationship between risk genes and dysfunction in specific neural systems that underlie symptoms is one way in which further progress may be made.

FURTHER READING

Howes, O. D., & Kapur, S. (2009). The dopamine hypothesis of schizophrenia: Version III – the final common pathway. *Schizophrenia Bulletin*, *35*(3), 549–62.

Plots the development of the dopamine hypothesis of schizophrenia.

Belmaker, R. H., & Agam, G. (2008). Major depressive disorder. *New England Journal of Medicine*, *358*(1), 55–68.

Provides a critical discussion of the monoamine hypothesis of depression and other approaches to understanding the biological mechanisms underlying major depression.

Russo, S. J. & Nestler, E. J. (2013). The brain reward circuitry in mood disorders. *Nature Reviews Neuroscience*, *14*(9), 609–25.

Reviews recent advances in research in depression, and discusses avenues for future research.

Tyrer, P. & Baldwin, D. (2006). Generalised anxiety disorder. *The Lancet*, *368*(9553), 2156–66.

Provides a clear overview of the clinical features and treatment of GAD.

SPOTLIGHT 9A
SCHIZOPHRENIA

KEY ISSUES AND CONTROVERSIES

- Does adolescent cannabis use cause schizophrenia?
- How effective are drug treatments for schizophrenia and are new antipsychotic medications better than older drugs?
- Is there a common underlying neurochemical disturbance that might explain the range of symptoms seen in schizophrenia?

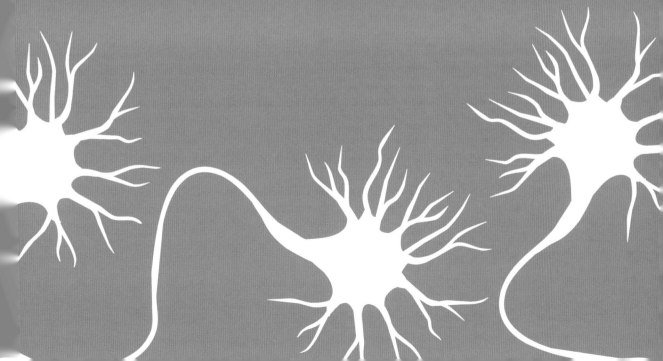

INTRODUCTION

In Chapter 9 we discovered that schizophrenia is a psychological disorder that is characterised by disturbances in perception, emotion and cognition. We explored how the onset of schizophrenia is affected by genetic and environmental factors. We also learned that the symptoms of schizophrenia are related to changes in neurotransmission in the brain and that drugs acting as dopamine antagonists can provide relief from some symptoms. In this spotlight, our aim is to delve deeper into schizophrenia research and shine a light on some key issues that are the topic of current research and controversy. We will explore three issues in depth and along the way we will analyse some key research papers and critically appraise methods and findings. Over the last few years, studies assessing the relationship between cannabis and psychosis have attracted considerable attention in research literature, popular media, and the community. Many young people report using cannabis and so whether or not cannabis use can cause schizophrenia is an important issue. We will examine adolescent cannabis use as a risk factor for schizophrenia and analyse in detail the evidence on this issue. We will also look in more detail at the actions of drugs that are used to treat schizophrenia and analyse their clinical effectiveness and associated side effects. Drugs are commonly prescribed to treat schizophrenia but there has been debate about whether drug development in schizophrenia has been effective. We will answer the question of whether the newer drugs that have come on the market in recent years are an improvement on the older drugs in terms of their clinical effects and side effect profile. Finally, we will go beyond the dopamine hypothesis of schizophrenia and investigate the possibility that dysfunction in glutamate systems might be a common underlying mechanism that explains the range of symptoms seen in schizophrenia. This research is likely to inform new approaches to the treatment of schizophrenia and push forward our understanding of the nature of the disorder.

CANNABIS USE AND SCHIZOPHRENIA

Cannabis use has been linked with progression to chronic schizophrenia in some young people. This has led to the suggestion that cannabis use during adolescence is a causal factor in the development of the disorder. The question of whether cannabis use actually causes schizophrenia in some people is not an easy issue to resolve and has been a topic of great debate. In this section, we will think about how the relationship between cannabis use and schizophrenia has been investigated and what can be concluded based on the evidence.

If there is a causal relationship between cannabis use and onset of schizophrenia then we would expect that any trends towards an increase in cannabis use would be accompanied by an increase in the incidence of schizophrenia. No clear evidence has emerged here (Degenhardt et al., 2003) but it may be that recent trends towards an increase in cannabis use have yet to emerge (Hickman et al., 2007). Controlled trials of the effect of cannabis cannot be conducted in adolescents for ethical reasons and so most studies investigating links between cannabis use and schizophrenia have used what is known as a prospective cohort design.

In a prospective cohort design, a large group of participants are tested at a specific baseline time point for various disorder risk factors and then there is a follow-up assessment for schizophrenia some years later. In this way, it is possible to find out if there is a relationship between cannabis use and future likelihood of a schizophrenia diagnosis. Studying a large cohort is important because of the relatively low incidence of schizophrenia in the population. However, a problem when studying large samples over time is the number of people who drop out from the study (attrition rate). Bias can be introduced if some people are more likely to drop out than others thus affecting the follow-up results. Some studies have tracked individuals from a young age or even from birth and this is useful because it allows researchers to control for the confounding effects of early childhood and family risk factors (Arseneault et al., 2002).

A number of cohort studies have found that cannabis use, particularly during adolescence, is associated with a greater likelihood of schizophrenic symptoms at follow-up (Andréasson et al., 1987; Zammit et al., 2002; van Os et al., 2002; Henquet et al., 2005). But just because a cohort study reveals an association between cannabis use and later onset of schizophrenia, this does not mean that cannabis use actually causes schizophrenia. In fact, the reverse might be true. It may be that people who are already experiencing sub-clinical signs of schizophrenia are more likely to use cannabis, perhaps to self-medicate their symptoms. Cannabis use might not cause schizophrenia but rather the signs of schizophrenia cause cannabis use.

Another possibility is that cannabis users are more likely to use other drugs such as amphetamines and it is the other drug use rather than the cannabis use that explains the later onset of schizophrenia. Similarly, maybe cannabis use is associated with other factors linked to the development of schizophrenia such as living in an urban environment. We would want to find out whether studies have taken into account these confounding factors.

We would also want to know about the psychological outcome measures that have been used. How are schizophrenic symptoms being diagnosed? Are the measures clear and quantifiable? Could any symptoms be explained by acute effects of cannabis intoxication? Maybe people who use cannabis when they are younger continue to use the drug when they are older and report schizophrenic symptoms that can be explained by acute pharmacological effects of the drug.

Another question is how drug use is assessed. Drug use in cohort studies is usually assessed by self-reports and these measures may not reflect actual drug use. People may either over- or under-report their drug use to create a particular impression of themselves. Because of the illegal nature of cannabis use some people may be prone to under-reporting their use whereas others may wish to convey an impression of rebelliousness by over-reporting their use. If these same people are also prone to over- or under-reporting psychological symptoms then associations can arise merely due to the fact that some people are more willing to complain than others. For example, associations between self-reported stress and self-reported chest pain have been reported in middle-aged men but stress was not associated with actual hospital admission for heart problems. The lack of relationship between self-reported stress and an objective measure of disease, hospital admission, may be because people who report stress are also biased towards reporting symptoms (Macleod et al., 2002). In other words, the positive relationship arises from a willingness of some people to report feeling symptoms rather than a real relationship between stress and heart disease. Associations between self-reported measures that arise due to such reporting biases are difficult to control for but on the other hand other measures such as urine testing for drug use would be very difficult to implement in large cohorts. Bearing these issues in mind, let's critically analyse the results from a cohort study.

KEY STUDY
Andréasson, S. et al. (1987). Cannabis and schizophrenia: A longitudinal study of Swedish conscripts. *The Lancet, 330(8574),* 1483–6

Andreasson and colleagues analysed data from a survey of Swedish men who were conscripted to military service. The cohort comprised just over 45,000 men born in 1951 so it was a sufficiently large sample to allow for drop-outs and for detecting rates of schizophrenia. The men completed various questionnaires at baseline about their drug use and upbringing, school, and personal relationships. The questionnaires were anonymous, which might have encouraged participants to be truthful about their drug use, but we should bear in mind the limitation of drug self-reports.

The conscripts were initially assessed for psychiatric symptoms by a psychologist using a diagnostic manual, which gives us some reassurance on the reliability of the assessment. They were then followed over 15 years using a national register of psychiatric care which means they would have been diagnosed by a clinician. The researchers used statistical methods to calculate the risk of having a diagnosis of schizophrenia at follow-up depending upon how much cannabis use was reported at baseline.

Those conscripts who reported using cannabis more than 50 times by the age of 18 were six times more likely to be hospitalised for schizophrenia by the age of 33 than those who had not used cannabis. Furthermore, the risk was dose-related such that young people using a large amount of cannabis were at greater risk than those with less drug exposure. However, the researchers also found that there were other factors such as other drug use and family background that were associated with cannabis use and so they conducted some additional statistical tests to see which of these correlated factors was the best predictor of being hospitalised for schizophrenia. They found that already having a psychiatric diagnosis at baseline predicted hospitalisation for schizophrenia at follow-up, which is not surprising. Family divorce was also a predictor, emphasising the role of early environmental factors in schizophrenia. But independent of these factors, cannabis use was the third best predictor of hospitalisation for schizophrenia.

If we analyse the strengths of the study we can pinpoint that the assessments were conducted by a clinician and so we know whether there was a diagnosis of schizophrenia both at baseline and follow-up. It was also good that the researchers were able to control for confounding factors. However, a problem for the study is that there was no information gathered about whether the recruits were using drugs in between the baseline and follow-up assessments. This means it is possible that some of the people who were hospitalised might have been suffering from the effects of recent cannabis use and not that previous cannabis use was causing the development of chronic schizophrenia. Another limitation to consider is that although the conscripts were assessed for a diagnosis of schizophrenia at baseline, there was no assessment of the presence of psychotic symptoms that might indicate the presence of the schizophrenia prodrome. Hence, it is possible that those conscripts who went on to be hospitalised for schizophrenia were self-medicating for early sub-clinical signs of the disorder. An interesting discussion point in the paper is that although the data presented show an association between cannabis use and onset of schizophrenia, they also show that cannabis use accounts for only a minority of cases of schizophrenia, suggesting that cannabis use is likely to be just one of many risk factors.

We can also note that only a small number of the cannabis users developed schizophrenia. There are various factors that might explain this. Age of first use might be important, perhaps because there is a period of vulnerability to the effects of cannabis (Arseneault et al., 2002). So what can we conclude from the results of this study? The finding that cannabis use preceded the onset of symptoms and was related to the amount of cannabis used, even when controlling for likely confounding factors, suggests there is a causal relationship between cannabis use and onset of schizophrenia. Nevertheless, because it is impossible to control for all possible confounding factors, the possibility that the relationship between cannabis use and schizophrenia onset is explained by risk factors correlated with cannabis use cannot be totally ruled out. Given that only a relatively small number of cannabis users developed schizophrenia, we might also conclude that cannabis use may be causally linked to development of schizophrenia but only in individuals that are genetically vulnerable.

Implications

Since the study by Andreasson and colleagues was conducted, many other similar types of studies have been published and many have addressed the limitations of the original study (Zammit et al., 2002; van Os et al., 2002; Henquet et al., 2005). While longitudinal cohort studies can never prove beyond doubt that cannabis causes schizophrenia, looking at the results of many studies together one can see a consistent pattern, which is that there is an increase in incidence of schizophrenia in people who had used cannabis (Moore et al., 2007). This kind of research has implications for information given to young people about cannabis and whether or not warnings based on the evidence should be communicated to young people.

THE EFFECTIVENESS OF ANTIPSYCHOTIC DRUGS

Since the discovery of the first antipsychotic medication, chlorpromazine, over 60 new drugs have been developed for the treatment of schizophrenia. Drug therapy is the mainstay of treatment for the disorder although it is usually more effective when combined with psychological and social support (Marshall and Lockwood, 2000). The goal of antipsychotic drug development is to produce drugs that can treat the cognitive and negative symptoms of schizophrenia as well as the positive symptoms and which are not associated with significant serious side effects. But has this been achieved? Let's take a closer look at the clinical effects and side effects of first and second generation antipsychotic drug treatments to find out.

First generation or typical antipsychotics

Chlorpromazine and haloperidol are examples of first generation antipsychotics. First generation drugs are generally effective at treating the positive symptoms of schizophrenia but they are minimally effective at treating the negative and cognitive symptoms (Nasrallah and Tandon, 2013) and may even worsen cognitive impairments (Bilder, 1997). Furthermore, a third of patients fail to respond at all to treatment with first generation drugs.

As outlined in Chapter 9, the first generation drugs are all antagonists at dopamine D2 receptors, and this action is likely to be related to their therapeutic effects. Evidence suggests that schizophrenia is associated with overactivity in dopamine neurotransmission, and the ability of first generation drugs to block dopamine is related to their clinical efficacy. Both immediate dopamine D2 receptor blockade and delayed inactivation of dopamine-neuron firing may contribute to the effects of first generation drugs (Grace et al., 1997; Kapur et al., 2005).

Dopamine D2 receptors are located in the nigrostriatal, mesolimbic, mesocortical and thalamic dopamine systems but for antipsychotic effects, most interest has been focused on the role of receptors located in the mesolimbic system, in particular the ventral striatum. This is in line with the importance of the mesolimbic system in emotion and motivation (see Chapter 8). However, more recent evidence also suggests a potential role for dorsal areas of the striatum, particularly the caudate nucleus (Kegeles et al., 2010). Molecular imaging studies, including PET, provide evidence that at clinical doses, the occupancy of dopamine D2 receptors achieved by all first generation drugs in the striatum is around 60%, suggesting that this level of occupancy is associated with antipsychotic effects (Farde et al., 1992; Kapur et al., 2000).

A problem is that when drug receptor occupancy reaches around 80%, side effects begin to emerge. This means there is only a small margin between therapeutic doses and doses associated with undesirable effects. These side effects are disturbances of motor function due to dopamine D2 receptor blockade in the nigrostriatal dopamine system that projects from the substantia nigra to the dorsal striatum. The nigrostriatal system forms part of a motor control system known as the extra-pyramidal system because it is distinct from motor fibres relayed through the pyramids of the medulla. Impaired motor behaviours due to blockade of dopamine D2 receptors in the nigrostriatal system are therefore known as extra-pyramidal symptoms (EPSs).

There are three types of EPS that can develop after acute drug treatment. The first type resembles the symptoms of Parkinson's disease, a condition that is also caused by reduced dopamine function in the nigrostriatal dopamine system. The second is akathesia, which is a syndrome involving feelings of anxiety and restlessness. A patient with akathesia may be unable to stop themselves constantly fidgeting and may be unable to keep still for long, feeling the need to pace around or rock back and forth. Dystonia is the third EPS that is characterised by involuntary muscle movements such as tics and jerky arm or leg movements.

Tardive dyskinesia is another movement disorder associated with antipsychotic treatment but it has a later onset, only emerging after chronic treatment and in older patients (Jeste et al., 1999). Tardive dyskinesia is usually characterised by involuntary movements of the face, such as lip smacking, and slow, writhing movements of the limbs. It can be very debilitating and stigmatising yet the precise cause is unknown. Likely mechanisms are changes in dopamine, GABA or acetylcholine function in the basal ganglia as a result of long term dopamine D2 antagonism (Margolese et al., 2005).

First generation antipsychotic drugs bind to dopamine D2 receptors in the striatum but also to D2 receptors in other areas of the brain such as the hypothalamus and pituitary, and this causes additional side effects such as problems with temperature regulation, suppression of menstruation, and impotence. They also have actions at receptors other than dopamine receptors and these actions are associated with side effects; for example: histamine antagonism, which can cause in drowsiness; blockade of acetylcholine receptors, which can cause dry mouth; and blockade of noradrenaline receptors, which can cause tachycardia (fast resting heart rate).

Overall, whilst the introduction of first generation antipsychotics resulted in many more people with schizophrenia being able to leave long term care in institutions due to management of the positive symptoms, there were many problems with adverse effects of the drug treatments and failure to deal adequately with the full range of symptoms associated with the disorder. Initially the development of less problematic drugs was hampered by the belief that the motor side effects could not be dissociated from the therapeutic effects of antipsychotics, but then a drug was discovered that bucked this trend (Shen, 1999). We will next consider the wave of drug treatments that started with the second generation antipsychotic clozapine.

Second generation or atypical drugs

The first drug to show a different profile to the first generation antipsychotics was the drug clozapine, which was discovered in the 1960s and first marketed in some European countries in the 1970s. Clozapine does not cause EPS, which is one reason why it and other second generation drugs are known as atypical. In addition, patients who fail to respond to first generation drugs will often show a response to clozapine (although a proportion do not respond to any drug treatment). However, clozapine is no more effective than the first generation drugs in dealing with the negative and cognitive symptoms of schizophrenia. It was initially thought that clozapine was effective in reducing negative symptoms but any benefits were probably because alleviating positive symptoms has a secondary effect to improve some aspects of social functioning (Breier et al., 1991). Clozapine also has serious side effects. Notably, some patients taking clozapine in Finland developed fatal agranulocytosis, which is a failure to produce sufficient white blood cells to fight infections (Amsler et al., 1977). The discovery that clozapine can cause agranulocytosis prevented its use in many countries for about 15 years, but the drug was reintroduced in the 1990s because it was realised that the blood disorder could be caught early through monitoring and then treated. The benefits of clozapine over previous antipsychotics in terms of its ability to treat non-responders and its lack of EPSs also contributed to its re-evaluation and subsequent licensing by the US Federal Drug Administration (FDA) (Crilly, 2007). The development of a range of other second generation drugs such as risperidone, olanzapine and ziprasidone quickly followed.

There has been great interest in whether the second generation drugs warranted the early enthusiasm expressed about their potential for enhanced efficacy. Several large-scale studies and meta-analyses have now been conducted comparing the effect of first and second generation drugs both in terms of their clinical effectiveness and side effects. Analysis of the data from these clinical trials suggests that both categories of drugs are broadly similar in their effectiveness in treating the positive symptoms of schizophrenia and in reducing rates of relapse, but clozapine stands out in terms of its effectiveness in treating patients who do not respond to other drug treatments (Tandon et al., 2008). There is some evidence that second generation drugs may be more effective in alleviating negative symptoms, but this is probably related to their reduced liability for EPSs. The benefits of second generation drugs also has to be balanced with the finding that some have been shown to cause substantial weight gain and increased risk of diabetes, particularly olanzapine and clozapine and to some extent risperidone (Reynolds and Kirk, 2010). The amount of weight gained varies across patients but can be around 12kg over a year (Nasrallah, 2003). Excessive weight gain has clear implications for health but can also lead to discontinuation of treatment because of concerns about obesity.

An important question to answer, if better drugs are to be developed, is which drug actions contribute to an atypical profile? One way of approaching this problem is to compare the pharmacological mechanisms of action of typical and atypical drugs. As we have already noted, all effective drugs developed to date share a common mechanism of action as dopamine D2 receptor antagonists suggesting that this action is important for antipsychotic effects. However, analysis of D2 receptor occupancy suggests differences between drugs at clinical doses. Clozapine and quetiapine have therapeutic effects at much lower levels of D2 receptor occupancy than other antipsychotics drugs. This would appear to undermine the suggestion that a threshold of around 60% D2 receptor occupancy is a feature of antipsychotic effectiveness. One explanation is that dopamine D2 receptor antagonism is not necessary for an antipsychotic effect and that other mechanisms contribute. Antipsychotic effects are likely to be modulated by drug action at receptors for neurotransmitters other than dopamine, including serotonin (Meltzer et al., 1989) although a clear picture has yet to emerge here. A difficulty is that a common mechanism across drugs that relates to therapeutic efficacy has not been identified. It is possible that there is a primary mechanism of action that remains to be identified but another explanation is that dopamine D2 receptor antagonism is the critical feature of antipsychotic action but occupancy rates do not tell the whole story (Seeman, 2005).

It has been suggested that the way in which antipsychotic drugs interact with the dopamine D2 receptor is important to understanding the relationship between D2 receptor antagonism and clinical effects. In particular, it has been argued that sustained levels of dopamine D2 blockade are not necessary for antipsychotic effects and that transient blockade can be equally as effective (Seeman, 2005). The extent to which an antagonist provides sustained versus transient blockade of a receptor is affected by its affinity for the receptor. Some drugs have a high affinity and bind tightly to the receptor whereas others have a low affinity and bind to the receptor in the same way but just dissociate from it more quickly and so are bound more loosely. Drugs that bind tightly can maintain occupancy for long periods whereas occupancy levels for loosely bound drugs will decline more quickly. Attenuation of dopamine transmission can be achieved by drugs with low affinity as long as a high dose is administered. In fact clozapine and quetiapine have a low affinity for the D2 receptor but when given in appropriate doses can provide effective dopamine D2 antagonism even at low levels of receptor occupancy. Differences in how antipsychotic drugs interact with the D2 receptor may therefore explain why clinical effects can be achieved at different levels of receptor occupancy.

But does fast receptor dissociation explain why atypical drugs show reduced EPSs?

One suggestion is that there may be advantages of antagonism by loosely bound drugs in terms of avoiding EPSs. A loosely bound drug only transiently occupies a receptor because it is coming on and off the receptors rapidly. This means that the endogenous dopamine, which is also competing for access to the receptors, is still able to bind. Fast dissociation from receptors therefore allows for attenuation of dopamine transmission while maintaining responsiveness to changes in normal dopamine signalling. This might explain the lack of EPSs by atypicals because they achieve a more physiological 'turning down' of dopamine receptor signalling that causes less disruption to normal dopamine-related functioning. A similar effect is achieved by the partial dopamine D2 receptor agonist aripiprazole which stabilises dopamine transmission by acting as a functional antagonist in the presence of a hyperactive dopamine system and is an effective antipsychotic agent that lacks EPSs (Seeman, 2005).

IMPLICATIONS

First generation antipsychotic drugs were a breakthrough in treatment for schizophrenia but these drugs are only really effective in treating positive symptoms and they induce serious side effects. The second generation of antipsychotic drugs are no more effective than the first generation drugs in treating symptoms and just bring with them a different set of side effects. It appears that the best profile attained so far for antipsychotic medications is effectiveness in treating positive symptoms with reduced likelihood of EPS. This profile holds for some, but not all, second generation drugs and can be achieved with careful dosing of some first generation drugs. Dopamine D2 receptor blockade seems to be a requirement for relief of positive symptoms in schizophrenia, and this is consistent with the dopamine theory of schizophrenia. Some of the side effects associated with dopamine D2 receptor antagonism can be minimised by using drugs that stabilise dopamine transmission. However, it is important to remember that some people do not respond to drug therapy and available drug treatments do not reverse the underlying neuronal disturbances in schizophrenia. The development of more effective pharmacotherapy in the future will depend on further advances in understanding of the biological bases of the symptoms of schizophrenia so that these systems can be targeted by new drugs. In the next section we will find out more about how research into the biological bases of schizophrenia is going beyond the dopamine hypothesis and highlighting the involvement of glutamate systems.

BEYOND THE DOPAMINE HYPOTHESIS OF SCHIZOPHRENIA

We have seen that the cognitive and negative symptoms of schizophrenia are core features of the disorder that have a big impact on quality of life and yet have so far proven to be resistant to drug treatment with dopamine D2 receptor antagonists. This suggests that overactivity in dopamine systems cannot be the only neurochemical disturbance in schizophrenia. The NMDA receptor hypofunction hypothesis has been proposed to try to offer a common mechanism that might explain the whole range of symptoms of schizophrenia (Olney and Farber, 1995). The NMDA receptor hypofunction theory seeks to explain two other aspects of schizophrenia: the fact that the onset is usually in adolescence and that it is associated with structural changes to the brain. However, the NMDA hypofunction theory is not contradictory to the dopamine hypothesis because as we will find out, there are significant interactions between dopamine and glutamatergic neurotransmission in areas of the brain that are known to be altered in schizophrenia. It is possible that a deficit in NMDA receptor function could lead to overactivity in dopamine transmission and the other way round.

NMDA receptor hypofunction and schizophrenia

Several lines of evidence support the NMDA receptor hypofunction hypothesis of schizophrenia. We will examine three different types of evidence: 1) post-mortem and imaging studies of glutamate markers in the brains of people with schizophrenia; 2) the effects of drugs that act as NMDA receptor antagonists in humans and laboratory animals; and 3) the effects of genetically altering glutamate receptors in the brains of mice.

Imaging and post-mortem studies

Using techniques such as magnetic resonance spectroscopy and single photon emission computed tomography it is possible to examine glutamate neurotransmission in the living human brain. There is evidence of altered glutamate activity in the brains of non-medicated schizophrenic patients compared with healthy controls (Théberge, 2002) and in adolescents at high risk of schizophrenia (Tibbo et al., 2004). Patients with schizophrenia have also been shown to have fewer NMDA receptors in the hippocampus (Pilowsky et al., 2006). Interestingly, this deficit was partially reversed by treatment with antipsychotics. Post-mortem studies confirm that the expression of NMDA receptors in schizophrenia is altered compared to healthy controls although these changes are complex (Kristiansen et al., 2007).

Effects of NMDA receptor antagonists

Various studies have investigated the effects of administration of NMDA antagonists with the aim of finding out if inducing NMDA receptor hypofunction via acute or chronic blockade of NMDA receptors induces schizophrenia-like symptoms. Reliable effects of ketamine on memory and delusions have been reported (Honey et al., 2005; Pomarol-Clotet et al., 2006). A recent study found that the illusion that a rubber hand is one's own was enhanced after acute administration of ketamine, an effect that is also seen in patients with schizophrenia when compared with healthy controls (Morgan et al., 2011). There are methodological and ethical issues associated with examining the effects of NMDA receptor antagonists in healthy volunteers so let's analyse a key paper in this area.

KEY STUDY
Krystal, J. H. et al. (1994). Subanaesthetic effects of the non-competitive NMDA antagonist, ketamine, in humans: Psychotomimetic, perceptual, cognitive and neuroendocrine responses *Archives of General Psychiatry, 51*(3), 199

Krystal and colleagues tested the effects of ketamine in 12 men and seven women. The participants underwent a thorough screening session in which the researchers checked that they did not have any mental health problems and were not vulnerable to psychosis. This was for ethical reasons, to reduce the possibility that the drug might induce psychosis. The researchers also asked the participants not to take any psychoactive drugs before and during the experiment to avoid the possibility of the ketamine interacting with other drugs. Compliance was checked by analysing a urine sample. This is important both for the safety of the participants and for ruling out the possibility that the results of the study could be explained by the influence of drugs other than ketamine.

There were three conditions in the study and all participants experienced the three conditions on three separate test days (this is known as a repeated-measures design). Two of the test days were ketamine days. Testing the effects of two ketamine doses is useful because the researchers can find out whether any effects of ketamine are related to the dose that was administered: pharmacological principles predict that would be a relationship between dose and response. The ketamine was administered intravenously, which allows very good control of the doses via a pump that maintains a particular level of drug in the bloodstream. The researchers were careful to choose doses that would not have a dissociative anaesthetic effect so as not to 'knock out' the participants. The effects of the ketamine administration were compared with the effects on a placebo day when everything about the procedure was the same apart from the participants receiving an injection of saline rather than drug. Having a placebo condition controls for the possibility that the general drug administration procedure might affect how the participants behave. Also, if the participants are unsure about whether they will be getting placebo or drug on any given day then this helps to reduce the influence of expectancy effects on responding. If the participants knew that they were definitely receiving ketamine then this might mean that they behave in line with how they think people respond to ketamine.

The key measures in the study were ratings that were chosen to tap into symptoms characteristic of schizophrenia such as unusual thought content, delusions, mood alterations and hallucinations. Some of these measures were self-ratings and others were ratings made by the experimenter. The symptom measures were completed before the ketamine infusion started and then at fixed intervals during and after the drug infusion had finished to allow the time course of the effects to be characterised. The participants also completed measures of cognitive function such as general cognitive ability, memory (Mini-Mental State Examination), flexible thinking (Wisconsin Card Sorting Test), attention (continuous performance tasks) and verbal fluency. These cognitive tasks were completed 20 minutes after starting the ketamine infusion. The researchers noted that the effects of the drug wore off quite quickly after the infusion finished. In fact, three participants did not finish their verbal fluency test until after the infusion had finished so the researchers did not analyse those results. In addition to behavioural measures, the participants gave a blood sample and this was analysed for markers of drug action on neurotransmitters such as dopamine (HVA) and noradrenaline metabolites (MHPG) and hormones (cortisol and prolactin).

The data analysis involved using statistical methods to find out whether the ketamine conditions differed from the placebo on the key measures. The data were also analysed according to the time the measures were taken, to find out if any drug effects varied according to time. The researchers controlled for the effects of expectancy in their analyses by calculating how the participants responded to the placebo and then subtracting this response from the drug effect. The rationale here is that since the placebo is inactive then one would not expect it to have any effect so any change in the measures observed after the placebo will reflect the participant behaving in line with expectations.

The researchers found that the participants scored similarly on the symptom measures before they had the drug on each of the test days (baseline measurers). This suggests that the participants were in a similar state before any drug was given and so any differences between conditions observed after the drug cannot be explained by existing group differences, say for example if it just so happened that on one day the participants arrived in a rather anxious state. Effects of ketamine on the symptom measures were found and these effects were much higher after the higher dose than the lower dose of ketamine. The effects also varied over time such that for the placebo condition, the symptom ratings were continuously low at all time points, whereas for the ketamine doses there was an initial increase in ratings up to a maximum and then a decline. This pattern of results is reflected in a statistically significant interaction between condition and time. The pattern of results was similar across the different symptom measures (positive and negative symptoms) such that the highest dose of ketamine increased rated symptoms whereas the low dose ketamine sometimes had an effect and the placebo had no effect.

Ketamine did not have any effect on the general cognitive measures as measured by the Mini-Mental State Examination but the highest dose of ketamine impaired attention, delayed memory

(Continued)

(Continued)

recall, and impaired verbal fluency and some aspects of performance on the Wisconsin Card Sorting Test. For mood measure, the high dose of ketamine increased anxiety but the low dose decreased anxiety although when the placebo effect was taken into account this decreased anxiety disappeared as an effect. The high dose also was associated with increased rating of 'high' that peaked around 15 minutes after drug infusion. Ketamine increased most of the biochemical and physiological measures such as HVA. However, cortisol, prolactin and blood pressure these measures did not correlate with the effects of ketamine on symptoms, suggesting that changes in psychological parameters probably do not relate to the behavioural effects.

Overall, the highest dose of ketamine reliably increased ratings on measures tapping into the positive symptoms of schizophrenia. Ketamine also produced effects consistent with some of the negative symptoms of schizophrenia, such as decreased motivation. Finally, ketamine had selective effects on cognitive function similar to those observed in schizophrenia. However, ketamine did not induce the visual hallucinations associated with schizophrenia. These findings suggest that ketamine may mimic some aspects of schizophrenia. From the study findings it is not possible to say whether the exact same biological mechanisms underlie the effects of ketamine in healthy volunteers and the symptoms in schizophrenia patients. Nevertheless, the results are consistent with the suggestion that NMDA receptor hypofunction induced by the NMDA receptor antagonist ketamine may be a factor contributing to schizophrenia.

Effects of repeated administration of NMDA antagonists

The effects of repeated administration of ketamine to human volunteers have been examined but for ethical reasons this is usually assessed in people who are already abusing ketamine. Therefore, the results of such studies have to be interpreted carefully because of the fact that ketamine abusers may co-abuse other drugs, making it difficult to separate the effects of repeated ketamine dosing from the effects of dosing with other drugs. In addition, people who choose to use drugs may constitute a specific population of individuals who are at risk of psychopathology and therefore prone to poor emotional and cognitive function regardless of their level of drug use. Nevertheless, studies of cognitive function in chronic ketamine users provide evidence of memory impairments that are related to the lifetime amount of drug used (Morgan et al., 2010). Also, frequent users of ketamine are more likely to report that they have delusion-like experiences than a control group of users of drugs other than ketamine, suggesting that the increased delusions were not just a result of drug using *per se* (Morgan et al., 2010).

Because of the issues with studying current drug users, the effects of NMDA receptor antagonists on the cognition of laboratory animals has also been examined. Testing laboratory animals means that the effects of drug administration can be examined under tightly controlled conditions and allows for assessment of detailed aspects of neuronal function that are not currently possible in humans. Animal models also allow for more reliable testing of the effects of repeated drug dosing on performance. This is important because the effects of repeated dosing might mimic more closely the neuronal changes observed in schizophrenia than the effects of a one-off dose (Jentsch and Roth, 1999). Moreover, if the effects of prior, repeated drug doses are assessed then it is not necessary to perform the tests in the presence of the drug. This is useful because testing in the drug-free state avoids confounds owing to direct drug effects on, for example, the movements required for performing tasks.

Various tests have been devised to assess cognitive function in rodents and non-human primates, and the idea is that the tests assess specific aspects of cognition that are similar to those affected in schizophrenia. Tests of attention and learning and memory are most commonly employed. Overall, the pattern of results is mixed but repeated administration of PCP has been found to impair a range of cognitive functions that are known to be affected in schizophrenia (Amitai et al., 2007; Jentsch et al., 1997; Podhorna and Didriksen, 2005).

Implications

Overall, evidence from different types of studies suggests that pharmacological blockade of NMDA receptors induces schizophrenia-like symptoms. It has been suggested that ketamine produces a state that is more similar to that observed in schizophrenia than drugs like amphetamine which induce psychosis but do not induce schizophrenia-like disruptions in cognitive processes. But from these types of studies it is not possible to say anything about how it is that NMDA receptor hypofunction leads to schizophrenic symptoms and whether NMDA hypofunction is related in any way to other known features of the disorder such as structural and functional brain changes. Another important question in relation to the biological bases of schizophrenia is how NMDA might receptor hypofunction theory account for the fact that schizophrenia emerges during adolescence. Next we will consider evidence relating some of the symptoms of schizophrenia to the effects of NMDA receptor hypofunction on brain structure and function.

NMDA receptor hypofunction and excitotoxicity

Evidence suggests that the cognitive deficits in schizophrenia may be related to alterations in the structure and function of the prefrontal cortex that are usually evident before the experience of a first psychotic episode. An idea that links NMDA receptor hypofunction to these deficits is that a consequence of NMDA receptor hypofunction is excessive release of glutamate which causes neuronal damage via apoptosis. In support of this idea, chronic administration of PCP to rats has been shown to increase release of glutamate in the prefrontal cortex (Moghaddam et al., 1997) and induce neuronal damage in the cortex (Olney and Farber, 1995). Elevated glutamate release as a result of NMDA receptor hypofunction and associated excitotoxicity could explain the reductions in grey matter volume seen in schizophrenia. How might this occur? A model that has been proposed is that reduced function of NMDA receptors located on GABA interneurons leads to reduced inhibitory input from these GABA interneurons onto glutamatergic projection neurons. The result is disinhibition of these excitatory glutamatergic neurons and excessive release of glutamate, which causes excitotoxicity and neuronal damage.

NMDA receptor hypofunction and neurodevelopment

A hypothesis that has been put forward to explain why the onset of schizophrenia is usually in the late teens is that adolescence is a time when there are profound changes in the brain involving reorganisation of synapses and that these processes are disrupted in some people, leading to schizophrenic symptoms (Feinberg, 1983). Early brain development involves the birth of cells, their proliferation, and growth and migration to different parts of the brain to form synapses. Many more synapses are formed initially than are needed and weaker synapses are pruned away early in development. In the prefrontal cortex there is also proliferation of synapses at the onset of puberty (Bourgeois, Goldman-Rakic, and Rakic, 1994) which is followed by a reorganisation of synaptic connections in adolescence that involves a reduction in synapses. It has been argued that schizophrenia is due to an exaggerated form of this synaptic pruning process (Keshavan et al., 1994).

Another idea is that people prone to developing schizophrenia have a neurochemical abnormality from early on in development but this is only expressed when there is a period of brain reorganisation during adolescence (Weinberger, 1987). There is evidence that neurocognitive deficits in schizophrenia are apparent before the first onset of psychosis (Bilder et al., 2006) and that brain damage early in life increases the risk of psychosis, all of which is consistent with the early neurodevelopmental perspective of schizophrenia.

Relating these changes to the NMDA receptor hypofunction theory, it has been noted that brain alterations occurring during the teenage years involve changes to glutamatergic synapses. Furthermore many of the risk genes for schizophrenia are associated with NMDA receptor signalling (Harrison and Weinberger, 2004). In addition, early environmental factors such as birth trauma can result in degeneration of neurons expressing NMDA receptors (Olney et al., 1999). During early development NMDA receptors are in a hypersensitive state, and too much or too little glutamate can result in neurodegeneration of neurons (Ikonomidou et al., 1999). Indeed neonatal administration of ketamine and PCP causes neurodegeneration and long-lasting behavioural changes (Wang, C. et al., 2001).

It is possible that individuals with a genetically mediated glutamatergic defect are vulnerable to the effects of environmental insults such as hypoxia at birth. This insult may lead to a loss of glutamatergic neurons that is associated with the cognitive deficits that precede the onset of psychosis. When there is another stage of pruning of synapses during adolescence, hypofunction of NMDA receptors increases the risk of onset of schizophrenia due to neuronal loss through excessive pruning.

A question arises as to the potential sites of early neuronal damage that might lead to later deficits. It has been suggested that a primary site might be the cortex and involve the loss of GABAergic interneurons as a result of glutamate-induced excitotoxicity (Reynolds et al., 2004) but the hippocampus may also be involved in line with evidence of reduced hippocampal volume in patients with schizophrenia. In support of this idea, neonatal lesions of the ventral hippocampus have been shown to model many aspects of schizophrenia including the late onset of symptoms (Lipska, Khaing and Weinberger, 1993). There is evidence that neonatal ventral hippocampal lesions cause functional and structural dysfunction to the prefrontal cortex and disruption to dopamine and glutamate neurotransmission (Tseng et al., 2009). Similar effects are observed after administration of a toxin that alters development during gestation in rats (Lodge and Grace, 2009). These models suggest a mechanism whereby early developmental neuropathology might lead to dopamine dysregulation due to problems with glutamatergic/GABAergic signalling.

Glutamate and dopamine interactions

There is evidence from animal models that some of symptoms of schizophrenia could be due to interactions between glutamate and dopamine signalling in the brain. Over-expression of dopamine D2 receptors early in life can lead to deficits in cognitive functioning that are similar to those observed in schizophrenia (Bach et al., 2008). Mice that have been genetically modified to over-express dopamine D2 receptors in the striatum perform poorly on tests that rely on prefrontal cortex function, suggesting that dopamine hyper-function early in life could be a primary cause of cognitive deficits in schizophrenia owing to effects of overactive dopamine transmission on prefrontal glutamate systems (Bach et al., 2008). Hence, the picture is complex and changes in both glutamate and dopamine signalling could contribute to the cause of schizophrenia. Changes in glutamate function could lead to alterations in dopamine transmission, or changes in dopamine neurotransmission could lead to glutamate transmission deficit. In fact, it may be that glutamate/dopamine and dopamine/glutamate interactions are implicated in the pathology of schizophrenia. For example, a deficit in glutamate transmission may lead to overactivity in striatal dopamine systems and dopamine alterations might then reinforce glutamate transmission deficits in a vicious cycle (Laruelle et al., 2005).

Implications

The available data converge to suggest that NMDA receptor hypofunction is an underlying problem in schizophrenia. An implication of this is that there is potential in developing treatments that reverse this deficit. The addition of NMDA-enhancing agents to antipsychotics may result in improvements in the range of symptoms associated with schizophrenia.

FURTHER READING

Keshavan, M. S., Nasrallah, H. A., & Tandon, R. (2011). Schizophrenia, 'Just the Facts' 6. Moving ahead with the schizophrenia concept: From the elephant to the mouse. *Schizophrenia Research*, *127*, 3–13.

Tandon, R., Nasrallah, H. A., & Keshavan, M. S. (2010). Schizophrenia, 'Just the Facts' 5. Treatment and prevention past, present, and future. *Schizophrenia Research*, *122*, 1–23.

Two reviews by the same authors that provide a detailed and comprehensive overview of current animal models of schizophrenia, treatment options and future directions for research.

GLOSSARY

Actin   One of the proteins, with myosin, that are important in the contraction of muscle fibres.

Afferent   Neuron that conveys sensory information to the central nervous system.

Agonist (muscle)   One of a group of muscles that act together to achieve a specific movement of a joint.

Agonist   Substance that binds to the same receptors as a neurotransmitter and has a similar effect on neuronal function as that neurotransmitter.

Albedo   The proportion of incident light that a surface reflects. Sometimes called reflectance.

Allele   An alternative form of a gene.

Allosteric modulator   A substance which indirectly influences neurotransmission by acting at a site distinct from the primary binding site to modify receptor structure.

Alpha activity   A pattern of brain electrical activity that occurs with a rhythm of 8–13 cycles per second. Indicates relaxed wakefulness with eyes closed.

Alpha motoneuron   The final stage in the motor pathway. Motoneurons have cell bodies in the spinal cord and their axons project to muscle fibres.

Amnesic   Lacking in memory.

Amygdala   Brain area within the temporal lobe; involved in pavlovian conditioning and emotional processing.

Anorexia   Eating disorder characterised by low body weight and eating disturbances that cause clinical impairment to health.

Antagonist   A substance that binds to a receptor but does not have any physiological effects.

Antagonist (muscle)   One of a group of muscles that act together to resist a specific movement.

Anterograde amnesia   Failure to form new memories after brain damage.

Antipsychotic   Medication used to treat schizophrenia or psychosis.

Anxiolytic   A medication used to treat anxiety.

Apoptosis   The process of programmed cell death in which cells self-destruct to remove unwanted cells.

Arcuate nucleus   A nucleus of the hypothalamus containing cells that are important for nutrient monitoring.

Aspiration   Sucking out of a region of the brain.

Associative LTP   LTP that depends upon the co-activation of two inputs, and strengthens both pathways.

Astrocyte   A star-shaped glial cell of the central nervous system that limits the exchange of substances between the blood and the brain.

Autonomic   Relating to the autonomic (involuntary) nervous system.

Axon   A projection that extends from the cell body of a neuron to the terminal endings and transmits the neural signal.

Basal ganglia   A collection of subcortical nuclei important for the control of movement.

Basilar membrane   Membrane in the cochlea of the inner ear that vibrates in response to a sound and is important in exciting the hair cells that act as auditory receptors.

Beta activity   Irregular, high frequency but low amplitude brain waves of around 13–30 cycles per second, associated with waking.

Binocular disparity   The difference in the positions of the two images of an object in the two eyes. Acts as a depth cue in binocular stereopsis.

Bioavailability   The degree to which a drug is available at sites of action after administration.

Blood brain barrier   A network of blood vessels and cells that limits the exchange of substances between the blood and the brain.

Body schema   The sense of our body's position in space.

Brainstem   A stalk-like part of the brain consisting of medulla oblongata, the midbrain, and the pons, which joins the brain to the spinal cord.

Cannon–Bard Theory   Theory that emotional feelings and physiological responses occur in parallel.

Cellular consolidation   Time-dependent stabilisation of memory within a brain area, taking place over minutes to hours.

Central nervous system   Part of the nervous system that consists of the brain and spinal cord.

Cerebellum   The portion of the brain between the cerebrum and the brainstem. It is important for learning and coordinating complex movements.

Cerebrum   The largest portion of the brain, which is divided into two hemispheres.

Change blindness   The inability, under some circumstances, to be unable to detect quite major changes in the visual scene.

Chromatin   Part of the nucleus of a cell (consisting of DNA and histone proteins) that makes up chromosomes.

Circadian rhythm   A daily rhythmic activity cycle exhibited by many organisms.

Cochlea   The main auditory sensory organ located in the inner ear.

Concordance rate   The extent to which individuals, typically twins, share a particular trait.

Conditioned emotional response   Fear responses resulting from **fear conditioning**.

Conditioned stimulus (CS)   A previously neutral stimulus that is conditioned during **pavlovian conditioning** to predict an outcome.

Critical periods   Specific stages in development during which systems and behaviours are shaped and moulded for life.

Cytoarchitecture   Structure and organisation of neurons.

Declarative memory   Conscious retention of information; includes **episodic** and **semantic memory**.

Delirium tremens   A psychotic condition typical of withdrawal in chronic alcoholics, involving tremors, hallucinations, anxiety, and disorientation.

Delta wave   A high amplitude pattern of brain electrical activity that occurs with a rhythm of 4 cycles per second and occurs especially in **slow wave sleep**.

Delusion   A symptom of psychosis that is a belief maintained despite contradictory evidence.

Dementia   An umbrella term describing symptoms of cognitive decline that may include memory loss and difficulties with thinking, problem-solving or language.

Dendrite   A projection that conducts the electrochemical stimulation received from other neural cells to the cell body of a neuron.

Dizygotic twins   Non-identical or fraternal twins where each twin is derived from two separately fertilised eggs.

Down-regulation   The process by which a cell decreases the quantity of a cellular component, such as a receptor, in response to an external variable.

Dyskinesia   An impairment in the ability to control movements.

Efferent   Neuron that conveys information from the central nervous system to an organ of response.

Electrolytic lesions   Damage caused by delivery of an electric current through a probe inserted into a region of the brain.

Electrophysiology   Recording of electrical activity from neurons.

Emotional facial paresis   Disorder involving the inability to produce unconscious emotional facial expressions.

Endocrine   Relating to hormonal function.

Endorphins   Naturally occurring peptides in the brain that bind to the same receptors as opiates.

Epigenetic   Relating to changes that alter the expression of genes, but not involving a change in the genetic sequence.

Episodic memory   Retention of information for personal life events.

Excitotoxic lesions   Damage caused by the delivery of a toxin into the brain that over-excites neurons to death.

Extensor   A muscle that acts to straighten a joint.

Extrafusal muscle fibre   The main contractile element making up skeletal muscles.

Fear conditioning pavlovian conditioning   Involving an aversive fearful outcome.

Fetal alcohol syndrome   A syndrome associated with excessive consumption of alcohol by the mother during pregnancy. Babies are characterised by poor growth, delayed development and characteristic facial features such as a small head, narrow eyes and a smooth area between the nose and the lips with a thin upper lip.

First pass effect   The reduction in the amount of drug reaching sites of action due to metabolism of orally administered drugs by enzymes in the stomach and liver.

Flexor   A muscle that acts to bend a joint.

Frequency spectrum   The pattern of frequencies making up a stimulus.

Gene   The part of a chromosome that is the blueprint for a protein.

Genome   The complete set of genes in an organism.

Genome-wide association studies (GWAS)   An examination of genetic variants to see if any variant is associated with a trait. The method involves assessing whether gene variations, called single nucleotide polymorphisms or SNPs, occur more frequently in people with a particular disease than in people without the disease.

Genotype   The genetic makeup of an organism which is a combination of alleles responsible for determining characteristics and traits of an organism.

Ghrelin   A hormone produced by cells lining the stomach that stimulates appetite.

Gyrus   A ridge on the surface of a cerebral hemisphere caused by the infolding of the cerebral cortex.

Half-life   The period of time required for the concentration or amount of drug in the body to be reduced by one-half. A measure of duration of drug action.

Hallucination   A false or distorted perceptual experience that occurs in the absence of a sensory stimulus but appears to be a real perception.

Haptics   The active exploration of the world through touch, sometimes called 'active touch'.

Hedonic   Pleasurable sensation.

Hertz   The name of the unit (cycles/second) in which frequency is measured.

Hippocampus   Brain area within the temporal lobe; involved in **declarative memory**.

Homeostasis   The process by which the body maintains a stable internal environment in response to deviations from that environment.

Iconic memory   Very short-lasting retention of visual information.

Implicit learning   Unconscious learning; includes **pavlovian** and **instrumental conditioning**.

Imprinting   Differential expression of a gene as a function of whether it was inherited from the male or the female parent. Either the maternal or the paternal version of the allele is silenced through the addition of methyl groups during egg or sperm formation.

In vitro   Carried out not in a living body (e.g. in brain slices).

In vivo   Carried out in a living body.

Incentive   A stimulus that induces action or motivates effort.

Instrumental conditioning   Learning that associates an action with an outcome.

Insulin   A hormone produced in the pancreas, which regulates the amount of glucose in the blood.

Intrafusal muscle fibre   A type of muscle fibre that contracts weakly and ensures that muscle spindles are at the correct length to detect muscle stretch.

Inverse agonist   Substance that binds to the same receptors as a neurotransmitter and has the opposite effect on neuronal function to that neurotransmitter.

James–Lange Theory   Theory that emotional feelings are dependent on physiological responses.

Kinaesthesis   The ability to sense the movements of our limbs and body.

Klüver–Bucy syndrome   Pattern of symptoms associated with damage to the temporal lobe; includes loss of fear.

Korsakoff's syndrome   A syndrome associated with excessive alcohol consumption that is caused by lack of thiamine (vitamin B1) and results in cognitive impairments.

Lateral inhibition   Inhibition of one neuron by a neuron responding to a neighbouring spatial position.

Leptin   A hormone produced by fat cells that signals amounts of fat stored by the body.

Lesions   Damage to the brain (usually experimentally-induced).

Lightness constancy   The phenomenon of perceiving surfaces to have consistent reflectance despite changes in their illumination.

Lightness contrast   The phenomenon through which the perceived lightness of a surface depends upon its background. A given reflectance appears lighter against a dark background than it does against a light background.

Linkage analysis   A method that investigates whether there is an association between easily identifiable pieces of DNA (genetic markers) and a trait of interest or disease. If the marker is present in all affected individuals then this suggests that a gene close to the marker region is involved in the trait/disorder.

Lobe   A subdivision of the cerebral cortex.

Long-term depression (LTD)   Persistent reduction of postsynaptic response.

Long-term memory (LTM)   Retention of information over a period of greater than 24 hours and up to a lifetime.

Long-term potentiation (LTP)   Persistent enhancement of postsynaptic response.

Memory extinction Reduction in pavlovian or instrumental memory expression when the **CS** or action is no longer associated with the outcome.

Memory reconsolidation Restabilisation of a reactivated memory trace.

Mirror neurons Neurons that are active both when a monkey performs an action and when it perceives the same action. Also found in people.

Mnemonic Relating to memory processing.

Monozygotic From a single fertilised egg; relates to identical twins.

Motor pool The set of spinal motoneurons that innervate a single muscle.

Motor unit The set of muscle fibres and the single motoneuron that innervates them.

Muscimol GABA receptor agonist.

Muscle spindle Sensory cell that signals stretching of a muscle.

Myelin A white fatty material (enclosing the axons of some neurons) that insulates the neurons and permits the rapid transmission of electrical signals along the axon.

Myosin One of the proteins, with actin, responsible for the contraction of muscle fibres.

Narcolepsy A neurological disorder that affects the control of sleep and wakefulness.

Necrosis Cell death due to damage or trauma to cells.

Neophobia Fear of new objects.

Neural tube A hollow tube-like structure running the length of the vertebrate embryo that eventually forms the brain and spinal cord.

Neurofibrillary tangles Aberrant aggregation of a neuronal protein, tau, especially the cerebral cortex and hippocampus, which occurs in Alzheimer's disease.

Neurogenesis The process by which new nerve cells are generated.

Neuromuscular junction A synapse between a motoneuron and a muscle fibre.

Neuropathic pain Pain that cannot be attributed to the normal firing of nociceptors.

Neurotoxic Damaging to neurons.

Neurotransmitter A chemical that is released by a neuron and travels across the synapse to bind to receptors on the post-synaptic terminal of another neuron to change the electrical activity of the target cell.

Neurulation The formation of the embryonic neural plate and its transformation into the neural tube.

Non-associative LTP LTP that is induced by activity in a single input pathway.

Non-declarative memory Unconscious memory; includes **pavlovian** and **instrumental conditioning**.

NSAIDs Non-steroidal anti-inflammatory drugs. Act peripherally to reduce swelling and pain.

Obesity Having a body mass index greater than $30 kg/m^2$.

Oligodendrocyte   Type of glial cell that produces myelin.

Operant conditioning   see **Instrumental conditioning**.

Opioid   Class of chemicals with similar effects to morphine.

Opponency   A theory of colour vision in which colours are arranged in antagonistic pairs, with yellow the opponent of blue and green the opponent of red.

Pavlovian (classical) conditioning   Learning that associates a stimulus with an outcome.

Peripheral nervous system   The part of the nervous system that is outside the central nervous system, made up of the somatic nervous system and the autonomic nervous system.

Phenotype   The observable physical or biochemical characteristics of an organism, determined by both genetic makeup and environmental influences.

Photoreceptor   The rods and cones, which are the visual receptors.

Physiological   Relating to bodily function.

Placebo effect   A positive response to an inactive treatment like a sugar pill.

Plaques   Abnormal clusters of protein fragments that accumulate between neurons in Alzheimer's disease.

Polymorphism   Term used to describe the naturally occurring multiple forms of a single gene that can exist in an individual or among a group of individuals.

Prediction error   Difference between what is predicted on the basis of prior learning and what actually occurs; essential to the **Rescorla–Wagner rule**.

Psychedelic drug   A psychoactive drug that induces hallucinations or altered sensory experiences.

Psychoactive drug   A drug that can produce a psychological effect.

Psychopharmacology   The study of the effects of drugs on brain and behaviour.

Quantitative trait locus (QTL) analysis   The statistical analysis and identification of stretches of DNA that are linked to the genes that underlie a particular trait.

Rapid eye movement (REM) sleep   A sleep phase characterised by eye movements, paralysis and a desynchronised EEG.

Receptive field   The region of a receptive surface, such as the skin or the retina, which, when stimulated, changes a cell's response.

Refinement   The process by which non-active synaptic connections are lost during development.

Reinforcer   A reward that acts as a positive outcome to engage **pavlovian** or **instrumental conditioning**.

REM behaviour disorder   A sleep disorder in which the sufferer lacks muscle paralysis during sleep and appears to physically act out vivid, often unpleasant dreams.

Rescorla–Wagner rule   Rule that determines how much is learned on a given training trial; depends on the **Prediction Error**.

Retinal ganglion cell   The output stage of the retina. The axons of retinal ganglion cells form the optic nerve.

Retrograde amnesia   Memory loss for information prior to brain damage.

Reuptake inhibitor   A drug that blocks the re-uptake of a neurotransmitter from the neuron that released it.

Rhodopsin   The visual pigment found in photoreceptors that can be bleached by light to produce a neural response.

Saccule   Organ of the inner ear that, together with the utricle, detects linear acceleration of the head; is important in balance.

Satiety   The inhibition of appetite.

Schachter–Singer theory   Theory that **physiological** responses activate emotions, but cognitive interpretation determines the emotion felt.

Semantic memory   Retention of factual information.

Semi-circular canal   The three semi-circular canals in the inner ear detect rotational acceleration of the head, important in balance.

Sensitisation   Process whereby repeated administration of a stimulus results in a progressively stronger response.

Sensory specific satiety   Decreased motivation to consume a specific food that has been eaten to satiety.

Short-term memory   Retention of information over a period of minutes to hours.

Simple cell   Type of cell in the visual cortex that responds to an appropriately oriented feature of an image that falls within its receptive field.

Single nucleotide polymorphisms (SNPs)   A variation in DNA sequence that occurs when a single nucleotide is altered.

Sleep paralysis   Temporary inability to move due to muscle paralysis either when falling asleep or wakening.

Slow wave sleep   Stages 3 and 4 of sleep.

Soma   The cell body.

Somnambulism   Sleep walking.

STM   see **Short-term memory**.

Subliminal   Below conscious threshold.

Sulcus   A shallow furrow on the surface of the brain.

Surface reflectance   The proportion of light falling upon a surface that it reflects. See also **albedo**.

Sympathetic nervous system   Part of the **autonomic** nervous system; involved in emotional **physiological** responses.

Synapse   The junction between two neurons where neurons communicate by chemical means.

Synaptic plasticity   Alteration in the strength of a synapse (i.e. the likelihood of the post-synaptic neuron being activated by presynaptic activity).

Synaptogenesis   The formation of synapses between neurons.

Synaptopathy   Dysfunction in synapse function.

Systems consolidation   Time-dependent transformation of memory, resulting in a change in the dependence upon different brain areas.

Tardive dyskinesia   A movement disorder that affects a person's ability to perform voluntary muscular movements, resulting from long term use of some antipsychotic medications.

TENS   Transcutaneous electrical nerve stimulation; electrical stimulation of the skin used to reduce pain.

Teratogen   An agent that causes malformation of an embryo or foetus.

Tetanic contraction   The smooth contraction of a muscle fibre that results when individual twitches fuse during rapid stimulation.

Tetrodotoxin   Toxin from the puffer fish that blocks sodium channels and thus prevents neuronal activity.

Therapeutic index   The ratio between the toxic dose and the *therapeutic dose* of a drug; a measure of drug safety.

Theta wave activity   A pattern of brain electrical activity that occurs with a rhythm of 3–7 cycles per second, associated with Stage 1 sleep.

Tolerance   Process whereby repeated administration of a stimulus results in a progressively weaker response. In the context of drug administration, more of a drug will be required to achieve the same response.

Tract   Bundles of neurons.

Transcription   The process of making a copy of genetic information stored in a DNA strand into a complementary strand of RNA.

Transgenic   An organism that has a segment of foreign DNA incorporated into their genome.

Translocation   Transfer of a chromosomal segment to a new position.

Ultradian cycle   A biorhythm having a period of less than 24 hours.

Unconditioned stimulus (US)   The outcome that drives learning in **pavlovian and instrumental conditioning**.

Urbach–Wiethe disease   Degenerative disease resulting in selective damage to the amygdala.

Utricle   Organ of the inner ear that, together with the saccule, detects linear acceleration of the head and is important in balance.

Ventromedial prefrontal cortex   Brain area within the prefrontal cortex; involved in **memory extinction** and emotional decision making.

Volitional facial paresis   Disorder involving the inability to move facial muscles voluntarily.

Withdrawal   State associated with the cessation of drug taking.

Working memory   Short-term store of information in an online state for current processing and use.

Zeitgeber   A stimulus or event that sets a biological clock.

REFERENCES

Abbott, C. R., Monteiro, M., Small, C. J., Sajedi, A., Smith, K. L., Parkinson, J. R., & Bloom, S. R. (2005). The inhibitory effects of peripheral administration of peptide YY 3–36 and glucagon-like peptide-1 on food intake are attenuated by ablation of the vagal–brainstem–hypothalamic pathway. *Brain Research*, *1044*(1), 127–31.

AbdelMalik, P., Husted, J., Chow, E. W., & Bassett, A. S. (2003). Childhood head injury and expression of schizophrenia in multiply affected families. *Archives of General Psychiatry*, *60*(3), 231.

Abel, E. L. (1971). Marihuana and memory: Acquisition or retrieval? *Science*, *173*(4001), 1038–40.

Abi-Dargham, A., Gil, R., Krystal, J., Baldwin, R. M., Seibyl, J. P., Bowers, M., & Laruelle, M. (1998). Increased striatal dopamine transmission in schizophrenia: Confirmation in a second cohort. *American Journal of Psychiatry*, *155*(6), 761–67.

Abi-Dargham, A., Rodenhiser, J., Printz, D., Zea-Ponce, Y., Gil, R., Kegeles, L. S., ... & Laruelle, M. (2000). Increased baseline occupancy of D2 receptors by dopamine in schizophrenia. *Proceedings of the National Academy of Sciences*, *97*(14), 8104–09.

Abood, M. E., & Martin, B. R. (1992). Neurobiology of marijuana abuse. *Trends in Pharmacological Sciences*, *13*, 201–6.

Adamantidis, A. R., Zhang, F., Aravanis, A. M., Deisseroth, K., & De Lecea, L. (2007). Neural substrates of awakening probed with optogenetic control of hypocretin neurons. *Nature*, *450*(7168), 420–4.

Adams, J., Hennessy-Priest, K., Ingimarsdottir, S., Sheeshka, J., Østbye, T., & White, M. (2009). Food advertising during children's television in Canada and the UK. *Archives of Disease in Childhood*, *94*(9), 658–62.

Adams, W., Kendell, R. E., Hare, E. H., & Munk-J, P. (1993). Epidemiological evidence that maternal influenza contributes to the aetiology of schizophrenia: An analysis of Scottish, English, and Danish data. *British Journal of Psychiatry*, *163*(4), 522–34.

Addy, P. H. (2012). Acute and post-acute behavioral and psychological effects of salvinorin A in humans. *Psychopharmacology*, *220*(1), 195–204.

Aglioti, S. M., Cesari, P., Romani, M., & Urgesi, C. (2008). Action anticipation and motor resonance in elite basketball players. *Nature Neuroscience, 11,* 1109–16.

Agurell, S., Halldin, M., Lindgren, J. E., Ohlsson, A., Widman, M., Gillespie, H., et al. (1986). Pharmacokinetics and metabolism of delta 1-tetrahydrocannabinol and other cannabinoids with emphasis on man. *Pharmacology Review*, *38*, 21–43.

Ahima, R. S., & Lazar, M. A. (2013). The health risk of obesity – better metrics imperative. *Science*, *341*(6148), 856–8.

Åkerstedt, T. (1979). Altered sleep/wake patterns and circadian rhythms: Laboratory and field studies of sympathoadrenomedullary and related variables. *Acta Physiologica Scandinavica, Supplementum*, *469*, 1.

Akimova, E., Lanzenberger, R., & Kasper, S. (2009). The serotonin-1A receptor in anxiety disorders. *Biological Psychiatry*, *66*(7), 627–35.

Albrecht, S., Ihmsen, H., Hering, W., Geisslinger, G., Dingemanse, J., Schwilden, H., & Schüttler, J. (1999). The effect of age on the pharmacokinetics and pharmacodynamics of midazolam. *Clinical Pharmacology & Therapeutics*, *65*(6), 630–39.

Aleman, A., Kahn, R. S., & Selten, J. P. (2003). Sex differences in the risk of schizophrenia: Evidence from meta-analysis. *Archives of General Psychiatry*, *60*(6), 565.

Allan, L. E., Petit, G. H., & Brundin, P. (2010). Cell transplantation in Parkinson's disease: Problems and perspectives. *Current Opinion in Neurology, 23*(4), 426–32.

Allebeck, P. (1989). Schizophrenia: a life-shortening disease. *Schizophrenia Bulletin*, *15*(1), 81.

Allen, N. C., Bagade, S., McQueen, M. B., Ioannidis, J. P., Kavvoura, F. K., Khoury, M. J., ... & Bertram, L. (2008). Systematic meta-analyses and field synopsis of genetic association studies in schizophrenia: The SzGene database. *Nature Genetics*, *40*(7), 827–34.

Alsene, K., Deckert, J., Sand, P., & de Wit, H. (2003). Association between A2a receptor gene polymorphisms and caffeine-induced anxiety. *Neuropsychopharmacology*, *28*(9), 1694–702.

Altar, C. A., Whitehead, R. E., Chen, R., Wörtwein, G., & Madsen, T. M. (2003). Effects of electroconvulsive seizures and antidepressant drugs on brain-derived neurotrophic factor protein in rat brain. *Biological Psychiatry*, *54*(7), 703–09.

Amaral, D. G., Price, J. L., Pitkänen, A., & Carmichael, S. T. (1992). Anatomical Organisation of the Primate Amygdaloid Complex, in Aggleton, J. P. (ed.), *The Amygdala: Neurobiological Aspects of Emotion, Memory and Mental Dysfunction*. New York: Wiley-Liss, pp. 1–66.

Amitai, N., Semenova, S., & Markou, A. (2007). Cognitive-disruptive effects of the psychotomimetic phencyclidine and attenuation by atypical antipsychotic medications in rats. *Psychopharmacology, 193*(4), 521–37.

Amorapanth, P., LeDoux, J. E., & Nader, K. (2000). Different lateral amygdala outputs mediate reactions and actions elicited by a fear-arousing stimulus. *Nature Neuroscience, 3*(1), 74–9.

Amsler, H. A., Teerenhovi, L., Barth, E., Harjula, K., & Vuopio, P. (1977). Agranulocytosis in patients treated with clozapine. *Acta Psychiatrica Scandinavica, 56*(4), 241–8.

Anand, B. K., & Brobeck, J. R. (1951). Hypothalamic control of food intake in rats and cats. *Yale Journal of Biology and Medicine, 24*(2), 123.

Ancoli-Israel, S., & Kripke, D. F. (1991). Prevalent sleep problems in the aged. *Biofeedback and Self-Regulation, 16*(4), 349–59.

Andréasson, S., Engström, A., Allebeck, P., & Rydberg, U. (1987). Cannabis and schizophrenia: A longitudinal study of Swedish conscripts. *The Lancet, 330*(8574), 1483–6.

Andrews, P. (1997). Cocaethylene toxicity. *Journal of Addictive Diseases, 16*(3), 75–84.

Anglada-Figueroa, D., & Quirk, G. J. (2005). Lesions of the basal amygdala block expression of conditioned fear but not extinction. *Journal of Neuroscience, 25*(42), 9680–5.

Antelman, S. M., Caggiula, A. R., Knopf, S., Kocan, D. J., & Edwards, D. J. (1992). Amphetamine or haloperidol 2 weeks earlier antagonized the plasma corticosterone response to amphetamine: Evidence for the stressful/foreign nature of drugs. *Psychopharmacology (Berl), 107*(2–3), 331–6.

Antoniadis, E. A., Winslow, J. T., Davis, M., & Amaral, D. G. (2007). Role of the primate amygdala in fear-potentiated startle: Effects of chronic lesions in the rhesus monkey. *Journal of Neuroscience, 27*(28), 7386–96.

Arbib, M.A. (2005). From monkey-like action recognition to human language: An evolutionary framework for neurolinguistics. *Behavioral & Brain Sciences, 28,* 105–67.

Arbib, M. A., & Rizzolatti, G. (1997). Neural expectations: A possible evolutionary path from manual skills to language. *Communication and Cognition, 29,* 393–423.

Arendt, D., & Nübler-Jung, K. (1996). Common ground plans in early brain development in mice and flies. *BioEssays, 18,* 255–9.

Ariyasu, H., Takaya, K., Tagami, T., Ogawa, Y., Hosoda, K., Akamizu, T., … & Nakao, K. (2001). Stomach is a major source of circulating ghrelin, and feeding state determines plasma ghrelin-like immunoreactivity levels in humans. *Journal of Clinical Endocrinology & Metabolism, 86*(10), 4753–8.

Arseneault, L., Cannon, M., Poulton, R., Murray, R., Caspi, A., & Moffitt, T. E. (2002). Cannabis use in adolescence and risk for adult psychosis: Longitudinal prospective study. *BMJ, 325*(7374), 1212–13.

Asakawa, A., Inui, A., Kaga, O., Yuzuriha, H., Nagata, T., Ueno, N., … & Kasuga, M. (2001). Ghrelin is an appetite-stimulatory signal from stomach with structural resemblance to motilin. *Gastroenterology, 120*(2), 337–45.

Aserinsky, E., & Kleitman, N. (1953). Regularly occurring periods of eye motility, and concomitant phenomena, during sleep. *Science, 118*(3062), 273–4.

Aston-Jones, G., & Bloom, F. E. (1981). Activity of norepinephrine-containing locus coeruleus neurons in behaving rats anticipates fluctuations in the sleep-waking cycle. *Journal of Neuroscience, 1*(8), 876–86.

Atack, J. R. (2010). Preclinical and clinical pharmacology of the GABAA receptor α5 subtype-selective inverse agonist α5IA. *Pharmacology & Therapeutics, 125*(1), 11–26.

Atha, M.J., & Blanchard, S. (1997). *Regular Users. Self-Reported Drug Consumption Patterns and Attitudes Towards Drugs Among 1333 Regular Cannabis Users*. Wigan: Independent Drug Monitoring Unit.

Avena, N. M., Rada, P., & Hoebel, B. G. (2008a). Evidence for sugar addiction: Behavioral and neurochemical effects of intermittent, excessive sugar intake. *Neuroscience & Biobehavioral Reviews, 32*(1), 20–39.

Avena, N. M., Bocarsly, M. E., Rada, P., Kim, A., & Hoebel, B. G. (2008b). After daily bingeing on a sucrose solution, food deprivation induces anxiety and accumbens dopamine/acetylcholine imbalance. *Physiology & Behavior, 94*(3), 309–15.

Avramopoulos, D. (2009). Genetics of Alzheimer's disease: Recent advances. *Genome Medicine, 1*(3), 34.

Ayas, N. T., White, D. P., Al-Delaimy, W. K., Manson, J. E., Stampfer, M. J., Speizer, F. E., … & Hu, F. B. (2003). A prospective study of self-reported sleep duration and incident diabetes in women. *Diabetes Care, 26*(2), 380–4.

Azevedo, F. A., Carvalho, L. R., Grinberg, L. T., Farfel, J. M., Ferretti, R. E., Leite, R. E., Jacob Filho, W., Lent, R. and Herculano-Houzel, S. (2009). Equal numbers of neuronal and nonneuronal cells make the human brain an isometrically scaled-up primate brain. *Journal of Comparative Neurology, 513*(5), 532–41.

Babor, T. F., Berglas, S., Mendelson, J. H., Ellingboe, J., & Miller, K. (1983). Alcohol, affect, and the disinhibition of verbal behavior. *Psychopharmacology*, *80*(1), 53–60.

Bach, M. E., Simpson, E. H., Kahn, L., Marshall, J. J., Kandel, E. R., & Kellendonk, C. (2008). Transient and selective overexpression of D2 receptors in the striatum causes persistent deficits in conditional associative learning. *Proceedings of the National Academy of Sciences*, *105*(41), 16027–32.

Baeyens, F., Vansteenwegen, D. E. B., De Houwer, J. A. N., & Crombez, G. (1996). Observational conditioning of food valence in humans. *Appetite*, *27*(3), 235–50.

Bailey, D. G., Arnold, J. M. O., & Spence, J. D. (1994). Grapefruit juice and drugs. *Clinical Pharmacokinetics*, *26*(2), 91–8.

Bailey, P. L., Lu, J. K., Pace, N. L., Orr, J. A., White, J. L., Hamber, E. A., & Rollins, D. E. (2000). Effects of intrathecal morphine on the ventilatory response to hypoxia. *New England Journal of Medicine*, *343*(17), 1228–34.

Baker, D. G., West, S. A., Nicholson, W. E., Ekhator, N. N., Kasckow, J. W., Hill, K. K., … Geracioti, T. D., Jr. (1999). Serial CSF corticotropin-releasing hormone levels and adrenocortical activity in combat veterans with posttraumatic stress disorder. *American Journal of Psychiatry*, *156*(4), 585–8.

Bakker, P. R., van Harten, P. N., & van Os, J. (2006). Antipsychotic-induced tardive dyskinesia and the Ser9Gly polymorphism in the DRD3 gene: A meta analysis. *Schizophrenia Research*, *83*(2), 185–92.

Balleine, B. W., & Killcross, S. (2006). Parallel incentive processing: An integrated view of amygdala function. *Trends in Neuroscience*, 29(5), 272–9.

Baran, B., Pace-Schott, E. F., Ericson, C., & Spencer, R. M. (2012). Processing of emotional reactivity and emotional memory over sleep. *Journal of Neuroscience*, *32*(3), 1035–42.

Barch, D. M., Carter, C. S., Braver, T. S., Sabb, F. W., MacDonald, A., III, Noll, D. C., & Cohen, J. D. (2001). Selective deficits in prefrontal cortex function in medication-naive patients with schizophrenia. *Archives of General Psychiatry*, *58*(3), 280.

Barense, M. D., Bussey, T. J., Lee, A. C., Rogers, T. T., Davies, R. R., Saksida, L. M., & Graham, K. S. (2005). Functional specialization in the human medial temporal lobe. *Journal of Neuroscience*, *25*(44), 10239–46.

Barnes, J. (2013). *Essential Biological Psychology*. London: SAGE.

Barney, L. J., Griffiths, K. M., Christensen, H., & Jorm, A. F. (2009). Exploring the nature of stigmatising beliefs about depression and help-seeking: Implications for reducing stigma. *BMC Public Health*, *9*(1), 61.

Barr, C. S., & Goldman, D. (2006). Non-human primate models of inheritance vulnerability to alcohol use disorders. *Addiction Biology*, *11*(3–4), 374–85.

Barrett, D., Shumake, J., Jones, D., & Gonzalez-Lima, F. (2003). Metabolic mapping of mouse brain activity after extinction of a conditioned emotional response. *Journal of Neuroscience*, *23*(13), 5740–49.

Baskin, D. G., Figlewicz Lattemann, D., Seeley, R. J., Woods, S. C., Porte, D., Jr, & Schwartz, M. W. (1999). Insulin and leptin: Dual adiposity signals to the brain for the regulation of food intake and body weight. *Brain Research*, *848*(1), 114–23.

Basner, M., Fomberstein, K. M., Razavi, F. M., Banks, S., William, J. H., Rosa, R. R., & Dinges, D. F. (2007). American time use survey: Sleep time and its relationship to waking activities. *Sleep*, *30*(9), 1085.

Battaglia, G., Brooks, B. P., Kulsakdinun, C., & De Souza, E. B. (1988). Pharmacologic profile of MDMA (3,4-methylenedioxymethamphetamine) at various brain recognition sites. *European Journal of Pharmacology*, *149*(1), 159–63.

Batterink, L., Yokum, S., & Stice, E. (2010). Body mass correlates inversely with inhibitory control in response to food among adolescent girls: An fMRI study. *Neuroimage*, *52*(4), 1696–703.

Bauer, E. P., Schafe, G. E., & LeDoux, J. E. (2002). NMDA receptors and L-type voltage-gated calcium channels contribute to long-term potentiation and different components of fear memory formation in the lateral amygdala. *Journal of Neuroscience*, *22*(12), 5239–49.

Bayer, L., Eggermann, E., Serafin, M., Saint-Mleux, B., Machard, D., Jones, B., & Mühlethaler, M. (2001). Orexins (hypocretins) directly excite tuberomammillary neurons. *European Journal of Neuroscience*, *14*(9), 1571–5.

Baylen, C. A., & Rosenberg, H. (2006). A review of the acute subjective effects of MDMA/ecstasy. *Addiction*, *101*(7), 933–47.

Beal, J. E., Olson, R., Lefkowitz, L., Laubenstein, L., Bellman, P., Yangco, B., & Shepard, K. V. (1997). Long-term efficacy and safety of dronabinol for acquired immunodeficiency syndrome-associated anorexia. *Journal of Pain and Symptom Management*, *14*(1), 7–14.

Bechara, A., & Damasio, H. (2002). Decision-making and addiction (part I): Impaired activation of somatic states in substance dependent individuals when pondering decisions with negative future consequences. *Neuropsychologia*, *40*(10), 1675–89.

Bechara, A., Damasio, A. R., Damasio, H., & Anderson, S. W. (1994). Insensitivity to future consequences following damage to human prefrontal cortex. *Cognition*, *50*(1–3), 7–15.

Bechara, A., Tranel, D., Damasio, H., Adolphs, R., Rockland, C., & Damasio, A. R. (1995). Double dissociation of conditioning and declarative knowledge relative to the amygdala and hippocampus in humans. *Science, 269*(5227), 1115–18.

Bechara, A., Damasio, H., Damasio, A. R., & Lee, G. P. (1999). Different contributions of the human amygdala and ventromedial prefrontal cortex to decision-making. *Journal of Neuroscience, 19*(13), 5473–81.

Bechara, A., Damasio, H., Tranel, D., & Damasio, A. R. (1997). Deciding advantageously before knowing the advantageous strategy. *Science, 275*(5304), 1293–5.

Bechara, A., Damasio, H., Tranel, D., & Damasio, A. R. (2005). The Iowa Gambling Task and the somatic marker hypothesis: Some questions and answers. *Trends in Cognitive Sciences, 9*(4), 159–162.

Becker, R. C., Brobert, G. P., Johansson, S., Jick, S. S., & Meier, C. R. (2011). Risk of incident depression in patients with Parkinson disease in the UK. *European Journal of Neurology, 18*(3), 448–53.

Bell, C., Abrams, J., & Nutt, D. (2001). Tryptophan depletion and its implications for psychiatry. *British Journal of Psychiatry, 178*(5), 399–405.

Bellisle, F., Dalix, A. M., & Slama, G. (2004). Non food-related environmental stimuli induce increased meal intake in healthy women: Comparison of television viewing versus listening to a recorded story in laboratory settings. *Appetite, 43*(2), 175–80.

Benedetti, F., Mayberg, H. S., Wager, T. D., Stohler, C. S., & Zubieta, J. K. (2005). Neurobiological mechanisms of the placebo effect. *Journal of Neuroscience, 25*(45), 10390–402.

Benedetti, F., Carlino, E., & Pollo, A. (2011). How placebos change the patient's brain. *Neuropsychopharmacology, 36*(1), 339–54.

Benoit, S. C., Clegg, D. J., Seeley, R. J., & Woods, S. C. (2004). Insulin and leptin as adiposity signals. *Recent Progress in Hormone Research, 59*(1), 267–85.

Benowitz, N. L. (1996). Pharmacology of nicotine: Addiction and therapeutics. *Annual Review of Pharmacology and Toxicology, 36*(1), 597–613.

Benson, D. F., & Blumer, D. (1975). Personality changes with frontal and temporal lobe lesions, in Blumer, B. D. F., & Blumer, D. (eds), *Psychiatric Aspects of Neurological Disease*. New York: Grune and Stratton.

Berns, G. S., McClure, S. M., Pagnoni, G., & Montague, P. R. (2001). Predictability modulates human brain response to reward. *Journal of Neuroscience, 21*(8), 2793–8.

Berridge, C. W., & Waterhouse, B. D. (2003). The locus coeruleus–noradrenergic system: Modulation of behavioral state and state-dependent cognitive processes. *Brain Research Reviews, 42*(1), 33–84.

Berridge, K. C. (1996). Food reward: Brain substrates of wanting and liking. *Neuroscience & Biobehavioral Reviews, 20*(1), 1–25.

Berridge, K. C. (2003). Pleasures of the brain. *Brain and Cognition, 52*(1), 106–28.

Berridge, K. C. (2004). Motivation concepts in behavioral neuroscience. *Physiology & Behavior, 81*(2), 179–209.

Berridge, K. C., Ho, C. Y., Richard, J. M., & DiFeliceantonio, A. G. (2010). The tempted brain eats: Pleasure and desire circuits in obesity and eating disorders. *Brain Research, 1350*, 43–64.

Berridge, V. (1977). Opium and the historical perspective. *The Lancet, 310*(8028), 78–80.

Berthoud, H. R. (2011). Metabolic and hedonic drives in the neural control of appetite: Who is the boss? *Current Opinion in Neurobiology, 21*(6), 888–96.

Bertilsson, L., Dahl, M. L., Dalén, P., & Al-Shurbaji, A. (2002). Molecular genetics of CYP2D6: Clinical relevance with focus on psychotropic drugs. *British Journal of Clinical Pharmacology, 53*(2), 111–22.

Bilder, R. M. (1997). Neurocognitive impairment in schizophrenia and how it affects treatment options. *Canadian Journal of Psychiatry, 42*(3), 255–64.

Bilder, R. M., Reiter, G., Bates, J., Lencz, T., Szeszko, P., Goldman, R. S., ... & Kane, J. M. (2006). Cognitive development in schizophrenia: Follow-back from the first episode. *Journal of Clinical and Experimental Neuropsychology, 28*(2), 270–82.

Bin, Y. S., Marshall, N. S., & Glozier, N. (2012). Secular trends in adult sleep duration: A systematic review. *Sleep Medicine Reviews, 16*(3), 223–30.

Birak, K. S., Terry, P., & Higgs, S. (2010). Effect of cues associated with an alcoholic beverage on executive function. *Journal of Studies on Alcohol and Drugs, 71*(4), 562.

Birak, K. S., Higgs, S., & Terry, P. (2011). Conditioned tolerance to the effects of alcohol on inhibitory control in humans. *Alcohol and Alcoholism, 46*(6), 686–93.

Birch, L. L. (1990). Development of food acceptance patterns. *Developmental Psychology, 26*(4), 515.

Bird, T. D., Jarvik, G. P., & Wood, N. W. (2001). Genetic association studies: Genes in search of diseases. *Neurology, 57*, 1153–4.

Birmaher, B., Ryan, N. D., Williamson, D. E., Brent, D. A., Kaufman, J., Dahl, R. E., ... & Nelson, B. (1996). Childhood and adolescent depression: A review of the past 10 years. Part I. *Journal of the American Academy of Child & Adolescent Psychiatry, 35*(11), 1427–39.

Blair, P. S., Humphreys, J. S., Gringras, P., Taheri, S., Scott, N., Emond, A., ... & Fleming, P. J. (2012). Childhood sleep duration and associated demographic characteristics in an English cohort. *Sleep, 35*(3), 353.

Blakemore, S. J. (2008). The social brain in adolescence. *Nature Reviews Neuroscience, 9*(4), 267–77.

Bliss, T. V., & Lømo, T. (1973). Long-lasting potentiation of synaptic transmission in the dentate area of the anaesthetized rabbit following stimulation of the perforant path. *Journal of Physiology, 232*(2), 331–56.

Blundell, J. E., & Finlayson, G. (2011). Food addiction not helpful: The hedonic component –implicit wanting – is important. *Addiction, 106*(7), 1216–18.

Blundell, J. E., & Latham, C. J. (1979). Serotonergic influences on food intake: Effect of 5-hydroxytryptophan on parameters of feeding behaviour in deprived and free-feeding rats. *Pharmacology Biochemistry and Behavior, 11*(4), 431–7.

Boggiano, M. M., & Chandler, P. C. (2006). Binge eating in rats produced by combining dieting with stress. *Current Protocols in Neuroscience*, 9–23.

Boissard, R., Gervasoni, D., Schmidt, M. H., Barbagli, B., Fort, P., & Luppi, P. H. (2002). The rat ponto-medullary network responsible for paradoxical sleep onset and maintenance: A combined microinjection and functional neuroanatomical study. *European Journal of Neuroscience, 16*(10), 1959–73.

Bolla, K. I., Eldreth, D. A., London, E. D., Kiehl, K. A., Mouratidis, M., Contoreggi, C., ... Ernst, M. (2003). Orbitofrontal cortex dysfunction in abstinent cocaine abusers performing a decision-making task. *Neuroimage, 19*(3), 1085–94.

Booth, D. A., Lee, M., & McAleavey, C. (1976). Acquired sensory control of satiation in man. *British Journal of Psychology, 67*(2), 137–47.

Borbely, A. A., & Achermann, P. (1999). Sleep homeostasis and models of sleep regulation. *Journal of Biological Rhythms, 14*(6), 559–70.

Borbely, A. A., & Tobler, I. (1985). Homeostatic and circadian principles in sleep regulation in the rat. In McGinty, D. J., Drucker-Colin, R., Morrison, A., Parmeggiani, L. (eds), *Brain Mechanisms of Sleep*. New York: Raven Press, pp. 35–44.

Bostwick, J. M., & Pankratz, V. S. (2000). Affective disorders and suicide risk: A reexamination. *American Journal of Psychiatry, 157*(12), 1925–32.

Bourgeois, J. P., Goldman-Rakic, P. S., & Rakic, P. (1994). Synaptogenesis in the prefrontal cortex of rhesus monkeys. *Cerebral Cortex, 4*(1), 78–96.

Bourgeron, T. (2009). A synaptic trek to autism. *Current Opinion in Neurobiology 19*, 231–4.

Braak, H., Del Tredici, K., Rüb, U., de Vos, R. A. I., Jansen Steur, E. N. H., & Braak, E. (2003). Staging of brain pathology related to sporadic Parkinson's disease. *Neurobiology of Aging, 24*, 197–211.

Bradley, R. G., Binder, E. B., Epstein, M. P., Tang, Y., Nair, H. P., Liu, W., ... & Ressler, K. J. (2008). Influence of child abuse on adult depression: Moderation by the corticotropin-releasing hormone receptor gene. *Archives of General Psychiatry, 65*(2), 190.

Brandon, N. J., Millar, J. K., Korth, C., Sive, H., Singh K. K. and Sawa, A. (2009). Understanding the role of DISC1 in psychiatric disease and during normal development. *Journal of Neuroscience, 29*(41), 12768–75.

Branthwaite, A., & Cooper, P. (1981). Analgesic effects of branding in treatment of headaches. *British Medical Journal (Clinical Research edition), 282*(6276), 1576.

Breier, A., Schreiber, J. L., Dyer, J., & Pickar, D. (1991). National Institute of Mental Health longitudinal study of chronic schizophrenia: Prognosis and predictors of outcome. *Archives of General Psychiatry, 48*(3), 239.

Bremner, J. D., Randall, P., Scott, T. M., Bronen, R. A., Seibyl, J. P., Southwick, S. M., ... Innis, R. B. (1995). MRI-based measurement of hippocampal volume in patients with combat-related posttraumatic stress disorder. *American Journal of Psychiatry, 152*(7), 973–81.

Brody, A. L., Mandelkern, M. A., London, E. D., Olmstead, R. E., Farahi, J., Scheibal, D., & Mukhin, A. G. (2006). Cigarette smoking saturates brain {alpha} 4beta2 nicotinic acetylcholine receptors. *Archives of General Psychiatry, 63*(8), 907.

Brooks, D. J. (2004). Neuroimaging in Parkinson's Disease. *NeuroRX, 1(2),* 243–54.

Brooks, S. J., Cedernaes, J., & Schiöth, H. B. (2013). Increased prefrontal and parahippocampal activation with reduced dorsolateral prefrontal and insular cortex activation to food images in obesity: A meta-analysis of fMRI studies. *PloS ONE, 8*(4), e60393.

Brower, M. C., & Price, B. H. (2001). Neuropsychiatry of frontal lobe dysfunction in violent and criminal behaviour: A critical review. *Journal of Neurology, Neurosurgery and Psychiatry, 71*(6), 720–6.

Brown, R. E., Sergeeva, O. A., Eriksson, K. S., & Haas, H. L. (2002). Convergent excitation of dorsal raphe serotonin neurons by multiple arousal systems (orexin/hypocretin, histamine and noradrenaline). *Journal of Neuroscience, 22*(20), 8850–9.

Brownell, K. D., & Frieden, T. R. (2009). Ounces of prevention – The public policy case for taxes on sugared beverages. *New England Journal of Medicine, 360*(18), 1805–08.

Bruch, H. (1962). Perceptual and conceptual disturbances in anorexia nervosa. *Obstetrical & Gynecological Survey, 17*(5), 730–2.

Brunet, A., Orr, S. P., Tremblay, J., Robertson, K., Nader, K., & Pitman, R. K. (2008). Effect of post-retrieval propranolol on psychophysiologic responding during subsequent script-driven traumatic imagery in post-traumatic stress disorder. *Journal of Psychiatric Research, 42*(6), 503–6.

Brunet, A., Ashbaugh, A. R., Saumier, D., Nelson, M., Pitman, R. K., Tremblay, J., … Birmes, P. (2011). Does reconsolidation occur in humans? A reply. *Frontiers in Behavioral Neuroscience, 5*, 74.

Brunet, A., Poundja, J., Tremblay, J., Bui, E., Thomas, E., Orr, S. P., … Pitman, R. K. (2011). Trauma reactivation under the influence of propranolol decreases posttraumatic stress symptoms and disorder: 3 open-label trials. *Journal of Clinical Psychopharmacology, 31*(4), 547–50.

Brunstrom, J. M., Shakeshaft, N. G., & Scott-Samuel, N. E. (2008). Measuring 'expected satiety' in a range of common foods using a method of constant stimuli. *Appetite, 51*(3), 604–14.

Bryant, P. A., Trinder, J., & Curtis, N. (2004). Sick and tired: Does sleep have a vital role in the immune system? *Nature Reviews Immunology, 4*(6), 457–467.

Büchel, C., Morris, J., Dolan, R. J., & Friston, K. J. (1998). Brain systems mediating aversive conditioning: An event-related fMRI study. *Neuron, 20*(5), 947–57.

Buchert, R., Thomasius, R., Wilke, F., Petersen, K., Nebeling, B., Obrocki, J., & Clausen, M. (2004). A voxel-based PET investigation of the long-term effects of 'ecstasy' consumption on brain serotonin transporters. *American Journal of Psychiatry, 161*(7), 1181–9.

Buchsbaum, M. S., & Hazlett, E. A. (1998). Positron emission tomography studies of abnormal glucose metabolism in schizophrenia. *Schizophrenia Bulletin, 24*(3), 343–64.

Bulik, C. M., & Tozzi, F. (2004). Genetics in eating disorders: State of the science. *CNS Spectrums, 9*, 511–15.

Bullock, R. (2004). Future directions in the treatment of Alzheimer's disease. *Expert Opinions on Investigational Drugs, 13*, 303–14.

Bullock, W. M., Cardon, K., Bustillo, J., Roberts, R. C., & Perrone-Bizzozero, N. I. (2008). Altered expression of genes involved in GABAergic transmission and neuromodulation of granule cell activity in the cerebellum of schizophrenia patients. *American Journal of Psychiatry, 165*, 1594–603.

Burgos-Robles, A., Vidal-Gonzalez, I., & Quirk, G. J. (2009). Sustained conditioned responses in prelimbic prefrontal neurons are correlated with fear expression and extinction failure. *Journal of Neuroscience, 29*(26), 8474–82.

Buschert, V., Bokde, A. L. W. & Hampel, H. (2010). Cognitive intervention in Alzheimer disease. *Nature Reviews Neurology, 6*, 508–17.

Bushey, D., Tononi, G., & Cirelli, C. (2011). Sleep and synaptic homeostasis: Structural evidence in Drosophila. *Science, 332*(6037), 1576–81.

Buysse, D. J., Frank, E., Lowe, K. K., Cherry, C. R., & Kupfer, D. J. (1997). Electroencephalographic sleep correlates of episode and vulnerability to recurrence in depression. *Biological Psychiatry, 41*(4), 406–18.

Cabanac, M. (1971). Physiological role of pleasure. *Science, 173*(4002), 1103–7.

Caggiula, A. R., Donny, E. C., White, A. R., Chaudhri, N., Booth, S., Gharib, M. A., & Sved, A. F. (2001). Cue dependency of nicotine self-administration and smoking. *Pharmacology Biochemistry and Behavior, 70*(4), 515–30.

Cahill, L., Prins, B., Weber, M., & McGaugh, J. L. (1994). Beta-adrenergic activation and memory for emotional events. *Nature, 371*(6499), 702–4.

Calvo-Merino, B., Glaser, D.E., Grezes, J., Passingham, R.E., & Haggard, P. (2005). Action observation and acquired motor skills: An fMRI study with expert dancers. *Cerebral Cortex, 15*, 1243–9.

Calvo-Merino, B., Grezes, J., Glaser, D.E., Passingham, R.E., & Haggard, P. (2006). Seeing or doing? Influence of visual and motor familiarity in action observation. *Current Biology, 16*, 1905–10.

Campeau, S., & Davis, M. (1995). Involvement of the central nucleus and basolateral complex of the amygdala in fear conditioning measured with fear-potentiated startle in rats trained concurrently with auditory and visual conditioned-stimuli. *Journal of Neuroscience, 15*(3), 2301–11.

Cannon, W. B. (1927). The James–Lange theory of emotions: A critical examination and an alternative theory. *American Journal of Psychology, 39*(1), 106–24.

Cannon, W. B. (1932). *The Wisdom of the Body.* New York: Norton.

Cano, G., Mochizuki, T., & Saper, C. B. (2008). Neural circuitry of stress-induced insomnia in rats. *Journal of Neuroscience, 28*(40), 10167–84.

Cantor-Graae, E., & Selten, J. P. (2005). Schizophrenia and migration: A meta-analysis and review. *American Journal of Psychiatry, 162*(1), 12–24.

Carelli, R. M., Ijames, S. G., & Crumling, A. J. (2000). Evidence that separate neural circuits in the nucleus accumbens encode cocaine versus 'natural' (water and food) reward. *Journal of Neuroscience, 20*(11), 4255–66.

Carhart-Harris, R. L., Erritzoe, D., Williams, T., Stone, J. M., Reed, L. J., Colasanti, A., & Nutt, D. J. (2012). Neural correlates of the psychedelic state as determined by fMRI studies with psilocybin. *Proceedings of the National Academy of Sciences, 109*(6), 2138–43.

Carlezon Jr, W. A., Duman, R. S., & Nestler, E. J. (2005). The many faces of CREB. *Trends in Neurosciences, 28*(8), 436–45.

Carlsson, A. (1977). Does dopamine play a role in schizophrenia? *Psychological Medicine, 7*(4), 583–97.

Carroll, B. J., Cassidy, F., Naftolowitz, D., Tatham, N. E., Wilson, W. H., Iranmanesh, A., ... & Veldhuis, J. D. (2007). Pathophysiology of hypercortisolism in depression. *Acta Psychiatrica Scandinavica, 115*(s433), 90–103.

Carroll, M. E., & Stotz, D. C. (1983). Oral d-amphetamine and ketamine self-administration by rhesus monkeys: Effects of food deprivation. *Journal of Pharmacology and Experimental Therapeutics, 227*(1), 28–34.

Carroll, M. E., Roth, M. E., Voeller, R. K., & Nguyen, P. D. (2000). Acquisition of oral phencyclidine self-administration in rhesus monkeys: Effect of sex. *Psychopharmacology, 149*(4), 401–8.

Carter, M. E., Adamantidis, A., Ohtsu, H., Deisseroth, K., & de Lecea, L. (2009). Sleep homeostasis modulates hypocretin-mediated sleep-to-wake transitions. *Journal of Neuroscience, 29*(35), 10939–49.

Caspi, A., Sugden, K., Moffitt, T. E., Taylor, A., Craig, I. W., Harrington, H., ... & Poulton, R. (2003). Influence of life stress on depression: Moderation by a polymorphism in the 5-HTT gene. *Science Signaling, 301*(5631), 386.

Caspi, A., Moffitt, T. E., Cannon, M., McClay, J., Murray, R., Harrington, H., ... & Craig, I. W. (2005). Moderation of the effect of adolescent-onset cannabis use on adult psychosis by a functional polymorphism in the catechol-O-methyltransferase gene: Longitudinal evidence of a gene X environment interaction. *Biological psychiatry, 57*(10), 1117–27.

Castrén, E. (2005). Is mood chemistry? *Nature Reviews Neuroscience, 6*(3), 241–6.

Catmur, C., Gillmeister, H., Bird, G., Liepelt, R., Brass, M., & Heyes, C. (2008). Through the looking glass: Counter-mirror activation following incompatible sensorimotor learning. *European Journal of Neuroscience, 28,* 1208–15.

Chait, L. D., & Johanson, C. E. (1988). Discriminative stimulus effects of caffeine and benzphetamine in amphetamine-trained volunteers. *Psychopharmacology, 96*(3), 302–8.

Chaput, J. P., Despres, J. P., Bouchard, C., & Tremblay, A. (2011). Longer sleep duration associates with lower adiposity gain in adult short sleepers. *International Journal of Obesity, 36*(5), 752–6.

Charney, D. S., Heninger, G. R., & Jatlow, P. I. (1985). Increased anxiogenic effects of caffeine in panic disorders. *Archives of General Psychiatry, 42*(3), 233.

Chatzitheochari, S., & Arber, S. (2009). Lack of sleep, work and the long hours culture: Evidence from the UK Time Use Survey. *Work, Employment & Society, 23*(1), 30–48.

Chaudhuri, K. R., & Schapira, A. H. (2009). Non-motor symptoms of Parkinson's disease: Dopaminergic pathophysiology and treatment. *Lancet Neurology, 8*(5), 464–74.

Chee, M. W., & Chuah, L. Y. (2008). Functional neuroimaging insights into how sleep and sleep deprivation affect memory and cognition. *Current Opinion in Neurology, 21*(4), 417–23.

Chen, J. F., Xu, K., Petzer, J. P., Staal, R., Xu, Y. H., Beilstein, M., ... & Schwarzschild, M. A. (2001). Neuroprotection by caffeine and A (2A) adenosine receptor inactivation in a model of Parkinson's disease. *Journal of Neuroscience, 21*(10), 143.

Chevaleyre, V., & Castillo, P. E. (2004). Endocannabinoid-mediated metaplasticity in the hippocampus. *Neuron, 43,* 871–81.

Chiara, G. D., & North, R. A. (1992). Neurobiology of opiate abuse. *Trends in Pharmacological Sciences, 13,* 185–93

Childress, A. -R., Hole, A. V., Ehrman, R. N., Robbins, S. J., McLellan, A. T., & O'Brien, C. P. (1993). Cue reactivity and cue reactivity interventions in drug dependence. *NIDA Research Monograph, 137,* 73.

Childress, A. R., Mozley, P. D., McElgin, W., Fitzgerald, J., Reivich, M., & O'Brien, C. P. (1999). Limbic activation during cue-induced cocaine craving. *American Journal of Psychiatry, 156*(1), 11–18.

Childs, E., & de Wit, H. (2006). Subjective, behavioral, and physiological effects of acute caffeine in light, nondependent caffeine users. *Psychopharmacology, 185*(4), 514–23.

Chou, T. C., Scammell, T. E., Gooley, J. J., Gaus, S. E., Saper, C. B., & Lu, J. (2003). Critical role of dorsomedial hypothalamic nucleus in a wide range of behavioral circadian rhythms. *Journal of Neuroscience, 23*(33), 10691–702.

Cipolotti, L., Shallice, T., Chan, D., Fox, N., Scahill, R., Harrison, G., & Rudge, P. (2001). Long-term retrograde amnesia: The crucial role of the hippocampus. *Neuropsychologia, 39*(2), 151–72.

Cirelli, C., & Tononi, G. (2008). Is sleep essential? *PLoS Biology, 6*(8), e216.

Clark, R. E., Broadbent, N. J., & Squire, L. R. (2007). The hippocampus and spatial memory: Findings with a novel modification of the water maze. *Journal of Neuroscience, 27*(25), 6647–54.

Clarke, M. C., Harley, M., & Cannon, M. (2006). The role of obstetric events in schizophrenia. *Schizophrenia Bulletin, 32*(1), 3–8.

Clarren, S. K., & Smith, D. W. (1978). The fetal alcohol syndrome. *New England Journal of Medicine,* 298, 1063–7.

Colantuoni, C., Schwenker, J., McCarthy, J., Rada, P., Ladenheim, B., Cadet, J. L., ... & Hoebel, B. G. (2001). Excessive sugar intake alters binding to dopamine and mu-opioid receptors in the brain. *Neuroreport, 12*(16), 3549–52.

Colantuoni, C., Rada, P., McCarthy, J., Patten, C., Avena, N. M., Chadeayne, A., & Hoebel, B. G. (2002). Evidence that intermittent, excessive sugar intake causes endogenous opioid dependence. *Obesity Research, 10*(6), 478–88.

Collier, G. H. (1985). Satiety: An ecological perspective. *Brain Research Bulletin, 14*(6), 693–700.

Collishaw, S., Maughan, B., Natarajan, L., & Pickles, A. (2010). Trends in adolescent emotional problems in England: A comparison of two national cohorts twenty years apart. *Journal of Child Psychology and Psychiatry, 51*(8), 885–94.

Colloca, L., & Benedetti, F. (2009). Placebo analgesia induced by social observational learning. *Pain, 144*(1), 28–34.

Cone, R. D., Cowley, M. A., Butler, A. A., Fan, W., Marks, D. L., & Low, M. J. (2001). The arcuate nucleus as a conduit for diverse signals relevant to energy homeostasis. *International Journal of Obesity and Related Metabolic Disorders, 25,* S63–7.

Conrad, C. D., LeDoux, J. E., Magarinos, A. M., & McEwen, B. S. (1999). Repeated restraint stress facilitates fear conditioning independently of causing hippocampal CA3 dendritic atrophy. *Behavioural Neuroscience, 113*(5), 902–13.

Cook, T. A., Luczak, S. E., Shea, S. H., Ehlers, C. L., Carr, L. G., & Wall, T. L. (2005). Associations of ALDH2 and ADH1B genotypes with response to alcohol in Asian Americans. *Journal of Studies on Alcohol and Drugs, 66*(2), 196.

Corcoran, K. A., & Maren, S. (2001). Hippocampal inactivation disrupts contextual retrieval of fear memory after extinction. *Journal of Neuroscience, 21*(5), 1720–26.

Corlett, P. R., Frith, C. D., & Fletcher, P. C. (2009). From drugs to deprivation: A Bayesian framework for understanding models of psychosis. *Psychopharmacology, 206*(4), 515–30.

Corssen, G., & Domino, E. F. (1966). Dissociative anesthesia further pharmacologic studies and first clinical experience with the phencyclidine derivative Cl-581. *Anesthesia & Analgesia, 45*(1), 29–40.

Corti, O., Lesage, S., & Brice A. (2011). What genetics tells us about the causes and mechanisms of Parkinson's Disease. *Physiological Reviews,* 91, 1161–218.

Corwin, R. L., & Buda-Levin, A. (2004). Behavioral models of binge-type eating. *Physiology & Behavior, 82*(1), 123–30.

Corwin, R. L., Avena, N. M., & Boggiano, M. M. (2011). Feeding and reward: Perspectives from three rat models of binge eating. *Physiology & Behavior, 104*(1), 87–97.

Costa, E., Dong, E., Grayson, D. R., Guidotti, A., Ruzicka, W., &Veldic, M. (2007). Reviewing the role of DNA (cytosine-5) methyltransferase overexpression in the cortical GABAergic dysfunction associated with psychosis vulnerability. *Epigenetics, 2,* 29–36.

Courchesne, E., Chisum, H. J., Townsend, J., Cowles, A., Covington, J., Egaas, B., Harwood, M., Hinds, S., & Press, G. A. (2000). Normal brain development and aging: Quantitative analysis at in vivo MR imaging in healthy volunteers. *Radiology,* 672–82.

Courtney, S. M., Ungerleider, L. G., Keil, K., & Haxby, J. V. (1997). Transient and sustained activity in a distributed neural system for human working memory. *Nature, 386*(6625), 608–11.

Crews, F. T., Morrow, A. L., Criswell, H., & Breese, G. (1996). Effects of ethanol on ion channels. *International Review of Neurobiology, 39,* 283–367.

Crilly, J. (2007). The history of clozapine and its emergence in the US market: A review and analysis. *History of Psychiatry, 18*(1), 39–60.

Critchley, H. D., Wiens, S., Rotshtein, P., Öhman, A., & Dolan, R. J. (2004). Neural systems supporting interoceptive awareness. *Nature Neuroscience, 7*(2), 189–95.

Cummings, D. E., Purnell, J. Q., Frayo, R. S., Schmidova, K., Wisse, B. E., & Weigle, D. S. (2001). A preprandial rise in plasma ghrelin levels suggests a role in meal initiation in humans. *Diabetes, 50*(8), 1714–19.

Cummings, D. E., Clement, K., Purnell, J. Q., Vaisse, C., Foster, K. E., Frayo, R. S., ... & Weigle, D. S. (2002). Elevated plasma ghrelin levels in Prader–Willi syndrome. *Nature Medicine, 8*(7), 643–44.

Cunha-Oliveira, T., Rego, A. C., Cardoso, S. M., Borges, F., Swerdlow, R. H., Macedo, T., & de Oliveira, C. R. (2006). Mitochondrial dysfunction and caspase activation in rat cortical neurons treated with cocaine or amphetamine. *Brain Research, 1089*(1), 44–54.

Cunha-Oliveira, T., Rego, A. C., Garrido, J., Borges, F., Macedo, T., & Oliveira, C. R. (2007). Street heroin induces mitochondrial dysfunction and apoptosis in rat cortical neurons. *Journal of Neurochemistry, 101*(2), 543–54.

Curran, H. V., & Morgan, C. (2000). Cognitive, dissociative and psychotogenic effects of ketamine in recreational users on the night of drug use and 3 days later. *Addiction, 95*(4), 575–90.

Curran, H. V., & Travill, R. A. (1997). Mood and cognitive effects of ±3, 4-methylenedioxy methamphetamine (MDMA, 'ecstasy'): Week-end 'high' followed by mid-week low. *Addiction, 92*(7), 821–31.

Czeisler, C. A., Shanahan, T. L., Klerman, E. B., Martens, H., Brotman, D. J., Emens, J. S., ... & Rizzo, J. F. (1995). Suppression of melatonin secretion in some blind patients by exposure to bright light. *New England Journal of Medicine, 332*(1), 6–11.

Czeisler, C. A., Duffy, J. F., Shanahan, T. L., Brown, E. N., Mitchell, J. F., Rimmer, D. W., ... & Kronauer, R. E. (1999). Stability, precision, and near-24-hour period of the human circadian pacemaker. *Science, 284*(5423), 2177–81.

D'Ausilio, A., Pulvermüller, F., Salmas, P., Bufalari, I., Begliomini, C., & Fadiga, L. (2009). The motor somatotopy of speech perception. *Current Biology, 19*, 381–5.

Da Prada, M., Kettler, R., Keller, H. H., Burkard, W. P., Muggli-Maniglio, D., & Haefely, W. E. (1989). Neurochemical profile of moclobemide, a short-acting and reversible inhibitor of monoamine oxidase type A. *Journal of Pharmacology and Experimental Therapeutics, 248*(1), 400–14.

Dalgleish, T. (2004). The emotional brain. *Nature Reviews Neuroscience, 5*(7), 583–9.

Dallman, M. F. (2010). Stress-induced obesity and the emotional nervous system. *Trends in Endocrinology & Metabolism, 21*(3), 159–65.

Damasio, H., Grabowski, T., Frank, R., Galaburda, A. M., & Damasio, A. R. (1994). The return of Phineas Gage: Clues about the brain from the skull of a famous patient. *Science, 264*(5162), 1102–05.

Darwin, C. R. (1872). *The expression of the emotions in man and animals.* London: John Murray.

Dauer, W. & Przedborski, S. (2003). Parkinson's disease: Mechanisms and models. *Neuron, 39*(6), 889–909.

Davey, C. G., Allen, N. B., Harrison, B. J., Dwyer, D. B., & Yucel, M. (2010). Being liked activates primary reward and midline self-related brain regions. *Human Brain Mapping, 31*(4), 660–68.

Davidson, T. L., Chan, K., Jarrard, L. E., Kanoski, S. E., Clegg, D. J., & Benoit, S. C. (2009). Contributions of the hippocampus and medial prefrontal cortex to energy and body weight regulation. *Hippocampus, 19*(3), 235–52.

Davis, C., Curtis, C., Levitan, R. D., Carter, J. C., Kaplan, A. S., & Kennedy, J. L. (2011). Evidence that 'food addiction' is a valid phenotype of obesity. *Appetite, 57*(3), 711–17.

Davis, C., Loxton, N. J., Levitan, R. D., Kaplan, A. S., Carter, J. C., & Kennedy, J. L. (2013). 'Food addiction' and its association with a dopaminergic multilocus genetic profile. *Physiology & Behavior, 13*(118), 63–9.

Davis, M. (1992). The role of the amygdala in fear and anxiety. *Annual Review of Neuroscience, 15*, 353–75.

Davis, M. (1997). Neurobiology of fear responses: The role of the amygdala. *Journal of Neuropsychiatry and Clinical Neurosciences, 9*(3), 382–402.

Dawson, D., & Reid, K. (1997). Fatigue, alcohol and performance impairment. *Nature, 388*(6639), 235

de Castro, J. M., & Brewer, E. M. (1992). The amount eaten in meals by humans is a power function of the number of people present. *Physiology & Behavior, 51*(1), 121–5.

de Craen, A. J., Roos, P. J., De Vries, A. L., & Kleijnen, J. (1996). Effect of colour of drugs: Systematic review of perceived effect of drugs and of their effectiveness. *British Medical Journal, 313*(7072), 1624–6.

de Kloet, C. S., Vermetten, E., Geuze, E., Kavelaars, A., Heijnen, C. J., & Westenberg, H. G. (2006). Assessment of HPA-axis function in posttraumatic stress disorder: Pharmacological and non-pharmacological challenge tests, a review. *Journal of Psychiatric Research, 40*(6), 550–67.

de Weijer, B. A., van de Giessen, E., van Amelsvoort, T. A., Boot, E., Braak, B., Janssen, I. M., & Booij, J. (2011). Lower striatal dopamine D2/3 receptor availability in obese compared with non-obese subjects. *EJNMMI Research, 1*(1), 1–5.

de Wit, H., Dudish, S., & Ambre, J. (1993). Subjective and behavioral effects of diazepam depend on its rate of onset. *Psychopharmacology, 112*(2–3), 324–30.

Debiec, J., & LeDoux, J. E. (2004). Disruption of reconsolidation but not consolidation of auditory fear conditioning by noradrenergic blockade in the amygdala. *Neuroscience, 129*(2), 267–72.

Debiec, J., Bush, D. E., & LeDoux, J. E. (2011). Noradrenergic enhancement of reconsolidation in the amygdala impairs extinction of conditioned fear in rats – A possible mechanism for the persistence of traumatic memories in PTSD. *Depression and Anxiety, 28*(3), 186–93.

Degenhardt, L., Hall, W., & Lynskey, M. (2003). Testing hypotheses about the relationship between cannabis use and psychosis. *Drug and Alcohol Dependence, 71*(1), 37–48.

DeJong, W. (1980). The stigma of obesity: The consequences of naive assumptions concerning the causes of physical deviance. *Journal of Health and Social Behavior*, 75–87.

Delaville, C., De Deurwaerdère, P., & Benazzouz, A. (2011) Noradrenaline and Parkinson's Disease. *Frontiers in Systems Neuroscience, 5*, 31.

Dement, W., & Kleitman, N. (1957). Cyclic variations in EEG during sleep and their relation to eye movements, body motility, and dreaming. *Electroencephalography and Clinical Neurophysiology, 9*(4), 673–90.

Depue, R. A., & Collins, P. F. (1999). Neurobiology of the structure of personality: Dopamine, facilitation of incentive motivation, and extraversion. *Behavioral and Brain Sciences, 22*(3), 491–517.

Després, J. P., & Lemieux, I. (2006). Abdominal obesity and metabolic syndrome. *Nature, 444*(7121), 881–7.

Devane, W. A., Dysarz, F. A., III, Johnson, M. R., Melvin, L. S., & Howlett, A. C. (1988). Determination and characterization of a cannabinoid receptor in rat brain. *Molecular Pharmacology, 34*, 605–13.

Devane, W. A., Hanus, L., Breuer, A., Pertwee, R. G., Stevenson, L. A., Griffin, G., et al. (1992). Isolation and structure of a brain constituent that binds to the cannabinoid receptor. *Science, 258*, 1946–9.

Di Chiara, G. (1999). Drug addiction as dopamine-dependent associative learning disorder. *European Journal of Pharmacology, 375*(1), 13–30.

Di Chiara, G., & Imperato, A. (1988). Drugs abused by humans preferentially increase synaptic dopamine concentrations in the mesolimbic system of freely moving rats. *Proceedings of the National Academy of Sciences, 85*(14), 5274–8.

Di Pellegrino, G., Fadiga, L., Fogassi, L., Gallese, V., & Rizzolatti, G. (1992). Understanding motor events: A neurophysiological study. *Experimental Brain Research, 91*, 176–80.

Diekelmann, S., & Born, J. (2010). The memory function of sleep. *Nature Reviews Neuroscience, 11*(2), 114–26.

Dinges, D. F., Pack, F., Williams, K., Gillen, K. A., Powell, J. W., Ott, G. E., ... & Pack, A. I. (1997). Cumulative sleepiness, mood disturbance and psychomotor vigilance performance decrements during a week of sleep restricted to 4–5 hours per night. *Sleep: Journal of Sleep Research & Sleep Medicine, 20*(4), 267–77.

Dinstein, I., Hasson, U., Rubin, N. & Heeger, D. J. (2007). Brain areas selective for both observed and executed movements. *Journal of Neurophysiology, 98,* 1415–27.

Doll, R., Peto, R., Wheatley, K., Gray, R., & Sutherland, I. (1994). Mortality in relation to smoking: 40 years' observations on male British doctors. *British Medical Journal, 309*(6959), 901–11.

Dougherty, D. D., Baer, L., Cosgrove, G. R., Cassem, E. H., Price, B. H., Nierenberg, A. A., ... Rauch, S. L. (2002). Prospective long-term follow-up of 44 patients who received cingulotomy for treatment-refractory obsessive-compulsive disorder. *American Journal of Psychiatry, 159*(2), 269–75.

Doyon, J., Gaudreau, D., Laforce, R., Jr., Castonguay, M., Bedard, P. J., Bedard, F., & Bouchard, J. P. (1997). Role of the striatum, cerebellum, and frontal lobes in the learning of a visuomotor sequence. *Brain and Cognition, 34*(2), 218–45.

Drevets, W. C., Gautier, C., Price, J. C., Kupfer, D. J., Kinahan, P. E., Grace, A. A., & Mathis, C. A. (2001). Amphetamine-induced dopamine release in human ventral striatum correlates with euphoria. *Biological Psychiatry, 49*(2), 81–96.

Dudai, Y. (2002). Molecular bases of long-term memories: A question of persistence. *Current Opinion in Neurobiology, 12*(2), 211–16.

Dudley, R. (2004). Ethanol, fruit ripening, and the historical origins of human alcoholism in primate frugivory. *Integrative and Comparative Biology, 44,* 315–23.

Duman, R. S., & Monteggia, L. M. (2006). A neurotrophic model for stress-related mood disorders. *Biological Psychiatry, 59*(12), 1116–27.

Dunn, J. D., & Whitener, J. (1986). Plasma corticosterone responses to electrical stimulation of the amygdaloid complex: Cytoarchitectural specificity. *Neuroendocrinology, 42*(3), 211–17.

Dunnett, S. B., Lane, D. M., & Winn, P. (1985). Ibotenic acid lesions of the lateral hypothalamus: Comparison with 6-hydroxydopamine-induced sensorimotor deficits. *Neuroscience, 14*(2), 509–18.

Duty, S., & Jenner, P. (2011). Animal models of Parkinson's disease: A source of novel treatments and clues to the cause of the disease. *British Journal of Pharmacology, 164*(4), 1357–91.

Eggermann, E., Serafin, M., Bayer, L., Machard, D., Saint-Mleux, B., Jones, B. E., & Mühlethaler, M. (2001). Orexins/hypocretins excite basal forebrain cholinergic neurones. *Neuroscience, 108*(2), 177–81.

Ekman, P. (1993). Facial expression and emotion. *American Psychologist, 48*(4), 384–92.

Ekman, P., & Friesen, W. V. (1971). Constants across cultures in the face and emotion. *Journal of Personality and Social Psychology, 17*(2), 124–9.

Ekman, P., Levenson, R. W., & Friesen, W. V. (1983). Autonomic nervous system activity distinguishes among emotions. *Science, 221*(4616), 1208–10.

El Mansari, M., Sakai, K., & Jouvet, M. (1989). Unitary characteristics of presumptive cholinergic tegmental neurons during the sleep-waking cycle in freely moving cats. *Experimental Brain Research, 76*(3), 519–29.

Elgh, E., Domellöf, M., Linder, J., Edström, M., Stenlund, H., & Forsgren, L. (2009). Cognitive function in early Parkinson's disease: A population-based study. *European Journal of Neurology, 16*(12), 1278–84.

Emmorey, K., Xu, J., Gannon, P., Goldin-Meadow, S., & Braun, A. (2010). CNS activation and regional connectivity during pantomime observation: No engagement of the mirror neuron system for deaf signers. *NeuroImage, 49*, 994–1005.

Emsley, J. G., Mitchell, B. D., Kempermann, G., & Macklis, J. D. (2005). Adult neurogenesis and repair of the adult CNS with neural progenitors, precursors, and stem cells. *Progress in Neurobiology, 75*(5), 321–41.

Epstein, D. H., & Shaham, Y. (2010). Cheesecake-eating rats and the question of food addiction. *Nature Neuroscience, 13*(5), 529.

Eriksson, P. S., Perfilieva, E., Björk-Eriksson, T., Alborn, A. M., Nordborg, C., Peterson, D. A., & Gage, F. H. (1998). Neurogenesis in the adult human hippocampus. *Nature Medicine, 4*(11), 1313–17.

Eskelinen, M. H., & Kivipelto, M. (2010). Caffeine as a protective factor in dementia and Alzheimer's disease. *Journal of Alzheimer's Disease, 20*, 167–74.

Etkin, A., Egner, T., & Kalisch, R. (2011). Emotional processing in anterior cingulate and medial prefrontal cortex. *Trends in Cognitive Sciences, 15*(2), 85–93.

Evans, W. E., & Johnson, J. A. (2001). Pharmacogenomics: The inherited basis for interindividual differences in drug response. *Annual Review of Genomics and Human Genetics, 2*(1), 9–39.

Fadiga, L., Craighero, L., Buccino, G., & Rizzolatti, G. (2002). Speech listening specifically modulates the excitability of tongue muscles: A TMS study. *European Journal of Neuroscience, 15*, 399–402.

Fahy, F. L., Riches, I. P., & Brown, M. W. (1993). Neuronal activity related to visual recognition memory: Long-term memory and the encoding of recency and familiarity information in the primate anterior and medial inferior temporal and rhinal cortex. *Experimental Brain Research, 96*(3), 457–72.

Fairburn, C. G., & Harrison, P. J. (2003). Eating disorders. *The Lancet, 361*(9355), 407–16.

Fantegrossi, W. E., Woolverton, W. L., Kilbourn, M., Sherman, P., Yuan, J., Hatzidimitriou, G., & Winger, G. (2004). Behavioral and neurochemical consequences of long-term intravenous self-administration of MDMA and its enantiomers by rhesus monkeys. *Neuropsychopharmacology, 29*(7), 1270–81.

Farde, L., Nordstrom, A. L., Wiesel, F. A., Pauli, S., Halldin, C., & Sedvall, G. (1992). Positron emission tomographic analysis of central D1 and D2 dopamine receptor occupancy in patients treated with classical neuroleptics and clozapine: Relation to extrapyramidal side effects. *Archives of General Psychiatry, 49*(7), 538.

Farooqi, I. S., & O'Rahilly, S. (2008). Mutations in ligands and receptors of the leptin–melanocortin pathway that lead to obesity. *Nature Clinical Practice Endocrinology & Metabolism, 4*(10), 569–77.

Fatemi, S. H., Earle, J. A., & McMenomy, T. (2000). Reduction in Reelin immunoreactivity in hippocampus of subjects with schizophrenia, bipolar disorder and major depression. *Molecular Psychiatry, 5*(6), 654–63, 571.

Fava, M., & Kendler, K. S. (2000). Major depressive disorder. *Neuron, 28*(2), 335–41.

Fazel, S., Gulati, G., Linsell, L., Geddes, J. R., & Grann, M. (2009). Schizophrenia and violence: Systematic review and meta-analysis. *PLoS Medicine, 6*(8), e1000120.

Feinberg, A.P. (2007). Phenotypic plasticity and the epigenetics of human disease. *Nature, 447*, 433–40.

Feinberg, I. (1983). Schizophrenia: Caused by a fault in programmed synaptic elimination during adolescence? *Journal of Psychiatric Research, 17*(4), 319–34.

Feinstein, J. S., Adolphs, R., Damasio, A., & Tranel, D. (2011). The human amygdala and the induction and experience of fear. *Current Biology, 21*(1), 34–8.

Felleman, D. J. & Van Essen, D. C. (1991). Distributed hierarchical processing in the primate cerebral cortex. *Cerebral Cortex, 1*(1), 1–47.

Feng, Y., Crosbie, J., Wigg, K., Pathare, T., Ickowicz, A., Schachar, R., Tannock, R., Roberts, W., Malone, M., Swanson, J., Kennedy, J. L., & Barr, C. L. (2005). The SNAP25 gene as a susceptibility gene contributing to attention-deficit hyperactivity disorder. *Molecular Psychiatry, 10*, 998–1005.

Fergusson, D. M., Horwood, L. J., & Ridder, E. M. (2005). Tests of causal linkages between cannabis use and psychotic symptoms. *Addiction, 100*(3), 354–66.

Ferrari, P. F., Visalberghi, E., Paukner, A., Fogassi, L., Ruggiero, A., & Suomi, S.J. (2006). Neonatal imitation in rhesus macaques. *PLoS Biology, 4*(9), e302.

Ferré, S., Fuxe, K., Von Euler, G., Johansson, B., & Fredholm, B. B. (1992). Adenosine-dopamine interactions in the brain. *Neuroscience, 51*(3), 501–12.

Ferrie, J. E., Shipley, M. J., Cappuccio, F. P., Brunner, E., Miller, M. A., Kumari, M., & Marmot, M. G. (2007). A prospective study of change in sleep duration: Associations with mortality in the Whitehall II cohort. *Sleep, 30*(12), 1659.

Field, M., & Cox, W. M. (2008). Attentional bias in addictive behaviors: A review of its development, causes, and consequences. *Drug and Alcohol Dependence, 97*(1), 1–20.

Figlewicz, D. P., Evans, S. B., Murphy, J., Hoen, M., & Baskin, D. G. (2003). Expression of receptors for insulin and leptin in the ventral tegmental area/substantia nigra (VTA/SN) of the rat. *Brain Research, 964*(1), 107–15.

Fillmore, K. M., Stockwell, T., Chikritzhs, T., Bostrom, A., & Kerr, W. (2007). Moderate alcohol use and reduced mortality risk: Systematic error in prospective studies and new hypotheses. *Annals of Epidemiology, 17*(5), S16–S23.

Fischer, S., & Born, J. (2009). Anticipated reward enhances offline learning during sleep. *Journal of Experimental Psychology: Learning, Memory, and Cognition, 35*(6), 1586.

Fleckenstein, A. E., Volz, T. J., Riddle, E. L., Gibb, J. W., & Hanson, G. R. (2007). New insights into the mechanism of action of amphetamines. *Annual Review of Pharmacology and Toxicology, 47*, 681–98.

Flegal, K. M., Kit, B. K., Orpana, H., & Graubard, B. I. (2013). Association of all-cause mortality with overweight and obesity using standard body mass index categories: A systematic review and meta-analysis all-cause mortality using BMI categories. *JAMA, 309*(1), 71–82.

Fletcher, P. C., & Frith, C. D. (2008). Perceiving is believing: a Bayesian approach to explaining the positive symptoms of schizophrenia. *Nature Reviews Neuroscience, 10*(1), 48–58.

Fogassi, L., Gallese, V., Fadiga, L., & Rizzolatti, G. (1998). Neurons responding to the sight of goal directed hand/arm actions in the parietal area PF (7b) of the macaque monkey. *Society for Neuroscience, 24*, 257.5 (Abstract).

Folstein, S., & Rutter, M. (1977). Genetic heritability and shared environmental factors among twin pairs with autism. *Journal of Child Psychology and Psychiatry, 18*, 297–321.

Forcato, C., Rodriguez, M. L., Pedreira, M. E., & Maldonado, H. (2010). Reconsolidation in humans opens up declarative memory to the entrance of new information. *Neurobiology of Learning and Memory, 93*(1), 77–84.

Förster, E., Bock, H. H., Herz, J., Chai, X., Frotscher, M., & Zhao, S. (2010). Emerging topics in Reelin function. *European Journal of Neuroscience, 31*(9), 511–8.

Fox K., & Wong, R.O.L. (2005). A comparison of experience-review dependent plasticity in the visual and somatosensory systems. *Neuron, 48*, 465–77.

Fox, S. H., Chuang, R., & Brotchie, J. M. (2009). Serotonin and Parkinson's disease: On movement, mood, and madness. *Movement Disorders, 24*, 1255–66.

Fox, S. H., Katzenschlager, R., Lim, S.-Y., Ravina, B., Seppi, K., Coelho, M., Poewe, W., Rascol, O., Goetz, C. G., & Sampaio, C. (2011). The Movement Disorder Society Evidence-Based Medicine Review Update: Treatments for the motor symptoms of Parkinson's disease. *Movement Disorders Supplement: Evidence-Based Medicine, 26 (S3)*, S2–S41.

Frankland, P. W., & Bontempi, B. (2005). The organization of recent and remote memories. *Nature Reviews Neuroscience, 6*(2), 119–30.

Franklin, T. R., Acton, P. D., Maldjian, J. A., Gray, J. D., Croft, J. R., Dackis, C. A., ... Childress, A. R. (2002). Decreased gray matter concentration in the insular, orbitofrontal, cingulate, and temporal cortices of cocaine patients. *Biological Psychiatry, 51*(2), 134–42.

Frayling, T. M., Timpson, N. J., Weedon, M. N., Zeggini, E., Freathy, R. M., Lindgren, C. M., ... & McCarthy, M. I. (2007). A common variant in the FTO gene is associated with body mass index and predisposes to childhood and adult obesity. *Science, 316*(5826), 889–94.

Freo, U., & Ori, C. (2002). Opioid pharmacology of ketamine. *ACTA Anaesthesiologica Italica, 53*(3), 149–64.

Frezza, M., di Padova, C., Pozzato, G., Terpin, M., Baraona, E., & Lieber, C. S. (1990). High blood alcohol levels in women: The role of decreased gastric alcohol dehydrogenase activity and first-pass metabolism. *New England Journal of Medicine, 322*(2), 95–9.

Frieden, T. R., & Bloomberg, M. R. (2007). How to prevent 100 million deaths from tobacco. *The Lancet, 369*(9574), 1758–61.

Froehlich, J. C., & Li, T. K. (1994). Opioid involvement in alcohol drinking. *Annals of the New York Academy of Sciences, 739*(1), 156–67.

Fuchs, R. A., & See, R. E. (2002). Basolateral amygdala inactivation abolishes conditioned stimulus- and heroin-induced reinstatement of extinguished heroin-seeking behavior in rats. *Psychopharmacology (Berl), 160*(4), 425–33.

Fugh-Berman, A. (2000). Herb–drug interactions. *The Lancet, 355*(9198), 134–8.

Fuller, P. M., Saper, C. B., & Lu, J. (2007). The pontine REM switch: Past and present. *Journal of Physiology, 584*(3), 735–41.

Fulton, S., Pissios, P., Manchon, R. P., Stiles, L., Frank, L., Pothos, E. N., ... & Flier, J. S. (2006). Leptin regulation of the mesoaccumbens dopamine pathway. *Neuron, 51*(6), 811–22.

Gabbay, F. H. (2003). Variations in affect following amphetamine and placebo: Markers of stimulant drug preference. *Experimental and Clinical Psychopharmacology, 11*(1), 91.

Gage, F. H. (2000). Structural plasticity: Cause, result, or correlate of depression. *Biological Psychiatry, 48*(8), 713–14.

Gale, G. D., Anagnostaras, S. G., Godsil, B. P., Mitchell, S., Nozawa, T., Sage, J. R., & Fanselow, M. S. (2004). Role of the basolateral amygdala in the storage of fear memories across the adult lifetime of rats. *Journal of Neuroscience, 24*(15), 3810–15.

Gallese, V., Gernsbacher, M. A., Heyes, C., Hickok, G. & Iacoboni, M. (2011). Mirror neuron forum. *Perspectives on Psychological Science, 6*, 369–407.

Gallicchio, L., & Kalesan, B. (2009). Sleep duration and mortality: A systematic review and meta-analysis. *Journal of Sleep Research, 18*(2), 148–58.

Garcia, J., Kimeldorf, D. J., & Koelling, R. A. (1955). Conditioned aversion to saccharin resulting from exposure to gamma radiation. *Science, 122*(3160), 157–8.

Garner, D. M., & Garfinkel, P. E. (1980). Socio-cultural factors in the development of anorexia nervosa. *Psychological Medicine, 10*(4), 647–56.

Garrett, B. (2011). *Brain and Behavior: An Introduction to Biological Psychology*, 3rd edition. Thousand Oaks, CA: SAGE.

Garthwaite, J. (2008). Concepts of neural nitric oxide-mediated transmission. *European Journal of Neuroscience, 27*, 2783–802.

Gaus, S. E., Strecker, R. E., Tate, B. A., Parker, R. A., & Saper, C. B. (2002). Ventrolateral preoptic nucleus contains sleep-active, galaninergic neurons in multiple mammalian species. *Neuroscience, 115*(1), 285–94.

Gearhardt, A. N., Corbin, W. R., & Brownell, K. D. (2009). Preliminary validation of the Yale food addiction scale. *Appetite, 52*(2), 430–36.

Gearhardt, A. N., Davis, C., Kuschner, R., & Brownell, K. D. (2011a). The addiction potential of hyperpalatable foods. *Current Drug Abuse Reviews, 4*, 140–45.

Gearhardt, A. N., Grilo, C. M., DiLeone, R. J., Brownell, K. D., & Potenza, M. N. (2011b). Can food be addictive? Public health and policy implications. *Addiction, 106*(7), 1208–1212.

Gearhardt, A. N., Yokum, S., Orr, P. T., Stice, E., Corbin, W. R., & Brownell, K. D. (2011c). Neural correlates of food addiction. *Archives of General Psychiatry, 68*(8), 808.

Geers, A. L., Wellman, J. A., Fowler, S. L., Helfer, S. G., & France, C. R. (2010). Dispositional optimism predicts placebo analgesia. *Journal of Pain, 11*(11), 1165–71.

Gerashchenko, D., Wisor, J. P., Burns, D., Reh, R. K., Shiromani, P. J., Sakurai, T., ... & Kilduff, T. S. (2008). Identification of a population of sleep-active cerebral cortex neurons. *Proceedings of the National Academy of Sciences, 105*(29), 10227–32.

Gessa, G. L., Muntoni, F., Collu, M., Vargiu, L., & Mereu, G. (1985). Low doses of ethanol activate dopaminergic neurons in the ventral tegmental area. *Brain Research, 348*(1), 201–03.

Gewirtz, J. C., Falls, W. A., & Davis, M. (1997). Normal conditioned inhibition and extinction of freezing and fear-potentiated startle following electrolytic lesions of medical prefrontal cortex in rats. *Behavioral Neuroscience, 111*(4), 712–26.

Geyer, M. A., & Vollenweider, F. X. (2008). Serotonin research: Contributions to understanding psychoses. *Trends in Pharmacological Sciences, 29*(9), 445–53.

Gibbs, J., Young, R. C., & Smith, G. P. (1973). Cholecystokinin decreases food intake in rats. *Journal of Comparative and Physiological Psychology, 84*(3), 488.

Gilbertson, M. W., Shenton, M. E., Ciszewski, A., Kasai, K., Lasko, N. B., Orr, S. P., & Pitman, R. K. (2002). Smaller hippocampal volume predicts pathologic vulnerability to psychological trauma. *Nature Neuroscience, 5*(11), 1242–7.

Gillespie, N. A., Whitfield, J. B., Williams, B. E. N., Heath, A. C., & Martin, N. G. (2005). The relationship between stressful life events, the serotonin transporter (5-HTTLPR) genotype and major depression. *Psychological Medicine, 35*(1), 101–11.

Gilman, S.L., & Xun, Z. (2004). (eds) *Smoke: A Global History of Smoking*. London: Reaktion Books.

Giroud, C., Felber, F., Augsburger, M., Horisberger, B., Rivier, L., & Mangin, P. (2000). Salvia divinorum: An hallucinogenic mint which might become a new recreational drug in Switzerland. *Forensic Science International, 112*(2), 143–50.

Glass, M., Brotchie, J. M., & Maneuf, Y. P. (1997). Modulation of neurotransmission by cannabinoids in the basal ganglia. *European Journal of Neuroscience, 9*, 199–203.

Glenberg, A. M., Lopez-Mobilia, G., McBeath, M., Toma, M., Sato, M., & Cattaneo, L. (2010). Knowing beans: Human mirror mechanisms revealed through motor adaptation. *Frontiers in Human Neuroscience, 4*, 206.

Goetz, C. G. (2011). The history of Parkinson's disease: Early clinical descriptions and neurological therapies. *Cold Spring Harbor Perspectives in Medicine, 1*(1): a008862. Doi: 10.1101/cshperspect.a008862.

Goldman-Rakic, P. S., Castner, S. A., Svensson, T. H., Siever, L. J., & Williams, G. V. (2004). Targeting the dopamine D1 receptor in schizophrenia: Insights for cognitive dysfunction. *Psychopharmacology, 174*(1), 3–16.

Gonnissen, H. K., Hursel, R., Rutters, F., Martens, E. A., & Westerterp-Plantenga, M. S. (2012). Effects of sleep fragmentation on appetite and related hormone concentrations over 24 h in healthy men. *British Journal of Nutrition*, 1–9.

Gooley, J. J., Lu, J., Chou, T. C., Scammell, T. E., & Saper, C. B. (2001). Melanopsin in cells of origin of the retinohypothalamic tract. *Nature Neuroscience, 4*(12), 1165.

Goosens, K. A., & Maren, S. (2001). Contextual and auditory fear conditioning are mediated by the lateral, basal, and central amygdaloid nuclei in rats. *Learning & Memory, 8*(3), 148–55.

Gottesmann, C., & Gottesman, I. (2007). The neurobiological characteristics of rapid eye movement (REM) sleep are candidate endophenotypes of depression, schizophrenia, mental retardation and dementia. *Progress in Neurobiology, 81*(4), 237–50.

Gouzoulis-Mayfrank, E., Fischermann, T., Rezk, M., Thimm, B., Hensen, G., & Daumann, J. (2005). Memory performance in polyvalent MDMA (ecstasy) users who continue or discontinue MDMA use. *Drug and Alcohol Dependence*, *78*(3), 317–23.

Grace, A. A., Bunney, B. S., Moore, H., & Todd, C. L. (1997). Dopamine-cell depolarization block as a model for the therapeutic actions of antipsychotic drugs. *Trends in Neurosciences*, *20*(1), 31–7.

Grafman, J., Schwab, K., Warden, D., Pridgen, A., Brown, H. R., & Salazar, A. M. (1996). Frontal lobe injuries, violence, and aggression: A report of the Vietnam Head Injury Study. *Neurology, 46*(5), 1231–8.

Graham, K., & West, P. (2001). Alcohol and crime, in Heather, N., Peters, T. J., & Stockwell, T. (eds), *International Handbook of Alcohol Dependence and Problems*. London: John Wiley and Sons, pp. 439–70.

Graham, K. S., Simons, J. S., Pratt, K. H., Patterson, K., & Hodges, J. R. (2000). Insights from semantic dementia on the relationship between episodic and semantic memory. *Neuropsychologia, 38*(3), 313–24.

Grant, S., Contoreggi, C., & London, E. D. (2000). Drug abusers show impaired performance in a laboratory test of decision making. *Neuropsychologia, 38*(8), 1180–87.

Gray, J. A., Feldon, J., Rawlins, J. N. P., Hemsley, D. R., & Smith, A. D. (1991). The neuropsychology of schizophrenia. *Behavioral and Brain Sciences, 14*(01), 1–20.

Green, B., Kavanagh, D., & Young, R. (2003). Being stoned: A review of self-reported cannabis effects. *Drug and Alcohol Review, 22*, 453–60.

Green, M. F. (1996). What are the functional consequences of neurocognitive deficits in schizophrenia? *American Journal of Psychiatry*, 153, 321–30.

Green, M. F., Kern, R. S., Braff, D. L., & Mintz, J. (2000). Neurocognitive deficits and functional outcome in schizophrenia. *Schizophrenia Bulletin*, *26*(1), 119–36.

Greenberg, H. S., Werness, S. A., Pugh, J. E., Andrus, R. O., Anderson, D. J., & Domino, E. F. (1994). Short-term effects of smoking marijuana on balance in patients with multiple sclerosis and normal volunteers. *Clinical Pharmacology & Therapeutics, 55*(3), 324–8.

Greenberg, P. E., Sisitsky, T., Kessler, R. C., Finkelstein, S. N., Berndt, E. R., Davidson, J. R., … & Fyer, A. J. (1999). The economic burden of anxiety disorders in the 1990s. *Journal of Clinical Psychiatry*, *60*(7), 427–35.

Griffiths, R. R., Bigelow, G. E., Liebson, I., & Kaliszak, J. E. (1980). Drug preference in humans: Double-blind choice comparison of pentobarbital, diazepam and placebo. *Journal of Pharmacology and Experimental Therapeutics, 215*(3), 649–61.

Griffiths, R. R., Richards, W. A., McCann, U., & Jesse, R. (2006). Psilocybin can occasion mystical-type experiences having substantial and sustained personal meaning and spiritual significance. *Psychopharmacology, 187*(3), 268–83.

Grill, H. J. (2010). Leptin and the systems neuroscience of meal size control. *Frontiers in Neuroendocrinology, 31*(1), 61–78.

Grill, H. J., & Hayes, M. R. (2012). Hindbrain neurons as an essential hub in the neuroanatomically distributed control of energy balance. *Cell Metabolism*, 16(3), 296–309.

Grill, H. J., & Norgren, R. (1978). The taste reactivity test. I. Mimetic responses to gustatory stimuli in neurologically normal rats. *Brain Research*, *143*(2), 263–79.

Grinberg, L. T., Rueb, U., Alho, A. T. L., & Heinsen, H. (2010). Brainstem pathology and non-motor symptoms in PD. *Journal of the Neurological Sciences, 289*(1–2), 81–8.

Grob, C. S., Danforth, A. L., Chopra, G. S., et al. (2011). Pilot study of psilocybin treatment for anxiety in patients with advanced-stage cancer. *Archives of General Psychiatry, 68*, 71–8.

Groeger, J. A., Zijlstra, F. R. H., & Dijk, D. J. (2004). Sleep quantity, sleep difficulties and their perceived consequences in a representative sample of some 2000 British adults. *Journal of Sleep Research, 13*(4), 359–71.

Grønbæk, M., Deis, A., Becker, U., Hein, H. O., Schnohr, P., Jensen, G., & Sørensen, T. I. (1998). Alcohol and mortality: Is there a U-shaped relation in elderly people? *Age and Ageing, 27*(6), 739–44.

Grothe, M., Zaborszky, L., Atienza, M., Gil-Neciga, E., Rodriguez-Romero, R., Teipel, S. J., Amunts, K., Suarez-Gonzalez, A., & Cantero, J. L. (2010). Reduction of basal forebrain cholinergic system parallels cognitive impairment in patients at high risk of developing Alzheimer's disease. *Cerebral Cortex, 20*(7), 1685–95.

Gunnell, D., Harrison, G., Rasmussen, F., Fouskakis, D., & Tynelius, P. E. R. (2002). Associations between premorbid intellectual performance, early-life exposures and early-onset schizophrenia cohort study. *British Journal of Psychiatry, 181*(4), 298–305.

Gurvits, T. V., Shenton, M. E., Hokama, H., Ohta, H., Lasko, N. B., Gilbertson, M. W., … Pitman, R. K. (1996). Magnetic resonance imaging study of hippocampal volume in chronic, combat-related posttraumatic stress disorder. *Biological Psychiatry, 40*(11), 1091–9.

Hagan, M. M., Wauford, P. K., Chandler, P. C., Jarrett, L. A., Rybak, R. J., & Blackburn, K. (2002). A new animal model of binge eating: Key synergistic role of past caloric restriction and stress. *Physiology & Behavior, 77*(1), 45–54.

Hahn, C. G., Wang, H. Y., Cho, D. S., Talbot, K., Gur, R. E., Berrettini, W. H., ... & Arnold, S. E. (2006). Altered neuregulin 1–erbB4 signaling contributes to NMDA> receptor hypofunction in schizophrenia. *Nature Medicine, 12*(7), 824–8.

Haist, F., Bowden Gore, J., & Mao, H. (2001). Consolidation of human memory over decades revealed by functional magnetic resonance imaging. *Nature Neuroscience, 4*(11), 1139–45.

Halaas, J. L., Gajiwala, K. S., Maffei, M., Cohen, S. L., Chait, B. T., Rabinowitz, D., ... & Friedman, J. M. (1995). Weight-reducing effects of the plasma protein encoded by the obese gene. *Science, 269*(5223), 543–6.

Halassa, M. M., Florian, C., Fellin, T., Munoz, J. R., Lee, S. Y., Abel, T., ... & Frank, M. G. (2009). Astrocytic modulation of sleep homeostasis and cognitive consequences of sleep loss. *Neuron, 61*(2), 213–19.

Halgren, E., Walter, R. D., Cherlow, D. G., & Crandall, P. H. (1978). Mental phenomena evoked by electrical stimulation of the human hippocampal formation and amygdala. *Brain, 101*(1), 83–117.

Hall, J., Thomas, K. L., & Everitt, B. J. (2001). Fear memory retrieval induces CREB phosphorylation and Fos expression within the amygdala. *European Journal of Neuroscience, 13*(7), 1453–58.

Hallmayer, J., Cleveland, S., Torres, A., Phillips, J., Cohen, B., Torigoe, T., Miller, J., Fedele, A., Collins, J.,Smith, K., Lotspeich, L., Croen, L.A., Ozonoff, S., Lajonchere, C., Grether, J.K., & Risch, N. (2011). Genetic heritability and shared environmental factors among twin pairs with autism. *Archives of General Psychiatry*, 68(11), 1095–102.

Halpern, J. H., & Pope, H. G. (2003). Hallucinogen persisting perception disorder: What do we know after 50 years? *Drug and Alcohol Dependence*, 69(2), 109–19.

Haltia, L. T., Rinne, J. O., Merisaari, H., Maguire, R. P., Savontaus, E., Helin, S., ... & Kaasinen, V. (2007). Effects of intravenous glucose on dopaminergic function in the human brain in vivo. *Synapse, 61*(9), 748–56.

Hamidovic, A., Dlugos, A., Palmer, A. A., & de Wit, H. (2010). Catechol-O-methyltransferase val158met genotype modulates sustained attention in both the drug-free state and in response to amphetamine. *Psychiatric Genetics, 20*(3), 85.

Hancock, P. J., & Stamford, J. A. (1999). Stereospecific effects of ketamine on dopamine efflux and uptake in the rat nucleus accumbens. *British Journal of Anaesthesia*, 82(4), 603–8.

Haney, M., Comer, S. D., Ward, A. S., Foltin, R. W., & Fischman, M. W. (1997). Factors influencing marijuana self-administration by humans. *Behavioural Pharmacology*, 8(2–3), 101–12.

Hare, T. A., O'Doherty, J., Camerer, C. F., Schultz, W., & Rangel, A. (2008). Dissociating the role of the orbitofrontal cortex and the striatum in the computation of goal values and prediction errors. *Journal of Neuroscience, 28*(22), 5623–5630.

Harmer, C., O'Sullivan, U., Favaron, E., Massey-Chase, R., Ayres, R., Reinecke, A. and Cowen, P. (2009). Effect of acute antidepressant administration on negative affective bias in depressed patients. *American Journal of Psychiatry, 166*(10), 1178–84.

Harris, D. S., Everhart, E. T., Mendelson, J., & Jones, R. T. (2003). The pharmacology of cocaethylene in humans following cocaine and ethanol administration. *Drug and Alcohol Dependence, 72*(2), 169–82.

Harrison, G., Glazebrook, C., Brewin, J., Cantwell, R., Dalkin, T., Fox, R., ... & Medley, I. (1997). Increased incidence of psychotic disorders in migrants from the Caribbean to the United Kingdom. *Psychological Medicine, 27*(04), 799–806.

Harrison, P. J. (2002). The neuropathology of primary mood disorder. *Brain, 125*(7), 1428–49.

Harrison, P. J., & Weinberger, D. R. (2004). Schizophrenia genes, gene expression, and neuropathology: On the matter of their convergence. *Molecular Psychiatry, 10*(1), 40–68.

Harrow, M., & Jobe, T. H. (2007). Factors involved in outcome and recovery in schizophrenia patients not on antipsychotic medications: A 15-year multifollow-up study. *Journal of Nervous and Mental Disease, 195*(5), 406–14.

Härter, M. C., Conway, K. P., & Merikangas, K. R. (2003). Associations between anxiety disorders and physical illness. *European Archives of Psychiatry and Clinical Neuroscience, 253*(6), 313–320.

Hattar, S., Liao, H. W., Takao, M., Berson, D. M., & Yau, K. W. (2002). Melanopsin-containing retinal ganglion cells: Architecture, projections, and intrinsic photosensitivity. *Science, 295*(5557), 1065–70.

He, G., Luo, W., Li, P., Remmers, C., Netzer, W., Hendrick, J., Bettayeb, K., Flajolet, M., Gorelick, F., Wennogle, L.P., & Greengard, P. (2010). Gamma-secretase activating protein, a therapeutic target for Alzheimer's disease. *Nature, 467*(7311), 95–8.

He, Y., Jones, C. R., Fujiki, N., Xu, Y., Guo, B., Holder, J. L., ... & Fu, Y. H. (2009). The transcriptional repressor DEC2 regulates sleep length in mammals. *Science, 325*(5942), 866–70.

Hebb, D. O. (1947). The effects of early experience on problem solving at maturity. *American Psychologist, 2*, 306–7.

Hebb, D. O. (1949). *The Organization of Behavior*. New York: Wiley.

Heider, F., & Simmel, M. (1944). An experimental study of apparent behavior. *American Journal of Psychology, 57*, 243–59.

Heim, C., & Nemeroff, C. B. (2001). The role of childhood trauma in the neurobiology of mood and anxiety disorders: Preclinical and clinical studies. *Biological Psychiatry, 49*(12), 1023–39.

Heishman, S. J., Stitzer, M. L., & Yingling, J. E. (1989). Effects of tetrahydrocannabinol content on marijuana smoking behavior, subjective reports, and performance. *Pharmacology, Biochemistry and Behavior*, *34*(1), 173–9.

Heishman, S. J., Taylor, R. C., & Henningfield, J. E. (1994). Nicotine and smoking: A review of effects on human performance. *Experimental and Clinical Psychopharmacology*, *2*(4), 345.

Helmich, R. C., Hallett, M., Deuschl, G., Toni, I., & Bloem, B. R. (2012). Cerebral causes and consequences of parkinsonian resting tremor: A tale of two circuits? *Brain*, *135*(11), 3206–26.

Henquet, C., Murray, R., Linszen, D., & van Os, J. (2005). The environment and schizophrenia: The role of cannabis use. *Schizophrenia Bulletin*, *31*(3), 608–12.

Henry, J. P. (1986). Neuroendocrine patterns of emotional response, in R. Plutchik & H. Kellerman (eds), *Emotion – Theory, Research and Experience. Vol. 3: Biological Foundations of Emotion*. Orlando: Academic Press, pp. 37–60.

Hensch, T. K. (2004). Critical period regulation. *Annual Review of Neuroscience*, *27*, 549–79.

Herkenham, M., Lynn, A. B., Little, M. D., Johnson, M. R., Melvin, L. S., de Costa, B. R., et al. (1990). Cannabinoid receptor localization in brain. *Proceedings of the National Academy of Sciences*, *87*, 1932–6.

Herman, C. P., & Mack, D. (1975). Restrained and unrestrained eating. *Journal of Personality*, *43*(4), 647–60.

Hernandez, L., & Hoebel, B. G. (1988). Food reward and cocaine increase extracellular dopamine in the nucleus accumbens as measured by microdialysis. *Life Sciences*, *42*(18), 1705–12.

Heston, L. L. (1966). Psychiatric disorders in foster home reared children of schizophrenic mothers. *British Journal of Psychiatry*, *112*(489), 819–25.

Hetherington, A. W., & Ranson, S. W. (1942). The spontaneous activity and food intake of rats with hypothalamic lesions. *American Journal of Physiology – Legacy Content*, *136*(4), 609–17.

Hettema, J. M., Neale, M. C., & Kendler, K. S. (2001). A review and meta-analysis of the genetic epidemiology of anxiety disorders. *American Journal of Psychiatry*, *158*(10), 1568–78.

Heyes, C. (2009). Where do mirror neurons come from? *Neuroscience & Biobehavioral Reviews*, *34*(4), 575–83.

Hickman, M., Vickerman, P., Macleod, J., Kirkbride, J., & Jones, P. B. (2007). Cannabis and schizophrenia: Model projections of the impact of the rise in cannabis use on historical and future trends in schizophrenia in England and Wales. *Addiction*, *102*(4), 597–606.

Hicks, R. E., Gualtieri, C. T., Mayo, J. P., Jr, & Perez-Reyes, M. (1984). Cannabis, atropine, and temporal information processing. *Neuropsychobiology*, *12*(4), 229–37.

Higgs, S., & Cooper, S. J. (1996). Hyperphagia induced by direct administration of midazolam into the parabrachial nucleus of the rat. *European Journal of Pharmacology*, *313*(1), 1–9.

Higgs, S., & Woodward, M. (2009). Television watching during lunch increases afternoon snack intake of young women. *Appetite*, *52*(1), 39–43.

Higgs, S., Williams, C. M., & Kirkham, T. C. (2003). Cannabinoid influences on palatability: Microstructural analysis of sucrose drinking after Δ9-tetrahydrocannabinol, anandamide, 2-arachidonoyl glycerol and SR141716. *Psychopharmacology*, *165*(4), 370–77.

Higgs, S., Williamson, A. C., Rotshtein, P., & Humphreys, G. W. (2008). Sensory-specific satiety is intact in amnesics who eat multiple meals. *Psychological Science*, *19*(7), 623–8.

Hirsch, E. C., & Hunot, S. (2009). Neuroinflammation in Parkinson's disease: A target for neuroprotection? *The Lancet Neurology*, *8*, 382–97.

Hobson, J. A. (2005). Sleep is of the brain, by the brain and for the brain. *Nature*, *437*(7063), 1254–6.

Hobson, J. A., & Pace-Schott, E. F. (2002). The cognitive neuroscience of sleep: Neuronal systems, consciousness and learning. *Nature Reviews Neuroscience*, *3*(9), 679–93.

Hoevenaar-Blom, M. P., Spijkerman, A. M., Kromhout, D., van den Berg, J. F., & Verschuren, W. M. (2011). Sleep duration and sleep quality in relation to 12-year cardiovascular disease incidence: The MORGEN study. *Sleep*, *34*(11), 1487.

Hofmann, A. (1994). Notes and documents concerning the discovery of LSD. *Inflammation Research*, *43*(3), 79–81.

Hohmann, G. W. (1966). Some effects of spinal cord lesions on experienced emotional feelings. *Psychophysiology*, 3(2), 143–56.

Holliday, J., Tchanturia, K., Landau, S., Collier, D., & Treasure, J. (2005). Is impaired set-shifting an endophenotype of anorexia nervosa? *American Journal of Psychiatry*, *162*(12), 2269–75.

Holtmaat, A. J., Trachtenberg, J. T., Wilbrecht, L., Shepherd, G. M., Zhang, X., Knott, G. W., & Svoboda, K. (2005). Transient and persistent dendritic spines in the neocortex in vivo. *Neuron*, *45*(2), 279–91.

Honey, G. D., O'Loughlin, C., Turner, D. C., Pomarol-Clotet, E., Corlett, P. R., & Fletcher, P. C. (2005). The effects of a subpsychotic dose of ketamine on recognition and source memory for agency: Implications for pharmacological modelling of core symptoms of schizophrenia. *Neuropsychopharmacology*, *31*(2), 413–23.

Hopf, H. C., Muller-Forell, W., & Hopf, N. J. (1992). Localization of emotional and volitional facial paresis. *Neurology*, *42*(10), 1918–23.

Horne, J. (1988). *Why We Sleep: The Functions of Sleep in Humans and Other Mammals*. Oxford University Press.

Horne, J. (2008). Short sleep is a questionable risk factor for obesity and related disorders: Statistical versus clinical significance. *Biological Psychology*, *77*(3), 266–76.

Horne, J. (2011). The end of sleep: 'Sleep debt' versus biological adaptation of human sleep to waking needs. *Biological Psychology*, *87*(1), 1–14.

Horne, J. (2012). Working throughout the night: Beyond 'sleepiness'-impairments to critical decision making. *Neuroscience & Biobehavioral Reviews*, *36*(10), 2226–31.

Horne, J. A., & Reyner, L. A. (1995). Sleep related vehicle accidents. *British Medical Journal*, *310*(6979), 565–7.

Horne, J. A., & Wilkinson, S. (1985). Chronic sleep reduction: Daytime vigilance performance and EEG measures of sleepiness, with particular reference to 'practice' effects. *Psychophysiology*, *22*(1), 69–78.

Horvath, T. L., Diano, S., & van den Pol, A. N. (1999). Synaptic interaction between hypocretin (orexin) and neuropeptide Y cells in the rodent and primate hypothalamus: A novel circuit implicated in metabolic and endocrine regulations. *Journal of Neuroscience*, *19*(3), 1072–87.

Horváth, S., & Mirnics, K. (2009). Breaking the gene barrier in schizophrenia. *Nature Medicine*, *15*(5), 488–90.

Hoschl, C., & Hajek, T. (2001). Hippocampal damage mediated by corticosteroids – A neuropsychiatric research challenge. *European Archives of Psychiatry and Clinical Neuroscience, 251*(2), II81–8.

Hradetzky, E., Sanderson, T. M., Tsang, T. M., Sherwood, J. L., Fitzjohn, S. M., Lakics, V., Malik, N., Schoeffmann, S., O'Neill, M. J., Cheng, T. M., Harris, L. W., Rahmoune, H., Guest, P. C., Sher, E., Collingridge, G. L., Holmes, E., Tricklebank, M. D., & Bahn, S. (2012). The methylazoxymethanol acetate (MAM-E17) rat model: Molecular and functional effects in the hippocampus. *Neuropsychopharmacology 37*, 364–77.

Hu, P., Stylos-Allan, M., & Walker, M. P. (2006). Sleep facilitates consolidation of emotional declarative memory. *Psychological Science*, *17*(10), 891–8.

Huang, H. S., Allen, J. A., Mabb, A. M., King, I. F., Miriyala, J., et al. (2011). Topoisomerase inhibitors unsilence the dormant allele of Ube3a in neurons. *Nature, 481*(7380), 185–9.

Hungund, B. L., Szakall, I., Adam, A., Basavarajappa, B. S., & Vadasz, C. (2003). Cannabinoid CB1 receptor knockout mice exhibit markedly reduced voluntary alcohol consumption and lack alcohol-induced dopamine release in the nucleus accumbens. *Journal of Neurochemistry*, *84*(4), 698–704.

Hupbach, A., Gomez, R., Hardt, O., & Nadel L. (2007). Reconsolidation of episodic memories: A subtle reminder triggers integration of new information. *Learning and Memory*, *14*(1–2), 47–53.

Hupbach, A., Hardt, O., Gomez, R., & Nadel, L. (2008). The dynamics of memory: Context-dependent updating. *Learning and Memory, 15*(8), 574–9.

Hupbach, A., Gomez, R. L., Bootzin, R. R., & Nadel, L. (2009). Nap-dependent learning in infants. *Developmental Science*, *12*(6), 1007–12.

Huttunen, M. O. (1989). Maternal stress during pregnancy and the behavior of the offspring. In *Early Influences Shaping the Individual*, Springer, pp. 175–82.

Hyman, S. E. (2009). How adversity gets under the skin. *Nature Neuroscience*, *12*(3), 241–3.

Iacoboni, M., Molnar-Szakacs, I., Gallese, V., Buccino, G., Mazziotta, J.C., & Rizzolatti, G. (2005). Grasping the intentions of others with one's own Mirror Neuron System. *PLoS Biology*, *3*(3), e79.

Ibrahim, H. M., Hogg, A. J., Healy, D. J., Haroutunian, V., Davis, K. L., & Meador-Woodruff, J. H. (2000). Ionotropic glutamate receptor binding and subunit mRNA expression in thalamic nuclei in schizophrenia. *American Journal of Psychiatry, 157*(11), 1811–23.

Ikonomidou, C., Bosch, F., Miksa, M., Bittigau, P., Vöckler, J., Dikranian, K., ... & Olney, J. W. (1999). Blockade of NMDA receptors and apoptotic neurodegeneration in the developing brain. *Science*, *283*(5398), 70–74.

Inda, M. C., Muravieva, E. V., & Alberini, C. M. (2011). Memory retrieval and the passage of time: From reconsolidation and strengthening to extinction. *Journal of Neuroscience, 31*(5), 1635–43.

Isbell, H. (1959). Comparison of the reactions induced by psilocybin and LSD-25 in man. *Psychopharmacologia*, *1*(1), 29–38.

Ito, M. (2000). Mechanisms of motor learning in the cerebellum. *Brain Research, 886*(1–2), 237–45.

Iwata, J., Chida, K., & LeDoux, J. E. (1987). Cardiovascular responses elicited by stimulation of neurons in the central amygdaloid nucleus in awake but not anesthetized rats resemble conditioned emotional responses. *Brain Research, 418*(1), 183–8.

Izquierdo, L. A., Barros, D. M., Vianna, M. R., Coitinho, A., deDavid e Silva, T., Choi, H., & Izquierdo, I. (2002). Molecular pharmacological dissection of short- and long-term memory. *Cellular and Molecular Neurobiology, 22*(3), 269–87.

Jaffe, J. H. (1990). Drug addiction and drug abuse, in Goodman, A. G., Rall, T. W., Nies, A. S., & Taylor, P. (eds) *Goodman and Gilman's the Pharmacological Basis of Therapeutics*. New York: McGraw-Hill, pp. 522–73.

James, J. E. (1997). *Understanding Caffeine: A Biobehavioral Analysis*. Thousand Oaks, CA: Sage Publications.

James, J. E., & Rogers, P. J. (2005). Effects of caffeine on performance and mood: Withdrawal reversal is the most plausible explanation. *Psychopharmacology, 182*(1), 1–8.

James, W. (1890). *The Principles of Psychology.* New York: H. Holt and Company.

Jansen, K. L. (1997). The ketamine model of the near-death experience: A central role for the N-methyl-D-aspartate receptor. *Journal of Near-Death Studies, 16*(1), 5–26.

Jansen, K. L. (2000). A review of the nonmedical use of ketamine: Use, users and consequences. *Journal of Psychoactive Drugs, 32*(4), 419–33.

Janssen, I., Katzmarzyk, P. T., & Ross, R. (2004). Waist circumference and not body mass index explains obesity-related health risk. *American Journal of Clinical Nutrition, 79*(3), 379–84.

Jenkins, J. G., & Dallenbach, K. M. (1924). Obliviscence during sleep and waking. *American Journal of Psychology, 35*(4), 605–12.

Jentsch, J. D., & Roth, R. H. (1999). The neuropsychopharmacology of phencyclidine: From NMDA receptor hypofunction to the dopamine hypothesis of schizophrenia. *Neuropsychopharmacology, 20*(3), 201–25.

Jentsch, J. D., Redmond, D. E., Elsworth, J. D., Taylor, J. R., Youngren, K. D., & Roth, R. H. (1997). Enduring cognitive deficits and cortical dopamine dysfunction in monkeys after long-term administration of phencyclidine. *Science, 277*(5328), 953–5.

Jeste, D. V., Lacro, J. P., Bailey, A., Rockwell, E., Harris, M. J., & Caligiuri, M. P. (1999). Lower incidence of tardive dyskinesia with risperidone compared with haloperidol in older patients. *Journal of the American Geriatrics Society, 47*(6), 716–9.

Jimenez, S. A., & Maren, S. (2009). Nuclear disconnection within the amygdala reveal a direct pathway to fear. *Learning & Memory, 16*(12), 766–8.

Jobe, T. H., & Harrow, M. (2010). Schizophrenia course, long-term outcome, recovery, and prognosis. *Current Directions in Psychological Science, 19*(4), 220–25.

Johansen, J. P., Hamanaka, H., Monfils, M. H., Behnia, R., Deisseroth, K., Blair, H. T., & LeDoux, J. E. (2010). Optical activation of lateral amygdala pyramidal cells instructs associative fear learning. [Research Support, N.I.H., Extramural Research Support, Non-U.S. Gov't]. *Proceedings of the National Academy of Sciences USA, 107*(28), 12692–7.

Johansson, I., Lundqvist, E., Bertilsson, L., Dahl, M. L., Sjöqvist, F., & Ingelman-Sundberg, M. (1993). Inherited amplification of an active gene in the cytochrome P450 CYP2D locus as a cause of ultrarapid metabolism of debrisoquine. *Proceedings of the National Academy of Sciences, 90*(24), 11825–9.

Johns, T. (1990). *With Bitter Herbs They Shall Eat It: Chemical Ecology and the Origins of Human Diet and Medicine.* University of Arizona Press.

Johnson, M. W., MacLean, K. A., Reissig, C. J., Prisinzano, T. E., & Griffiths, R. R. (2011). Human psychopharmacology and dose-effects of salvinorin A, a kappa opioid agonist hallucinogen present in the plant Salvia divinorum. *Drug and Alcohol Dependence, 115*(1), 150–55.

Johnson, P. M., & Kenny, P. J. (2010). Dopamine D2 receptors in addiction-like reward dysfunction and compulsive eating in obese rats. *Nature Neuroscience, 13*(5), 635–41.

Jones, B. E. (2003). Arousal systems. *Frontiers in Bioscience, 8*(5), 438–51.

Jones, B. E. (2004). Activity, modulation and role of basal forebrain cholinergic neurons innervating the cerebral cortex. *Progress in Brain Research, 145*, 157–69.

Jones, B. T., Corbin, W., & Fromme, K. (2001). A review of expectancy theory and alcohol consumption. *Addiction, 96*(1), 57–72.

Jones, P. B., Rantakallio, P., Hartikainen, A. L., Isohanni, M., & Sipila, P. (1998). Schizophrenia as a long-term outcome of pregnancy, delivery, and perinatal complications: A 28-year follow-up of the 1966 north Finland general population birth cohort. *American Journal of Psychiatry, 155*(3), 355–64.

Joormann, J. (2010). Cognitive inhibition and emotion regulation in depression. *Current Directions in Psychological Science, 19*(3), 161–66.

Jouvet, M. (1962). Research on the neural structures and responsible mechanisms in different phases of physiological sleep. *Archives Italiennes de Biologie, 100*, 125.

Juliano, L. M., & Griffiths, R. R. (2004). A critical review of caffeine withdrawal: Empirical validation of symptoms and signs, incidence, severity, and associated features. *Psychopharmacology, 176*(1), 1–29.

Justice, A. J., & de Wit, H. (1999). Acute effects of d-amphetamine during the follicular and luteal phases of the menstrual cycle in women. *Psychopharmacology, 145*(1), 67–75.

Kähler, A. K., Djurovic, S., Kulle, B., Jönsson, E. G., Agartz, I., Hall, H., Opjordsmoen, S., Jakobsen, K. D., Hansen, T., Melle, I., Werge, T., Steen, V. M., & Andreassen, O. A. (2008). Association analysis of schizophrenia on 18 genes involved in neuronal migration: MDGA1 as a new susceptibility gene. *American Journal of Medical Genetics Part B: Neuropsychiatric Genetics, 147B*(7), 1089–100.

Kalat, J. W., & Rozin, P. (1973). 'Learned safety' as a mechanism in long-delay taste-aversion learning in rats. *Journal of Comparative and Physiological Psychology*, *83*(2), 198.

Kalisch, R., Korenfeld, E., Stephan, K. E., Weiskopf, N., Seymour, B., & Dolan, R. J. (2006). Context-dependent human extinction memory is mediated by a ventromedial prefrontal and hippocampal network. *Journal of Neuroscience*, *26*(37), 9503–11.

Kamaya, H., & Krishna, P. R. (1987). Ketamine addiction. *Anesthesiology*, *67*(5), 861–2.

Kamin, L. (1969). Predictability, surprise, attention and conditioning, in Campbell, B., & Church, R. (eds), *Punishment and Aversive Behavior*. New York: Appleton-Century-Crofts, pp. 279–96.

Kanoski, S. E., Zhao, S., Guarnieri, D. J., DiLeone, R. J., Yan, J., De Jonghe, B. C., ... & Grill, H. J. (2012). Endogenous leptin receptor signaling in the medial nucleus tractus solitarius affects meal size and potentiates intestinal satiation signals. *American Journal of Physiology – Endocrinology And Metabolism*, *303*(4), E496–E503.

Kaptchuk, T. J., Stason, W. B., Davis, R. B., Legedza, A. R., Schnyer, R. N., Kerr, C. E., ... & Goldman, R. H. (2006). Sham device v inert pill: Randomised controlled trial of two placebo treatments. *British Medical Journal*, *332*(7538), 391–7.

Kaptchuk, T. J., Kelley, J. M., Conboy, L. A., Davis, R. B., Kerr, C. E., Jacobson, E. E., ... & Lembo, A. J. (2008). Components of placebo effect: Randomised controlled trial in patients with irritable bowel syndrome. *British Medical Journal*, *336*(7651), 999–1003.

Kapur, S., Zipursky, R., Jones, C., Remington, G., & Houle, S. (2000). Relationship between dopamine D2 occupancy, clinical response, and side effects: A double-blind PET study of first-episode schizophrenia. *American Journal of Psychiatry*, *157*(4), 514–20.

Kapur, S., Mizrahi, R., & Li, M. (2005). From dopamine to salience to psychosis – Linking biology, pharmacology and phenomenology of psychosis. *Schizophrenia Research*, *79*(1), 59–68.

Karban, R., & Agrawal, A. A. (2002). Herbivore offense. *Annual Review of Ecology and Systematics*, 641–64.

Karban, R., & Baldwin, I. T. (1997). *Induced Responses to Herbivory*. Chicago: University of Chicago Press.

Karege, F., Bondolfi, G., Gervasoni, N., Schwald, M., Aubry, J. M., & Bertschy, G. (2005). Low brain-derived neurotrophic factor (BDNF) levels in serum of depressed patients probably results from lowered platelet BDNF release unrelated to platelet reactivity. *Biological Psychiatry*, *57*(9), 1068–72.

Katzman, D. K., Lambe, E. K., Mikulis, D. J., Ridgley, J. N., Goldbloom, D. S., & Zipursky, R. B. (1996). Cerebral gray matter and white matter volume deficits in adolescent girls with anorexia nervosa. *Journal of Pediatrics*, *129*(6), 794–803.

Kaye, W. H., Frank, G. K., Bailer, U. F., Henry, S. E., Meltzer, C. C., Price, J. C., ... & Wagner, A. (2005). Serotonin alterations in anorexia and bulimia nervosa: New insights from imaging studies. *Physiology & Behavior*, *85*(1), 73–81.

Kaye, W. H., Fudge, J. L., & Paulus, M. (2009). New insights into symptoms and neurocircuit function of anorexia nervosa. *Nature Reviews Neuroscience*, *10*(8), 573–84.

Keel, P. K., & Brown, T. A. (2010). Update on course and outcome in eating disorders. *International Journal of Eating Disorders*, *43*(3), 195–204.

Kegeles, L. S., Abi-Dargham, A., Frankle, W. G., Gil, R., Cooper, T. B., Slifstein, M., ... & Laruelle, M. (2010). Increased synaptic dopamine function in associative regions of the striatum in schizophrenia. *Archives of General Psychiatry*, *67*(3), 231.

Keller, G. B., & Hahnloser, R. H. (2009). Neural processing of auditory feedback during vocal practice in a songbird. *Nature*, *457*, 187–90.

Kendler, K. S., & Diehl, S. R. (1993). The genetics of schizophrenia. *Schizophrenia Bulletin*, *19*(2), 261–85.

Kendler, K. S., Karkowski, L. M., & Prescott, C. A. (1999). Causal relationship between stressful life events and the onset of major depression. *American Journal of Psychiatry*, *156*(6), 837–41.

Kennedy, B. L., & Schwab, J. J. (1997). Utilization of medical specialists by anxiety disorder patients. *Psychosomatics*, *3 8*(2), 109–12.

Kenny, P. (2013). The food addiction. *Scientific American Magazine*, *309*(3), 44–9.

Keshavan, M. S., Anderson, S., & Pettergrew, J. W. (1994). Is schizophrenia due to excessive synaptic pruning in the prefrontal cortex? The Feinberg hypothesis revisited. *Journal of Psychiatric Research*, *28*(3), 239–65.

Kessler, R. C., Borges, G., & Walters, E. E. (1999). Prevalence of and risk factors for lifetime suicide attempts in the National Comorbidity Survey. *Archives of General Psychiatry*, *56*(7), 617.

Kessler, R. C., Chiu, W. T., Demler, O., & Walters, E. E. (2005). Prevalence, severity, and comorbidity of 12-month DSM-IV disorders in the National Comorbidity Survey Replication. *Archives of General Psychiatry*, *62*(6), 617.

Kessler, R. C., Aguilar-Gaxiola, S., Alonso, J., Chatterji, S., Lee, S., & Üstün, T. B. (2009). The WHO World Mental Health (WMH) Surveys. *Psychiatrie (Stuttgart, Germany)*, *6*(1), 5.

Kety, S. S. (1956). Human cerebral blood flow and oxygen consumption as related to aging. *Journal of Chronic Diseases*, *3*(5), 478–86.

Kety, S. S., Rosenthal, D., Wender, P. H., & Schulsinger, F. (1968). The types and prevalence of mental illness in the biological and adoptive families of adopted schizophrenics. *Journal of Psychiatric Research, 6,* 345–62.

Keys, A., Fidanza, F., Karvonen, M. J., Kimura, N., & Taylor, H. L. (1972). Indices of relative weight and obesity. *Journal of Chronic Diseases, 25*(6), 329–43.

Keysers, C., & Gazzola, V. (2006). Towards a unifying neural theory of social cognition. *Progress in Brain Research, 156,* 379–401.

Keysers, C., Wicker, B., Gazzola, V., Anton, J. L., Fogassi, L., & Gallese, V. (2004). A touching sight: SII/PV activation during the observation and experience of touch. *Neuron, 42,* 335–46.

Kilkus, J. M., Booth, J. N., Bromley, L. E., Darukhanavala, A. P., Imperial, J. G., & Penev, P. D.(2012). Sleep and eating behavior in adults at risk for type 2 diabetes. *Obesity, 20*(1), 112–17.

Killcross, S., Everitt, B. J., & Robbins, T. W. (1997a). Different types of fear-conditioned behaviour mediated by separate nuclei within amygdala. *Nature, 388*(6640), 377–80.

Killcross, S., Everitt, B. J., & Robbins, T. W. (1997b). Reply to Nader et al. (1997). *Trends in Cognitive Sciences, 1*(7), 244–6.

Killgore, W. D. (2010). Effects of sleep deprivation on cognition. *Progress in Brain Research, 185,* 105.

Kim, E. J., & Dimsdale, J. E. (2007). The effect of psychosocial stress on sleep: A review of polysomnographic evidence. *Behavioral Sleep Medicine, 5*(4), 256–78.

Kim, M. J., & Whalen, P. J. (2009). The structural integrity of an amygdala-prefrontal pathway predicts trait anxiety. *Journal of Neuroscience, 29*(37), 11614–18.

King, B. M., Cook, J. T., Rossiter, K. N. & Rollins, B. L. (2003). Obesity-inducing amygdala lesions: Examination of anterograde degeneration and retrograde transport. *American Journal of Physiology – Regulatory, Integrative and Comparative Physiology, 284*(4), R965–82.

Kirschenbaum, B., & Goldman, S. A. (1995). Brain-derived neurotrophic factor promotes the survival of neurons arising from the adult rat forebrain subependymal zone. *Proceedings of the National Academy of Sciences, 92*(1), 210–14.

Kleim, B., Wilhelm, F. H., Temp, L., Margraf, J., Wiederhold, B. K., & Rasch, B. (2013). Sleep enhances exposure therapy. *Psychological Medicine, 10,* 1–9.

Klein, S., Allison, D. B., Heymsfield, S. B., Kelley, D. E., Leibel, R. L., Nonas, C., & Kahn, R. (2007). Waist circumference and cardiometabolic risk: A consensus statement from shaping America's health (Association for Weight Management and Obesity Prevention; NAASO, the Obesity Society; the American Society for Nutrition; and the American Diabetes Association). *Obesity, 15*(5), 1061–7.

Klüver, H., & Bucy, P. C. (1939). Preliminary analysis of the temporal lobe in monkeys. *Archives of Neurology and Psychiatry, 42,* 979–1000.

Koob, G. F. (1992). Neural mechanisms of drug reinforcement. *Annals of the New York Academy of Sciences, 654,* 171–91.

Kosten, T. A., Miserendino, M. J., & Kehoe, P. (2000). Enhanced acquisition of cocaine self-administration in adult rats with neonatal isolation stress experience. *Brain Research, 875*(1), 44–50.

Kringelbach, M. L., O'Doherty, J., Rolls, E. T., & Andrews, C. (2003). Activation of the human orbitofrontal cortex to a liquid food stimulus is correlated with its subjective pleasantness. *Cerebral Cortex, 13*(10), 1064–71.

Kristiansen, L. V., Huerta, I., Beneyto, M., & Meador-Woodruff, J. H. (2007). NMDA receptors and schizophrenia. *Current Opinion in Pharmacology, 7*(1), 48–55.

Kronstrand, R., Roman, M., Thelander, G., & Eriksson, A. (2011). Unintentional fatal intoxications with mitragynine and O-desmethyltramadol from the herbal blend Krypton. *Journal of Analytical Toxicology, 35*(4), 242–7.

Krueger, J. M., & Majde, J. A. (1994). Microbial products and cytokines in sleep and fever regulation. *Critical Reviews in Immunology, 14*(3), 355–80.

Krueger, P. M., & Friedman, E. M. (2009). Sleep duration in the United States: A cross-sectional population-based study. *American Journal of Epidemiology, 169*(9), 1052–63.

Krystal, J. H., Karper, L. P., Seibyl, J. P., Freeman, G. K., Delaney, R., Bremner, J. D., ... & Charney, D. S. (1994). Subanesthetic effects of the noncompetitive NMDA antagonist, ketamine, in humans: Psychotomimetic, perceptual, cognitive, and neuroendocrine responses. *Archives of General Psychiatry, 51*(3), 199.

Kubota, K. (1989). Kuniomi Ishimori and the first discovery of sleep-inducing substances in the brain. *Neuroscience Research, 6*(6), 497–518.

Kufahl, P. R., Zavala, A. R., Singh, A., Thiel, K. J., Dickey, E. D., Joyce, J. N., & Neisewander, J. L. (2009). c-Fos expression associated with reinstatement of cocaine-seeking behavior by response-contingent conditioned cues. *Synapse, 63*(10), 823–35.

Kumar, A. et al. (2008). Chromatin remodeling is a key mechanism underlying cocaine-induced plasticity in striatum. *Neuron, 48,* 303–14.

Kupfer, D. J. (1991). Long-term treatment of depression. *Journal of Clinical Psychiatry, 52*(Suppl), 28–34.

Kurdziel, L., Duclos, K., & Spencer, R. M. (2013). Sleep spindles in midday naps enhance learning in preschool children. *Proceedings of the National Academy of Sciences, 110*(43), 17267–72.

Kurina, L. M., McClintock, M. K., Chen, J. H., Waite, L. J., Thisted, R. A., & Lauderdale, D. S. (2013). Sleep duration and all-cause mortality: A critical review of measurement and associations. *Annals of Epidemiology, 23*(6), 361–70.

Kwapis, J. L., Jarome, T. J., Lonergan, M. E., & Helmstetter, F. J. (2009). Protein kinase Mzeta maintains fear memory in the amygdala but not in the hippocampus. *Behavioral Neuroscience, 123*(4), 844–50.

LaBar, K. S., Gatenby, J. C., Gore, J. C., LeDoux, J. E., & Phelps, E. A. (1998). Human amygdala activation during conditioned fear acquisition and extinction: A mixed-trial fMRI study. *Neuron, 20*(5), 937–45.

Langston, J. W., Ballard, P., Tetrud, J. W., & Irwin, I. (1983) Chronic Parkinsonism in humans due to a product of meperidine-analog synthesis. *Science, 219*(4587), 979–80.

Laruelle, M., Abi-Dargham, A., Van Dyck, C. H., Gil, R., D'Souza, C. D., Erdos, J., ... & Innis, R. B. (1996). Single photon emission computerized tomography imaging of amphetamine-induced dopamine release in drug-free schizophrenic subjects. *Proceedings of the National Academy of Sciences, 93*(17), 9235–40.

Laruelle, M., Frankle, W. G., Narendran, R., Kegeles, L. S., & Abi-Dargham, A. (2005). Mechanism of action of antipsychotic drugs: From dopamine D2 receptor antagonism to glutamate NMDA facilitation. *Clinical Therapeutics, 27,* S16–S24.

Lasser, K., Boyd, J. W., Woolhandler, S., Himmelstein, D. U., McCormick, D., & Bor, D. H. (2000). Smoking and mental illness. *Journal of the American Medical Association, 284*(20), 2606–10.

Latner, J. D., & Schwartz, M. B. (2005). Weight bias in a child's world. Weight bias: *Nature, Consequences, and Remedies,* 54–67.

Lawrie, S. M., Whalley, H., Kestelman, J. N., Abukmeil, S. S., Byrne, M., Hodges, A., ... & Johnstone, E. C. (1999). Magnetic resonance imaging of brain in people at high risk of developing schizophrenia. *The Lancet, 353*(9146), 30–33.

Lazarini, F., & Lledo, P. M. (2011). Is adult neurogenesis essential for olfaction? *Trends in Neuroscience, 34*(1), 20–30.

LeDoux, J. E., Cicchetti, P., Xagoraris, A., & Romanski, L. M. (1990). The lateral amygdaloid nucleus – Sensory interface of the amygdala in fear conditioning. *Journal of Neuroscience, 10*(4), 1062–9.

Lee, A. M., Kanter, B. R., Wang, D., Lim, J. P., Zou, M. E., Qiu, C., & Messing, R. O. (2013). Prkcz null mice show normal learning and memory. *Nature, 493*(7432), 416–19.

Lee, D. N. & Lishman, J. R. (1975). Visual proprioceptive control of stance. *Journal of Movement Studies, 1,* 87–95.

Lee, H., & Kim, J. J. (1998). Amygdalar NMDA receptors are critical for new fear learning in previously fear-conditioned rats. *Journal of Neuroscience, 18*(20), 8444–54.

Lee, J. L. C. (2008). Memory reconsolidation mediates the strengthening of memories by additional learning. *Nature Neuroscience, 11*(11), 1264–6.

Lee, J. L. C. (2009). Reconsolidation: Maintaining memory relevance. *Trends in Neuroscience, 32*(8), 413–20.

Lee, J. L. C. (2010). Memory reconsolidation mediates the updating of hippocampal memory content. *Frontiers in Behavioral Neuroscience, 4,* 168.

Lee, J. L. C., Dickinson, A., & Everitt, B. J. (2005). Conditioned suppression and freezing as measures of aversive Pavlovian conditioning: Effects of discrete amygdala lesions and overtraining. *Behavioural Brain Research, 159*(2), 221–33.

Lee, J. L. C., Milton, A. L., & Everitt, B. J. (2006). Cue-induced cocaine seeking and relapse are reduced by disruption of drug memory reconsolidation. *Journal of Neuroscience, 26*(22), 5881–7.

Lee, M. A., Flegel, P., Greden, J. F., & Cameron, O. G. (1988). Anxiogenic effects of caffeine on panic and depressed patients. *American Journal of Psychiatry, 145*(5), 632–5.

Lees, A. J., Hardy, J., & Revesz, T. (2009). Parkinson's disease. *Lancet, 373*(9680), 2055–66.

Leinninger, G. M., Jo, Y. H., Leshan, R. L., Louis, G. W., Yang, H., Barrera, J. G., ... & Myers, M. G., Jr, (2009). Leptin acts via leptin receptor-expressing lateral hypothalamic neurons to modulate the mesolimbic dopamine system and suppress feeding. *Cell Metabolism, 10*(2), 89–98.

Le Marquand, D., Pihl, R. O., & Benkelfat, C. (1994). Serotonin and alcohol intake, abuse, and dependence: Clinical evidence. *Biological psychiatry, 36*(5), 326–37.

Levin, B. E. (2002). Metabolic sensors: Viewing glucosensing neurons from a broader perspective. *Physiology & Behavior, 76*(3), 397–401.

Levine, A. S., Kotz, C. M., & Gosnell, B. A. (2003). Sugars and fats: The neurobiology of preference. *Journal of Nutrition, 133*(3), 831S–834S.

Levine, D. G. (1974). 'Needle freaks': Compulsive self-injection by drug users. *American Journal of Psychiatry, 131*(3), 297–300.

Levine, J., Gordon, N., & Fields, H. (1978). The mechanism of placebo analgesia. *The Lancet, 312*(8091), 654–7.

Lewinsohn, P. M., Hops, H., Roberts, R. E., Seeley, J. R., & Andrews, J. A. (1993). Adolescent psychopathology: I. Prevalence and incidence of depression and other DSM-III–R disorders in high school students. *Journal of Abnormal Psychology*, *102*(1), 133.

Lewinsohn, P. M., Rohde, P., Klein, D. N., & Seeley, J. R. (1999). Natural course of adolescent major depressive disorder: I. Continuity into young adulthood. *Journal of the American Academy of Child & Adolescent Psychiatry*, *38*(1), 56–63.

Lewis, A., Miller, J. H., & Lea, R. A. (2007). Monoamine oxidase and tobacco dependence. *Neurotoxicology*, *28*(1), 182–95.

Leyton, M., Boileau, I., Benkelfat, C., Diksic, M., Baker, G., & Dagher, A. (2002). Amphetamine-induced increases in extracellular dopamine, drug wanting, and novelty seeking: A PET/[11C] raclopride study in healthy men. *Neuropsychopharmacology*, *27*(6), 1027–35.

Li, X., Lu, Z. L., D'Argembeau, A., Ng, M., & Bechara, A. (2010). The Iowa Gambling Task in fMRI images. *Human Brain Mapping*, *31*(3), 410–23.

Lichtenstein, P., Yip, B. H., Bjork, C. P., Pawitan, Y., Cannon, T. D., Sullivan, P. F, & Hultman, C.M. (2009). Common genetic determinants of schizophrenia and bipolar disorder in Swedish families: A population-based study. *The Lancet*, *373*, 234–9.

Liddle, R. A., Goldfine, I. D., Rosen, M. S., Taplitz, R. A., & Williams, J. A. (1985). Cholecystokinin bioactivity in human plasma: Molecular forms, responses to feeding, and relationship to gallbladder contraction. *Journal of Clinical Investigation*, *75*(4), 1144.

Liberman, A. M., Cooper, F. S., Shankweiler, D. P., & Studdert-Kennedy, M. (1967). Perception of the speech code. *Psychological Review*, *74*, 431–61.

Lieberman, H. R., Wurtman, R. J., Emde, G. G., Roberts, C., & Coviella, I. L. G. (1987). The effects of low doses of caffeine on human performance and mood. *Psychopharmacology*, *92*(3), 308–12.

Lieberman, J. A., Perkins, D., Belger, A., Chakos, M., Jarskog, F., Boteva, K., & Gilmore, J. (2001). The early stages of schizophrenia: Speculations on pathogenesis, pathophysiology, and therapeutic approaches. *Biological Psychiatry*, *50*(11), 884–97.

Lilenfeld, L. R., Wonderlich, S., Riso, L. P., Crosby, R., & Mitchell, J. (2006). Eating disorders and personality: A methodological and empirical review. *Clinical Psychology Review*, *26*(3), 299–320.

Lim, J., & Dinges, D. F. (2008). Sleep deprivation and vigilant attention. *Annals of the New York Academy of Sciences*, *1129*(1), 305–22.

Lin, M., Hrabovsky, A., Pedrosa, E., Wang, T., Zheng, D., & Lachman, H. M. (2012). Allele-biased expression in differentiating human neurons: Implications for neuropsychiatric disorders. *PLoS (Public Library of Science) ONE*, *7*(8), e44017.

Lindvall, O., & Kokaia, Z. (2010). Stem cells in human neurodegenerative disorders — Time for clinical translation? *Journal of Clinical Investigation*, *120*(1), 29–40.

Linnoila, M. I. (1990). Benzodiazepines and alcohol. *Journal of Psychiatric Research*, *24*, 121–7.

Lipska, B. K., Jaskiw, G. E., & Weinberger, D. R. (1993). Postpubertal emergence of hyperresponsiveness to stress and to amphetamine after neonatal excitotoxic hippocampal damage: A potential animal model of schizophrenia. *Neuropsychopharmacology*, *9*(1), 67–75.

Liu, J. S. (2011). Molecular genetics of neuronal migration disorders. *Current Neurology and Neuroscience Reports, 11*, 171–8.

Liu, A., & Niswander, L. A. (2005). Bone morphogenetic protein signalling and vertebrate nervous system development. *Nature Reviews Neuroscience*, *6*(12), 945–54.

Lock, E. A., Zhang, J., & Checkoway, H. (2013). Solvents and Parkinson disease: A systematic review of toxicological and epidemiological evidence. *Toxicology and Applied Pharmacology*, *266*(3), 345–55.

Lodge, D. J., & Grace, A. A. (2009). Gestational methylazoxymethanol acetate administration: A developmental disruption model of schizophrenia. *Behavioural Brain Research*, *204*(2), 306–12.

Loftus, E. F. (2005). Planting misinformation in the human mind: A 30-year investigation of the malleability of memory. *Learning and Memory*, *12*(4), 361–6.

Lorant, V., Deliège, D., Eaton, W., Robert, A., Philippot, P., & Ansseau, M. (2003). Socioeconomic inequalities in depression: A meta-analysis. *American Journal of Epidemiology*, *157*(2), 98–112.

Lovinger, D. M., White, G., & Weight, F. F. (1989). Ethanol inhibits NMDA-activated ion current in hippocampal neurons. *Science*, *243*(4899), 1721–4.

Lu, J., Greco, M. A., Shiromani, P., & Saper, C. B. (2000). Effect of lesions of the ventrolateral preoptic nucleus on NREM and REM sleep. *Journal of Neuroscience*, *20*(10), 3830–42.

Lund, T. B., Sandøe, P., & Lassen, J. (2011). Attitudes to publicly funded obesity treatment and prevention. *Obesity*, *19*(8), 1580–85.

Lyubomirsky, S., Caldwell, N. D., & Nolen-Hoeksema, S. (1998). Effects of ruminative and distracting responses to depressed mood on retrieval of autobiographical memories. *Journal of Personality and Social Psychology, 75*(1), 166.

Machado-Vieira, R., Manji, H. K. and Zarate, C. A. (2009). The role of the tripartite glutamatergic synapse in the pathophysiology and therapeutics of mood disorders. *Neuroscientist, 15*(5), 525–39.

Mackiewicz, M., Zimmerman, J. E., Shockley, K. R., Churchill, G. A., & Pack, A. I. (2009). What are microarrays teaching us about sleep? *Trends in Molecular Medicine, 15*(2), 79–87.

MacLean, K. A., Johnson, M. W., & Griffiths, R. R. (2011). Mystical experiences occasioned by the hallucinogen psilocybin lead to increases in the personality domain of openness. *Journal of Psychopharmacology, 25*(11), 1453–61.

Macleod, J., Smith, G. D., Heslop, P., Metcalfe, C., Carroll, D., & Hart, C. (2002). Psychological stress and cardiovascular disease: Empirical demonstration of bias in a prospective observational study of Scottish men. *British Medical Journal, 324*(7348), 1247.

Maffei, M., Halaas, J., Ravussin, E., Pratley, R. E., Lee, G. H., Zhang, Y., ... & Friedman, J. M. (1995). Leptin levels in human and rodent: Measurement of plasma leptin and ob RNA in obese and weight-reduced subjects. *Nature Medicine, 1*(11), 1155–61.

Magee, C. A., Iverson, D. C., Huang, X. F., & Caputi, P. (2008). A link between chronic sleep restriction and obesity: Methodological considerations. *Public Health, 122*(12), 1373–81.

Magee, C. A., Holliday, E. G., Attia, J., Kritharides, L., & Banks, E. (2013). Investigation of the relationship between sleep duration, all-cause mortality, and preexisting disease. *Sleep Medicine, 14*(7), 591–6.

Magee, L., & Hale, L. (2012). Longitudinal associations between sleep duration and subsequent weight gain: A systematic review. *Sleep Medicine Reviews, 16*(3), 231–41.

Maguire, E. A., Burgess, N., Donnett, J. G., Frackowiak, R. S., Frith, C. D., & O'Keefe, J. (1998). Knowing where and getting there: A human navigation network. *Science, 280*(5365), 921–4.

Maher, B. J., & LoTurco, J. J. (2012). Disrupted-in-schizophrenia (DISC1) functions presynaptically at glutamatergic synapses. *PLoS (Public Library of Science) ONE, 7*(3), e34053.

Maldonado, R., Valverde, O., & Berrendero, F. (2006). Involvement of the endocannabinoid system in drug addiction. *Trends in Neurosciences, 29*(4), 225–32.

Malhotra, A. K., Correll, C. U., Chowdhury, N. I., Muller, D. J., Gregersen, P. K., Lee, A. T., & Kennedy, J. L. (2012). Association between common variants near the melanocortin 4 receptor gene and severe antipsychotic drug-induced weight gain. *Archives of General Psychiatry, 69*(9), 904–12.

Malhotra, A. K., Pinals, D. A., Weingartner, H., Sirocco, K., Missar, C. D., Pickar, D., & Breier, A. (1996). NMDA receptor function and human cognition: The effects of ketamine in healthy volunteers. *Neuropsychopharmacology, 14*(5), 301–7.

Malizia, A. L., Cunningham, V. J., Bell, C. J., Liddle, P. F., Jones, T., & Nutt, D. J. (1998). Decreased brain GABAA-benzodiazepine receptor binding in panic disorder: Preliminary results from a quantitative PET study. *Archives of General Psychiatry, 55*(8), 715.

Malpass, D., & Higgs, S. (2007). Acute psychomotor, subjective and physiological responses to smoking in depressed outpatient smokers and matched controls. *Psychopharmacology, 190*(3), 363–72.

Mander, B. A., Rao, V., Lu, B., Saletin, J. M., Ancoli-Israel, S., Jagust, W. J., & Walker, M. P. (2013). Impaired prefrontal sleep spindle regulation of hippocampal-dependent learning in older adults. *Cerebral Cortex*, bht188.

Manfredsson, F. P., Okun, M. S., & Mandel, R. J. (2009). Gene therapy for neurological disorders: Challenges and future prospects for the use of growth factors for the treatment of Parkinson's disease. *Current Gene Therapy, 9*(5), 375–88.

Manno, J. E., Kiplinger, G. F., Haine, S. E., Bennett, I. F., & Forney, R. B. (1970). Comparative effects of smoking marihuana or placebo on human motor and mental performance. *Clinical Pharmacology and Therapeutics, 11*(6), 808–15.

Mao, Y., Ge, X., Frank, C. L., Madison, J. M., Koehler, A. N., Doud, M. K., Tassa, C., Berry, E. M., Soda, T., Singh, K. K., Biechele, T., Petryshen, T. L., Moon, R. T., Haggarty, S. J., & Tsai, L. H. (2009). DISC-1 regulates neuronal progenitor proliferation via modulation of GSK3beta/beta-catenin signaling. *Cell, 136*(6), 1017–31.

Maquet, P. (2000). Functional neuroimaging of normal human sleep by positron emission tomography. *Journal of Sleep Research, 9*(3), 207–32.

Maquet, P., Ruby, P., Maudoux, A., Albouy, G., Sterpenich, V., Dang-Vu, T., ... & Laureys, S. (2005). Human cognition during REM sleep and the activity profile within frontal and parietal cortices: A reappraisal of functional neuroimaging data. *Progress in Brain Research, 150*, 219–27.

Marañon, G. (1924). Contribution a l'etude de l'action emotive de l'adrenaline. *La Revue Francaise d'Endocrinologie Clinique, Nutrition, et Metabolisme, 2*, 301–25.

Marczewski, A. E., & Kamrin, M. (1991). *Toxicology for the Citizen*, 2nd edition. East Lansing, MI: Michigan State University, Center for Integrative Toxicology.

Maren, S. (1999). Neurotoxic basolateral amygdala lesions impair learning and memory but not the performance of conditional fear in rats. *Journal of Neuroscience, 19*(19), 8696.

Maren, S. (2005). Synaptic mechanisms of associative memory in the amygdala. *Neuron, 47*(6), 783–6.

Maren, S., Ferrario, C. R., Corcoran, K. A., Desmond, T. J., & Frey, K. A. (2003). Protein synthesis in the amygdala, but not the auditory thalamus, is required for consolidation of Pavlovian fear conditioning in rats. *European Journal of Neuroscience, 18*(11), 3080–88.

Margolese, H. C., Chouinard, G., Kolivakis, T. T., Beauclair, L., & Miller, R. (2005). Tardive dyskinesia in the era of typical and atypical antipsychotics. Part 1: pathophysiology and mechanisms of induction. *Canadian Journal of Psychiatry, 50*(9), 541.

Marona-Lewicka, D., Thisted, R. A., & Nichols, D. E. (2005). Distinct temporal phases in the behavioral pharmacology of LSD: Dopamine D2 receptor-mediated effects in the rat and implications for psychosis. *Psychopharmacology, 180*(3), 427–35.

Marrazzi, M. A., & Luby, E. D. (1986). An auto-addiction opioid model of chronic anorexia nervosa. *International Journal of Eating Disorders, 5*(2), 191–208.

Marshall, M., & Lockwood, A. (2000) Assertive community treatment for people with severe mental disorders. *Cochrane Library*, issue 2. Oxford: John Wiley.

Martin, H. L., & Teismann, P. (2009). Glutathione – a review on its role and significance in Parkinson's disease. *FASEB Journal, 23*(10), 3263–72.

Martin-Ruiz, C., Graham, A., & Perry, E. (2000). Nicotinic receptors in human brain: Topography and pathology. *Journal of Chemical Neuroanatomy, 20*(3), 281–98.

Masterson, E., & O'Shea, B. (1984). Smoking and malignancy in schizophrenia. *British Journal of Psychiatry, 145*(4), 429–32.

Mastroeni, D., Grover, A., Delvaux, E., Whiteside, C., Coleman, P. D., & Rogers, J. (2011). Epigenetics mechanisms in Alzheimer's disease. *Neurobiology of Aging, 32*(7), 1161–80.

Mathews, A., & MacLeod, C. (2005). Cognitive vulnerability to emotional disorders. *Annual Review of Clinical Psychology, 1*, 167–95.

Matricciani, L. A., Olds, T. S., Blunden, S., Rigney, G., & Williams, M. T. (2012). Never enough sleep: A brief history of sleep recommendations for children. *Pediatrics, 129*(3), 548–56.

Matsumoto, D., & Willingham, B. (2009). Spontaneous facial expressions of emotion of congenitally and non-congenitally blind individuals. *Journal of Personality and Social Psychology, 96*(1), 1–10.

Mauk, M. D., Garcia, K. S., Medina, J. F., & Steele, P. M. (1998). Does cerebellar LTD mediate motor learning? Toward a resolution without a smoking gun. *Neuron, 20*(3), 359–62.

Maxwell, H., Dubois, S., Weaver, B., & Bédard, M. (2010). The additive effects of alcohol and benzodiazepines on driving. *Canadian Journal of Public Health, 101*(5), 353–57.

McAuley, P. A., Artero, E. G., Sui, X., Lee, D. C., Church, T. S., Lavie, C. J., ... & Blair, S. N. (2012, May). The obesity paradox, cardiorespiratory fitness, and coronary heart disease. In *Mayo Clinic Proceedings*, 87(5), 443–51.

McCarley, R. W., & Hobson, J. A. (1975). Neuronal excitability modulation over the sleep cycle: A structural and mathematical model. *Science, 189*(4196), 58–60.

McClure, E. B., Adler, A., Monk, C. S., Cameron, J., Smith, S., Nelson, E. E., ... & Pine, D. S. (2007). fMRI predictors of treatment outcome in pediatric anxiety disorders. *Psychopharmacology, 191*(1), 97–105.

McCormick, D. A. (1989). Cholinergic and noradrenergic modulation of thalamocortical processing. *Trends in Neurosciences, 12*(6), 215–21.

McCoy, J. G., & Strecker, R. E. (2011). The cognitive cost of sleep lost. *Neurobiology of Learning and Memory, 96*(4), 564–82.

McDonald, A. J. (1998). Cortical pathways to the mammalian amygdala. *Progress in Neurobiology, 55*(3), 257–332.

McDonald, A. J., Shammah-Lagnado, S. J., Shi, C., & Davis, M. (1999). Cortical afferents to the extended amygdala. *Annals of the New York Academy of Sciences, 877*, 309–38.

McEwen, B. S. (2001). Plasticity of the hippocampus: Adaptation to chronic stress and allostatic load. *Annals of the New York Academy of Sciences, 933*(1), 265–77.

McEwen, B. S. (2007). Physiology and neurobiology of stress and adaptation: Central role of the brain. *Physiological Reviews, 87*(3), 873–904.

McFarlane, A. C., Atchison, M., & Yehuda, R. (1997). The acute stress response following motor vehicle accidents and its relation to PTSD. *Annals of the New York Academy of Sciences, 821*, 437–41.

McGlothlin, W. H., & Arnold, D. O. (1971). LSD revisited: A ten-year follow-up of medical LSD use. *Archives of General Psychiatry, 24*(1), 35.

McGrath, J., Saha, S., Chant, D., & Welham, J. (2008). Schizophrenia: A concise overview of incidence, prevalence, and mortality. *Epidemiologic Reviews*, *30*(1), 67–76.

McGurk., H., & MacDonald, J. (1976). Hearing lips and seeing voices. *Nature, 264*(5588), 746–8.

McIntyre, C.C., & Hahn, P.J. (2010). Network perspectives on the mechanisms of deep brain stimulation. *Neurobiology of Disease, 38*(3), 329–37.

Mechoulam, R. (Ed.). (1986). *Cannabinoids as Therapeutics*. Heidelberg: Springer.

Mechoulam, R., & Gaoni, Y. (1967). The absolute configuration of delta-1-tetrahydro cannabinol, the major active constituent of hashish. *Tetrahedron Letters*, *12*, 1109–11.

Meddis, R. (1977). *The Sleep Instinct*. London: Routledge and Kegan Paul.

Meewisse, M. L., Reitsma, J. B., de Vries, G. J., Gersons, B. P., & Olff, M. (2007). Cortisol and post-traumatic stress disorder in adults: Systematic review and meta-analysis. *British Journal of Psychiatry*, 191, 387–92.

Meil, W. M., & See, R. E. (1997). Lesions of the basolateral amygdala abolish the ability of drug associated cues to reinstate responding during withdrawal from self-administered cocaine. *Behavioural Brain Research, 87*(2), 139–48.

Meister, I. G., Weidemann, J., Foltys, H., Brand, H., Willmes, K., Krings, T., & Boroojerdi, B.(2005). The neural correlate of very-long-term picture priming. *European Journal of Neuroscience, 21*(4), 1101–06.

Meltzer, H. Y., Matsubara, S., & Lee, J. C. (1989). Classification of typical and atypical antipsychotic drugs on the basis of dopamine D-1, D-2 and serotonin2 pKi values. *Journal of Pharmacology and Experimental Therapeutics, 251*(1), 238–46.

Melzack, R., & Wall, P. D. (1996). *The Challenge of Pain*, 2nd edition. London: Penguin Books.

Menz, M. M., Rihm, J. S., Salari, N., Born, J., Kalisch, R., Pape, H. C., ... & Büchel, C. (2013). The role of sleep and sleep deprivation in consolidating fear memories. *NeuroImage*, 75, 87–96.

Meyer, J. H., Ginovart, N., Boovariwala, A., Sagrati, S., Hussey, D., Garcia, A., ... & Houle, S. (2006). Elevated monoamine oxidase A levels in the brain: An explanation for the monoamine imbalance of major depression. *Archives of General Psychiatry, 63*(11), 1209.

Michaelides, M., Thanos, P. K., Kim, R., Cho, J., Ananth, M., Wang, G. J., & Volkow, N. D. (2012). PET imaging predicts future body weight and cocaine preference. *Neuroimage, 59*(2), 1508–13.

Miczek, K. A., Yap, J. J., & Covington, H. E. (2008). Social stress, therapeutics and drug abuse: Preclinical models of escalated and depressed intake. *Pharmacology & Therapeutics, 120*(2), 102–28.

Milad, M. R., & Quirk, G. J. (2002). Neurons in medial prefrontal cortex signal memory for fear extinction. *Nature, 420*(6911), 70–74.

Milad, M. R., Vidal-Gonzalez, I., & Quirk, G. J. (2004). Electrical stimulation of medial prefrontal cortex reduces conditioned fear in a temporally specific manner. *Behaviourial Neuroscience, 118*(2), 389–94.

Milad, M. R., Wright, C. I., Orr, S. P., Pitman, R. K., Quirk, G. J., & Rauch, S. L. (2007). Recall of fear extinction in humans activates the ventromedial prefrontal cortex and hippocampus in concert. *Biological Psychiatry, 62*(5), 446–54.

Milad, M. R., Quirk, G. J., Pitman, R. K., Orr, S. P., Fischl, B., & Rauch, S. L. (2007). A role for the human dorsal anterior cingulate cortex in fear expression. *Biological Psychiatry, 62*(10), 1191–4.

Milad, M. R., Pitman, R. K., Ellis, C. B., Gold, A. L., Shin, L. M., Lasko, N. B., & Rauch, S. L. (2009). Neurobiological basis of failure to recall extinction memory in posttraumatic stress disorder. *Biological Psychiatry, 66*(12), 1075–82.

Miles, C., & Wayne, M. (2008). Quantitative trait locus (QTL) analysis. *Nature Education 1*(1), 208.

Mileykovskiy, B. Y., Kiyashchenko, L. I., & Siegel, J. M. (2005). Behavioral correlates of activity in identified hypocretin/orexin neurons. *Neuron, 46*(5), 787–98.

Millar, J. K., James, R., Brandon, N. J., & Thomson, P. A. (2004). DISC1 and DISC2: Discovering and dissecting molecular mechanisms underlying psychiatric illness. *Annals of Medicine, 36*(5), 367–78.

Miller, E. K., & Desimone, R. (1994). Parallel neuronal mechanisms for short-term memory. *Science, 263*(5146), 520–22.

Miller, G. E., & Blackwell, E. (2006). Turning up the heat: Inflammation as a mechanism linking chronic stress, depression, and heart disease. *Current Directions in Psychological Science, 15*(6), 269–72.

Miller, N. E. (1973). How the project started, in Valenstein, E. S. (ed.), *Brain Stimulation and Motivation: Research and Commentary*. Glenview, IL: Scott, Foresman and Company, pp. 53–68.

Mills, J. N., Minors, D. S., & Waterhouse, J. M. (1978). Adaptation to abrupt time shifts of the oscillator(s) controlling human circadian rhythms. *Journal of Physiology, 285*(1), 455–70.

Milton, A. L., Lee, J. L. C., Butler, V. J., Gardner, R., & Everitt, B. J. (2008). Intra-amygdala and systemic antagonism of NMDA receptors prevents the reconsolidation of drug-associated memory and impairs subsequently both novel and previously acquired drug-seeking behaviors. *Journal of Neuroscience, 28*(33), 8230–37.

Ming, G. L., & Song, H. (2005). Adult neurogenesis in the mammalian central nervous system. *Annual Review of Neuroscience, 28*, 223–50.

Mirenowicz, J., & Schultz, W. (1994). Importance of unpredictability for reward responses in primate dopamine neurons. *Journal of Neurophysiology, 72*(2), 1024–7.

Miserendino, M. J., Sananes, C. B., Melia, K. R., & Davis, M. (1990). Blocking of acquisition but not expression of conditioned fear-potentiated startle by NMDA antagonists in the amygdala. *Nature, 345*(6277), 716–18.

Mistlberger, R. E., & Skene, D. J. (2005). Nonphotic entrainment in humans? *Journal of Biological Rhythms, 20*(4), 339–52.

Mithoefer, M. C., Wagner, M. T., Mithoefer, A. T., Jerome, L., & Doblin, R. (2011). The safety and efficacy of ±3,4-methylenedioxymethamphetamine-assisted psychotherapy in subjects with chronic, treatment-resistant post-traumatic stress disorder: The first randomized controlled pilot study. *Journal of Psychopharmacology, 25*(4), 439–52.

Mittermeyer, G., Christine, C. W., Rosenbluth, K. H., Baker, S. L., Starr, P., Larson, P., Kaplan, P. L., Forsayeth, J., Aminoff, M. J., & Bankiewicz, K. S. (2012). Long-term evaluation of a phase 1 study of AADC gene therapy for Parkinson's disease. *Human Gene Therapy, 23*(4), 377–81.

Mogg, K., & Bradley, B. P. (1998). A cognitive-motivational analysis of anxiety. *Behaviour Research and Therapy, 36*(9), 809–48.

Mogg, K., Bradley, B. P., Williams, R., & Mathews, A. (1993). Subliminal processing of emotional information in anxiety and depression. *Journal of Abnormal Psychology, 102*(2), 304.

Mogg, K., Bradley, B. P., Field, M., & De Houwer, J. (2003). Eye movements to smoking-related pictures in smokers: Relationship between attentional biases and implicit and explicit measures of stimulus valence. *Addiction, 98*(6), 825–36.

Moghaddam, B., Adams, B., Verma, A., & Daly, D. (1997). Activation of glutamatergic neurotransmission by ketamine: A novel step in the pathway from NMDA receptor blockade to dopaminergic and cognitive disruptions associated with the prefrontal cortex. *Journal of Neuroscience, 17*(8), 2921–7.

Moir, D., Rickert, W. S., Levasseur, G., Larose, Y., Maertens, R., White, P., & Desjardins, S. (2007). A comparison of mainstream and sidestream marijuana and tobacco cigarette smoke produced under two machine smoking conditions. *Chemical Research in Toxicology, 21*(2), 494–502.

Molenberghs, P., Cunnington, R., & Mattingley, J. B. (2012). Brain regions with mirror properties: A meta-analysis of 125 human fMRI studies. *Neuroscience & Biobehavioral Reviews, 36*, 341–9.

Monk, C. S., Telzer, E. H., Mogg, K., Bradley, B. P., Mai, X., Louro, H., ... & Pine, D. S. (2008). Amygdala and ventrolateral prefrontal cortex activation to masked angry faces in children and adolescents with generalized anxiety disorder. *Archives of General Psychiatry, 65*(5), 568.

Montague, C. T., Farooqi, I. S., Whitehead, J. P., Soos, M. A., Rau, H., Wareham, N. J., ... & O'Rahilly, S. (1997). Congenital leptin deficiency is associated with severe early-onset obesity in humans. *Nature, 387*(6636), 903–08.

Moore, R. Y., Speh, J. C., & Card, J. P. (1995). The retinohypothalamic tract originates from a distinct subset of retinal ganglion cells. *Journal of Comparative Neurology, 352*(3), 351–66.

Moore, T. H., Zammit, S., Lingford-Hughes, A., Barnes, T. R., Jones, P. B., Burke, M., & Lewis, G. (2007). Cannabis use and risk of psychotic or affective mental health outcomes: A systematic review. *The Lancet, 370*(9584), 319–28.

Moran, T. H., Baldessarini, A. R., Salorio, C. F., Lowery, T., & Schwartz, G. J. (1997). Vagal afferent and efferent contributions to the inhibition of food intake by cholecystokinin. *American Journal of Physiology – Regulatory, Integrative and Comparative Physiology, 272*(4), R1245–R1251.

Moreno, J. A., Radford, H., Peretti, D., Steinert, J. R., Verity, N., Martin, M. G., Halliday, M., Morgan, J., Dinsdale, D., Otori, C. A., Barrett, D. A., Tsaytler, P., Bertolotti, A., Willis, A. E., Bushell, M., & Mallucci, G. R. (2012). Sustained translational repression by eIF2α-P mediates prion neurodegeneration. *Nature, 485*(7399), 507–11.

Morey, R. A., Gold, A. L., LaBar, K. S., Beall, S. K., Brown, V. M., Haswell, C. C., ... Mid-Atlantic, M. W. (2012). Amygdala volume changes in posttraumatic stress disorder in a large case-controlled veterans group. *Archives of General Psychiatry, 69*(11), 1169–78.

Morgan, C. J., Monaghan, L., & Curran, H. V. (2004a). Beyond the K-hole: A 3-year longitudinal investigation of the cognitive and subjective effects of ketamine in recreational users who have substantially reduced their use of the drug. *Addiction, 99*(11), 1450–61.

Morgan, C. J., Riccelli, M., Maitland, C. H., & Curran, H. V. (2004b). Long-term effects of ketamine: Evidence for a persisting impairment of source memory in recreational users. *Drug and Alcohol Dependence, 75*(3), 301–08.

Morgan, C. J., Muetzelfeldt, L., & Curran, H. V. (2010a). Consequences of chronic ketamine self-administration upon neurocognitive function and psychological wellbeing: A 1-year longitudinal study. *Addiction, 105*(1), 121–33.

Morgan, C. J., Schafer, G., Freeman, T. P., & Curran, H. V. (2010b). Impact of cannabidiol on the acute memory and psychotomimetic effects of smoked cannabis: Naturalistic study. *British Journal of Psychiatry, 197*(4), 285–90.

Morgan, D., Grant, K. A., Gage, H. D., Mach, R. H., Kaplan, J. R., Prioleau, O., & Nader, M. A. (2002). Social dominance in monkeys: Dopamine D2 receptors and cocaine self-administration. *Nature Neuroscience, 5*(2), 169–74.

Morgan, H. L., Turner, D. C., Corlett, P. R., Absalom, A. R., Adapa, R., Arana, F. S., ... & Fletcher, P. C. (2011). Exploring the impact of ketamine on the experience of illusory body ownership. *Biological Psychiatry, 69*(1), 35–41.

Morgan, M. A., Romanski, L. M., & LeDoux, J. E. (1993). Extinction of emotional learning: Contribution of medial pre-frontal cortex. *Neuroscience Letters, 163*(1), 109–13.

Morgan, M. A., Schulkin, J., & LeDoux, J. E. (2003). Ventral medial prefrontal cortex and emotional perseveration: The memory for prior extinction training. *Behavioural Brain Research, 146*(1–2), 121–30.

Morgan, M. J., McFie, L., Fleetwood, L., & Robinson, J. (2002). Ecstasy (MDMA): Are the psychological problems associated with its use reversed by prolonged abstinence? *Psychopharmacology, 159*(3), 294–303.

Mori, E., Ikeda, M., Hirono, N., Kitagaki, H., Imamura, T., & Shimomura, T. (1999). Amygdalar volume and emotional memory in Alzheimer's disease. *American Journal of Psychiatry, 156*(2), 216–22.

Morris, R. G., Inglis, J., Ainge, J. A., Olverman, H. J., Tulloch, J., Dudai, Y., & Kelly, P. A. (2006). Memory reconsolidation: Sensitivity of spatial memory to inhibition of protein synthesis in dorsal hippocampus during encoding and retrieval. *Neuron, 50*(3), 479–89.

Morrison J. H., & Baxter M. G. (2012). The ageing cortical synapse: Hallmarks and implications for cognitive decline. *Nature Reviews Neuroscience, 13*, 240–50.

Moruzzi, G., & Magoun, H. W. (1949). Brain stem reticular formation and activation of the EEG. *Electroencephalography and Clinical Neurophysiology, 1*(1), 455–73.

Mottonen, R., & Watkins, K. E. (2009). Motor representations of articulators contribute to categorical perception of speech sounds. *Journal of Neuroscience, 29*, 9819–25.

Mukamel, R., Ekstrom, A. D., Kaplan, J., Iacoboni, M., & Fried, I. (2010). Single-neuron responses in humans during execution and observation of actions. *Current Biology, 20*(8), 750–56.

Mukhametov, L. M., Supin, A. Y., & Polyakova, I. G. (1977). Interhemispheric asymmetry of the electroencephalographic sleep patterns in dolphins. *Brain Research, 134*(3), 581–4.

Muller, J., Corodimas, K. P., Fridel, Z., & LeDoux, J. E. (1997). Functional inactivation of the lateral and basal nuclei of the amygdala by muscimol infusion prevents fear conditioning to an explicit conditioned stimulus and to contextual stimuli. *Behavioral Neuroscience, 111*(4), 683–91.

Munro, S., Thomas, K. L., & Abu-Shaar, M. (1993). Molecular characterization of a peripheral receptor for cannabinoids. *Nature, 365*, 61–5.

Muntaner, C., Cascella, N. G., Kumor, K. M., Nagoshi, C., Herning, R., & Jaffe, J. (1989). Placebo responses to cocaine administration in humans: Effects of prior administrations and verbal instructions. *Psychopharmacology, 99*(2), 282–6.

Murphy, K. C. (2002). Schizophrenia and velo-cardio-facial syndrome. *The Lancet, 359*, 426–30.

Murray, G. K., Corlett, P. R., Clark, L., Pessiglione, M., Blackwell, A. D., Honey, G., ... & Fletcher, P. C. (2007). Substantia nigra/ventral tegmental reward prediction error disruption in psychosis. *Molecular Psychiatry, 13*(3), 267–76.

Murray, R. M., Jones, P., & O'Callaghan, E. (1991). Fetal brain development and later schizophrenia. *Ciba Foundation Symposium, 156*, 155–70.

Musselman, D. L., Evans, D. L., & Nemeroff, C. B. (1998). The relationship of depression to cardiovascular disease: Epidemiology, biology, and treatment. *Archives of General Psychiatry, 55*(7), 580.

Nadel, L., & Land, C. (2000). Memory traces revisited. *Nature Reviews Neuroscience, 1*(3), 209–12.

Nadel, L., & Moscovitch, M. (2001). The hippocampal complex and long-term memory revisited. *Trends in Cognitive Sciences, 5*(6), 228–30.

Nader, K., & LeDoux, J. E. (1997). Is it time to invoke multiple fear learning systems in the amygdala? *Trends in Cognitive Sciences, 1*(7), 241–4.

Nader, K., Schafe, G. E., & Le Doux, J. E. (2000). Fear memories require protein synthesis in the amygdala for reconsolidation after retrieval. *Nature, 406*(6797), 722–6.

Nader, K., Majidishad, P., Amorapanth, P., & LeDoux, J. E. (2001). Damage to the lateral and central, but not other, amygdaloid nuclei prevents the acquisition of auditory fear conditioning. *Learning & Memory, 8*(3), 156–63.

Nagatsu, T., & Sawada, M. (2009). L-dopa therapy for Parkinson's disease: Past, present, and future. *Parkinsonism & Related Disorders, 15*(1), S3–S8.

Naimi, T. S., Brown, D. W., Brewer, R. D., Giles, W. H., Mensah, G., Serdula, M. K., & Stroup, D. F. (2005). Cardiovascular risk factors and confounders among nondrinking and moderate-drinking US adults. *American Journal of Preventive Medicine, 28*(4), 369–73.

Nasrallah, H. (2003). A review of the effect of atypical antipsychotics on weight. *Psychoneuroendocrinology, 28*, 83–96.

Nasrallah, H. A., & Tandon, R. (2013). Classic antipsychotic medications. In *Essentials of Clinical Psychopharmacology*, 3rd edition. Arlington, VA: American Psychiatric Publishing Inc, pp. 219–36.

Nedergaard, J., Bengtsson, T., & Cannon, B. (2007). Unexpected evidence for active brown adipose tissue in adult humans. *American Journal of Physiology – Endocrinology And Metabolism, 293*(2), E444–E452.

Neel, J. V. (1962). Diabetes mellitus: A 'thrifty' genotype rendered detrimental by 'progress'? *American Journal of Human Genetics*, *14*(4), 353.

Nesse, R. M., & Berridge, K. C. (1997). Psychoactive drug use in evolutionary perspective. *Science*, *278*(5335), 63–6.

Nestler, E. J. (2005). Is there a common molecular pathway for addiction? *Nature Neuroscience*, *8*(11), 1445–9.

Nestoros, J. N. (1980). Ethanol specifically potentiates GABA-mediated neurotransmission in feline cerebral cortex. *Science*, *209*(4457), 708–10.

Neumark-Sztainer, D., Falkner, N., Story, M., Perry, C., Hannan, P. J., & Mulert, S. (2002). Weight-teasing among adolescents: Correlations with weight status and disordered eating behaviors. *International Journal of Obesity*, *26*(1), 123–31.

Neumeister, A., Young, T., & Stastny, J. (2004). Implications of genetic research on the role of the serotonin in depression: Emphasis on the serotonin type 1. A receptor and the serotonin transporter. *Psychopharmacology*, *174*(4), 512–24.

Newbold, R. R., Padilla-Banks, E., & Jefferson, W. N. (2009). Environmental estrogens and obesity. *Molecular and Cellular Endocrinology*, *304*(1), 84–9.

Ngo, H. V. V., Claussen, J. C., Born, J., & Moelle, M. (2013). Induction of slow oscillations by rhythmic acoustic stimulation. *Journal of Sleep Research*, *22*(1), 22–31.

Nibuya, M., Morinobu, S., & Duman, R. S. (1995). Regulation of BDNF and trkB mRNA in rat brain by chronic electroconvulsive seizure and antidepressant drug treatments. *Journal of Neuroscience*, *15*(11), 7539–47.

Nielsen, L. S., Danielsen, K. V., & Sørensen, T. I. A. (2011). Short sleep duration as a possible cause of obesity: Critical analysis of the epidemiological evidence. *Obesity Reviews*, *12*(2), 78–92.

Nixon, P. D., & Passingham, R. E. (2000). The cerebellum and cognition: Cerebellar lesions impair sequence learning but not conditional visuomotor learning in monkeys. *Neuropsychologia, 38*(7), 1054–72.

Nofzinger, E. A., Buysse, D. J., Germain, A., Price, J. C., Miewald, J. M., & Kupfer, D. J. (2004). Functional neuroimaging evidence for hyperarousal in insomnia. *American Journal of Psychiatry*, *161*(11), 2126–28.

Nolen-Hoeksema, S. (1990). *Sex Differences in Depression*. Stanford, CA: Stanford University Press.

Nolen-Hoeksema, S., Larson, J., & Grayson, C. (1999). Explaining the gender difference in depressive symptoms. *Journal of Personality and Social Psychology*, *77*(5), 1061.

Northoff, G., Grimm, S., Boeker, H., Schmidt, C., Bermpohl, F., Heinzel, A., ... Boesiger, P. (2006). Affective judgment and beneficial decision making: Ventromedial prefrontal activity correlates with performance in the Iowa Gambling Task. *Human Brain Mapping, 27*(7), 572–87.

Nutt, D. J., & Malizia, A. L. (2001). New insights into the role of the GABAA–benzodiazepine receptor in psychiatric disorders. *British Journal of Psychiatry*, *179*(5), 390–96.

O'Brien, C. P., Childress, A. R., Ehrman, R., & Robbins, S. J. (1998). Conditioning factors in drug abuse: Can they explain compulsion? *Journal of Psychopharmacology*, *12*(1), 15–22.

O'Brien, M., Singleton, N., Bumpstead, R., & Office for National Statistics (2001). *Psychiatric Morbidity Among Adults Living in Private Households, 2000*. London: The Stationery Office.

Odegaard, O. (1932). Emigration and insanity: A study of mental disease among the Norwegian-born population of Minnesota. *Acta Psychiatrica Scandinavica, 7*(suppl 4), 1–206.

Ogden, J., & Wardle, J. (1990). Control of eating and attributional style. *British Journal of Clinical Psychology*, *29*(4), 445–6.

Oliveri, M., Turriziani, P., Carlesimo, G. A., Koch, G., Tomaiuolo, F., Panella, M., & Caltagirone, C. (2001). Parieto-frontal interactions in visual-object and visual-spatial working memory: Evidence from transcranial magnetic stimulation. *Cerebral Cortex, 11*(7), 606–18.

Olney, J. W., & Farber, N. B. (1995). Glutamate receptor dysfunction and schizophrenia. *Archives of General Psychiatry*, *52*(12), 998–1007.

Olney, J. W., Newcomer, J. W., & Farber, N. B. (1999). NMDA receptor hypofunction model of schizophrenia. *Journal of Psychiatric Research*, *33*(6), 523–33.

Onishi, B. K., & Xavier, G. F. (2010). Contextual, but not auditory, fear conditioning is disrupted by neurotoxic selective lesion of the basal nucleus of amygdala in rats. *Neurobiology of Learning and Memory, 93*(2), 165–74.

Ostroff, L. E., Cain, C. K., Jindal, N., Dar, N., & LeDoux, J. E. (2012). Stability of presynaptic vesicle pools and changes in synapse morphology in the amygdala following fear learning in adult rats. *Journal of Comparative Neurology, 520*(2), 295–314.

Owen, M. J., Craddock, N., & O'Donovan, M. C. (2010). Suggestion of roles for both common and rare risk variants in genome-wide studies of schizophrenia. *Archives of General Psychiatry, 67*(7), 667.

Palop, J. J., & Mucke, L. (2010). Amyloid-β induced neuronal dysfunction in Alzheimer's disease: From synapses toward neural networks. *Nature Neuroscience, 13*(7), 812–18.

Paneda, C., Winsky-Sommerer, R., Boutrel, B., & De Lecea, L. (2005). The corticotropin–releasing factor–hypocretin connection: Implications in stress response and addiction. *Drug News Perspect, 18*(4), 250.

Parent, M., & Parent, A. (2010). Substantia nigra and parkinson's disease: A brief history of their long and intimate relationship. *Canadian Journal of Neurological Sciences, 37*(3), 313–19.

Parker, G. (2007). Head to head: Is depression overdiagnosed? Yes. *British Medical Journal, 335*(7615), 328.

Parsons, R. G., & Davis, M. (2011). Temporary disruption of fear-potentiated startle following PKMzeta inhibition in the amygdala. *Nature Neuroscience, 14*(3), 295–6.

Pascoe, J. P., & Kapp, B. S. (1985). Electrophysiological characteristics of amygdaloid central nucleus neurons during pavlovian fear conditioning in the rabbit. *Behavioural Brain Research, 16*(2–3), 117–33.

Pastalkova, E., Serrano, P., Pinkhasova, D., Wallace, E., Fenton, A. A., & Sacktor, T. C. (2006). Storage of spatial information by the maintenance mechanism of LTP. *Science, 313*(5790), 1141–4.

Paulus, M. P., & Stein, M. B. (2006). An insular view of anxiety. *Biological Psychiatry, 60*(4), 383–7.

Pavlov, I. P. (1927). *Conditioned Reflexes: An Investigation of the Physiological Activity of the Cerebral Cortex.* Translated and Edited by G. V. Anrep. London: Courier Dover Publications.

Peciña, S., & Berridge, K. C. (2000). Opioid site in nucleus accumbens shell mediates eating and hedonic 'liking' for food: Map based on microinjection Fos plumes. *Brain Research, 863*(1), 71–86.

Peciña, S., Cagniard, B., Berridge, K. C., Aldridge, J. W., & Zhuang, X. (2003). Hyperdopaminergic mutant mice have higher 'wanting' but not 'liking' for sweet rewards. *Journal of Neuroscience, 23*(28), 9395–402.

Pedersen, C. B., & Mortensen, P. B. (2001). Evidence of a dose–response relationship between urbanicity during upbringing and schizophrenia risk. *Archives of General Psychiatry, 58*(11), 1039.

Pelchat, M. L., Johnson, A., Chan, R., Valdez, J., & Ragland, J. D. (2004). Images of desire: Food-craving activation during fMRI. *Neuroimage, 23*(4), 1486–93.

Peleg, G., Katzir, G., Peleg, O., Kamara, M., Brodsky, L., Hel-Or, H., ... Nevo, E. (2006). Hereditary family signature of facial expression. *Proceedings of the National Academy of Sciences, 103*(43), 15921–6.

Pelloux, Y., Dilleen, R., Economidou, D., Theobald, D., & Everitt, B. J. (2012). Reduced forebrain serotonin transmission is causally involved in the development of compulsive cocaine seeking in rats. *Neuropsychopharmacology, 37*(11), 2505–14.

Perera, T. D., Coplan, J. D., Lisanby, S. H., Lipira, C. M., Arif, M., Carpio, C., ... & Dwork, A. J. (2007). Anti-depressant-induced neurogenesis in the hippocampus of adult nonhuman primates. *Journal of Neuroscience, 27*(18), 4894–901.

Perera, T. D., Park, S., & Nemirovskaya, Y. (2008). Cognitive role of neurogenesis in depression and antidepressant treatment. *Neuroscientist,* 326–38.

Perl, D. P. (2010) Neuropathology of Alzheimer's disease. *Mount Sinai Journal of Medicine, 77*(1), 32–42.

Perrett, D., Rolls, E. T., & Cann, W. (1982) Visual neurons responsive to faces in the monkey temporal cortex. *Experimental Brain Research, 47*, 329–42.

Perrett, D., Smith, P. A. J., Mistlin, A. J., Chitty, A. J., Head, A. S., Potter, D. D, Broenniman, R., Milner, A. P., & Jeeves, M. A. (1985). Visual analysis of body movements by neurones in the temporal cortex of the macaque monkey. *Behavior and Brain Research, 16*(2–3), 153–70.

Pert, C. B., & Snyder, S. H. (1973). Opiate receptor: Demonstration in nervous tissue. *Science, 179*(77), 1011–14.

Pertwee, R. G. (2006). Cannabinoid pharmacology: The first 66 years. *British Journal of Pharmacology, 147*(S1), S163–71.

Pescosolido, B. A., Martin, J. K., Long, J. S., Medina, T. R., Phelan, J. C., & Link, B. G. (2010). 'A disease like any other'? A decade of change in public reactions to schizophrenia, depression, and alcohol dependence. *American Journal of Psychiatry, 167*(11), 1321–30.

Peters, J., Dieppa-Perea, L. M., Melendez, L. M., & Quirk, G. J. (2010). Induction of fear extinction with hippocampal-infralimbic BDNF. *Science, 328*(5983), 1288–90.

Petrovich, G. D., Hobin, M. P., & Reppucci, C. J. (2012). Selective Fos induction in hypothalamic orexin/hypocretin, but not melanin-concentrating hormone neurons, by a learned food-cue that stimulates feeding in sated rats. *Neuroscience, 224*, 70–80.

Pfaff, D., & Banavar, J. R. (2007). A theoretical framework for CNS arousal. *Bioessays, 29*(8), 803–10.

Phelps, E. A. (2006). Emotion and cognition: Insights from studies of the human amygdala. *Annual Review of Psychology, 57*, 27–53.

Phelps, E. A., O'Connor, K. J., Gatenby, J. C., Gore, J. C., Grillon, C., & Davis, M. (2001). Activation of the left amygdala to a cognitive representation of fear. *Nature Neuroscience, 4*(4), 437–41.

Pilowsky, L. S., Bressan, R. A., Stone, J. M., Erlandsson, K., Mulligan, R. S., Krystal, J. H., & Ell, P. J. (2006). First *in vivo* evidence of an NMDA receptor deficit in medication-free schizophrenic patients. *Molecular Psychiatry, 11*(2), 118–19.

Pilowsky, D. J., Keyes, K. M., & Hasin, D. S. (2009). Adverse childhood events and lifetime alcohol dependence. *American Journal of Public Health, 99*(2), 258.

Pineda J. A. (2008). Sensorimotor cortex as a critical component of an 'extended' mirror neuron system: Does it solve the development, correspondence, and control problems in mirroring? *Behavioral and Brain Functions, 4,* 47.

Piness, G., Miller, H., & Alles, G. A. (1930). Clinical observations on phenylaminoethanol sulphate. *Journal of the American Medical Association, 94*(11), 790–91.

Pirona, A., & Morgan, M. J. (2010). An investigation of the subacute effects of ecstasy on neuropsychological performance, sleep and mood in regular ecstasy users. *Journal of Psychopharmacology, 24*(2), 175–85.

Pitkänen, A. (2000). Connectivity of the rat amygdaloid complex, in Aggleton, J. P. (ed.), *The Amygdala: A Functional Analysis.* Oxford: OUP, pp. 31–115.

Pitkänen, A., Savander, V., & LeDoux, J. E. (1997). Organization of intra-amygdaloid circuitries in the rat: An emerging framework for understanding functions of the amygdala [published erratum appears in *Trends in Neurosciences* (1998) *21*(2), 52; [see comments]. *Trends in Neurosciences, 20*(11), 517–23.

Pitman, R. K., Sanders, K. M., Zusman, R. M., Healy, A. R., Cheema, F., Lasko, N. B., ... Orr, S. P. (2002). Pilot study of secondary prevention of posttraumatic stress disorder with propranolol. *Biological Psychiatry, 51*(2), 189–92.

Plassmann, H., O'Doherty, J., Shiv, B., & Rangel, A. (2008). Marketing actions can modulate neural representations of experienced pleasantness. *Proceedings of the National Academy of Sciences, 105*(3), 1050–54.

Plaznik, A., Palejko, W., Nazar, M., & Jessa, M. (1994). Effects of antagonists at the NMDA receptor complex in two models of anxiety. *European Neuropsychopharmacology, 4*(4), 503–12.

Plihal, W., & Born, J. (1997). Effects of early and late nocturnal sleep on declarative and procedural memory. *Journal of Cognitive Neuroscience, 9*(4), 534–47.

Pliner, P. (1982). The effects of mere exposure on liking for edible substances. *Appetite, 3*(3), 283–90.

Pliner, P., & Chaiken, S. (1990). Eating, social motives, and self-presentation in women and men. *Journal of Experimental Social Psychology, 26*(3), 240–54.

Ploski, J. E., Pierre, V. J., Smucny, J., Park, K., Monsey, M. S., Overeem, K. A., & Schafe, G. E. (2008). The activity-regulated cytoskeletal-associated protein (Arc/Arg3.1) is required for memory consolidation of pavlovian fear conditioning in the lateral amygdala. *Journal of Neuroscience, 28*(47), 12383–95.

Pobric, G., & Hamilton, A. F. (2006). Action understanding requires the left inferior frontal cortex. *Current Biology, 16*(5), 524–9.

Podhorna, J., & Didriksen, M. (2005). Performance of male C57BL/6J mice and Wistar rats in the water maze following various schedules of phencyclidine treatment. *Behavioural Pharmacology, 16*(1), 25–34.

Pohorecky, L. A. (1981). The interaction of alcohol and stress: A review. *Neuroscience & Biobehavioral Reviews, 5*(2), 209–29.

Pomarol-Clotet, E., Honey, G. D., Murray, G. K., Corlett, P. R., Absalom, A. R., Lee, M., ... & Fletcher, P. C. (2006). Psychological effects of ketamine in healthy volunteers: Phenomenological study. *British Journal of Psychiatry, 189*(2), 173–79.

Pomerleau, O. F., & Pomerleau, C. S. (1985). Neuroregulators and the reinforcement of smoking: Towards a biobehavioral explanation. *Neuroscience & Biobehavioral Reviews, 8*(4), 503–13.

Postuma, R. B., Gagnon, J. F., & Montplaisir, J. (2010). Clinical prediction of Parkinson's disease: Planning for the age of neuroprotection. *Journal of Neurology, Neurosurgery & Psychiatry, 81,* 1008–13.

Prinz, W. (1990). A common coding approach to perception and action, in Neumann, O., & Prinz, W. (eds), *Relationships Between Perception and Action.* Heidelberg: Germany: Springer-Verlag, pp. 167–210.

Puhl, R. M., & Heuer, C. A. (2009). The stigma of obesity: A review and update. *Obesity, 17*(5), 941–64.

Puhl, R. M., & Latner, J. D. (2007). Stigma, obesity, and the health of the nation's children. *Psychological Bulletin, 133*(4), 557.

Pulvermüller, F., Huss, M., Kherif, F., del Prado Martin, F. M., Hauk, O., & Shtyrov, Y. (2006). Motor cortex maps articulatory features of speech sounds. *Proceedings of the National Academy of Sciences, USA, 103,* 7865–70.

Quirk, G. J., & Mueller, D. (2008). Neural mechanisms of extinction learning and retrieval. *Neuropsychopharmacology, 33*(1), 56–72.

Quirk, G. J., Repa, C., & LeDoux, J. E. (1995). Fear conditioning enhances short-latency auditory responses of lateral amygdala neurons: Parallel recordings in the freely behaving rat. *Neuron, 15*(5), 1029–39.

Quirk, G. J., Russo, G. K., Barron, J. L., & Lebron, K. (2000). The role of ventromedial prefrontal cortex in the recovery of extinguished fear. *Journal of Neuroscience, 20*(16), 6225–31.

Radulovic, J., Kammermeier, J., & Spiess, J. (1998). Relationship between fos production and classical fear conditioning: Effects of novelty, latent inhibition, and unconditioned stimulus preexposure. *Journal of Neuroscience, 18*(18), 7452–61.

Raichle, M. E., & Snyder, A. Z. (2007). A default mode of brain function: A brief history of an evolving idea. *Neuroimage, 37*(4), 1083–90.

Raine, A., Buchsbaum, M., & LaCasse, L. (1997). Brain abnormalities in murderers indicated by positron emission tomography. *Biological Psychiatry, 42*(6), 495–508.

Raine, A., Lencz, T., Bihrle, S., LaCasse, L., & Colletti, P. (2000). Reduced prefrontal gray matter volume and reduced autonomic activity in antisocial personality disorder. *Archives of General Psychiatry, 57*(2), 119–27; discussion 119–27.

Ralph, M. R., Foster, R. G., Davis, F. C., & Menaker, M. (1990). Transplanted suprachiasmatic nucleus determines circadian period. *Science, 247*(4945), 975–8.

Ramachandran, V. S. (2000). Mirror neurons and imitation learning as the driving force behind 'the great leap forward' in human evolution. http://www.edge.org/3rd_culture/ramachandran/ramachandran_index.html. Retrieved 28/09/2012.

Ramnani, N. (2006). The primate cortico-cerebellar system: Anatomy and function. *Nature Reviews Neuroscience, 7*(7), 511–22.

Rasch, B., & Born, J. (2013). About sleep's role in memory. *Physiological Reviews, 93*(2), 681–766.

Rasch, B., Büchel, C., Gais, S., & Born, J. (2007). Odor cues during slow-wave sleep prompt declarative memory consolidation. *Science, 315*(5817), 1426–9.

Rasmussen, N. (2008). America's first amphetamine epidemic 1929–1971: A quantitative and qualitative retrospective with implications for the present. *American Journal of Public Health, 98*(6), 974–85.

Rauch, S. L., Shin, L. M., & Wright, C. I. (2003). Neuroimaging studies of amygdala function in anxiety disorders. *Annals of the New York Academy of Sciences, 985*(1), 389–410.

Rauch, S. L., Shin, L. M., & Phelps, E. A. (2006). Neurocircuitry models of posttraumatic stress disorder and extinction: Human neuroimaging research – past, present, and future. *Biological Psychiatry, 60*(4), 376–82.

Rauch, S. L., Whalen, P. J., Shin, L. M., McInerney, S. C., Macklin, M. L., Lasko, N. B., ... Pitman, R. K. (2000). Exaggerated amygdala response to masked facial stimuli in posttraumatic stress disorder: A functional MRI study. *Biological Psychiatry, 47*(9), 769–76.

Rechtschaffen, A., Gilliland, M. A., Bergmann, B. M., & Winter, J. B. (1983). Physiological correlates of prolonged sleep deprivation in rats. *Science, 221*(4606), 182–4.

Reich, D. L., & Silvay, G. (1989). Ketamine: An update on the first twenty-five years of clinical experience. *Canadian Journal of Anaesthesia, 36*(2), 186–97.

Reichmann, H., Schneider. C., & Löhle, M. (2009). Non-motor features of Parkinson's disease: Depression and dementia. *Parkinsonism & Related Disorders, 15(3)*, S87–S92.

Reis, D. J., & Oliphant, M. C. (1964). Bradycardia and tachycardia following electrical stimulation of the amygdaloid region in monkey. *Journal of Neurophysiology, 27*, 893–912.

Repp, B.H., & Knoblich, G. (2009). Performed or observed keyboard actions affect pianists' judgements of relative pitch. *Quarterly Journal of Experimental Psychology, 62*(11), 2156–70.

Rescorla, R. A., & Wagner, A. R. (1972). A theory of Pavlovian conditioning: Variations in the effectiveness of reinforcement and nonreinforcement. In A. H. B. W. F. Prokasy (Ed.), *Classical Conditioning II: Current Research and Theory.* New York: Appleton-Century-Crofts, pp. 64–99.

Ressler, K. J., Rothbaum, B. O., Tannenbaum, L., Anderson, P., Graap, K., Zimand, E., Hodges, L., & Davis, M. (2004). Cognitive enhancers as adjuncts to psychotherapy: Use of D-cycloserine in phobic individuals to facilitate extinction of fear. *Archives of General Psychiatry, 61*(11), 1136–44.

Reynolds, G. P., & Kirk, S. L. (2010). Metabolic side effects of antipsychotic drug treatment –Pharmacological mechanisms. *Pharmacology & Therapeutics, 125*(1), 169–79.

Reynolds, G. P., Abdul-Monim, Z., Neill, J. C., & Zhang, Z. J. (2004). Calcium binding protein markers of GABA deficits in schizophrenia – Post mortem studies and animal models. *Neurotoxicity Research, 6*(1), 57–61.

Rhodes, S. E., & Killcross, A. S. (2007). Lesions of rat infralimbic cortex enhance renewal of extinguished appetitive Pavlovian responding. *European Journal of Neuroscience, 25*(8), 2498–503.

Ricardo, J. A., & Koh, E. T. (1978). Anatomical evidence of direct projections from the nucleus of the solitary tract to the hypothalamus, amygdala, and other forebrain structures in the rat. *Brain Research, 153*(1), 1–26.

Riemann, D., Berger, M., & Voderholzer, U. (2001). Sleep and depression – Results from psychobiological studies: An overview. *Biological Psychology, 57*(1), 67–103.

Rimm, E. B., Klatsky, A., Grobbee, D., & Stampfer, M. J. (1996). Review of moderate alcohol consumption and reduced risk of coronary heart disease: Is the effect due to beer, wine, or spirits? *British Medical Journal, 312*(7033), 731–6.

Robbins, T. W., Ersche, K. D., & Everitt, B. J. (2008). Drug addiction and the memory systems of the brain. *Annals of the New York Academy of Sciences, 1141*, 1–21.

Robicsek, F. (2004). Ritual smoking in Central America, in Gilman, S. L., & Xun, Z. (eds) *Smoke: A Global History of Smoking*. London: Reaktion Books.

Robinson, D., Woerner, M. G., Alvir, J. M. J., Bilder, R., Goldman, R., Geisler, S., ... & Lieberman, J. A. (1999). Predictors of relapse following response from a first episode of schizophrenia or schizoaffective disorder. *Archives of General Psychiatry*, *56*(3), 241.

Robinson, T. E., & Berridge, K. C. (1993). The neural basis of drug craving: An incentive-sensitization theory of addiction. *Brain Research Reviews*, *18*(3), 247–91.

Robinson, T. E., & Berridge, K. C. (2001). Incentive-sensitization and addiction.*Addiction*, *96*(1), 103–114.

Rocha, B. A., Fumagalli, F., Gainetdinov, R. R., Jones, S. R., Ator, R., Giros, B., & Caron, M. G. (1998). Cocaine self-administration in dopamine-transporter knockout mice. *Nature Neuroscience*, *1*(2), 132–7.

Rodriguez-Romaguera, J., Sotres-Bayon, F., Mueller, D., & Quirk, G. J. (2009). Systemic propranolol acts centrally to reduce conditioned fear in rats without impairing extinction. *Biological Psychiatry*, *65*(10), 887–92.

Rogan, M. T., & LeDoux, J. E. (1995). LTP is accompanied by commensurate enhancement of auditory-evoked responses in a fear conditioning circuit. *Neuron, 15*(1), 127–36.

Rogan, M. T., Stäubli, U. V., & LeDoux, J. E. (1997). Fear conditioning induces associative long-term potentiation in the amygdala. *Nature, 390*(6660), 604–07.

Rogers, P. J., & Smit, H. J. (2000). Food craving and food 'addiction': A critical review of the evidence from a bio-psychosocial perspective. *Pharmacology, Biochemistry and Behavior*, *66*(1), 3–14.

Roiser, J. P., Rogers, R. D., Cook, L. J., & Sahakian, B. J. (2006). The effect of polymorphism at the serotonin transporter gene on decision-making, memory and executive function in ecstasy users and controls. *Psychopharmacology*, *188*(2), 213–27.

Rolls, B. J., Rolls, E. T., Rowe, E. A., & Sweeney, K. (1981). Sensory specific satiety in man. *Physiology & Behavior*, *27*(1), 137–42.

Rolls, B. J., Roe, L. S., & Meengs, J. S. (2007). The effect of large portion sizes on energy intake is sustained for 11 days. *Obesity*, *15*(6), 1535–43.

Rolls, E. T., Critchley, H. D., Browning, A., & Hernadi, I. (1998). The neurophysiology of taste and olfaction in primates, and umami flavora. *Annals of the New York Academy of Sciences*, *855*(1), 426–37.

Romanski, L. M., Clugnet, M. C., Bordi, F., & LeDoux, J. E. (1993). Somatosensory and auditory convergence in the lateral nucleus of the amygdala. *Behavioral Neuroscience, 107*(3), 444–50.

Ronald, A., & Hoekstra, R. A. (2011). Autism spectrum disorders and autistic traits: A decade of new twin studies. *American Journal of Medical Genetics Part B: Neuropsychiatric Genetics*, *156*(3), 255–74.

Rose, J. E., Behm, F. M., Westman, E. C., & Johnson, M. (2000). Dissociating nicotine and nonnicotine components of cigarette smoking. *Pharmacology, Biochemistry and Behavior*, *67*(1), 71–81.

Rosen, J. B., & Davis, M. (1988). Enhancement of acoustic startle by electrical stimulation of the amygdala. *Behavioral Neuroscience, 102*(2), 195–202, 324.

Rosenthal, N. E., Sack, D. A., Gillin, J. C., Lewy, A. J., Goodwin, F. K., Davenport, Y., ... & Wehr, T. A. (1984). Seasonal affective disorder: A description of the syndrome and preliminary findings with light therapy. *Archives of General Psychiatry*, *41*(1), 72.

Roth, B. L., Baner, K., Westkaemper, R., Siebert, D., Rice, K. C., Steinberg, S., & Rothman, R. B. (2002). Salvinorin A: A potent naturally occurring nonnitrogenous κ opioid selective agonist. *Proceedings of the National Academy of Sciences*, *99*(18), 11934–9.

Rottenberg, J., Kasch, K. L., Gross, J. J., & Gotlib, I. H. (2002). Sadness and amusement reactivity differentially predict concurrent and prospective functioning in major depressive disorder. *Emotion*, *2*(2), 135.

Roy-Byrne, P. P., Davidson, K. W., Kessler, R. C., Asmundson, G. J., Goodwin, R. D., Kubzansky, L., ... & Stein, M. B. (2008). Anxiety disorders and comorbid medical illness. *General Hospital Psychiatry*, *30*(3), 208–25.

Rozin, P. (1996). Sociocultural influences on human food selection, in Capaldi, E.D. (ed.), *Why We Eat What We Eat: The Psychology of Eating*. American Psychological Association, pp. 233–63.

Rozin, P., Dow, S., Moscovitch, M., & Rajaram, S. (1998). What causes humans to begin and end a meal? A role for memory for what has been eaten, as evidenced by a study of multiple meal eating in amnesic patients. *Psychological Science*, *9*(5), 392–6.

Ruhé, H. G., Mason, N. S., & Schene, A. H. (2007). Mood is indirectly related to serotonin, norepinephrine and dopamine levels in humans: A meta-analysis of monoamine depletion studies. *Molecular Psychiatry*, *12*(4), 331–59.

Russo, E. B. (2011). Taming THC: Potential cannabis synergy and phytocannabinoid-terpenoid entourage effects. *British Journal of Pharmacology*, *163*(7), 1344–64.

Russo, S. J., & Nestler, E. J. (2013). The brain reward circuitry in mood disorders. *Nature Reviews Neuroscience*, *14*(9), 609–25.

Russo-Neustadt, A. A., Beard, R. C., Huang, Y. M., & Cotman, C. W. (2000). Physical activity and antidepressant treatment potentiate the expression of specific brain-derived neurotrophic factor transcripts in the rat hippocampus. *Neuroscience, 101*(2), 305–12.

Ryan, L., Nadel, L., Keil, K., Putnam, K., Schnyer, D., Trouard, T., & Moscovitch, M. (2001). Hippocampal complex and retrieval of recent and very remote autobiographical memories: Evidence from functional magnetic resonance imaging in neurologically intact people. *Hippocampus, 11*(6), 707–14.

Ryback, R. S., & Lewis, O. F. (1971). Effects of prolonged bed rest on EEG sleep patterns in young, healthy volunteers. *Electroencephalography and Clinical Neurophysiology, 31*(4), 395–9.

Sacktor, T. C. (2011). How does PKMzeta maintain long-term memory? *Nature Reviews Neuroscience, 12*(1), 9–15.

Sadler T. W., (1998). Mechanisms of neural tube closure and defects. *Mental Retardation and Developmental Disabilities Research Reviews, 4,* 247–53.

Sadzot, B., Baraban, J. M., Glennon, R. A., Lyon, R. A., Leonhardt, S., Jan, C. R., & Titeler, M. (1989). Hallucinogenic drug interactions at human brain 5-HT2 receptors: Implications for treating LSD-induced hallucinogenesis. *Psychopharmacology, 98*(4), 495–9.

Sakurai, T., Amemiya, A., Ishii, M., Matsuzaki, I., Chemelli, R. M., Tanaka, H., … & Yanagisawa, M. (1998). Orexins and orexin receptors: A family of hypothalamic neuropeptides and G protein-coupled receptors that regulate feeding behavior. *Cell, 92*(4), 573–85.

Samaha, A. N., & Robinson, T. E. (2005). Why does the rapid delivery of drugs to the brain promote addiction? *Trends in Pharmacological Sciences, 26*(2), 82–7.

Samson, H. H., Pfeffer, A. O., & Tolliver, G. A. (1988). Oral ethanol self-administration in rats: Models of alcohol-seeking behavior. *Alcoholism: Clinical and Experimental Research, 12*(5), 591–8.

Sananes, C. B., & Davis, M. (1992). N-Methyl-D-Aspartate lesions of the lateral and basolateral nuclei of the amygdala block fear-potentiated startle and shock sensitization of startle. *Behavioral Neuroscience, 106*(1), 72–80.

Santarelli, L., Saxe, M., Gross, C., Surget, A., Battaglia, F., Dulawa, S., … & Hen, R. (2003). Requirement of hippocampal neurogenesis for the behavioral effects of antidepressants. *Science, 301*(5634), 805–09.

Saper, C. B., Chou, T. C., & Scammell, T. E. (2001). The sleep switch: Hypothalamic control of sleep and wakefulness. *Trends in Neurosciences, 24*(12), 726–31.

Saper, C. B., Scammell, T. E., & Lu, J. (2005). Hypothalamic regulation of sleep and circadian rhythms. *Nature, 437*(7063), 1257–63.

Saper, C. B., Fuller, P. M., Pedersen, N. P., Lu, J., & Scammell, T. E. (2010). Sleep state switching. *Neuron, 68*(6), 1023–42.

Sato, M., Tremblay, P., & Gracco, V. L. (2009). A mediating role of the premotor cortex in phoneme segmentation. *Brain & Language, 111,* 1–7.

Scammell, T. E., Gerashchenko, D. Y., Mochizuki, T., McCarthy, M. T., Estabrooke, I. V., Sears, C. A., … & Hayaishi, O. (2001). An adenosine A2a agonist increases sleep and induces Fos in ventrolateral preoptic neurons. *Neuroscience, 107*(4), 653–63.

Schachter, S., & Singer, J. E. (1962). Cognitive, social, and physiological determinants of emotional state. *Psychological Review, 69,* 379–99.

Schafe, G. E., & LeDoux, J. E. (2000). Memory consolidation of auditory pavlovian fear conditioning requires protein synthesis and protein kinase A in the amygdala. *Journal of Neuroscience, 20*(18), RC96.

Schafe, G. E., Atkins, C. M., Swank, M. W., Bauer, E. P., Sweatt, J. D., & LeDoux, J. E. (2000). Activation of ERK/MAP kinase in the amygdala is required for memory consolidation of pavlovian fear conditioning. *Journal of Neuroscience, 20*(21), 8177–87.

Schifano, F., Oyefeso, A., Webb, L., Pollard, M., Corkery, J., & Ghodse, A. H. (2003). Review of deaths related to taking ecstasy, England and Wales, 1997–2000. *British Medical Journal, 326*(7380), 80–81.

Schiller, D., & Phelps, E. A. (2011). Does reconsolidation occur in humans? *Frontiers in Behavioral Neuroscience, 5,* 24.

Schmidt-Kastner, R., van Os, J., Steinbusch, H. M. W., & Schmitz, C. (2006). Gene regulation by hypoxia and the neurodevelopmental origin of schizophrenia. *Schizophrenia Research, 84,* 253–71.

Schomerus, G., Lucht, M., Holzinger, A., Matschinger, H., Carta, M. G., & Angermeyer, M. C. (2011). The stigma of alcohol dependence compared with other mental disorders: A review of population studies. *Alcohol and Alcoholism, 46*(2), 105–12.

Schultes, R. E., & Hofmann, A. (1979). *Plants of the Gods*: *Origins of Hallucinogenic Use*. New York: Alfred van der Marck Editions.

Schultz, W. (2007). Behavioral dopamine signals. *Trends in Neurosciences, 30*(5), 203–10.

Schultz, W., Dayan, P., & Montague, P. R. (1997). A neural substrate of prediction and reward. *Science, 275*(5306), 1593–9. Doi:10.1126/science.275.5306.1593.

Schurov, I. L., Handford, E. J., Brandon, N. J., & Whiting, P. J. (2004). Expression of disrupted in schizophrenia 1 (DISC1) protein in the adult and developing mouse brain indicates its role in neurodevelopment. *Molecular Psychiatry, 9*(12), 1100–10.

Schütze, M., Boeing, H., Pischon, T., Rehm, J., Kehoe, T., Gmel, G., & Bergmann, M. M. (2011). Alcohol attributable burden of incidence of cancer in eight European countries based on results from prospective cohort study. *British Medical Journal, 342.*

Schwartz, R. C., & Cohen, B. N. (2001). Psychosocial correlates of suicidal intent among patients with schizophrenia. *Comprehensive Psychiatry, 42*(2), 118–23.

Sclafani, A. (1995). How food preferences are learned: Laboratory animal models. *Proceedings of the Nutrition Society, 54*(02), 419–27.

Seely, K. A., Lapoint, J., Moran, J. H., & Fattore, L. (2012). Spice drugs are more than harmless herbal blends: A review of the pharmacology and toxicology of synthetic cannabinoids. *Progress in Neuro-Psychopharmacology and Biological Psychiatry, 39*(2), 234–43.

Seeman, P. (2005). An update of fast-off dopamine D2 atypical antipsychotics. *American Journal of Psychiatry, 162*(10), 1984-a.

Segal, N. L., & Allison, D. B. (2002). Twins and virtual twins: Bases of relative body weight revisited. *International Journal of Obesity and Related Metabolic Disorders, 26*(4), 437.

Seidman, L. J., Thermenos, H. W., Poldrack, R. A., Peace, N. K., Koch, J. K., Faraone, S. V., & Tsuang, M. T. (2006). Altered brain activation in dorsolateral prefrontal cortex in adolescents and young adults at genetic risk for schizophrenia: An fMRI study of working memory. *Schizophrenia Research, 85*(1), 58–72.

Serretti, A., Kato, M., De Ronchi, D., & Kinoshita, T. (2006). Meta-analysis of serotonin transporter gene promoter polymorphism (5-HTTLPR) association with selective serotonin reuptake inhibitor efficacy in depressed patients. *Molecular Psychiatry, 12*(3), 247–57.

Sessa, B., & Nutt, D. J. (2007). MDMA, politics and medical research: Have we thrown the baby out with the bathwater? *Journal of Psychopharmacology 21,* 787–91.

Shafey, O., Dolwick, S., & Guindon, G. E. (2003). Tobacco control country profiles. *Atlanta: American Cancer Society, 356.*

Shalev, A. Y., Sahar, T., Freedman, S., Peri, T., Glick, N., Brandes, D., ... Pitman, R. K. (1998). A prospective study of heart rate response following trauma and the subsequent development of posttraumatic stress disorder. *Archives of General Psychiatry, 55*(6), 553–9.

Shapiro, A. P., & Nathan, P. E. (1986). Human tolerance to alcohol: The role of Pavlovian conditioning processes. *Psychopharmacology, 88*(1), 90–95.

Sheline, Y. I., Price, J. L., Yan, Z., & Mintun, M. A. (2010). Resting-state functional MRI in depression unmasks increased connectivity between networks via the dorsal nexus. *Proceedings of the National Academy of Sciences, 107*(24), 11020–25.

Shema, R., Sacktor, T. C., & Dudai, Y. (2007). Rapid erasure of long-term memory associations in the cortex by an inhibitor of PKM zeta. *Science, 317*(5840), 951–3.

Shema, R., Haramati, S., Ron, S., Hazvi, S., Chen, A., Sacktor, T. C., & Dudai, Y. (2011). Enhancement of consolidated long-term memory by overexpression of protein kinase Mzeta in the neocortex. *Science, 331*(6021), 1207–10.

Shen, W. W. (1999). A history of antipsychotic drug development. *Comprehensive Psychiatry, 40*(6), 407–14.

Shenton, M. E., Dickey, C. C., Frumin, M., & McCarley, R. W. (2001). A review of MRI findings in schizophrenia. *Schizophrenia Research, 49*(1), 1–52.

Sherin, J. E., Shiromani, P. J., McCarley, R. W., & Saper, C. B. (1996). Activation of ventrolateral preoptic neurons during sleep. *Science, 271*(5246), 216–19.

Sherin, J. E., Elmquist, J. K., Torrealba, F., & Saper, C. B. (1998). Innervation of histaminergic tuberomammillary neurons by GABAergic and galaninergic neurons in the ventrolateral preoptic nucleus of the rat. *Journal of Neuroscience, 18*(12), 4705–21.

Shirayama, Y., Chen, A. C. H., Nakagawa, S., Russell, D. S., & Duman, R. S. (2002). Brain-derived neurotrophic factor produces antidepressant effects in behavioral models of depression. *Journal of Neuroscience, 22*(8), 3251–61.

Siebert, D. J. (1994). Salvia divinorum and salvinorin A: New pharmacologic findings. *Journal of Ethnopharmacology, 43*(1), 53–56.

Siegel, S. (1977). Morphine tolerance acquisition as an associative process. *Journal of Experimental Psychology: Animal Behavior Processes, 3*(1), 1.

Siegel, S. (1999). Drug anticipation and drug addiction: The 1998 H. David Archibald lecture. *Addiction, 94*(8), 1113–24.

Siegel, S. (2001). Pavlovian conditioning and drug overdose: When tolerance fails. *Addiction Research & Theory, 9*(5), 503–13.

Sierra-Mercado, D., Jr, Corcoran, K. A., Lebron-Milad, K., & Quirk, G. J. (2006). Inactivation of the ventromedial pre-frontal cortex reduces expression of conditioned fear and impairs subsequent recall of extinction. *European Journal of Neuroscience, 24*(6), 1751–8.

Sierra-Mercado, D., Jr, Padilla-Coreano, N., & Quirk, G. J. (2011). Dissociable roles of prelimbic and infralimbic cortices, ventral hippocampus, and basolateral amygdala in the expression and extinction of conditioned fear. *Neuropsychopharmacology, 36*(2), 529–38.

Sikorski, C., Luppa, M., Kaiser, M., Glaesmer, H., Schomerus, G., König, H. H., & Riedel-Heller, S. (2011). The stigma of obesity in the general public and its implications for public health – A systematic review. *BMC Public Health, 11*(1), 661.

Singer, T., Seymour, B., O'Doherty, J., Kaube, H., Dolan, R. J., & Frith, C. D. (2004). Empathy for pain involves the affective but not sensory components of pain. *Science, 303,* 1157–62.

Smith, G. P., & Epstein, A. N. (1969). Increased feeding in response to decreased glucose utilization in the rat and monkey. *American Journal of Physiology – Legacy Content, 217*(4), 1083–7.

Smith, R. L., Barrett, R. J., & Sanders-Bush, E. (1999). Mechanism of tolerance development to 2,5-dimethoxy-4-iodoamphetamine in rats: Down-regulation of the 5-HT2A, but not 5-HT2C, receptor. *Psychopharmacology, 144*(3), 248–54.

Söderpalm, A. H., & Berridge, K. C. (2000). The hedonic impact and intake of food are increased by midazolam microinjection in the parabrachial nucleus. *Brain Research, 877*(2), 288–97.

Sotres-Bayon, F., & Quirk, G. J. (2010). Prefrontal control of fear: More than just extinction. *Current Opinion in Neurobiology, 20*(2), 231–5.

Speakman, J. R. (2008). Thrifty genes for obesity, an attractive but flawed idea, and an alternative perspective: The 'drifty gene' hypothesis. *International Journal of Obesity, 32*(11), 1611–17.

Spence, C., Shankar, M. U., & Blumenthal, H. (2010). 'Sound bites': Auditory contributions to the perception and consumption of food and drink. *Art and the Senses,* 207–38.

Sperling, G. (1960). The information available in brief visual presentations. *Psychological Monographs, 74,* 1–29.

Spiegel, K., Leproult, R., & Van Cauter, E. (1999). Impact of sleep debt on metabolic and endocrine function. *The Lancet, 354*(9188), 1435–9.

Spiegel, K., Tasali, E., Penev, P., & Van Cauter, E. (2004). Brief communication: Sleep curtailment in healthy young men is associated with decreased leptin levels, elevated ghrelin levels, and increased hunger and appetite. *Annals of Internal Medicine, 141*(11), 846–50.

Spiegel, K., Tasali, E., Leproult, R., & Van Cauter, E. (2009). Effects of poor and short sleep on glucose metabolism and obesity risk. *Nature Reviews Endocrinology, 5*(5), 253–61.

Squire, L. R., Clark, R. E., & Knowlton, B. J. (2001). Retrograde amnesia. *Hippocampus, 11*(1), 50–55.

Stairs, D. J., & Bardo, M. T. (2009). Neurobehavioral effects of environmental enrichment and drug abuse vulnerability. *Pharmacology Biochemistry and Behavior, 92*(3), 377–82.

Steele, C. M., & Josephs, R. A. (1990). Alcohol myopia: Its prized and dangerous effects. *American Psychologist, 45*(8), 921.

Stein, M., Simmons, A., Feinstein, J., & Paulus, M. (2007). Increased amygdala and insula activation during emotion processing in anxiety-prone subjects. *American Journal of Psychiatry, 164*(2), 318–27.

Steiner, J. E., Glaser, D., Hawilo, M. E., & Berridge, K. C. (2001). Comparative expression of hedonic impact: Affective reactions to taste by human infants and other primates. *Neuroscience & Biobehavioral Reviews, 25*(1), 53–74.

Stice, E., Figlewicz, D. P., Gosnell, B. A., Levine, A. S., & Pratt, W. E. (2013). The contribution of brain reward circuits to the obesity epidemic. *Neuroscience & Biobehavioral Reviews, 37*(9), 2047–58.

Stice, E., Yokum, S., & Burger, K. S. (2013). Elevated reward region responsivity predicts future substance use onset but not overweight/obesity onset. *Biological Psychiatry, 73*(9), 869–76.

St-Onge, M. P. (2013). The role of sleep duration in the regulation of energy balance: Effects on energy intakes and expenditure. *Journal of Clinical Sleep Medicine (JCSM), 9*(1), 73–80.

Stranger, B. E., Stahl, E. A., & Raj, T. (2011). Progress and promise of genome-wide association studies for human complex trait genetics. *Genetics, 187,* 367–83.

Stricker, E. M., Swerdloff, A. F., & Zigmond, M. J. (1978). Intrahypothalamic injections of kainic acid produce feeding and drinking deficits in rats. *Brain Research, 158*(2), 470–73.

Strober, M., Freeman, R., Lampert, C., Diamond, J., & Kaye, W. (2000). Controlled family study of anorexia nervosa and bulimia nervosa: Evidence of shared liability and transmission of partial syndromes. *American Journal of Psychiatry, 157*(3), 393–401.

Stunkard, A. J., Faith, M. S., & Allison, K. C. (2003). Depression and obesity. *Biological Psychiatry, 54*(3), 330–37.

Subiaul, F., Cantlon, J. F., Holloway, R. L., & Terrace, H. S. (2004). Cognitive imitation in rhesus macaques. *Science, 305,* 407–10.

Sullivan, P. F., Kendler, K. S., & Neale, M. C. (2003). Schizophrenia as a complex trait: Evidence from a meta-analysis of twin studies. *Archives of General Psychiatry, 60*, 1187–92.

Sultana, R., & Butterfield, D. A. (2010). Role of oxidative stress in the progression of Alzheimer's disease. *Journal of Alzheimer's Disease, 19*, 341–53.

Sun, D., Phillips, L., Velakoulis, D., Yung, A., McGorry, P. D., Wood, S. J., ... & Pantelis, C. (2009). Progressive brain structural changes mapped as psychosis develops in 'at risk' individuals. *Schizophrenia Research, 108*(1), 85–92.

Sweatt, J. D. (2009). Experience-dependent epigenetic modifications in the central nervous system. *Biological Psychiatry, 65*, 191–7.

Swenson, R. M., & Vogel, W. H. (1983). Plasma catecholamine and corticosterone as well as brain catecholamine changes during coping in rats exposed to stressful footshock. *Pharmacology, Biochemistry and Behavior, 18*(5), 689–93.

Swinburn, B. A., Sacks, G., Hall, K. D., McPherson, K., Finegood, D. T., Moodie, M. L., & Gortmaker, S. L. (2011). The global obesity pandemic: Shaped by global drivers and local environments. *The Lancet, 378*(9793), 804–14.

Szymusiak, R., Alam, N., Steininger, T. L., & McGinty, D. (1998). Sleep–waking discharge patterns of ventrolateral pre-optic/anterior hypothalamic neurons in rats. *Brain Research, 803*(1), 178–88.

Taheri, S. (2006). The link between short sleep duration and obesity: We should recommend more sleep to prevent obesity. *Archives of Disease in Childhood, 91*(11), 881–4.

Taheri, S., Lin, L., Austin, D., Young, T., & Mignot, E. (2004). Short sleep duration is associated with reduced leptin, elevated ghrelin, and increased body mass index. *PLoS Medicine, 1*(3), e62.

Tai, Y. F., Hoshi, R., Brignell, C. M., Cohen, L., Brooks, D. J., Curran, H. V., & Piccini, P. (2010). Persistent nigrostriatal dopaminergic abnormalities in ex-users of MDMA ('Ecstasy'): An 18F-dopa PET study. *Neuropsychopharmacology, 36*(4), 735–43.

Takahashi, Y. K., Roesch, M. R., Stalnaker, T. A., Haney, R. Z., Calu, D. J., Taylor, A. R., & Schoenbaum, G. (2009). The orbitofrontal cortex and ventral tegmental area are necessary for learning from unexpected outcomes. *Neuron, 62*(2), 269–80.

Tanabe, J., Thompson, L., Claus, E., Dalwani, M., Hutchison, K., & Banich, M. T. (2007). Prefrontal cortex activity is reduced in gambling and nongambling substance users during decision-making. *Human Brain Mapping, 28*(12), 1276–86

Tanabe, J., Tregellas, J. R., Dalwani, M., Thompson, L., Owens, E., Crowley, T., & Banich, M. (2009). Medial orbitofrontal cortex gray matter is reduced in abstinent substance-dependent individuals. *Biological Psychiatry, 65*(2), 160–64.

Tanda, G., Pontieri, F. E., & Di Chiara, G. (1997). Cannabinoid and heroin activation of mesolimbic dopamine transmission by a common µ1 opioid receptor mechanism. *Science, 276*(5321), 2048–50.

Tandon, R., Belmaker, R. H., & Gattaz, W. F. (2008). World Psychiatric Association Pharmacopsychiatry Section statement on comparative effectiveness of antipsychotics in the treatment of schizophrenia. *Schizophrenia Research, 100*(1), 20–38.

Tang, B., Dean, B., & Thomas, E. A. (2011). Disease- and age-related changes in histone acetylation at gene promoters in psychiatric disorders. *Translational Psychiatry, 1*(12), e64. DOI: 10.1038/tp.2011.6110.1038/tp.2011.6110.1038/tp.2011.61.

Tang, D. W., Fellows, L. K., Small, D. M., & Dagher, A. (2012). Food and drug cues activate similar brain regions: A meta-analysis of functional MRI studies. *Physiology & Behavior, 106*(3), 317–24.

Teff, K. L., Mattes, R. D., & Engelman, K. A. R. L. (1991). Cephalic phase insulin release in normal-weight males: Verification and reliability. *American Journal of Physiology – Endocrinology and Metabolism, 261*(4), E430–E436.

Teixeira, C. M., Pomedli, S. R., Maei, H. R., Kee, N., & Frankland, P. W. (2006). Involvement of the anterior cingulate cortex in the expression of remote spatial memory. *Journal of Neuroscience, 26*(29), 7555–64.

Terry, M., Steelman, K. L., Guilderson, T., Dering, P., & Rowe, M. W. (2006). Lower Pecos and Coahuila peyote: New radiocarbon dates. *Journal of Archaeological Science, 33*(7), 1017–21.

Terry, P., & Wright, K. A. (2005). Self-reported driving behaviour and attitudes towards driving under the influence of cannabis among three different user groups in England. *Addictive Behaviors, 30*(3), 619–26.

Terry, R. D., et al. (1991) Physical basis of cognitive alterations in Alzheimer's disease: Synapse loss is the major correlate of cognitive impairment. *Annals of Neurology, 30*, 572–80.

Thannickal, T. C., Moore, R. Y., Nienhuis, R., Ramanathan, L., Gulyani, S., Aldrich, M., ... & Siegel, J. M. (2000). Reduced number of hypocretin neurons in human narcolepsy. *Neuron, 27*(3), 469–74.

Théberge, J., Bartha, R., Drost, D. J., Menon, R. S., Malla, A., Takhar, J., ... & Williamson, P. C. (2002). Glutamate and glutamine measured with 4.0 T proton MRS in never-treated patients with schizophrenia and healthy volunteers. *American Journal of Psychiatry, 159*(11), 1944–6.

Thompson, P. M., Hayashi, K. M., Simon, S. L., Geaga, J. A., Hong, M. S., Sui, Y., & London, E. D. (2004). Structural abnormalities in the brains of human subjects who use methamphetamine. *Journal of Neuroscience, 24*(26), 6028–36.

Tibbo, P., Hanstock, C., Valiakalayil, A., & Allen, P. (2004). 3-T proton MRS investigation of glutamate and glutamine in adolescents at high genetic risk for schizophrenia. *American Journal of Psychiatry, 161*(6), 1116–18.

Ticku, M. K., Lowrimore, P., & Lehoullier, P. (1986). Ethanol enhances GABA-induced 36Cl-influx in primary spinal cord cultured neurons. *Brain Research Bulletin, 17*(1), 123–6.

Tiihonen, J., Kuikka, J., Räsänen, P., Lepola, U., Koponen, H., Liuska, A., ... & Karhu, J. (1997). Cerebral benzodiazepine receptor binding and distribution in generalized anxiety disorder: A fractal analysis. *Molecular Psychiatry, 2*(6), 463.

Tiwari, A. K., Zai, C. C., Müller, D. J., & Kennedy, J. L. (2010). Genetics in schizophrenia: Where are we and what next? *Molecular Psychiatry, 17*(1), 36–48.

Tkachev, D., Mimmack, M. L., Ryan, M. M., Wayland, M., Freeman, T., Jones, P. B., Starkey, M., Webster, M. J., Yolken, R. H., & Bahn, S. (2003). Oligodendrocyte dysfunction in schizophrenia and bipolar disorder. *The Lancet, 362*, 798–805.

Toates, F. M. (1986). *Motivational Systems* (Vol. 4). Cambridge: Cambridge University Press Archive.

Toni, I., Krams, M., Turner, R., & Passingham, R. E. (1998). The time course of changes during motor sequence learning: A whole-brain fMRI study. *Neuroimage, 8*(1), 50–61.

Torrey, E. F., Miller, J., Rawlings, R., & Yolken, R. H. (1997). Seasonality of births in schizophrenia and bipolar disorder: A review of the literature. *Schizophrenia Research, 28*(1), 1–38.

Tracey, I. (2010). Getting the pain you expect: Mechanisms of placebo, nocebo and reappraisal effects in humans. *Nature Medicine, 16*(11), 1277–83.

Trachtenberg, J. T., Chen, B. E., Knott, G. W., Feng, G., Sanes, J. R., Welker, W. and Svoboda, K. (2002). Long-term in vivo imaging of experience-dependent synaptic plasticity in adult cortex. *Nature, 420*, 788–94.

Tranel, D., Kemmerer, D., Adolphs, R., Damasio, H., & Damasio, A. R. (2003). Neural correlates of conceptual knowledge for actions. *Cognitive Neuropsychology, 20*(3), 409–32.

Tremblay, L., & Schultz, W. (2000). Modifications of reward expectation-related neuronal activity during learning in primate orbitofrontal cortex. *Journal of Neurophysiology, 83*(4), 1877–85.

Tronel, S., Milekic, M. H., & Alberini, C. M. (2005). Linking new information to a reactivated memory requires consolidation and not reconsolidation mechanisms. *PLoS Biology, 3*(9), e293.

Tsang, T. M., Huang, J. T. J., Holmes, E., & Bahn, S. (2006). Metabolic profiling of plasma from discordant schizophrenia twins: Correlation between lipid signals and global functioning in female schizophrenia patients. *Journal of Proteome Research, 5*(4), 756–60.

Tsankova, N., Renthal, W., Kumar, A., & Nestler, E. J. (2007). Epigenetic regulation in psychiatric disorders. *Nature Reviews Neuroscience, 8*(5), 355–67.

Tseng, K. Y., Chambers, R. A., & Lipska, B. K. (2009). The neonatal ventral hippocampal lesion as a heuristic neurodevelopmental model of schizophrenia. *Behavioural Brain Research, 204*(2), 295–305.

Turner, L. H., Solomon, R. L., Stellar, E., & Wampler, S. N. (1975). Humoral factors controlling food intake in dogs. *Acta Neurobiologiae Experimentalis, 35*, 491–8.

Tyrka, A. R., Price, L. H., Marsit, C., Walters, O. C., & Carpenter, L. L. (2012). Childhood adversity and epigenetic modulation of the leukocyte glucocorticoid receptor: Preliminary findings in healthy adults. *Public Library of Science (PLoS) One, 7*(1), e30148.

Umilta, M. A., Kohler, E., Gallese, V., Fogassi, L., Fadiga, L., Keysers, C., & Rizzolatti, G. (2001). I know what you are doing: A neurophysiological study. *Neuron, 31*, 155–65.

UNODC, (2012). *United Nations Office on Drugs and Crime World Drug Report.* Vienna: United Nations.

Valdés, L. J. (1994). Salvia divinorum and the unique diterpene hallucinogen, Salvinorin (divinorin) A. *Journal of Psychoactive Drugs, 26*(3), 277–83.

Valenstein, E. S. (1969). Behavior elicited by hypothalamic stimulation. *Brain, Behavior and Evolution, 2*(4), 295–316.

Vallbo, A. B., & Johansson, R. S. (1984). Properties of cutaneous mechanoreceptors in the human hand related to touch sensation. *Human Neurobiology, 3*(1), 3–14.

Vallee, B. L. (1998). Alcohol in the Western world. *Scientific American, 278*, 80–85.

Van Cauter, E., Spiegel, K., Tasali, E., & Leproult, R. (2008). Metabolic consequences of sleep and sleep loss. *Sleep Medicine, 9*, S23–S28.

Van der Laan, L. N., De Ridder, D. T. D., Viergever, M. A., & Smeets, P. A. (2011). The first taste is always with the eyes: A meta-analysis on the neural correlates of processing visual food cues. *Neuroimage, 55*(1), 296–303.

Van Dongen, H. P. A., Baynard, M. D., Maislin, G., & Dinges, D. F. (2004). Systematic interindividual differences in neurobehavioral impairment from sleep loss: Evidence of trait-like differential vulnerability. *Sleep, 27*(3), 423–33.

van Os, J., Bak, M., Hanssen, M., Bijl, R. V., De Graaf, R., & Verdoux, H. (2002). Cannabis use and psychosis: A longitudinal population-based study. *American Journal of Epidemiology, 156*(4), 319–27.

Van Praag, H., Kempermann, G., & Gage, F. H. (2000). Neural consequences of environmental enrichment. *Nature Reviews Neuroscience 1*, 191–8.

van Turennout, M., Ellmore, T., & Martin, A. (2000). Long-lasting cortical plasticity in the object naming system. *Nature Neuroscience, 3*(12), 1329–34.

Vandekar, L. D., Piechowski, R. A., Rittenhouse, P. A., & Gray, T. S. (1991). Amygdaloid-lesions – Differential effect on conditioned stress and immobilization-induced increases in corticosterone and renin secretion. *Neuroendocrinology, 54*(2), 89–95.

Vanderwolf, C. H. (1992). The electrocorticogram in relation to physiology and behavior: A new analysis. *Electroencephalography and Clinical Neurophysiology, 82*(3), 165–75.

Velakoulis, D., Pantelis, C., McGorry, P. D., Dudgeon, P., Brewer, W., Cook, M., ... & Copolov, D. (1999). Hippocampal volume in first-episode psychoses and chronic schizophrenia: A high-resolution magnetic resonance imaging study. *Archives of General Psychiatry, 56*(2), 133.

Verret, L., Goutagny, R., Fort, P., Cagnon, L., Salvert, D., Léger, L., ... & Luppi, P. H. (2003). A role of melanin-concentrating hormone producing neurons in the central regulation of paradoxical sleep. *BMC Neuroscience, 4*(1), 19.

Vianna, D. M., Graeff, F. G., Brandao, M. L., & Landeira-Fernandez, J. (2001). Defensive freezing evoked by electrical stimulation of the periaqueductal gray: Comparison between dorsolateral and ventrolateral regions. *Neuroreport, 12*(18), 4109–12.

Vidal-Gonzalez, I., Vidal-Gonzalez, B., Rauch, S. L., & Quirk, G. J. (2006). Microstimulation reveals opposing influences of prelimbic and infralimbic cortex on the expression of conditioned fear. *Learning & Memory, 13*(6), 728–33.

Vincent, B. J., McQuiston, D. J., Einhorn, L. H., Nagy, C. M., & Brames, M. J. (1983). Review of cannabinoids and their antiemetic effectiveness. *Drugs, 25*(1), 52–62.

Viola, A. U., Archer, S. N., James, L. M., Groeger, J. A., Lo, J. C., Skene, D. J., ... & Dijk, D. J. (2007). PER3 polymorphism predicts sleep structure and waking performance. *Current Biology, 17*(7), 613–18.

Vitousek, K., & Manke, F. (1994). Personality variables and disorders in anorexia nervosa and bulimia nervosa. *Journal of Abnormal Psychology, 103*(1), 137.

Vogels, N., Brunt, T. M., Rigter, S., Van Dijk, P., Vervaeke, H., & Niesink, R. J. (2009). Content of ecstasy in the Netherlands: 1993–2008. *Addiction, 104*(12), 2057–66.

Voisey, J., Swagell, C. D., Hughes, I. P., Connor, J. P., Lawford, B. R., Young, R. M., & Morris, C. P. (2010). A polymorphism in the dysbindin gene (DTNBP1) associated with multiple psychiatric disorders including schizophrenia. *Behavioral and Brain Functions, 6*, 41.

Volk, L. J., Bachman, J. L., Johnson, R., Yu, Y., & Huganir, R. L. (2013). PKM-zeta is not required for hippocampal synaptic plasticity, learning and memory. *Nature, 493*(7432), 420–23.

Volkow, N. D., & O'Brien C. P. (2007). Issues for DSM-V: Should obesity be included as a brain disorder? *American Journal of Psychiatry, 164*(5), 708–10.

Volkow, N. D., Wang, G. J., Fischman, M. W., Foltin, R. W., Fowler, J. S., Vitkun, S., Logan, J., Gatley, S. J., Pappas, N., Hitzemann, R., & Shea, K. (1997). Relationship between subjective effects of cocaine and dopamine transporter occupancy. *Nature, 386*, 827–30.

Volkow, N. D., Wang, G. J., Fowler, J. S., Logan, J., Jayne, M., Franceschi, D., ... & Pappas, N. (2002). 'Nonhedonic' food motivation in humans involves dopamine in the dorsal striatum and methylphenidate amplifies this effect. *Synapse, 44*(3), 175–80.

Volkow, N. D., Wang, G. J., Ma, Y., Fowler, J. S., Zhu, W., Maynard, L., & Swanson, J. M. (2003). Expectation enhances the regional brain metabolic and the reinforcing effects of stimulants in cocaine abusers. *Journal of Neuroscience, 23*(36), 11461–8.

Volkow, N. D., Wang, G. J., Telang, F., Fowler, J. S., Thanos, P. K., Logan, J., & Pradhan, K. (2008). Low dopamine striatal D2 receptors are associated with prefrontal metabolism in obese subjects: Possible contributing factors. *Neuroimage, 42*(4), 1537–43.

Volkow, N. D., Wang, G. J., Tomasi, D., & Baler, R. D. (2013). The addictive dimensionality of obesity. *Biological Psychiatry, 73*(9), 811–18.

Vollenweider, F. X., Gamma, A., Liechti, M., & Huber, T. (1998). Psychological and cardiovascular effects and short-term sequelae of MDMA ('ecstasy') in MDMA-naive healthy volunteers. *Neuropsychopharmacology, 19*(4), 241–51.

Vollenweider, F. X., Vollenweider-Scherpenhuyzen, M. F., Bäbler, A., Vogel, H., & Hell, D. (1998). Psilocybin induces schizophrenia-like psychosis in humans via a serotonin-2 agonist action. *Neuroreport, 9*(17), 3897–902.

von Economo, C. (1930). Sleep as a problem of localization. *Journal of Nervous and Mental Disease, 71*(3), 249–59.

Voon, V., & Fox, S. H. (2007). Medication-related impulse control and repetitive behaviors in Parkinson Disease. *Archives of Neurology, 64*(8), 1089–96.

Waber, R. L., Shiv, B., Carmon, Z., & Ariely, D. (2008). Commercial features of placebo and therapeutic efficacy. *Journal of the American Medical Association, 299*(9), 1016–17.

Wade, D. T., Makela, P., Robson, P., House, H., & Bateman, C. (2004). Do cannabis-based medicinal extracts have general or specific effects on symptoms in multiple sclerosis? A double-blind, randomized, placebo-controlled study on 160 patients. *Multiple Sclerosis*, *10*(4), 434–41.

Wager, T. D., Rilling, J. K., Smith, E. E., Sokolik, A., Casey, K. L., Davidson, R. J., & Cohen, J. D. (2004). Placebo-induced changes in FMRI in the anticipation and experience of pain. *Science*, *303*(5661), 1162–7.

Wagner, A., Aizenstein, H., Mazurkewicz, L., Fudge, J., Frank, G. K., Putnam, K., ... & Kaye, W. H. (2007). Altered insula response to taste stimuli in individuals recovered from restricting-type anorexia nervosa. *Neuropsychopharmacology*, *33*(3), 513–23.

Wagner, U., Hallschmid, M., Rasch, B., & Born, J. (2006). Brief sleep after learning keeps emotional memories alive for years. *Biological Psychiatry*, *60*(7), 788–90.

Wagner, D., Becker, B., Koester, P., Gouzoulis-Mayfrank, E., & Daumann, J. (2013). A prospective study of learning, memory, and executive function in new MDMA users. *Addiction*, *108*(1), 136–45.

Walker, D. L., & Davis, M. (1997). Double dissociation between the involvement of the bed nucleus of the stria terminalis and the central nucleus of the amygdala in startle increases produced by conditioned versus unconditioned fear. *Journal of Neuroscience*, *17*(23), 9375–83.

Walker, M. P., & van der Helm, E. (2009). Overnight therapy? The role of sleep in emotional brain processing. *Psychological Bulletin*, *135*(5), 731.

Walker, M. P., Brakefield, T., Hobson, J. A., & Stickgold, R. (2003). Dissociable stages of human memory consolidation and reconsolidation. *Nature*, *425*(6958), 616–20.

Wall, T. L., Thomasson, H. R., Schuckit, M. A., & Ehlers, C. L. (1992). Subjective feelings of alcohol intoxication in Asians with genetic variations of ALDH2 alleles. *Alcoholism: Clinical and Experimental Research*, *16*(5), 991–5.

Walsh, T., McClellan, J. M., McCarthy, S. E., Addington, A. M., Pierce, S. B., Cooper, G. M., ... & Sebat, J. (2008). Rare structural variants disrupt multiple genes in neurodevelopmental pathways in schizophrenia. *Science*, *320*(5875), 539–43.

Wang, C., McInnis, J., Ross-Sanchez, M., Shinnick-Gallagher, P., Wiley, J. L., & Johnson, K. M. (2001). Long-term behavioral and neurodegenerative effects of perinatal phencyclidine administration: Implications for schizophrenia. *Neuroscience*, *107*(4), 535–50.

Wang, G. J., Volkow, N. D., Logan, J., Pappas, N. R., Wong, C. T., Zhu, W., ... & Fowler, J. S. (2001). Brain dopamine and obesity. *The Lancet*, *357*(9253), 354–7.

Wang, H., & Sun, X. (2005). Desensitized nicotinic receptors in brain. *Brain Research Reviews*, *48*(3), 420–37.

Wang, Y. C., McPherson, K., Marsh, T., Gortmaker, S. L., & Brown, M. (2011). Health and economic burden of the projected obesity trends in the USA and the UK. *The Lancet*, *378*(9793), 815–25.

Warburton, D. M. (1994). Psychological resources from nicotine. *Journal of Smoking-Related Disorders*, *5*(1), 149–55.

Ward, J., Hall, W., & Mattick, R. P. (1999). Role of maintenance treatment in opioid dependence. *The Lancet*, *353*(9148), 221–6.

Wardle, J., & Cooke, L. (2005). The impact of obesity on psychological well-being. *Best Practice & Research Clinical Endocrinology & Metabolism*, *19*(3), 421–40.

Wardle, J., Llewellyn, C., Sanderson, S., & Plomin, R. (2008). The FTO gene and measured food intake in children. *International Journal of Obesity*, *33*(1), 42–5.

Webb, W. B., & Agnew, H. W. Jr, (1965). Sleep: Effects of a restricted regime. *Science*, *150*(3704), 1745–7.

Webb, W. B., & Agnew, H. W. Jr, (1975). Are we chronically sleep deprived? *Bulletin of the Psychonomic Society*, *6*(1), 47–8.

Webster, H. H., & Jones, B. E. (1988). Neurotoxic lesions of the dorsolateral pontomesencephalic tegmentum-cholinergic cell area in the cat. II. Effects upon sleep-waking states. *Brain Research*, *458*(2), 285–302.

Weike, A. I., Hamm, A. O., Schupp, H. T., Runge, U., Schroeder, H. W., & Kessler, C. (2005). Fear conditioning following unilateral temporal lobectomy: Dissociation of conditioned startle potentiation and autonomic learning. *Journal of Neuroscience*, *25*(48), 11117–24.

Weinberger, D. R. (1987). Implications of normal brain development for the pathogenesis of schizophrenia. *Archives of General Psychiatry*, *44*(7), 660.

Weingarten, H. P. (1983). Conditioned cues elicit feeding in sated rats: A role for learning in meal initiation. *Science*, *220*(4595), 431–3.

Weingarten, H. P., & Elston, D. (1991). Food cravings in a college population. *Appetite*, *17*(3), 167–75.

Weiskrantz, L. (1956). Behavioural changes associated with ablations of the amygdaloid complex in monkeys. *Journal of Comparative and Physiological Psychology*, *49*, 381–91.

Weissman, M. M., & Klerman, G. L. (1977). The chronic depressive in the community: Unrecognized and poorly treated. *Comprehensive Psychiatry*, *18*(6), 523–32.

Weissman, M. M., Warner, V., Wickramaratne, P., Moreau, D., & Olfson, M. (1997). Offspring of depressed parents: 10 years later. *Archives of General Psychiatry, 54*(10), 932.

Welchman, A. E., Stanley, J., Schomers, M. R., Miall, R. C., & Bülthoff, H. H. (2010). The quick and the dead: When reaction beats intention. *Proceedings of the Royal Society, B: Biological Sciences, 277*(1688), 1667–74.

Westerterp, K. R., & Speakman, J. R. (2008). Physical activity energy expenditure has not declined since the 1980s and matches energy expenditures of wild mammals. *International Journal of Obesity, 32*(8), 1256–63.

White, T. L., Lott, D. C., & de Wit, H. (2005). Personality and the subjective effects of acute amphetamine in healthy volunteers. *Neuropsychopharmacology, 31*(5), 1064–74.

Wicker, B., Keysers, C., Plailly, J., Royet, J. P., Gallese, V., & Rizzolatti, G. (2003). Both of us disgusted in my insula: The common neural basis of seeing and feeling disgust. *Neuron, 40*, 655–64.

Wildman, R. P., Muntner, P., Reynolds, K., McGinn, A. P., Rajpathak, S., Wylie-Rosett, J., & Sowers, M. R. (2008). The obese without cardiometabolic risk factor clustering and the normal weight with cardiometabolic risk factor clustering: Prevalence and correlates of 2 phenotypes among the US population (NHANES 1999–2004). *Archives of Internal Medicine, 168*(15), 1617–24.

Wilensky, A. E., Schafe, G. E., Kristensen, M. P., & LeDoux, J. E. (2006). Rethinking the fear circuit: The central nucleus of the amygdala is required for the acquisition, consolidation, and expression of Pavlovian fear conditioning. *Journal of Neuroscience, 26*(48), 12387–96.

Wilhelm, I., Diekelmann, S., Molzow, I., Ayoub, A., Mölle, M., & Born, J. (2011). Sleep selectively enhances memory expected to be of future relevance. *Journal of Neuroscience, 31*(5), 1563–9.

Wilhelm, I., Prehn-Kristensen, A., & Born, J. (2012). Sleep-dependent memory consolidation – What can be learnt from children? *Neuroscience & Biobehavioral Reviews, 36*(7), 1718–28.

Williams, H. J., Owen, M. J., & O'Donovan, M. C. (2007). Is COMT a susceptibility gene for schizophrenia? *Schizophrenia Bulletin, 33*(3), 635–41.

Williams, H. J., Owen, M. J., & O'Donovan, M. C. (2009). Schizophrenia genetics: New insights from new approaches. *British Medical Bulletin, 91*(1), 61–74.

Wilson, M. A., & McNaughton, B. L. (1994). Reactivation of hippocampal ensemble memories during sleep. *Science, 265*(5172), 676–9.

Winkielman, P., & Berridge, K. C. (2004). Unconscious emotion. *Current Directions in Psychological Science, 13*(3), 120–23.

Winter, J. C. (1971). Tolerance to a behavioral effect of lysergic acid diethylamide and cross-tolerance to mescaline in the rat: Absence of a metabolic component. *Journal of Pharmacology and Experimental Therapeutics, 178*(3), 625–30.

Wittchen, H. U., Zhao, S., Kessler, R. C., & Eaton, W. W. (1994). DSM-III–R generalized anxiety disorder in the National Comorbidity Survey. *Archives of General Psychiatry, 51*(5), 355–64.

Wittchen, H. U., Carter, R. M., Pfister, H., Montgomery, S. A., & Kessler, R. C. (2000). Disabilities and quality of life in pure and comorbid generalized anxiety disorder and major depression in a national survey. *International Clinical Psychopharmacology, 15*(6), 319–28.

Wolf, S. G., & Wolff, H. G. (1943). *Human Gastric Function: An Experimental of a Man and His Stomach.* Oxford: Oxford University Press.

Wonnacott, S. (1997). Presynaptic nicotinic ACh receptors. *Trends in Neurosciences, 20*(2), 92–8.

Woods, J. H., & Winger, G. (1997). Abuse liability of flunitrazepam. *Journal of Clinical Psychopharmacology, 17*(3), 1S–57S.

Woods, S. C. (1991). The eating paradox: How we tolerate food. *Psychological Review, 98*(4), 488.

Woods, S. C., & Ramsay, D. S. (2007). Homeostasis: Beyond Curt Richter. *Appetite, 49*, 388–98.

World Alzheimer Report (2009). Available at: http://www.alz.co.uk/research/fi les/WorldAlzheimerReport.pdf.

Wray, N. R., Pergadia, M. L., Blackwood, D. H. R., Penninx, B. W. J. H., Gordon, S. D., Nyholt, D. R., Ripke, S., MacIntyre, D. J., McGhee, K. A., Maclean, A. W., Smit, J. J., Hottenga, J. H., Willemsen, G., Middeldorp, C. M., de Geus, E. J. C., Lewis, C. M., McGuffin, P., Hickie, I. B., van den Oord, E. J. C. G., Liu, J. Z., Macgregor, S., McEvoy, B. P., Byrne, E. M., Medland, S. E., Statham, D. J., Henders, A. K., Heath, A. C., Montgomery, G. W., Martin, N. G., Boomsma, D. I., Madden, P. A. -F., & Sullivan, P. F. (2012). Genome-wide association study of major depressive disorder: New results, meta-analysis, and lessons learned. *Molecular Psychiatry, 17*, 36–48.

Wulff, K., Gatti, S., Wettstein, J. G., & Foster, R. G. (2010). Sleep and circadian rhythm disruption in psychiatric and neurodegenerative disease. *Nature Reviews Neuroscience, 11*(8), 589–99.

Xue, Y. X., Luo, Y. X., Wu, P., Shi, H. S., Xue, L. F., Chen, C., ... Lu, L. (2012). A memory retrieval-extinction procedure to prevent drug craving and relapse. *Science, 336*(6078), 241–5.

Yamanaka, A., Beuckmann, C. T., Willie, J. T., Hara, J., Tsujino, N., Mieda, M., ... & Sakurai, T. (2003). Hypothalamic orexin neurons regulate arousal according to energy balance in mice. *Neuron, 38*(5), 701–13.

Yang, A., Palmer, A. A., & de Wit, H. (2010). Genetics of caffeine consumption and responses to caffeine. *Psychopharmacology, 211*(3), 245–57.

Yehuda, R. (2002). Post-traumatic stress disorder. *New England Journal of Medicine, 346*(2), 108–14.

Yehuda, R., Kahana, B., Binder-Brynes, K., Southwick, S. M., Mason, J. W., & Giller, E. L. (1995). Low urinary cortisol excretion in holocaust survivors with posttraumatic stress disorder. *American Journal of Psychiatry, 152*(7), 982–6.

Yehuda, R., Schmeidler, J., Wainberg, M., Binder-Brynes, K., & Duvdevani, T. (1998). Vulnerability to posttraumatic stress disorder in adult offspring of Holocaust survivors. *American Journal of Psychiatry, 155*(9), 1163–71.

Yehuda, R., Siever, L. J., Teicher, M. H., Levengood, R. A., Gerber, D. K., Schmeidler, J., & Yang, R. K. (1998). Plasma norepinephrine and 3-methoxy-4-hydroxyphenylglycol concentrations and severity of depression in combat post-traumatic stress disorder and major depressive disorder. *Biological Psychiatry, 44*(1), 56–63.

Yehuda, R., Bierer, L. M., Schmeidler, J., Aferiat, D. H., Breslau, I., & Dolan, S. (2000). Low cortisol and risk for PTSD in adult offspring of holocaust survivors. *American Journal of Psychiatry, 157*(8), 1252–9.

Yehuda, R., Morris, A., Labinsky, E., Zemelman, S., & Schmeidler, J. (2007). Ten-year follow-up study of cortisol levels in aging holocaust survivors with and without PTSD. *Journal of Traumatic Stress, 20*(5), 757–61.

Yeomans, M. R., & Gray, R. W. (1997). Effects of naltrexone on food intake and changes in subjective appetite during eating: Evidence for opioid involvement in the appetizer effect. *Physiology & Behavior, 62*(1), 15–21.

Yeomans, M. R., Chambers, L., Blumenthal, H., & Blake, A. (2008). The role of expectancy in sensory and hedonic evaluation: The case of smoked salmon ice-cream. *Food Quality and Preference, 19*(6), 565–73.

Yip, S. W., Doherty, J., Wakeley, J., Saunders, K., Tzagarakis, C., de Wit, H., & Rogers, R. D. (2012). Reduced subjective response to acute ethanol administration among young men with a broad bipolar phenotype. *Neuropsychopharmacology, 37*(8), 1808–15.

Yiu, G. and He, Z. (2006). Glial inhibition of CNS axon regeneration. *Nature Reviews Neuroscience, 7*(8), 617–27.

Yokum, S., Ng, J., & Stice, E. (2011). Attentional bias to food images associated with elevated weight and future weight gain: An fMRI study. *Obesity, 19*(9), 1775–83.

Yonkers, K. A., Dyck, I. R., Warshaw, M., & Keller, M. B. (2000). Factors predicting the clinical course of generalised anxiety disorder. *British Journal of Psychiatry, 176*(6), 544–9.

Yoo, S. S., Gujar, N., Hu, P., Jolesz, F. A., & Walker, M. P. (2007). The human emotional brain without sleep – a prefrontal amygdala disconnect. *Current Biology, 17*(20), R877–R878.

Youdim, M. B. H., Edmondson, D., & Tipton, K. F. (2006). The therapeutic potential of monoamine oxidase inhibitors. *Nature Reviews Neuroscience, 7*(4), 295–309.

Young, E., & Korszun, A. (2009). Sex, trauma, stress hormones and depression. *Molecular Psychiatry, 15*(1), 23–8.

Zajicek, J., Fox, P., Sanders, H., Wright, D., Vickery, J., Nunn, A., & Thompson, A. (2003). Cannabinoids for treatment of spasticity and other symptoms related to multiple sclerosis (CAMS study): Multicentre randomised placebo-controlled trial. *The Lancet, 362*(9395), 1517–26.

Zammit, S., Allebeck, P., Andreasson, S., Lundberg, I., & Lewis, G. (2002). Self-reported cannabis use as a risk factor for schizophrenia in Swedish conscripts of 1969: Historical cohort study. *British Medical Journal, 325*(7374), 1199.

Zampini, M., & Spence, C. (2004). The role of auditory cues in modulating the perceived crispness and staleness of potato chips. *Journal of Sensory Studies, 19*(5), 347–63.

Zellner, D. A., Rozin, P., Aron, M., & Kulish, C. (1983). Conditioned enhancement of human's liking for flavor by pairing with sweetness. *Learning and Motivation, 14*(3), 338–50.

Ziauddeen, H., & Fletcher, P. C. (2013). Is food addiction a valid and useful concept? *Obesity Reviews, 14*(1), 19–28.

Ziauddeen, H., Farooqi, I. S., & Fletcher, P. C. (2012). Obesity and the brain: How convincing is the addiction model? *Nature Reviews Neuroscience, 13*(4), 279–86.

Zimmerman, J. M., Rabinak, C. A., McLachlan, I. G., & Maren, S. (2007). The central nucleus of the amygdala is essential for acquiring and expressing conditional fear after overtraining. *Learning & Memory, 14*(9), 634–44.

Zola-Morgan, S., Squire, L. R., Amaral, D. G., & Suzuki, W. A. (1989). Lesions of perirhinal and parahippocampal cortex that spare the amygdala and hippocampal formation produce severe memory impairment. *Journal of Neuroscience, 9*(12), 4355–70.

Zorawski, M., Cook, C. A., Kuhn, C. M., & LaBar, K. S. (2005). Sex, stress, and fear: Individual differences in conditioned learning. *Cognitive, Affective, & Behavioral Neuroscience, 5*(2), 191–201.

Zubieta, J. K., Bueller, J. A., Jackson, L. R., Scott, D. J., Xu, Y., Koeppe, R. A., ... & Stohler, C. S. (2005). Placebo effects mediated by endogenous opioid activity on μ-opioid receptors. *Journal of Neuroscience, 25*(34), 7754–62.

Zuckerman, L., Rehavi, M., Nachman, R., & Weiner, I. (2003). Immune activation during pregnancy in rats leads to a postpubertal emergence of disrupted latent inhibition, dopaminergic hyperfunction, and altered limbic morphology in the offspring: A novel neurodevelopmental model of schizophrenia. *Neuropsychopharmacology, 28*(10), 1778–89.

INDEX